THE ACTIVE READER

SECOND EDITION

THE *ACTIVE READER*

STRATEGIES FOR ACADEMIC READING AND WRITING

ERIC HENDERSON

OXFORD

UNIVERSITY PRESS

OXFORD
UNIVERSITY PRESS

Oxford University Press is a department of the University of Oxford.
It furthers the University's objective of excellence in research, scholarship,
and education by publishing worldwide. Oxford is a registered trade mark of
Oxford University Press in the UK and in certain other countries.

Published in Canada by
Oxford University Press
8 Sampson Mews, Suite 204,
Don Mills, Ontario M3C 0H5 Canada

www.oupcanada.com

Copyright © Oxford University Press Canada 2012

The moral rights of the author have been asserted

Database right Oxford University Press (maker)

First Edition published in 2008

Library and Archives Canada Cataloguing in Publication

Henderson, Eric, 1951–
The active reader: strategies for academic reading and writing / Eric Henderson. — 2nd ed.

Includes bibliographical references and index.
ISBN 978-0-19-543974-8

1. English language—Rhetoric—Textbooks. 2. Academic writing—Textbooks. 3. Report writing—Textbooks.
4. Reading comprehension—Textbooks. 5. College readers. I. Title.

PE1408.H385 2011   808′.042   C2011-905212-1

Cover image: Paul Harizan/Getty

This book is printed permanent (acid-free) paper ∞.

Printed and bound in Canada

1 2 3 4 — 15 14 13 12

CONTENTS

PART III   THE ACTIVE READER   165

PREFACE

Academic Writing and the New Realists

The future turns out to be a work-in-progress, not a set of map coordinates but the product of a never-ending argument between the inertia as things-as-they-are and the energy inherent in the hope of things-as-they-might-become.

Lewis Lapham, Editor, *Harper's Magazine*
Convocation Address, Queen's University

All life is problem solving. All organisms are inventors and technicians, good or not so good, successful or not so successful, in solving technical problems. This is how it is among animals—spiders, for example. Human technology solves human problems such as sewage disposal, or the storage and supply of food and water, as, for example, bees already have to do.

Philosopher Karl Popper

A decade ago ago, I watched first-year students tapping hesitantly on keyboards in a computer lab at my university, completing a simple early-term assignment: a short essay on what they considered the major challenge humans face today. Predictably, I read about dwindling oil supplies, overpopulation, pollution, the Middle East battleground, and terrorism. Today, the fruits of their labours are different: their responses are more thoughtful, paradoxically less concrete. Typical problems identified include "our lack of concern for the world around us," "lack of cooperation," "loss of faith in our ability to act," "problems communicating," "flawed human perception," "hatred," "evasion of important issues," "intolerance," "humanity itself," "*we* are the problem."

If this does, indeed, suggest a trend, these students could be called the "new realists." They are willing to confront underlying causes, unlike the idealists of the 1960s who "dropped out," blaming another generation, or the idealists of the 1980s, many of whom were too busy envisioning "the good life" of material success to even think about causes. Certainly, most students today are well aware of the challenges that their generation and future ones face. They also understand the role that communication, especially written communication, will play in meeting these challenges. This book was designed in response to the need both for problem-solvers and for good communicators; the two are intertwined.

One of the sustaining purposes in studying the conventions of academic reading and writing is to direct the human need to explore and learn, to express and create, to discuss and debate, in writing, into useful and fulfilling channels. Although the immediate result might be a level of competence that will help students in their other courses and lead to improved grades, the acquisition of writing and reading skills serves many long-term goals. Language is one of the most powerful tools—possibly the most powerful—for ensuring our survival as individuals, as a society, and as a species. Through the medium of language, we can read about contemporary problems, ask a range of pertinent questions, and propose practical solutions to these problems. *The Active Reader: Strategies for Academic Reading and Writing* seeks to provide student readers, writers, and researchers with the training to question, investigate, analyze, and communicate.

For the Second Edition

The words above, written for the first edition, resound even more urgently three years later in a world increasingly beset by challenges both to the quality of life and to sustaining the diversity of life in the generations to come. It is for the "new realists" mentioned above—students and instructors—that the second edition has been prepared.

This edition includes several necessary adaptations of the first. Most important is the increase in the proportion of scholarly to journalistic essays in Part III. This means that the essays cover a wider spectrum of disciplines and topics than before. Selection criteria, however, have remained the same: essays of high interest, relevance, and accessibility to today's student have been chosen.

While popular academic essays have been retained from the first edition, the replacement of some 20 informal, non-academic essays gives a new prominence to the academic review essay and the editorial/argumentative essay, both highly suitable formats for study. The academic review essay affords an apt model for the research essay, in which students investigate sources on a topic, organize them logically, and evaluate their contribution, forming conclusions or answering questions posed in their introductions. Like student writers, academic writers often have opinions on the topics they investigate, and may make recommendations based on their findings. By studying the essays in Part III, students should find assurance that scholarly writing is a place for informed discussion and enlivened debate, thus providing an efficacious model for argumentation.

The 39 readings, all recently published in academic journals or books, are divided into seven categories of interest to today's students: "University Issues," Canada in the World," "Identity and Citizenship," "Gender and Sexuality," Media and Image," "Society of Excess," and "The Human Face of Science." They embrace diverse disciplines, from economics to environmental studies, history to health sciences. The essays are integrated with a well-developed rhetoric—nine chapters covering the conventions of academic writing and reading, critical thinking, summarizing, argumentation, and writing rhetorical analyses and research papers. Plentiful examples from student writing, many of which include explanatory comments, illustrate material covered. Using many resources to assist in comprehension, *The Active Reader* actively challenges the stereotype that academic writing is dry and inaccessible to students today. In sum, the pages that follow will fully equip students to successfully read and write about challenging texts, the kinds of texts they will often be called on to read, understand, and model in many of their upper-level assignments.

Other new or expanded features of the second edition include the following:

- The number of chapter divisions has increased to nine, with wide coverage of areas related to academic reading and writing. Many new sections have been included; others have been updated or expanded;
- New subject categories for Part III reflect our changing world and the interests of students;
- In addition to the questions, activities, and vocabulary lists accompanying each reading, useful websites and suggested library reading are now featured;
- Short sample academic essays with annotations have been introduced, enabling students to connect terms and other material covered with real examples;
- Ancillaries, such as charts, have been added to help students understand content; the number and diversity of exercises in the rhetoric have been increased;
- Terms and important concepts are now reinforced by marginal annotations;
- Updated and expanded research sections with detailed information about reliability of sources, electronic research, and plagiarism, along with coverage of the most current APA, MLA, CMS, and CSE formats, are included.

As in the first edition, throughout the rhetoric chapters and in the appendix, experts, including instructors and writing professionals, and students (see below) offer their perspectives in a feature entitled "The Active Voice." These essays, on topics ranging from disciplinary writing to environmental activism, alert students to issues of vital concern today. Some of the essays flow seamlessly from the text, while others elaborate on or demonstrate the application of a point mentioned in the text. Many can be treated as mini-essays that can be discussed and analyzed.

The Active Voice

A Journey Inspired

Although it is true that many people on this planet are privileged to take part in interesting adventures and journeys, what concerns me is how people change as a result. This is of particular interest to me after getting back from one of the most inspirational adventures I'd ever been on. My trip to the Arctic with the organization Students on Ice took place in the summer of 2005. This international expedition brought together 65 youth from all over the world for a two-week educational experience whose purpose was to teach us the effects that climate change is having on the Arctic environment.

Even though each day on this expedition had many inspirational or moving moments, one in particular stood out for me. This moment was listening to an elder from a village called Pangnirtung, located on the eastern coast of Baffin Island. Here, we learned of the suffering that the Inuit people were going through as a result of climate change in the area. More specifically, the elder explained how the warming of the area was causing the ice to become thinner and more dangerous to hunt on, and also how it led to increasing unpredictability of the already extreme weather that the town experienced. In addition, we learned the reason why Inuit women's breast milk contained some of the highest numbers of PCBs and other contaminants of any of the world's peoples.

What does a moment like this do to a person? For me, aside from feeling a great deal of grief and sorrow, it reinstated a sense of injustice: it was not the fault of these people that they are having to try to adapt to these changing conditions and circumstances. This is why, upon coming to university, I vowed to bring light to these issues and injustices. I did this in what I thought was the simplest way possible: by doing presentations on my trip, mostly to the local university community. Although many of these presentations were merely to friends of mine, two of them were highly successful. One was at a conference with the BCSEA (BC Sustainable Energy Association) in Victoria, which I had found out about through Guy Dauncey, the director of the organization, who was at a presentation by Elizabeth May, executive director of the Sierra Club of Canada, back in October 2005. The other presentation, which I was grateful to be able to make, was at the Western Division of the Canadian Association of Geographers (WDCAG) Conference in Kamloops, BC. Here, I was actually able to do my presentation in front of about 30 professors and graduate students from across the country.

In hindsight, I realize how fortunate I was to have such a moving learning experience. However, I also realize that an experience such as this can not only inspire one but also work to eliminate apathy in people of my generation. This is why I believe that it should be imperative that youth like me be given this opportunity, regardless of their financial or social status.

Ben Tannenbaum, environmental studies/
political science major

Acknowledgements

I wish to gratefully acknowledge the editorial staff at Oxford University Press Canada for their enthusiasm and expertise. I would particularly like to thank Peter Chambers for charting the course of the new edition; Eric Sinkins for his ongoing support and adept problem-solving skills in this as in all my textbooks; and Steven Hall for making the proofing and production stages virtually frustration free! Thanks also to Amy Hick for her thoughtful copyediting.

I much appreciate the help of my colleagues at the University of Victoria. I am especially indebted to Susan Doyle for her leadership; Monika Rydygier Smith has contributed to both editions in numberless ways. I am grateful to suggestions and other input from Elizabeth Grove-White, Richard Pickard, Brian Day, Celeste Derksen, Candace Neveu, Leina Pauls, Harb Sanghara, and Madeline Walker. I would also like to gratefully acknowledge Anthony Barrett, formerly of UBC, whose guiding hand allowed me to venture, with some confidence, on the thin ice of English etymology.

I am indebted to the generosity of those individuals who took the time to update their original contributions for the second edition: Bradley Anholt, Jim Henderson, Danielle Forster, and Monika Rydygier Smith. All "Active Voice" contributors have enlarged the scope of this book significantly, imbuing it with their knowledge of and passion for their subject.

From its inception to the completion of the second edition, *The Active Reader: Strategies for Academic Reading and Writing* has been rooted in my teaching life at UVic, particularly the teaching of academic reading and writing to first-year students. I am indebted to the many students who allowed their writing to be represented in this book.

Above all, Madeline Sonik has been a constant and sustaining presence in my life, in which the aspirations for and planning of this book occupy a small—but vital—part.

In memory of Danielle Forster

PART I

Academic Reading – An Introduction

As students, you will be introduced to many different kinds of writing during your post-secondary education. The goal usually is to interact with these texts in various ways, such as the following:

- discuss the issues they raise with your classmates;
- respond to them in writing, agreeing or disagreeing with the argument;
- learn the ways they are put together and/or the rhetorical strategies used;
- acquire the specialized knowledge they contain or become familiar with the procedures through which this knowledge can be acquired;
- use them as "models" for your own writing, perhaps in preparation for other undergraduate courses.

As you proceed in your program of study, the nature of this interaction will likely increase in complexity. For example, early in the term you might focus on discussing and responding; later, as the texts become more familiar, you may be asked to summarize or analyze them. New skill acquisition invites new challenges. By rising to these challenges early in your university career, you will be better prepared for the discipline-specific reading and writing challenges that lie ahead. Inevitably, some of these challenges will present themselves as academic readings, researched and documented essays by experts who seek to advance knowledge in their discipline.

The pages that follow are designed to help you interact with these essays, which range considerably in their level of difficulty and accessibility. Chapters 1 and 2 introduce the kinds of reading tasks you perform at the post-secondary level. They attempt to answer the questions: What can you expect when you read academic essays? Who are they written for and how are they written? In what ways is academic writing a distinct genre with its own rules and procedures? What do academic readings across the disciplines have in common?

After looking at common features of academic prose, in Chapter 3 we consider three distinct formats of academic essays. What can you look for when you read a humanities essay? How does an essay in the humanities differ from one in the social sciences or the sciences?

Of course, reading academic prose involves much more than identifying its main features and where to find them. Chapters 4 and 5 highlight the unique engagement between writers and readers of academic texts and the strategies that can enhance this engagement. Chapter 4 focuses on applying critical thinking skills to academic reading. Although we exercise critical thinking in many everyday activities, the complex and diverse nature of academic writing requires us to be conscious of critical thinking before, during, and after reading academic texts. The material in Chapter 5 is designed to facilitate your understanding of challenging essays, enabling you not only to become familiar with their rules and procedures but also to be able to use them in practical ways throughout your university career. Questions addressed include: What kinds of thinking does academic reading require of you? What kinds of reading skills are required? What specific strategies can you use to make the reading process easier, increase comprehension of content, and give you the skills to analyze the text and the author's rhetorical strategies?

Chapter 1

An Introduction to Academic Prose

What Is Academic Writing?

For some people, "academic writing" is a euphemism for dense, abstract writing, so highly specialized as to be virtually impenetrable to non-specialists. However, successful academic writing is not intended to baffle the reader but is customized for an audience familiar with a given discipline's conventions and modes of discourse, its central ideas, and ways of presenting and analyzing them.

> "Successful academic writing is not intended to baffle the reader but is customized for an audience familiar with a given discipline's conventions and modes of discourse, its central ideas, and ways of presenting and analyzing them."

Roadblocks to Reading

Like most other writing, academic writing has a distinct purpose, in this case, to advance knowledge in a discipline. It is also intended for a specific audience: knowledgeable and interested readers. In most kinds of writing, including the kinds you will do in many of your courses, **purpose** and **audience** are two key variables that you must consider before you begin.

However, language and/or problems with discipline-specific concepts can be barriers to understanding for the uninitiated reader. To become a competent reader of an academic document, then, might require working to understand vocabulary, including specialized terms, and establishing a firmer grounding in key concepts and their uses.

In order to be prepared for the kinds of sophisticated reading tasks that lie ahead, you need to become acquainted with academic discourse: its conventions and vocabulary, as well as the critical thinking skills that enable you to respond fully to its challenges.

PURPOSE
why you are writing; variables affecting purpose include your topic and your audience.

AUDIENCE
whom you are writing to; includes one or more readers with common interests, knowledge level, and/or expectations.

What Are Conventions?

Fortunately, students beginning to engage as academic readers and writers usually do not have to deal with highly complex language or concepts. Much academic writing is accessible to a wider audience than students tend to assume; most of the "barriers" of academic discourse are far from insurmountable and can be overcome by paying careful attention to its formal conventions.

You can think of conventions (the word means "come together") as a set of implicit instructions. **Conventions** are recurrent patterns that direct and organize the behaviour of specific groups of people. One reason we follow conventions is to help us communicate with one another. For example, it is a convention in some cultures to bow respectfully when being introduced to a stranger or simple acquaintance. In formal letter-writing, it is conventional to use a form of salutation like "Dear Sir/Madam"; however, in email a more appropriate salutation might be "Hello" or "Hi." A convention must continue to be functional (i.e., serve a specific purpose); otherwise, it may be considered outdated and be replaced by a newer, more useful convention.

Academic writing also has its conventions, which vary somewhat from discipline to discipline. Conventions help direct the reader and organize the essay. They help him or her respond appropriately and knowledgeably. They also open up an effective channel of communication between writer and reader. The next section focuses on general information applicable to most academic writing as well as several of the accepted conventions—we discuss the conventions of academic writing in more detail in Chapter 2.

CONVENTIONS
recurrent patterns that direct and organize the behaviour of specific groups of people and that, applied appropriately, help us communicate with our audience.

General Features of Academic Writing

Knowledge Across the Disciplines

Although academic writing is generally written for knowledgeable readers, knowledge itself differs somewhat across the disciplines, as the following definitions suggest. (See Chapter 9 for more information on which research methods and procedures are best suited to the various disciplines.)

Humanities: The branch of knowledge concerned with examining the cultural tools that humans use to express and represent themselves. Humanities writing focuses on how ideas and values are used to interpret human experience, analyzing primary sources to draw conclusions about their literary themes, language, art and culture, historical significance, theoretical basis, or universality. Typical humanities disciplines are classical studies, history, linguistics, literature, modern languages, Native studies, philosophy, and religious studies, among others.

Social sciences: The branch of knowledge concerned with the study of human behaviour within a well-defined order or system (e.g., society, human mind, economics, political system). Social science disciplines include anthropology, economics, geography, political science, psychology, and sociology, among others.

Sciences: The branch of knowledge concerned with the study of natural phenomena using empirical methods to determine or validate their laws. The natural and applied sciences include biology, chemistry, engineering, environmental sciences, health sciences, mathematics, and many more.

Audience: Who Reads Academic Writing?

It will come as no surprise that the largest audience for academic writing is scholars, people with knowledge about and interest in the discipline or subject area. However, not all writing in academic books and journals is intended for the same audience. The expert in cell biology will not necessarily speak the same language as the expert in theoretical physics. The biologist may be an ardent reader of the academic journal *Cell* while the physicist may read every issue of *Communications in Mathematical Physics*. Yet both may faithfully subscribe to scientific journals like *Nature* or *Science* that publish articles of interest in the broad field of science and the social sciences as well as the results of rigorous research. Academic journals and many academic presses vary in their readership, from highly knowledgeable readers to those with a general knowledge.

One way of gauging the intended audience is to note what, if any, criteria are used to determine the suitability of a given article for publication. The most reliable academic journals are **peer-reviewed** (refereed). In other types of journals that are not peer-reviewed, authors may summarize and rewrite technical prose for interested but not highly knowledgeable readers. (See below, "Where Academic Writing is Found," for different categories of journals and magazines.) Such journals are not usually considered academic and may even be sold through retail outlets: their stress is less on original research and more on making this research accessible to the literate non-specialist. However, they are different from consumer-type *magazines* in which writers must often adopt strategies to attract and maintain the interest of a general reader.

The aims of academic publications are well summarized by John Fraser, a columnist for *The Globe and Mail*:

> [T]he best academic publications extend our understanding of who we are in ways that trade publications and magazines and newspapers have largely abandoned. Canada's collective memory, our understanding of our social and economic conditions, aboriginal challenges to national complacency, the actual consequences of de-linking ourselves from the realities of our past . . . all find provocative and highly useful resonances from our academic publishers. (Fraser. "Academic Publishers Teach Mainstream Ones a Lesson." *The Globe and Mail* 4 June 2005: F9)

The Purposes of Academic Writing

The most obvious function of academic journals, particularly those in the social sciences and sciences, is to publish the results of experiments. However, not all articles in journals are concerned with **original research**. Many articles in humanities journals refer to previous studies and interpret them in light of a specific theory or framework. Depending on the purpose of the author(s), the focus may be on generating new knowledge through experimentation or on modifying the way future researchers interpret this knowledge. Still others review what is currently known about a particular topic and what remains to be known, summarizing what has been written to date and its significance.

These distinctions suggest three basic kinds of academic articles: 1) those that *present the results* of original research, 2) those that *build on* existing research, offering new interpretations, and 3) those that *review and analyze* the current state of knowledge about a topic. (See Chapter 3.)

An Exchange of Ideas

Academic writing operates as a shared or "open" system, *a medium for the exchange of ideas among informed and interested experts*, in order to explore an idea, concept, or text; to answer an important question; to test a hypothesis; or to solve a problem. In spite of

PEER-REVIEWED
type of journal in which submissions are reviewed by experts before publication; authoritative source for scholarly research.

ORIGINAL RESEARCH
research in which the author(s) conducts an experiment to generate raw data or uses available data to prove/disprove a hypothesis or answer a research question. Such research includes methodology, results, and discussion of results.

the occasional inconsistencies in results and disagreements among experts, it is this common objective to help us better understand ourselves and our world that unites those working in specialized fields. This objective undermines the stereotype of the "isolated scholar." Scholars, especially those involved in experimentation, seldom work alone; more often, they work in collaborative teams in which breakdowns in communication or a lack of cooperation could endanger the experiment's validity and damage their own credibility.

Analysis, Synthesis, and Academic Writing

Analysis

Another basic feature separates most academic writing from other kinds of specialized writing and from most journalistic writing: the emphasis on analysis. When you analyze, you "loosen [something] up." Analysis can be applied to all the disciplines: an earth scientist may literally "loosen up," or break down, the constituents of a soil sample to determine the concentration of its elements, while a molecular physicist may study the behaviour of atoms in a particle accelerator as they reach very high speeds and begin to break down into smaller units. A literary analysis could involve breaking down a poem's stanzas or a novel's narrative to study smaller units, such as metre (in a poem) or point of view (in fiction).

Analysis can serve several functions, as suggested by the examples above. Thus, there are various ways that an analysis can proceed:

ANALYSIS
In analysis, you break up a whole in order (1) to closely examine each part individually and/or (2) to investigate the relationships among the parts.

- by careful attention to detail (description),
- by applying a timeline to events (chronology),
- by comparing and contrasting,
- by dividing and perhaps subdividing a whole (division and classification), or
- by looking at the pros and cons of something. There are many other methods as well (see "Rhetorical Patterns and Paragraph Development," p. 85).

A **rhetorical analysis** involves breaking down an idea or a statement, such as a claim, and subjecting it to critical thinking in order to test its validity. In the rhetorical analysis of an argumentative essay, you assess a line of reasoning in order to test each link in the reasoning chain; you probably also test for consistency and coherence. (See Chapter 4, "Critical Thinking," p. 35.)

RHETORICAL ANALYSIS
writing that breaks down an idea, claim, or essay into parts, which are analyzed in relation to the main idea or claim and/or in relation to other parts.

Sometimes, a journal publishes editorials or commentaries in which an editor or writer "takes a stand," analyzing the strengths and weaknesses of a controversial or debatable issue. Such essays rely on analysis and can be much like the argumentative or persuasive essays you might be assigned.

Of course, analysis is not unique to academic writing. The media often employ analysts, and many businesses and governments use consultants who analyze data and give recommendations. Commentaries and editorials are features of most forms of media—newspapers, magazines, television, and the Internet—in which the writer uses analysis to support his or her view of or opinion on a subject. Although most academic writers avoid directly stating their opinion, they, too, sometimes write argumentatively on issues of concern to them (see, for example, "The Active Voice: Climate Change and the Integrity of Science," below).

Synthesis

Just as in the academic essays of experts, in most research essays you write, you do not just break down; you also synthesize. **Synthesis** is the act of "putting together." The writer(s) of a scientific experiment presents the raw data that emerged in the study of a particular phenomenon. However, the data alone are not meaningful or relevant until they are placed within a larger context—the hypothesis that the experiment was intended to test, for example, or results from similar experiments. In the final section of the write-up, the writer attempts to synthesize his or her findings by connecting them with the hypothesis and/or the results of similar studies.

Some humanities and social science essays may employ a different analysis/synthesis pattern. In these essays, the activities of analysis and synthesis are not confined to distinct sections of the essay but are part of the essay's evolving structure. Writers of review essays use synthesis throughout the essay, categorizing the research using a systematic method, summarizing each study, and showing how it relates to other, similar studies.

When you organize the sources you have used in your research essays, you, too, will be synthesizing, combining the results of your research to reflect your purpose and approach to your topic. Part of the synthesizing process will involve decisions about whether to quote your sources directly, summarize the findings, or paraphrase important passages. Synthesis can also take place on two levels: the ideas you use and the language you use to express them. (See Chapter 9.)

> **SYNTHESIS**
> writing in which elements of a work or other studies about a work are brought together, usually in order to draw a conclusion or interpret a claim you wish to assert about the work.

Where Academic Writing Is Found

Academic writing is published in academic journals and in books published by academic (university) presses. When searching for research sources, you should pay particular attention to *who* publishes the work.

University presses are generally run by non-profit, university-affiliated organizations; they exist primarily to disseminate the research of scholars in diverse fields. Although the decision to publish usually rests with the editors, they are guided by the comments of "readers," or peer-reviewers, experts in the same subject as the work's author, who evaluate the manuscript. They may recommend rejecting the work, publishing it, or publishing it with changes. Although the work may be controversial—for example, if it challenges previous findings or interpretations—you can be confident that it is a credible source. University presses also produce **monographs**, the term for a highly specialized scholarly work or treatise in book form.

Trade books, published for profit and usually to appeal to a wider audience than books published by academic presses, may also be reliable academic sources, particularly if they have been commented on favourably by noted authorities. The best way to assess their reliability is by looking for reviews from independent sources. Many journals regularly include book reviews relevant to their content; in fact, some journals are devoted primarily to reviewing current books in their field.

Academic (scholarly) journals are not sold at retail outlets; university libraries subscribe to them and make them available to faculty and students in hard-copy versions (i.e., they can be found on library shelves) and/or through electronic databases and indexes. (Do not assume, however, that every article you locate in your library's database is an academic source. Databases often include both scholarly and non-scholarly material.) They are often more current sources than book-length studies because

> **UNIVERSITY PRESS**
> university-affiliated publisher, usually of books or journals; authoritative sources for scholarly research.
>
> **MONOGRAPH**
> term for a highly specialized scholarly work or treatise in book form.

> **TRADE BOOK**
> book published by non-academic press for general readers about topics of interest to them.
>
> **ACADEMIC (SCHOLARLY) JOURNAL**
> type of periodical containing scholarly content (articles, reviews, and commentaries) by experts for a knowledgeable audience in related fields of study.

journals publish several times a year—a few publish weekly—and the pre-publication process is quicker than with longer works, so journals can provide "leading-edge" research in rapidly developing fields.

An increasing number of academic journals publish only in online formats. **Open-access journals** permit free access by users. The publishers of such journals may wish to promote the use of their studies' findings in the interests of a more informed and knowledgeable public. As with everything you encounter online, however, you should scrutinize such sources for their reliability before using them in your essay. (The Directory of Open Access Journals lists more than 5,000 international open access journals, many of them peer-reviewed: www.doaj.org).

For complete information about source reliability, see pp. 145–147.

Figure 1.1 summarizes some of the different classifications of academic and non-academic writing. However, the categories are not always clear-cut; for example, some academic journals include material intended for a more general audience. (Note that a **periodical** is a general term for the kind of publication that is issued periodically, at regular or semi-regular intervals.)

In this text, essays written for a prospective audience comprised of scholars, researchers, and professors are referred to as *academic* or *scholarly essays*, whether they are in book or journal format, while essays written for an audience comprised of non-specialists who share certain interests, beliefs, or ideologies are referred to as *journalistic essays*. Articles in mass circulation magazines or newspapers are usually written for an audience with varied knowledge and interest levels.

Although the essays in this text are primarily scholarly, a few are written for a literate audience of non-specialists and do not conform in all respects to the conventions of scholarly writing. Furthermore, not all your assignments may be modelled on scholarly conventions or require you to use scholarly discourse. For example, you may be asked to respond online with other class members to an essay and be permitted to write more informally. In some of your assignments, your instructor may ask you to begin with a "hook," a deliberate strategy to engage a reader, such as a catchy phrase, question, or brief narrative, a technique less used in scholarly writing. Understanding the strategies professional writers use to "spice up" their prose or make it more concise when space is at a premium will give you more options when scholarly conventions are less crucial.

The Influence of the Academic Community

While some students may interact with the academic community throughout their careers, most eventually leave school and the academy behind. What have the "isolated" interests of the scholarly community to do with those outside this community, whose everyday lives may be focused on the struggle to get or keep a job?

In fact, the academy and the world outside it benefit from one another in unmistakable ways. The rigour of academia provides training for those who take the skills they acquired in university out into the world. They are better equipped to confront problems, both in their personal lives and in dealing with the larger concerns of our society and world because of their exposure to the specialized skills, along with the general reading, writing, and critical thinking skills that the academy seeks to instill.

OPEN-ACCESS JOURNAL
kind of journal (usually scholarly) that is available online without a fee.

PERIODICAL
kind of publication that is issued periodically, at regular or semi-regular intervals; academic journals and magazines are examples of periodicals.

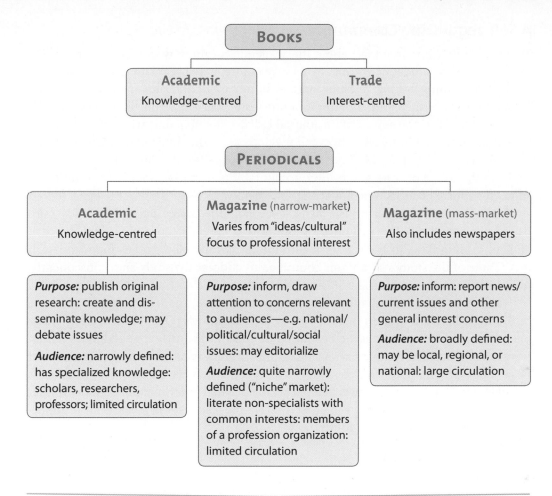

FIGURE 1.1   PUBLISHED TEXTS CAN BE DIVIDED INTO CATEGORIES DEPENDING ON THEIR PURPOSE AND AUDIENCE.

In less obvious ways, the influence of academic research is far-reaching and consequential. For one thing, the results of major academic studies often help shape our future by influencing the policies of governments. Government agencies and independent think tanks may consult scholars or commission scholarly research before making recommendations about a particular course of action; they may even provide the funds for research in areas of interest or concern.

Since 1990, governments and scientists, including many with connections to universities, have joined forces to produce four assessment reports and many special reports on climate change through the agency of the Intergovernmental Panel on Climate Change (IPCC). The creation of these non-binding but highly influential reports on "the current state of knowledge on climate change" suggests that, notwithstanding the tensions that can exist between governments and researchers, the relationship between them is symbiotic. Furthermore, the role of the media in disseminating the content of these reports underscores its vital relationship with the academic community.

A Self-regulating Community

There is another important fact about the academic community that helps to make it a true community: academic writing, by its very nature, is self-regulating. Researchers are always questioning, testing, retesting, and, in some cases, criticizing one another's work. Even a well-established journal is not immune from criticism, as one incident dramatically shows: in 2005 the editors of the journal *Cell* decided to retract without explanation an article published in its own pages the previous year. The decision unleashed a furor. What the critics objected to was not the retraction per se but the failure to give a reason for it. In the world of academic writing, accountability is crucial, and, in the opinion of some, the journal editors were not acting responsibly.

More recently, a major British medical journal, *The Lancet*, retracted a study published a dozen years before that linked a common vaccine with an increased incidence of autism, finding flaws in the study's methodology as follow-up studies found no such link. Three of the study's 13 authors continued to endorse the study and, consequently, found their careers as physicians in jeopardy.

Academic writers often anticipate criticism or, at least, challenges to their methods or findings. To assure readers that they are aware of a study's possible weaknesses, authors often include a section at the beginning or end of the article that addresses limitations, such as a small sample size. A small sample might mean that the findings cannot be generalized. This does not necessarily mean that the study is flawed but rather extends an invitation to future researchers to replicate the original experiment or conduct similar studies using a larger sample size in order to make the results more reliable, more applicable to larger or more diverse groups.

ACADEMIC WRITERS
The academic writer as a specialist in his or her subject area is familiar with what has been written and is able to assess the strengths as well as the limitations of others' work. He or she can discriminate between a study that satisfies its objectives and one that does not, and between one whose methods are consistent with its aims and one whose methods are not. In other words, self-criticism is built into the model of research-oriented scholarship.

The Active Voice

Although self-criticism is fundamental to the scientific model, ensuring that only well-tested and reliable results are presented to the public and governments, the scientific community has sometimes reacted to criticism from those outside that community. In 2010, 255 scientists, including at least 11 Nobel laureates, wrote an open letter that was published in a prominent academic journal. In it, they explained how scientific theories become facts, how the attacks of "climate deniers" on scientists distort these facts, and why it is vital to act now against the consequences of global warming.

CLIMATE CHANGE AND THE INTEGRITY OF SCIENCE
edited by Jennifer Sills

1   We are deeply disturbed by the recent escalation of political assaults on scientists in general and on climate scientists in particular. All citizens should understand some basic scientific facts. There is always some uncertainty associated with scientific conclusions; science never absolutely proves anything. When someone says that society should wait until scientists are absolutely certain before taking any action, it is the same as saying society should never take action. For a problem as potentially catastrophic as climate change, taking no action poses a dangerous risk for our planet.

2   Scientific conclusions derive from an understanding of basic laws supported by laboratory experiments, observations of nature, and mathematical and computer modeling. Like all human beings, scientists make mistakes, but the scientific process is designed to find and correct them. This process is inherently adversarial—scientists build reputations and gain recognition not only for supporting conventional wisdom, but even more so for demonstrating that the scientific consensus is wrong and that there is a better explanation. That's what Galileo, Pasteur, Darwin, and Einstein did.

But when some conclusions have been thoroughly and deeply tested, questioned, and examined, they gain the status of "well-established theories" and are often spoken of as "facts."

3   For instance, there is compelling scientific evidence that our planet is about 4.5 billion years old (the theory of the origin of Earth), that our universe was born from a single event about 14 billion years ago (the Big Bang theory), and that today's organisms evolved from ones living in the past (the theory of evolution). Even as these are overwhelmingly accepted by the scientific community, fame still awaits anyone who could show these theories to be wrong. Climate change now falls into this category: There is compelling, comprehensive, and consistent objective evidence that humans are changing the climate in ways that threaten our societies and the ecosystems on which we depend.

4   Many recent assaults on climate science and, more disturbingly, on climate scientists by climate change deniers are typically driven by special interests or dogma, not by an honest effort to provide an alternative theory that credibly satisfies the evidence. The Intergovernmental Panel on Climate Change (IPCC) and other scientific assessments of climate change, which involve thousands of scientists producing massive and comprehensive reports, have, quite expectedly and normally, made some mistakes. When errors are pointed out, they are corrected. But there is nothing remotely identified in the recent events that changes the fundamental conclusions about climate change:

(i)   The planet is warming due to increased concentrations of heat-trapping gases in our atmosphere. A snowy winter in Washington does not alter this fact.

(ii) Most of the increase in the concentration of these gases over the last century is due to human activities, especially the burning of fossil fuels and deforestation.

(iii) Natural causes always play a role in changing Earth's climate, but are now being overwhelmed by human-induced changes.

(iv) Warming the planet will cause many other climatic patterns to change at speeds unprecedented in modern times, including increasing rates of sea-level rise and alterations in the hydrologic cycle. Rising concentrations of carbon dioxide are making the oceans more acidic.

(v)   The combination of these complex climate changes threatens coastal communities and cities, our food and water supplies, marine and freshwater ecosystems, forests, high mountain environments, and far more.

5   Much more can be, and has been, said by the world's scientific societies, national academies, and individuals, but these conclusions should be enough to indicate why scientists are concerned about what future generations will face from business-as-usual practices. We urge our policy-makers and the public to move forward immediately to address the causes of climate change, including the unrestrained burning of fossil fuels.

6   We also call for an end to McCarthy-like threats of criminal prosecution against our colleagues based on innuendo and guilt by association, the harassment of scientists by politicians seeking distractions to avoid taking action, and the outright lies being spread about them. Society has two choices: We can ignore the science and hide our heads in the sand and hope we are lucky, or we can act in the public interest to reduce the threat of global climate change quickly and substantively. The good news is that smart and effective actions are possible. But delay must not be an option.

—*Science* 328, 689–90.

QUESTIONS TO CONSIDER:

1. In your own words, explain what is meant by the statement, "When someone says that society should wait until scientists are absolutely certain before taking any action, it is the same as saying society should never take action" (paragraph 1).

2. What is the difference between a theory and a fact? (paragraph 2)

3. According to the authors, what is the fundamental difference between those who "gain recognition . . . for demonstrating that the scientific consensus is wrong" (paragraph 2) and those who believe that the theory of climate change is wrong?

4. Among the opponents of the climate change theory, to whom do you believe the authors are referring in paragraph 6? What shows you this?

5. Do you think the authors produced a strong argument in the letter? Why or why not? (For more information about argumentative strategies, see pp. 124–127.)

Chapter 2

Conventions of Academic Writing

Some of the conventions of academic writing described below apply more to scholarly journals than to books. However, academic essays on a related topic are often collected in edited volumes and follow formats similar to those described. Although essays in edited books are not preceded by abstracts (see "Abstracts," p. 18), editors often summarize the purpose and content of each essay in a book's introduction and indicate how it contributes to the field of study.

Authors

EMPIRICALLY BASED STUDY
data or information based on an experiment or on observation; can be verified.

Collaborative research is very common in the sciences and social sciences. This is due to the nature of **empirically based study**, such as experimentation, which relies on direct observation under controlled conditions. Many people may be needed to observe and record the data or to perform statistical operations on the raw data; members of the research team contribute their expertise, as well as having input in the final version. For example, as is clear from the "contributors" section at the end of "Roadblocks to laws for healthy eating and activity" (p. 435), each author was assigned one or more special responsibilities in the project.

A study's authors may be colleagues from the same institution, or they may conduct their research at different institutions or research centres. In some studies, it is necessary to sample varied populations, so the authors may work in different provinces or countries. For example, a 2005 study on national stereotypes published in the journal *Science* lists 65 authors from 43 different countries; interestingly, the complete article is only five pages long! Most academic writing could be considered collaborative, in a sense, because the authors draw heavily on the work of their predecessors in the field.

Length

Academic essays vary in length. It is a truism, however, that good science writing is straightforward and concise. Scientific studies, in particular, may be as short as two or three pages; others are longer (see "The Active Voice: How to Write a Scientific Paper," p. 92, and "Academic language and the challenge of reading for learning about science,"

p. 166). Writing in some humanities disciplines, such as philosophy, history, and English, is more **discursive** (i.e., covers a wide area), partly because of the way that knowledge is defined in these disciplines: many fundamental ideas and concepts have been debated for generations, and writers continue to explore new subtleties in and variations on them. Writers may therefore draw out the implications of a concept as they apply them to a close reading of a literary or philosophical text.

Length is often a function of the depth and detail expected in academic writing. Many science and social science essays use tables, graphs, charts, and other illustrative matter to simplify content. In other essays, particularly in the humanities, length may be governed by the need throughout the essay to summarize the work of other researchers and integrate it with the author's own investigations. In addition, writers in the humanities often make extensive use of primary sources, quoting from these texts to support their points (see below, "Research Sources").

> **DISCURSIVE**
> expansive, or covering a wide area.

Research

Research Sources

The use of sources is a hallmark of academic writing. The most authoritative research sources for an academic writer are previously published studies on the topic. Academic writers depend on the writing of scholars in their fields; however, this does not mean that all academic writing is concerned only with what has been written previously in academic journals/books or delivered at academic conferences. Nor does academic writing consist mostly of summaries of other scholars' work. Thus, when you are asked to write a research paper, you too must do more than summarize.

Most research, whether conducted by scholars or by scholars-in-training—students—involves analysis, which is often centred on first-hand or **primary sources**, *original material in a field of study*. Much research begins with primary source material; for example, it would be logical to study a literary work (primary source) before you looked at what other people had to say about it (secondary source). "Primary," then, means *first in order*, not necessarily first in importance. **Secondary sources**, by contrast, *comprise commentary on or interpretation of primary material*.

Kinds of primary sources vary from discipline to discipline. Here are a few examples from various disciplines:

> **PRIMARY SOURCES**
> original material in a field of study; examples include literary texts, historical documents, and interviews.
>
> **SECONDARY SOURCES**
> commentary on or interpretation of primary material; examples include academic studies, reports, and presentations.

- *Anthropology and archaeology:* artifacts, fossils, original field notes, reports resulting from direct observations.
- *Literature:* poems, plays, fiction, diaries/letters of writers.
- *Fine arts:* sheet music, recordings, photographs, sketches, paintings, sculpture, films.
- *History:* contemporary documents from the period being studied—e.g., newspaper accounts, letters, speeches, photographs, treaties, diaries, autobiographies.
- *Natural sciences:* data from experimentation, field/laboratory notes, original research reports.
- *Sociology:* interviews, questionnaires, surveys, the raw data from these sources.

Many scientific journals publish only original research, just as many arts and humanities journals publish only research that interprets primary or secondary source material. Still other journals publish both. For example, the *Canadian Journal of Psychiatry* publishes various kinds of articles but includes headings such as "original research" to inform its readers about the nature of the research that follows.

Of course, it is not just writers of scholarly articles who use research. Magazine writers, including journalists writing for a "niche" market or for the mass market, may conduct extensive research. But a journalist, unlike a scholarly writer, does not usually provide a citation for the source, whether primary or secondary. *Documenting sources by using citations is a feature of academic writing.*

Academic writers seek to add to the store of knowledge in their discipline; to do so, they analyze the findings of previous studies. In turn, future researchers will attempt to use the findings of these current studies to help answer a question, test a hypothesis, or solve a problem of their own. It would be very difficult to locate important studies if the writer failed to say where they appeared. Thus, the writer provides a bibliographic "trail" that future researchers can follow to the source.

Documenting Sources

An academic publication usually employs one documentation method consistently, using a set of established standards (conventions) for citing sources. The method varies from publisher to publisher, and academic journals in similar disciplines may not always use the identical documentation method. However, there are four basic formats preferred by most book and journal publishers, which are described in detail in the major manuals published by university presses and research organizations:

- *MLA Style Manual and Guide to Scholarly Publishing*, 3rd ed. Published by the Modern Language Association of America (MLA). The MLA also publishes a manual designed for student writers and researchers: *MLA Handbook for Writers of Research Papers*, 7th ed.
- *Publication Manual of the American Psychological Association*, 6th ed.
- *The Chicago Manual of Style*, 16th ed. Published by the University of Chicago Press.
- *Scientific Style and Format: The CSE Manual for Authors, Editors, and Publishers*, 7th ed. Published by the Council of Science Editors.

See pages 155–160 for a summary of major documentation methods and formats.

Although it is not unusual for scholarly bibliographies (the alphabetical list of sources at the end of the essay) to be many pages long, articles in the field of history typically include extensive notes as well, either at the foot of the page (footnotes) or at the end of the essay (endnotes), suggesting the unique engagement of the historical researcher with other scholars in the field. The following essay focuses on academic historical writing, although some of the comments about using research sources apply across the disciplines.

The Active Voice

THE HISTORIAN'S CRITICAL APPARATUS

1   The heart of most academic writing in a field such as history lies not in the text on the page but hidden away either at the bottom of the page or at the end of the book in the references. Here, the whole story is told about the writer, the audience, the subject, and the standards of the discipline. Certainly references serve to document sources: to provide the origin of a quote, to substantiate a fact that might otherwise be disputed, to guide readers to find their place in the original source material. So much more than that is being revealed, however, and that is why many historians prefer notes to the more abbreviated "in-text" reference system that is favoured in some social science and science disciplines.

2   A text with no notes (or what we might also call a critical apparatus) has been written with a particular audience in mind. The author has assumed a position of absolute authority on the subject being discussed and is saying to the reader that he or she is to be trusted as a source. Such writing is often deemed "popular" in academic circles. It suggests that the historical "facts" are known for certain and that there are accepted ways of understanding the flow of history that need no debate.

3   A few footnotes or endnotes providing direct sources of information or quotes do not indicate much about the writer's imagined audience, but they do reflect honesty on the part of the researcher in disclosing his or her debts to other scholars. For the reader, they give a few hints of a different nature: they tell you about other relevant sources for this topic of discussion, names of authoritative writers in the field, and sometimes the theoretical perspective that is implicit in the essay being read. Academics tend to work within a single intellectual trend of their discipline. The sources indicated in authors' notes give the first hint of the genealogy of their ideas and perspective. History is being revealed to be more complex; these notes suggest that writing history is not just a recounting of data but an intellectual reconstruction through a framework built upon theoretical generalizations.

4   It is in the essay with an elaborate note apparatus that a scholar's full range is displayed. Not only will you find a bibliography on the topic and its related aspects packed into these notes, but you will also find the traces of the debates that the discipline of history engenders and the methodological issues that produce divergent perspectives. Such documentation tells the reader—especially one who is approaching a field for the first time—a good deal about the extent to which the essay being considered has a particular perspective or even bias that needs to be taken account of in using it as a source.

5   The full experience of scholarly reading incorporates the aptly called footnote: it is the foundation and the support of the entire endeavour, the key to decoding the values of the writer and the value of the writing. That said, a question lingers. What is the best way for the reader to tackle an essay laden with notes, whether the latter be brief, long, or a combination of the two? As surprising as it may seem, one way is to skim the notes first. For this to be a fully meaningful exercise, it is necessary for you to know something of the subject about which you are reading first. If you do, then the notes can reveal quite quickly all the hidden secrets that are their very purpose. By reading the notes first, you can make an initial and rapid assessment of whether the essay is relevant to your research topic. If it is, then you can turn to the text and read it through, ignoring most of the notes except where a quick glance might suggest that the note has something relevant to tell. That completed, your critical reflection upon the whole essay is possible. Certainly this is a process which takes practice. It also does not work as well if you are learning a subject for the first time. In that situation, there is little alternative to the opposite strategy of reading the text without the notes first and then reviewing them subsequently for their hints for further reading and the like. With practice and some immersion in your topic of research, however, that initial quick skim of the notes will prove rewarding.

6   Such are the joys of historical writing. The same set of data is repeated in different essays, but the picture that emerges varies in the hands of different writers. The notes can frequently be the key to understanding the hows, whys, and wherefores of the discipline.

—Andrew Rippin, Professor, Department of History,
University of Victoria

Voice and Style

The voice in academic essays is generally objective and analytical. Although the authors may express an opinion, it will be seen as arising out of the findings of the study and the possible consequences or as a result of their careful analysis of the subject of investigation. It will be closely linked to their own research, in other words, and not based on their attitude toward the subject itself. In this sense, academic writing can be considered expository rather than argumentative writing, since academic writers do not usually try to persuade their audience of the rightness of a system of values or of a course of action.

(The exception is editorials and commentaries that have a clear argumentative purpose; even here, however, the author's voice and tone usually remain objective.)

On the other hand, academic studies often set out to investigate a real-life problem, and their authors may propose solutions to the problem at the end of the study. This may take the form of specific recommendations or areas that future research could focus on.

Furthermore, academic writing can be considered persuasive in that it seeks to convince its reader of the accuracy and validity of the findings. And, of course, academic writers do have opinions and a stake in what they are investigating. Objectivity, then, is not synonymous with a lack of involvement but refers to the degree of detachment that ensures the writer will not be swayed by contrary or faulty evidence or by imprecise reasoning. Such a guarantee is necessary if the author is to be seen as reliable and the findings as credible.

Objectivity and Style: As observers and recorders of natural phenomena, scientists must assume a distance from the object of study to avoid influencing the results or raising the perception of bias. Thus, these writers may use voice in specific ways to convey this distance. Writers may use **passive constructions**, in which the subject of the sentence is acted upon, rather than acting itself. Student writers may be told to avoid the passive voice in their writing—for good reason, because it often results in a weaker sentence. However, if the purpose is to de-emphasize the subject, such as the researcher, or to stress the object (receiver of the action), such as that which is being studied, then a passive construction may be preferred to an active one. Note the difference between passive and active in the following example:

Active voice: Researchers have carried out several studies to assess psychiatric risk factors in motor vehicle accidents.

"Researchers" is the active subject, but in this case, the "studies" (object of the verb) that assess risk factors are more important than the generic subject, "researchers." By changing the construction of this sentence to the passive, the writer can replace an active but unimportant subject with a passive but more important subject. Note that in passive constructions, the active subject may not even be expressed. In the sentence below, the original, unimportant subject is indicated by the use of brackets.

Passive voice: Several studies have been carried out [by researchers] to assess psychiatric risk factors in motor vehicle accidents.

If an **active construction** is used, writers may displace themselves as the subject, substituting "this study shows" or "the research confirmed." When the article is multi-authored, as it often is in the sciences, the writer may use the exclusive "we" point of view. By contrast, in many argumentative essays, the writer deliberately uses the inclusive "we" or "us" to appeal to values that writer and readers hold in common; these latter forms of the first-person pronoun, then, include both author and reader.

Abstracts, which precede many journal articles in the natural and social sciences, typically use the above strategies to convey detachment and objectivity. The first abstract, below, from the journal *Child Development*, uses the passive voice and displaces the authors of the study. The second example, from the *Canadian Journal of Forest Research*, uses the displaced subject and the exclusive "we." The passive voice is italicized, the displaced subject is bolded, and the exclusive "we" is underlined.

PASSIVE CONSTRUCTION (PASSIVE VOICE)
way of constructing a sentence to show that the subject is being acted upon.

ACTIVE CONSTRUCTION (ACTIVE VOICE)
way of constructing a sentence to show that the subject performs the action of the verb.

ABSTRACT
condensed summary used in empirical studies; is placed before the essay begins and includes at a minimum purpose, methods, and results.

Using a genetic design of 234 six-year-old twins, **this study examined** (a) the contribution of genes and environment to social versus physical aggression, and (b) whether *the correlation between social and physical aggression can be explained by* similar genetic or environmental factors or by a directional link between the phenotypes. For social aggression, *substantial (shared and unique) environmental effects but only weak genetic effects were found*. For physical aggression, *significant effects of genes and unique environment were found*. . . . (M. Brendgen, G. Dionne, A. Girard, M. Boivin, F. Vitaro, & D. Pérusse. 2005. "Examining genetic and environmental effects on social aggression: a study of 6-year-old twins." *Child Development*, 76: 930–46.)

This paper considers the question of whether sustainable forest management (SFM) should continue to incorporate sustained yield (SY) requirements. . . . <u>We</u> evaluate the extent to which SY and SFM are consistent with notions of weak and (or) strong sustainability. . . . (M.K. Luckert, & T.B. Williamson, T.B. 2005. "Should sustained yield be part of sustainable forest management?" *Canadian Journal of Forest Research*, 35: 356–64.)

> Academic studies, particularly in the sciences, may use various strategies to convey objectivity, such as passive constructions and displaced subjects. They may also include direct references to the authors. Such strategies are usually not appropriate in student essays.

Language and Academic Writing: Many readers can identify scholarly writing simply by the level of the language itself. Academic writers may also use specialized diction, or jargon. Compared to literary writing, however, academic writing is characterized by a lack of ornamentation. Writing in the sciences, in particular, is marked by direct, straightforward prose with minimal use of modifiers (adjectives and adverbs). (See "The Active Voice: How to Write a Scientific Paper," p. 92.) Academic writers are also much less likely to use figurative language, such as metaphors, similes, personification, and the like, than literary writers. They may, however, use analogies to help explain a point. An **analogy** is a systematic comparison between one item and another one that is otherwise unlike the first one. Analogies can be used to make the first item more easily understood.

> **ANALOGY**
> systematic comparison between one item and another one that is otherwise unlike the first one; can be used to make the first item more easily understood.

In spite of this lack of ornamentation, academic writing may strike ordinary readers as hard to follow. Although jargon and language level can be obstacles to understanding, other elements of style, such as complex sentence and paragraph structure, and intrusive documentation, can hinder comprehension. Many of these obstacles can be overcome, though, by frequent exposure to this kind of writing and by learning the conventions of the various disciplines. Undeniably, however, inexperienced readers must read more closely, more slowly, and more consciously than they have to do when presented with simpler material. In spite of this, new reading habits can be cultivated by adopting specific strategies, such as learning to differentiate more important ideas from less important ones and using context to identify crucial words and concepts. Fortunately, clarity is a major aim of all successful academic writers, as it should be for writers in general, and academic writers employ deliberate techniques to make this goal attainable. Inexperienced readers, with patience and diligence, can overcome the legitimate difficulties they encounter.

The three-pronged approach to reading challenging essays is summarized below:

- Learn the conventions of academic writing and of your discipline (Chapters 2 and 3)
- Develop an effective large-scale reading strategy based on the conventions and reading purpose (Chapter 5, pp. 47–58)
- Learn to recognize words by their context; look up jargon and other words essential to meaning (Chapter 5, pp. 59–66)

See also "Academic language and the challenge of reading for learning about science," p. 166.

Strategies for Approaching Academic Essays

Previewing Content

True to their purpose as "knowledge-based" rather than "interest-based" writing, academic texts usually provide a "preview" of the article's content through an informative, often lengthy, title and an abstract. In addition, many include structural markers such as headings.

Titles

Academic titles are often

- Lengthy and informative,
- Divided into two parts with a colon separating them, and
- Composed mostly of nouns, many of them specific to the discipline.

"The title of a scholarly article is designed to give the reader important information about content at a glance. This is helpful not only for experts but also for student researchers because it enables them to gauge an article's potential usefulness by a scan of a journal issue's contents. Typically, key terms in the article appear in the title."

The title of a scholarly article is designed to give the reader important information about content at a glance. This is helpful not only for experts but also for student researchers because it enables them to gauge an article's potential usefulness by a scan of a journal issue's contents. Typically, key terms in the article appear in the title; thus, searching by "keyword" in an electronic database often yields useful entries.

Although it is difficult to generalize when it comes to titles, many include two parts separated by a colon. In this example from the *Journal of Clinical Child and Adolescent Psychology*, the first part summarizes the study's finding while the second part reveals the method: "School connectedness is an underemphasized parameter in adolescent mental health: Results of a community prediction study." In this example from *Essays on Canadian Writing*, an attention-grabbing phrase precedes the colon while the second phrase focuses more on content: "Venus Envy: The Depiction of the Feminine Sublime in Gayla Reid's *All the Seas of the World*."

If you turn to Part III, "The Active Reader," in this book's table of contents, you will often be able to predict an essay's topic and perhaps its findings or conclusion by looking at the detail included in the title.

Abstracts

The function of the abstract is not to introduce the essay but to provide a concise overview so that readers can determine whether they should read the entire article.

An abstract is a kind of summary or condensed version of an article. Abstracts precede most journal articles in the sciences and social sciences, giving a preview of content by focusing on the study's purpose, method, results, and conclusion. They may also briefly explain background (for example, the need for the study) or consider the findings' significance. Abstracts are increasingly being used in humanities articles as well. They often include keywords, which enable a researcher to find the article electronically when searching for words and phrases related to the topic. Abstracts are usually written by the study's author(s) and range in length from 100 to 250 words but can be longer.

Section Markers

Section markers can be used to *re*view or to *pre*view content. Because of the complex organizational scheme of many academic essays, writers may use markers throughout the essay, including in the introductory section where they preview the essay's organizational scheme (see "essay plan" in the next section). They may also review where he or she has been. Section markers, in effect, "mark" specific places in an essay where readers can get their bearings. Used after complex material, they recapitulate content before the writer moves on to a new area. The following is the first sentence from the end of a section in "Moral panic and the Nasty Girl," p. 327, and acts as a review:

> In summary, we have drawn on the moral panic literature to examine the recent preoccupation with the violent girl.

This excerpt is from the first sentence of a section in "Listening to the voices of *hijab*," p. 291, and acts as a preview:

> Before illustrating the participants' views about the *hijab*, I would like to outline some of the concepts of the *hijab* in the Muslim context, because many participants referred to them.

Writers often announce upcoming content by using headings. In empirical studies, these markers serve a *formal function* by dividing the essay into conventional categories, each having a particular purpose: for example, "introduction," "methods," "results," "discussion," and "conclusion." In longer essays, writers may include subsection markers as well.

In other kinds of academic writing, the markers serve a *descriptive function*, enabling readers to preview content. Descriptive section markers are one way that writers can make essay structure clearer to their readers. **Descriptive headings** are especially useful in orienting the reader of long academic essays or those that deal with complex material. Because the essays students write for class are usually much shorter, such markers are seldom necessary. However, if you are writing a scientific, engineering, or business report, you may be required to use formal markers to designate the standardized sections of your report (see "The Active Voice: Report Writing," p. 91).

> EMPIRICAL STUDIES USE FORMAL HEADINGS Introduction, Methods, Results, and Discussion. Authors of other kinds of studies may use **descriptive** or **content headings**, which make it easy for readers to determine the essay's main points or areas of discussion.

Activity

A good way to prepare for reading academic essays is to look at specific articles and see how they make use of the general academic conventions discussed so far. Browse current issues of periodicals on your library's shelves or use a periodical index or electronic database (your library's home page can likely guide you to listings of both), and evaluate a sample issue of a humanities, social sciences, and natural sciences journal, noting some of the differences among them. You can answer the following questions by scanning the table of contents and a representative number of essays—say, three or four.

What kinds of articles did the journal contain? How long were they? What were some typical titles? Were most articles written by a single author or by multiple authors? Did the articles include abstracts? How many articles were there per issue? Were book reviews included? Were there editorials? How were the essays laid out (for example, the use of formal/standardized or content/descriptive headings or other markers)? Typically, how many sources were used per article (you can determine this by looking at the last pages of the article where references are listed alphabetically)? Was specialized language used? Was the level of language difficult?

Features of Introductions in Academic Writing

Most of the discussion so far has focused on general characteristics of academic writing and on the kind of information you can get when you preview an essay. This section discusses some common characteristics of introductions of academic essays, usually the first part of the essay you read after you preview or "pre-read" the whole essay for content. They include the **essay plan**, the **justification**, and the **literature review**.

Like virtually all essays, academic essays begin with an introductory section. It may be titled "introduction" or "background" or have no heading, but its purpose is to set the scene for the body of the essay by introducing important concepts or summarizing previous studies on the topic. If the purpose is primarily to summarize scholarship, a review of relevant literature might be included. Literature reviews are a general characteristic of academic writing.

Thesis Statements: Student writers are familiar with the common practice of including a thesis statement in their introductions. Academic writers refer to their thesis near the end of their introductions, but the form that the thesis takes can vary. For students, it is a claim that is supported in the body of the essay and reiterated in the conclusion. It must go beyond a simple statement of what they will be writing about: it must include a comment about the topic or focus on the specific approach to be taken toward the topic.

In experiments, the thesis may consist of a **hypothesis** that will be tested or a question that will be answered. One common academic form for a thesis to take is an essay plan, a detailed statement of intent. An essay plan outlines the areas to be explored in the order they will appear. Authors may refer to the plan throughout the essay; in this way, it is used to orient the reader as he or she is conducted through the different stages of the essay's development.

An essay plan sounds like, and in effect is, an announcement, signalling where the writer intends to go. Since it announces where as much as what, it is rather like a map with directional arrows. Students may ask why essay plans can be used in academic essays but may not be acceptable in their own essays. The answer is simple: academic essays are longer and more complex than most undergraduate student essays; they have more parts. Announcing a plan in the introduction of an essay that will be only 1,000 to 1,500 words long is usually unnecessary.

Justification: Academic essays, unlike student essays, usually include a justification; in other words, the author will explicitly state or implicitly convey the reason for the study. While students generally write essays to become more proficient planners, researchers, and writers (as well as to satisfy a course requirement and receive a grade, of course), academic authors need to convince their peers that their essay is worth consideration. And although student writers should be clear about their purpose in writing before composing, academic writers usually need to go one step further and announce this purpose to justify it in light of how their work will contribute to the field of study. The justification answers questions like: Why was the study undertaken? Why is it important? What will it add to the field of study? How will it advance knowledge about the topic?

As mentioned earlier, academic essays are always written with a view toward what has been written; if an academic writer naively jumped right in and ignored previous studies, he or she would be dismissed as uninformed. In justifying the study, the writer is announcing why the investigation is necessary or beneficial. He or she also establishes credibility in appearing informed about what other scholars have written. The literature review, in turn, provides support for the justification.

ESSAY PLAN
form a thesis can take in which main points are outlined in the order they will occur in the essay.

JUSTIFICATION
announces reason for undertaking the study; may focus on what it will add to previous research or what gap in the research it will fill.

LITERATURE REVIEW
condensed survey of articles on the topic arranged in a logical order usually ending with the article most relevant to the author's study.

The term "literature" in this context does not refer to literary works but to the broader meaning of something written —it comes from the Latin *littera*, "letter"— so "literature review" refers to a focused survey of the related scholarship in the field of study.

HYPOTHESIS
prediction about an outcome; used in Type B (empirical) essays in which an experiment is set up to prove/disprove the prediction.

Literature Review (Review of the Literature): By reviewing related studies on the topic, the author demonstrates where his or her contribution fits in and how it furthers knowledge about the subject. Here, the writer summarizes the findings of scholars, often but not always in chronological order, and either ends with the most recent studies or those most closely related to the author's approach. Having a clear structure is vital because, typically, the literature review presents many studies concisely in a short space, perhaps only one or two paragraphs. Surveying what has been written underscores the interdependence between the current study and previous scholarly studies in the field, an interdependence at the heart of most academic writing.

All in all, academic writers must be concerned with presenting their credentials for the work they undertake; the justification and the literature review serve as a kind of badge of membership in the academic community.

Two essay plans from articles in *The Active Reader* are reproduced below, one in the sciences and the other in the humanities. In the first one, note that the justification for the study lies in the absence of such studies in Canada; therefore, no review of the literature is included. Academic writers often make it clear as part of their justification that the reason for undertaking the study is the neglect of scholars or their failure to investigate an area thoroughly.

> The epidemiological knowledge regarding heavy drinking in the US is longstanding, but the history of such studies in Canada is recent, sparse, and regionalized, and no study has been conducted nationally. This paper will describe the prevalence and frequency of heavy drinking among a nationally representative sample of Canadian undergraduates and assess the character of subgroup differences related to key demographic and campus lifestyle factors. (Gliksman et al. "Heavy drinking on Canadian campuses," p. 202)

> In this case study of Victoria, British Columbia, using records from the 1891 census and the 1901 census, I show how brothelkeepers and brothel prostitutes can be identified in manuscript census schedules, how the records might be used to construct a prosopographical profile of these sex-trade workers, and how the records can assist in mapping the geography of sexual commerce in a nineteenth-century city. In the process, I raise questions about the prima facie value of census records. (Dunae. "Sex, charades and census records: Locating female sex trade workers in a Victorian city," p. 341)

In the excerpt below, from the introduction of an article dealing with conduct codes in secondary schools, the author includes a thorough literature review. Because she uses a parenthetical citation style, novice readers may find the passage difficult to read. However, this difficulty can be overcome by making a conscious effort to read "between the parentheses," following the meaning of the text by ignoring the names and numbers mentioned in the sources. It takes some practice to learn to read this way because, in the literature review section, the information is often very compressed to make it as comprehensive as possible.

> Current literature on school rules focuses primarily on two areas: zero tolerance policies and uniforms. Zero tolerance policies delineate specific, inevitable consequences ranging from suspension to expulsion for a series of behaviours, including bringing a weapon to school. Uniforms and zero tolerance policies are often introduced in the interest of

violence prevention in the school (Casella, 2003; Sughrue, 2003; Day et al., 1995). For example, Shannon and McCall's (2003) overview of school codes of conduct and zero tolerance policies in Canada was created to assist schools in developing discipline policies to address violence. Zero tolerance policies have been introduced in Ontario and in a number of American schools with the argument that they increase school safety. Recent researchers and popular commentators have responded critically, however (Sughrue, 2003; Casella, 2003; Insley, 2001; Gabor, 1995), with particular emphasis on inappropriate and unfair applications to learning disabled and non-white students (Boyle, 2003; Keleher, 2000). (Rebecca Raby. 2005. "Polite, well-dressed and on time: Secondary school conduct codes and the production of docile citizens." *Canadian Review of Sociology 42*.)

Chapter 3

Three Common Kinds of Academic Essays

Although academic writing shares many characteristics, most academic essays can be divided into one of three categories. You can think of them as Type A (for "*arts*," often referred to as the humanities), Type B (for "*biology*," an example of a discipline within the natural sciences), and Type C (for "*critical review*"). Since formats and other conventions vary among these different kinds of essays, being able to identify their type will enable you to access information more efficiently.

Type A

Type A is common in the arts/humanities disciplines and in other disciplines in which an author's methodology is not one of direct experimentation. Type A essays use a *qualitative* methodology, often concerned with ideas, values, or theories, rather than with data that can be measured and quantified. Typically, Type A essays include a thesis, an essay plan, or questions that the writer will attempt to answer. Descriptive headings may be used to summarize section content. See "Characteristics of Type A, Type B, and Type C Essays" in Appendix B, and the excerpt from a Type A essay, p. 26, for more details.

Authors of Type A essays use a qualitative methodology, concerned with the interpretation of ideas, values, or theories, which they may apply to specific primary sources.

Type B

In Type B essays, the writer's research design involves an experiment or some other empirical process through which primary sources, such as raw data, are generated. If the researcher analyzes data that already exist in order to address a problem or answer a question, the writer might also use a Type B format. Research of this kind is sometimes called original research to distinguish it from the kind of research that depends heavily on underlying theories and perspectives.

In addition to using quantitative methods, these essays also use standardized divisions (indicated by formal headings). These divisions, in effect, replicate the chronological stages of the experiment, beginning with "introduction," followed by "methods" (or "materials"), "results," and "discussion" and/or "conclusion." The divisions may then be subdivided. For example, "methods"/"materials" may be divided into "subjects,"

Authors of Type B essays use quantitative data, often generated through an experiment, to prove a hypothesis or answer a question.

"participants," "measures," "procedures," "statistical analyses used," and so on. Other sections, too, may be divided into formal or descriptive categories with corresponding subheadings. See "Characteristics of Type A, Type B, and Type C Essays" in Appendix B, and the sample Type B essay, p. 28, for more details.

Type B Subgenre: Qualitative Methodologies

An increasing number of essays use conventional Type B formats while employing qualitative methods to gather and analyze raw data—for example, unstructured interviews, focus groups, and forums. As contrasted with the sometimes artificial setting of the psychology "lab," qualitative methods enable the researcher to examine human motivations and interactions within a range of naturally occurring contexts. For example, Furgal and Seguin analyze the results of community-based dialogue to assess northern communities' vulnerability to health issues caused by climate change (p. 468). The authors of "An exploratory study of cyberbullying with undergraduate university students" (p. 181) discuss their qualitative results along with the quantitative ones.

In spite of the advantages of qualitative studies, data generated through these methods are usually harder to generalize to larger populations than data generated through quantitative methods. In addition, data analysis requires careful and skilled interpretation to avoid researcher bias. In their discussion section, researchers who use qualitative methods may suggest the need for quantitative studies to help validate their findings.

Type C

Authors of Type C essays synthesize and critically evaluate published studies to reveal the progress toward solving a problem.

Common in the social sciences—especially psychology—and in the sciences, Type C essays synthesize and critically evaluate previously published studies. Type C essays reveal the progress toward solving a problem; they may also draw attention to inconsistencies or gaps in the research. In this sense, they look back to see how far social scientists have come and look ahead to future directions for research. Review essays may be occasioned by a specific phenomenon, such as the prevalence of online gaming among adolescents (see p. 382), or a significant social concern, such as "Enhancing democratic citizenship," p. 262. In their formats, Type C essays resemble Type A essays with a thesis/essay plan and content divisions. See "Characteristics of Type A, Type B, and Type C Essays" in Appendix B, and the sample Type C essay, p. 31, for more details.

Type C Subgenre: Meta-analyses

In a meta-analysis, the findings of empirical research are combined to yield quantitative data, which is then analyzed with goals similar to those of other review essays. The following excerpt from the introduction of a review explains why the study was necessary (i.e., its justification) and the way that meta-analysis uses previous studies, such as qualitative ones, to provide quantitative answers to a problem:

> A number of literature reviews conclude that salmonid abundance typically increases following restoration. . . . However, traditional literature reviews, while qualitatively describing the results of many individual case studies, do not allow statistical testing of

overall trends (Roberts et al. 2006). Meta-analysis overcomes this problem by allowing the formal combination of results from a large number of case studies (Gates 2002). (Whiteway et al. 2010. "Do in-stream restoration structures enhance salmonid abundance? A meta-analysis." *Canadian Journal of Fisheries Aquatic Science, 67*: 831–41.)

Although not all academic essays conform precisely to the characteristics outlined here and in Appendix B, the vast majority do conform in most respects to either Type A, Type B, or Type C. Works published in books generally follow the formats of Type A or Type C, whereas experimental results (Type B) typically appear in journals. As well as much scientific writing, several kinds of public writing, such as case studies, proposals, and business and other kinds of formal reports commonly use the methodology and structure of Type B essays.

Argumentative essays, such as editorials and commentaries, are discussed in Chapter 8.

Tables, Graphs, and Other Visuals

A **table** presents detailed information in matrix format, in columns and rows that are easily scanned. **Graphs** represent relationships between two variables. *Line graphs* show a relationship over time while *bar graphs* show values or trends within the data.

Writers may use tables, graphs, and charts (the last two are often represented by the abbreviation "Fig.," for "Figure") to present their raw data. They are especially common in the "results" section of Type B essays where their primary function is to concisely summarize the quantitative results of the experiment. Writers may explain the most significant results in the text of the essay, reserving detail for the table to which the reader will be directed in the explanatory text.

Type C (review) essays may also present data through tables, graphs, and charts. The information in the table or graph may be taken from one of the studies analyzed in the essay; sometimes (see, for example, Godfray et al., p. 482), the authors use aggregate data from several sources to summarize key information.

> TABLES
> present detailed information in matrix format, in columns and rows that are easily scanned.
>
> GRAPHS
> represent relationships between two variables.

Reading Tables and Graphs

- Read the text material first. This way you will understand specific terms and/or abbreviations used in the table/figure.
- If there is a heading, read it carefully; headings are sometimes given above the figure and explanatory material below it. At other times, the information is all in one place, and the first sentence summarizes the table's/figure's purpose, the following sentence(s) giving further explanation.
- If the table/figure is particularly detailed or complex, reread the relevant section(s) in the text. Text material will often direct you to specific parts of the table/figure deemed most significant by the author(s).
- Read labels carefully, but don't be distracted by superscript numbers, letters, or symbols, which often refer to statistical significance of specific items.

For use of graphs in student reports, see "How to Write a Scientific Paper," p. 92.

Academic Essay Formats and Student Assignments

In your career as a student, you will be asked to write essays and reports that conform to one or another of the essay types discussed. For example, you may be asked to write a lab report as a result of a specific experiment you performed in order to satisfy a course learning objective in a science or social science discipline. Such empirically based reports resemble the Type B academic essay. For information on how to write reports, see "The Active Voice: Report Writing," p. 91; for information on how to write a scientific paper, see "The Active Voice: How to Write a Scientific Paper," p. 92.

Inevitably, you will write essays in several of your classes in which you generate a position about a literary text, historical event, or philosophical system and defend that position, citing from primary sources; the classic/traditional essay format, as it has been taught for many years in university, resembles the Type A academic essay format.

However, the use of research, synthesis, summarizing, and critical evaluation makes the student research essay much like the Type C essay. Students in a humanities discipline such as English literature may be asked to write a critical review, in which case they might critically evaluate significant studies on an author's work—for example, one of Shakespeare's plays, dividing the studies in a logical way, such as by chronology or critical approach.

The following samples demonstrate key features of the types of essays discussed in this chapter.

Type A

The introduction of the essay on p. 307 is excerpted here in order to illustrate some of the conventions of Type A essays.

Type A essays often have a two-part title that includes key words from the essay. The phrase "the new man" recurs throughout the essay and is the title of a major section.

Humanities essays may begin with a brief narrative, such as an anecdote or, occasionally, a personal experience that introduces the subject. Another common pattern is to begin by referring to a key study. The author may then expand on, qualify, or disagree with this study.

At the end of the second paragraph, the authors concisely state the result of their investigation. Although the statement applies to the entire essay, the thesis occurs later in the introduction in the form of an essay plan.

Excerpt from "Post-Princess Models of Gender: The New Man in Disney/Pixar"

1   Lisping over the Steve McQueen allusion in Pixar's *Cars* (2006), our two-year-old son, Oscar, inadvertently directed us to the definition(s) of masculinity that might be embedded in a children's animated film about NASCAR. The film overtly praises the "good woman" proverbially behind every successful man: the champion car, voiced by Richard Petty, tells his wife, "I wouldn't be nothin' without you, honey." But gender in this twenty first-century bildungsroman is rather more complex, and Oscar's mispronunciation held the first clue. To him, a member of the film's target audience, the character closing in on the title long held by "The King" is not "Lightning McQueen" but "Lightning the queen"; his chief rival, the always-a-bridesmaid runner-up "Chick" Hicks.

2   Does this nominal feminizing of male also-rans (and the simultaneous gendering of success) constitute a meaningful pattern? Piqued, we began examining the construction of masculinity in major feature films released by Disney's Pixar studios over the past thirteen years. Indeed, as we argue here, Pixar consistently promotes a new model of masculinity, one that matures into acceptance of its more traditionally "feminine" aspects.

3   Cultural critics have long been interested in Disney's cinematic products, but the gender critics examining the texts most enthusiastically gobbled up by the under-six set have so far generally focused on their retrograde representations of women. As Elizabeth Bell argues, the animated Disney features through *Beauty and the Beast* feature a "teenaged heroine at the idealized height of puberty's graceful promenade, [f]emale wickedness . . . rendered as middle-aged beauty at its peak of sexuality and authority [and] [f]eminine sacrifice and nurturing . . . drawn in pear-shaped, old women past menopause" (108). Some have noted the models of masculinity in the classic animated films, primarily the contrast between the ubermacho Gaston and the sensitive, misunderstood Beast in *Beauty and the Beast*,[1] but the male protagonist of the animated classics, at least through *The Little Mermaid*, remains largely uninterrogated.[2] For most of the early films, this critical omission seems generally appropriate, the various versions of Prince Charming being often too two-dimensional to do more than inadvertently shape the definition of the protagonists' femininity. But if the feminist thought that has shaped our cultural texts for three decades now has been somewhat disappointing in its ability to actually rewrite the princess trope (the spunkiest of the "princesses," Ariel, Belle, Jasmine, and, arguably, even *Mulan*, remain thin, beautiful, kind, obedient or punished for disobedience, and headed for the altar), it has been surprisingly effective in rewriting the type of masculine power promoted by Disney's products.[3]

4   Disney's new face, Pixar studios, has released nine films—*Toy Story* (1995) and *Toy Story 2* (1999); *A Bug's Life* (1998); *Finding Nemo* (2003); *Monsters, Inc.* (2001); *The Incredibles* (2004); *Cars* (2006); *Ratatouille* (2007); and now *WALL•E* (2008)—all of which feature interesting male figures in leading positions. Unlike many of the princesses, who remain relatively static even through their own adventures, these male leads are actual protagonists; their characters develop and change over the course of the film, rendering the plot. Ultimately these various developing characters particularly Buzz and Woody from *Toy Story*, Mr. Incredible from *The Incredibles*, and Lightning McQueen from *Cars*—experience a common narrative trajectory, culminating in a common "New Man" model[4]: they all strive for an alpha-male identity; they face emasculating failures; they find themselves, in large part, through what Eve Sedgwick refers to as "homosocial desire" and a triangulation of this desire with a feminized object (and/or a set of "feminine" values); and, finally, they achieve (and teach) a kinder, gentler understanding of what it means to be a man.

Type A essays do not always include a thorough review of the literature. In this paragraph, only one critic is mentioned; however, several more are referred to in the notes (see p. 314).

The justification of this study is the absence of critical studies focusing on male protagonists in Disney films. The rest of this paragraph elaborates on this statement, explaining the reason for the gap. Like many essays in the humanities, the Modern Language Association (MLA) documentation method is used to cite sources. MLA encourages the use of notes in cases where excess detail could interfere with the essay's flow or distract from the topic. Notes 1 and 2 refer to other studies related to the points raised here. (See p. 156 for common MLA formats.)

This lengthy, but understandable, sentence illustrates several stylistic features of humanities writing. For example, the sentence is balanced by repeated verb phrases (has been . . . has been; to rewrite . . . in rewriting). It includes an example of jargon, "trope," and a parenthetical independent clause made memorable by the balanced descriptive words and phrases: "thin, beautiful, kind, obedient or punished for disobedience, and headed for the altar." It is a rhetorically effective sentence that is not difficult to follow in spite of its length and complexity.

The three-part essay plan begins here. The order of points is repeated in the section headings (see pp. 309–312).

At the end of their introduction, the authors refer to gender studies critic Eve Sedgwick. Type A essays often draw on theory. The terms mentioned here are amplified in the section "Homosociality, Intimacy, and Emotion," p. 311.

Type B

A short example of a Type B essay, illustrating some of the conventions of this kind of essay.

As is often the case in Type B essays, the two-part title includes the result of the study (following the colon). The first part of the title identifies the area studied. Unlike most Type B essays, there is no abstract. As this article appeared as a "Short Report" in the journal, its editors may have felt that an abstract was unnecessary.

The literature review is a major focus in the introductions of most Type B essays. Here it begins in the first sentence and continues for much of the introduction.

Typically, the last study mentioned by the authors in the literature review is the one most relevant to their own research. Note: In the American Psychological Association (APA) documentation method, a study with three or more authors can be shortened in subsequent references by adding "et al." after the first author's name. The Pickett et al. study was cited in paragraph 1 with all authors' names. (See p. 156 for common APA formats.)

In this sentence, the dependent clause summarizes the results of an important study while the independent clause suggests a gap in the research. The complete sentence justifies the need for the current study.

The hypothesis (prediction) occurs at the end of the introduction in most Type B essays. It arises out of previous research and the attempt to extend or refine the results of earlier studies in order to explain a phenomenon or solve a problem.

Adaptive Responses to Social Exclusion: Social Rejection Improves Detection of Real and Fake Smiles

Michael J. Bernstein, Steven G. Young, Christina M. Brown, Donald F. Sacco, and Heather M. Claypool

1   Being excluded from social relationships poses numerous immediate and long-term threats (e.g., Baumeister & Leary, 1995). Consequently, it is not surprising that people are sensitive to cues that indicate potential rejection (Pickett & Gardner, 2005). For example, individuals who are dispositionally high in need to belong are better than others at identifying facial expressions and vocal tones (Pickett, Gardner, & Knowles, 2004), and ostracized participants have better memory for socially relevant information than do nonostracized participants (Gardner, Pickett, & Brewer, 2000). In both cases, individuals either fearing rejection or suffering actual rejection show increased attention to social cues.

2   Facial expressions of emotion can act as such social cues. A Duchenne smile, for example, involves the automatic activation of two facial muscles in response to the experience of pleasure and is generally considered a "true" smile (Ekman, Davidson, & Friesen, 1990), indicative of cooperation and affiliation (Brown & Moore, 2002). In contrast, non-Duchenne, or "masking," smiles can conceal the experience of negative emotions (Ekman, Friesen, & O'Sullivan, 1988). Knowing whether a facial expression is conveying an honest affiliation signal should help rejected individuals identify targets who are likely to offer the greatest opportunity for reconnection.

3   Although research has shown that individuals with greater belongingness needs (Pickett et al., 2004) are more accurate at discriminating among true, diagnostic facial-expression signals (e.g., discriminating between expressions of anger and happiness), no research has examined the extent to which rejected individuals are able to determine whether the expression being identified is genuine in the first place. Although being able to identify the qualitative emotional category of a facial display is of value to socially excluded individuals, distinguishing real from fake emotions seems especially important to ensure that reaffiliation efforts are maximally distributed toward people displaying genuine affiliative cues. Indeed, directing resources toward an individual faking an affiliative display would likely be a costly error for socially rejected individuals, who already find themselves in a perilous situation. Accordingly, we hypothesized that rejected individuals would show an enhanced ability to discriminate between real and fake smiles, presumably because they are more attuned than others to subtle social cues, including those present in Duchenne smiles (involuntary signals of cooperation) as opposed to non-Duchenne smiles (controllable and unreliable indicators of cooperation).

Method

4   Participants were randomly assigned to social-inclusion, social-exclusion, or control conditions. They were then shown faces exhibiting Duchenne or non-Duchenne smiles and were asked to decide whether each was "real" or "fake."

Participants

5   Thirty-two undergraduates (17 females, 15 males) participated in the study for course credit.

Materials

6   The facial stimuli were located on the BBC Science & Nature Web site (BBC, n.d.).[1] Respondents were asked to watch 20 color videos (approximately 4 s each) one at a time. Each depicted an individual who had an initially neutral expression and then smiled before returning to a neutral expression. Which faces exhibited real/fake smiles remained constant for all participants. Thus, there were 20 faces, 10 of which were always exhibiting real smiles and 10 of which were always exhibiting fake smiles. Thirteen men and seven women were depicted in the videos.[2]

Procedure

7   Participants were informed that they were to perform two ostensibly unrelated tasks concerning memory and face perception. The first was an essay task that constituted the manipulation of social status. Participants, having been randomly assigned, wrote about a time they felt "rejected or excluded," a time they felt "accepted or included," or their morning the day before the study (control condition). This manipulation has been used previously with success (e.g., Gardner et al., 2000). As a manipulation check, participants responded to a scale assessing the degree to which they felt a threat to their sense of belonging, a common measure used to confirm the effectiveness of rejection manipulations (Williams, Cheung, & Choi, 2000).

8   Finally, participants watched each video and indicated, on a response sheet next to the computer, whether the smile was "genuine" or "fake." Upon completion of this task, participants responded to demographic questions before being probed for suspicion, thanked, and debriefed.

Results

Manipulation Check

9   To examine whether the manipulation of social rejection was successful, we conducted a one-way between-subjects analysis of variance (ANOVA) on the belongingness measure.

10   Results indicated that the manipulation had the intended effect (prep > .99); rejected participants experienced a greater threat to their sense of belonging.

Discrimination Scores

11   We calculated d0, a signal detection measure examining the ability to discriminate stimuli—in this case, the ability to discriminate Duchenne smiles from non-Duchenne smiles. This measure simultaneously considers hits (correctly identifying a Duchenne smile as genuine) and false alarms (incorrectly identifying a non-Duchenne smile as genuine) in the calculation. The one-way *ANOVA* on these scores was significant, F(2, 29) 5 5.63, prep 5 .97; compared with control participants (M51.05, SD50.56) and included participants (M51.34, SD 5 0.56), rejected participants (M 51.88, SD5 0.62) exhibited greater discriminability, t(29) 5 3.33, prep 5 .98, d 5 1.35, and t(29) 5 2.12, prep 5 .92, d 5 0.87, respectively. Discrimination ability did not differ between included and control participants (p > .25; see Fig. 1).

12   There was no effect of target or participant sex. Thus, these variables are not discussed further.

---

1   The faces were pretested for equivalency of attractiveness and positivity. Ratings of neutral expressions of targets showing Duchenne smiles versus neutral expressions of targets showing non-Duchenne smiles revealed no differences (p > .2).

2   The stimuli included three minority-group individuals. Removing data for these targets from analyses did not change any findings.

The "Method" section is divided into three short subsections, "Participants" (*who* took part), "Materials," (*what* was used), and "Procedure," (*how* the experiment was done). The precise detail is needed so that future researchers can replicate the study or build on it by varying the research methods.

The citation underscores the reliance of researchers on prior studies. By utilizing an established procedure, the authors add to their credibility.

The result of the manipulation check confirms that the manipulation worked as it was designed to do. If it had failed to confirm the validity of the social status manipulation, the researchers would probably have had to redesign their experiment. The check, then, acted as a backup, confirming the validity of the methodology.

Researchers often present their data by referring to complex statistical methods, and the "Results" section may be written by a specialist in statistics. Non-specialists, including students, can learn to read such sections carefully to extract the most important information while ignoring unneeded detail. The key finding, which is discussed more fully in the next section, is highlighted here. For more information about statistics, see Appendix A, "A Note on Statistics" p. 497.

Most Type B essays are accompanied by tables, graphs, or charts that summarize the study's results. In this case, a bar graph shows the relationship between social status and the ability to tell fake from genuine smiles. Note the clear labelling of both axes and the brief explanation below the graphic.

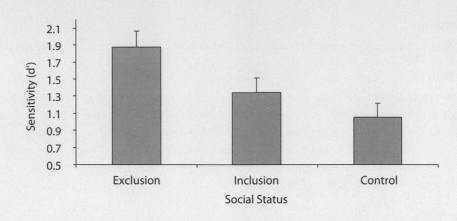

FIGURE 1 MEAN ABILITY TO DISCRIMINATE (SENSITIVITY, D') DUCHENNE AND NON-DUCHENNE SMILES AS A FUNCTION OF SOCIAL-STATUS CONDITION. ERROR BARS INDICATE STANDARD ERRORS.

Discussion

In the first sentence, the authors indicate that the hypothesis was proven. The next sentence discusses the significance of the results.

13 We found that socially rejected individuals have enhanced ability to determine whether the "happy" facial expression of a target individual is genuine (a true indication of an affiliative opportunity) or deceptive (feigning the appearance of positive affect). This suggests that motivation to reaffiliate increases rejected individuals' sensitivity to other social cues indicating belongingness opportunities—specifically, facial displays that are honest signals of cooperation and affiliation.

14 Although the results of the current study are congruent with some of the rejection literature showing reaffiliative responses to social exclusion (Lakin & Chartrand, 2005; Maner, DeWall, Baumeister, & Schaller, 2007), these results are among the first to show that rejection can lead to increases in performance at a perceptual level, provided that the performance supports opportunities for affiliation. Once rejected, people are left with a strong desire to be accepted, which leads them toward interaction partners with whom they might affiliate. Therefore, it seems essential to detect legitimate signs of positivity that indicate possible reaffiliation with other people. Otherwise, rejected individuals could miss out on new chances for acceptance or "waste" affiliation efforts on people who are not receptive.

After discussing the significance of the findings in the larger, "real world" context, the authors suggest areas for future research, in effect extending an invitation to others to build on their conclusions. Researchers often discuss possible limitations of their study in the "Discussion" section. Bernstein et al. do not do so, possibly because of the study's brevity.

Future research should examine whether other faked emotions can be differentiated from true emotions, as well as how these perceptual skills may guide subsequent behavioral choices.

References

Baumeister, R.F., & Leary, M.R. (1995). The need to belong: Desire for interpersonal attachments as a fundamental human motivation. *Psychological Bulletin*, 117, 497–529.

BBC. (n.d.). Spot the fake smile. Retrieved October 1, 2007, from http://www.bbc.co.uk/science/humanbody/mind/surveys/smiles

Brown, W.M., & Moore, C. (2002). Smile asymmetries and reputation as reliable indicators of likelihood to cooperate: An evolutionary analysis. In. S.P. Shohov (Ed.). *Advances in psychology research* (Vol. 11, pp. 59–78). Huntington, NY: Nova Science Publishers.

Ekman, P., Davidson, R.J., & Friesen, W.V. (1990). The Duchenne smile: Emotional expression and brain physiology II. *Journal of Personality and Social Psychology 58*, 342–353.

Ekman, P., Friesen, W.V., & O'Sullivan, M. (1988). Smiles when lying. *Journal of Personality and Social Psychology, 54*, 414–420.

Gardner, W.L., Pickett, C.L., & Brewer, M.B. (2000). Social exclusion and selective memory: How the need to belong influences memory for social events. *Personality and Social Psychology Bulletin, 26*, 486–496.

Lakin, J.L., & Chartrand, T.L. (2005). Exclusion and nonconscious behavioral mimicry. In K.D. Williams, J.P. Forgas, & W. von Hippel (Eds.), *The social outcast: Ostracism, social exclusion, rejection, and bullying* (pp. 279–296). New York: Psychology Press.

Maner, J.K., DeWall, C.N., Baumeister, R.F., & Schaller, M. (2007). Does social exclusion motivate interpersonal reconnection? Resolving the "porcupine problem." *Journal of Personality and Social Psychology, 92*, 42–55.

Pickett, C.L., & Gardner, W.L. (2005). The social monitoring system: Enhanced sensitivity to social cues and information as an adaptive response to social exclusion and belonging need. In K.D. Williams, J.P. Forgas, & W. von Hippel (Eds.), *The social outcast: Ostracism, social exclusion, rejection, and bullying* (pp. 213–226). New York: Psychology Press.

Pickett, C.L., Gardner, W.L., & Knowles, M. (2004). Getting a cue: The need to belong and enhanced sensitivity to social cues. *Personality and Social Psychology Bulletin, 30*, 1095–1107.

Williams, K.D., Cheung, C.K.T., & Choi, W. (2000). Cyberostracism: Effects of being ignored over the Internet. *Journal of Personality and Social Psychology, 79*, 748–762.

Type C

A short example of a Type C essay.

Why Ordinary People Torture Enemy Prisoners

by Susan T. Fiske, Lasana T. Harris and Amy J. C. Cuddy

1   As official investigations and courts-martial continue, we are all taking stock of the events at Abu Ghraib last year. Initial reactions were shock and disgust. How could Americans be doing this to anyone, even Iraqi prisoners of war? Some observers immediately blamed "the few bad apples" presumably responsible for the abuse. However, many social psychologists knew that it was not that simple. Society holds individuals responsible for their actions, as the military court-martial recognizes, but social psychology suggests we should also hold responsible peers and superiors who control the social context.

2   Social psychological evidence emphasizes the power of social context; in other words, the power of the interpersonal situation. Social psychology has accumulated a century of knowledge about how people influence each other for good or ill [1]. Meta-analysis, the quantitative summary of findings across a variety of studies, reveals the size and consistency of such empirical results. Recent meta-analyses document reliable experimental evidence of social context effects across 25,000 studies of 8 million participants [2]. Abu Ghraib resulted in part from ordinary social processes, not just extraordinary individual evil. This Policy Forum cites meta-analyses to describe how the right (or wrong) social context can make almost anyone aggress, oppress, conform, and obey.

3   Virtually anyone can be aggressive if sufficiently provoked, stressed, disgruntled, or hot [3–6]. The situation of the 800th Military Police Brigade guarding Abu Ghraib prisoners fit all the social conditions known to cause aggression. The soldiers were certainly provoked and stressed: at war, in constant danger, taunted and harassed by some of the very citizens they were sent to save, and their comrades were dying daily and unpredictably. Their morale suffered, they were untrained for the job, their

Titles of Type C essays are often shorter than those of other types, containing a statement of the problem under investigation.

The authors of this study introduce the problem in the first paragraph, understanding the behaviour of American troops at an Iraqi prison. In the next paragraph, they explain how social psychology can help us understand the complexities of the factors involved.

The paragraph begins by briefly outlining the study's methodology and concludes with the simple thesis.

The review is divided into four categories or sub-topics. Typically, categories in Type C essays include content headings; however, because three of the categories are only one paragraph long, the authors probably thought headings were unnecessary.

The Council of Science Editors (CSE) documentation method, used here, consists of numbers in the text, which correspond to a list of sources at the end of the essay arranged by their order in the text. The CSE method allows several sources to be cited in one reference. (See p. 157 for common CSE formats.)

The category or sub-topic of outgroups is analyzed in this and the following two paragraphs.

Review essays contain a large number of concise summaries.

command climate was lax, their return home was a year overdue, their identity as disciplined soldiers was gone, and their own amenities were scant [7]. Heat and discomfort also doubtless contributed.

4   The fact that the prisoners were part of a group encountered as enemies would only exaggerate the tendency to feel spontaneous prejudice against outgroups. In this context, oppression and discrimination are synonymous. One of the most basic principles of social psychology is that people prefer their own group [8] and attribute bad behavior to outgroups [9]. Prejudice especially festers if people see the outgroup as threatening cherished values [10–12]. This would have certainly applied to the guards viewing their prisoners at Abu Ghraib, but it also applies in more "normal" situations. A recent sample of U.S. citizens on average viewed Muslims and Arabs as not sharing their interests and stereotyped them as not especially sincere, honest, friendly, or warm [13–15].

5   Even more potent predictors of discrimination are the emotional prejudices ("hot" affective feelings such as disgust or contempt) that operate in parallel with cognitive processes [16–18]. Such emotional reactions appear rapidly, even in neuroimaging of brain activations to outgroups [19,20]. But even they can be affected by social context. Categorization of people as interchangeable members of an outgroup promotes an amygdala response characteristic of vigilance and alarm and an insula response characteristic of disgust or arousal, depending on social context; these effects dissipate when the same people are encountered as unique individuals [21,22].

6   According to our survey data [13,14], the contemptible, disgusting kind of outgroup—low-status opponents—elicits a mix of active and passive harm: attacking and fighting, as well as excluding and demeaning. This certainly describes the Abu Ghraib abuse of captured enemies. It also fits our national sample of Americans [14] who reported that allegedly contemptible outgroups such as homeless people, welfare recipients, Turks, and Arabs often are attacked or excluded [14].

In this paragraph, the authors introduce two important research areas to help explain the prevalence of prisoner mistreatment. The first, "conformity to peers," is analyzed in this paragraph; the second, "obedience to authority," is discussed in the following one. Clear organization is vital in Type C essays.

7   Given an environment conducive to aggression and prisoners deemed disgusting and subhuman [23], well-established principles of conformity to peers [24,25] and obedience to authority [26] may account for the widespread nature of the abuse. In combat, conformity to one's unit means survival, and ostracism is death. The social context apparently reflected the phenomenon of people trying to make sense of a complex, confusing, ambiguous situation by relying on their immediate social group [27]. People rioted at St. Paul's Church, Bristol UK, in 1980, for example, in conformity to events they saw occurring in their immediate proximity [28]. Guards abuse prisoners in conformity with what other guards do, in order to fulfill a potent role; this is illustrated by the Stanford Prison Study, in which ordinary college students, randomly assigned to be full-time guards and prisoners in a temporary prison, nevertheless behaved respectively as abusers and victims [29]. Social psychology shows that, whatever their own good or bad choices, most people believe that others would do whatever they personally chose to do, a phenomenon termed false consensus [30,31]. Conformity to the perceived reactions of one's peers can be defined as good or bad, depending on how well the local norms fit those of larger society.

Compare and contrast, a common pattern of development in Type C essays, is used in this paragraph.

8   As every graduate of introductory psychology should know from the Milgram studies [32], ordinary people can engage in incredibly destructive behavior if so ordered by legitimate authority. In those studies, participants acting as teachers frequently followed an experimenter's orders to punish a supposed learner (actually a confederate) with electric shock, all the way to administering lethal levels. Obedience to authority sustains every culture [33]. Firefighters heroically rushing into the flaming World Trade Center were partly obeying their superiors, partly conforming to extraordinary group loyalty, and partly showing incredibly brave self-sacrifice. But obedience and conformity also motivated the terrorist hijackers and the Abu Ghraib guards, however much one might abhor their (vastly different) actions. Social conformity and obedience themselves are neutral, but their consequences can be heroic or evil. Torture is partly a crime of socialized obedience [34]. Subordinates not only do what they are ordered to do, but what they think their superiors would order them to do, given their understanding of the authority's overall goals. For example, lynching represented ordinary people going beyond the law to enact their view of the community's will.

9   Social influence starts with small, apparently trivial actions (in this case, insulting epithets), followed by more serious actions (humiliation and abuse) [35–37], as novices overcome their hesitancy and learn by doing [38]. The actions are always intentional, although the perpetrator may not be aware that those actions constitute evil. In fact, perpetrators may see themselves as doing a great service by punishing and or eliminating a group that they perceive as deserving ill treatment [39].

10   In short, ordinary individuals under the influence of complex social forces may commit evil acts [40]. Such actions are human behaviors that can and should be studied scientifically [41,42]. We need ◄— to understand more about the contexts that will promote aggression. We also need to understand the basis for exceptions—why, in the face of these social contexts, not all individuals succumb [43]. Thus, although lay-observers may believe that explaining evil amounts to excusing it and absolving people of responsibility for their actions [44], in fact, explaining evils such as Abu Ghraib demonstrates scientific principles that could help to avert them.

> The focus of this paragraph is on research needed in specific areas. Identifying gaps in the literature is a common feature of Type C essay conclusions.

11   Even one dissenting peer can undermine conformity [24]. For example, whistle-blowers not only ◄— alert the authorities but also prevent their peers from continuing in unethical behavior. Authorities can restructure situations to allow communication. For example, *CEO*s can either welcome or discourage a diversity of opinions. Contexts can undermine prejudice [1]. Individual, extended, equal-status, constructive, cooperative contact between mutual outgroups (whether American blacks and whites in the military or American soldiers and Iraqi civilians) can improve mutual respect and even liking. It would be harder to dehumanize and abuse imprisoned Iraqis if one had friends among ordinary Iraqis. A difficult objective in wartime, but as some Iraqis work alongside their American counterparts, future abuse is less likely. The slippery slope to abuse can be avoided. The same social contexts that provoke and permit abuse can be harnessed to prevent it. To quote another report [(45), p. 94]: "All personnel who may be engaged in detention operations, from point of capture to final disposition, should participate in a professional ethics program that would equip them with a sharp moral compass for guidance in situations often riven with conflicting moral obligations."

> Type C essays usually have a clear practical focus on the progress of research in clarifying and solving a problem. Authors may address possible research applications at the end of specific sections or at the end of the essay, as Fiske et al. do here.

References and Notes

> Typically, Type C essays include more sources than other types, as the purpose is to critically analyze all studies in the field in order to fully show how researchers have investigated a problem.

1. S. T. Fiske, Social Beings (Wiley, New York, 2004).
2. F. D. Richard, C. F. Bond, J. J. Stokes-Zoota, Rev. Gen. Psychol. 7, 331 (2003).
3. B. A. Bettencourt, N. Miller, Psychol. Bull. 119, 422 (1996).
4. M. Carlson, N. Miller, Sociol. Soc. Res. 72, 155 (1988).
5. M. Carlson, A. Marcus-Newhall, N. Miller, Pers. Soc. Psychol. Bull. 15, 377 (1989).
6. C.A. Anderson, B. J. Bushman, Rev. Gen. Psychol. 1, 19 (1997).
7. A. Taguba, "Article 15-6. Investigation of the 800th Military Police Brigade," accessed 30 June 2004 from www.npr.org/iraq/2004/prison%5fabuse%5freport.pdf
8. B. Mullen, R. Brown, C. Smith, fur. J. Soc. Psychol. 22, 103(1992).
9. B. Mullen, C. Johnson, Br. J. Soc. Psychol. 29, 11 (1990).
10. J. Duckitt, in Advances in Experimental Social Psychology, M. P. Zanna, Ed. (Academic Press, New York. 2001).
11. When their own mortality is salient, as in wartime, people particularly punish those from outgroups seen to threaten basic values (12).
12. S. Solomon, J. Creenberg, T. Pyszczynski, Curr. Dir. Psychol. Sci. 9. 200 (2000).
13. S. T. Fiske, A. J. Cuddy, P. Click, J. Xu, J. Person. Soc. Psychol. 82. 878 (2002).
14. A. J. Cuddy, S. T. Fiske, P. Click, "The BIAS map: Behaviors from intergroup affect and stereotypes," unpublished manuscript (Princeton University, Princeton, NJ, 2004).
15. L J. Heller, thesis. Princeton University, 2002.
16. H. Schütz, B. Six, Int. J. Intercuit. Relat. 20, 441 (1996).
17. J. F. Dovidio et al., in Stereotypes and Stereotyping, C. N. Macrae, C. Stangor, M. Hewstone, Ed. (Guilford, New York, 1996).

18. C. A. Talaska, S. T. Fiske, S. Chaiken, "Predicting discrimination: A meta-analysis of the racial attitudes — behavior literature," unpublished manuscript (Princeton University, Princeton, NJ, 2004).

19. A. J. Hart et al., Neuroreport 11, 2351 (2000).

20. E. A. Phelps et al., J. Cogn. Neurosci. 12, 729 (2000).

21. Neuroimaging data represent college student reactions to photographs of outgroup members. These data should not be interpreted to mean that such reactions are innate or "wired in"; they result from long-term social context [9] and vary depending on short-term social context [46].

22. M. E. Wheeler. S.T. Fiske, Psychol. Sci., in press.

23. J. P. Leyens et at., Eur. J, Soc. Psychol. 33, 703 (2003).

24. R. Bond, P. B. Smith, Psychol. Bull. 119, 111 (1996).

25. S. Tanford, S. Penrod, Psychol. Bull. 95, 189 (1984).

26. J. Tata et al., J. Soc. Behav. Pers. 11, 739 (1996).

27. J. C. Turner, Social Influence (Brooks/Cole, Pacific Grove, CA, 1991).

28. S. D. Reicher, Eur. J. Soc. Psychol. 14, 1 (1984).

29. C. Haney. C. Banks, P. Zimbardo, Int. J. Criminol. Penol. 1, 69(1973).

30. B. Mullen et at., J. Exp. Soc. Psychol. 21, 262 (1985).

31. B. Mullen, L. Hu, Br. J. Soc. Psychol. 27, 333 (1988).

32. S. Milgram, Obedience to Authority (Harper & Row, New York, 1974).

33. T. Blass, J. Appl. Soc. Psychol. 29, 955 (1999).

34. H. C. Kelman, in The Politics of Pain: Torturers and Their Masters, R. D. Crelinsten, A. P. Schmidt, Eds. (Univ. of Leiden, Leiden, NL, 1991).

35. A. L. Beaman et al., Pers. Soc. Psychol. Bull. 9, 181 (1983).

36. A. L. Dillard, J. E. Hunter, M. Burgoon, Hum. Commun. Res. 10, 461 (1984).

37. E. F. Fern, K. B. Monroe, R.A. Avila, J. Mark. Res. 23, 144 (1986).

38. E. Staub, Pers. Soc. Psychol. Rev. 3, 179 (1999).

39. A. Bandura, Pers. Soc. Psychol. Rev. 3, 193 (1999).

40. L. Berkowitz, Pers. Soc. Psychol. Rev. 3, 246 (1999).

41. J. M. Darley. Pers. Soc. Psychol. Rev. 3, 269 (1999).

42. A. G. Miller, Ed., The Social Psychology of Good and Evil (Guilford, New York, 2004).

43. Although social context matters more than most people think, individual personality also matters, in accord with most people's intuitions: Social Dominance Orientation (SDO) describes a tough-minded view that it is a zero-sum, dog-eat-dog world, where some groups justifiably dominate other groups. People who score low on SDO tend to join helping professions, be more tolerant, and endorse less aggression: they might be less inclined to abuse. People choosing to join hierarchical institutions such as the military tend to score high on SDO, in contrast [47]. Right-Wing Authoritarianism (RWA) entails conforming to conventional values, submitting to authority, and aggressing as sanctioned by authority. People who score low on RWA would be less prone to abuse. [48] High SDO and RWA both predict intolerance of outgroups social groups outside one's own.

44. A. G. Miller, A. K. Gordon, A. M. Buddie, Pers. Soc. Psychol. Rev. 3. 254 (1999).

45. J. R. Schlesinger, H. Brown, T. K. Fowler, C.A. Homer, J. A. Blackwell Jr., Final Report of the Independent Panel to Review DoD Detention Operations, accessed 8 November 2004, from www.informationclearinghouse.info/article6785.htm

46. L. T. Harris, S. T. Fiske, unpublished data.

47. J. Sidanius. F. Pratto, Social Dominance: An Intergroup Theory of Social Hierarchy and Oppression (Cambridge Univ. Press, New York. 1999).

48. B. Altemeyer, Enemies of Freedom: Understanding Right-Wing Authoritarianism (Jossey-Bass, San Francisco, 1988).

Chapter 4

Critical Thinking

Although the focus of this chapter and the next is on reading academic writing, the strategies discussed apply to both the essays in *The Active Reader* and to many of the other readings you will undertake as part of your education. As the previous chapters stress, there is no mystique about scholarly writing: conventions exist to ensure effective communication and ease in understanding, not to privilege this kind of discourse over other genres or to segregate the writing in one discipline from the writing in another. Consistently applying the thinking and reading strategies discussed in these two chapters will make you a more conscious and active reader and, in the end, make reading less a matter of overcoming challenges and more a matter of personal satisfaction.

Academic essays call on the reader's use of critical thinking skills. Other kinds of writing, such as literary works, do this as well, but exercising the range of critical thinking skills is crucial when you read academic prose because academic arguments are frequently based on tight logic or a series of unfolding claims that increase in complexity or significance. Various assumptions and premises underlie the claims of academic writers. Questioning and testing these assumptions is at the heart of critical thinking.

Writing at the post-secondary level also requires readers to make inferences, to draw valid conclusions based on evidence. What is common to all forms of interactive reading is a reliance on critical thinking, which can involve any of the following:

> Critical thinking is a process of engagement. It consists of a series of logical mental processes that lead to a conclusion.

- Analyzing
- Questioning
- Hypothesizing
- Evaluating
- Comparing
- Judging
- Reconsidering
- Synthesizing
- Weighing the evidence
- Drawing a conclusion

If you look up the words "critical," "critic," or "criticism" in a dictionary, you will see that each word has several meanings. One meaning of "critical" is to make a negative judgment, to criticize. However, the root of "critical" comes from a Greek word that means to *judge* or *discern*, to weigh and evaluate evidence. It is this meaning that is implied in the term *critical thinking*.

Much of what we do today is done quickly. This is true not only of video games, text messages, Twitter, and email but also in business where "instant" decisions are valued (especially if they turn out to be good decisions!). However, because critical thinking involves many related activities, speed is not usually an asset. Leaders may sometimes need to make quick decisions, but more often, their decisions arise after carefully weighing an issue and receiving input from diverse sources. Since critical thinking is a process, the best way to succeed is to slow down, to be more deliberate in your thinking so you can complete each stage of the process.

When Do You Use Critical Thinking?

In many of your assignments you will have to form conclusions about what you have read. You might employ critical thinking to decide whether to use a secondary source in your research essay. As well as deciding whether the topic and the writer's approach to the topic are close to your own, you will need to judge the reliability of the source and the validity of the findings—critical thinking, again.

It might seem that summarizing a text does not involve critical thinking. However, summaries require you to carefully discriminate among ideas, judging which are most important, so critical thinking *is* involved. Critical thinking skills are also triggered whenever you read a work in order to comment on it; this could be in the form of a classroom discussion or debate or a written assignment, such as a review or rhetorical analysis. When you use research, you will have to assess the reliability and usefulness of your sources, compare their claims, and organize them logically in your essay.

However, critical skills do not apply just to reading and writing: they are used in many everyday situations, like those described below ("Inferences and Critical Thinking"), and in fieldwork projects, like those discussed in "The Active Voice: Silent Witnesses to the Past" (p. 43) in which the fieldworker observes phenomena in their surroundings and draws conclusions from these observations.

For a writer, critical thinking is stimulated whenever analysis is involved, as it is in most kinds of problem-solving. A writer asks a question about a relevant topic in his or her discipline and uses the methods and processes of the discipline to answer it. For example, criminologists Christie Barron and Dany Lacombe question the phenomenon of the "nasty girl," account for its general acceptance, and draw on related literature and social policy to propose their own theory for its popularity ("Moral panic and the Nasty Girl," p. 327). Using critical thinking in an argument, as Joel Lexchin does in "Pharmaceutical innovation: Can we live forever? A commentary on Schnittker and Karandinos" (p. 396), involves challenging the conclusions of a scholarly study; he uses questioning, evaluating, comparing, and weighing the evidence to help him reach his conclusion.

Although critical thinking involves typical activities, they vary somewhat from discipline to discipline:

- Empirical studies in the natural and social sciences often identify problems, generate hypotheses, predict occurrences, create raw data, analyze using cause and effect, and attempt to generalize on the basis of their findings.

Summaries, reviews, critical analyses, research, and many everyday activities involve critical thinking.

- Studies in the arts/humanities often identify problems, ask questions, propose a thesis (which is supported by a theoretical framework), interpret primary and secondary sources in light of the thesis, and analyze using definitions, examples, compare/contrast, and other patterns.

Inferences and Critical Thinking

Context clues can be used to infer the meaning of an unfamiliar word (see "Word Meanings," p. 60). More broadly, **inferences** apply to ideas and the way we use them to form conclusions. Writers do not always explicitly state their points but leave it to the reader to infer meaning.

Many research methods rely on inferences: astronomers, for example, study the phenomenon of black holes by observing the behaviour of the matter that surrounds them. They know that before gas is swallowed up by a black hole, it is heated to extreme temperatures and accelerates. In the process, X-rays are created, which escape the black hole and reveal its presence. Scientists cannot actually *see* black holes, but they can *infer* their existence through the emission of X-rays.

We practice critical thinking in our daily lives, inferring probable causes or consequences from what we observe—the evidence—and our interpretation of this evidence. For example, say you are jogging while wearing headphones. Another jogger catches your eye and points to her wrist. What is the probable reason (cause)? You might infer that she is asking for the time. Other inferences are possible too, but the most valid inference is the one with the greatest probability of being correct. If you shouted out the time and she looked puzzled, you might then infer that your original inference was incorrect.

If you are impatiently waiting for a bus and someone at the bus stop tells you that the buses are running 15 minutes late, you might be more interested in inferring the consequence than the cause: you will be late for class. However, if the bus immediately arrives, you might revise your original conclusion, which was based on the testimony of the person at the bus stop. You might also infer that this person is not a reliable source.

You use critical thinking as you read whenever you evaluate evidence and draw conclusions about claims (assertions) or the source of these claims, the writer. Although critical thinking can involve all the activities mentioned above, there are three general activities that will promote critical thinking skills as you read a text: reading closely and objectively, asking questions, and drawing logical conclusions. However, although most texts are linear (that is, we read them from beginning to end), our engagement with them is not always linear. It is important to remember that critical thinking is a *process of rigorous but flexible engagement* with a text (or a non-textual situation) that may change as you read (or learn more about the non-textual situation).

More than one inference might be possible in a given situation—i.e., an inference could be a *possible* conclusion, but not the *most probable* one, such as the examples above about the jogger and the person at the bus stop. A more probable inference is said to be a better one. However, an inference can also be incorrect. This could occur if you drew a hasty conclusion without thinking something through or if you had a bias (for example, if you prejudged someone based on appearance). In reading, you might make an incorrect inference if you failed to read the instructions for an assignment or read them too quickly.

INFERENCE
a conclusion based on what the evidence shows or points to. More than one inference might be possible in a given situation, but the most probable one is said to be the best inference.

Activity

The passages below contain specific statements from which readers may be able to make inferences either about the information presented or about the writer's attitude toward the subject. Choose the most valid (most probable) conclusion:

1. [The students at the school] work in isolated workstations; their desks face the walls. Social interaction is structured and supervised. Time-out rooms are small, windowless areas without furniture or carpeted floors; the doors have keyed locks. The cells are painted bright colors: pink, yellow, and blue; the light switch for each cubicle is on the outside.[1]

    a.   The students at the school are thoroughly dedicated to their studies.
    b.   School designers have provided the optimal conditions for study.
    c.   The school has been designed for students with behavioural problems.
    d.   No inference is possible about the students or their school.

2. Jen was hired as the manager of Cilantro due to her competence and high ethical standards. It was a stressful time because a new staff team had been hired to complete a company project. Jen, who was in charge of the project, was particularly annoyed when one of the team members told her they needed two more weeks to work on samples before they could begin production. After listening to team concerns, she left the room saying, "Well, if we keep going at this pace, we're not going to complete production in the projected three weeks." However, the following day, she submitted a report to her supervisors, indicating that the project was running smoothly.

    a.   She lied in the report to protect her job with the company.
    b.   She has decided to change her team and hire new members.
    c.   She found a solution to the problem and did not want to complain needlessly.
    d.   No inference is possible about the reason for Jen's statement.

3. All was not eager anticipation for Meghan. She chose to attend the largest university in the province, and she found herself frequently feeling lost, both geographically and socially. She had to take a campus bus to get to some of her classes on time. Most of her classes were large with well over 100 students; one class had 250 students. She was used to smaller class sizes in high school, with support from her resource teacher. Although she arranged for support through the university's Office of Disability Services, Meghan realized that she would have to approach the professors to describe her learning problems and request accommodations. . . . Meghan also felt disorganized. Although her roommates had purchased their texts, yearly organizational calendars, and other materials, Meghan had no idea where to begin; her fear of failure was increasing by the moment.[2]

    a.   Meghan will likely face many challenges at the university.
    b.   Meghan will likely give up and go home.
    c.   Meghan's fears are likely unfounded, since the many resources available at the university will help her adjust to her new life.
    d.   No inference is possible about Meghan's future at the university.

4. Two recent studies have found that those arrested for property or financial crimes (such as embezzlement) were disproportionately likely to have used marijuana. However, when the researchers looked at crime rates rather than arrest rates, the connection disappeared entirely. (These correlations are determined by comparing a community's rate of pot use with its overall crime and arrest rates.)[3]

a. Marijuana users are more likely to break the law but are less likely to get caught.

b. Marijuana users are less likely to break the law and less likely to get caught.

c. Marijuana users are more likely to break the law and more likely to get caught.

d. Marijuana users are less likely to break the law but are more likely to get caught.

5. Binkley paid for all the travel and expenses, and what was only 12 months ago a very new and controversial transaction has today left Binkley a healthy man—and the first of 16 people who have successfully received organs through MatchingDonors.com.[4]

a. The author believes that this method of soliciting donors is wrong.

b. The author believes that this method of soliciting donors is, at the very least, ethically questionable.

c. The author sees nothing wrong with this method of soliciting donors.

d. No inference is possible about the author's beliefs.

Writers may not directly state their reason for writing or their attitude to their subject. Instead, they may use deliberate strategies to embed their meaning or tone in the work and expect readers to "read between the lines" to infer this meaning. As a reader, you must pay careful attention to the language, to nuances (implications), and other specific cues, or you might misunderstand a passage and, possibly, the entire essay.

Collaborative Exercise: Reading for Meaning

1. After reading the first passage, below, discuss the author's use of linguistic strategies (such as word choice), exaggeration, and similar cues to suggest that he does not actually believe what he says. Some areas for discussion are underlined, but other parts of the essay may also be relevant.

When I was a youngster, I spent the bulk of my Saturday mornings in front of the television, entertained by the hand-drawn shenanigans of a host of animated cartoon characters. I remember so many of them fondly, like family members or good friends: Bugs Bunny, Tweety Bird, Scrooge McDuck, Ronald Reagan. It's only now, armed with the wisdom and hindsight that comes with age, that I realize how dangerous an indulgence this may have been. For this, I have the good Dr. James Dobson, founder of Focus on the Family, to thank. He noticed the effete tendencies of a pant-wearing sponge on a video entitled *We Are Family: A Musical Message For All*. (The video bears the name of the infamous disco song that hinted at the indiscriminate inclusiveness of vice-ridden dens such as Studio 54.) *We Are Family* is a video that was distributed to school groups all over the United States and, by all accounts (no, I have not seen it), it can make people either tolerant, open-minded and/or homosexual. . . . Dobson, with characteristic sharpness of mind and tongue, has opened up a Pandora's box, and the torrent subsequently unleashed will change the face of popular entertainment. Forever.

Or, at the very least, for several weeks.

(Richard Poplak. 2005. "Fear and Loathing in Toontown," *This* May/June: 39–40. © Richard Poplak)

2. Discuss the writer's attitude in the following passage. Is it one more of amusement or of contempt? Reading closely, determine the writer's tone and explain, using specific words and phrases, how you came to your decision.

> They're the impulse buys piled up next to the cash register. They're the books stocked by Urban Outfitters and hipster gift stores. They're the books you pick up, laugh at, and figure would be just about right for that co-worker who's into sci-fi (*The Space Tourist's Handbook*) [or] the friend who watches too much TV (*Hey! It's That Guy!: the Fametracker.com Guide to Character Actors*). . . .
>
> Pop-culture-inspired handbooks for situations you're never going to face featuring information you're never going to need, these gimmicky, kooky, sometimes just plain stupid books have at least one thing in common: There are more and more of them out there, because they sell. (Hal Niedzviecki. 2005. "Publishers feel smart about selling people stupid books." *The Globe and Mail*, 17 Dec.: R1.)

Critical Thinking and Skepticism

"Reading closely means becoming conscious of more than just content but also of how you interact with a text—for example, being open to challenges to your own ways of thinking but not being swayed by other views unless they stand up to the tests of logic and consistency. One attitude often used to describe this state of readiness is *skepticism*."

Focused reading is a systematic method that can be used in reading for content (see "Focused Reading," p. 52). By reading a text very closely, by attending objectively to its claims, to the details that support these claims, and to the writer's language and tone, you will be in a position to go beyond simple comprehension and apply critical thinking skills.

Reading closely, then, means becoming conscious of more than just content but also of how you interact with a text—for example, being open to challenges to your own ways of thinking but not being swayed by other views unless they stand up to the tests of logic and consistency. One attitude often used to describe this state of readiness is *skepticism*. Adopting an attitude of healthy skepticism does not mean you are obliged to mistrust everything you read. A skeptic is very different from a cynic, as explained in the philosophical statement of the Skeptics Society, a group of scholars who publish the quarterly magazine *Skeptic*:

> Some people believe that skepticism is the rejection of new ideas, or worse, they confuse "skeptic" with "cynic" and think that skeptics are a bunch of grumpy curmudgeons unwilling to accept any claim that challenges the status quo. This is wrong. *Skepticism is a provisional approach to claims.* It is the application of reason to any and all ideas—no sacred cows allowed. In other words, skepticism is a method, not a position. Ideally, skeptics do not go into an investigation closed to the possibility that a phenomenon might be real or that a claim might be true. When we say we are "skeptical," we mean that we must see compelling evidence before we believe. (www.skeptic.com/about_us/)

In critical thinking, you constantly test and assess the evidence presented, considering how it is being used and where the writer is going with it. Key activities in a close reading of a text are questioning, evaluating, and reconsidering.

The Spirit of Inquiry

The popular tabloid the *National Enquirer* promotes itself as a magazine "for enquiring minds." In fact, it is nothing of the sort: a more typical tabloid reader is one who believes anything he or she is told or at least finds humour in having his or her credulity stretched to the breaking point.

A truly inquiring mind analyzes what it reads and does not take everything at face value. The critical thinker questions assumptions, tests the evidence, and accepts (or rejects) conclusions after careful analysis. When questions arise, the critical thinker first seeks for answers within the text itself but may also consider relevant knowledge from outside sources or from personal experience. How might such sources address or answer the question? Are these answers consistent with or different from those found in the text being read?

In analyzing arguments, the critical thinker should ask, does the writer reason consistently, does he or she do justice to the argument's complexity, or are there inconsistencies or oversimplifications? (See "Failures in Reasoning," Chapter 8, p. 122). The critical thinker should also be aware of the potential force of counter-arguments, especially those unacknowledged by the writer. Is the writer avoiding or minimizing certain issues by not mentioning them? By considering all sides and angles and by questioning all easy or glib answers, the critical thinker sets firm and logical boundaries within which the text can be understood.

Critical Situations for Critical Thinking

As we read along in a text, we may not even be aware that we are thinking critically until we take particular note of something we have read and that skill is brought to the fore. A writer might make a claim that directly contradicts what our knowledge or common sense tells us—for example, that cats are more intelligent than humans. Another example might be a writer making a claim about a topic that experts have been debating for years—for example, that cats are smarter than dogs. Although you would probably just dismiss the first claim, the second claim would probably cause you to use critical thinking to evaluate the following:

- *The writer's credibility:* Is the writer considered an expert? What is the nature of his or her expertise? A researcher into animal behaviour? A veterinarian? An animal trainer? Someone who has owned dogs and cats? Someone who has owned dogs only? Could the writer have a bias? Are there any logical fallacies in the argument? Has fact been carefully distinguished from opinion?
- *Nature of the claim (assertion):* Specific claims are stronger than general ones and often easier to prove. Since variability has been found among dog breeds, it would be difficult to generalize about the intelligence of all dogs.
- *Basis of the claim:* Some claims are more straightforward than others. A claim may depend on an underlying assumption, such as a particular definition. There are different ways to define and measure intelligence: physiologically (e.g., the weight of the brain in proportion to the weight of the body) and behaviourally

(e.g., trainability, adaptability, independence). Advocates of a dog's superior intelligence may point to trainability as the intelligence factor, while advocates of cat intelligence may point to adaptability or independence. Both could be valid criteria, but by themselves they do not offer proof.

- *Method:* How does the writer attempt to prove the claim? Is the method compatible with the claim? Intelligence can be measured (but see previous point). Therefore, a method that sought to measure intelligence scientifically would be more credible than one that relied on personal observation— especially since many pet-lovers are quite opinionated about their pets' intelligence and may not always distinguish between fact and opinion.

- *Support:* A credible writer needs to provide more than opinion or personal observation to back up a claim. In critical thinking, you must evaluate the nature of the evidence and the way the writer uses it. Typical questions might include the following: What kind of evidence did the writer use? Has the writer relied too much on one kind of evidence or one source? How many sources were used? Were they current sources (recent studies may be more credible than older ones)? Did the writer ignore or minimize some sources (e.g., those that found dogs more intelligent than cats)?

- *Conclusion:* See below, "Drawing Conclusions."

There is another scenario in which critical thinking is inevitably involved: comparing the arguments of two writers who arrive at different or even contradictory conclusions, even though both appear to reason logically and bolster their points with the use of solid evidence. The kinds of analysis employed in these cases will be primarily those of relating, comparing, and weighing the evidence on both sides.

Expository writing as well as argumentative writing can produce disagreement and contradictory findings. For example, researchers conducting experiments to determine the effectiveness of a new drug or to investigate the connection between television viewing and violence may arrive at very different conclusions although their various methods appear credible. A researcher's attempts to replicate an experiment may fail in spite of the care taken to follow the precise methods of the original experiment. What can account for the differing results? Attempting to answer this question, to account for variation, involves critical thinking. Critical thinking is a necessary part of problem-solving.

Drawing Conclusions

"Drawing a conclusion about a work you have read involves more than making one inference; it results from the *incremental process of reading critically.* In arriving at a conclusion, you weigh the various factors involved in your analysis of the text."

Remember that an inference can be defined as a conclusion drawn from the evidence. However, drawing a conclusion about a work you have read involves more than making one inference; it results from the *incremental process of reading critically.* In arriving at a conclusion, you weigh the various factors involved in your analysis of the text. But while analysis and its associated activities were paramount when you were reading the work, as you complete your reading, you are synthesizing this information in order to say something definitive about it, about its presentation, and/or about the writer.

To form conclusions, you might assess the way that the parts relate to the whole, assigning relative significance to these different parts. Obviously, some points are more important than others, and some evidence is more effective than other evidence. *Your goal is to determine whether the accumulated weight of evidence supports the writer's claim*, or, as members of the Skeptics Society would ask: Is the weight of evidence "compelling"? You might consider how weaker or less substantiated points affect the validity of the findings. Were there any gaps or inconsistencies in the chain of reasoning? Was the writer's conclusion logically prepared for? Ultimately, you are determining whether the writer's findings/conclusion reflect what he or she set out to investigate. Was the original hypothesis proved or disproved? Was the original question answered?

If you have been using your critical thinking skills to write a rhetorical analysis of a work, you will need to make explicit the critical thinking that led to your conclusion. In a rhetorical analysis, you use critical thinking not just to analyze another text but to demonstrate your own abilities to think critically. See p. 104. For a critical thinking assignment involving research, see Chapter 9, p. 145.

The two essays below, from the disciplines of classical studies and women's studies, demonstrate how critical thinking can be used to make or challenge constructions of reality, enabling us to revise inaccurate perceptions or limited "truths." The questions that follow "Silent Witnesses to the Past" stress the application of critical thinking to the essay itself.

Clearly, the effects of critical thinking, whether applied to small practical problems or to fundamental social issues, allow us to better understand our past and radically transform our future.

The Active Voice

SILENT WITNESSES TO THE PAST

1   No academic subject can claim a greater longevity in the Western educational system than the study of Greek and Latin. From the Renaissance on, it was thought that the mastery of these two difficult languages would provide a mental training without equal. The consequences of this belief were still apparent until quite recently. During the Second World War, for instance, classicists came second only to mathematicians in the recruitment of code-breakers, having intellectual capabilities, it was believed, perfectly honed to tackle complex problems. That said, despite their formidable reputation, classical languages have of late suffered an astonishingly rapid decline. Dominant for some 500 years, the study of Latin all but disappeared from schools in a single generation, while Greek is in an even more perilous state.

2   University departments of classics (now usually called something along the lines of "Greek and Roman Studies") have generally shown themselves to be highly adept at adjusting to the changing circumstances. Their new mission is to introduce students to classical civilization through non-linguistic media. None has proved more successful than archaeology.

3   Classical archaeology is, of course, much more than an inferior substitute for the ancient languages. It is a highly effective way for students to gain a direct and tangible connection with antiquity, in many ways far more direct than they ever could from the written text. I might illustrate this from my own experience with a training excavation conducted on behalf of the University of British Columbia. The practicum, conducted for academic credit at the Lunt Roman Fort, near Coventry, England, from 1985 to 2002, was in each of those years attended by 35 or so students from UBC and elsewhere in North America.

4   The Lunt Fort was first built in the early sixties AD (during the reign of Nero) and remained under occupation for about 30 years. Our work concentrated on its defensive system, in the form of a turf rampart fronted by a series of ditches. In the course of excavation, the students brought to light objects that had remained untouched since they were discarded nearly 2,000 years ago by the fort's original occupants. The term "discarded" is deliberate, since most of the material was there because its owners had thrown it away: pieces of pot, old nails, a belt buckle, a broken brooch, and the like. For students sensitive to the spirit of history, the thrill of gaining this direct physical contact with the ancient Romans proved to be a life-transforming experience.

5   Archaeology is not, of course, a mere treasure hunt. The students, usually from faculties of arts, were obliged to acquire a whole new set of skills. They were given thorough training in the techniques required of the modern archaeologist. They learned to plan, to survey, to enter items into a systematic database. They were taught to date fragments of pottery, to identify different types of corroded metal, to distinguish between natural strata in sandy soil and deposited material compacted over hundreds of years. This last is not an easy task but a crucial one on a site like ours, where no stone construction was used and the residual material is often detectable only through variations in the colour of the soil.

6   More importantly, however, beyond these essentially technical skills, the students developed crucial expertise in applying logical thought processes to the investigation of complex evidence. Archaeological remains are silent witnesses to the past. Like other witnesses, they surrender their testimony only under skilful cross-examination. Let me illustrate this with a concrete example. The most useful features on any Roman fort are the "V"-shaped defensive ditches. When forts were demolished to give way to civilian settlements, the ditches were filled, and the material deposited in them came primarily from the fort's upper structures. In the ensuing centuries, the surface area would almost invariably be subject to human activity, usually ploughing. The evidence at ground level would thus often be destroyed or damaged. But the fill of the ditches would survive intact, and much of the history of the site can be recovered from it. Students noticed when they drew a plan of a section of a ditch that there was, at the bottom, at the point of the "V," a roughly square-shaped slot. What had caused this? They soon learned to dismiss such fanciful ideas such as "ankle-breakers" by observing what happened

in the newly excavated ditches when it rained: they filled with silt.

7   The slots were clearly made by Roman soldiers dragging buckets along the ditch-bottom to remove the silt. Students were then told to observe whether the excavated slot was silt-free or full of silt. What could that observation tell us? We made the students try to think in Roman terms. In the case of a silted-up ditch, why would the Romans have stopped removing silt from the bottom of the ditch? Almost certainly, it means that the occupants anticipated that they would be abandoning the fort at some point in the near future and saw no need to keep the ditch clean. In other words, it suggests an orderly redeployment. Conversely, a meticulously cleaned ditch suggests that the fort was abandoned and the ditches filled in as the immediate result of an order to move, perhaps because of some military crisis.

8   Archaeology thus involves not only the collection of material from which evidence is derived but, most importantly, the interpretation of that evidence by a series of logical mental sequences. It is a never-ending process. Examination of surviving material will reveal the size and nature of wall foundations. Foundations of a certain size token walls of a certain size. Why do walls have to be so high, so thick? Would that size have been needed for storage? If not, it presumably means that the walls were needed for defence. But, let us suppose, the period was peaceful and the region settled, at least according to Tacitus and the like. Does the evidence on the ground suggest that we have to question the literary evidence (written, after all, in Rome, usually by historians who never set foot in a military camp and almost certainly had never been to Britain)? There are numerous permutations of this kind of questioning.

9   Interestingly, the very mental discipline that the detailed knowledge of the ancient languages reputedly bestowed on previous generations is now well matched by what archaeology offers the students of today. The vast majority will not become professional archaeologists. But after their training, they see their world differently and will have developed considerable proficiency as problems-solvers, acquiring broad skills that stand them in excellent stead in their chosen future careers.

—Anthony Barrett, Professor, Department of Classical,
Near Eastern and Religious Studies,
University of British Columbia

QUESTIONS:

1. Why do you think that the study of classical languages was considered "a mental training without equal"? Can you infer reasons for its decline after the Second World War?

2. Explain how the specialized skills mentioned in paragraph 5 equip students to draw more accurate conclusions about the objects they will be studying? How do the skills described in paragraph 6 differ from those in paragraph 5?

3. What are "ankle-breakers," and why does the writer dismiss them as "fanciful"?

4. What is the function of the questions in paragraph 8? Does the writer answer the last question in this paragraph? Why or why not?

5. Paraphrase (put in your own words) the last sentence, in which the writer summarizes the value of the skills students gain through the experience at the excavation of the Lunt Fort.

The Active Voice

FEMINIST THINKING IN COMPOSITION AND LITERATURE CLASSES

1   Feminist thinking has revolutionized the way we write, as well as the way we read, in university English classes. A feminist approach to these activities encourages us to investigate the (sometimes unconscious) assumptions about gender that inform both our own writing and the array of cultural "texts" we encounter every day: the television and movies we watch, the advertising we take in, the music we listen to, the books we read, the world around us. The human body itself constitutes another example of a text; intentionally or not, whenever we dress, speak, move, or adorn our bodies (or not), we present ourselves to others for interpretation. All such texts, we have come to realize, are charged with meaning, and a feminist approach encourages us to become active, rather than passive, interpreters of them.

2   In other words, feminism encourages us to practise critical thinking in the study of both composition and literature. Indeed, feminism itself constitutes a primary example of how critical thinking can produce wholesale change, both inside and outside the university. Particularly since its grassroots upsurge in the women's liberation movement of the 1970s, feminist thinking has questioned the authority of conventional gender hierarchies, calling attention to the inequity (and the impossibility) of forcing individuals to comply with stereotypical notions of masculinity and femininity.

3   Feminism has come a long way since then, becoming first of all academically legitimate—in the establishment of women's studies departments at all major universities—and then more theoretically sophisticated, evolving into the study of gender more generally. The popular stereotype of feminists as man-haters, albeit persistent, has generally given way to an understanding of gender as a cultural construct and of feminism as a means of critiquing this construct. Masculinity, as well as femininity, has become the object of intellectual scrutiny, and the possibility and/or desirability of maintaining a binary gender system has been called into question.

4   Closely related to questions about gender are questions about sexuality, another concept that has been rigorously examined by feminist thinking. Is there any necessary connection between gender and sexuality? Is an individual's sexuality always unambiguous, and does it remain constant over time? The gay/straight binary, like the masculine/feminine binary, has come under scrutiny, giving rise to the branch of gender studies known as "queer theory." Such a questioning of identity binaries constitutes a post-modern theoretical move that has become indispensable to the study of all cultural texts, including literary texts and our own writing. The automatic classification of individuals or concepts into binary oppositions, we have come to realize—oppositions such as self/other, black/white, culture/nature, as well as man/woman and hetero-/homosexual—misses many of the groups and nuances that do not fall neatly into one category or the other.

5   This critical approach has given rise to exciting new interpretations of traditional texts, as well as an expansion in the category of texts available for literary study. Asking why texts written by women were traditionally excluded or ignored in the study of literature, feminist scholarship has transformed the canon—the body of literary texts considered worthy of study—to include a much more equitable propor-tion of women's writing. Following this, texts by women (and men) of colour, by women (and men) of all socio-economic groups, and by gays, lesbians, and bisexuals have become legitimate objects of literary study along with the "great litera-ture" of the past—which has itself been subjected to rigorous feminist critique.

6   Discussions of texts in twenty-first-century literature and composition classrooms, accordingly, encourage readers to ask searching questions about gender and sexuality. How are male and female characters represented in any given text—including those we write? Is gender represented as a fixed or fluid category of identity? Is the sexuality of the char-acters represented as definite or ambiguous? What is the atti-tude of the narrator, speaker, or implied author to such issues? Most importantly, what are the ideological implications of the answers to these questions?

7   At the very least, an awareness of gender issues requires us to regard our own writing as a culturally significant activity, one that produces results that readers will interpret in light of cultural norms. Gender-neutral terminology such as inclusive pronouns ("he/she" or "they" instead of "he") and designations ("humanity" instead of "mankind"; "firefighter" instead of "fireman") sends a message, as do the images we create, the figurative language we use, and the humour we draw on. Texts, we have come to realize, are not interpreted "neutrally" but in the context of the culture in which they are produced or consumed.

8   Along with an awareness of issues of class and race, our awareness of gender issues has profoundly influenced the way we write, the way we read literature, and our understand-ing of literature itself. In our post-modern world, we have become aware that the texts a culture produces and con-sumes command enormous power, the power to affect the beliefs and behaviours of individuals in that culture. Feminist thinking in university English classrooms can help us to develop the critical skills we need in order to create and inter-pret the texts that shape our world.

—Judith Mitchell, Associate Professor,
Department of English, University of Victoria

CHAPTER ENDNOTES

1. Groves, J., & Huber, T. (2003). Art and anger management. *The Clearing House, 76*(4), 186.
2. Skinner, M.E., & Lindstrom, B.D. (2003). Bridging the gap between high school and college: Strategies for the successful transition of students with learning disabilities. *Preventing School Failure, 47*(3), 132–138.
3. Reefer dumbness. (2004, March). *The Atlantic Monthly, 293*(2), 48–50.
4. Desai, J. (2006). Google yourself an organ donor. *Science & Spirit, 17*(1), 46–52.

Chapter 5

Reading Strategies

Interacting with Texts

As suggested in Chapter 4, reading is not a passive process in which you simply register the meanings of words and, aided by your knowledge of English syntax and other rules, combine words, phrases, and clauses to construct meaning. Although reading does rely on such competencies, it is also an *interactive* process involving a relationship *between* you and the text you are reading ("inter" is a prefix meaning "between"), which often changes as you read and apply critical thinking skills. That is why when you read a text for the second time, you uncover new meanings, make new inferences, and become aware of new things.

Each reader approaches a text, like an essay, in a different way: your ideas, beliefs, and specific knowledge about the topic reflect who you are and your unique experiences. You will therefore interact with the text in a unique way.

In addition, the nature of the text itself, the purpose of the author in writing, the audience it was intended to reach, and the reason for reading it all play a role in the way you interact with it, as do the author's own ideas, beliefs, background, and the specific choices—in diction, style, and tone—that he or she makes.

Consider, for example, what you might find yourself thinking about as you began reading an essay by David Suzuki on wind power (wind farms) as an alternative source of energy.

> Off the coast of British Columbia in Canada is an island called Quadra, where I have a cabin that is as close to my heart as you can imagine. From my porch on a good day you can see clear across the waters of Georgia Strait to the snowy peaks of the rugged Coast Mountains. It is one of the most beautiful views I have seen. And I would gladly share it with a wind farm.
>
> But sometimes it seems like I'm in the minority. All across Europe and North America, environmentalists are locking horns with the wind industry over the location of wind farms. (Suzuki. 2005. "The beauty of wind farms." *New Scientist, 186* (2495): 20–21.)

Questions about the subject itself: What do I know about wind farms? Where did my knowledge come from (the media, teachers or textbooks, conversations with friends, my own observation)? Have I any personal experience that might have a bearing on my reading? Do I have opinions about the topic? Are they open to change? What could cause them to change?

Questions about the writer: Is the author's name familiar? What do I associate with him and his writing? Where did these associations come from (previous work by the author or by another author, something mentioned in class or in general conversation)? Do I consider him an authority? Why or why not? How would the average Canadian respond to an essay written by this writer? How do I know this?

While many readers have different knowledge and opinions about wind farms, most know something about the author, a noted Canadian scientist and environmentalist. The following comments on his essay illustrate the different ways that reader and writer can interact based on prior knowledge and experience. What they reveal is that each reader's point of view is coloured, at least somewhat, by his or her experience with the subject of wind farms and, in one case, with the author. Each reader, therefore, has likely approached the essay in a different way. Canvassing your knowledge of the subject and author(s) is a practical pre-reading activity because it will make you more conscious of the background, opinions, and possible biases that could come into play as you read.

Student comments

Katherine W.: I wasn't very knowledgeable about the "windmill issue" before I read this article, but by the end, I was pretty much convinced that it is an important issue. Of course, my viewpoint might have been a little biased because I've always been a fan of windmills (no practical reason) and have a lot of respect for David Suzuki. I guess that's the main reason I was convinced.

Tristan H.: Since I grew up in southern Alberta, I am no stranger to windmills, but I never imagined they were an issue with certain groups. Whenever we talked about windmills, it wasn't to say how ugly or unpleasant they were. They were more of an accent to the background. Without reading this essay, I would never have thought they were an environmental issue at all.

Andrew M.: In the first paragraph, David Suzuki speaks of his cabin on Quadra Island and the fact he would "gladly share it with a wind farm." I have flown over and around Quadra Island numerous times as well as across the Georgia Strait to the Coastal Mountains referred to in his article. The island is covered by forest, as are the mountains across the strait. I have seen wind farms in various parts of Alberta, all of them in non-forested areas. I don't see his point as credible, as it is impractical to set up wind farms in forested areas.

As you continue to read an essay, of course, many other factors arise. Your initial impressions or preconceptions may intensify or weaken through the accumulating evidence the writer presents. A simple issue may begin to appear more complex, or the level of detail may make it increasingly difficult to follow the writer's points; on the other hand, points could become clearer. Whatever the case, some general reading strategies can make the reading process more manageable, ensuring that you remain in control of the reading situation.

Annotating Texts

One simple way of responding to an essay is to reflect on what the author has written. If your purpose for reading is to prepare for a general discussion of a topic for the next class, this might be adequate preparation. On the other hand, if the discussion is two days away or if you are to write a rhetorical analysis of the essay, simply thinking about it is probably not sufficient. You will need to jot your ideas down, to **annotate** the essay— annotate = *ad* (to) + *nota* (note).

Making annotations about the text you are reading is an important (perhaps the *most* important) reading strategy, not just because it enables you to return to the essay later and have your questions and other responses fresh in your mind but also because your written response, your annotation, will almost certainly be more complete than a mere thought would have been. When you annotate an essay, you are *beginning your actual work on the assignment*: you are translating abstract ideas and impressions into concrete language, solidifying those ideas.

> ANNOTATION
> (VERB *ANNOTATE*)
> note that explains, expands, or comments on a written text.

Pre-Reading Strategies: Reading Purpose

It is important to know why you are reading a text; the reason affects the way you respond to it. This advice might seem obvious. Yet there are many different reasons for reading— beyond the obvious one of satisfying a course requirement. Are you reading it to determine whether the essay is related to your topic? To extract the main ideas? To use the text as a secondary source in your essay? To write a critical response to the text? To write a rhetorical analysis? Each of these questions affects the way you respond to the essay and necessitates a conscious reading strategy.

Reading to determine whether the essay is related to your topic (to explore)
When you search for potential sources for a research essay, you are looking for essays that seem promising, perhaps on the basis of their title or the fact that they are listed in bibliographies of general works such as textbooks or in encyclopedias, indexes, or subject directories. If you are using an online resource, you might want to search for articles or books by keywords related to your topic. Since you are reading for exploratory purposes, you do not want to waste time by closely reading each text, so a different strategy is essential.

Once you find a potentially useful essay, you can read the abstract, if available, the introduction, and headings. If you are encouraged by what you read, turn your attention to the main parts of the essay, scanning for topic sentences and other content clues (See "Reading Paragraphs: Locating Main Ideas," p. 54). Finally, read the concluding section. Scanning prevents wasting time on what might not be useful, giving you more time to apply these reading techniques to other potential sources. Underlining and annotation can be minimal at this stage since you are assessing the essay to determine whether it will be useful.

It is vital, however, that you record all relevant bibliographic information for every potential source—title, author, journal or book title (and include names of editors if the source is an edited book), journal volume and issue numbers, and page range, or website details. This information will enable you to access the source quickly when you are ready.

It often happens that you end up using some information you recall from a source you were not planning to use. Having the bibliographic information at hand can be a life-saver for late-stage additions to your essay.

Reading to extract main ideas (to summarize)

You might read an essay in order to write a formal summary, or précis (see p. 98). In this case, you identify the important points, perhaps by underlining them. However, do not underline until you have read the text through once. Since most formal summaries include *only* the main points, you do not want to confuse yourself by excessive underlining; you may not know which are the main and which the sub-points until you have completed your reading. (This practice applies to other reading purposes too: save the underlining for later readings—after you have become familiar with the entire contents of the essay, its purpose, its tone, and so on.)

Reading to use the text as a secondary source in your essay (to synthesize)

After you have explored to find out what research is available on your topic, you need to flesh out the general areas of each article that you identified as potentially useful. Thus, you must now read closely, take careful notes, and think of how each point relates to your thesis. If your source is borrowed from the library, you should make a photocopy of the article or relevant chapters of a book; in the case of a journal or magazine article, you can check your library databases to see whether a full-text version exists. If so, you can download the pages and print them.

How much you annotate depends on the importance of the source to the essay you are writing, so your initial task is to attempt to answer this question. It may be that after scanning the entire essay, you decide that only one section directly pertains to your topic. You may then wish to summarize this section to use in your essay. If a phrase or sentence is particularly significant or expressed in a memorable way, you can record its wording exactly for future use. (See "Integrating Your Sources," p. 150.) Make sure that you record the page numbers of every potential source whether you are quoting directly, summarizing, or making a brief reference.

Reading to respond and analyze

Reading to respond critically to a text is very different from reading to summarize content or to synthesize information. The goal is to look for possible connections between the text and your own thoughts and opinions. Annotation is therefore important. Writing speculative comments in the margin can help with this engagement. Asking basic questions like "what have I heard about this topic before?" or "how does this relate to me or others I know?" can provide starting points. It is also important in critical responses that you frequently refer to the text. By keeping the text front and centre, by citing it specifically, your essay becomes truly a response to the *text* and not just to the *topic*.

Although simply responding to a work may or may not be an assignment at the university level, **rhetorical analyses** are common because they reveal how an essay is put together, making them useful as models for your own writing. While, typically, in a response you will use your own experience and the first-person voice, at least partly, in an analysis you are concerned with breaking down (analyzing) the text to determine the author's premises, to test the validity of the claims and conclusion, and to examine the specific methods and strategies used. Thus, your interaction with the text will involve

RHETORICAL ANALYSIS writing activity concerned with breaking down a text to examine its structure, rhetorical strategies, significance, and other features.

such activities as identifying and evaluating; it will involve critical thinking and objective analysis. (See "Critical Thinking," p. 35, and "The Rhetorical Analysis: Explaining the How and Why," p. 104).

Of course, there are other reasons for reading: to write a review of a book or film, to prepare an informational or evaluative report, to compare/contrast two essays, to study for an exam, to see whether an essay topic interests you, for pure pleasure, and many more. Asking "how am I going to use the text?" before you begin can orient you appropriately and help you select the most useful approaches and strategies from among those discussed below.

Reading Strategies: The Big Picture

People often assess their own strengths by saying, "I like to look at the big picture" or "I'm a detail person." Many of us do seem to have a natural aptitude—or at least a preference—for one or the other. In order to complete many tasks, both skills are required. In much scientific research, a professor or senior researcher will oversee an experiment; the success of the experiment, however, depends just as much on the painstaking work of graduate students or junior researchers, all of whom may be mentioned among the study's authors. Successful essay writing, too, requires attention to the large and the small: while large-scale concerns relating to essay organization and paragraph structure (sometimes referred to as *macro-composing*) tend to occupy the writer in the early and middle stages of the process, by the final-draft stage, the focus will have changed to detail-oriented tasks (*micro-composing*), such as sentence construction, word choice, grammar, and source integration. These details increasingly become the focus throughout the revision process. This general pattern applies to reading as well, with some significant differences.

Selective Reading: Scanning and Focused Reading

In **selective reading**, your reading strategy is governed by your pre-reading choices, which can depend on what you are reading (for example, an introduction, a book chapter, an academic essay, or a book review) and your purpose for reading, as discussed above. It is therefore very different from simply sitting down with a book or essay and closely reading every word from beginning to end. Unlike reading for pleasure, selective reading, then, is planned, conscious reading.

Scanning

Scanning is a form of selective reading. In a *general scan*, you read to get the gist of a text. You read rapidly, keeping an eye out for content markers, such as headings and places in which the author summarizes material (in academic Type B essays, this summary could include tables, graphs, and other visual representations used to condense textual explanation). You try to identify main ideas in the essay by locating topic sentences within major paragraphs; topic sentences are often, but not always, the first sentence of the paragraph. Thesis statements, plans, or hypotheses are found in academic essays at the end of the introductory section. You proceed to skim, skipping detail such as examples or explanatory matter. General scanning is a good way to start reading a text since it will

SELECTIVE READING
reading strategy designed to meet a specific objective, such as scanning for main points or reading for detail.

SCANNING
form of selective reading in which you skim sections or an entire text. In a general scan, you try to determine the gist of a text—for example, by locating main ideas; in a targeted scan, you look for specific concepts or topics by keywords or phrases. In research, a targeted scan typically occurs after you have narrowed your general topic.

give you an overview of content. From a general scan, you might then move on to another selective reading method.

In a specific scan, or *targeted scan*, you look for specific content. You might use this method if you are trying to determine whether a text will be useful. Say, for example, that the text is mentioned in a source that you definitely plan on using. You then look up the title of the potentially useful text and read its abstract, but neither the title nor the abstract confirms its usefulness. To investigate further, you *target scan* the entire text for specific content: you look for words and phrases related to your topic.

If you are looking for information in a book, you are likely able to locate it by referring to the **subject index** (or author index), a standard feature of most full-length reference and scholarly texts. These indexes, found at the back of books after any appendices or bibliographies, may give you many page references, so you may have to scan a number of pages in order to access the information you seek.

If your source is a journal article involving original research, you may not need to target scan the whole article—only the appropriate sections. But if your potential source is a journal article that is not divided into formal sections, you may have to scan the entire text. If you are accessing a text online, however, you can use your word processing program's "Find" function under "Edit" to locate significant words or phrases in the text.

A *general scan* is helpful if you know you will be using the whole text since it can give you an overview of content—for example, if you are going to summarize a work or refer to it often in your essay. A *targeted scan* is helpful if you want to assess the usefulness of a text; if you decide that it does contain relevant content, you can then apply another method of selective reading, such as focused reading.

Reading Hypothesis

After scanning an essay's title, abstract, headings, list of sources, and introduction (if appropriate), one strategy is to construct a reading hypothesis that can guide you throughout a first reading of an essay. In essence, a reading hypothesis is a prediction about the essay's content or other elements, such as the writer's style or tone. Its main purpose is to solidify your expectations about the essay and shape the way you approach your reading of it.

It can be useful to make the hypothesis concrete by writing it up as a short paragraph of, perhaps, three to four sentences. Essentially, the reading hypothesis answers questions like What is the essay about? What is the author trying to prove and how does he or she accomplish this? How might the essay be similar to/different from others on the same topic? Of course, your hypothesis is a starting point and may well change as you read more closely.

Focused Reading

Because focused reading is time-consuming, you will probably have scanned the essay beforehand to find the most relevant portions of the text, which you then read in detail. University-level reading across the disciplines often involves both scanning and focused reading.

As the term **focused reading** implies, you read the text closely line by line and word by word. You may want to analyze the text for rhetorical strategies, tone, or stylistic elements. You may want to subject it to a rhetorical analysis by testing the author's premises or questioning the conclusions he or she draws from the evidence, or you may simply want to extract the text's main ideas. Many of the strategies for focused reading are discussed below under "Dividing the Whole"; "Reading Strategies: The Detail Work" is also applicable.

In order to successfully scan academic essays, you must be familiar with their conventions —in particular, where to find important information. See Chapter 2.

SUBJECT INDEX
list of important words in a text, ordered alphabetically and usually placed at the end of the text.

FOCUSED READING
reading strategy in which close attention is paid to sentences and words in order to extract detail, tone, style, relevance, etc.

Below are several reading situations with two variables for each—reading purpose and kind of text. Consider how the variables would help you decide on the most appropriate reading strategy(ies) to use in each situation.

Reading Purpose	Kind of Text	Reading Strategy(ies)?
To provide an overview or general summary	journalistic essay	
To see whether the topic interests you sufficiently to write an essay on it	informative essay	
To summarize results	journal study that describes original research (an experiment)	
To write a character or thematic analysis	novel	
To prepare for an exam question with a topic assigned in advance	essay you have never read	
To study for a final exam	your class notes	
To write a critical response to an essay about a recent controversial topic (e.g., face transplants)	journalistic essay accessed online	
Compare/contrast two essays (e.g., two tax systems)	edited collection of essays with differing points of view published by an academic press	
To write a critical analysis	argumentative essay	
To pass the time before your dentist appointment	popular magazine	
To check the accuracy of a direct quotation you used in your essay	academic essay	

In a focused reading, you often concentrate on one or more short or medium-length passages and relate them to a main idea or to other sections of the text. For example, if you are writing an essay for a history class, you might concentrate on specific passages from a primary text, such as a historical document, in order to connect key ideas in the passage to a historical event or other historical element. The purpose of analyzing the specific passage(s) is to support your thesis about the significance or interpretation of the event.

Dividing the Whole

Information is more easily grasped if it is separated into logical divisions. Empirical studies (Type B academic essays) are divided into formal categories, each labelled according to convention; formal reports also use standardized headings. Such conventional categories are useful in telling you where specific kinds of information can be found; for example, in the "methods" section, the writer describes how the study was set up, the number of participants, how they were chosen, what measurements were applied, and similar details. If you are interested in whether the author proved a hypothesis or answered a question, you would read the abstract or the introduction and then read the "discussion" and/or "conclusion."

However, not all academic essays clearly indicate how they are broken down. In Type A and Type C essays, descriptive headings may be used, but you might want to subdivide the essay further to create more manageable content subcategories. Some writers do not use descriptive headings but may nevertheless separate sections by leaving additional spaces between the end of one section and the beginning of the next.

One way to figure out an academic essay's structure is to return to the introduction and reread the thesis or essay plan in which the author announces the essay's organization. Fortunately, most academic writers are aware of the importance of structure and organize content in the body of their essays logically. In the absence of an essay plan, headings, additional spacing, or similar aids, your job is to determine that logic and use it to create manageable subdivisions. As well as making the essay easier to read, when you do this you are also familiarizing yourself with the parts of the essay that are going to be useful to you.

Information can often be organized by specific **rhetorical patterns**. Identifying these patterns makes the text easier to follow. For example, in the chronological method, the writer traces a development over time, usually from old to new. In the spatial method, the writer describes an object or scene in a systematic way, from top to bottom, for example, or from one side to another. In enumeration, points are listed in a numbered sequence (see "Rhetorical Patterns and Paragraph Development," p. 85).

In addition, the relationship between ideas is often shown through **transitional words and phrases**. These transitions can indicate whether an idea is going to be expanded or more fully explained or whether there will be a shift from one idea to another one. Transitions can occur between one paragraph and the next (as shown below) or between parts of a paragraph, linking smaller parts of the text (for examples, see pp. 83–84). Paying attention to organizational patterns and transitions can help you break down an essay into smaller and more manageable units. In the passage below, the writers use enumeration to indicate the development of one point and the transitional phrase "in addition" to indicate what could be either a new point or a major expansion of the earlier point. (Ellipses show that sentences in between have been omitted.)

> So, what can be done to reduce the start-up costs for young Canadians? *First*, political parties have a role to play. . . .
>
> *Second*, the problems with the permanent voters list need to be resolved. . . .
>
> *In addition* to these short-term solutions, various long-term solutions should be considered. (Gidengil et al. "Enhancing democratic citizenship")

Reading Paragraphs: Locating Main Ideas

Scanning paragraphs for important information is not just a mechanical process. The paragraphs in much academic writing may be long and detailed; sentences may also be long and complex. Furthermore, although student writers are often encouraged to announce their main idea in the first sentence of the paragraph, in academic or

RHETORICAL PATTERN
method of organization and developing content of essays and paragraphs; examples include cause-effect, chronology, comparison and contrast, and definition.

TRANSITIONAL WORDS AND PHRASES
words and phrases that connect ideas in a sentence or paragraph, or between paragraphs.

journalistic prose, topic sentences can occur later in the paragraph, or not at all. A **topic sentence** states the main idea of the paragraph. It is usually the most general statement (although it should not be vague or overly broad), which can be developed by examples or analysis throughout the rest of the paragraph. Although it is less common in academic writing, a writer may build *toward* the central idea, in which case the topic sentence may be a middle or even the last sentence in the paragraph. The function of topic sentences is partly structural—providing a foundation for the paragraph; this anchoring can occur in different places in the paragraph.

> **TOPIC SENTENCE**
> sentence that contains the main idea in the paragraph.

The following paragraphs illustrate different methods of paragraph construction. In the first, the opening sentence announces the paragraph's main idea; it is the topic sentence, which is developed though statistics in the next sentence. This paragraph can be said to have been developed *deductively*: the topic sentence makes a general statement after which more specific statements are used for support.

> *Even though there is a growing tendency for the population to congregate in large urban centres and people have access to better public transportation services, dependence on the automobile increased between 1992 and 2005.* According to data from the General Social Survey (GSS) on time use, the proportion of people aged 18 and over who went everywhere by car—as either a driver or a passenger—rose from 68 per cent in 1992, to 70 per cent in 1998, and then 74 per cent in 2005. (Turcotte, "Life in metropolitan areas: Dependence on cars in urban neighbourhoods," p. 407)

In contrast to the first example, the paragraph below, from a journalistic essay, begins with a personal observation, which is explored until its significance is revealed in the final (topic) sentence. The paragraph can be said to have been developed *inductively*: the topic sentence is a general statement arrived at after specific "evidence" has been considered.

> Lately I've discovered a British series called "Playing Shakespeare" in which John Barton of the Royal Shakespeare Company works through a few scenes with half a dozen actors. Together they unlock a text, discovering what words and phrases to stress, where to breathe, what meaning Shakespeare encoded in the words, how the actors should react to each other. Barton comes across as a master teacher and a bit of a TV star (like Buddy Rich, he forgets the camera). What makes this historic is that the lessons take place in 1982 and the actors he works with—Ben Kingsley, Judi Dench, Ian McKellan—are among the best of their generation, all caught relatively early in their distinguished careers. *It offers a privileged glimpse of a long-ago reality.* (Fulford, Robert. "A Box Full of History: TV and Our Sense of the Past." *Queen's Quarterly 112*.1 (2005): 89–97.)

In the final example, the topic sentence is neither the first nor the last sentence. It can be determined by asking which sentence best describes what the paragraph is about. Clearly, the first sentence is not the focus of the paragraph, but the sentence that names the writer's methodology, the way she found Muslim women for her research. Reading carefully would enable you to identify the second sentence as the topic sentence.

> There is a small population of immigrant Muslim women in Saskatoon (the geographical location of my research), and most of them know each other. *I have personal contact with many of these Muslim women, and through the use of the "snowball technique," I was*

able to identify participants. The "snowball" or "chain" method occurs when "sampling identifies cases of interest from people who know other people with relevant cases" (Bradshaw & Straford, 2000: 44). In recruiting the sample, the Islamic Association of Saskatchewan played a particularly important role. Along with Friday prayers, weekly gatherings in the mosque facilitated meetings with diverse groups of women and provided opportunities to talk with them about my research project. (Ruby, "Listening to the voices of *hijab*," p. 291)

Activity

Identify the topic sentences in the following paragraphs. If you wish to get a sense of paragraph context, page numbers have been given.

1. The extent to which citizens are informed is not a function of their own abilities and motivation alone: "Voters are not fools. . . . The electorate behaves about as rationally and responsibly as we should expect, given the clarity of the alternatives presented to it and the character of the information available to it" (Key 1966, 7). The main sources of information for citizens are the media and political actors, neither of which necessarily have a vested interest in disseminating the objective facts. Politicians and other political actors may be tempted to deploy facts in self-serving ways to build support for their preferred positions. If politicians obfuscate and political parties fail to articulate clear alternatives, is there reason to be surprised if many citizens end up with only a vague or confused sense of what the politicians stand for? (p. 265)

2. Sexual commerce in Victoria was located principally, but not exclusively, in three areas: around Broad Street in the commercial centre of the city; around the lower (western) end of Herald Street and Chatham Street in an industrial part of the city; and on Fisguard Street in Chinatown. Prostitution on Fisguard Street was confined almost exclusively to the Chinese community, which was virtually closed to outsiders, including moral regulators like the police. Since Fisguard Street was outside the mainstream of sexual commerce, it is not considered here. Instead, we focus on the denizens of Victoria's better-known and more accessible red-light districts, starting with Broad Street. (p. 349).

3. "My dear brothers in Jihad," wrote a man who identified himself as Abu Jendal, "I have a kilo of Acetone Peroxide. I want to know how to make a bomb from it in order to blow up an army jeep; I await your quick response." About an hour later the answer came: "My dear brother Abu Jendal," answered a Hamas supporter who called himself Abu Hadafa, "I understand that you have 1,000 grams of *Om El Abad*. Well done! There are several ways to change it into a bomb" . . . . Th[is] exchange was not encoded or concealed, but was published completely openly on the website of the *Izz al din al Kassam* Brigades, the military faction of the Hamas. (p. 388)

4. While most students engaged in some heavy drinking while in university, more compelling is the frequency of heavy drinking. As seen in Table IV, on average, drinkers reported consuming 5-plus drinks per occasion 4.7 times since September, and 8-plus drinks 1.9 times. Generally the same factors that predict prevalence of heavy drinking also predict the frequency of heavy drinking. Five variables are significantly related to the frequency of both 5-plus and 8-plus heavy drinking: gender, living arrangements, academic orientation, recreational orientation, and academic hours. (p. 205)

5. Does this nominal feminizing of male also-rans (and the simultaneous gendering of success) constitute a meaningful pattern? Piqued, we began examining the construction of masculinity in major feature films released by Disney's Pixar studios over the past thirteen years. Indeed, as we argue here, Pixar consistently promotes a new model of masculinity, one that matures into acceptance of its more traditionally "feminine" aspects. (p. 308)

Using Transitions and Repetitions in Reading

Does the variety of paragraph construction mean that every paragraph needs to be closely read to determine its main idea? It is useful to scan first sentences of paragraphs not just because they may contain the main idea but also because they may suggest the paragraph's development. Also, typically, important words and phrases recur throughout related paragraphs in an essay, and since topic sentences anchor the thought in the paragraph, they often contain these recurring words. The first place to look is the first sentence of the paragraph.

Rhetorical patterns, transitions, repetitions, and topic sentences give structural and content cues about where important information can be found. **Prompts** are another kind of cue that direct readers to important content to be found in the next sentence or paragraph. Thus, brief summaries and questions can act as prompts to what lies ahead.

In the following paragraph excerpt, the first sentence, which summarizes the previous paragraph, provides a transition as well as a prompt for the topic sentence (italicized), which follows immediately:

> The new rationality and concern over bullying is not only targeting the aggressive girl. *It also actively seeks the participation of school authorities in the informal control of girls.* (Barron & Lacombe, "Moral panic and the Nasty Girl," p. 327.)

In the following excerpts from the same essay, the authors provide cues through transitional and repeated words and phrases to guide the reader to the main ideas in the paragraphs. Note that in the first paragraph, the reader would need to read beyond the generalization to find the topic sentence, which follows the semicolon in the second sentence; the first sentence and the first clause in the second, then, act as a prompt. In the interests of efficiency, several of the middle sentences in the paragraphs are omitted. If you were scanning these paragraphs, you might not read these middle sentences at all since they do not contain main ideas but are expansions on the topic sentences. (Main ideas are italicized, and transitional and repeated words are bolded.)

> Girl violence is not a new phenomenon. A glimpse at newspaper articles in 1977 reveals that acts of girl violence are not new; *rather, the attention paid to them is novel.* **For example**, one article reports a violent confrontation between a group of teenage girls who had been feuding for a week. . . .
>
> **Despite** a rich description of violent details, *the tone of the article is non-threatening.* The title, "Teenager girl in knife feud says: 'We're friends again,'" certainly prepares the reader for an account of violence, but it also emphasizes the fact that the dispute has been

When you scan an essay, a section, or a paragraph, try to identify the topic sentence(s)—usually, but not always the first sentence of paragraphs.

PROMPT
word, phrase, or clause that directs readers to important content rather than containing important content itself.

resolved amicably. . . . The article ends with the assurance that this violent incident is not typical of girl behaviour, a conclusion justified by the knowledge that the weapon used in the girl feud did, after all, belong to a boy. In the **wake of fear** created by Virk's murder, the relationship between girls and violence is presented differently.

Also *central to the creation of a* **climate of fear** *is statistical manipulation of crime data to establish the amplitude of girl violence. . . .*

However, *most articles failed to recognize that the increase was in reference to minor assaults*, such as pushing or slapping, which did not cause serious injury. . . .

Thinking of transitions, repeated words, prompts, and other strategies for reading reiterates the importance of using them to create coherence in your own writing. In fact, they are usually discussed as writing rather than as reading strategies, ways to ensure that your ideas are communicated clearly to your readers.

Looking at them as reading strategies highlights the essential relationship between writing and reading: writing consciously by using strategies for coherence facilitates conscious readers in their decoding of a difficult text. Less conscious writers who do not focus on strategies to make their writing coherent put their readers at a distinct disadvantage, possibly frustrating them. See "Writing Middle Paragraphs" (p. 82), which discusses strategies for producing coherent writing.

Note that the transitional words/phrases "for example," "despite," "also," and "however" suggest specific relationships between what has preceded and what follows (respectively, relationships of illustration, contrast, addition, and qualification). By attending carefully to prompts, along with transitional and repeated words in these paragraphs, a reader could quickly find the most important ideas and focus on them.

It is important to realize that the hints above serve as rough guides to where the main ideas in any text can be found. The best way to become familiar with the reading process is to read frequently and to be conscious both of the author's attempts to create coherence through specific strategies and your own attempts to find coherence by being aware of these strategies.

Activity

Analyze the following paragraphs, identifying comprehension strategies such as rhetorical patterns, topics sentences, transitions, repetitions, and prompts.

1. Many people do resist the temptation to engage in self-serving behaviours that contribute to climate change. Yet, admittedly, many do yield to the temptation. What will it take to change these people's behaviour? As a start—but only a start—understanding environment-related motivations, attitudes, social and organisational perceptions, rationales, biases, habits, barriers to change, life-context, and trust in government will help. Certainly, psychologists are already engaged in the effort on their own. For example, some have investigated the psychological dimensions of global warming (e.g., Dresner, 1989–90; Heath & Gifford, 2006; Nilsson, von Borgstede, & Biel, 2004). However, the major thesis of the present article is that we psychologists must do more. (p. 457)

2. A working definition of *alpha male* may be unnecessary; although more traditionally associated with the animal kingdom than the Magic Kingdom, it familiarly evokes ideas of dominance, leadership, and power in human social organizations as well. The phrase "alpha male" may stand for all things stereotypically patriarchal: unquestioned authority, physical power and social dominance, competitiveness for positions of status and leadership, lack of visible or shared emotion, social isolation. An alpha male, like Vann in *Cars*, does not ask for directions . . . . These models have worked in Disney for decades. The worst storm at sea is no match for *The Little Mermaid*'s uncomplicated Prince Eric—indeed, any charming prince need only ride in on his steed to save his respective princess. But the post-feminist world is a different place for men, and the post-princess Pixar is a different place for male protagonists. (p. 309)

Reading Strategies: The Detail Work

As useful as it is to think in terms of the big picture and to be able to identify important information in essays and paragraphs, sooner or later you will find yourself grappling with the elements of the sentence—words, phrases, and clauses. When you look more closely at a text, you may be confronted with problems in any of the three areas listed below, but the last two typically present most of the challenges for student readers:

1. The relationships among words and the other syntactical units in a sentence, phrases and clauses (grammar and sentence structure).
2. The variety of linguistic resources used by the author (you can think of this as the way that the author uses words or the range of linguistic options at a writer's disposal).
3. Word meanings (vocabulary).

Grammar and Sentence Structure

Knowing the meaning of words is not going to help with comprehension unless you are familiar with the conventions that govern the arrangement of these words in a sentence, that determine the order of words and other relationships among the syntactical units in a sentence (syntax refers to the *order of words, phrases, and clauses in a sentence*). Fortunately, most English speakers entering university have been practising these conventions for years, albeit unconsciously, in their daily speech and writing.

English sentence structure and rules of grammar are governed largely by these syntactical relationships, and when you write in English, it is necessary to know them well. Poor grammar or sentence structure undermines your credibility as a writer.

Connotations and Denotations

All readers need to know *how* a writer is using words before they can make assumptions about the meaning of a text. Individual words carry **connotations**, or implications, beyond those of their dictionary meanings, or **denotations**. Paying careful attention to context—the surrounding words—can help you determine a word's connotation and orient you to the intended meaning. Sometimes dictionaries suggest a word's connotations, although often, when you look up a word in a dictionary, you find one or more of its common definitions and have to look at the passage itself to know exactly how it is being used (its connotation). Dictionaries are often not the "final word" on meaning but necessary starting places.

A word can acquire different connotations through its use over time or within a specific group. In some cases, positive or negative values have become associated with the word. Many common words have several connotations. Consider, for example, the implications of the words *slender, slim, lean, thin, skinny, underweight, scrawny,* and *emaciated*, which suggest a progression from positive (graceful, athletic . . .) to negative (. . . weak, sickly). Sometimes only context will make a word's connotation clear.

CONNOTATION
(VERB *CONNOTE*)
the implications or additional meanings of a word; a word's context may suggest its connotations.

DENOTATION
(VERB *DENOTE*)
the meaning of a word, for example, as defined in a dictionary.

Activity

In groups or individually, make a list of ten common adjectives. Then, for each word, come up with five words similar but not identical in meaning to the original word and use them in sentences. The sentences should reveal the word's connotation, so ensure that you provide adequate context for each word's exact meaning in the sentence. This exercise could also be done after reading "Word Meanings," below.

Linguistic Resources

Writers may indirectly signal their true or deeper intentions to their readers, and if readers fail to pick up the signals, they will fail to "read" the work as intended. Finding the purpose or intended meaning of a passage or an essay might involve more than figuring out contextual clues: it might involve asking questions like *What response is the author looking for from me? Does the author want me to read literally, or does the surface level of the words hide another meaning?* Although these kinds of questions relate to the author's purpose, their answers are inevitably embedded in the language of the text. Therefore, the author's use of language is the place to find answers.

Such questions are more pertinent to essays written to persuade or entertain than to those written to explain. Thus, writers might adopt an ironic tone to make the reader question a commonly accepted or simplistic perspective. In **irony**, you look beyond the literal meaning of words to their deeper or "true" meaning. The object might be to make you aware of another perspective, to poke fun at a perspective, or to advocate change.

Authors whose primary purpose is to entertain may do so by using humour. Although some humour engages us directly, other kinds of humour rely on subtle linguistic techniques revealed through implication or through devices like word play or **allusion**; many essays, of course, use humour not just to entertain but to criticize people or institutions, employing irony as well. Literary works present yet another way in which writers seek to encode multiple meanings and resonances beyond those of literal representation. You would not read a novel or short story in the same way you would read an essay; your approach to these two kinds of texts varies with the author's purpose.

Word Meanings

Dictionaries are an indispensable part of the writing life whether you are a professional writer or a student writer. They are also an essential part of the reading life, and every student needs at least one good dictionary—two are preferable: one mid-sized dictionary for the longer, more complex writing you do at home and a portable one for the classroom or school computing station (you may also be able to access reliable online dictionaries through your library). But while a good dictionary is part of the key to understanding challenging texts, it is not the only one—often it is not even the best one.

This is because the texts you read at the post-secondary level may be a good deal more challenging than you are used to. To look up every word when the meaning is unclear would require too much time; as well, if you interrupt your reading too often, it

---

IRONY
the existence in a text of two levels of meaning, one surface and literal, the other deeper and non-literal.

ALLUSION
indirect reference to outside source in order to clarify a point or get the reader to look at it in a new light.

will be hard to maintain continuity, reducing your understanding and retention of the material. Thankfully, you do not need to know the precise meaning of every word you read; you need to know the exact meanings of the most important words but only approximate meanings for many of the others.

We all have three vocabularies: a speaking vocabulary, a writing vocabulary, and a reading, or *recognition*, vocabulary. The speaking vocabulary is the smallest, and 2,000 words can be considered sufficient for most conversations. Our recognition vocabulary is the largest, but it includes words we would not use in our writing. That is why, if you are asked the meaning of a word from your recognition vocabulary, you might struggle to define it, even though you might *think* you know what it means; you probably know it only within the contexts in which you have read or heard it.

Since relying *only* on a dictionary is both inefficient and unreliable, you should cultivate reading practices that minimize—not maximize—the use of a dictionary. Use a dictionary if you have to, but first try to determine meanings by utilizing contextual clues. In the following passage, the omission of first words in the lines has very little effect on comprehension:

___ controversy over Wikipedia	*The* controversy over Wikipedia
___ library circles has died down over	*in* library circles has died down over
___ last few months, as our attention	*the* last few months, as our attention
___ moved on to other representations	*has* moved on to other representations
___ the new "Web 2.0" environment.	*of* the new "Web 2.0" environment.

Context Clues

In the passage above, the missing words are small words—prepositions, articles, and an auxiliary verb. However, important nouns, verbs, adjectives, and adverbs are also often revealed through context—the words around them. Writers may define difficult words or may use synonyms or rephrasing to make their meanings easy to grasp; such strategies are used if the author thinks the typical reader may not know them. On the other hand, authors may, without conscious effort, use an unfamiliar word in such a way that the meanings of the surrounding words clarify the meaning and connotation of the unfamiliar word. There are various ways of using these context clues, as we see in the examples below.

Specialized words, such as words borrowed from another language or culture, are defined for general audiences:

> Ibe-al-Jawzi . . . argues that the debate on the hijab among classical and contemporary scholars is fundamentally rooted in the idea of *fitnah* (temptation). (Ruby, "Listening to the voices of the *hijab*," p. 291)

Even in highly specialized writing, the writer may define terms the reader might not know:

> Young female larvae of bees, wasps, and ants are usually *totipotent*, that is, they have the potential to develop into either a queen or a worker.[1]

Rather than being stated directly in a clause or phrase that follows, a word's meaning may be inferred from a word or phrase elsewhere in the sentence:

> Minoxidil has some benefit in male pattern *alopecia*, but baldness is not a fatal disease. (Lexchin, "Pharmaceutical innovation: Can we live forever? A commentary on Schnittker and Karandinos," p. 396).

When a writer does not define a word, you may be able to infer its meaning by determining the idea the writer is trying to express. In the following example, the preceding word, "parts," and the following word, "whole," help reveal the word's meaning as *touching* or *adjoining*. The previous part of the sentence also suggests something stronger than "linked":

> Since at least the end of the 19th century, cartoonists in Canada . . . have depicted North America as a collection of territories whose identities are linked, and sometimes even as parts of a *contiguous* whole.[2]

In addition to looking at nearby words to guide you to meaning, you can often look at relationships expressed in the sentence or a previous one, like those showing contrasts. In the sentence below, a contrastive relationship can help you infer the meaning of the italicized word:

> The availability of pornographic material at the library . . . represents the *defilement* of something regarded by Mali'hah as "pure." (Ruby, "Listening to the voices of the *hijab*," p. 291.)

Similarly, if a writer uses examples, they can sometimes be used to infer the meaning of a previous word. In this sentence, the author gives the example of "dressmaker" used as a substitute for "prostitute"; a *euphemism* is a kind of substitution:

> When prostitutes were recorded on nominal census schedules, the space beside their names for "occupation, trade or calling" was left blank, or some innocuous term or *euphemism*—such as dressmaker—was entered in the space. (Dunae, "Sex, charades, and census records: Locating female sex trade workers in a Victorian city," p. 341).

What follows *innocuous* could also help define that word, especially if it occurs to you that *innocuous* has the same first five letters as the word "innocent" (see "Family Resemblances," below).

In the passage below, examples of *changes across* the spectrum of light are given (it also helps to look at the etymology of the word; see "Word Puzzles," below: *trans* = across + *mutare* = change):

> [N]atural philosophers assumed that coloured rays of light were *transmutable*. To change blue into red, white into yellow, or orange into violet, they reckoned that one simply had to find a way to quicken or retard the speed at which the pulses moved through the aether.[3]

Reading carefully to determine both the immediate context and the encompassing idea of the passage can help you determine a word's meaning. Remember that the object is not necessarily to make the word part of your writing vocabulary but to enable you to know how the author is using it—to recognize its connotation. Of course, if you are still in doubt, you should look up the word. By examining a word's denotations and at least one of its connotations (the way it is used by the author in a particular context), you are well on the way to making it part of your writing vocabulary.

Family Resemblances

If context does not help you to determine a word's meaning, you can look for resemblances, recalling words that look similar and whose meanings you know. Many words in English come from Greek or Latin (most English words of more than one syllable are derived from Latin). A "family" of words may arise from the same Latin or Greek root. While it is helpful to know some of these roots (see below), you may be able to infer the meaning of a new word by recalling a known word with the same word element. For example, you can easily see a family resemblance between the word "meritocracy" and the familiar word "merit." You can take this a step further by looking at the second element and recalling that "meritocracy" and "democracy" contain a common element. In a *democracy*, the *people* determine who will govern them. In a *meritocracy*, then, *merit* determines who governs.

Word puzzles: In the following sentences, it is difficult to determine meaning either by context or by family resemblance:

> The scientist's authoritative stance. . . derives from membership in a community committed to a shared *epistemology* (Snow, "Academic language and the challenge of reading for learning about science," p. 166)

> The government asked one of the Liberal party's retired *luminaries* . . . to head up an Independent Panel on Canada's future Role in Afghanistan. (Chapin, "Into Afghanistan: The transformation of Canada's international security policy since 9/11," p. 233)

Using a dictionary in such instances is a good idea, but another way of determining a word's meaning is to break it down to discover its *root* (its base) and, if applicable, its *affixes* (its prefix and/or suffix). A *prefix* precedes a root, changing or qualifying the word's meaning; a *suffix* follows the root, changing or qualifying the word's meaning and indicating its grammatical function. Not all words have prefixes and suffixes, and some contain more than one root. Assembling the "pieces" of an unfamiliar word is much like putting together a puzzle; it can enable you to make an educated guess about the word's meaning, which is often sufficient for reading purposes.

The study of the origin of roots can be a mystifying process that is bound up in the complex development of the English language. Often, the basic root of a word does not much resemble the form it takes in an English word. For example, in the word "tactile," the basic root is "tang," the past participle of a Latin verb, while "tact" is a secondary root formed from "tang," Thus, the charts below give the secondary root or roots when applicable because that makes it easier to see the connection between the root's meaning and the meaning of the English word that contains the root. Some of the roots, prefixes, and suffixes can be used to help define the key and difficult words that follow the essays in *The Active Reader*.

Examples

antecedent: *ante* (before) + *cede* (goes) + *ent* (noun). An antecedent of an event occurs before the event (and is usually a cause); it is also the grammatical term for the noun that a pronoun replaces (so it "goes before" the pronoun).

autocratic: *auto* (self) + *crat* (power) + *ic* (adjective). An autocratic ruler does not share power with others but rules absolutely (and usually harshly). The word is formed from two roots plus a suffix indicating its function as an adjective.

Specialized Language

The strategies discussed above for understanding unfamiliar words apply to all kinds of writing. However, the academic disciplines have their own specialized vocabularies that scholars use to communicate with each other. This language is known as **jargon**, and even the jargon of two subdisciplines, such as plant sciences and zoology, can vary considerably. When you take undergraduate courses in a discipline, you begin to acquire this specialized vocabulary, which has developed along with the discipline itself. To acquire knowledge about a subject is to simultaneously acquire its language, in addition to the other conventions of the discipline.

Although some highly technical articles may use jargon that is beyond the reach of the undergraduate, both novice and more experienced readers can make use of the variety of discipline-specific dictionaries, encyclopedias, and research guides that can be accessed through many libraries. For example, Oxford University Press publishes a series of subject dictionaries in art and architecture, the biological sciences, classical studies, computing, earth and environmental sciences, and many other disciplines.

JARGON
discipline-specific language used to communicate among members of the discipline.

Prefix	Meaning	Root	Meaning	Suffix	Meaning/Use[1]
a; an before vowel/*h*	*not, absence of*	alter	*other (of two)*	-able/ ible	*capable of* (adj.)
ab; a before *v*; abs before *c, t*	*away, from*	amphi/ ampho	*both, on both sides*	-acy/ ocracy	*government* (n.)
ad; may add first letter of root (*allude/ affix*); usually assimilates with first letter of root	*to(ward)*	ann	*year*	-ade	*result of action* (n.)
ante	*before (in temporal sense)*	anthrop	*human being*	-age	*result, act* (n.)
anti; elides before vowel	*against*	arch	*beginning, old, ruler*	-al/ial	*relating to* (adj.)
bi; bin before vowel	*double*	aud	*hear, listen*	-an/ian	*pertaining to* (adj.)
circum	*around*	auto	*self*	-ance	*state of, action* (n.)
con; co before vowel/*h*; assimilates with *l* and *m*	*together, with*	bi	*life*	-ant	*agent, cause* (n.)

Prefix	*Meaning*	Root	*Meaning*	Suffix	*Meaning/Use*[1]
contra	*against*	capit	*head, chief, leader*	-arium	*place, housing* (n.)
de	*away, from, down*	cathar	*purge, purify*	-ary	*relating to, place where* (n.)
di	*two, double, separate*	ced	*go, yield, surrender*	-ate	*associated with* (n.) (adj.) (v.)
dia	*through, across*	chron	*time*	-cule	*small* (n.) (adj.)
dis	*take away, not, deprive of*	cid	*kill*	-dom	*quality, state* (n.)
e (Latin); ex before vowel, *h, c, p, q, s*; ef before *f*; ec (Greek); ex before vowel, *h*	*out, from*	clud	*shut*	-eer	*one who* (n.)
en; em before *b, m, p*	*into*	cis	*cut*	-ed/en	*past participle* (adj.)
hyper	*over, above, excessive*	cord	*heart*	-en	*consisting of* (adj.)
in; im before *b, m, p*	*not, into*	crat	*power*	-ent	*quality of* (n.) (adj.)
inter	*between, among*	cosm	*world*	-ence/ ency	*state of, action* (n.)
macr	*large*	cred	*believe*	-er/or	*doer* (n.)
mal	*bad, evil*	dem	*people*	-ese	*native/language of* (n.) (adj.)
ob	*facing*	dic	*speak*	-ful(l)	*full of* (n.) (adj.)
pan	*all*	dogm	*belief, opinion*	-ic	*like, nature of* (adj.)
per	*through*	epistem	*knowledge*	-ion/ sion/ tion	*act, result, state of* (n.)
post	*after, behind*	fac	*make*	-ism	*system, condition* (n.)
pre	*before*	fort	*strong*	-ize/ise	*make* (v.)
pro	*forward, forth, before*	grad/gress	*step, degree, walk*	-ness	*state of* (n.)
re	*again, back*	greg	*crowd, group*	-ory	*place* (n.)
sub	*under*	heur	*find*	-ous	*full of* (adj.)
syn; sym before *b, m, p*	*with, together*	icon	*image*	-ster	*one who is, belongs to* (n.)
trans	*across*	log	*word, study*	-ure	*state of, act, process* (n.)

1 (n.) = noun; (adj.) = adjective; (v.) = verb

Thirty Additional Roots

luc/lum/lun	*light*	man	*by hand*	met	*measure*
mis	*hate*	mitt	*send*	mut	*(ex)change*
nasc/nat	*born*	omni	*all*	palp	*touch*
path	*feel, suffer, disease*	phil	*love*	phren	*mind, brain*
pleb	*people*	port	*carry*	punct	*point*
put	*think*	rect	*straight, right*	rid/ris	*laughter*
semin	*seed*	tax	*order*	tel	*end*
sci	*know*	scrib	*write*	simil/simul	*like, resembling*
stru	*build*	tact/tang	*touch*	taut	*identical*
trib	*pay, bestow*	ven	*come*	vert	*turn*

Activity

Using the lists above, determine the meanings of the italicized words in the two sentences on p. 63 (Word Puzzles). When you've done this, check a dictionary to confirm their meanings.

Activity

Using contextual, word resemblance, or word puzzle strategies whenever necessary, determine the meanings of the italicized words in the following passages, all of which are taken from readings in Part III of this book:

1. Social networking websites allow terrorists to *disseminate* propaganda to an impressionable age bracket that might *empathize* with their cause.
2. These influences [on a person's decisions] are presumed to determine the different strategies or *heuristics* that individuals as decision-makers actually employ.
3. Although industry and government describe the tar sands as "Canada's new economic engine," the project has in reality given Canada a bad case of the Dutch Disease. This economic *malaise* . . . takes its name from a 1977 article that detailed how a natural gas boom hollowed out the manufacturing base of the Netherlands.
4. Implicit features of a task include information students might be expected to *extrapolate* beyond the assigned description.
5. The BBC helped pioneer the *hybridization* of documentary and entertainment.
6. If one takes an *unflinching* look at Canadian conduct in the world, the evidence permits no conclusion other than that the country has lately been engaged in a *liquidation* of its internationalism.
7. At first, the reception of the Chinese was relatively *cordial*: "Colonial British Columbians were initially remarkably tolerant of the thousands of Chinese who came."

8. In 2005, the *autonomous* Inuit region on Nunatisavut was established via a *tripartite* agreement between the federal and provincial governments and the Inuit of Labrador.

9. Composed of 3,000 troops, the international force was *mandated* to ensure an orderly *plebiscite* on the future of the Saar territory.

10. Despite our finding of an association between fast food restaurant density and deprivation, the *directionality* of the relationship is *equivocal*. For example, community characteristics could be shaped by the type of food outlets and other services available which make the community more or less desirable. Likewise marketers and restaurant owners may establish restaurants in communities with specific *demographic* and socio-economic profiles with the aims of reaching target consumers and maximizing profits.

CHAPTER ENDNOTES

1. Ratnieks, F.L.W., & Wenseleers, T. (2005). Policing insect societies. *Science, 307* (5706), 54.

2. Green, A.J. (2007). Mapping North America: Visual representation of Canada and the United States in recent academic work and editorial cartoons. *The American Review of Canadian Studies, 37*(2), 134.

3. Waller, J. (2004). *Leaps in the Dark: The Forging of Scientific Reputations.* Oxford: Oxford University Press.

PART II

Academic Writing

Academic discourse can be thought of as *a set of oral and written procedures used to generate and disseminate ideas within the academic community*. Most of the classes you take in college or university focus on written discourse: by writing down your thoughts, you are recording them to be analyzed by others (and, yes, usually graded). Familiarity with the conventions of written discourse will be valuable to you throughout your academic career and beyond because it is primarily through writing that knowledge is transmitted. Compared to written discourse, oral discourse lacks staying power, though modern technology has lessened this distinction.

By the time students approach university, most are familiar with the rudiments of reading and writing. They probably know the ground rules for writing essays, though they may find the requirements of reading and writing at the post-secondary level somewhat alien. Thus, you may find that some of the essays you are asked to read and respond to seem more challenging than you are used to.

You will probably be writing essays and reports in most of your courses, which, while they share similarities, may be markedly different. To write a lab report for a chemistry class, for example, you use different standards and procedures, or conventions, from those you use in a literary analysis for an English class, which, in turn, are different from those you use to write a marketing plan for a business class or a feasibility study for an engineering class.

Despite these differences, there are two relatively distinct forms that academic writing can take: the essay and the report. You will be required to write essays in many of your undergraduate courses. Writing reports may be limited to your science courses, some of your social sciences courses, along with business, engineering, or health sciences courses. Chapter 6 reviews the fundamentals of writing academic essays, followed by an overview of report writing ("The Active Voice: Report Writing," p. 91) and a step-by-step guide to writing science papers ("The Active Voice: How to Write a Scientific Paper," p. 92).

Chapters 7–9 discuss specific kinds of writing assignments. When you write a rhetorical analysis—discussed in Chapter 7—you use your critical thinking skills to analyze one or more specific texts. Learning summarization skills enables you to represent in your essays the ideas and words of other writers. When you summarize, then, you focus more on *re-presenting* than on analyzing.

In Chapter 8 you will learn about applying general academic writing skills to the mode of argument: in argumentative essays, you assert and defend a claim, usually one of value or policy. When you try to convince someone that something is good or bad or to adopt a particular action, you consider the use of specific strategies in order to support your claim; outside sources may also strengthen your claim.

Research papers, discussed in Chapter 9, display the fullest range of skills for student readers and writers because they combine various skills, including representation, analysis, synthesis, and critical thinking. Although they sometimes use argument, they *always* call on what is for many students one of the most challenging of skills at the post-secondary level: research—locating, evaluating, and integrating outside sources.

Chapter 6

An Overview of the Essay

There are two major models of essay writing: the sequential (or chronological) model and the structural model. Each approaches the essay in a distinct way, although you will no doubt use both at different times.

The Sequential Model

The sequential model quite logically implies that essays, like most projects, are written in chronological stages. Although academic writing may emphasize revising and editing the rough draft or research more than you are used to, students approach academic writing with the knowledge that it is a chronological process that usually begins with a broad topic.

Formulating a Thesis

Using pre-writing techniques, you explore the topic, asking what you know and what you want to find out about it. The objective is to narrow the topic to express your specific focus or approach, which you formulate as a **thesis statement**. Some students find this the most difficult stage: intimidated by a blank page or screen, they may feel frustrated. Fortunately, there are several pre-writing techniques that help to ease the transition from blank to written page.

Students who are assigned a topic of their choice may find the task more daunting than those who are given specific topics on which to write. Although they may be relieved when the instructor offers as preliminary guidance "write on what you're inter-ested in," they may nonetheless feel that many of their interests do not seem to lend themselves to the kind of writing they are being asked to produce at the university level; for example, how does an interest in cats, comics, or classical music translate into a topic for a research essay?

Let us say that you are interested in dance, having taken classes for several years in jazz and hip hop. To refine this broad area, try the "subject test": dance is considered a subject or subdiscipline within the fine or performing arts, yet this subject could be explored from a number of different angles within other disciplines:

THESIS STATEMENT includes the main point of your essay or what you will attempt to prove; it is placed at the end of your introduction.

- dance as self-expression (humanities—fine arts);
- dance as entertainment (humanities—fine arts);
- the history of dance (humanities—history);
- the function of dance in other cultures (humanities—cultural studies; social sciences—anthropology);
- dance as the expression of a collective identity (social sciences—sociology);
- dance as therapy (social sciences—psychology);
- dance as physical movement (science—kinesiology);
- dance as an area of skill acquisition and study (education).

Each of these approaches suggests a way of narrowing the broad subject of dance in order to write on it for different classes or as an assignment for your English class. In fact, the approaches could already be considered topics, but they are, as yet, undeveloped. *What would you like to know about it?* Let us say that you are planning to major in psychology. Therefore, the topic of dance as therapy is something you would like to know more about. One option is to begin your research now by finding out what has been written about this topic. Accordingly, you could check out your library's databases, such as *Humanities Index* or *Periodical Contents Index*, which cover journals focusing on the performing arts. However, there are other techniques you can use to narrow your topic further before you commit yourself to research. These techniques can also be used when you have only a broad subject (such as dance) and want to make it more specific.

Pre-writing Techniques

Freewriting utilizes your associations with something. To freewrite, begin with a blank piece of paper or a blank screen and start recording your associations with a subject. Do not stop to reflect on your next thought or polish your writing: simply write continuously for a predetermined time—such as five or 10 minutes. A good starting point is a sentence that includes the subject you want to find out more about, such as a tentative definition: "Dance as therapy is. . . ."

After you are done, look back at what you have written. You may find much of it repetitive or that you have started thinking about one thing and suddenly switched to something else. That is to be expected. But it is also possible that your writing reveals consistencies or subtleties you had not considered before or were not aware of when you were writing. Underline potentially useful points. You can take the best one and use it as a starting point for another freewriting session, or you could summarize one significant section in a sentence and use that sentence as a new starting point. The sample below is the result of one freewriting session. The writer might have continued by summarizing the last three lines in one sentence and attempted to refine her topic further by a second session.

Dance as therapy is i don't really know what it is as i've never thought about dance that way but i know that my dancing can be therapeutic in that i lose myself self self as i spin or split leap and once the teacher had everyone look at me as i was doing a fouette and i was not even aware only of concentrating on one spot as you're supposed to and i was blocking out everything else and not thinking about what i'm going to wear the next day or my problems at work getting more hours so i can pay for these classes so therapy is healing and there must be a method to follow to heal yourself just as there is a method or technique for learning different kinds of dance i would like to learn about integrating healing into my dancing but i think i do anyway so maybe i am learning about therapy as i dance. (student writer Madison Mauberly)

In the questioning technique, you ask questions pertinent to the topic. Initially, these questions could be the basic *who, what, where, when, why, how.*

- What is dance therapy? What are its basic elements/divisions/stages? What are its goals?
- Who would use dance as therapy? Who would benefit from it?
- Where can you go to study dance therapy? Where is it practised?
- When did dance therapy begin? Why?
- How does it work? How is it similar to/different from other kinds of creative healing techniques?

Each question suggests a different approach to the topic and a different rhetorical pattern. For example, the first question might lead you to the definition pattern; the second question might lead you to divide dance therapy into different types or other subcategories (division/classification). The last question could lead you to focus on comparison and contrast (e.g., dance therapy versus music therapy) or to analyze the costs and benefits of different creative healing techniques (see "Rhetorical Patterns and Paragraph Development," p. 85).

Brainstorming and **clustering** (mapping) work by generating associations. In brainstorming, which can be done either collaboratively or individually, you list your associations with a topic, writing down words and phrases until you feel you have covered the topic thoroughly. Although you do not intentionally look for connections when you generate your list, you can look back after to explore possible connections between the items.

While brainstorming works linearly, clustering is a spatial technique that generates associations and seeks connections among them. You begin by writing a word or phrase in the middle of a blank page and circling it. As associations occur to you, you write them down and circle them, connecting them by a line to the word/phrase that gave rise to the association. As you continue this process beyond the first words/phrases surrounding the original word/phrase, you will develop larger clusters in some places than in others. The well-developed clusters may suggest the most promising ways to develop your topic. The spatial organization of the individual clusters themselves may suggest connections, but you may also be able to draw lines to connect one item in a cluster to another item in a separate cluster. These clusters and interconnecting lines can suggest ways to extend your topic (which is circled in the centre of the page) and develop your essay's structure in the process.

The thesis statement you come up with should always reflect your purpose in writing. For example, if you were writing a personal essay on dance as part of your application to a performing arts program it would be very different from what you would write for a research essay.

BRAINSTORMING
prewriting technique in which you list your associations with a subject in the order they occur to you.

CLUSTERING
prewriting technique that works spatially to generate associations with a subject and connections among them.

Activity

Three sample thesis statements on dance follow. Determine which one would be applicable to a) a personal essay; b) an argumentative essay that attempts to persuade the reader to take a particular course of action; c) a research essay concerned with the historical development of dance therapy:

1. With its roots in modern dance and its stress on self-expression over performance, dance therapy has evolved into a vibrant profession that today serves such diverse groups as disabled people and employees of large corporations.

2. One of my earliest memories is of pulling myself up close to the TV so I could follow the intricate moving shapes before my eyes, trying to make sense of the patterns they formed. Now, at 18, I want to personally explore what it is like to be a part of the visual pattern called dance.

3. Cuts to the operating budgets of performing arts programs at this university must be curtailed so these students can feel the security they need to succeed in their studies and the university community can experience the benefits of the performing arts on campus.

Finding Support

SUPPORT
consists of evidence to help prove a claim.

In the next stage, you attempt to back up your thesis. Thesis statements are claims of some kind. A claim must have **support**; otherwise, it is an empty statement that will be disregarded. For example, although you could claim that the dog ate your homework, your instructor is not likely to take such a claim seriously. But if you produced your vet bill, the claim would at least have some support and may merit your instructor's consideration. If you were writing a critical analysis of a poem, the support would need to come from the poem itself (a primary source). If you were writing a research paper, you would need to find out what other people have said or written about the topic as it relates to your thesis (secondary sources).

Your general claim (thesis statement) must be supported by more specific claims (main points), which, in turn, require support in the form of references to primary sources (English or history essay) or factual information such as statistics or secondary sources (research essay). If, during this stage, it becomes clear that you cannot support your thesis, you can consider adapting the thesis to be in line with the support you have found; occasionally, you may have to abandon the thesis and begin again. (See "Kinds of Evidence," p. 88; see also "Kinds of Evidence in Argumentative Essays," p. 119, and "Selecting Resources" in "The Active Voice: A Beginner's Guide to Researching in the Digital Age," p. 139.)

Relating Parts and Discovering Structure

OUTLINE
linear or graphic representation of main and sub-points, showing an essay's structure.

When you have found enough support, it is time to begin thinking about how you will use it in your essay—how, in other words, you will connect the general claim (thesis statement) to the specific claims (main ideas related to the thesis). With this in mind, you begin organizing claims and support in a logical and consistent way, one that clearly expresses the relationship between each claim and its support. One way to clarify these relationships is to construct an **outline**, a diagrammatic representation of the essay and a plan you can use in the composing stage so you stay on-track.

An outline can be a brief listing of your main points, a *scratch* or *sketch outline*, often used for in-class or exam essays when you do not have the time for much more than a rudimentary sketch of your essay. With longer essays, an outline can be extensively developed to include levels of sub-points (developments of main points) along with details and examples. The *formal outline* uses a number/letter scheme to represent the essay's complete structure. The conventional scheme goes like this:

I. First main point (topic sentence of paragraph)
    A. First sub-point (development of main point)
        1. first sub-sub-point (development of sub-point: detail or example)
        2. second sub-sub-point
    B. Second sub-point
        1. first sub-sub-point
        2. second sub-sub-point

This example represents a paragraph with a three-level outline—that is, one main point and two sub-points—presumably, a very important paragraph in the essay. Not all paragraphs are developed this much; in fact, such a paragraph might be too long to hold a reader's attention, and it might be advisable to divide it into two paragraphs.

When you are considering your outline, especially if it is a formal outline, remember that it serves as the blueprint for the essay itself. Therefore, to construct a useful outline, you should ask questions like the following:

- How do the main points in my outline relate to my thesis statement?
- How do the sub-points relate to my main points?
- Do I have enough main points to support my thesis?
- Do I have enough sub-points (at least two) for each main point?
- Are there any points that seem either irrelevant or out of place? (If the latter, where do they belong?)
- What is the most effective order for my points? (In argumentative essays, you should order points according to their persuasiveness—for example, least to most persuasive, the climax order. In expository essays, you often order them according to a consistent organizational method—for example, compare/contrast, cause/effect, chronology.)
- Are my points logically related to each other (i.e., each one should naturally follow from the previous point)? Will these relationships result in a coherent essay (one that is easy to follow)?
- Can points be expanded? Have I covered everything my reader would expect me to cover?

Composing

Making the commitment to the first draft is difficult for many people—students and non-students alike. It is important to realize that a first draft is inevitably "drafty"—incomplete, uneven, and in need of revising. Its tentative nature should not hold you back from fully recording your thoughts on paper—imperfectly expressed as they may be. See "The Structural Model" (below), which considers the drafting of introductions, middle paragraphs, and conclusions.

Revising

Most essays require more than one draft before you begin to think about the final stage in which you train a critical eye on what you have written. In composing the first, "rough" drafts, your focus is on getting ideas down, explaining, clarifying, integrating, and ordering. During the revision stage, however, you should not expect to be simply dotting i's and crossing t's. The word "revise" means to "see again." First, you should take a hard, objective look at your essay's purpose and audience, its structure, solidity of ideas, connection to your thesis, and clarity of expression. Review these areas as if you are seeing them for the first time. Waiting at least several hours after you have completed a rough draft before revising is sensible. Ask the kinds of questions you originally asked when you were creating an outline (see above, p. 75), and see if you are satisfied with the results.

Next, check for grammatical correctness and stylistic efficiency. *Then*, it will be time to dot the i's and cross the t's—checking for spelling errors and typos and ensuring that the essay conforms to the format your instructor requires.

The importance of these end-stage activities cannot be underestimated, although it is understandable that they sometimes are. After all, when you have finished the rough draft, the paper looks physically complete. It has a beginning, middle, and end; it makes a claim in the thesis statement that is supported through various kinds of evidence. At this time, try to see your essay through the eyes of your instructor. What often strikes a marker first are the very things you may have glossed over as your deadline approached: grammatical errors, lack of coherence, faulty word choice, wordiness, typos, and mechanical errors that could easily have been fixed.

Though nothing will replace careful attention to every detail, here is a checklist that will help you "re-see" your essay:

Content and Structure

- Is the essay's purpose clear? Is it conveyed in the introduction, consistent throughout the middle paragraphs, and reinforced in the conclusion?
- Is it written for a specific audience? What would show a reader this (for example, level of language, voice or tone, kinds of evidence used, citation format)?
- Is the thesis statement aligned with the focus of the essay and its main points? If not, consider adjusting the thesis—sometimes a word or phrase will clarify this alignment.
- Are all paragraphs adequately developed and focused on one main idea?
- Are any paragraphs noticeably shorter or longer than others? If so, can you combine short paragraphs, ensuring a logical transition between them, or break up longer paragraphs, ensuring each can, in fact, stand on its own?
- Have different kinds of evidence been used for support? Does any part of the essay seem less well supported than other parts?
- Would an example, illustration, or analogy make an abstract point more concrete or a general point more specific?
- Is there a possibility a reader could misunderstand any part of the essay? If so, would this be due to the complexity of a point or the way it is expressed? If your draft has been commented on/edited by a peer, pay particular attention to any

passages noted as unclear. If one reader has difficulties in comprehension, others will too.

Grammar and Style

- Are there sentence fragments (i.e., "sentences" missing a subject or predicate), run-on sentences (two "sentences," or independent clauses, with no punctuation between them), or comma splices (two "sentences" separated only by a comma)?
- Is punctuation used correctly? For example, are commas used (1) to separate independent clauses with a coordinating conjunction (*and, or, but, for, nor, yet, so*) and to separate an introductory word, phrase, or clause from a following independent clause; (2) to separate items in a list or series; (3) to separate parenthetical or nonessential words and phrases from more important (essential) information? Are semicolons and colons used correctly? Are dashes and parentheses used correctly and sparingly (dashes for emphasis, parentheses for asides)?
- Are apostrophes used correctly to indicate possession and similar relationships in nouns and indefinite pronouns (e.g., the book's author—one book; the books' authors—more than one book; anyone's opinion—indefinite pronoun)?
- Do verbs agree in number with their subjects and pronouns with their antecedents (the noun they replace)?
- Is the relationship between a noun and its antecedent clear (i.e., every pronoun should refer back to a specific noun)?
- Has the principle of pronoun consistency been maintained (i.e., pronouns should not arbitrarily change from third person [he/she, they/them] to first or second person [I/me, we/us, you])?
- Is parallelism present in sentences with elements that must be parallel (lists, compounds, correlative conjunctions, and comparisons)?
- Are there any misplaced or dangling modifiers, confusing sentence meaning?
- Are you satisfied that every word you have used is the best word and expresses precisely what you want to say? Is the level of language appropriate and have you avoided contractions and slang?
- Have you avoided repetition? Have you managed to eliminate unnecessary words and phrases? Doing so will greatly help you achieve clarity and concision.

Mechanics

- Have all outside references been cited correctly? Have you used the documentation style favoured by your instructor or by your discipline?
- Have you met word length, essay/page format, and other specific requirements?
- Have you proofread the essay at least twice (once for content and flow, once for minor errors such as typos—breaking each word into syllables and reading syllabically throughout is the best way to catch minor errors)?

The Process-Reflective Method

Most essays are not written mechanically using the sequential model: you may often find yourself going back and forth—from composing to outline, for example, if you find you need to rethink your original structure, or from composing back to the research stage if you need to check on a source or find more support for a point. In fact, it is a sign of your maturity as a writer if you *do* go back and reconsider changes as the writing process is ongoing.

Many writers, including professionals, do not follow a traditional-linear process but instead write more discursively; that is, they begin composing without any firm plan in place, trusting to their instincts and realizing that it is sometimes only by writing something down and taking the risk of going off-topic occasionally that they can discover what they really want to say. In the exploratory model discussed below, your intentions and goals are revealed through the act of writing itself, and an outline is less important than in the linear, highly planned approach. Below, Frans de Waal, primatologist and author of *Our Inner Ape*, describes his personal process. Few instructors would recommend it, but it does illustrate the importance of revising and the necessity of finding the approach that works best for you:

> I write my books without much of an outline except for the chapter titles. My main strategy is to just start writing and see what happens. From one topic follows another, and before you know it I have a dozen pages filled with stories and thoughts. . . . I have a very visual memory, and remember events in great detail. When I write, my desk fills up with ever higher piles of papers and books used for reference, until it is a big mess, which is something I cannot stand. I am very neat. So, at some point I put all that stuff away, print out the text I've written, and sit down comfortably with a red pen. By that time I have already gone over the text multiple times. With pen in hand, I do a very rigorous rereading and again change things around. (http://www.emory.edu/LIVING_LINKS/OurInnerApe/book.html)

PROCESS-REFLECTIVE DRAFT
draft that emerges from a
flexible engagement with what
you are writing, one that reflects
the connections between
thinking and writing.

The **process-reflective draft** involves a self-conscious approach to what you are writing. When de Waal reveals, above, that he has "gone over the text multiple times" before he stops to consider large-scale changes, he is revealing his preference for a writing process in which he pauses to reflect, re-examine, and change, if necessary, before continuing—a kind of revision on the fly, or paragraph-by-paragraph approach. As with the traditional-linear approach, however, you should not be concerned with mechanical correctness as you write.

Typical activities in process-reflective drafts are rephrasing, clarifying, evaluating, amplifying, and connecting: you concern yourself with making logical transitions from one thought to the next and checking to see that your developing points are consistent with your general plan. You should begin with a few rough points and "reminders," such as important authors or quotations you want to use, but you do not need to have a detailed plan. Rather, the plan evolves as you write. Process-reflective writing can also be used for in-class and exam essays in which there is seldom time to outline your points in detail.

The Structural Model

Like the sequential model, the structural model is familiar to most students because it is often stressed in high school. The essay is divided into an introduction, middle or body paragraphs, and a conclusion. Each part contributes in a different way to the essay.

Writing Introductions

Introductions are more than just starting places. Their primary function is to inform the reader about the essay's purpose and topic and what the writer's approach to the topic will be (usually through the thesis statement); sometimes, they also mention the essay's main points. As well, introductions may indicate the primary organizational pattern for the essay. In all these ways, the introduction previews what is forthcoming.

Good introductions are inherently persuasive: they must sufficiently interest the reader, encouraging him or her to read on, perhaps by conveying the importance of the topic. As science writer Bradley Anholt puts it, "You need to convince your readers to care enough about the subject to invest their time in reading your paper."

Introductions not only introduce the essay but also introduce its writer; therefore, you must come across as credible and reliable. Nobody, except a college or university instructor, is going to continue reading an essay if the writer has not come across as credible. (See "Issues of Credibility," p. 89.)

Student writers are often advised to write their introductions last because they will not know precisely how the topic will develop until the body of the essay is written. On the other hand, many writers like to have a concrete starting point. If the latter describes you best, you should return to the introduction after you have completed drafting your middle paragraphs to ensure that it fits well with them.

Thesis Statements

The Greek word *thesis* refers to the act of placing or setting down. *A thesis statement, then, is a formal assertion, a generalization that is applicable to the entire essay*. However, this generalization can take different forms depending on purpose and audience. Student and academic writers usually place the thesis statement in their introductions; journalistic writers often do not. For kinds of theses in academic essays, see Chapter 2 (p. 20).

The thesis announces the topic and includes a comment about the topic (*simple thesis statement*). Thesis statements may also incorporate the major points to be discussed in the essay (*expanded thesis statement* or *essay plan*). The thesis statement usually embodies a **claim**, the nature of which depends on the essay's purpose. Typical argumentative claims are ones of *value* or *policy*. *Fact-based* claims are common in expository essays in the sciences and social sciences, while *interpretive* claims are used in many humanities essays in which the writer sets out to analyze one or more primary sources by using a specific frame of reference, such as a critical theory of some kind, or a set of discipline-related standards that are announced in the claim. For example, a poem could be analyzed through the lens of feminist theory or by looking at its literary motifs.

CLAIM
assertion about the topic appearing in the thesis statement and topic sentences.

For comparative purposes, the following statements illustrate the different forms that theses can take:

Conventional thesis statement from an expository student essay (fact-based claim): Xenotransplantation, the transplantation of organs across a species barrier, is emerging as a possible alternative to transplants from human donors.

Conventional thesis statement from an argumentative student essay (policy claim): Despite the variety of equipment, aerobic classes, and availability of personal trainers, joining a fitness club will not meet a person's complete needs today. Canadians need to step out into their backyards to find the many wonders the outdoors and sports have to offer.

Thesis in the form of a question: In Europe, stirrups changed the warfare of the time, but could they have also had an impact on society beyond the battlefield?

Thesis in the form of a hypothesis from an academic essay: It was hypothesized that obsessive passion, but not harmonious passion, would be related to greater gambling involvement and greater problem gambling severity. (A.A. Skitch & D.C. Hodgins. 2005. "A passion for the game: Problem gambling and passion among university students." *Canadian Journal of Behavioural Science, 37*: 193–197.)

Creating Reader Interest

Although thinking about techniques to generate reader interest is especially important when you are writing for a general audience, all readers need to be convinced at the outset that your essay is worth reading. The most traditional way to generate interest and persuade your reader of the topic's importance is to use a **logical opening**: to begin with a universal statement that becomes more specific and ends with the most specific claim, the thesis itself; this method is referred to as the inverted triangle method.

One risk in this approach is that in making the first sentence too broad or familiar, it fails to interest the reader. Therefore, student writers are often encouraged to use a **dramatic opening**. Examples of dramatic openings include the use of personal experience, description, or narration, or asking a pertinent question that intrigues the reader. An opening could also make an emotional appeal; however, use these appeals cautiously because you cannot always assume that a typical reader will respond in the way you wish. The following paragraphs illustrate two different ways of attracting reader interest. Note that, in both cases, the last sentence is the thesis statement.

Logical: The writer begins with a statement about the beginning of World War I and proceeds to discuss Canada's contribution to the war effort. He then briefly refers to Canadians of British descent before focusing on the contribution of Aboriginal peoples.

> Canada was only 47 years old when it entered World War I on the same day as Britain in August 1914. Canada saw the war as an opportunity to define itself as a great nation and contributed by supplying, among other things, materials and soldiers. By the time peace was declared, over 400,000 Canadians had fought in World War I, of whom approximately 60,000 lost their lives (Gaffen 15). Canadians of direct British descent were not the only people willing to help their country; Aboriginals also enlisted, eager to prove their right to be called British subjects. Early on, there was some question as to whether or not Aboriginals should be allowed to participate in the war. Their lack of British lineage, together with the false stereotypes of violence created by books like *The Last of the Mohicans*, initially made the Canadian government reluctant to officially accept them into the army. Eager to disprove any previous stereotypes, and with a desire to be accepted as British subjects, Aboriginals fought hard and contributed immensely during World War I. (student writer Mike Mason)

Dramatic (questions): The writer begins with two questions, referring to the popular connotation of perfectionism. Using the reversal strategy, she then cites the definition of experts. Her final sentence makes it clear that her essay will focus on the problems of the "maladaptive perfectionist."

What does it mean to say that one is a perfectionist? Does it mean that one does everything perfectly? In common language, the term "perfectionist" carries the connotation that the perfectionistic individual does everything perfectly, but according to perfectionism experts in social psychology, perfectionism is a term referring to a mentality, or set of cognitions, that are characteristic of certain people. According to Hollender (as cited in Slade & Owens, 1998), perfectionism refers to "the practice of demanding of oneself or others a higher quality of performance than is required by the situation" (p. 384). Although the name suggests to the layperson that perfectionism would be a desirable trait, this quality is in fact often unrecognized for its detrimental effects on the lives of people who are maladaptively perfectionistic. Perfectionism is associated with mental illness and can contribute to problems in areas of life such as academic success and intimate relationships. (student writer Erin Walker)

Activity

In the following paragraphs, a) identify the method for creating interest; b) discuss how the writer establishes his or her credibility; c) identify the thesis statement and whether it is a simple thesis or an expanded one. You can also pre-read "Rhetorical Patterns and Paragraph Development," p. 85, to determine the essay's main organizational method.

1. Women in society have come a long way, from earning the right to vote to becoming political leaders, and from riding horses side saddle to riding motorcycles. Today, with more dual income families and an increasing number of wives whose salaries are more than their husbands, the gender wage gap has improved significantly. However, women are still not treated equally in the workplace, and women's salaries remain a very relevant issue as, on average, women make only seventy two cents for every dollar that men make (Drolet, "Why has the gender wage gap narrowed?"). In a society that has promoted gender pay equality since 1956 by implementing the *Female Employees Equal Pay Act* (Canadian Human Rights Commission "Federal Government adopts the *Female Employees Equal Pay Act*".), how can such a large disparity still exist? By examining the gender wage gap and its causes, the problem is clear, but what are the solutions? Action must be taken to overcome this disparity by an extensive education program that informs society about the gender wage gap and its contributing factors. (student writer Jacqueline Greenard)

2. On April 6, 1994, the plane transporting Rwandan President Juvenal Habyarimana was shot down, killing everyone on board. This tragedy was only the beginning; the death of President Habyarimana set in motion a violent genocide that had been brewing for more than a century. The dominant Hutus feared an uprising of the oppressed Tutsis and sought to avoid the threat by exterminating them. The Rwandan capital of Kigali was engulfed in violence within minutes of the president's death, and the presidential guard embarked on a "campaign of retribution." A massive Hutu civilian mob known as the Interahamwe, meaning "*those who attack together*," rampaged across the country for the next three months as anti-Tutsi propaganda pumped through the airwaves. The Rwanda Patriotic Front (RPF) eventually launched an organized counterattack in July and regained control of Kigali, but by the time the last shot was fired, nearly 800,000 Tutsis had lost

their lives. In the aftermath of this mass murder, experts began analyzing how a tragedy of this magnitude could have happened and have isolated three main factors: the long-standing Rwandan struggle for racial dominance, the ineffective pre-emptive mediation during the years preceding the genocide, and the absence of foreign aid and intervention once the massacre had begun (Walker & Zajtman, 2004). (student writer Alec Page)

Writing Middle Paragraphs

The structure of middle paragraphs is often said to mirror that of the essay itself: the paragraph begins with a generalization that is supported by the sentences that follow. In its structure and function, the essay's thesis statement is equivalent to the **topic sentence** of a paragraph, which announces the main idea (topic) of that paragraph. This is a useful, if somewhat restrictive, analogy—useful because it stresses the importance of a predictable order for both essays and paragraphs but also somewhat limiting because, in reality, paragraphs are not always constructed this way.

When a writer uses a topic sentence to announce the central idea, the rest of the paragraph provides support, such as examples, reasons, statistical data, or other kinds of evidence. In some way, it illustrates, expands on, or reinforces the topic sentence. In the following paragraph, student writer Leslie Nelson expands on the main idea, first by explaining the function of talking therapies and then by dividing them into three different subcategories and explaining the function of each (the topic sentence is italicized):

> *Talking therapies—especially when combined with medication—are common to treatment of adolescent depression.* There are several kinds of talking therapies, including cognitive and humanistic approaches, and family and group sessions. Each of these therapy types confronts depression in a different way, and each is useful to adolescent treatment. Cognitive therapies confront illogical thought patterns that accompany depression; humanistic therapies provide support to the patient, stressing unconditional acceptance. Group therapies, on the other hand, encourage depressed patients to talk about their feelings in a setting with other people who are undergoing treatment for similar problems. This therapy can inspire different coping strategies, and it allows people to realize that they are not alone in their problems.

However, in the following paragraph, the writer uses his first sentence to set up a common opinion with which he disagrees. His own position is not fully explained until the final sentence, the paragraph's topic sentence, italicized below:

> Some suggest that we should actively limit our reliance on technological props and aids, not just to protect our privacy but to control our own destinies and preserve our essential humanity. Here, the title of the book gives me away. Human-machine symbiosis, I believe, is simply what comes naturally. It lies on a direct continuum with clothes, cooking, bricklaying, and writing. *The capacity to creatively distribute labour between biology and the designed environment is the very signature of our species, and it implies no real loss of control on our part,*

TOPIC SENTENCE
states the main idea in the paragraph, usually the first sentence.

for who we are is in large part a function of the webs of surrounding structure in which the conscious mind exercises at best a kind of gentle, indirect control. (Andy Clark. *Natural Born Cyborgs.*)

You can experiment by trying different placements for your topic sentences. The common placement as the first sentence tends to make for a coherent paragraph, while a succession of such paragraphs contributes to a readable, coherent essay, but students should choose the order that best reflects the paragraph's purpose. For example, in the first paragraph above, the writer is dividing a general category into subcategories, while in the second paragraph, the writer is raising a point in order to counter it with his own point. These purposes require contrastive approaches to paragraph construction.

Writing Strong Paragraphs

Effective paragraphs are unified, coherent, and well-developed. A **unified** paragraph focuses on only one main idea; when you move to another main idea, you begin a new paragraph. If, however, a paragraph is lengthy, you should consider dividing it into two paragraphs even if each contains the same idea. Look for the most logical place to make the division; for example, you could divide the paragraph where you begin an important sub-point.

A **coherent** paragraph is easy to follow. Coherent paragraphs are both clear and carefully arranged to place the emphasis where you want it to be. Compositional theorists use the term **reader-based prose** to suggest a focus on the concerns of the reader. In reader-based prose, the writer carefully designs the paragraph for a specific audience by using understandable and well-organized prose, stressing what is most important and omitting what is irrelevant, and clarifying the relationships among the points and sub-points. Coherence can be achieved by considering the following points:

UNITY
principle of paragraph construction in which only one idea is developed throughout the paragraph.

COHERENCE
principle of paragraph construction in which ideas are logically laid out with clear connections between them.

READER-BASED PROSE
clear, accessible writing designed for an intended reader.

1. *Logical sentence order:* In logical sentence order, one sentence follows naturally from the preceding one, and there are no sentences out of order or off-topic (an off-topic sentence would not result in a unified paragraph); there are no gaps in thought that the reader has to try to fill.
2. *Organizational patterns:* You can order the paragraph according to specific patterns (see "Rhetorical Patterns and Paragraph Development," below).
3. *Precise language:* When you consider what words to use, remember that it is not always a case of the right word versus the wrong word. Always choose the *best word for the given context.* Whenever you use a word that is not part of your everyday vocabulary, you should confirm its meaning by looking it up in a dictionary.
4. *Appropriate adverbial transitions:* Transitional words and phrases enable you to convey precise relationships between one idea and the next.
5. *Selective rephrasing and reiteration:* Knowing the knowledge level of your audience will determine whether and when you should rephrase in order to clarify difficult concepts.
6. *Repetition of key words/phrases or the use of synonyms:* Repetition can be used to emphasize important ideas. Of course, *needless* repetition should always be avoided.

7. *Parallel/balanced structures:* Employing parallel/balanced structures creates coherence, in part, through the use of familiar syntactic patterns. William Shakespeare and Charles Dickens are two acknowledged literary masters of balanced structures, which makes their words memorable and easy to recall.

Being aware of organizational and syntactical patterns as you write will make you a more conscious writer, focused on the needs of your readers. In the excerpt below, after defining the term "nanotechnology," student writer Jeff Proctor makes effective use of transitions (noted by italics) to help explain a difficult concept to general readers. He uses a balanced structure in sentence 4 to make a comparison understandable and repeats the key word "precision" at strategic points in the paragraph (the beginning, middle, and end); other words, too, can be considered near-synonyms for "precision" (synonyms and repetition are underlined):

> Nanotechnology will allow the construction of compounds at nanometre precision. *Essentially*, this capability would allow scientists to form a substance one atom at a time and to put each atom exactly where it needs to be. *Consequently*, any chemical structure that is stable under normal conditions could theoretically be produced. In comparison to semiconductor lithography, which could be imagined as the formation of electrical circuits by joining large heaps of molecules, the techniques of nanotechnology could be imagined as the careful arrangement of molecules with a pair of tweezers. With this incredible degree of precision, electrical circuits could be designed to be smaller than ever before. *Currently*, each component in a computer is the size of thousands of atoms; *however*, if nanotechnological processes were used to produce it, one component could be on the scale of several atoms. This fact alone emphasizes the potential efficiency of next-generation computer circuits, for smaller components are closer together and, *thus*, able to communicate with each other in less time. *Furthermore*, it could be guaranteed that products are reproducible and reliable as a result of the absolute precision of these formation processes.

Transitions in the paragraph above convey various relationships: *essentially* (transition of summary), *consequently*, *thus* (cause/effect), *currently* (time), *however* (contrast), *furthermore* (addition). Other relationships include concession or limit (e.g., *admittedly*, *although*, *though*, *it is true that*, *of course*), illustration (e.g., *for example*, *for instance*, *such as*), sequence (e.g., *first*, *second . . .; then*, *next*), and emphasis (e.g., *certainly*, *especially*, *in fact*, *indeed*, *undoubtedly*).

Striving for coherence throughout the writing process should not just enable a reader to follow you but also assist you in clarifying your train of thought as you write. Successful writing is the result of a complex process that utilizes varied cognitive activities at different times. To clarify your own thoughts, it is useful to consciously rephrase ideas and specific passages as you write. Without crossing out what you wrote, follow it with transitions like *in other words*, *in short*, *in summary*, *to reiterate*, *that is* and a paraphrase or expansion of the original. If your "second attempt" is clearer—and it often is—you can then consider crossing out the original to avoid needless repetition.

For more information on paragraphs, see "Dividing the Whole," p. 53, and "Reading Paragraphs: Locating Main Ideas," p. 54.

Sidebar:

Striving for coherence throughout the writing process should not just enable a reader to follow you but also assist you in clarifying your train of thought as you write. Successful writing is the result of a complex process that utilizes varied cognitive activities at different times. To clarify your own thoughts, it is useful to consciously rephrase ideas and specific passages as you write. Without crossing out what you wrote, follow it with transitions like *in other words*, *in short*, *in summary*, *to reiterate*, *that is* and a paraphrase or expansion of the original. If your "second attempt" is clearer—and it often is—you can then consider crossing out the original to avoid needless repetition.

Rhetorical Patterns and Paragraph Development

Rhetorical patterns are systematic ways to organize and present information; they apply to both the essay itself and to individual paragraphs. All the claims you make in your essay—your general claim, or thesis, and your specific claims, which are usually made in your topic sentences—must be well-supported or they will not be convincing. You can support a general claim by using one primary rhetorical pattern, which will depend on your essay's purpose. For example, the first of the thesis statements above, p. 79, on xeno-transplantation, will likely be organized through the problem/solution pattern (this transplantation method offers a possible solution to a problem); the second will likely use cost/benefit, with the writer arguing for the benefits of exercising outdoors, although perhaps acknowledging that exercising in gyms is also beneficial; the third and fourth examples will use the cause/effect pattern.

Writers also use these and other patterns to help organize and develop individual paragraphs, supporting the specific claims in the topic sentences. Part of an essay's success lies in choosing the most appropriate rhetorical pattern(s) to develop a claim.

> RHETORICAL PATTERN
> method for organizing and presenting information in essays and paragraphs; examples include cause-effect, classification, compare and contrast, cost-benefit, and definition.

Purpose	Rhetorical Pattern	Description/Explanation
To create an image or picture of something	Description	Uses images related to sight or the other senses to create immediacy and involve the reader; uses modifiers (adjectives and adverbs) to add detail; may systematically focus on a scene, using a logical method such as from left to right, top to bottom, etc.
To tell a story	Narration	Relates an occurrence, usually in chronological order; stresses action through the use of strong verbs; anecdotes are brief narratives that introduce or illustrate a point.
To show how something works or is done	Process analysis	Breaks down a (usually) complex process into a sequence of successive steps, making it more understandable; provides instructions or directions.
To show the way something changed/ developed	Chronology	Uses time order to trace something, often from its beginning to the present day; can be applied to people, objects (like inventions), or situations.
To particularize the general or concretize the abstract	Example	Gives particular instances of a larger category, enabling readers to better understand the larger category; gives immediacy and concreteness to what can seem otherwise broad or abstract.
To analyze why something happened or a result/ outcome	Cause/effect	Uses inductive methods to draw conclusions; works from causes to effects or from effects to causes; for example, to determine whether smoking leads to (causes) heart disease or to determine whether heart disease results from (is an effect of) smoking.
To account for or justify something	Reasons	Uses deductive methods that draw on one's knowledge or experience (which may ultimately be derived from inductive findings); for example, you should not smoke because it often leads to heart disease (reason derived via empirical evidence).

Purpose	Rhetorical Pattern	Description/Explanation
To analyze by dividing into subcategories	Classification/division	Classification: groups according to shared characteristics (e.g., types of bottled water: purified, mineral, sparkling). Division: separates large category into constituent parts (e.g., the essay into introduction, middle paragraphs, conclusion).
To look at two sides/views of something	Cost/benefit analysis	Weighs the pros and cons of an issue, question, or action, usually to decide which is stronger; in argument, cost/benefit analysis is used to support a value or policy claim and/or refute an opposing claim.
To identify a problem or solve/resolve it	Problem/solution	Analyzes or explains a problem or proposes a solution; may incorporate other methods, such as reasons, cause/effect, or cost/benefit analysis.
To better understand something	Analogy	Shows how one subject is similar to another to clarify the nature or a feature of the first subject.

Most topics can be developed by using one or more of the methods above or the two methods discussed below. For example, if you were looking for ways to develop the topic "fighting in hockey," you could use description or narration to convey the excitement of a hockey brawl; conversely, you could use either method to convey it as an unseemly spectacle. You could use the process analysis pattern to depict the step-by-step procedures officials use to break up a fight, the chronological pattern to trace the history of rules governing fighting, or the pattern by example to call attention to notorious fighting incidents in recent years.

Definition

Using definition as a rhetorical pattern is common in expository essays written for a general audience who would be unfamiliar with specialized terms. Thus, definitions often precede large sections that focus on explaining or analyzing, as in this introduction to an essay on the effects of trans fat on human health:

> In the early 1900s, William Normann invented the hydrogenation process in which trans fat, short for trans-fatty acid, is the byproduct. A tiny amount of trans fat is found naturally, usually in animal fat; however, the majority of trans fats are made when hydrogen is added to vegetable oil in a process called hydrogenation. Hydrogenation is the modification of vegetable oil to allow it to be a solid at room temperature. The way the atoms of the fatty acids are bonded shows whether the fat is saturated or unsaturated: saturated fats have only single bonds while unsaturated fats have double bonds. A trans fat is a fat that was once an unsaturated fat but has had its double bonds weakened through the process of hydrogenation. (student writer Kim Snyder)

Using definition can also be an effective strategy in argument. Value claims, in particular, often rely on definition: after explaining what you mean by something, you can support the claim by demonstrating the validity of the definition through various kinds of evidence. For example, if you were arguing that gymnastics should or should not be considered a sport, you would need to state what you meant by a "sport." Ensuring that this was a definition with which most readers would agree, you could then use the definition as a springboard into your claim and main points by showing how gymnastics does or does not fit this definition.

Comparison and Contrast

Comparison and contrast can be used to develop one or more paragraphs or to organize an entire essay. When you compare, you look at how two items are similar; when you contrast, you consider their differences. However, the term *compare* is generally used to refer to both similarities and differences. You can compare ideas, issues, people, places, objects, or events—as long as bases of comparison exist to make such comparisons valid. For example, you can compare two jobs by looking at their salaries, workweeks, levels of responsibility, and so on. However, if you were comparing two things in order to evaluate them, you would have to ensure that the same evaluation standards could be fairly applied to each. For example, you could not evaluate two universities that were vastly different in size. That is why the compilers of *Maclean's Guide to Canadian Universities* categorize universities by their size before applying their performance measures, such as student body, classroom size, and calibre of faculty, which serve as the bases of comparison.

> "When you compare, you look at how two items are similar; when you contrast, you consider their differences. However, the term *compare* is generally used to refer to both similarities and differences."

Organizing a comparison and contrast essay can be more complicated than organizing essays that use another primary rhetorical pattern. Consider using the three-step approach when organizing these kinds of essays.

1. Determine whether the two items you want to compare *can* logically be compared. The health care system in the US cannot be compared to the education system in Canada. Although the health care systems in the two countries are comparable, such a large undertaking might prove unmanageable. More reasonable would be a comparison between two provincial health care or education systems.

2. Carefully select the bases of comparison, or criteria for comparing (choosing at least three should help make the comparison valid); each basis can serve as a main point in your essay.

3. Choose one of two possible methods for organizing your main points: the *subject-by-subject (block)* method or the *point-by-point (topics)* method. In the first, you begin with the first subject of comparison and apply your bases of comparison to it; you then do the same for the second subject, keeping your points (criteria) in the identical order. In the more commonly used point-by-point method, you begin with a basis of comparison and apply it to the first, then the second subject. You continue to do this until you have represented all your bases of comparison.

> "In the block method, you begin with the first subject of comparison and apply your bases of comparison to it; you then do the same for the second subject, keeping your points (criteria) in the identical order. In the more commonly used point-by-point method, you begin with a basis of comparison and apply it to the first, then the second subject. You continue to do this until you have represented all your bases of comparison."

Which is the better method? The block method stresses the subjects themselves, while the point-by-point method stresses the criteria for comparison. If there seems no compelling reason to prefer one over the other, consider that the point-by-point method can be more efficient and easier to follow because in the block method, the reader needs to keep in mind each basis of comparison as it has been applied to the first subject while it is being raised for the second subject. For this reason, essays that use the block method can be more challenging to write and to read.

The following paragraphs use one basis of comparison, human health benefits, as part of an essay that compares organic and locally grown foods to determine which is better for human and ecosystem health. The paragraph that discusses the benefits of organic food is longer because more studies have been done on this. Nevertheless, the second paragraph on locally grown foods is well-developed through logical reasoning. Notice that both paragraphs present different contrasts: the first between organic and non-organic food and the second between locally grown and imported foods. Thus, the essay's main organizational method is compare and contrast, while individual paragraphs are also developed through this pattern:

> The demand for organically produced food in supermarkets across North America has steadily increased over the past decade (USDA, 2008). A big reason for this is the widely held belief that organic food is better for our health than "conventional" food, largely based on differences in how the food is grown. Organic food is produced naturally and has no contact with synthetic inputs, such as pesticides, chemical food additives, or chemical fertilizers. "Conventional" food, by contrast, is grown in conditions where synthetic chemicals are used. Naturally, this has led many people to believe that there is more nutritional value in organic than in non-organic food (Williams, 2002). However, a critical review of past research shows an inconsistency in data regarding the relationship between organic food and increased nutrients (Magkos, Arvaniti, Zampelas, 2006). Short-term studies have shown mixed results regarding the health benefits of conventional and organic food; long-term studies, due to time and money constraints, have been too difficult to undertake. It remains unclear if organic is indeed more nutritious than conventionally grown food.
>
> There have been substantially fewer scientific studies on the health effects of eating local food, but it has garnered no shortage of public awareness. In a wave of new food initiatives, regimens that stress eating locally, like the 100-mile diet, have become extremely popular. Although people tend to buy local food for political reasons, it can be argued that it is actually better for your health than exotic food. Fruits and vegetables that travel a great distance before being consumed are harvested early to allow time to ripen during transportation. Local food travels a very short distance before being consumed, which allows for it to ripen in its natural environment. With shortened food chains (Feagen, 2007), produce that is ripened by the sun and consumed soon after harvest will not only taste better but also retain more nutrients than produce grown at a distance. (student writer Stephen Littleford)

For examples of essays in *The Active Reader* that employ different rhetorical patterns, including definition and comparison and contrast, see "Classification by Rhetorical Mode/Pattern or Style," (inside back cover).

Kinds of Evidence

Although it is good to use various kinds of evidence in your essay, some are likely going to be more important than others. The choices you make depend on your purpose, audience, topic and claim, and the type of essay you are writing. For example, if you are writing a rhetorical analysis, it will focus on the essay you're analyzing as a primary source; if you are writing a research essay, your focus will likely be on secondary sources. For kinds of evidence typically used in argumentative essays, see p. 119.

Common kinds of evidence may vary from discipline to discipline: humanities writing often uses extensive direct quotation from primary sources; social sciences writing tends to focus on statistics, interviews, questionnaires, case studies, and interpersonal observation, while the sciences rely on direct methods that involve experimentation.

Some kinds of evidence can be more authoritative than others. In fact-based writing, "hard" evidence—facts, statistics, and the findings of empirical research—provides the strongest grounds for support. Various kinds of "soft" evidence, such as expert opinion, examples, illustrations, and analogies, may also be important to help explain a concept but will likely be less important than "hard" evidence. Argumentative essays may use analogies, precedents, expert opinion, and even, perhaps, personal experience.

One kind of example that is often pertinent to fact-based social sciences writing, as well as writing in business and education, is the **case study**, a detailed exploration of one particular case, such as a real-life situation, in order to gain a depth of understanding of the issue being investigated. Case studies use empirical methods of observing and recording, although typically, the data produced and then analyzed is qualitative rather than quantitative, based, for example, on interviews, questionnaires, and personal observation. Because of their systematic methodology and the wealth of detail that is analyzed, the findings from case studies can often be generalized, while ordinary examples cannot.

> CASE STUDY
> carefully selected example that is analyzed in detail in order to support a writer's claim.

Issues of Credibility

Credibility factors include *knowledge, reliability*, and *fairness*. You exhibit your knowledge by appearing well-informed about your topic and supporting each claim with solid and substantial evidence. You convey reliability in many ways:

> CREDIBILITY
> along with evidence helps support a claim. Credibility can be demonstrated by an author's knowledge, reliability, and fairness.

- by using the accepted conventions of the discipline in which you are writing; this includes using the appropriate citation style, being aware of the specialized language of the discipline, and adhering to format requirements, such as the use of an abstract and formal sections (report writing);
- by writing effectively and following the rules of grammar, punctuation, syntax, sentence structure, and spelling; writing efficiently, using words that express exactly what you want them to;
- by using credible and authoritative sources (research essays);
- by reasoning logically and avoiding logical fallacies (argumentative essays).

Although fairness applies particularly to argumentative essays, it can also be important in research essays, since synthesis could involve acknowledging sources whose findings contradict your claim or hypothesis; this entails accounting for contrary evidence. The following criteria, however, apply mostly to argument. You convey fairness in several ways:

- by using an objective voice and not showing bias;
- by acknowledging and accurately representing the opposing view;
- by looking for common ground;
- by avoiding slanted language and emotional fallacies.

Writing Conclusions

CONCLUSION
the last paragraph or section of an essay whose function is to summarize the thesis and/or main points in the body of the essay. Circular conclusions reinforce the thesis; spiral conclusions suggest applications or further research.

Like introductions, **conclusions** can vary depending on the kind of essay and other factors. While conclusions are always a vital part of essays, their functions differ. In student essays, the conclusion refers back to the thesis statement, reasserting its importance and usually rephrasing it. The conclusion may also look ahead by considering a way that the thesis can be applied or the ways that it could be further explored.

Although essay conclusions may both look back to the thesis statement and look ahead to the thesis's implications, the stress often falls on one or the other. *Circular conclusions* are primarily concerned with reminding the reader of your thesis and with reinforcing it. Even so, if you want to emphasize these functions, you should not repeat the thesis word for word, nor should you simply summarize what you have already said in your introduction. You should draw attention to the significance of the paragraphs that follow your introduction and precede your conclusion—after all, they are probably the most substantial part of the essay. One way you can do this is to summarize the most important point, connecting it to your thesis.

Spiral conclusions refer to the thesis but are more concerned with looking beyond it by considering its larger importance. In argumentative essays, you may want to make an emotional or ethical appeal or, especially if your purpose is to reach a compromise, to suggest common ground between your view and the opposing one. Other strategies in spiral conclusions include ending with a relevant anecdote or personal experience (informal essays) or a question or hypothesis that extends from your findings or that of the research you have used (formal essays or reports). If your focus has been on a problem, this may be the time to suggest ways to solve it; thus, you could end by making recommendations. If your topic was applicable to a relatively small number of people, you can suggest how it could be generalized to a larger group, one that would include the reader.

The paragraph below uses the circular pattern. Although it repeats some information from the introduction, it uses different words and introduces a new term, "adaptive perfectionism," from the middle paragraphs of the essay. In the final sentence, the writer advocates further research in the field to benefit people who are maladaptive perfectionists. You can compare the conclusion to the introduction, above on page 81.

As an infiltrating personality characteristic, perfectionism is often deleterious and psychologically harmful. Although adaptive perfectionism has been associated with positive elements such as a proclivity for excellence, it has also been associated with increased levels of depression as compared to non-perfectionists. Maladaptive perfectionism is that much more detrimental to an individual's life in that it is associated with more elements of mental illness and with difficulty in academics and intimate relationships. Since, as Costa and McCrae (1986) point out, personality is relatively stable, research on perfectionism is a warranted endeavour to better understand, and to better help people suffering from, this quality. (Student writer Erin Walker)

The following "Active Voice" essays, "Report Writing" and "How to Write a Scientific Paper," give guidelines relevant to students writing reports and papers in the sciences, social sciences, engineering, and other disciplines in which an adaptation of the Type B essay is required. Note the emphasis in both essays on clear, direct, and active writing.

The Active Voice

REPORT WRITING – AIMS AND GOALS

1   Of all types of writing, report writing is the most categorically active. It's built on *doing something*, then writing about what was discovered as a result of doing it—a lab experiment, for instance, or a survey, or a site visit. "Planned," "designed," "measured," "saw," "researched," "interviewed," "calculated," "analyzed," "evaluated," "solved": verbs—dynamic action or "doing" words—lie at the heart of all report writing. That's because reports record the results of a study undertaken to *find out something specific*: answer a question, clarify an issue, solve a problem, analyze a policy, establish a cause or consequence, decide on a course of action, evaluate possible outcomes, make a recommendation, or give an update on a project. In all these cases, reports "write up" the results of a study conducted to yield specific, concrete information that's otherwise missing, unknown, or incomplete.

2   Original findings based on original research—that's what reports typically deal with. In fact, "Report of original research" is a common name for this type of writing in the science and social science disciplines, where the principal goal is to expand the field of knowledge— to fill gaps in the current state of research. The audience for such reports is typically other scientists or scholars. The report writer's job is to convince experts in the field that the findings are valid, making an original contribution to knowledge.

3   In other situations, however, report writing may answer more practical goals. Engineers, for example, may write investigative reports, recommendation reports, feasibility reports, or progress reports. The information compiled in these types of reports is usually intended to promote a specific course of action—for example, to implement (or scrap) a policy, develop a community program, approve an expansion of medical facilities, upgrade a highway, purchase new educational software, build a new gas line, or restore polluted waterways. As a result, they tend to be written for a mixed audience—other engineers as well as managers, policy-makers, public administrators, budgeting personnel, or company clients. Consequently, while they're generally technical in scope, they're often written so as to make sense to non-experts as well, with the goal of persuading them to act on the findings.

Organizing Reports

4   We've said that the goal of report writing is to provide specialized, concrete information, based on empirical research, in response to a question, problem, or project. At the same time, to ensure the report is sufficiently persuasive—allowing important decisions to be made on the information presented—reports also record *how* the information was compiled. They provide a methodology. This is a key way in which science and much social science writing differs from humanities writing. It explains not only the facts but how the facts were derived. This is important because knowing *how* the data was compiled means readers can gauge its trustworthiness for themselves.

5   Report writers therefore organize reports with an eye to showing *how* the information was found so they can demonstrate its reliability. Luckily, organizational *templates* make this a relatively easy task. Formal reports have a rigidly defined structure that report writers are expected to follow to meet disciplinary demands for clarity and accountability. The American Psychological Association (APA), the disciplinary body that regulates report writing in the social sciences and some of the sciences, requires an IMRAD style of organization: introduction, methods, results, and discussion, with each section clearly signalled by headings.

Introduction

6   Introductions provide context and needed background, explaining topic and purpose, describing what the study was intended to find out and why. In the academic disciplines, this

usually involves giving an opening literature review, an overview of current research in the field. A research question that the study is designed to answer may also be stipulated.

7   The introduction often ends with a hypothesis, a "prediction" about expected results that the study is designed to test.

Methodology

8   This section explains *how* the study was conducted. It outlines steps taken to compile the data, giving details about *where*, *when*, and *how*. In many cases, this section may also explain *why* the study was designed the way it was. The methodology section, in short, stipulates the techniques used to gather information:

- lab experiment;
- fieldwork;
- "on-site" observations;
- tests, surveys, or questionnaires;
- primary and secondary sources (print and electronic);
- interviews;
- technical descriptions or specifications;
- mathematical formulas or calculations;
- computer modelling.

Results

9   This section objectively describes the findings yielded by the study. The focus is on presenting the "raw data": no discussion of its significance takes place yet. What the data *means* (interpretation and evaluation) is reserved for the next section.

Discussion

10   The *APA Publication Manual* is very specific about key functions of a conclusion (usually called "discussion") of an APA report. Primarily, this is where the study's findings are evaluated or interpreted. Their significance is explained. This section answers the questions: What do the results mean? What conclusions can we derive from them? If a hypothesis has been presented, the discussion should likewise state whether it's been confirmed or not, always bearing in mind that a negative result can be as valuable as a positive one. In either case, something new has been discovered.

11   Finally, a discussion worth its salt ends with a closing peroration, a final "heightened appeal" for the significance or worth of the study. The goal here is to avoid a "so what?" response. The *APA Manual* suggests that report writers should aim to answer the following questions:

- What have I contributed here?
- What has my study helped resolve?
- What broader theoretical implications can I draw from my study?
- Can meaningful generalizations be drawn?
- Does further research need to be done to clarify any remaining uncertainties?

—Monika Rydygier Smith, Instructor, Technical Writing, Department of English, University of Victoria

The Active Voice

HOW TO WRITE A SCIENTIFIC PAPER

1   The scientific enterprise requires that ideas and results be subject to scrutiny by others. Errors are thus recognized and genuine advances can be incorporated into current thinking. No matter how brilliant your theory or experiments might be, if you don't write them up in accessible form, you might as well not have done the work.

2   Editors and reviewers for scientific journals are busy people, just as your professors are. If they can't understand your paper they will reject it (or, in the case of your professor, give it a low grade).

Rule 1: Apply bum to chair

3   Writing is simply hard work. No amount of inspiration is going to generate beautiful, pleasing, elegant prose. Waiting for the muses to inspire you is a guaranteed way of never submitting your paper. The goal of the scientific paper is to

accurately transfer information to the reader. If it is done elegantly and gracefully, so much the better, but this isn't the object of the exercise. Start by writing the paper accurately; let inspiration come along the way.

Rule 2: Remember your audience

4   Although your scientific report will be submitted to your instructor, it helps if you think of your audience as the editors and reviewers of a journal in your subject area. Journals have stylistic conventions, so read the "Instructions to Authors." Then, read a few of the papers in that journal to see how successful authors have presented their work. You should avoid obscure words and complex sentence constructions. You won't become famous by writing obscure papers no one can understand. It is your responsibility to write as clearly as possible to communicate your results. Don't make reading painful for your audience.

Rule 3: Begin with an outline

5   This may seem obvious, but many people neglect this step. The scientific paper has four main sections: Introduction (What is the question?), Methods (What did I do?), Results (What did I find?), and Discussion (What does it mean?). Sections are sometimes combined, called something else, or placed in a different order, but these four elements are found in every paper.

6   If you create a point-form outline of what should be in each section, you will have the topic sentence of almost every paragraph in the paper. Obviously, the outline will change as you write. You will likely reorder it, add topics and drop others, expand in some places and simplify in others—this is called editing—but the structure that an outline provides will still be invaluable. Spend more time editing your paper than writing the first draft.

Rule 4: A scientific paper isn't a diary

7   You should only include those things necessary to understand the paper. All of the failed ideas and apparatus will only confuse the reader. So begin by deciding what message you are trying to convey. This can often be summarized in a single sentence. Include only results that contribute to a fair understanding of how you came to this conclusion. You can't exclude inconvenient or contrary data, but you should exclude irrelevant data. You only need a description of the methods for the data you include, and the introduction and discussion need only include material that is relevant to the message of the paper.

Rule 5: Tell a story but don't write a mystery

8   Tell the reader what you have learned in the order that is easiest to follow. This might not be the order in which you learned them. Tell the reader early on what will follow in the paper. Often, this will entail telling the reader what you have concluded in the last paragraph of the Introduction. The perfect paper would only need to be read once. A bad, confusing paper needs to be read several times looking for the clues that support the conclusions. State your rationale clearly and don't build up to a surprise ending.

Rule 6: Write the Methods first

9   This isn't a hard and fast rule but is usually the easiest. The Methods outline what you did: The experimental or sampling design, study subjects, protocols, any chemical analyses that had to be done, the data analysis, and so on. Use the active voice whenever feasible. This varies markedly among disciplines and journals. Some journals prefer the passive voice "the samples were collected" as opposed to the active voice "I collected the samples." The active voice is almost always simpler and more direct than the passive. It also places responsibility on the person who performed the action. For example, the sentence "I broke the lamp" places responsibility in a way that "The lamp was broken" never could.

Rule 7: Write about your Results

10   Write the Results after the Methods. Remember that you are telling a story; the figures and tables are illustrations. You don't need to include all of the tables and figures you generated, just enough to adequately illustrate the story. Tell your readers what you found and then refer to the figure. "Females were 10% heavier than males (Figure 1)" is shorter and clearer than "The data plotted in Figure 1 show that females were 10% heavier than males." Data should only be presented once in one table or in one figure, but not both. Too many tables and figures are confusing. Remember, the Results are a description; leave interpretation for the Discussion.

11   The results are more important than the statistical analyses so avoid making them the subject of a sentence. A common fault is to write "There was a significant difference between group A and group B." This contains no information on the size of the difference or even the direction! It is much more informative to write "Individuals of Group A were 15% larger than those of Group B (t = 7.5; df = 28; P < 0.001; Figure 1)." The second sentence tells you which group was larger, by how much, and the supporting statistics are found in the parentheses.

Rule 8: Explain how to understand a Figure or Table in its caption

12   Your readers should be able to get the gist of a paper by reading the Introduction and looking at the Figures and Tables. Briefly summarize the results presented in the figure even if this seems redundant to the text.

Rule 9: Tell the reader in the Discussion what you learned

13   Begin by restating your most important results and put them into context of what has been reported before. This means being able to draw conclusions based on what you did. Your readers want to know what you learned: is it the same or different from what has been reported before, what are the limitations of the study, and what needs to be done next? Avoid over-interpretation and wild speculation.

Rule 10: Introductions are difficult

14   So write them last. A good introduction sets the general context for a paper. You need to convince your readers to care enough about the subject to invest their time in reading your paper. You do this by explaining the general context of your study and by summarizing current understanding of the problem. Explain how your study will address a general theory or problem and what is novel about your hypothesis or approach. At the end of the introduction, outline your main results. Readers will evaluate your conclusions as they read the methods and results. They won't have to go back and reread your entire paper to determine whether they agree with you. They will have been thinking about it while they are reading. Explain why your paper is interesting and give your readers a roadmap to your paper.

Rule 11: Focus on ideas, not authorities

15   "Anholt and Werner (1995) found that food level affected predation mortality" takes the emphasis away from the result and puts it on the citation. This is sometimes good when you want to emphasize that this is an old problem, but usually you want to emphasize the result. In contrast, "food level can affect predation mortality (Anholt & Werner 1995)" is shorter, and the citation doesn't get in the way of the presentation.

Rule 12: Use parallel construction

16   Set up the Results to follow the same order as the Methods. Cover subjects in the Discussion in the same order in which they are presented in the Introduction. If there are four explanations for a result, explain them in the same order you first mentioned them. If you refer to two things in a sentence or paragraph, don't change the order later in the paper. In the same vein, don't use two different words to describe or refer to the same thing. Using the same wording allows your readers to make connections throughout the paper. If you use different wording, your readers will wonder whether you are referring to a different observation. You can enhance the parallel construction among sections by using subheadings to guide the reader. When your reader is going through topic X of the results he or she should be able to easily find topic X in the methods, rather than being forced to reread the entire section. Be consistent in your presentation.

Rule 13: Revise, revise, revise… and revise again

17   When I submit a paper for publication, it typically has had 10 to 15 drafts. Even so, it will come back from the journal with requests for revision. Most of those questions can be resolved by more careful writing because the reviewers did not understand exactly what I meant. The secret of great writing is editing and revision. After you finish a draft, give it a few days rest before going back. You will be appalled at the horrors you have committed in the rush to get everything written down. It is difficult to edit your own work, especially at the beginning; get someone else to read it. If they ask a question about anything, then the writing is not clear enough. Don't be offended, but, rather, benefit from their comments and questions.

Rule 14: Make copies of your work

18   Writing papers is hard work. Make back-up copies. I emphasize cop*ies*. Put them someplace other than where you keep your computer. There is nothing more miserable than losing days or weeks of work to a dog, electrical storm, demonic possession, virus, or theft. Don't be careless.

19   These rules are subject to bending and interpretation. Different disciplines have their own conventions, as do different instructors. No matter the discipline, the goal is the same: to write a comprehensible account of your research so that anyone in your discipline, with even an imperfect grasp of English, can understand and repeat it. With practice, your writing will also become more compelling and graceful.

—Bradley R. Anholt, Professor, Department of Biology, University of Victoria

Activity

Choose a scientific article in an area of interest or one of the Type B essays in this book, and write a short analytical report using the four divisions mentioned in Anholt's essay (if your instructor permits, you could omit "Methodology").

Objective: to determine whether the study satisfies the requirements discussed in Anholt's essay (not all the requirements will apply).

In your introduction, you should mention your purpose and include a hypothesis based on what you expect to find (i.e., whether the article you are analyzing will meet specific criteria). Your Methodology section (if used) should outline the criteria you used to evaluate the study, such as some of the questions below or other relevant ones. Your Results should include a brief summary of your findings, while your Discussion should focus on the significance of your findings.

Questions to consider for your report:

1. Does the study meet the formal requirements of a scientific paper? Has it been designed for its intended audience?
2. Does the writer use the headings that Anholt suggests? Are there subheadings?
3. Is the writing clear and the content accessible?
4. Does the writer focus more on ideas than on authorities (see Rule 11)?
5. Is only essential information included, that which directly relates to the essay's purpose, what the hypothesis is testing, or what the question is answering? Are there sentences (paragraphs?) that the writer could have omitted?
6. Does the writer provide adequate context for his or her study? Is the author's approach unique? Does it aim to add to the body of knowledge about the subject? Does the writer provide a "roadmap for the paper" in the introduction?
7. When does the author reveal the results of his or her study? In the introduction? The Results section?
8. Does the writer use parallel structure and repetition for reading ease (see rule 12)? Give examples.
9. Does the writer use the active voice (see rule 6)? How often are passive constructions used? Give examples.
10. Were tables and figures used? Were they overused? Did they effectively summarize or did they confuse?
11. In the Discussion section, did the writer clearly identify the most important results and place them in an understandable context? Was the conclusion concrete and specific or speculative? Were the study's limitations mentioned? Did the writer suggest what related areas future researchers should investigate?

Chapter 7

Summaries and Rhetorical Analyses

Writing Summaries

Student researchers are often told that when they use secondary sources in their research essays, they must do more than simply summarize them. Similarly, when students analyze literature, they may be advised to "avoid plot summary." From these examples, it might seem that summarization should play a minor role in academic discourse. Nothing could be further from the truth: although there are specific times and places for summaries, they are a major part of research-related writing.

Just how important summaries are depends on writing purpose and audience. For example, in book or film reviews written for a general audience, some summary is essential. On the other hand, if you are writing a rhetorical analysis of an essay for your professor, you would probably include minimal summary. In the former case, readers need to know the gist of the work being reviewed, perhaps the basic plot and a description of the main characters, since you cannot assume that your readers will have read or seen the work. In the latter case, you can usually assume that your instructor is familiar with the work, so inessential summarizing would waste space. However, research never occurs in a vacuum; it is part of a collaborative effort. Even the most novel theories and innovative research must be placed within the context of what has been thought and written before. And that is often where summarization comes in.

Times and Places for Summaries

"Summarization is a broadly inclusive term for an activity concerned with representing the ideas of a writer in a condensed form, using mostly your own words."

Summarization is a broadly inclusive term for an activity concerned with representing the ideas of a writer in a condensed form, using mostly your own words. The key words in this definition are "represent"—*re-present*—and "condensed"—concentrated. A summary does no more than re-present; it does not interpret or analyze, for example. What a summary re-presents is the essence of the original. Summaries are more concentrated than the work being summarized because they contain only the main ideas, and sometimes only *the* main idea, of the original.

There are many occasions when you will be called on to represent the main ideas of a source. As mentioned, if you are reviewing a work, you will typically summarize its plot or characters before you begin your analysis. If you are critiquing a specific text in order to argue against the author's position, you might begin by summarizing the author's arguments before replying with your own points. Similarly, in a rhetorical analysis, you will likely briefly summarize a point before applying your critical thinking skills to it. (See an example of a student rhetorical analysis on page 108.)The following are specialized summaries; their various functions are discussed below:

- Abstract
- Literature review
- Annotated bibliography

In many academic essays, concentrated summaries called **abstracts** precede the essay, giving an overview of what follows. Unlike most other summaries, however, academic writers may lift entire phrases directly from the essay itself (see p. 18). Another form of summary is the **literature review**, in which the author, often in a phrase or sentence for each, summarizes the relevant studies in the field, before stating his or her own thesis or hypothesis (see p. 21).

However, not all summaries come at the beginning of an essay. Sometimes they occur at the end. Students are familiar with summaries that conclude the traditional "five-paragraph essay." In the conclusion, according to the conventions of this essay type, you reiterate your thesis, using different words but in essence summarizing what you have already told your reader. Academic writers may occasionally use this kind of circular conclusion as well.

Another special kind of summary is the **annotated bibliography**, an expanded bibliography that includes not only the information of standard bibliographies but also highly condensed summaries of related works. These include studies referred to in the text, but they may also include significant studies not cited there. Typically, each entry in the bibliography includes the main point, or thesis, and a comment on what it contributes to the field as a whole—where it fits in. Annotated bibliographies may form appendices to book-length studies.

Some authorities in a subject compile such bibliographies as independent projects. For example, *The World Shakespeare Bibliography Online* is a massive compilation of annotated entries for "all important books, articles, book reviews, dissertations, theatrical productions, reviews of productions, audiovisual materials, electronic media, and other scholarly and popular materials related to Shakespeare" created in the last 40 years. It includes more than 40,000 articles, 18,000 books, and 500 films in various languages. Students may be assigned a more modest annotated bibliography as part of a research project or as an independent project. In either case, the purpose will be to demonstrate your ability to research and summarize relevant works on a topic.

The following is an example of an entry in an annotated bibliography by the student writer whose completed essay appears on page 161. Lorinda Fraser summarizes one of the studies she used in her research essay and provides a brief assessment of its value.

Sublette and Mullan analyzed 471 studies on Massively Multiplayer Online Games (MMOGs) addiction or "problematic game play," narrowing themselves down to only 16 studies that they felt met their criteria for unbiased data to evaluate the reliability of the evidence. These studies were then combined, compared, and discussed; recommendations for future research directions were proposed. In their review, Sublette and Mullan

ABSTRACT
condensed summary used in empirical studies; is placed before the essay begins and includes at a minimum purpose, methods, and results.

LITERATURE REVIEW
condensed survey of articles on the topic arranged in a logical order usually ending with the article most relevant to the author's study.

ANNOTATED BIBLIOGRAPHY
expanded bibliography that includes not only the information of standard bibliographies but also highly condensed summaries of related works.

satisfy an important need by providing an extensive, objective review of current evidence-based research removed from the fear-based hype and sensationalism frequently offered in this field today.

Summarizing and Research

Summary is an important feature of scholarly discourse, whether practised by students or academics, because it enables writers to situate their own points relative to those of others. By presenting the main idea(s) of your sources and synthesizing them with your own ideas, you are developing and supporting your thesis. Writers of academic essays, especially Types A and C, rely on this form of development. Academic writers summarize the ideas of other writers:

- to support their own point;
- to disagree with a relevant study;
- to explain a concept or theory relevant to their topic; or
- to compare/contrast a study's findings with those of other studies.

Student writers may be reluctant to summarize a source, particularly a scholarly one, in order to disagree with the writer, but academic writers often summarize a point, which they proceed to critique, as a way of setting up their own point. After all, critical thinking, an indispensable reading skill, involves questioning and evaluating, and a full engagement with the text you are using for your research goes well beyond the passive acceptance of its methods and its results.

The amount of space you devote to a summary depends on how you want to use it and on its importance to your thesis. In the case of a book or movie review, you want to provide enough plot to enable your reader to grasp what the work was about. If you are summarizing an author's position with which you disagree, you do not want to do more than briefly sketch the main arguments on the other side, unless your purpose in arguing is to reach a compromise. If one source is particularly important to your research essay, your summary should be longer than those of less important sources. Summaries, then, can range greatly in length, as well as in purpose.

The Stand-alone Summary: The Précis

"A stand-alone summary, sometimes called a précis (meaning something precise), represents all the main points in a complete work or section(s) of a work. In effect, it is a miniature version of the original, following the same order of points as the original but omitting less important sub-points and all detail."

Summaries can also serve as ends in themselves. A stand-alone summary, sometimes called a précis (meaning something precise), represents all the main points in a complete work or section(s) of a work. In effect, it is a miniature version of the original, following the same order of points as the original but omitting less important sub-points and all detail. The specific guidelines that apply to stand-alone summaries do not apply to all types of summaries, but learning these guidelines and practising them is the best way to learn the exacting art of summary writing. The important skills required in précis writing include the following:

Comprehension skills: Because précis summaries, like most summaries, require you to change the wording of the original, you focus more closely on comprehension than if you quoted the words of the source directly: you have to be clear on content in order to write a successful summary. If you are unsure of a writer's meaning, you need to work at deciphering it before you can re-present it in summary form. This could mean using contextual clues to determine a word's meaning or looking it up in a dictionary. It could also mean understanding relevant concepts. You can hardly express another's ideas clearly if you are not clear on their meaning yourself.

Prioritizing skills (establishing a hierarchy of importance): Distinguishing the main ideas from the less important ideas is a fundamental part of the reading process. In précis writing, you often have to go further than this: if you are assigned to write a summary that is 20 to 25 per cent the length of the original (the average range for a précis), you may have to include one or more important sub-points or a key example in addition to the main points in order to achieve the word quota; on the other hand, if your summary is too long, you may have to omit a main point or an important sub-point. In effect, you need to think about the importance of a point relative to other points, the importance of a sub-point relative to other sub-points, and so on.

Concision skills: A crucial principle applies to précis writing: the more economical your writing, the more content you can include and the more informed your reader will be. Therefore, you should strive for concision in your own writing. Wherever possible, too, you should try to tighten up the writing of the original without sacrificing clarity. Focusing on conciseness will serve you well in any writing you do, making you a more conscious and disciplined writer.

> Stand-alone summaries help develop three main skills basic to reading and writing at the university level: comprehension, prioritizing, and concision skills.

Nine Pointers for Précis Writing

When writing précis-style summaries, you should keep the following guidelines in mind:

1. Follow the exact order of the original. Points out of order will not result in a summary that mirrors the source. Begin the summary with the thesis or first main point, not a generalization.
2. Include only the most important points (the thesis and its major developments). You may include the most important sub-point(s) as well, depending on space. Most sub-points develop or expand a main point.
3. Avoid detail. Detail can be important for support, but in a summary you want only the essence; if a reader wants more information, he or she can read the original. Do not include examples unless they are very important, in which case, the writer will probably mention them more than once.
4. Avoid repetition. Writers often rephrase points to make them clearer. For your summary, choose either the point as first expressed or the rephrasing, not both. However, writers may emphasize a point by repeating it. Ideas stressed in the original should be stressed in your summary too, but without creating redundancy.
5. Do not repeat the author's name or the work's title any more than necessary.
6. Do not add your own opinions. Do not analyze or interpret—simply re-present. Summaries require you to be objective, not to judge the writer or his/her views.
7. Use your own words, keeping direct quotations to a minimum. If a brief passage does not lend itself to paraphrasing, you may quote it directly, but *ensure that you use quotation marks to show the reader that those exact words occurred in*

the source. You can also use direct quotation if a word/phrase is significant or memorably expressed. Common everyday words from the original do not have to be placed in quotation marks unless they occur in a phrase of four words or more (the number of words necessitating quotation marks can vary; check with your instructor).

8. Write economically. Rephrase the original concisely and check that you use no more words than you must; use basic words—nouns and verbs, adjectives and adverbs if they are important and can be expressed concisely, and transitions (sparingly) to create a logical flow between one idea and the next.

9. Ensure that the verbs you use reflect the author's rhetorical purpose. For example, if the writer is arguing rather than explaining a point, use a verb that reflects this: The author *argues . . . claims . . . criticizes . . .* (argument); the author *states . . . explains . . . discusses . . .* (exposition).

When summarizing, space is at a premium, so remember to be SPACE conscious. Be . . .

Specific

Precise

Accurate

Clear

Efficient

A How-to of Précis Writing

Reading strategies: Reading to summarize means you should use the forms of selective reading appropriate for this activity. Begin by scanning the text to get its gist—its thesis—and to determine its structure—that is, how the author has divided the text. Determining structure is vital if you use method 2 below, but it is also important in method 1, as can be seen in the sample précis that follows. You can use one of these methods to construct your summary:

1. *Outline method:* Identify main ideas by double underlining them. In *paragraphs*, for important ideas, look for topic sentences (often, but certainly not always, the first sentence of the paragraph). In *sentences*, look for independent clauses, which usually contain the main idea in the sentence. Identify the most important sub-points (developments) by single underlining. For information about using contextual cues, such as transitions and prompts to lead you to main ideas, see "Reading Paragraphs: Locating Main Ideas," p. 54. Next, prepare an outline with all main points and important sub-points. If you wish, you can indent sub-points as in a formal outline. Then write your summary from the outline, using your own words as much as possible and adding transitions to create coherent prose. If the summary exceeds the allowable length, omit the least important sub-point(s). *This method is particularly useful for shorter summaries.*

2. *Section summary method:* Prepare a section-by-section breakdown. Sections can be determined by headings or additional spacing between paragraphs. If there are none, try to determine where the writer has shifted focus or introduced a new concept. Summarize each section in your own words. Aim for one sentence for short sections, two sentences for mid-length sections, and two or three sentences for longer sections. As in the outline method, look for main ideas by trying to identify topic sentences. However, since you are dividing the text differently from the way you would in the outline method, pay strict attention to the opening paragraph of each section, where the main idea(s) in the section may be introduced. Then combine your section sentences to write your summary, adding transitions to create coherent prose. If the summary exceeds the allowable length, omit the least important sub-point(s). *This method is particularly useful for longer summaries.*

Some Summary Writing Strategies

In addition to the guidelines discussed above, you might find the following summarization strategies helpful:

- Read through the essay at least twice before beginning to identify main points and important sub-points.
- If you find it difficult to identify what is important in a passage, ask whether or how it connects with or contributes to the thesis. Main points usually provide support for the thesis or expand it in some way. If you are summarizing part of a complete work and not all of it, you may not find a thesis; still, every section should contain a controlling idea.
- You might find it easier to identify main ideas after you have first put parentheses around what you know are unimportant details and examples. Eliminating the non-essential can make it easier to identify the essential.
- For longer works, pay particular attention to the writer's own summaries, which may occur in the introduction, in the conclusion, or toward the end of long or complex sections.
- Remember that there is not necessarily a mechanical relationship between ideas and paragraphs. Not all paragraphs are equally important, and not all contain topic sentences. In addition, the introductory paragraph(s) will not necessarily contain important information. In much journalistic writing, for example, opening paragraphs may serve to attract the reader's interest; they may contain little of substance and should, in that case, be omitted.

The following is a section from a book chapter. In the chapter (entitled "Bad borgs?"), the author, Andy Clark, categorizes what he calls "spectres," possible threats to our autonomy posed by today's technology. Read the passage and consider strategies for summarization. The passage is 488 words; a 97-word summary would represent 20 per cent of the original, a typical length for a précis summary.

Overload

1   One of the most fearsome spectres . . . is that of plain simple overload—the danger of slowly drowning in a sea of contact. As I write, I am painfully aware of the unread messages that will have arrived since I last logged in yesterday evening. By midday there will be around 60 new items, about 10 of which will require action. Ten more may be pure junk mail, easy to spot or filter, but it is the rest that are the real problem. These I read, only to discover they require no immediate thought or action. I call this e-stodge. It is filling without being necessary or nourishing, and there seems to be more of it every day.

2   The root cause of e-stodge, Neil Gershenfeld has suggested, is a deep but unnoticed shift in the relative costs, in terms of time and effort, of *generating* messages and of *reading* them. Once upon a time, it cost much more—again in terms of time and effort—to create and send a message than to read one. Now, the situation is reversed. It is terribly easy to forward a whole screed to someone else, or to copy a message to all and sundry, just in case they happen to have an opinion or feel they should have been consulted. The length of the message grows as more and more responses get cheaply incorporated. Other forms of overload abound. The incoming messages aren't all e-mail; there are phone calls (on mobile and land lines) and text messages, even the occasional physical letter. There is the constant availability, via the Google-enhanced web, of more information about just about everything at the click of a mouse.

3   One cure for overload is, of course, simply to unplug. Several prominent academics have simply decided that "e-nough is e-nough" and have turned off their e-mail for good or else redirected it to assistants who sift, screen, and filter. Donald Knuth, a computer scientist who took this very step, quotes the novelist Umberto Eco, "I have reached an age where my main purpose is not to receive messages." Knuth himself asserts that "I have been a happy man since January 1, 1990, when I no longer had an e-mail address."

4   We won't all be able to unplug or to avail ourselves of intelligent secretarial filters. A better solution, the one championed by Neil Gershenfeld, is to combine intelligent filtering software (to weed out junk mail) with a new kind of business etiquette. What we need is an etiquette that reflects the new cost/benefit ratio according to which the receiver is usually paying the heaviest price in the exchange. That means sparse messages, sent only when action is likely to be required and sent only to those who really need to know—a 007 principle for communication in a densely interconnected world. E-mail only what is absolutely necessary, keep it short, and send it to as few people as possible. (Clark, Andrew. *Natural-born Cyborgs: Minds, Technologies, and the Future of Human Intelligence*. New York: Oxford University Press, 2004.)

Preparing to summarize: If you read the essay carefully, you will see that it is divided into two parts: the first two paragraphs describe a problem, while the last two present possible solutions. The summary, too, should be equally weighted. Unfamiliar words in this section might include "stodge" and "screed," examples of informal diction, meaning, respectively, "something dull or stupid" and "a long piece of writing." Since the passage to be summarized is relatively short, it is best to use the outline method to focus on the main ideas and important developments. These might include the following:

Para. 1: *Main point* (topic sentence): "One of the most fearsome spectres . . . is that of plain simple overload—the danger of slowly drowning in a sea of contact." This is the controlling idea in this section.

Very important development: Email that creates the "real problem" is that which "require[s] no immediate thought or action. I call this e-stodge. It is filling without being necessary or nourishing, and there seems to be more of it every day."

Para. 2: *Main point* (topic sentence): "The root cause of e-stodge, Neil Gershenfeld has suggested, is a deep but unnoticed shift in the relative costs, in terms of time and effort, of *generating* messages and of *reading* them."

Sub-point 1: It is easy today to "forward a whole screed to someone else, or to copy a message to all and sundry."

Sub-point 2: In addition to email, "[o]ther forms of overload abound."

Para. 3: *Main point* (topic sentence): "One cure for overload is, of course, simply to unplug."

Sub-point: "Several prominent academics have simply decided that 'e-nough is e-nough' and have turned off their e-mail for good or else redirected it to assistants who sift, screen, and filter."

Para. 4: *Main point* (topic sentence): "A better solution, the one championed by Neil Gershenfeld, is to combine intelligent filtering software (to weed out junk mail) with a new kind of business etiquette." Note that the first sentence in paragraph 4 connects the main idea in paragraph 3 to paragraph 4, serving as a prompt for the topic sentence in paragraph 4, the second sentence.

Very important development: "E-mail only what is absolutely necessary, keep it short, and send it to as few people as possible." Note that the last three sentences become progressively more specific. The best choice, then, is the final sentence—the most specific.

An important consideration is Clark's reliance on Neil Gershenfeld. The references to Gershenfeld occur in two important points. In constructing the summary, then, it would be advisable to specifically mention Gershenfeld.

What follows is a summary based on the outline above but using different words. Note that the summary does not include sub-point 2 in paragraph 2, because this development is not specifically about the problem of *email*. The sub-point in paragraph 3 is an example that supports the main point in this paragraph but which was deemed relatively unimportant. Of course, there is more than one way to summarize this essay. To check its effectiveness, you can refer to the summarization pointers on page 99.

Summary of "Overload," by Andy Clark

Users of today's technology are in danger of being overwhelmed by unimportant email, which Clark calls "e-stodge." While creating messages used to take longer than reading them, today's problem results from the ease with which one can forward or copy an email to numberless contacts. Although it is possible to sever connection with email entirely or let subordinates handle the problem, Clark favours Neil Gershenfeld's solution, one that uses sophisticated spam filtering with "a new kind of business etiquette." Such a protocol requires that all emails be essential, concise, and carefully directed to a select few. (96 words)

The Rhetorical Analysis: Explaining the How and Why

In a rhetorical analysis, you break down a work in order to examine its parts and the author's rhetorical strategies, using your critical thinking skills and your knowledge of texts themselves.

Like a full-length summary, a rhetorical analysis is usually focused on one text. But while a summary should only represent the ideas in the original, when you analyze a work, you break it down in order to examine its parts and the author's rhetorical strategies, using your critical thinking skills and your knowledge of texts themselves. The rhetorical analysis assumes you are a knowledgeable reader familiar with how such texts are written and capable of evaluating the author's success in achieving his or her objectives. The main purposes of rhetorical analyses are (1) to explain and (2) to evaluate/critique the text. They should be objective both in content and voice.

Analyses need to be planned carefully; for example, it is often a good idea to outline your points before beginning your draft. The reader of your analysis should not get the impression that spontaneity has been your organizing principle.

Writing a rhetorical analysis makes you more conscious of the way that texts written by academics and other professionals are put together, as well as the kinds of strategies that can be used to make content clear and accessible. In this sense, you critically analyze a text in order to see what works and what does not—and why. Honing your analytical abilities in this way helps you use the essays you analyze as models for your own writing. Of course, the text under consideration could also serve as a negative model in some respects.

Rhetorical Analysis and Essay Type

A critical response differs from a rhetorical analysis in being focused more on your own opinions or observations about an issue raised in a text. Writing a response enables you to explore your views on a topic. Although responses are usually more informal than rhetorical analyses, they should clearly demonstrate your critical thinking skills.

Rhetorical analyses can be approached in different ways, depending on the nature of the source text.

One kind of critical analysis applies to literary works. The literary analysis breaks down the elements of the text—in the case of fiction, such elements would include plot, character, setting, point of view, and language—showing how they relate to one another. Of course, such texts contain no thesis or hypothesis but rather themes, which can be inferred from the interconnections among these elements. Like other kinds of texts, literary texts can be analyzed according to their conventions, which vary by genre (poetry, drama, fiction, creative non-fiction) and by subgenre (lyric, dramatic, and narrative poetry, for example).

Type A essays: Because these essays usually make interpretive rather than fact-based claims, they are often assigned for a rhetorical analysis. Although students may believe that they lack the expertise to address the writers on their own terms, it is helpful to remember that rhetorical analyses do not necessarily involve a negative critique of the author or his or her methods. For example, they could focus on why an author organizes his or her material in a certain way or on the variety of evidence provided for support.

Type B essays: If the source text presents the findings of original research, your analysis might mainly involve evaluating the essay according to the formal conventions of this kind of writing. Further, when original research appears in academic journals today, it often includes a section that discusses the study's limitations. In such cases, your analysis should mention these limitations, but the analysis itself might consist mostly of explanation and include minimal evaluation.

Type C essays: Although Type C essays are written by experts in their field, their readers are not necessarily specialists. Because these essays offer overviews of many studies, they often do not include the detail or depth of knowledge demonstrated in other essay types. Furthermore, a non-specialist reader may be perfectly able to evaluate the effectiveness of an essay's organization or its clarity without being an expert in the subject. Although in some cases you may not be able to tell whether the writer has accurately represented a problem or answered a question, it may appear that he or she has not addressed all sides of the issue or all implications of the question. In such cases, you could point to undeveloped areas, suggesting why it would have been beneficial to expand on a point and what it could have contributed to the essay. For example, Gidengil et al. in "Enhancing democratic citizenship" (p. 262) review the literature in order to suggest ways of raising the level of participation in Canada's democratic process. You could ask yourself whether they have failed to consider other methods than those mentioned. Pointing out what a writer has not said is as much a critique as pointing out flaws in an essay's presentation or in the author's reasoning.

Argumentative essays: In a rhetorical analysis of an argumentative essay, you might question the validity of an author's assumptions or premises (premises underlie many kinds of thinking, especially deductive reasoning in which conclusions can be drawn from specific premises). One conclusion that might be drawn (inferred) from the previous statement is that essays employing argument are more easily critiqued than those that do not because in most arguments, an author's assumptions are clearly expressed in the form of an argumentative claim; argumentative claims are debatable. Remember, though, that a rhetorical analysis of an argumentative essay should focus on the hows and whys of the author's methods and strategies. *They should not be used as a forum for expressing your personal agreement or disagreement with the author's opinions but for evaluating the logic and effectiveness of the argument itself.*

Organizing a Rhetorical Analysis

Most rhetorical analyses begin with an introduction that includes a generalization about the essay and/or the topic, such as its importance or relevance in today's world. They must also include a summary of the author's thesis or what questions he or she tried to answer. If a reader of your analysis might be unfamiliar with the source text, you should briefly summarize the essay or at least give enough detail so that your reader will understand its essence. Summarization can be an important part of a rhetorical analysis, but rhetorical analyses are much more than simple summaries.

At the end of your introduction, include your thesis statement. The form of the thesis will depend on the kind of text you are analyzing and your purpose. Essentially, though, it should address whether the text, for example, an essay, successfully fulfills its purpose and supports its own claims. If the essay is argumentative, your thesis might summarize the essay's strengths and weaknesses, concluding whether it is effective or not.

In the body paragraphs, your analysis should break down the most relevant features of the essay, attempting to explain how these features, such as the author's methods and rhetorical strategies, reflect his or her purpose, objectives, and audience. The aim is to explain and evaluate the how and the why of the source text: How does the author explore the subject, prove the claim, and support the main points? Why are those particular methods and strategies used and not other ones? What are the essay's strengths and weaknesses? How could the text be improved?

In any analysis, being specific is vital. Support all claims you make about a text by referring specifically to examples that illustrate your point. The best critical analyses proceed from a close and detailed reading of the source text (see "Focused Reading," p. 52).

The questions below, organized according to purpose, can be used as a basis for a rhetorical analysis. Note that many of the questions and activities that follow individual essays in *The Active Reader* are the kinds of questions you can ask of a text as you read it in order to analyze it. The nature of the text itself and other factors will help determine which questions of those below are the most relevant to your analysis; for example, the author(s) of an empirical study appearing in an academic journal article do not need to consider special strategies in order to create reader interest.

Explaining

- When was the essay written relative to similar studies in the field?
- Why was it written? Is it intended to inform, explain, persuade?
- For what kind of audience is it written? How do you know this?
- What do you know about the author(s)? Does he/she appear to be an expert in his/her field or otherwise qualified to write on the topic? How is this apparent (if it is)?
- Is there an identifiable introduction? What is the writer's thesis or central question? What is the justification for the study? In what way(s) does the author propose to add to his/her field of knowledge? Is there a literature review?
- Is there an essay plan? How does the author convey essay structure?
- What are its main points?
- What format does the essay follow? How does the text reflect the conventions of the discipline for which it was written? Does it follow these conventions exactly, or does it depart from them in any way?
- What kinds of evidence does the author use? Which are used most extensively?
- Is there a stress on either analysis or synthesis in the essay? On both equally?
- What inferences are readers called on to make?
- How is the essay organized? Is there a primary rhetorical pattern? What other kinds of patterns are used?
- What level of language is used? Does the author include any particular stylistic features (e.g., analogies, metaphors, imagery, unusual/unconventional sentence structure)?
- Is there an identifiable conclusion? What is its primary purpose?

Evaluating/Critiquing

- Does the author successfully prepare the reader for what is to follow in the essay? Generally speaking, authors prepare their readers by revealing the essay's thesis in an introduction and/or abstract.
- Does the author manage to create interest in the topic? How is this done? Would other strategies have worked better?
- Main points: Are they identifiable (in topic sentences, for example)? Are they well supported? Is supporting detail specific and relevant?
- If secondary sources are used, are there an adequate number? Are most of them current references?

- What kinds of sources were used? Books? Journal articles? Websites? Have the author(s) published related works in the field of study?
- Are some sources more important than others—for example, are they used more often? Is there an overreliance on a particular source or kind of source? For example, could the essay benefit from a greater use of primary sources?
- Does the author adequately respond to findings that are at odds with his/her own? How does he/she do this?
- Are the kinds of evidence used relevant to the topic, audience, and discipline? Are examples and illustrations used to make points more concrete?
- What kinds of strategies and techniques does the author use to facilitate understanding? Are they effective? Are there other ways that organization or content could have been made clearer?
- Is the voice or tone appropriate, given the kind of essay and the audience? Does the author make it clear that he/she is using a distinctive voice/tone for a specific purpose?
- Does the conclusion answer the question that the author sets out to investigate? Does it explain the relevance of the study, what it contributes to the field? In various ways, the writer should use the conclusion to look beyond the immediate context and consider where the study fits into the whole. One way to do this is to propose directions for future research.

The following questions are particularly relevant to argument:

- Is it clear in the introduction that the essay will focus on argument rather than on exposition? Is the claim one of value or policy?
- Does the author appear reasonable? Has he/she used reason effectively, establishing a chain of logic throughout? Are there failures in logic (logical fallacies)?
- Does the author succeed in making the issue relevant to the reader? Does he/she appeal to the reader's concerns and values?
- Does the essay appear to focus on exposing a problem, critiquing a text, or another purpose? Is this focus the best one, given the nature of the topic and the audience?
- Is the order of points appropriate? From weakest to strongest (climax order) or strongest to weakest (reverse climax)?
- Does the essay appear free of bias? Is the voice as objective as possible, given the argumentative stance? Has slanted language been avoided? Authors sometimes openly declare their opinions. If this is the case, do you think it was a good strategy?
- Has the author acknowledged the other side? How has he/she responded to the opposing viewpoint? Limited rebuttal? Full rebuttal? Has the author tried to establish common ground with the reader?
- Does the author make emotional or ethical appeals? Are they extreme or manipulative? Are there any emotional fallacies?
- Is the conclusion strong and effective? What makes it so (or does not)?

Sample Rhetorical Analysis

A rhetorical analysis like the one below on "University wars: The corporate administration vs. the vocation of learning," by John McMurtry (see p. 191), highlights some of the main features of the source text, using summary, explanation, and evaluation. The annotations refer to some of the points discussed above.

A Critical Analysis of "University Wars: The Corporate Administration vs. the Vocation of Learning," by John McMurtry

by Simon Barer

1   In "University Wars," John McMurtry discusses the flaws inherent in the corporatization of the university system by juxtaposing the government-mandated goals of academia with the goals of corporations. McMurtry describes how academia is antithetical to corporate goals, then outlines the dangers of the current system and what measures must be taken to fix the crisis. Writing for an audience of educators, administrators and, presumably, students, McMurtry starkly portrays the dilemma faced by universities today: should they operate for profit or for the greater good? With his opinion heavily slanted in academia's favour, McMurtry reveals what happens when academic institutions crave a wealth of capital over a wealth of knowledge. Although his critique is effective, it is undermined in places by unsubstantiated claims and somewhat fanciful remedies.

2   In his introduction, McMurtry identifies many of the critical problems with the current university system. First, he points out that "university presidents now conceive of themselves as corporate CEOs," (192) whose main objective is to amass large profits, quite far from the noble pursuit of knowledge for its own sake. Next, the essay examines the illogical system of having copyrights on academic papers and journals. The author eloquently raises the paradox of universities funding studies and then publishing them in corporate-owned journals, relinquishing royalty rights, then buying those journals from companies for inflated prices. McMurtry lists the properties of corporate administrations and the way in which their aims directly contradict the purported aims and ideals of universities themselves. Focus is then drawn to the lack of funding now provided by universities and the resulting power corporations hold: only research that "reduces money costs and increases money revenues for money managers and possessors" (193) is funded, while studies for the greater good, such as advancements in organic agriculture, go without sponsorship. This inevitably leads to a system more effective than censorship, as those who attempt to defy the corporations are persecuted. Consequently, those within the system, namely professors, are prevented from speaking out and addressing the problem. The essay ends with McMurtry suggesting ways to fix the problem. An "independent faculty board of academic review" (194) must be put in place to ensure that finances don't go into greedy pockets, rather where they should go: research grants and student education.

3   On the matter of credibility, McMurtry sometimes fails to convey an authoritative grasp on the topic. Although many sources are used effectively in the article, some bold claims are made without proper substantiation. For example, when discussing Larry Summer's equation relating basic values to market growth, McMurtry expresses himself through a simple equation: "[if] life itself is of no value . . . so too [are] research and knowledge. If they are not marketable, they do not exist." (193) However, even those with a first-year economics education know that factors such as research and expertise do, indeed, have monetary value. Later, McMurtry uses the controversial Professor Denis Rancourt as an example of what happens when a radical teacher defies his corporate masters. Unfortunately, this

Barer's first paragraph meets the objectives of successful introductions by concisely outlining the main points of the text he is analyzing and, in his last sentence, revealing his thesis. Furthermore, Barer's prose is rhetorically effective. He uses balanced structures and precise phrasing: the reader easily grasps the essay's main thrust and Barer's own.

In this paragraph, Barer relies heavily on summary, thoroughly representing McMurtry's points and his attitude to his topic. In addition to straight summary, Barer combines significant direct quotations with his own words. In the paragraphs that follow, he turns to analysis.

Here Barer raises a general criticism, illustrates it by a specific example, and finishes by providing a direct critique. Critical analyses must be more than just summaries.

example considerably weakens his claim, as the firing of Rancourt was attributed to his slandering the president of the university, as well as giving A+s to all students in his fourth-year physics courses, which covered topics such as quantum mechanics and solid state physics.[1]

4   Despite some misleading statements and exaggerated claims, McMurtry succeeds in forming a convincing argument decrying the pitfalls of university commercialization. When he articulately states that where corporations "follow the global market program of self-maximizing strategies in conditions of scarcity at minimum costs for the self with no productive contribution," and that when academics value "learning advancement and dissemination by knowledge sharing without limit for truth at any cost of difficulty" (193), it is practically impossible to disagree with him since these seem to contradict the principles on which universities were founded. Indeed, with the noted exceptions, McMurtry's claims are well considered, supported by evidence, and concisely compiled into a convincing essay.

5   Unfortunately, McMurtry's proposals to fix the problem, ideas that are easy to implement and almost sure to work, will likely never see the light of day. In fact, the people the proposals intend to depose are the ones whose approval is needed in order to establish the initiatives. Though seeing this himself, McMurtry offers a glimmer of hope: "Once the facts on the systematic misallocation of public education funds on anti-educative salaries, privileges, and offices are flushed into the open, they will not be accepted by the public. Those in the university who follow more money as their ruling goal are then free to leave the academy, where they do not belong" (195).

6   McMurtry's essay presents an interesting and penetrating look into the current state of academia, as well as the problems universities face in retaining their goal to acquire and disseminate knowledge. Although the situation seems bleak, the paper offers ways in which the problem can be solved, however difficult the implementation may be. McMurtry states that only a fiery public outcry will fix the problem; his essay may just be the kindling to light that fire.

Using critical thinking and a quick web search, the writer argues that McMurtry's example is misleading.

Clear organization is vital in rhetorical analyses. Having pointed out weaknesses in the argument, Barer focuses on strengths in this paragraph. In the final body paragraph, Barer comments on McMurtry's conclusion, discussing a possible weakness but acknowledging that McMurtry himself is aware of it. Barer's own conclusion takes the form of a generalization about the essay, made effective partly by his use of an analogy. Although there are many other ways to write a successful rhetorical analysis of this essay, Barer's analysis will leave most readers with a positive impression of his analytical skills.

---

1. University of Ottawa. "Statement: Recommendation for the Dismissal with Cause of Mr. Denis Rancourt." 6 Feb. 2009. Web. 12 Mar. 2011. <www.media.uottawa.ca/mediaroom/news-details_1610.html>.

Chapter 8

Kinds of Specialized Essays

Writing Argumentative Essays

Classical argument has its origins among the ancient Greeks. To prove that a wrong or injustice was done to them, Greek citizens had to appear before a tribunal of fellow citizens and argue their case. This was a formal process in which the accuser and the accused tried to establish their credibility, exchanged claims and counterclaims, and ended with a rhetorical flourish. In the absence of compelling evidence, the more persuasive speaker often won the day.

Another kind of oral discourse using argument, the formal debate, was considered a training ground for men seeking public professions during the nineteenth century, and debating societies are still alive on the campuses of many North American universities (with female debaters now as prominent as males, of course). Successful debaters are thought to exhibit life skills such as mental dexterity, verbal adeptness, and poise. In the classical Western tradition, however, argument often went hand in hand with an "us versus them," "winner take all" divisiveness.

Today, argument can serve several purposes:

- to state or defend your point of view;
- to seek to change a situation;
- to critique a viewpoint, position, text, etc.;
- to expose a problem or raise awareness of a problem;
- to consolidate an opinion;
- to reach a compromise.

The most straightforward kind of argument is one in which you state and defend your point of view—that is, you take a position on an arguable topic and support it. However, argumentative purpose can extend beyond simply stating your position and defending it. For example, arguing to reach a compromise involves an objective appraisal of both sides of the debate; furthermore, it often constitutes a more realistic purpose than arguing to defend your point of view. Thus, in her essay on a section of the Criminal Code that permits corporal punishment "if the force does not exceed what is reasonable under the circumstances," student writer Danielle Gudgeon steers a middle ground between those who want the law upheld and those who want it abolished. Her middle position makes it likely that an audience on both sides will consider her points, making her argumentative goal more attainable:

> Section 43 of the Criminal Code has a social utility for both teachers and parents, but it is an old law that must be amended to reflect society's progression. The addition of clear guidelines to the law regarding the severity of discipline and the use of objects as weapons will create a distinction between abuse and discipline. This will prevent subjectivity within the courts and discourage future abuse, while affording parents the option of disciplining their children.

The kinds of evidence and the argumentative strategies you use depend on your purpose in arguing, your audience, and the topic itself. It is useful to look at three diverse forms that written argument can take in the media in order to see how these elements interact: the letter to the editor, the review, and the editorial (see the table on p. 112). Each has a different purpose, which is reflected in its structure, voice, language, kinds of evidence, and typical reader/viewer. The letter to the editor is the most subjective, in which writers can "have their say"; most published reviews reflect the informed opinions of experts; the voice of the editorial writer is usually the most objective and formal of the three. Within these categories, there can be much variation; for example, editorials do not always represent a collective viewpoint: "op-eds" (opinion-editorials) are usually written by one person, a "guest" editor or representative of an involved group. And certainly not all letters to the editor contain inflamed rhetoric.

An equivalent to the letter to the editor today is the blog; "bloggers" range from opinionated novices to informed experts. Unlike letters to the editor, blogs often take the form of entries and are not restricted by length requirements. Another obvious difference is that bloggers can incorporate interactive elements in the design of their site, including direct feedback. Blogs have become a major part of many online publications, as well as print publications that desire an online "presence."

Which of the forms of argument (table, p. 112) is most like the kind of argumentative essay you are likely to be assigned? Structurally, the argumentative essay resembles the review. In your language and use of voice, you should aspire to the objectivity of an editorial; however, letters to the editor are sometimes more interesting than editorials, and you should look for ways to interest your readers—especially neutral readers, those who have no strong position one way or the other.

Argumentative essays can be challenging to write because the methods and strategies that go into planning them vary depending not only on your writing purpose but also on the topic itself and the audience you are writing for. Furthermore, several common misconceptions surround argument today, so before beginning to plan, you need a clear picture of what argument is and what it is not.

Misconception 1: "I never argue"

People who say this may be thinking more of conflict than of reasoned debate. However, consider the following scenario: you have moved into a residence at your university only to find the rules and regulations there particularly unfair (a 10 p.m. curfew for social functions, for example). You might well discuss your disagreement with other residents

Letter to the Editor	Book/Film Review	Editorial
Purpose: to sound off, state your viewpoint; other purposes are possible as well.	*Purpose:* to critique a text, film, or some other type of material. The subjective nature of reviewing is assumed; thus, if you were reading reviews to decide whether to see a film, you would likely read several.	*Purpose:* to critique a position, expose a problem, or reach a compromise. Editorials in niche publications (e.g., a union newsletter) may attempt to consolidate an opinion.
Writer: anyone may write a letter to the editor, which may be published if it is not libellous and the writer provides name and contact information.	*Writer:* is named; is knowledgeable in the field; may have a degree or other credentials; may make a living as a reviewer.	*Writer:* member of an editorial board; writer's name is not given; represents the views of the publication.
Audience: no particular audience in mind but often appeals to those with similar values and views.	*Audience:* written for book readers, film-goers, readers with an interest in the subject matter, etc.	*Audience:* educated readers, often the politically informed.
Structure: usually short; might be edited for length and for style; might not be highly structured or well-organized.	*Structure:* varies in length; usually follows conventional structure of argument: generalization with value claim followed by supporting evidence from the film/book.	*Structure:* usually short; tight structure: focused on one issue.
Claim: may be of value or policy; argument may present only one side.	*Claim:* of value; will consider the pros and cons but will come down on one side or the other—"thumbs up" or down.	*Claim:* often of policy; will carefully weigh both sides; may argue for one side, but argument characterized by careful, scrupulous reasoning.
Voice: subjective—"I."	*Voice:* sometimes uses first person—"I."	*Voice:* objective—the "editorial we."
Language/tone: variable; may be colourful, emotional, or volatile: "I'm appalled by our political leaders"; conversational, informal.	*Language/tone:* may use some specialized words and terms; may be ironic or sarcastic, direct or evocative.	*Language/tone:* elevated, sophisticated; formal, detached.
Evidence: personal opinion may predominate.	*Evidence:* mostly expert opinion on primary source (text); may refer to other books/films; evaluates according to agreed-on standards of excellence.	*Evidence:* facts and figures; precedents—reason-based evidence.

and write a petition that argues for more reasonable rules—you are arguing your case, rather than engaging in conflict. The impulse to argue can easily arise if we perceive our values or beliefs challenged; similarly, we may argue to defend our self-interest or those of a group with which we identify, such as our family, school, or community.

Whenever you send a resumé to a prospective employer, you are implicitly arguing that you are the best person for the job and supporting your claim by facts about your knowledge and experience. If you are asked during the interview why you believe you should be hired, you will have to marshal your strongest persuasive skills in response. Argument in its myriad forms is engrained not only in our society—in our legal and legislative systems, for example—but also in our daily lives.

Misconception 2: "All opinions are equal"

Once declared, opinions reveal a great deal about the speaker or writer. For example, a racist opinion reveals the speaker as intolerant or misinformed at best. It is difficult to argue against someone who holds racist views because they are not grounded in either logic or reasoned experience; they lack credible support. An informed opinion, especially one based on various kinds of evidence—for example, statistics, personal experience, and research findings—is much more likely to be credible. On the other hand, a person may hold the opposite opinion, which may be equally informed. An *opinion*, then, is not the same as a *fact*, which can be verified by observation or research; opinions are challengeable.

As you will see, you cannot argue a position on a topic that has no opposing view—in other words, which cannot be challenged—yet facts can be interpreted differently and used for different purposes. Facts, therefore, can be used to support the thesis of an argumentative essay. However, effective arguers are always clear about when they are using facts and when they are using opinion. In reading, use your critical thinking skills to ask if the writer always clearly separates facts from opinion. If not, he or she might be guilty of faulty reasoning (see page 122).

Fact:

- The moon is 378,000 kilometres from earth's equator.

Now consider the following two pairs of statements, each consisting of a fact and a related opinion:

Fact:

- According to moon landing conspiracy theories, the 1969 Apollo moon landing was faked.

Opinion:

- The Apollo moon landing didn't actually take place; it was all a hoax.

Fact:

- On November 13, 2009, NASA announced that water had been found on the moon.

Opinion:

- Now that water has been found on the moon, humans should set up colonies at the moon's poles by 2050.

Collaborative Exercise

Consider the two pairs of statements above on the topic of humans on the moon. Discuss the ways that fact differs from opinion in each case. Come up with two other topics and write two statements for each, one of which represents a fact and the other of which represents an opinion.

Although what is accepted as fact by a community of experts, such as scientists, cannot usually be challenged, the *basis of a fact* can change, and if the basis changes, what was once considered a "fact" may no longer be so. The basis for the "fact" that the planetary bodies revolved around the Earth was the Ptolemaic system, which was influential until the seventeenth century when the Copernican system changed the nature of this "fact." From Pluto's discovery in 1930 until August 2006, it had been a "fact" that our solar system had nine planets. However, the basis of this fact changed when astronomers declared that Pluto did not fit the newly revised definition of a planet.

The *interpretation of facts*, too, can be challenged. Interpreting facts in light of the claim that the arguer makes is an important strategy in argument. For example, the fact that just over 50 per cent of lung transplant recipients have a five-year survival rate could be used to support a claim that more resources should be allocated to boost this rate. The same statistic could be used to support a claim that fewer resources should be allocated to this procedure since the result is less promising than for other kinds of transplants in Canada (see "Connecting Claim to Evidence," p. 118).

Misconception 3: "Arguments are boring"

Some kinds of argument are, indeed, boring for many people. However, the tedium of a subject is often synonymous with a lack of personal investment in it. For example, political speeches may be boring for a neutral observer but exciting for a member of the same political party as the speaker. Undoubtedly, one reason that media analysts focus attention on externals such as a politician's posture and expression, as well as on gaffes or hesitant responses to questions, is their effort—some would say a misguided one—to make up for the typical viewer's lack of interest in content by stressing human interest.

Many people find TV commercials boring. Over the years, some advertisers have attempted to infuse greater novelty into their commercials, making each one more outlandish than the previous. Although commercials that appeal to our sense of surprise may amuse us, even exotic commercials become boring if we see them too often. Numbing repetition is anathema in advertising, as it is in other forms of argument. The aim of commercials is simple: to persuade members of the audience to buy a product. Not all arguments are designed to persuade their audience to act directly, of course, but the challenges of both the media analyst and the advertiser are similar in some ways to the challenges of the writer of argumentative essays: to interest and involve the reader in order to make him or her more receptive to the argumentative claim (see "Giving Life to Logic," p. 124).

Claims in Argument

CLAIM
assertion that you will attempt to prove through evidence. Claims occur in thesis statements; many topic sentences also assert a claim about the topic of the paragraph.

The term **claim** is particularly appropriate to argumentation: when you set up your position in the introduction of your argumentative essay, you are doing more than *stating* a thesis: you are *actively asserting* one. When you claim something, you assert your right to it. The claim is the assertion that you will actively attempt to prove through logic and various kinds of evidence in the body of the essay. However, simply claiming something does not entitle you to it: you must convince people that the claim is merited, which is what you do when you argue effectively. Recall that a thesis statement/claim is a generalization about the essay's content: it includes your topic and sums up your main point(s), approach to your topic, the thrust of your argument.

An argumentative claim is usually one of value or policy. In a **value claim**, you would argue that something is good or bad, right or wrong, fair or unfair, and so on. A **policy claim** advocates an action. In this sense, a policy claim goes further than a value claim on which it often rests. However, value claims may be appropriate if you wish to make your audience consider something in a more positive light. For example, if you argue in favour of euthanasia to a general or unreceptive audience, you might not want to use a policy claim, one that focuses on changing laws. A value claim instead would focus on changing attitudes, getting the reader to see, as a first step, perhaps, that euthanasia relieves the suffering of a terminally ill patient. Value claims are especially relevant if you are critiquing a viewpoint or text (as book or movie reviews do) or trying to reach a compromise (i.e., to arrive at a middle ground).

For the purposes of an academic essay—outside of formal arguments, of course, people can and will debate anything—successful argumentative claims must be *arguable, substantial, specific, realistic,* and *manageable.*

> VALUE CLAIM
> assertion about a topic that appeals to its ethical nature (e.g., good/bad or fair/unfair).
>
> POLICY CLAIM
> assertion about a topic that advocates an action (e.g., to fix a problem or improve a situation).

> "Successful argumentative claims must be *arguable, substantial, specific, realistic,* and *manageable.*"

Arguable Claims

Most factual claims are not arguable in a formal way because, as mentioned, a fact is different from an opinion. Facts can be questioned, and their interpretation is sometimes open to debate, but it is difficult for facts themselves to serve as the basis of an argumentative claim, though they may be used to support that claim. For example, you could not easily argue against the fact that the closest star to Earth is 4.2 light years away. However, you could use this fact as evidence to support a policy claim, say, for allocating more financial resources to the space program.

In addition, a belief—for example, that God exists—is not arguable in a formal way, although you could argue the merits or interpretation of something within a given belief system, such as the meaning of a passage from the Koran or other religious text. Similarly, you could not logically argue that one religion is better than another since there are no clear and objective standards that reasonable members of your audience could agree on (and on which to base your claim; see "Connecting Claim to Evidence," p. 118). *Arguable claims must be supported through objective evidence, not just opinion.*

Essays that set out to extol the benefits of something, for example, exercise, a clean environment, or a good diet, can also be difficult to properly ground in an argument. Where a general consensus exists about an item's value, you will find yourself arguing in a vacuum. You do not have a meaningful claim if your audience accepts an idea as self-evident and as something that does not need proving. *If you cannot think of a strong opposing view to the one you want to argue, consider revising the topic so that it is arguable, or choose another topic.*

Cost-benefit Essays

When you set out to argue that one method or system is better than another—for example, that the flat tax system is better than the progressive tax system—you may find yourself considering the pros and cons of each in a point-by-point rebuttal, although your purpose at the outset would be to argue in favour of one side. You could also write

"There can be a fine line between cost/benefit argumentative and cost/benefit expository essays; therefore, it is necessary to clearly announce your purpose—argumentative/persuasive or investigating/explaining—in your claim."

a comparison and contrast *expository* essay on this topic, but in that case, you would set the essay up as a question to be considered (e.g., which system most benefits taxpayers in the middle-income bracket?) and use factual evidence to evaluate the question. There can be a fine line between cost/benefit argumentative and cost/benefit expository essays; therefore, it is necessary to clearly announce your purpose—argumentative/persuasive or investigating/explaining—in your claim.

Substantial Claims

A reader has a right to expect you to argue about something of importance and may dismiss a claim perceived as trivial. Readers should see how the claim could affect them, their community, or their society. A relevant claim for one group may not be relevant for another. If you want to use the claim, you must make the reader see its relevance (see "Appeal to Reader Interests," p. 125).

Some claims are trivial by their very nature—for example, that one brand of deodorant is better than another. Of course, many commercials "argue" precisely this way, often using irrelevant or misleading "evidence." Needless to say, in such claims, specific detail is lacking or is couched in such general terms as to be meaningless: "Now 97 per cent improved!!!"

Be careful not to use an exaggerated or weak claim as the basis for your argument—for example, that all cellphones should be banned in public places because they are distracting when they go off. A stronger argument would be for banning hand-held phones in automobiles—it is stronger because it is more important and has a much better chance of being implemented, as it has been in several provinces and US states.

Specific Claims

A claim should not promise more than it is able to deliver. This applies particularly to claims that are too broad: "we need to change our attitude toward the environment"; "we need to do something about terrorism." On the other hand, if your claim relates to a problem that most people are not aware of, your argumentative purpose would be different—to draw attention to a problem—and it might be possible to argue a broad claim.

One way to narrow a general claim, or amend it so it is more specific, is to think about how it might apply to a subject you are knowledgeable about. If you have come up with a broad topic, you can ask how it might affect people you know. For example, if you wanted to argue that the media promotes unhealthy weight loss in teenagers, a very big topic, and you were an athlete, you could consider what rules or procedures can lead to unhealthy weight loss in your sport. Many sports, such as rowing, have weight categories. In some provinces, the junior female lightweight category is 135 pounds and under. As a rower, you may be aware of unhealthy eating habits that can develop in rowers seeking to remain in a lower weight category in order to be competitive. Your thesis statement might take this specific form: *To help prevent unhealthy and dangerous activities in young rowers, junior lightweight categories should be eliminated from provincial regattas.*

A broad claim can also be made more specific (and manageable) if you can apply it to a particular group. It might be unwieldy to apply an anti-smoking claim to Canada or even to an entire province, since municipalities may have their own smoking bylaws; you might therefore restrict the focus to your city or even your campus.

Realistic Claims

Unrealistic claims are usually policy claims that have little chance of being implemented. One could argue for almost anything that would make life easier or that would fulfill a need, but if it cannot be instituted, the argument becomes moot. You may be able to muster some points in favour of a return to Prohibition or the legalization of all currently illegal drugs, but since such arguments would not take account of social conditions today, the claim would not be realistic. Unenforceable policy claims are also unrealistic.

Manageable Claims

Like a broad claim, an overly complex claim may not appear doable within an essay of a reasonable length. You should take a realistic approach to your topic, ensuring that it can be convincingly argued within the assigned word length. As is the case with overly broad claims, you can make a complex topic more manageable by limiting its scope in some way.

Activity

In discussion groups, evaluate the 10 claims below, determining whether they would make good thesis statements for an argumentative essay. Are the claims arguable, substantial, specific, realistic, and manageable? If they are not, consider what changes would need to be made to make them arguable. Revise them accordingly.

1. Cloning should be prohibited because it will mean the end of natural selection.
2. In order to represent the interests of voters more accurately, give voters a wider selection of candidates, and provide a stronger voice for minority issues, the government should adopt the single transferable vote (STV) electoral model.
3. *Futurama* is a much funnier sitcom than *Family Guy*.
4. Email is a very useful form of communication today because it is accessible, fast, and far-reaching.
5. The Wii is a more popular gaming system than the Xbox 360 or PlayStation 3.
6. No-fault insurance is very beneficial because it has made it easier for insurance companies to stay in business.
7. Internet dating services are an innovative, convenient, and affordable alternative to the singles scene.
8. The culture of consumerism is responsible for many of the problems that our world faces today.
9. There need to be legal guidelines for genetic testing because it may threaten our privacy, lead to harmful gene therapy, and have dangerous social costs.
10. Because of the dangerousness of the sport utility vehicle, people should have to prove that they really need an SUV before being permitted to purchase one.

Connecting Claim to Evidence

Strong arguments do not simply consist of an arguable claim and supporting evidence: there needs to be a link between claim and evidence, showing why the evidence is relevant to or supports the claim. Philosopher Stephen Toulmin called this the **warrant**.

One way to test the logical connection between your claim (or any important point), and its support, then, is through the underlying rationale for the claim, the warrant. If the warrant is self-evident to the reader, it does not have to be announced. The following warrant is clear without being stated:

Claim: I have to buy a new watch.

Evidence: My current watch says the same time as it did 30 minutes ago.

Warrant: My watch is broken.

The evidence is sufficient support for the claim only because the reader would infer the link ("My watch is broken"). On the other hand, if someone used the same claim and offered as evidence "I just bought a new outfit to attend a wedding," a reader or listener might ask what that had to do with buying a new watch. The speaker might then reply, "I could never show up at a wedding with an accessory that didn't match the rest of my outfit!" which would be an attempt to link the claim to the evidence.

A warrant can arise from various sources, including physical laws, human laws, assumptions, premises, common knowledge, ethical principles, or, in the case, of the fashionable wedding guest, above, aesthetic values. For an argument to be successful, the reader must agree with the warrant, whether stated or implied.

The underlying assumption of Joseph Henrich, Steven J. Heine, and Ara Norenzayan in "Most people are not WEIRD" (p. 438) is also unstated but arises out of a basic empirical principle: to be worthwhile, the results of a scientific experiment should be applicable to large groups of people. Consider the warrants in the following example (referred to under "Misconception 2," above) in which the same evidence is used to support different claims. It is the underlying assumption, the warrant, which links evidence to the claim in each case.

Claim #1: More resources should be allocated to boost the survival rate of lung transplant recipients.

Warrant: The survival rate could be improved if we allocate more resources. (An assumption, it could be based on the economic principle that allocating more resources is likely to improve a result.)

Evidence: Just over 50 per cent of lung transplant recipients have a five-year survival rate.

Claim #2: Fewer resources should be allocated to this procedure since the result is less promising than for other kinds of transplants in Canada.

Warrants: The survival rate does not justify the allocation of the present level of resources for this procedure. (This is an ethical principle.) The resources could be better allocated to help more people. (This is an economic principle.)

Evidence: Just over 50 per cent of lung transplant recipients have a five-year survival rate.

Activity

What warrant(s) could be used to connect the following claim to the evidence?

Claim #3: The allocation of resources for lung transplant recipients should be maintained at its present level.

Warrant(s):

Evidence: Just over 50 per cent of lung transplant recipients have a five-year survival rate.

Kinds of Evidence in Argumentative Essays

Argumentative essays often make ideal in-class and exam assignments because they do not require research and you are not usually called on to demonstrate specialized knowledge about the topic. However, although an effective argument can be built around reasonable points with logical connections between them, specific kinds of evidence can bolster a claim. Some are more common to argument than to exposition, but most can be used in both.

Experts and Authorities

Experts are directly involved in the issue you are arguing. You will usually use expert testimony to support your claim; however, the occasional use of experts with whom you disagree can make your argument more balanced. Joseph Heath ("Did the banks go crazy?," p. 400) uses a variety of experts in his essay, which argues in favour of one explanation for the recent financial crisis. Heath focuses on experts with whom he agrees but also mentions those he disagrees with, demonstrating both his knowledge and his fairness. One way to stress experts who agree with you is to cite them directly (direct quotation), while putting the ideas of opposing experts in your own words (summarization or paraphrase), ensuring that you do so accurately and fairly. Because academic writers are often experts in their chosen field, they may refer to their own studies throughout their papers. Doing so gives them credibility. *Authorities* can also lend credibility by virtue of who they are and what they say: even if they do not have direct experience in the issue you are arguing, they may make the reader pay more attention to it. Citing Albert Einstein in an essay that argues for a vegetarian diet could strengthen your claim since Einstein advocated such a diet, though his expertise lies elsewhere.

Examples and Illustrations

Using examples—specific instances or cases—can make a general claim more concrete and understandable, enabling the reader to relate to it. An illustration could take the form of an *anecdote* (a brief informal story) or other expanded example. In his essay "The ugly Canadian" (p. 215), Amir Attaran begins by relating the story of two kidnapped Canadian diplomats; the expanded example leads directly to his thesis concerning Canada's international reputation. John Ralston Saul uses examples in the body paragraphs of his essay, "Listen to the North," p. 238, developing them extensively to help support his claim (see paragraphs 16–24).

PRECEDENT
kind of example that refers to
the way a situation was dealt
with in the past in order to
argue for its similar use in
the present.

Precedents

In law, a **precedent** is an important kind of example: it is a ruling that can apply to sub-sequent cases that involve similar facts or issues. To *set a precedent* means to establish a formal procedure for dealing with future cases. In argument, appealing to precedents—the way something was done in the past—can be particularly effective in policy claims. To use a precedent, you must show (1) that the current situation (what you are arguing) is similar to that of the precedent and (2) that following the precedent will be beneficial. (Of course, you can use a precedent as a negative example as well, showing that it has not produced beneficial results.) Precedents can be used to legitimize controversial issues, such as decriminalizing marijuana or prostitution, providing universal access to post-secondary education, or introducing needle exchange programs into Canadian prisons, as student writer Kate Newcombe argues (see p. 130). Timothy Krahn ("Where are we going with preimplantation genetic diagnosis?," p. 451) makes it clear in his first paragraph why he intends to use the precedent of British policy on preimplantation genetic diagnosis.

Personal Experience

The selective use of personal experience in argumentative essays can be a highly effective way to involve your reader. In some cases, it can also increase your credibility; for example, if you have worked with street people, you may be seen as better qualified to argue a claim about homelessness. Personal experience could take the form of direct experience, of observing something first-hand, or of reporting on something that happened to a friend. Some kinds of personal experience are less successful. Simply announcing that you experienced something and benefited by it does not necessarily make your argument stronger; for example, saying that you enjoyed physical education classes in high school is not going to convince many people that it should be a required subject in schools. What is important is the way you use personal experience: you should stress the ways that an occurrence or situation has been a learning experience for you and that, by mentioning it, the reader can learn something too. The following introduction serves as a compelling set-up for the carefully phrased value claim (italicized):

> On a Friday night in February 2005, many friends of mine, including Tommy Stanwood, decided to party in Esquimalt's Cairn Park. When the crowd decided to move to Gorge Kinsmen Park to merge with another party, five of my peers got in the car with a 17-year-old who had also been drinking. Tommy, among three other male high school seniors and two ninth-grade girls, was nearly killed when the intoxicated driver flipped his Buick by slamming it into a concrete divider at high speed. Miraculously, no one was killed. Both girls suffered broken limbs, the driver was badly injured, and Tommy broke his pelvis and had his left ear severed in the crash. Tommy's life was spared, but he now walks with a limp, has many scars and only one ear. More tragically, he seems like an entirely different person. *Although it is not possible to legislate perfect judgment into the young people of British Columbia, the current laws regarding youth driving and alcohol take the wrong approaches to try to prevent these tragedies, which often result in death.* (student writer Alex Smith)

Facts, Statistics, and Scientific Studies

Policy claims can often benefit from factual support. Make sure, however, that all factual data is accurate and clearly represented. You are no doubt familiar with the truism that "statistics lie"—that is, they can often be manipulated to suit the purpose of the arguer. Use the most current statistics available from the most reliable sources. Be especially wary of sources that do not reveal where the facts they cite come from or the methods used to obtain the statistical data. All secondary sources need to be acknowledged in your essay; your citations will reveal both the currency and the reliability of the source. Referring to a fact, statistic, or study that is outdated or otherwise lacking authority can damage your credibility (see "Issues of Credibility," p. 89).

Two Kinds of Reasoning

Two methods of reasoning are **inductive** and **deductive reasoning**. In inductive reasoning, you arrive at a probable truth by observing and recording specific occurrences. Flaws in inductive reasoning can occur if not enough observations have been made—that is, the evidence is insufficient to make a generalization—or if the method for gathering the evidence is faulty. Thus, researchers try to include as large a sample as possible within the population they draw from; this makes their findings more reliable (see Appendix A, "A Note on Statistics" p. 497). Similarly, researchers reveal the details of their experiment's methodology. They need to show that their evidence-gathering methods are thorough and free of bias.

While inductive reasoning works from detail to generalization, deductive reasoning begins with a major premise, which can be summed up by a general statement assumed to be true. A second premise, which is a subset or instance of the major premise, is then applied to the major premise. If both statements are, in fact, true and logically related, the conclusion follows as true. The deductive reasoning method can be set up in the form of a **syllogism**, a three-part structure that nicely illustrates how deductive reasoning works in forming conclusions. Syllogisms have very complex applications in logic and mathematics. However, in its simple form, the syllogism can be useful in sorting out the validity of a conclusion. The conclusion of the following is true because both premises are true and are logically related:

> *Major premise:*   All students who wish to apply for admission to the university must submit their grade transcripts.
> *Minor premise:*   Deanna wishes to apply for admission to the university.
> *Conclusion:*   Deanna must submit her grade transcripts.

Using Reason in Arguments

Most arguments rely on both inductive and deductive reasoning, although we may not be aware of it when we hear or read an argument. Instead, we may silently assent to a plausible premise or one that seems borne out by our own experience. Whatever the purpose in arguing—whether to settle an issue, expose a problem, or reach a compromise—getting the listener/reader to agree with your premises is vital. It is also vital to make a neutral or hostile reader receptive to what you have to say; thus, it can be important to use specific strategies like concessions and appeals to common ground. Emotional and ethical appeals are useful argumentative strategies as well. *But most successful arguments begin and end with your effective use of reason.*

INDUCTIVE REASONING
reasoning that relies on facts, details, and observations to make a generalization about a phenomenon.

DEDUCTIVE REASONING
reasoning based on a generalization, which is applied to a specific example or subset to form a conclusion.

SYLLOGISM
a logical three-part structure that can be used to illustrate how deductive conclusions are made.

However, reason can also be misused in arguments. Consider the following statements, the first of which illustrates the misuse of inductive reasoning because there is inadequate evidence to justify the conclusion; the second illustrates the misuse of deductive reasoning because a false premise has resulted in a faulty conclusion. Avoiding logical fallacies (failures in reasoning) in your own essays and pointing them out in the arguments of others will make your arguments stronger and more credible.

The premier broke a promise he made during his election campaign. He is a liar, and his word can no longer be trusted.

It is not reasonable to distrust a politician because he broke one promise. Politicians do not always deliver on their pre-election promises (this could almost be considered a generalization peculiar to campaigning politicians!). If the premier broke several promises, there would be much stronger grounds for the conclusion. Thus, in most people's minds, there is not enough inductive evidence to prove the claim.

Eduardo is the only one in our family who has a PhD. He's obviously the one who inherited all the brains.

Underlying this statement is the assumption that having a PhD indicates your intelligence. Possessing an advanced degree could be partly a measure of intelligence; it could also indicate persistence, a fascination with a particular subject, a love of learning, inspiring teachers, an ambitious nature, strong financial and/or familial support, and so on.

Failures in Reasoning

LOGICAL FALLACIES
categories of faulty reasoning.

Errors in reasoning fall into several categories, termed **logical fallacies**. To argue effectively and to recognize weak arguments when you read them, it is not necessary to be able to categorize every failure in logic. Most errors are the result of sloppy or simplistic thinking—the failure to do justice to the complexity of an issue (sometimes deliberate in the case of conscious distortions, but often unconscious). Developing your critical thinking skills will make you alert to errors of logic. A few examples of fallacious reasoning follow:

- *Oversimplification:* An arguer may consider only two possibilities, one of which may be clearly unacceptable (*either/or fallacy*):

  If you don't get a college degree, you might as well resign yourself to low-paying jobs.

- *Cause/effect fallacy:* Among the many cause/effect fallacies is the one that argues a claim on the basis of a coincidental (non-causal) relationship between two occurrences:

  Re-elect your prime minister; the economy grew by 4 per cent while she was in office.

- *Slippery slope fallacy:* The arguer claims that a challenge to the status quo will lead to a breakdown in order or of human values; it has been used as an argument against such practices as euthanasia, legalizing marijuana, and the screening of embryos. Of course, arguments can be made against these issues, but using "slippery slope" logic does not make for a sound argument:

If gay marriage is legalized, the next thing people will want to do is marry their pets!

- *Deductive fallacy:* The arguer constructs a faulty generalization and uses it to prove a claim. The following could be set up as a syllogism:

Major premise:	**It is human nature to take the easy way.**
Minor premise:	**Downloading music is the easy way.**
Conclusion:	**It is only human nature to download music from the Internet, so why fight human nature?**

- *Circular reasoning:* An arguer may assume something is true simply by citing the premise as if it validated the claim, for example by appealing to a premise that has yet to be proven:

I'm an "A" student. How can the teacher give me a B- on the assignment?

- *Irrelevance:* One type of fallacy of irrelevance is a non sequitur—literally, "it does not follow"—as the "evidence" (supposed questionable personal conduct) has no logical connection with the claim (trustworthiness as a public official); it does not *follow from* the claim:

He can't be trusted for public office. After all, he admitted to an extramarital affair.

Another fallacy of irrelevance is *name-dropping*, citing a famous person as if his/her personal opinion can have the strength of evidence; in the *guilt by association fallacy*, the arguer uses the fact that some allegedly disreputable person or group supports a view as an argument against it (or opposes it as an argument in its favour).

- *False analogy:* In a false analogy, you make a comparison between two things that are not comparable because they are, in fact, not alike or they differ greatly in one respect. In the heat of the moment (see "Emotional fallacies"), people sometimes compare a perpetrator of a minor crime to Adolf Hitler or another bona fide tyrant. In the example below, the writer compares animals in zoos to those in people's homes. Calling pet owners "hypocrites" is also an example of slanted language (see below):

People who complain about zoo animals but who also own pets are nothing but hypocrites.

- *Slanted language:* An arguer may use highly charged language to dismiss an opponent's claims. Simply characterizing an opponent as "ignorant" or "greedy" serves no constructive purpose. Of course, you may be able to show through unbiased evidence that the opponent has demonstrated these characteristics.

- *Emotional fallacies:* These statements appeal to the emotions of a reader in a manipulative or unfair way, such as a partisan appeal, guilt by association, name-calling (*ad hominem*), or dogmatism (simply asserting something without offering proof—often, over and over). They are very different from legitimate appeals to emotion:

  Don't believe the claims of those neo-liberals. They just want to take your hard-earned money away from you. (partisan appeal)

  A common emotional fallacy is the *bandwagon*, which asserts that because something is popular, it has value:

  All my friends' parents give them unrestricted curfews on Friday nights.

Giving Life to Logic: Strategies for Argument

Academic writers may sometimes use argument—for example, in editorials, commentaries and "opinion" pieces—and, like other arguers, they may use specific strategies to make their arguments more compelling. Although effective arguments depend heavily on the use of reasonable claims supported by convincing evidence, logic alone will not necessarily convince readers to change their minds or adopt the writer's point of view. Student writers should consider using the following strategies, depending on topic, purpose, and audience, to shape a logical and appealing argument, one that will make readers more responsive to the claim.

Dramatic introductions: Dramatic introductions are used more often in argument than in exposition because they may enable the reader to relate to a human situation. The introductory paragraph on page 120 illustrates a dramatic introduction to an essay on impaired driving.

*Establishing **common ground**:* Getting your readers to see that you share many of their values enables you to come across as open and approachable, making them potentially more receptive to your argument. Although familiarity with your audience is important in knowing where your values and those of your audience intersect, you can assume that most readers will respond favourably to universal qualities like generosity, decency, security, and a healthy and peaceful environment.

Making concessions: In granting **concessions**, you acknowledge the validity of an opposing point, demonstrating your fairness and willingness to accept other views, at least in part. After conceding a point, you should follow with a strong point of your own. In effect, you are giving some ground in an effort to get the reader to do the same. The concession can be made in a dependent clause and your own point in the independent clause that follows: "Although it is valid to say. . . [concession is made], the fact is. . . [your point]."

Concessions can be vital in cases in which there is a strong opposition or in which you wish to reach a compromise. Simon N. Young makes a concession in the first paragraph of his essay "Universities, governments and industry: Can the essential nature of universities survive the drive to commercialize?" (p. 196), acknowledging a positive change in the direction that universities are taking before mentioning what he sees as a recent, more damaging change.

COMMON GROUND
argumentative strategy in which you show readers that you share many of their values, making you appear open and approachable.

CONCESSION
argumentative strategy in which you concede or qualify a point, acknowledging its validity, in order to come across as fair and reasonable.

Appeal to reader interests: When you appeal to the interests of your readers, you show how they might be affected by your claim. For example, in a policy claim, it might consist of showing how they might benefit by the implementation of a particular policy—how it will be good for them—or what costs could be incurred if it is not implemented—how it will be bad for them. Arguing in favour of a costly social program may be a hard sell to those whose approval and support are vital, such as business leaders. Therefore, you could explain how the program could benefit these leaders—for example, by helping to prevent a bigger problem, such as increased health care costs or taxes. If you know the values and motivations of your readers, you may be able to use this knowledge to make your points directly relevant to them.

> "When you appeal to the interests of your readers, you show how they might be affected by your claim."

Emotional and ethical appeals: While dramatic openings can be successful in many argumentative essays, the success of an opening that includes an appeal to emotion depends greatly on your audience. Beginning an essay on animal testing by describing a scene of caged animals at a slaughterhouse may alienate neutral readers. If you do use such an opening, you need to ensure that a typical reader will respond in the way you wish. Emotional and ethical appeals, however, are commonly used in the conclusion of an essay. They provide an effective coda, a final way that the audience can reflect on the topic. In the following conclusion, student writer Mary McQueen appeals to landlords in order to subtly reinforce her claim advocating a more open policy toward pets in apartments:

> Appeals are designed to evoke emotional or ethical (morally grounded) responses from your reader.

> The human/animal bond is special and worth preserving and promoting. Landlords who allow pets make an important, generous contribution towards the solution of the pet-friendly housing problem and have the opportunity to make the partnerships of landlords, tenants, and companion animals so successful that they become role models to inspire others around the community, the province, and the country.

In the cases of neutral or opposing viewpoints, emotional and ethical appeals work best when they are subtle, not overstated. In the example above, the writer indirectly evokes the emotional bond that many owners have with their pets, showing how landlords can contribute to this bond. Ethical appeals focus on issues like fairness, equality, responsibility, and the like. Thus, the example also demonstrates a subtle ethical appeal since it evokes a hierarchical relationship (landlord and tenant) based on the demonstration of ethical qualities like respect.

Refutation Strategies

Since the existence of an opposing viewpoint is needed for an argumentative claim, it is advisable to refer to this viewpoint in your essay—otherwise, it may appear that you are avoiding the obvious. Although you may use concessions as part of your argument, you will mostly be concerned with refuting the claims on the other side. In your **refutation**, or *rebuttal*, you show the weaknesses or limitations of these claims. Here are three general strategies to consider. Which one you use depends on the three factors that you need to take into account when planning your argumentative essay: your topic, purpose, and audience. There may be additional factors involved too, such as essay length.

> REFUTATION
> argumentative strategy of raising opposing points in order to counter them with your own points.

Acknowledgement

You may need to do no more than simply acknowledge the opposing view. Such a strategy may be appropriate if the argument on the other side is straightforward or obvious. In the case of arguing for more open policies toward pets (above), the position of landlords is simple: allowing pets increases the potential for property damage. Similarly, this strategy would be a natural choice if the claim argued against the use of pesticides in lawn maintenance. Again, the opposing view is obvious: lawn owners use pesticides to make their lawns look attractive. After acknowledging the competing claim, the writer would go on to raise strong points that counter this claim without necessarily referring to it again.

Occasionally, there may not be a recognizable opposing view to acknowledge. For example, if your argumentative purpose is to raise awareness of an important issue, as Robert Gifford does in "Psychology's essential role in alleviating the impacts of climate change" (p. 455), there may be no clear adversarial view to refute. In his introduction, Gifford clearly states his thesis that psychology "has an important role to play in easing the pain caused by climate change" and that his essay is necessary because "the thesis is not broadly acknowledged."

Limited Rebuttal

In a limited rebuttal, you raise and respond to the major point(s) on the other side, then follow with your own points without mentioning minor competing claims. One obvious reason for using a limited rebuttal is that in a short essay, you will not have space to respond to all the competing claims. This strategy may also be appropriate if the strength of the opposing view is anchored by one or perhaps two very significant claims. You would not want to give strength to the other side by raising and refuting less important issues unless you are trying to reach a compromise when both strengths and weaknesses might be considered. When you are analyzing the main argument on the other side, however, it is important to represent that position fairly; concessions are often helpful in this regard.

Whether you adopt the limited rebuttal strategy can depend on your audience and purpose for arguing. For example, if your audience is only generally knowledgeable about an issue, mentioning less important points on the other side might be counter-productive since they might not have been aware of them.

Full Rebuttal

There are two ways to organize a full rebuttal. You may systematically raise competing claims and respond to them one at a time (*point-by-point rebuttal*). Although concessions could be involved, especially if your purpose is to arrive at a compromise, usually you point out the flaws in each before responding with your own counterclaim. Alternatively, you could summarize the competing claims before you present the support for your claim, right after your introduction or after you have presented that support, just before your conclusion (*block rebuttal*). In some essays, you will not have the space or the need for a full rebuttal, let alone the more systematic form, the point-by-point rebuttal—for example, when you are limited by word length or when you are asked simply to give your opinion on a topic.

Point-by-point rebuttals can be very effective if the competing claims of an argument are well-known, if there is strong opposition to your claim, or if you are responding to a specific viewpoint, as is Joel Karadinos in "Pharmaceutical innovation: Can we live forever? A commentary on Schnittker and Karandinos" (p. 396). When your purpose is to critique a viewpoint, position, or text, a full rebuttal is often needed. If your argumentative purpose is to reach a compromise, you might also choose to use the point-by-point strategy. Here, however, you would be attempting to reach out to the other side (or both sides), showing that you understand the points that define their position. This strategy would demonstrate your knowledge and fairness.

The paragraph below illustrates the effective use of the point-by-point strategy in an essay on mandatory physical education classes in high school. Notice how student writer Meghan Cannon skilfully uses a concession (sentence 2) to help turn a competing claim into a point in her favour:

> Some individuals argue against mandatory physical education because they believe that many teenagers feel self-conscious about their bodies and, therefore, self-conscious about physical activity. While the initiation of physical activity may be difficult for one suffering from body image issues, the long-term effect is invariably one of satisfaction. Students learn to appreciate what they can do with their bodies instead of being completely concerned with how it looks. Physical activity promotes self-awareness and acceptance. Self-confidence soars from participation in sport and the social interaction induced by sport.

Organizing Your Argument

Before you begin an outline or an audience plan (see below), you should decide on the **order of your points**. For most argumentative essays, this will mean choosing between two orders: the *climax order* or a *mixed order*. In the first, you begin with the weakest point and build toward the strongest; in the second, you could begin with a strong point—but not the strongest—follow with weaker points, and conclude with the strongest. It may not be advisable to begin with the weakest point if your audience opposes your claim, since an initial weak point may make your readers believe your entire argument is weak. Other orders are also possible. For example, if you are arguing to reach a compromise, you might need to focus the first part of your essay on one side of the debate, the second part on the opposite side, and the third on your compromise solution.

There is nothing inherently wrong in ending with your weakest point either *(inverted climax order)*, although some advise against it. If you have presented a strong argument, a weaker concluding point is not necessarily going to undo your work. The last point could contain something humorous, anecdotal, or personal, for example, and serve as a fitting transition to a strong conclusion. Whatever order you use, it should be identical to the order of points in your thesis statement, assuming you use an expanded thesis statement.

Whichever refutation strategy you use, you should consider outlining the points on the other side before writing the essay—constructing a theoretical argument, as it were. In particular, consider how someone who disagreed with your claim might respond to your main points. This could reveal the strengths on the other side and any weaknesses in your own argument. More important, perhaps, it should serve to keep the opposing view in focus as you write, causing you to reflect carefully on what you are saying and how you say it.

ORDER OF POINTS
climax order is the order of points that proceeds from the weakest to the strongest; other orders include inverted climax order and mixed order.

Collaborative Exercise: The Audience Plan

Taking the audience factor into account is very important as you prepare to write an argumentative essay. Constructing an audience plan will enable you to consider your approach to the essay, including the kinds of strategies to use. Team up with two other students and interview the other members of your group to determine their knowledge level, their interest level, and their orientation (agree, disagree, neutral, or mixed) toward your topic; they will serve as your "audience," the basis for an audience profile. Then, use this information to construct an audience plan based on your specific "audience," your topic, and argumentative purpose. Discuss strategies you would use to persuade this audience. Include your topic and your writing purpose in the plan.

Readers could agree with your argumentative claim, disagree with it, be neutral, or be composed of some who agree and some who disagree. The make-up of your audience will help determine which argumentative strategies are the most effective ones for your essay.

A sample argumentative plan follows. After interviewing two students, who served as her audience, Kate Newcombe considered which strategies of those mentioned above would strengthen her argument. Specifically, she refers to the use of precedents and appeals to reader interests, along with logical and ethical appeals; she also decides to use a limited rebuttal strategy.

Because she planned on using research, she later wrote a research proposal in which she narrowed the topic further and decided on a research strategy, including potential sources (see her proposal, Chapter 9, page 137). Having both a plan and a proposal in place, Newcombe completed her research and wrote a formal outline, which she used to help structure her essay. Her completed essay appears below, page 130.

Like most writers, Newcombe's essay looks different from its early planning stages. Yet the basis of her argument can be seen in her argumentative plan, especially her considerations of her topic and audience.

Argumentative Plan

by Kate Newcombe

Topic: The introduction of needle exchange programs in the Canadian prison system.

Argumentative Purpose: To convince readers that the introduction of needle exchange programs within Canadian prisons is beneficial to inmates and employees alike.

Audience Profile: Two students in the class were interviewed regarding their knowledge, interest, and orientation to my topic.

Knowledge: Neither student knew anything about needle exchange programs in prisons, Canadian or otherwise. However, both were aware of the recent safe injection site in downtown Vancouver, which suggests that they know how needle exchange programs work if not the way they work in the specific prison environment.

Interest: The topic was of moderate interest to both students. They asked questions and seemed interested in finding out more information about the benefits and risks of implementing such a system. One student was definitely more involved in asking questions about the topic, being specifically concerned that implementation of this system might increase the incidence of intravenous drug use in prison.

Orientation: Both students had a neutral opinion towards the topic. Since they lacked background information, they didn't feel able to argue for one side or the other. They seemed to initially stress the risks of implementing such a system, but admitted that with more information and knowledge, they thought it could be beneficial. One student said she might approve of it in theory but that she didn't really see how it could affect her.

Audience Plan

Since my audience members stated that their opinion could depend partly on having the knowledge to make an informed decision, it is important to objectively explain needle exchange programs and the way they work. Defining key terms (for example, what *is* a needle exchange program?) could provide a basis for this information. In addition, I will examine needle exchange programs and safe injection sites in North America, especially the controversial on-site program recently implemented in Vancouver. I will then use the chronology method to provide a brief history of these programs and their use within prisons. Although there are currently no prison-based needle exchange programs in North America, I will use a cross-cultural comparison of prisons in Europe and Australia, where successful needle exchange programs exist.

Since this is such a controversial topic, it will be best not to ignore the perceived risks but to mention only the most important ones and to stress that the proven benefits outweigh the possible risks. By using a limited rebuttal strategy, I can address the major risks of the program while not weakening the argument by raising comparatively minor objections of which my audience might be unaware. In particular, early in my essay I will raise the point about exchange programs leading to increased drug use as a common and inaccurate perception of the consequences of needle exchange programs.

Through an overview of the benefits and risks of needle exchange programs, I will give my audience a better understanding of what they are and how they work, equipping them with the knowledge to make an informed decision. An important consideration is showing my readers that the issue does affect them—if not directly, then as good citizens in today's society. Most prisoners will eventually leave prison; since needle exchange programs have been proven to reduce the incidence of illnesses and diseases, notably HIV infections, there is less risk that they will spread these diseases, cutting down on health costs. Furthermore, I can use the positive health outcomes of the Vancouver safe injection site as a precedent for implementing a similar project inside Canadian prisons. Finally, I will use logical appeals throughout and end with an ethical appeal, arousing a sense of civil responsibility in my audience.

Sample Student Argumentative Essay with Annotations

The essay below uses APA documentation style.

The Need for Implementing Prison-Based Needle Exchange Programs in Canadian Federal Prisons

by Kate Newcombe

1   Over the past few decades, a controversial approach for improving the well-being of prison inmates has caused debate among individuals and government alike: the creation of prison-based needle exchange programs throughout Canada. Advocates of individual safety, health, and harm reduction argue on one side, while supporters of the "zero tolerance" rule and strict education argue on the other. Those caught in the middle are the individuals most at risk of acquiring life-threatening conditions and diseases, including HIV/AIDS: intravenous drug users in the Canadian prison system.

2   Although prison inmates are physically separated from the rest of Canadian citizens, their personal health and safety remain important issues in both the prison system and the outside population. With the prevalence of drug-related behaviour in prisons today, the risks of disease, addiction, and violence have increased drastically (Dolan, Rutter & Wodak, 2003; Okie, 2007). Most Canadian inmates eventually rejoin society and may pass on the deadly diseases they acquired while in prison, affecting the health of society as a whole. The prevention of HIV/AIDS and other health risks within prisons is not just a specific problem for a controlled group because this disease affects the population outside the prison walls as well. Without intervention from health organizations, the effects from ongoing risks to inmates will go untreated. Ignoring the problem will benefit no one, neither the prisoners directly affected, who, without such a program, could die from the lack of sterile instruments to support their drug use, nor the Canadian population as a whole. Although many oppose prison-based needle exchange systems, arguing that they will only increase drug use among inmates (Okie, 2007), officials should implement them in order to control drug-related problems and the spread of HIV/AIDS. They are beneficial for the prison community, cost efficient, and effective for those both inside and outside prison.

3   In order to better understand the issues surrounding needle exchange systems, it is vital to define some important terms that are specific to institutions and diseases and that affect the lives of drug users. Needle exchange programs (NEP) allow drug users to obtain safe, sterile injecting equipment (Bayoumi & Zaric, 2008; Dolan et al., 2003; Wodak & Cooney, 2005). Clean needles are given to drug users in exchange for used equipment, supporting the philosophy of harm reduction. Safe injection sites (SIS) are medically supervised facilities that provide a hygienic and stress-free environment for drug users to inject safely; they also provide clean injection equipment and may even have treatment and therapy options available (Bayoumi & Zaric). The main drug users of interest in this essay are those who use injection drugs, called intravenous (IV) drugs. Since these individuals use needles to support their drug habit, they are most at risk of infections once in prison due to the lack of available resources.

The writer concisely introduces the topic in the first paragraph.

Although it delays her thesis, Newcombe evidently felt it was important to raise this point early, suggesting that her topic should be of concern to her essay's readers, even those not interested in prisoners' lives. In doing so, she subtly appeals to reader interests, as she does in her conclusion.

After Newcombe acknowledges the main opposing point in a dependent clause, she follows in an independent clause with her thesis, a policy claim, and three main points in the order she will discuss them. She has chosen a mixed order, beginning with a moderately strong point, a weaker one (notice that paragraph 5 is the shortest body paragraph), and the most-developed point, which focuses on the success of needle exchange programs.

Before she introduces her first claim concerning the benefits of needle exchange programs for inmates, Newcombe defines terms, along with their abbreviations, that her readers may not know. It is also important that she writes economically, proceeding as quickly as possible to her first point. Note that she does not define HIV/AIDS, assuming an educated audience would be familiar with it.

4   Injecting drugs is a major risk factor for contracting blood-borne viruses, such as the Human Immunodeficiency Virus (HIV) and the Hepatitis C Virus (HCV) (Bayoumi & Zaric, 2008; Dolan et al., 2003; Okie, 2007; Wodak & Cooney, 2005). NEPs can drastically improve the personal health of prison inmates with the use of sterile injection tools and medically supervised injections, both of which decrease the risk factors associated with IV drug use. Medical professionals are able to supervise inmates using injection drugs, offering advice on how to alternate veins and where the best sites to inject are located; they offer support and counselling advice if needed. Because of the scarcity of needles and syringes within prison, people who inject drugs are more likely to share injecting equipment than people in the community, significantly increasing their risk of contracting HIV. With prison-based NEPs, sterile needles and other injecting equipment are provided to inmates to reduce the risk of harmful blood transmission.

5   Implementing prison-based NEPs not only has provided benefits to inmate IV drug users but also has been proven cost efficient (Bayoumi & Zaric, 2008; Cabases & Sanchez, 2003; Dolan et al., 2003). For example, among the findings of the most recent study, Bayoumi and Zaric (2008), is that there would be a cost of $20,100 per case of HIV infection averted, whereas direct HIV-related treatment is ten times this figure (p. 1149). Reducing the dangers and disease within prisons before these inmates return to society also reduces the amount of work, medicine, and counselling needed for inmates after they leave prison (Cabases & Sanchez). Also, needle exchange programs are not costly policies to implement due to the limited provisions needed and the work of volunteer medical assistants.

6   Although many opponents of prison-based NEPs argue that these systems promote increased drug use among inmates, studies suggest otherwise (Dolan et al., 2003; Wodak & Cooney, 2005). Studies of international NEPs do not reveal any increase in the prevalence of IV drug users, and they have also reported reduced blood-borne pathogens among intravenous drug users (Dolan et al., p. 157). With reduced pathogens transmitted throughout the prison population, providing sterile injecting equipment to inmates offers a simple prevention solution to HIV/AIDS. By implementing prison-based NEPs, inmate health increases while a harm reduction strategy is used to reduce the risk of HIV transmission among the prison population.

7   In the debate, the health of inmates has received much of the attention, but international trial programs suggest that the use of NEPs in prisons is beneficial to the prison community as a whole (Dolan et al., 2003). Without the need to create homemade injection devices from unsanitary objects, the demand for these devices by inmates is dramatically reduced. The search for scarce homemade injection equipment frequently results in violence as inmates try to obtain these implements. The availability of free, sterile equipment reduces the instances of inmates using homemade injection devices as weapons to injure guards and fellow inmates (Dolan et al., p. 157; Okie, 2007, p. 105). With the ability to access clean needles, IV drug users are less likely to be angry or in withdrawal, resulting in fewer attacks on prison guards and employees and a reduced need for constant, time-consuming cell inspections. Finally, by reducing the stigma associated with IV drug use, prison inmates who inject drugs frequently are less likely to do so in a concealed and dangerous way (Okie, p. 105). In summary, the health benefits to prison employees and inmates alike strongly demonstrate the advantages of prison-based NEPs in the Canadian federal prison system.

8   Although Canadian policy does not advocate the American practice of "zero tolerance" towards drug use, it also does not fully embrace the harm reduction techniques used throughout Europe and Australia (Dolan et al., 2003; Wodak & Cooney, 2005). Even though Canada has gained international recognition for its successful NEPs, notably its SIS in the downtown east side of Vancouver, as well as 34 centres throughout Ontario (Ontario Harm Reduction Distribution Program, "About Us," 2011, para. 3),

---

Newcombe uses the APA documentation style, which does not include page numbers for general references. In many cases, Newcombe simply reports the findings of the study and does not include information from specific pages. Several sources can be included in one parenthetical citation with semicolons separating them; sources are arranged alphabetically. For more about APA style, see Chapter 9, p. 155.

In the topic sentence of this paragraph, Newcombe introduces her second point, anticipating an opposing argument that such programs are costly to taxpayers.

In this paragraph, Newcombe refutes the strongest opposing point, using international studies for support.

APA does not require the repetition of the study's year if the same study has been cited earlier in the paragraph.

The writer summarizes several points in her paragraph wrap, reinforcing the paragraph's topic sentence.

there has been no corresponding support for NEPs in Canadian prisons. The Vancouver SIS was established in 2003, and it has become a leader in harm reduction services throughout the country. This specific site has demonstrated the advantages of implementing such a system and shown benefits such as a decrease in overdose, effective use of health and social services, and the cost efficiency of this service for public health officials (Bayoumi & Zaric, 2008). With the undeniable success of the limited programs in use, why has this policy not been extended to our federal prisons? Factors affecting the slow progression of NEPs into the Canadian prison system include improper promotion by several UN agencies, the Conservative government's stance on these programs, and the limited amount of reliable information regarding HIV/AIDS (Okie, 2007, p. 106; Wodak & Cooney, S41).

9   Several community-based studies throughout the world have shown that prison-based NEPs are both cost-effective and a successful disease prevention strategy. Wodak and Cooney (2005) reported that as of 2004, NEPs had been introduced in 53 prisons in Europe, in Switzerland, Spain, Germany, Moldova, Kyrgyzstan, and Belarus, all resulting in positive outcomes (p. S39). Decreased rates of drug use, needle sharing, and HIV transmission have been recorded, while no cases of needles being used as weapons or increased drug use have been reported (Bayoumi & Zaric, 2008; Dolan et al., 2003; Wodak & Cooney). In an evaluation of the cost-effectiveness of NEPs in general, Wodak and Cooney summarized, "There is sufficient evidence to consider that the criterion of cost effectiveness has been fulfilled" (p. S37). More recently, researcher Rolf Jürgens (as cited in Chu & Elliott, 2009) found that needle exchange programs are currently in place in more than 60 prisons of varying sizes in at least 10 countries in Europe and Asia, with significant improvements in the health of prisoners, such as reductions in HIV infections and the safety of the prison environment (p. 6). In light of the positive findings, the study's authors strongly urge that Canadian governments implement NEPs in prisons countrywide.

10   Introducing NEPs into prisons across Canada will ensure that improved healthcare is provided for at-risk prison inmates, resulting in numerous advantages to their personal health and the prison community. It can also play a vital role in reducing the number of Canadian prisoners using shared IV injection instruments, minimizing the amount of prison-related violence. Therefore, it can greatly help medical staff control HIV/AIDS and other blood-borne diseases. Although opponents of NEPs in federal prisons have often been vocal, the evidence from international examples shows the many benefits of the program. In particular, the belief that implementing NEPs will increase drug-related behaviour is ill-founded: such programs have revealed no steady increase in IV drug use. The benefits of NEPs far outweigh their possible risks. The implementation of NEPs into federal prisons throughout Canada is essential for the health of both the prison inmates and Canadian society as a whole. Ignoring the challenges posed by prison-based NEPs and evading our responsibilities as citizens will benefit nobody, neither prisoners, prison workers, nor those outside the system; rather, it will surely lead to further preventable breaches of health and human rights. Canadians should support the implementation of NEPs for the good of all.

References

Bayoumi, A., & Zaric, G. (2008). The cost-effectiveness of Vancouver's Supervised Injection Facility. *Canadian Medical Association Journal, 179,* 1143–1151. doi: 10.1503/cmaj.080808

Cabases, J., & Sanchez, E. (2003). Cost effectiveness of a syringe distribution and needle exchange program for HIV prevention in a regional setting. *The European Journal of Health Economics, 4,* 203–208. doi: 10.1007/s10198-003-0172-7

Chu, S. K. H., & Elliott, R. (2009). *Clean switch: The case for prison needle and syringe programs in Canada.* Retrieved from www.aidslaw.ca/publications/ publicationsdocEN.php?ref=948

Dolan, K., Rutter, S., & Wodak, D. (2003). Prison-based syringe exchange programmes: A review of international research and development. *Addiction, 98*, 153–158. doi: 10.1046/j.1360-0443.2003.00309.x

Okie, S. (2007). Sex, drugs, prisons, and HIV. *The New England Journal of Medicine, 356*(2), 105–108. doi:10.1056/NEJMp068277

Ontario Harm Reduction Distribution Program. (2011). Needle exchange. Retrieved from www.ohrdp.ca/needle-exchange/

Wodak, A., & Cooney, A. (2005). Effectiveness of sterile needle and syringe programmes [Supplemental issue]. *International Journal of Drug Policy, 16*, 31–44. doi:10.1016 /j.drugpo.2005.02.004

For examples of essays in *The Active Reader* that use argument, see "Classification by Rhetorical Mode/Pattern or Style" (inside back cover).

Chapter 9

Writing the Research Paper

Research essays call on various kinds of reading and writing skills, many of which have been discussed in this text. The usual formats for academic research writing are the essay and the report, discussed in Chapter 6. Since research requires you to read your sources closely, it is wise to adopt specific strategies to make the most of your reading, as we discussed in Chapter 5. Further, comprehension of the material depends on your ability to utilize critical thinking skills, which was discussed in Chapter 4. Responding to texts in writing involves such processes as evaluating, assessing, and comparing sources. In addition, identifying which ideas from a source are the most relevant to your topic and integrating them into your own essay are key research skills essential in summarization. These kinds of activities were discussed in Chapter 7.

However, the fundamentals of research extend beyond these skills. In this chapter, we focus on (1) locating sources in the modern library; (2) assessing the reliability of sources, particularly those accessed electronically; and (3) integrating ideas and words smoothly and efficiently—summarization is only one means of doing so—and giving credit to your sources. But first, let us begin with some brief comments on the nature of the research process.

Coming Up with a Topic

For many students, finding a topic to write on is the first challenge to overcome (assuming you have the freedom to use a topic of your choosing). Here are some questions to consider if you need to come up with a topic from scratch:

- Where do your interests lie (hobbies, leisure pursuits, reading interests, extra-curricular activities)?
- What would you like to learn more about? Curiosity is a good motivator. A topic you are very familiar with does not always make a good one for a research essay, as you might not be motivated to fully explore the subject.
- What topic do you think readers might like to learn about? Thinking of *other* people's interests can guide you to a worthwhile topic. What topic could benefit society or a specific group in society (for example, students at your university)?
- Can you think of a new angle on an old topic? Neglected areas of older topics can be new opportunities for exploration.

Preparing for Research

Research often begins after you have come up with a research question or a statement of the problem to be investigated. Your statement could also take the form of a hypothesis, as it does in many scientific experiments where the researcher predicts the result of the experiment; the experiment is then set up to test the **hypothesis**. Student researchers, too, could conduct research to determine whether their prediction is valid. For example, you could hypothesize that there is a causal relationship between children playing violent video games and aggression. In fact, if no such causal relationship is discovered, your original hypothesis isn't considered faulty—whether hypotheses are proven or not, you have discovered something new about your topic.

However, your question, thesis, or hypothesis will likely not be clear until you have conducted preliminary research. Typically, this begins with narrowing a general topic. If you began with a topic like "energy sources in today's world" you will soon find that the topic is much too large; the information available would be overwhelming. However, you can use any of the pre-writing strategies discussed on page 72 to make the topic more manageable.

One way to narrow the topic of energy sources is to focus on alternatives to fossil fuels, for example nuclear power, with its safety and environmental concerns, or thermomechanical energy, which is often considered a less viable long-term energy source. Most of this research must be done either in the library or online using your library's electronic resources, since most reference material cannot be taken out of the library.

Your reading will narrow the topic further. It could lead you to three specific energy sources: bio-diesel, solar energy, and hydrogen. However, writing on all three sources in one essay would probably prevent you from going into detail about any of them. Although one option might be simply to randomly select one of the three alternative sources, a better option would be to ask what you or your potential readers might want to know about these energy sources: *Why are these sources important? Who would be interested in knowing about them, and what more do you need to find out about them in order to inform others? Whom could they benefit? What are the potential benefits? What are the potential costs?* Posing these kinds of questions can provide valuable direction and help focus your research. They may lead you directly to a research question, hypothesis, or thesis statement.

In this case, all these energy sources offer a potential global solution to the energy crisis. *Which of the three offers the best potential?* With this last question in mind, you can recall what you have read about each or continue to browse general works for more background information—in particular, information concerning the costs and benefits of these three energy sources. In the end, you might decide that the most promising is hydrogen. Your thesis might take this form:

> Current research into the development of alternative fuels provides hope for an oil- and nuclear-free future, but of the different types of alternative fuels, hydrogen is the most promising because it satisfies the requirements for a long-term energy plan.

It could also be phrased as a research question:

> Among the various alternative fuels being promoted today, does hydrogen live up to the claims of its proponents by being able to satisfy the requirements for a long-term energy plan?

HYPOTHESIS
prediction about an outcome; used in Type B (empirical) essays in which an experiment is set up to prove/disprove the prediction.

You could begin your research into alternative sources by consulting general reference works, such as textbooks, encyclopedias, or dictionaries, along with indexes and guides in the fields of applied science, engineering, and technology.

Now, with a tentative thesis and organizational pattern (cost/benefit analysis), you can conduct further research by turning to specific journals, especially **peer-reviewed journals** in which academics, scientists, and researchers publish their findings. This is where library search skills enter the picture. Knowing how the modern library works will save you a lot of time and help you find high-quality sources. By following the guidelines in "The Active Voice: A Beginner's Guide to Researching in the Digital Age," below, you will be able to locate specific sources directly relevant to a topic like energy sources in peer-reviewed journals such as *Renewable and Sustainable Energy Reviews*, *Applied Energy*, and *International Journal of Hydrogen Energy* or, if your instructor permits it, non-peer-reviewed but reliable magazines such as *New Scientist* and *Scientific American*.

As with most projects involving a combination of skills that develop through *doing them*, doubts, false starts, and occasional frustrations are inevitable. The information that follows on research methods and sources is designed to make this process a more comprehensible and satisfying learning experience.

Research Proposals

The main purpose of a research proposal is to convince a reader that the project you propose is worth doing and that you are the right person to do it. At a bare minimum, research proposals need two parts: (1) a description of what you are undertaking, including your thesis and main points and (2) your methodology, including the kinds of sources you will be using.

Before you undertake your major research, it is useful to write a research proposal, although it can also be written after your research but before you begin composing, in which case it may include an essay outline. The main purpose of a proposal, whether a research proposal for your instructor or the kind of fully developed proposal used in various professions, is to convince a reader that the project you propose is worth doing and that you are the right person to do it. For you, the student researcher, a successful proposal will persuade your instructor that you have done adequate preparation and are on the right track to a successful research paper.

At a bare minimum, research proposals need two parts: (1) a description of what you are undertaking and (2) your methodology. In the first part, you include your thesis and, if known, your main points. You could also include your reason for wanting to research the topic; thus, you could mention your interest in the area or summarize the importance of research in this field to others. You will not be held to the specific terms of your proposal if you discover on further research that you need to amend your thesis or your main points. The proposal represents a *probable* plan: your thesis and main points are tentative at this stage and can be revised if necessary.

In the second part of the proposal, you should include the sources you have found useful so far and the kinds of sources that you will be looking at as you continue your research. Be as specific as possible here as well. Give names of books, journals, websites, and so on, along with article titles. If you are planning other kinds of research, such as interviews or questionnaires, mention them too. The more detail you provide, the more your reader will be convinced. Being specific makes your proposal credible.

A final function of the research proposal is that it gives you a preliminary plan to follow; it solidifies your topic and your approach to the topic in your own mind.

A proposal may even include projected dates, such as the date you plan to begin your major research and the date you plan to complete it.

Sample Proposal

The sample research proposal below is by the writer of the argumentative essay on p. 130. (See also her argumentative plan, Chapter 8, p. 128, which focuses on argumentative strategies rather than research.) In contrast to outlines, which represent your essay's structure, proposals usually have an exploratory function. Therefore, not all the points in the proposal below were included in the essay itself. One way to present your main points is in the form of questions, which can be used to generate possible research directions.

Proposal for Research Essay on the Effects of Implementing Prison-Based Needle Exchange Programs in Canadian Federal Prisons

by Kate Newcombe

Topic: The benefits that introducing needle exchange programs into the Canadian federal prison system will have on inmates and employees.

Purpose: To investigate prison-based needle exchange programs and argue the benefits of implementing such a system in Canadian federal prisons.

Description: With the recent introduction of the safe injection site in downtown Vancouver, a growing interest in these sites has developed throughout the community, health services programs, and governments. Although it is a controversial topic, evidence from the Vancouver needle exchange site demonstrates the benefits of these programs. This issue is worth exploring because drug use continues to be widespread in Canadian prisons, and the increased health risks to intravenous drug users due to lack of proper injecting equipment are growing rapidly. Currently, no such programs exist in Canadian prisons. I am interested in discovering more about prison-based needle exchange programs and arguing for the benefits they provide to inmates as well as prison workers. The main organizational methods will be problem-solution and cause/effect.

Tentative Thesis Statement and Central Questions: Prison-based needle exchange programs are an effective, cost-efficient, and beneficial safety tool for public health officials to implement in Canadian prisons in efforts to control drug-related problems and the spread of HIV/AIDS.

- What are the health benefits to intravenous drug users by introducing a system such as this into Canadian prisons?
- Will the introduction of needle exchange systems increase drug use by inmates?
- How will its introduction affect prison employees? (i.e., will there be a physical threat to the health and safety of workers?)
- Have other countries implemented this system into their prisons? If so, what are the results?
- How, if at all, will the introduction of this system help control the spread of HIV/AIDS in the prison population?
- How has the Canadian government dealt with groups and individuals who argue for implementation?
- Is this truly a cost-effective system?

Methodology: In my preliminary research through my university database, I have found several reliable scholarly articles and reviews of prison-based needle exchange programs. They are peer-reviewed and diverse, from such journals as *Addiction, CMAJ, The Lancet*, and *The New England Journal of Medicine*. Tentative articles include Dolan, Rutter, and Wodak (2002), "Prison-Based Syringe Exchange Programmes: A Review of International Research and Development", and Bayoumi and Zaric (2008), "The Cost-Effectiveness of Vancouver's supervised Injection Facility"; other studies available also evaluate the success of the Vancouver program. The researchers' findings support the argument that the introduction of prison-based needle exchange programs is beneficial to inmates and employees, while it does not appear that the health benefits of clean syringes and needles increase intravenous drug use within prisons. Davies'"Prison's Second Death Row" (2004) also looks promising as the author accounts for the reluctance of some governments to institute harm reduction programs.

Recording Important Information

Keeping methodical and accurate records during the research phase of the essay-writing process allows you to read material efficiently as well as save time (and your sanity) when you write your paper. You should record notes as you research, ensuring that they include the following information:

Ensure that you keep your research notes, such as summaries and direct quotations, separate from your personal annotations. Use a method that clearly distinguishes between the two; otherwise, you could end up plagiarizing by failing to attribute the idea or words of a source, thinking they were your own.

- a direct quotation, a summary, or a paraphrase of the writer's idea (if it is a direct quotation, make sure you put quotation marks around it);
- the complete name(s) of the author(s), ensuring correct spelling;
- the complete name(s) of any editors or translators;
- the complete name of the book, journal, magazine, newspaper, or website;
- the title of the specific article, chapter, section, or webpage;
- full publication details, including date, edition, and translation (if appropriate);
- the name of the publisher and the company's location (including province or state) for books;
- in the case of an article accessed electronically, the day you viewed the page and either the URL or the **digital object identifier** (DOI); the date of the site or its most recent update should also be recorded;
- the call number of a library book or bound journal (to help you find it again if necessary);
- the page numbers you consulted, both those from which specific ideas came and the full page range of the work (or some other marker, such as section headings and paragraph numbers, for unnumbered Internet documents).

DIGITAL OBJECT IDENTIFIER (DOI)
number-alphabet sequence that begins with the number 10 often found on journal articles; serves as means of persistent link for digital material.

Organizing Research Notes

There are many ways to organize information from your research in order to use it later. The manual method is probably the most familiar to students: notecards, for example, are portable and practical. You can also record notes in a notebook or journal and use tabs to divide the book, using distinct subject headings. In addition, there are a number of software programs available designed to help with planning and organization. For example, *RefWorks* (www.refworks.com/) is an Internet-based "citation manager" that allows you to import references from popular databases like *Academic Search Complete*, *MLA Bibliography*, and *EconLit*. Others are databases, such as *EndNote* (www.endnote.com/), *Bibliographix* (www.bibliographix.com/), and *Nota Bene* (www.notabene.com/). Students can usually take a tutorial for these programs on their websites or even through their own institution if it has purchased licences allowing students to use them. These programs offer many benefits, such as automatic formatting for a great variety of citation and bibliographic systems.

The Active Voice

A BEGINNER'S GUIDE TO RESEARCHING IN THE DIGITAL AGE

1   The twenty-first century academic library can seem like an overwhelming conglomeration of print and electronic resources, especially to the undergraduate researcher. In addition to the "traditional" materials found in the library's online catalogue, there are numerous other online resources available, including databases, e-journals, e-books and other digital formats and media. The sheer volume of information resources in today's academic library need not be intimidating. On the contrary, an effective research strategy will enable you to take full advantage of the wealth of print and electronic information resources available to you. An effective strategy should include three important considerations:

1.   Your *topic* or research question
2.   The *resources* that are most likely to contain information about your topic
3.   The *search strategy* you will use to obtain information from those resources

2   When you understand how to choose a well-defined research topic, where to look for information on that topic, and how to construct an effective search in a catalogue or database, you will have the basic tools required for most research projects at the first year level. As you become a more confident researcher, you can expand on these basic strategies by exploring more specialized resources and experimenting with advanced search methods.

The Research Topic

3   The starting point for your research will invariably be your topic. If you are choosing your own topic, you will want to select one that is not too broad or too narrow. If your topic is too broad, you will have difficulty focusing your research and writing. If your topic is too narrow or obscure, you may not be able to find enough relevant information to support your thesis.

4   For instance, you may want to write about *homelessness* or *the homeless*. It would be difficult to write a focused paper on such a broad topic. To narrow your focus, you might want to research homelessness in a particular age group, such as teenagers. However, this would probably still be too broad. You could narrow your focus further by looking at particular health problems of homeless teens or risk factors associated with homelessness in teens, like poverty, addiction, abuse, and so on.

Selecting Resources

5   *Subject or Research Guides:* Once you have decided on a topic, you must then choose your resources. Most academic libraries provide subject or research guides on the library website. These guides are prepared by subject librarians with specialized knowledge of the information resources for their particular subject areas. Many subject guides provide valuable information on reference resources like dictionaries, encyclopedias, biographies and bibliographies, call number ranges for the subject and select books, key databases, scholarly websites, and primary source materials.

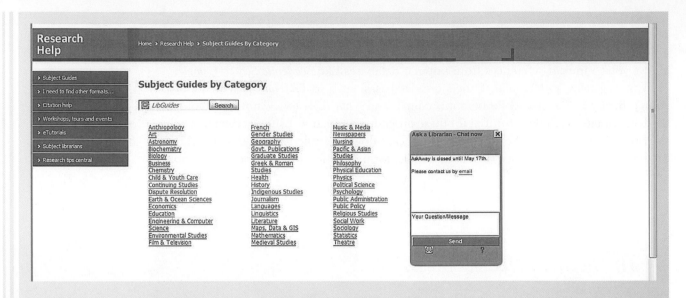

6   *Primary and Secondary Sources:* Your research may require that you investigate both primary and secondary source information. The meaning of primary and secondary sources can vary across the disciplines but in the Humanities and Social Sciences, primary sources generally provide *first-hand* information or data and may include literary and other original creative works, autobiographies, interviews, speeches, letters and diaries, unpublished manuscripts, data sources, government records, newspapers, etc. Secondary sources are works that analyze or provide criticism or interpretation of a primary work, source or experience from a *second-hand* perspective. They include textbooks, critical books, articles or essays, biographies, historical articles, or films, etc.

7   *The Library Catalogue:* The library catalogue is an important tool for finding secondary print sources like books, encyclopedias, dictionaries, and journals in your library as well as any electronic versions of these materials that are available. Encyclopedias and dictionaries provide concise, general information on your topic and are often useful for helping you to narrow your focus by highlighting key issues and concepts. Reference sources may also provide suggestions for further research. Scholarly books relevant to your topic are also important sources for you to explore. As well as covering a subject in more depth than a journal article can, they often provide important historical, biographical, literary,

or cultural context that may not be available in journal articles. Books also feature tables of contents that can help you to identify important aspects of the subject that you may want to explore further and bibliographies to help you locate other resources. E-books are especially useful for browsing tables of contents and bibliographies and for keyword searching within the full text of a book.

8   *Online Databases:* Scholarly journal articles are a key secondary source for your research. Journal articles review what other scholars have said about your topic and often provide important supportive or alternative perspectives relevant to your thesis. Online databases and indexes are your main tools for finding journal articles in both print and online formats. Your library's home page may provide a metasearch tool, such as *MetaLib* for searching the databases. The *Quick-Search* option will enable you to search for keywords for your topic within a pre-determined set of general, multidisciplinary, or subject-specific databases. Or you can create your own database sets using the *CustomSearch* option. The system retrieves a set number of relevant articles from each database in the set, and allows you to limit your search, save or export your results, or link to the full text. This method is useful for quickly finding information on your topic and to identify the best databases for more in depth searching—usually those that return the most results.

QuickSearch Results

Search for "homeless? teen?" in "Social Sciences (General)" found 3811 results

Table View Brief View Full View   Sort by: Rank

Summary

1- 10 of 122 records retrieved (retrieve more)   Custom Search   << <Previous Next> >>

No.	Rank	Author	Title	Year	Database	Action
1		Kasland, Karen	Out of Place. The article presents detailed information related to homeless teenagers, particularly in the U.S.	2010	Academic Search Complete (EBSCO)	
2			Agencies race to help 1.2 million homeless	2010	Academic Search Complete (EBSCO)	
3			Oregon Schools Support Homeless Students. The article discusses efforts in Oregon to help children and teens without permanent standard housing. It notes an increase during 2009 of 14 percent in homeless students. The state is committed to providing stability at school for ...	2010	Academic Search Complete (EBSCO)	
4		StephenWoolworth	Between the Wizard and the Deep Blue Sea: Notes on Homeless Youth Advocacy and Community Coalition Building. This article features a series of short self-reflective narrative vignettes about the experiences that led me to build and ultimately lead a coalition of homeless youth advocates who began the challenging work of calling attention to the ...	2010	Academic Search Complete (EBSCO)	
5		Nicoletti, Angela	The Homeless Teen Mom.	2009	Academic Search Complete (EBSCO)	
6		Moriarty, Sheila	Turbulent Transitions: A Day in the Life of a Homeless Teen. The short story "Turbulent Transitions: A Day in the Life of a Homeless Teen," by Sheila Moriarty is presented.	2009	Academic Search Complete (EBSCO)	
7		Scappaticci, Anne Lise Silveira	Homeless teen mothers: social and psychological aspects.	2009	Social Sciences Index (Wilson)	
8		Nicoletti, A	The Homeless Teen Mom.	2009	Web of Science (ISI)	

Topics
- Family (20)
- School (14)
- Youth (14)
- Mothers (10)
- Risk Factors (10)

Dates
- 2010 (16)
- 2009 (25)
- 2008 (6)
- 2007 (3)
- 2006 (8)

Authors
- Saewyc, Elizabeth M. (2)
- Other (120)

Journal Titles
- USA Today (10)

9   Another option is to start with a good multidisciplinary database like *Academic Search Complete* which should provide relevant information on most topics at the undergraduate level. However, you will also want to take advantage of the many subject and specialized databases available. Most subject areas feature a "core" database that indexes the key journals for that discipline, such as ERIC for Education, *Sociological Abstracts* for sociology or the *MLA International Bibliography* for language and literature. It is important to get to know the core databases in your subject area. If your library has subject guides, these will list the core databases or "best bets" for each subject. Most libraries will also allow you to select databases by subject in addition to providing an A–Z list. This is especially helpful if the database lists include information or abstract pages. These pages provide useful information on the kinds of resources indexed in the database, whether it includes full text, coverage dates available, whether it can be accessed remotely, and anything else that may be pertinent to that particular database.

10   You should also consider the type of information you require. For example, it is unlikely that you will find complex data or statistical information unless you search a statistical database. Again, the subject guides, "databases by subject" lists, and the database abstract or information pages will help you in determining which databases include the type of information you need.

11   *Bibliographic and Full Text Databases:* Bibliographic databases or indexes contain a bibliographic record or citation for each item indexed in the database. The record usually includes the title, author and other publication information, article type, and some subject headings or keywords. There

may also be a brief summary of the article, called an abstract. Full-text databases include the full text of the article or journal in HTML or PDF format along with the bibliographic record. Most bibliographic databases will also enable you to connect to the full text, the library's online catalogue, and the inter-library loan page through your library's link resolver system, so you may still be able to find the full text of the article even if you are not searching a "full text" database.

Search Strategies

12   *Determining Keywords:* Once you have chosen some relevant resources for your subject, the next step will be to identify the key concepts from your topic to use as keywords or search terms. For instance, if you want to search for information on risk factors associated with homelessness in youth, you will want to identify keywords that embody the concepts *risk factors*, *homelessness*, *youth*. Some risk factors might be *poverty*, *addiction*, *abuse*, etc. *Risk* or *factors* used as search terms would be far too broad and would not provide good search results. "*Risk factors*" combined as a single term would not find results unless the books or articles used this exact term as well.

13   *Boolean Operators:* The actual search process, to be effective, should employ some form of Boolean strategy. The most common Boolean operators, AND, OR, and NOT are used to combine, expand, or eliminate keywords in your search. For instance, AND combines the two different terms *homelessness* AND *youth*. A search conducted using AND will also narrow your results compared to searching for each of the keywords separately because sources retrieved must include both terms. The OR operator is used to expand your search results

by including other concepts. These may be synonymous concepts or different aspects of a broader concept. In this example, you might want to search for results that include the keywords *youth* OR *teens* OR *adolescents* which are synonymous concepts. Or you may want to search for *poverty* OR *abuse* OR *addiction* as different aspects of the risk factors such as *children*, if you don't want results that discuss young children. The NOT operator should be used judiciously, however, because you may eliminate an article that discusses both children and teens and therefore may be relevant to your topic.

14   The Boolean terms are capitalized here for readability but this is not necessary in most databases. Also, many databases will now allow you to combine your keywords without using the Boolean operators at all. You simply enter your terms and choose the correct search mode. Using Basic Search in *Academic Search Complete* as an example, the search mode *Find all of my search terms* is equivalent to AND, and the search mode *Find any of my search terms* is equivalent to OR. Many other databases and catalogues now work in a similar manner, including *Google Scholar*.

15   *Truncation and Wildcards:* Boolean search strategy is often used with truncation and/or wildcard symbols. Truncation symbols enable you to include all variants of a search term. Using the asterisk as the truncation symbol in *teen** will ensure that your search results include all the terms: *teen, teens*, and *teenager*. Wildcards are used within a word, for instance in *colo#r* to search for an alternative spelling (*colour* and *color*) or *wom?n* to search for any unknown characters (*woman* and *women*). Most databases and catalogues use the asterisk (*) or a question mark (?) for the truncation or wildcard symbol. Some databases may also use the pound sign (#) or another symbol. If you are not sure what symbol to use, check the help menu. This will usually be located in the upper right-hand corner of your screen. The help menu will also provide information on other advanced search strategies that can be used in that particular catalogue or database.

16   *Basic or Advanced Search:* Online catalogues and databases usually feature simple or basic search and advanced search options. The basic search field can be used to enter single terms, as described above, or more complex search statements using Boolean operators. However, to construct a search statement using Boolean strategy in a basic search field, you must use parentheses to separate the OR terms from the AND terms as indicated below. The database will search for the terms in parentheses first, then from left to right.

   (*Homeless** OR *runaway**) AND (*teen** OR *adolescen**
   OR *youth*) AND (*poverty* OR *abuse* OR *addict**)

17   Also, if you want to use a combined term such as *"risk factors,"* you must use quotation marks unless the field provides the option to search two or more words as a phrase.

18   The advanced search option is set up to allow you to insert your terms and then select AND, OR, or NOT to combine the fields and to add additional fields, if necessary. Advanced search also allows you to search for terms in various fields, such as *All Text, Author, Title, Subject Terms,* etc., or you can leave it on the default setting. By selecting a specific field, you limit the search for your term to that field alone. It is often best to try a search in the default field initially and then try other advanced strategies to refine your results, if necessary.

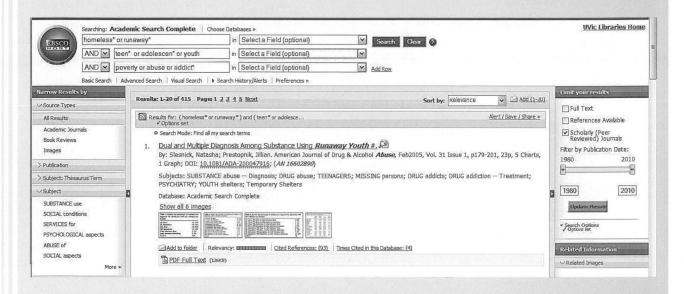

19   *Subject Headings or Descriptors:* Subject headings or descriptors are very useful for refining your search strategy. Subject headings have been applied to each bibliographic entry to describe what it is about. It is not merely a keyword found in the article or abstract, although it may be. Some databases will also enable you to search the subject *thesaurus* directly. This is a list of the specific subject terms used in that database. A thesaurus search can be useful for determining the best terms to use for your search initially, or if you have not had good results with your keyword searches. Subject headings within the results list are usually hyperlinked so that by clicking on the link, you either narrow the results of the current search to hits that all include that subject term or to all of the records in the database with that subject term.

19   Another strategy is to take note of the subject headings for your most relevant hits in your initial keyword searches. Combining these terms again in the *Subject Terms* field will often return more relevant results. Most online library catalogues also provide subject headings that are hyperlinked to other resources with the same heading. Additionally, there may be a hyperlink for the call number that will direct you to other items in the immediate call number range. This will enable you to easily "browse" the collection for other relevant materials.

20   *Limiters:* Another search strategy is using the limiters available to you in a particular database. This strategy is generally used to limit your results if there are too many or to limit to a particular date range, article type, format, or publication. One very useful limiter found in many databases is the scholarly or peer-reviewed limiter. Scholarly articles have been reviewed by a board or panel of scholars from the same discipline before being accepted for publication in academic journals. They are a more reliable source of information for your research than popular sources that are intended for a general audience. Some databases will limit to scholarly sources automatically and return the results under a *peer-reviewed* link or tab. *Academic Search Complete* provides a *Scholarly (Peer Reviewed) Journals* check box to the right of your search results list, or you can check the *Scholarly (Peer Reviewed) Journals* box in the *Limit your results* field before you execute your search and the database will return only scholarly articles.

21   *Marking and Saving:* Most databases and online catalogues provide a marking and saving feature. You can select your most relevant results, mark them by checking a box or adding them to a folder, and then choose from several options—usually print, email, save, or export. Export often includes an option to download or export to the bibliographic management software of your choice, such as *RefWorks* or *EndNote*. Some databases also allow you to create a personal account so that you can customize your preferences, save and retrieve your search history, organize your research in folders, or set up email alerts and RSS feeds. Again, the help menu for each database will provide information on all of the special features available to account holders.

22   *Refining your Strategy:* One final consideration for effective library research is refining your strategy throughout the process. It may be necessary to re-evaluate your topic,

choice of resources, or search strategy if your initial searches efforts are unfruitful. This is not an indication that your strategy is not a good one or has failed. On the contrary, the research process is naturally an iterative process. Therefore, it is important to start your library research early. This will allow you enough time to determine a manageable topic, explore as many resources as possible, refine your search strategy as necessary, and obtain any materials that are not readily available online or in your library.

—Danielle Forster, Reference Services Librarian:
English, French, Religious Studies,
Women's Studies, McPherson Library,
University of Victoria

Activity

Using one of your library's search engines or a general/science database, such as *Academic Search Complete* or *MEDLINE*, answer the questions below. To make your search more efficient, you can use the search limiters *journal article only* and *peer-reviewed journals only*; you can also set the publication date to 2004 and/or enter the main author's name "Tatem" in the Search window.

Access the academic journal *Nature* volume 432, issue 7014. Referring to the letter "Biology Students Find Holes in Gap Study" on page 147, answer the questions below, all of which stress the critical thinking skills discussed in Chapter 4:

1. How do these students establish their credibility to critique a study in an academic journal?
2. How do the students use the study by Whipp and Ward?
3. What year did Tatem et al. begin studying women's times? How can you infer this?
4. How many points do the students use to support their claim? Which do you consider the strongest? Why?
5. Following the letters, the authors of the study responded to the criticisms (see "Mind the Gap: Women Racers are Falling Behind," page 147). After reading all the letters on the page, along with the authors' response, consider whether the authors effectively answered the charges. What tone did they use in their response? Note: It is not necessary to be familiar with the models mentioned by the authors.

Using Credible Sources

In determining whether to use a source in your research essay, bear in mind the 4 "Re's" of research sources: reputable, reliable, recent, and relevant.

*Re*putable: Reputable sources are usually associated with well-known organizations or acknowledged experts in their field.

*Re*liable: Information from reliable sources can be trusted as accurate and free of bias.

*Re*cent: Although currency is more important to some topics than others, recent information is generally superior to older information.

*Re*levant: The information in relevant sources is directly related to your thesis and/or main points.

Credibility Issues in Online Sources

Of the four qualities mentioned above, the first two—reputable and reliable—are especially pertinent to online searches. The explosion of information via the Internet has made it more difficult to assess the authority of written information today. Because the boundaries are sometimes blurred between knowledge and speculation, fact and opinion, those who surf the net, reading indiscriminately, may not be able to distinguish readily between what is reliable information from a reputable source and what is not. (See "The Active Voice: Google and the Invisible Web—Using Library Resources for Deeper and Broader Research," p. 148.)

The Internet has increasingly become a forum for personal opinion, some of it informed, some of it uninformed. Today's student researcher must read carefully and ask questions about the source's sponsor(s) and/or author(s), along with the accuracy, currency, objectivity, and scope of the information.

The criteria below apply particularly to open-access resources, from Google Scholar to the enormously vast array of commercial, governmental, and personal websites that anyone sitting in front of a computer screen can view. In contrast to these are the more authoritative resources accessed through your institution's library home page. The way you use open-access resources, or *if* you use them in your research (your instructor may specify whether he or she considers them legitimate sources for your essay), depends on what kind of information you are looking for.

You should first consider your purpose for seeking out a source. Is it for reliable information from an objective source with evidence-gathering methods beyond reproach (Statistics Canada, for example), or is it to learn about a particular viewpoint? If the latter, it might be acceptable to use a website that advocates a position or supports a cause. If you were writing an essay on animal rights, you might want to access People for the Ethical Treatment of Animals (PETA) or Animal Rights Canada, since their advocacy of animal rights is clear and above board—which is not to say that their information is always factual or accurate.

> "Not all websites are forthcoming in acknowledging their true stake in an issue, nor do all websites use quality control to ensure the accuracy of their content. Even seemingly reliable and objective websites, such as those affiliated with governments, may be a source of misleading or outdated information."

Not all websites, however, are forthcoming in acknowledging their true stake in an issue, nor do all websites use quality control to ensure the accuracy of their content. Even seemingly reliable and objective websites, such as those affiliated with governments, may be a source of misleading or outdated information. The questions below are therefore relevant to most sources you access via the Internet.

Sponsors and Authors

- What group or individual has created the site or assumes responsibility for its content? If the organization/individual is unfamiliar, try to find (a) its parent organization, (b) affiliated organizations, or (c) a mission statement or similar claim concerning the organization's and/or website's purpose. If this information is not on the home page, it could be accessible from the home page. You should be suspicious of websites lacking these forms of self-identification.

- Who are the authors of the material on the site? Are names and affiliations given? Biographies? If the names of specific writers are not provided, what about names of the group's officers or officials? Is contact information provided? Mailing address, telephone number, email address? Note the domain of the website or email address: the most common ones in North America for educational institutions are ".edu" (US) and ".ca" (Canada), preceded by an abbreviated form of the school's name; ".gov" (a government source); ".org" (a non-profit organization); and ".com" (a commercial site).

Accuracy and Currency

- What is the source of the content? Are informational sources identified—by author, title, date? How has statistical information been calculated (e.g., through censuses, surveys, questionnaires by reliable organizations)? How are statistical information and other factual data being used? Does the use seem consistent with the website's purpose?
- Are all claims and other statements reasonable and well-supported?
- What is the original date of the site? Has it been updated recently? Does factual information appear verifiable? Can it be verified by checking a reliable and unaffiliated website? Does the website have a maintainer and a way to contact this person?

Objectivity

- Does the content seem presented without bias? Could it be considered politicized in any way? Does it seem to address a specific reader (e.g., is the voice familiar and informal?) or directed more toward a general reader? Do statements seem provocative? Is the tone neutral? Can you identify any slanted language or bias?
- If opinion exists, is it clearly differentiated from fact? Are other points of view besides those of the author/organization represented? How are they treated?
- Is there advertising on the site?

Scope and Comprehensiveness

- Does the site appear to include different views of and approaches to issues?
- Is there a menu or site map that provides an overview of content? (You could get an indication of scope from that.)
- Are there links to other sites? Do these sites appear reliable?
- Does content primarily consist of text, or are there photos or other graphics? What is the approximate proportion of text to graphics (it is not a hard and fast rule, but unless the purpose of the site is to display visual material, text should outweigh graphics)? Are there accompanying charts, graphs, or other illustrative material? If so, do they seem designed to explain and summarize (as opposed to having a merely decorative purpose)?

Other Issues

- Is the information on the website easy to access? Does it appear well-organized? What specific resources are designed to enhance accessibility or ease of site navigation? A site that is designed to facilitate access to information has at least thought about its potential readers.
- Is the site appealing and attractive rather than just glitzy?

In the following essay, the writer uses the techniques referred to in "The Active Voice: A Beginner's Guide to Researching in the Digital Age," above, to compare the effectiveness of the search engine Google with that of the resources of the "deep" web, such as bibliographic databases that can be accessed through your institution's library.

The Active Voice

Google and the Invisible Web: Using Library Resources for Deeper and Broader Research

1   The web is a window on many worlds. A few words in Google can lead to more than enough information on almost any topic. But is it a door to the "best" information? How complete is a Google search? Much of the "best," more scholarly information is not accessible, either hidden in private sources or available only for a fee.[1] These commercial and private sources represent much of the "deep" or "invisible" web,[2] the huge part of the web not reached comprehensively by the spiders of the search engines. This essay argues that Google and similar tools open up windows to only some of the worlds accessible via the web. It draws attention to the commercial bibliographic databases indexing the literature of specific subjects and providing retrieval tools more appropriate for the subject than Google. Libraries are licensing these databases for their clientele, opening up the "deep" web and the information inaccessible on the surface of the web through search engines.

Using Google

2   The web is indiscriminate, with no restrictions on what may be put up by whom. Web search engines rate sites using various criteria. Google uses word frequency counts and gives priority to sites that are linked on many others. In the scholarly literature, books and articles more highly cited are considered better, but this basic principle does not always apply to Google: because the web is so inclusive with commercial, popular, and self-published as well as scholarly sites all rated by popularity, much of the best scholarly material—especially on topics of wide interest—is not given priority because it is less popular than the material on non-scholarly sites.

3   Even though the web is undergoing rapid change and yet more information is becoming easily accessible, two unvarying features of the use for information mean that a Google search may never be enough. First is the need in searching for information for an adaptable view that brings together similar items, even if they don't use the same words for the same concepts. For example, computers do not recognize terms from their context; they are not able to tell if a hedge is a row of plants or a type of fund. Humans recognize

that information on Shakespeare and Chekhov would be relevant to a search on playwrights, but all terms, general and specific, must be input into Google to ensure a comprehensive search.

4   Second is the need for critical appraisal, bringing out more useful features than word frequency or popularity. The availability of tools for extracting the best items (peer-reviewed, in more important journals) and selection of what is indexed based on quality address this need. While Google pulls *more information*, these features lead to a focus on the *best information*.

Comparing Google and Library Databases

5   Bibliographic databases licensed by libraries for their users bring together and index items, print and electronic, from the literatures on particular topics. They give structure to this literature by using standard vocabulary and, often, concepts. Examples are *PsycInfo* for psychology and the MLA *(Modern Language Association) Bibliography* for literary criticism. As a health librarian, I use *Medline* daily, which indexes 19 million citations and gives structure to the literature of health sciences from research to clinical practice.

6   Comparing search results on Google vs. bibliographic databases makes the differences apparent. For example, a search[3] on "seasonal affective disorder" on *PsycInfo* led to 811 articles focusing on that topic (focused subject heading or with the phrase in the title). The particular interface I used, Ovid, allows limits to be applied, including to literature reviews as a methodology, leading to 37 articles, for many of which my university offered direct connections to the full text.[4] Google did provide useful information, mostly targeting patients, including a short article in Wikipedia, the cooperatively developed online encyclopedia. Google Scholar[5] did not work well for this topic, linking to older scholarly articles unless the date limit was used (I searched back to 2008), and then the articles were too specialized and less useful. Interestingly, my library's catalogue also provided good, recent printed books on this topic, which neither source retrieved. In summary, Google and *PsycInfo* both led to quality articles on seasonal

affective disorder, the difference being the purpose: Google provided information at a more basic level understandable to patients and *PsycInfo* gave access to more scholarly material.

7   I also tried a search on the portrayal of music in eighteenth century literature using Google and the *MLA Bibliography*. This search proved treacherous, particularly for Google, with retrieval including sites and articles discussing music and literature, not music in literature, in the eighteenth century. I tried the "Advanced Search" with "music in literature" as a phrase in Google. Although references to music in the work of specific authors was lost, a few hits looked useful, leading me to repeat in Google Scholar, which did not perform as well as in 2006 (the first version of this piece) because of less useful citations from the full text of books via Google Books. A basic search in *MLA Bibliography* pulled some good hits but also much dross. Using "Advanced Search" allows searches to be entered using "Period"—I used "1700–1799"—and "Literature Topic"—I used simply "music." All hits were relevant, 82 when I refined my search to English only. More specific topics—music in the writing of Blake and Goethe—suggested themselves. In this example, I found Google and Google Scholar generated more links that were irrelevant while *MLA Bibliography* enabled me to gain access to information specific to the topic.

8   Four similar examples were examined more carefully in a 2005 article.[6] The authors found that "Google is superior for coverage and accessibility. Library systems are superior for quality of results. . . . Improving the skills of the searcher is likely to give better results from the library systems, but not from Google."

9   There are hundreds of bibliographic databases, large and small, general and specific, reflecting the structure and communication patterns of the literatures of many subjects. A few of these databases are accessed via web search engines such as Google Scholar, as are some publisher sites. Access to the full text of articles retrieved is restricted to users verified as members of a library's clientele. While some interfaces are better than others, the various databases can generally be searched using techniques and vocabulary which suit the particular discipline indexed. Precise searches can be executed on specific topics. Databases collecting together and organizing the information of a discipline and made accessible with effective retrieval tools represent powerful adjuncts to the wide-ranging, indiscriminant search engines of the web.

Conclusion

10   So, Google away. But, are Google and friends good enough? As a librarian, I say "No!" Using Google or other search engines, you will find much useful information, much of high quality, even some of the "best" available. For complete and more precise searches, you will need to augment Google with the databases of the deep web that index the literature on the topic you are exploring.

11   How scholars communicate, even who are "scholars," is being changed by the web and the free flow of information. Google will turn up items made available outside the controlled world of scholarly communication. Databases indexing the published literature point to items beyond standard search engines using more varied concepts and interfaces adapted to the topic of the literature. As a librarian, I am pleased that a variety of tools is making information more accessible. I am thrilled that the value placed on using information, applying what is known, has increased. With the surface of the web readily accessible via Google and friends and with increasing understanding of the value of databases provided by libraries, more of the best information is going to reach and address the needs of more people.

—Jim Henderson, Liaison Librarian, McGill University

1 Since the 2006 first version of this article, Google has recognized the "deep web"—see Madhavan J et al. "Google's deep web crawl" Proceedings of the VLDB Endowment (2008), pp. 1241–1252. However, their efforts do not broaden access significantly.

2 For a bibliography, see Egger-Sider F, Devine J. "Beyond Google: the invisible web". May 2003, revised June 2010. http://library.laguardia.edu/invisibleweb/webography (accessed 22 July 2010). It includes the key paper, Bergman MK. "White Paper: The Deep Web: surfacing hidden value". *Journal of electronic publishing* 7(1) 2001. http://dx.doi.org/10.3998/3336451.0007.104 (accessed 27 July 2010).

3 All searches done July 2010.

4 In the past 5 years, many libraries have set up full-text links via Google.

5 Surprisingly, Google Scholar remains in beta (test) mode since the 2006 version of this piece.

6 Brophy J, Bawden D. "Is Google enough? Comparison of an internet search engine with academic library resources" Aslib proceedings: new information perspectives, 57(6) 2005: 498–512.

Integrating and Documenting Sources

When you integrate your research sources into your essay, you can use one or more of several methods to combine the source material with your own words. When you document these sources, you use a standardized format to show your readers where you obtained this material. Typically, you integrate, or synthesize, your sources as part of the composing process. Documenting your sources is often the final stage in the composing process—either of the rough draft or of a later draft. The value in documenting as early as possible in the process, however, is that it will give you ample time to check and double-check the accuracy of your information.

Integrating Your Sources: Summary versus Paraphrase

SUMMARY
method of extracting the main idea (or ideas) from an original source, expressing it in your own words.

PARAPHRASE
method of source integration in which you put someone else's ideas in your own words, keeping the length of the original.

When you **summarize** a source, you extract an idea (ideas) from the source that is directly relevant to your essay, expressing it in your own words. If you wanted to summarize a large portion of the original, you would follow the guidelines for précis summaries (see p. 99). What distinguishes a summary from a **paraphrase** is that summaries are selective: they focus on main ideas. When you paraphrase, you include *all of the original, putting it in your own words*. You could paraphrase anything from a part of a sentence to one or two paragraphs. Paraphrasing is reserved for very important information. Whereas a summary condenses and is thus an efficient method for synthesizing material, a paraphrased passage is not usually shorter than the original—in fact, it may be longer. Because you include so much in a paraphrase, you must be careful to use completely different wording or you may unknowingly be plagiarizing. Changing the order of the original will also help you avoid plagiarism (see "Plagiarism," below).

Direct Quotation and Mixed Format

Like a paraphrase, a direct quotation applies to specific content. When you represent a source by direct quotation, you use exactly the same words as the original, enclosing them within quotation marks. Authors of empirical studies make sparing use of direct quotations, but they are often used by authors of humanities essays, which analyze primary sources, such as literary or historical texts, and may depend on direct quotations for support. Researchers in the social sciences who use a qualitative methodology, such as interviews or focus groups, may also rely on direct quotations.

If there is no compelling reason to use direct quotation, use summary, paraphrase, or a mixed format instead.

With the exception of such discipline-related situations and the specific contexts outlined below, prefer summary or paraphrase to direct quotation. When you summarize or paraphrase, you concretely demonstrate your comprehension of a source by "translating" it into your own words. Quoting directly may demonstrate no more than your understanding of the relevance and importance of the source to your topic.

Direct quotation unnecessary or inappropriate: "Pilot error accounted for 34 per cent of major airline crashes between 1990 and 1996, compared with 43 per cent from 1983 to 1989." Statistical detail does not need be quoted directly.

Paraphrase: In the six-year period between 1990 and 1996, 34 per cent of major airline crashes were due to pilot error, a decrease of 9 per cent over the previous six-year period.

If factual material can be easily put in your own words, prefer summary or paraphrase to direct quotation.

"If factual material can be easily put in your own words, prefer summary or paraphrase to direct quotation."

> Direct quotation unnecessary: "Students often find ways to compensate for their symptoms of ADD in their earlier years so that the disorder reveals itself only with the increased intellectual and organizational demands of university."

> Summary: Because of the greater demands of university, compared to earlier schooling, students with ADD may not have to confront their disorder until university.

In a **mixed format**, you combine summary or paraphrase with direct quotation. Effective use of mixed format demonstrates both your understanding and polished writing skills since it requires you to seamlessly integrate the language of the source with your own language. You can use this format when you want to cite part of an important passage in which key words or phrases occur, carefully choosing the significant words and excluding the less important parts.

MIXED FORMAT
method of source integration in which you combine significant words of the source, placed in quotation marks, with your own words.

Specific contexts for using direct and mixed quotations: You can use direct or mixed quotations if you want to define something or if the exact wording is important for another reason—for example, to lend authority to your point or if the wording of the source is particularly significant or memorable:

> The Yerkes-Dodson law "predicts an inverted U relationship between arousal and performance and that the optimal level of arousal for a beginner is considerably less than that for an expert performing the same task" ("Yerkes-Dodson Law," 2002b, *The Oxford Dictionary of Sports Science and Medicine*).

The definition of a specialized term makes direct quotation a good choice.

> But how do we define our Canadian democracy? "The genius of a free and democratic people is manifested in its capacity and willingness to devise institutions and laws that secure fairness and equitable opportunities for citizens to influence democratic governance" (Royal Commission on Electoral Reform and Party Financing).

Using direct quotation is appropriate because the writer wants to stress the authority of the source.

> According to Sir Clifford Sifton, Prime Minister Wilfrid Laurier's interior minister, Canada was to be "a nation of good farmers," meaning Asian immigration was discouraged (Royal Commission 24).

Mixed format is useful here, quoting a significant phrase to reveal discrimination against Asians in the first decade of the twentieth century in Canada.

Integrating Quotations

When you incorporate direct quotations into your essay, you must do so grammatically and smoothly; you must also provide enough context for the reader to grasp their significance. The following shows a poorly integrated quotation and its well-integrated alternative:

> An unloving parent-child relationship can be characterized as "unaccepted, unacknowledged, or unloved" (Haworth-Hoeppner 216).

> Well-integrated: An unloving parent-child relationship exists when the child feels "unaccepted, unacknowledged, or unloved" (Haworth-Hoeppner 216).

Omitting, Adding, or Changing Material

"Whenever you alter a direct quotation, you must indicate these changes to the reader."

ELLIPSIS
the use of three or four spaced dots in a direct quotation, indicating one or more words have been omitted.

You may choose to omit quoted material in the interests of efficiency or add material in the interests of completeness or clarity. You may also have to make minor changes to a source for grammatical or stylistic reasons. Whenever you alter a direct quotation, you must indicate these changes to the reader.

Omitting: You may want to omit part of a sentence if it is irrelevant or unimportant for your purposes. To indicate an omission of one or more words in the middle of a sentence, use an **ellipsis** (the word means "omission"), which consists of three spaced dots. If you leave out all the words to the end of the sentence—and if you leave out the following sentence(s) as well—add a fourth dot, which represents the period at the end of the sentence:

> Original: The present thesis is that psychology, in concert with other disciplines, has an important role to play in easing the pain caused by climate change. Were this thesis widely recognised, the present article would be unnecessary. Unfortunately, the thesis is not broadly acknowledged. (Gifford, "Psychology's essential role in alleviating the impacts of climate change," p. 455).

> Words omitted in the middle of the first sentence: The present thesis is that psychology . . . has an important role to play in easing the pain caused by climate change.

> The second sentence omitted: The present thesis is that psychology, in concert with other disciplines, has an important role to play in easing the pain caused by climate change. . . . Unfortunately, the thesis is not broadly acknowledged.

Adding and changing: If you add or change material, you need to indicate this by using *brackets* (brackets are square; parentheses are rounded). Changes can be made for grammatical, stylistic, or clarification/explanation purposes. The following examples illustrate some of the different reasons for using brackets to add or change words:

> Grammatical (for pronoun consistency):

> > In affirming his oath, the enumerator promised "solemnly and sincerely" to "faithfully and exactly" discharge all of his duties "to the utmost of [his] skill and ability" (Dunae, "Sex, charades and census records: Locating female sex trade workers in a Victorian city," p. 341).

Stylistic (upper case "T" to begin a sentence):

> As Benjamin Barber argued in 1995, "[T]he true tutors of our children are not school-teachers or university professors but filmmakers, advertising executives and pop culture purveyors" (Gillam and Wooden, "Post-princess models of gender: The new man in Disney/Pixar," p. 307).

Clarification (to indicate words added to original):

> "Yes, [my playing is] very excessive" (Hussain & Griffiths, 2009, p. 749).

Explanation (to spell out an acronym):

> "WoW [World of Warcraft] takes a lot less priority now I'm in my final years at University" (Hussain & Griffiths, 2009, p. 748).

The chart below summarizes some of the main features of the four integration methods discussed above. Note that whatever method you use, documentation is usually required. See below, "Seven Questions about Source Citation."

Method	What It Includes	When and How to Use It
Summary	Only main ideas or most important points; is in your words.	When you want to refer to main idea in a paragraph, findings of a study, and similar uses; you can summarize as little as part of a sentence, as much as an entire article.
Paraphrase	All of the original in your own words, often with the structure changed.	When you want to refer to important material directly relevant to your point; paraphrases are used for small but significant passages.
Direct quotation	Words and punctuation taken directly from the source; put in quotation marks.	When material is both important to your point and memorably phrased or is difficult to paraphrase; must be integrated grammatically and smoothly.
Mixed format	Significant words from source with your own words (i.e., summary or paraphrase).	When you want to include *only* the most significant or memorable words, omitting the inessential; integrate words from the source grammatically and smoothly with your own prose, using brackets and ellipses as required.

Documenting Your Sources

Documenting sources serves several practical purposes: it enables a reader to distinguish between your ideas and someone else's, and it makes it possible for any reader to access the source itself, either to ensure its accuracy or to focus on its content. Documentation formats (called **documentation styles**) provide a coherent and consistent way for scholars to communicate with other scholars (and also with student researchers, who must learn the fundamentals of documentation formats in order to use them in their essays).

DOCUMENTATION STYLE guidelines for documenting sources put forth in style manuals and handbooks for researchers and other academic writers.

Plagiarism

Plagiarism is an extremely serious academic offence. A surprisingly large number of students approaching post-secondary study believe that plagiarism is limited to cases in which they use direct quotations and fail to cite their sources. In fact, plagiarism

> "You plagiarize if you use any material that is not your own—whether you quote directly, summarize, paraphrase, or refer to it in passing in your essay—without acknowledging it."

Other common forms of plagiarism include using the exact words of a source without putting them in quotation marks and following the structure of the original too closely.

encompasses much more than this: you plagiarize if you use any material that is not your own—whether you quote directly, summarize, paraphrase, or refer to it in passing in your essay—without acknowledging it. But it is not only lack of acknowledgement that constitutes plagiarism: you also plagiarize if you use the exact words of the source and do not put them in quotation marks; in the former case, you would be passing off someone else's ideas as your own, while in the latter, you are, in effect, passing their words off as your own. Finally, you plagiarize if you follow the structure of the original too closely.

Specifically, what kind of information must be acknowledged and what does not need to be? Two principles can guide you as you consider the question. You do not need to cite anything that falls under the category of *general knowledge*. If a typical reader is likely to know something, a citation may be unnecessary. Further, if a fact or idea is *easily obtainable*, a citation may also be unnecessary. (You may be told a specific number of sources that satisfies the "easily obtainable" factor—often three.) Both these categories depend on your audience; for example, if you were writing for an audience that is knowledgeable about the topic, your essay would probably contain fewer citations than if you were writing for a general audience that is less knowledgeable and would probably find it difficult to trace the information. If in doubt, err on the side of caution and make the citation.

The questions in the box below about citation are often asked by students beginning research projects at university.

Seven Common Questions about Source Citation

Q: Do you need to cite information that you do not quote directly in your essay?
A: Yes. Specific content requires a citation, whether you use direct quotation, paraphrase, or summary to integrate it into your essay. Even general information may necessitate a citation.

Q: If you already knew a fact and you encounter it in a secondary source, does it need to be cited?
A: Probably. The issue isn't whether you know something but whether your reader would know it. If you are writing for an audience familiar with your topic, you may not need to cite "common knowledge," that is, knowledge that all or almost all readers would be expected to know. If you're uncertain about the common knowledge factor, make the citation.

Q: What about specific information, such as a date, that is easy to look up, though it may not be common knowledge?
A: A fact that is easily obtained from a number of different sources (even if a typical reader wouldn't know it) may not need to be cited. Other factors could be involved (for example, would a typical reader know where to look?). Your instructor may be able to tell you how many sources constitute "easily obtainable" information; a minimum number often given is three (i.e., at least three common, easily accessible sources).

Q: If you use a source that you have already used earlier in the same paragraph, do you need to cite it a second time?
A: Yes, you do if another source, or your own point, has intervened. If all the content of the paragraph is from one source, you may not have to cite it until the end of the paragraph. However, always make it clear to the reader what is taken from a source.

Q: Is it necessary to cite "popular" quotations, for example, the kind that appear in dictionaries of quotations? What about dictionary definitions?

A: Yes, these kinds of quotations should be cited unless the quotation has entered everyday use. For example, the first quotation would not need a citation, though the second would—even though it's unlikely a reader would know either source: "When the going gets tough, the tough get going"; "Making your mark on the world is hard. If it were easy, everybody would do it." (Joan W. Donaldson is the author of the first quotation; Barack Obama is the author of the second). Dictionary definitions should be cited.

Q: Does a list of your sources on the final page of your essay mean that you don't have to cite the sources within the essay itself?

A: No. All major documentation methods require both in-text and final-page citations. (In some formats, the in-text citations consist only of numbers.)

Q: What can you do to guarantee that the question of plagiarism never arises in your essay?

A: Honesty alone may not be enough, but it is a good start. Knowledge about what needs to be and what may not need to be cited is also essential and can be learned. Finally, being conscious of "grey areas" and checking with your instructor or another expert, such as a librarian, should almost guarantee that this serious issue doesn't arise.

A good strategy for avoiding plagiarism (and consciously integrating the information) is to carefully study the passage you want to use; then, close the text and write the passage from memory completely in your own words. Finally, look at the passage again, ensuring that it is different in its structure as well as in its language—and that you have accurately restated the thought behind it.

Major Documentation Styles

There are four major documentation styles but many variants on these styles. The Modern Language Association (MLA) style is widely used in the humanities, including English literature. The American Psychological Association (APA) style is used in many social science disciplines and some science disciplines, as well as in education and business. Both are parenthetical styles, meaning that a brief citation including the author's name and page number (MLA) or name and publication year (APA) follows the reference in the text of an essay.

Both the Chicago Manual of Style (CMS), used in history, and the Council of Science Editors (CSE) style, used in mathematics, biology, health sciences, and some other science disciplines, follow a number/note method. Superscript (raised) numbers are placed after the in-text references; they correspond to the numbers at the end of the document where full bibliographical information is given (in the Chicago style, these notes can also be placed at the foot of the page). MLA, APA, and CMS styles also require a final-page listing of sources alphabetically by last name. CSE style requires a listing of sources that follows the order they were used in the text. Note: CSE also gives guidelines for an author/year system similar to that of the American Psychological Association; however, as the number/note method is more common, it is outlined below.

Students and teachers alike are sometimes frustrated by the many small differences among the styles, especially between the parenthetical styles, MLA and APA. This frustration may be compounded by the existence of variant style guides in disciplines like chemistry, engineering, law, and others. Many book publishers use a distinct "house" style, and different departments at your institution may publish their own set of guidelines applicable to students in that discipline. The major manuals are also constantly changing as new editions are brought out. Fortunately, there are an increasing number of online resources for those confused by the array of documentation styles; college or university library sources are the most reliable. Each organization that produces the manuals also maintains websites where updates are posted. Further, when you decide on an area of study, you will become familiar with the style prominent in your discipline.

Many of the distinguishing features of the styles are given below. Examples of the most common bibliographic formats are then provided. Note: A **signal phrase** names the author before the reference is given; thus, in MLA and APA styles, the parenthetical citation will not include the author's name if a signal phrase precedes it.

Electronic formats in all styles should include as much information as is available. If an author's name is not given, use the name of the organization or sponsoring group in its place. If there is no sponsor, use the work's title alphabetized by the first major word. MLA and CSE styles require you to include date of access for Internet citations; APA and CMS style do not. Paragraph number or section heading can sometimes be used to identify location, if necessary, in the absence of standard page numbering.

MLA (Modern Language Association) Style

- MLA uses an "author/number" referencing format. The basic parenthetical format includes author's last name and page number with no punctuation in between. e.g., (Slotkin 75); (Rusel and Wilson 122)
- If a signal phrase is used, only the page number will be in parentheses. e.g., Slotkin states, " . . ." (75).
- Block quotations should be used for important passages at least four typed lines long. They are indented 10 spaces from the left margin, double-spaced, and do not include quotation marks. The end period precedes the parenthetical citation.
- The final page, titled "Works Cited," alphabetically lists by author's last name all works used in the essay. Entries are double-spaced with the first line flush left and successive lines indented one-half inch. All major words in titles begin with a capital letter. Names of books and journals are italicized, and the medium of publication is included at the end of most entries.

APA (American Psychological Association) Style

- APA uses an "author/year" referencing format. One basic format includes author's last name and year of publication (general references and summaries); the other basic format also includes page number (direct quotations and paraphrases).
- Commas separate author's name from year and year from page number (if required); "p." or "pp." (for more than one page) precedes page number(s). e.g., (Huyer, 1997, p. 43); (Bryson & de Castell, 1998, pp. 542–544).
- If a signal phrase is used, the year will follow the author's name in parentheses. e.g., Huyer (1997) explains ". . ."; if a page number is required, it will be placed in parentheses after the reference: e.g., " . . . " (p. 43).
- Works by the same author(s) from the same year are assigned different letters—e.g., 2004a, 2004b. They are listed this way in "References" alphabetically by title.
- Block quotations should be used for important passages more than 40 words long. They are indented five spaces from the left margin, double-spaced, and do not include quotation marks. The end period precedes the parenthetical citation.

SIGNAL PHRASE
introduces a reference in a phrase that names the author(s) and usually includes a "signal verb" (e.g., *states*, *argues*, *explains*).

- The final page, titled "References," alphabetically lists by author's last name all works used in the essay; authors' initials are used, not given names. Entries are double-spaced with the first line flush left and successive lines indented five spaces. In article and book titles, only the first letter of first words, first words following colons, and proper nouns, along with all letters in acronyms, are capitalized.

CMS (Chicago Manual of Style) Style

- CMS uses the "note" referencing format with numbered footnotes (at the bottom of the page) or endnotes (at the end of the text) corresponding to superscript numbers in the text of the essay. Each entry is single-spaced with the first line indented five spaces and successive lines flush left.
- Full bibliographic details are given for first references, beginning with author's first name(s), followed by surname, work's title, and (in parentheses) place of publication, publisher, and date, and ending with page number(s).

  e.g., "As is well known, the sociobiologist E.O. Wilson has entitled one of his books *Consilience*."[15] The note would look like this:

  15. Edward O. Wilson, *Consilience: The Unity of Knowledge* (New York: Alfred A. Knopf, 1998).

  Successive references are condensed forms of the first citation:

  18. Wilson, *Consilience*, 55.

  Consecutive references to the same work:

  19. Ibid. (the page number would follow if different from preceding note)

- Block quotations should be used for important passages at least four typed lines long. They are indented five spaces from the left margin, double-spaced, and do not include quotation marks. The end period precedes the parenthetical citation.
- On the final page, titled "Bibliography," entries are listed alphabetically by author's last name. Entries are single-spaced with double-spacing between them; the first line is flush left, and successive lines are indented five spaces.

CSE (Council of Science Editors) Style

- CSE uses the "citation/sequence" referencing format with superscript or bracketed numbers corresponding to numbered sources at the end of the text in a separate section.
- To cite more than one source for a specific reference, each source number is included, followed by a comma with no space between; a dash is used to indicate consecutive sources (e.g., 2–5).

  e.g., "There is increasing evidence for the efficacy of exercise [10,11] and fish oils [12,13] in the treatment and prevention of depression."

- For references to a source for a second time or more, the number first assigned to the source continues to be used.
- On the final page, titled "References" or "Cited References," authors are listed beginning with author's last name followed by initial(s) with no spaces or periods between initials. The order of entries is based on their sequence in the text (i.e., the first cited source is assigned the number 1, the second one the number 2, etc.). Entries are single-spaced with double-spacing between them.

Common Formats: Sample Citations

Book (one author)

MLA: Berger, Arthur Asa. *Video Games: A Popular Culture Phenomenon.* New Brunswick: Transaction, 2002. Print.

APA: Heyd, D. (1992). *Genetics: Moral issues in the creation of people.* Berkeley, CA: University of California Press.

CMS: *Note:*

> 1. Keith D. McFarland, *The Korean War: An Annotated Bibliography* (New York: Garland, 1986), 91.

Bibliography:

McFarland, Keith D. *The Korean War: An Annotated Bibliography.* New York: Garland, 1986.

CSE: 1. Fleiss JL. The design and analysis of clinical experiments. New York (NY): John Wiley and Sons; 1986.

Book/journal (multiple authors)

MLA: Bolaria, B. Singh, and Peter S. Li. *Racial Oppression in Canada.* 2nd edn. Toronto: Garamond Press, 1988. Print. (second author's name is not reversed)

More than three authors: Give the name of the first author, followed by a comma and "et al."

APA: Sahalein, R., & Tuttle, D. (1997). *Creatine: Nature's muscle builder.* Garden City Park, NY: Avery Publishing Group. (second author's name is reversed.)

Three to seven authors: give all names; *more than seven:* list first six names followed by three points of ellipsis and the last author's name.

CMS: *Note:*

> 2. Bob Beal and Rod Macleod, *Prairie Fire: The 1885 North-West Rebellion* (Edmonton: Hurtig Publishers, 1984), 104.

More than three authors: name of first author given, followed by "and others."

Bibliography:

Beal, Bob, and Rod Macleod. *Prairie Fire: The 1885 North-West Rebellion.* Edmonton: Hurtig Publishers, 1984.

More than three authors: all authors are named (second author's name is not reversed).

CSE: 2.Thursby, JG, Thursby, MC. Intellectual property: university licensing and the Bayh-Dole Act. Science 2003; 301:1052.

More than 10 authors: names of 10 listed, followed by "and others."

Selection in edited work

All entries give page range; in-text citations in MLA, APA, and CMS give specific page(s) referenced.

MLA: Wright, Austin M. "On Defining the Short Story: The Genre Question." *Short Story Theory at a Crossroads.* Ed. Susan Lohafer and Jo Ellyn Clarey. Baton Rouge: Louisiana State UP, 1989. 46–63. Print. (UP is the abbreviation for *University Press*)

APA: Chesney-Lind, M. & Brown, M. (1999). Girls and violence: An overview. In D. Flannery & C. R. Huff (Eds.), *Youth violence: Prevention, intervention and social policy* (pp. 171–199). Washington, D.C.: American Psychiatric Press.

CMS: *Note:*

3. Marcia K. Lieberman, "'Some Day My Prince Will Come': Female Acculturation through the Fairy Tale," in *Don't Bet on the Prince*, ed. Jack Zipes and Ingrid Svendsen (New York: Routledge, 1987), 185–200.

Bibliography:

Lieberman, Marcia K. "'Some Day My Prince Will Come': Female Acculturation through the Fairy Tale." In *Don't Bet on the Prince*, edited by Jack Zipes and Ingrid Svendsen, 185–200. New York: Routledge, 1987.

CSE: 3. Saper CB, Iversen S, Frackowiak R. Integration of sensory and motor function: the association areas of the cerebral cortex and the cognitive capabilities of the brain. In: Kandel ER, Schwartz JH, Jessell TM, editors. Principles of neural science. 4th ed. New York (NY): McGraw-Hill; 2000. p. 349–380.

Journal article

MLA: Fetterley, Judith. "*Little Women*: Alcott's Civil War." *Feminist Studies* 5.2 (1979): 369–83. Print

Include both volume and issue number. For electronic articles in a database, include database name in italics before "Web."

APA: Clegg, S., Mayfield, W., & Trayhurn, D. (1999). Disciplinary discourses: A case study of gender in information technology and design courses. *Gender and Education, 11*(1), 43–55.

Volume number is italicized; issue number (required if each issue begins with page number "1") is not italicized. If available for print and electronic articles, include the DOI (digital object identifier) as last item; it is not followed by a period.

CMS: *Note:*

> 4. Robert Garner, "Political Ideologies and the Moral Status of Animals," *Journal of Political Ideologies* 8 (2003): 235.

If available, for electronic article, include the DOI as last item, followed by a period for both note and bibliographic entry. If no DOI, include a URL. Access date is optional for online article.

Issue number (required if each issue begins with page number "1"): 8, no. 1 (2003).

Bibliography:

Smith, John Maynard. "The Origin of Altruism." *Nature* 393 (1998): 639–40.

CSE: 4. Bayer R, Fairchild AL. The genesis of public health ethics. Bioethics. 2004;18(6):473–492. CSE uses abbreviations for most journal titles; for example, Can J Psychiatry is the abbreviation for *Canadian Journal of Psychiatry*.

Internet source

MLA: Environment Canada. "10 Things You Should Know About Climate Change." 12 Aug. 2009. Web. 15 Aug. 2010. <www.ec.gc.ca/cc/default.asp?lang=En&n=2F049262-1>.

The first date is that of the site; access date follows with publication medium between. Angle brackets enclose website address if the source would be hard to locate without it or if your instructor requires it.

APA: Statistics Canada (2010, March 26). Gasoline and fuel oil, price by urban centre. Retrieved from www40.Statcan.ca/101/cst01/econ154a.htm.

CMS: *Note:*

> 5. The Internet Encyclopedia of Philosophy, "Deductive and Inductive Arguments," www.iep.utm.edu/d/ded-ind.htm.

Bibliography entry would be listed alphabetically by first major word; if access date is required, it can be placed in parentheses—e.g., (accessed March 21, 2011).

CSE: 5. Health Canada. A report on mental illnesses in Canada [Internet]. Ottawa (ON): Health Canada; 2002. [modified 2002 Oct 15; cited 2006 Nov 28], Available from: www.phac-aspe.gc.ea/publicat/miic-mmae/.

Sample Student Research Essay

The essay below uses MLA documentation style.

The Price of Play? Social, Physical, and Mental Consequences of Video Game Addiction among Adults

by Lorinda Fraser

1   As the sophistication of technology and our dependency on computers increase so too does the amount of time spent on the Internet, and for some, playing computer video games. But how much game play is too much? Video games are no longer relegated to video arcades, and with the recent proliferation of mobile devices, games are accessible at any time and anywhere. While video game addiction is not currently a formally recognized term or disorder, concern about the amount of time spent on these pursuits is growing. Research and alarming reports regarding the addiction of children and adolescents appear to be readily available; however, much less research has been conducted on the impact of video game addiction on adults. "The video gaming world has been established, but the actual physical and psychosocial effects of video gaming [on adults] have not" (Sublette and Mullan). Despite the lack of consensus on whether the act of video game playing qualifies as a clinical addiction and a shortage of "[e]pidemiological surveys and clinical studies" (Flisher 559), there seems to be no debate that excessive video gaming by adult players can lead to addictive behaviour, resulting in adverse social, physical, and mental consequences.

2   Psychiatrist Dr van Goldberg was the first to use the term "Internet Addiction" (IA) in 1995 (Flisher 557). While the term "IA," or its sub-component "video game addiction," waits to be formally recognized by "reputable organization[s] responsible for defining disorders of the mind or body" (Wood 169), many experts have already begun establishing criteria for describing excessive video game playing based on existing criteria for gambling addiction. According to these experts, for video game playing to be considered an addiction, it would need to meet a minimum of three of the Diagnostic and Statistical Manual of Mental Disorders (DSM IV) and International Statistical Classification of Diseases (ICD-10) criteria for gambling addiction: "tolerance, salience, withdrawal symptoms, difficulty controlling use, continued use despite negative consequences, neglecting other activities, desire to cut down" (Flisher 557). Kimberly Young further adapted the criteria specifically for IA, and subsequently, video game addiction:

> preoccupation with use of the computer, thinking about previous online activity/anticipation of next online session; craving more and more time at the computer; making efforts to cut back on computer use or stop, and failing repeatedly; feelings of emptiness, depression, and irritation when not at the computer or when attempting to cut down; staying online longer than originally intended; jeopardizing significant relationships, job, career, or education because of the Internet; hiding the extent of computer/Internet use to family and friends; use of the Internet as a way of escaping from problems or of relieving a dysphoric mood (e.g. feelings of helplessness, guilt, anxiety, depression). (qtd. in Flisher 557)

Leading up to her thesis, Fraser justifies her approach to the topic, explaining, as the writers of scholarly essays often do, that the topic has not been adequately explored.

As this source appeared in pre-publication form without page numbers, they cannot be included in the citation. Use of current sources, however, is critical in an essay on such a recent topic.

Fraser's clear thesis states that she will be investigating three effects of "addictive behaviour" in adult video gamers.

MLA documentation style includes the author's name and page number with a space between. Later in the essay, Fraser names the author before the reference; the citation does not then repeat the author's name.

This quotation is set up in the block format—indented, double-spaced, and without quotation marks. This format should be reserved for lengthy and important content.

In the next two paragraphs, Fraser mediates the debate between Wood, who believes that excessive video gaming is not an addiction, and Turner, who believes that it is. Considering contradictory findings and viewpoints and drawing conclusions about their respective merits can be an important part of research.

3   Those labelling excessive video game playing as addictive have their challengers. Wood writes, "If people cannot deal with their problems, and choose instead to immerse themselves in a game, then surely their gaming behaviour is actually a symptom rather than the specific cause of their problem" (172). He lists four factors he feels need to be considered before video game playing can be labelled an "addiction":

1.   That some people are labelled "addicts" . . . when they have no problems with their game playing behaviour.
2.   That some people who have underlying problems may choose to play games to avoid dealing with those problems.
3.   That some people who are concerned about their own behaviour because of either 1 or 2 above end up labelling themselves as video game "addicts."
4.   That some people are not very good at managing how much time they spend playing video games. (176)

4   However, Turner argues that alcohol and gambling, among other addictions, could also meet these criteria. Furthermore, he questions Wood's assertion that if video games were "inherently addictive . . . a large[r] proportion of the population would be seriously addicted" to them (Turner 186). Again, if such an argument were applied to alcoholism and gambling, they too would no longer be considered addictions. However, Wood's contention that excessive game playing is a symptom of other problems rather than their cause also loses its validity when applied to addictions such as drug abuse, alcoholism, and gambling. Typically, well adjusted, stable people without underlying problems do not turn to addictive substances or avoidance activities in the first place. As Turner asks, "do happy people inject heroin?" (188).

5   The social consequences of video game addiction on adults' lives are numerous. Reports of an overall decrease in "the quality of interpersonal relationships" have led to social withdrawal, marital problems, and divorce (qtd. in Sublette and Mullan). Disturbed sleep patterns, physical ailments, and increased mental-health sick days can all negatively impact work performance resulting in job loss (Flisher 558). An international survey found that online video game players sacrificed "another hobby or pastime" (25 per cent), "socializing with friends, family and/or partner" (20 per cent), "sleep" (20 per cent), and/or "work and /or education" (less than 10 per cent) (Weaver et al. 300) in order to play their game of choice. As with other addictions, the effects on a video game addict's children would also likely show significant impact on their development and relationship with the addicted parent.

6   The physical repercussions of a sedentary pastime affect both male and female players; these can range from troublesome to life threatening. Flisher lists relatively mild complaints such as repetitive strain injury and back ache which can progress to more serious issues such as the development of deep vein thrombosis and pulmonary embolus (558). "Differences are [also] evident for three of the five measures in the health-assessment domain . . . [where] video game players report lower health status, a higher frequency of poor-mental-days, and higher BMI [body mass index]" (Weaver et al. 302) than non-players. Video game players also report poor sleep quality due to disturbed sleep schedules and the effects of withdrawal symptoms and cravings (qtd. in Sublette and Mullan) when video games are stopped. In a few alarmingly extreme cases, at least 10 Korean and Chinese video game players have collapsed and died as a result of multiple days of continuous video game playing (Flisher 558).

The writer uses brackets and an ellipsis to indicate changes to a direct quotation. However, it might have been more effective if she had paraphrased this passage instead.

7   In contrast to the physical and social repercussions associated with excessive video game playing, mental health issues effect male and female players differently. While both sexes experience depression, anger problems, anxiety disorders (Flisher 558), and reduced health status (Weaver et al. 303), male players experience more negative ramifications than their female counterparts with higher addiction scores, along with greater aggressive attitudes and reduced empathy (qtd. in Sublette and Mullan). Also, female players seem to use video games as a form of "digital self-medication", using their games to "take their minds off their worries" whereas male players "prefer video games that provide an impetus [stimulant] for socializing" (Weaver et al. 303–04). Noar, Benac, and Harris (qtd. in Weaver et al. 304) suggest "gender-based tailoring" for treatment options of the social effects of video game addiction.

8   Currently, no standardized test for identifying video game addiction exists. The development of a "theory-based clinical instrument" for measuring all addictions to technology (King, Delfabbro, and Zajac 74) would be beneficial to the study, treatment, and prevention of video game addiction. Previously, 30 hours of video game playing a week was considered "unhealthy." Today, video game playing for more than 50 hours per week is now considered a "highly prevalent activity" (75), but no definitive benchmark has been established (73). The Problem Video Game Playing Test (PVGT) was developed to identify the "core components" of addiction and investigate the negative personal and social consequences of extreme playing (76) and has shown initial success for gauging problem video game playing (85). Nevertheless, effective treatment options need to be established and standardized. Currently, in the US, psychological treatment programs, telephone counselling services, and treatment clinics using the 12-step program along with CBT [Cognitive Behavioural Therapy], family therapy, group therapy, social skills training, and addiction counselling have been offered. Chinese treatment clinics take a stricter approach, implementing regimented timetables, discipline, medication, and electric shock treatment (Flisher 558). Young proposes implementing "behavioural strategies" such as "practising the opposite, . . . external stoppers ,. . . setting clear goals, reminder cards, . . . personal inventory, . . . [and] abstinence" (Flisher 558). Due to the relatively new proliferation of technological addictions, long-term research on the effectiveness of these treatments needs to be conducted before any can be considered a success (559).

9   While moderate online video game play seems to have few negative consequences (Sublette and Mullan), it is reasonable to assume that any activity engaged in for prolonged periods of time will eventually affect one's social, physical, and mental health. Family and friends of avid video game players may experience the negative effects of game playing first-hand. As relationships develop and lifestyle choices become increasingly important beyond the adolescent years, concern for the player's physical and mental health proportionally escalates. As the popularity and accessibility of immersive environments increase, the need for evidence-based research becomes crucial to ensure an emphasis on prevention, education, and treatment of the negative costs of gaming. Future research needs to include consistency in data collection, inclusion and expansion of demographic information, and alternate forms of testing; research also must consider socio-economic implications (Sublette and Mullan). "[I]t is time for . . . standardized treatment protocols, [v]alidation of diagnostic instruments, and the establishment of a set of standard criteria . . . " (Flisher 559) to determine how much play is too much and when the consequences outweigh the entertainment.

> As the phrases in the last two sentences are memorable, use of a mixed format with direct quotation was a good choice. Notice the precise placement of citations throughout this paragraphto ensure that the sources are unambiguous.

> In her final paragraph, Fraser draws conclusions based on her synthesis of the major studies on her topic. Like the writers of scholarly essays, she applies these findings to society and families, and ends by suggesting further research.

> In the interests of efficiency in her last sentence, Fraser combines two sentences from the same page of her source. The original reads, "Arguably, it is time for the World Health Organization and health departments around the world to develop effective health polices to increase public awareness of IA and produce standardized treatment protocols. Validation of diagnostic instruments and the establishment of a set of standard criteria for IA will aid swift and accurate diagnosis."

Fraser has accessed her sources electronically so has followed the MLA guidelines for electronic sources from a database. See page 155.

For articles published online rather than in a database, MLA advises that as many publication details as possible should be given. In this case, neither page numbers nor volume/issue is available. Note the abbreviation for "no pagination."

When a work has more than three authors, all authors' names can be given or the first author only followed by *et al.* ("and others").

Works Cited

Flisher, Caroline. "Getting Plugged in: An Overview of Internet Addiction." *Journal of Paediatrics and Child Health* 46.10 (2010): 557–59. *Academic Search Complete*. Web. 10 Mar. 2011.

King, Daniel L., Paul H. Delfabbro, and Ian T. Zajac. "Preliminary Validation of a New Clinical Tool for Identifying Problem Video Game Playing." *International Journal of Mental Health and Addiction* 9.1 (2011): 72–87. *Academic Search Complete*. Web. 10 Mar. 2011.

Sublette, Victoria, and Barbara Mullan. "Consequences of Play: A Systematic Review of the Effects of Online Gaming." *International Journal of Mental Health and Addiction* (2010): n. pag. Web. 10 Mar. 2011.

Turner, Nigel. "A Comment on 'Problems with the Concept of Video Game 'Addiction': Some Case Study Examples.'" *International Journal of Mental Health and Addiction* 6.2 (2008): *186-90. Academic Search Complete*. Web. 10 Mar. 2011.

Weaver, James B., Darren Mays, Stephanie Sargent Weaver, Wendi Kannenberg, Gary L. Hopkins, Doğan Eroğlu, and Jay M. Bernhardt. "Health-Risk Correlates of Video-Game Playing Among Adults." *American Journal of Preventative Medicine* 37.4 (2009): 299-305. *Medline*. Web. 10 Mar. 2011.

Wood, Richard. "Problems with the Concept of Video Game 'Addiction': Some Case Study Examples." *International Journal of Mental Health and Addiction* 6.2 (2008): 169-78. *Academic Search Complete*. Web. 10 Mar. 2011.

PART III

The Active Reader

Academic language and the challenge of reading for learning about science

Catherine E. Snow

(2,409 words)

Pre-reading

1. What are your perceptions of or associations with "academic language" or "academic reading"? Write down some of these perceptions in point or bulleted form. Where do your perceptions come from (e.g., high school classes, university instructors, textbooks, general knowledge)? As a pre-reading activity, you could exchange your list with another person's and discuss some of the similarities and differences.

---

1   A major challenge to students learning science is the academic language in which science is written. Academic language is designed to be concise, precise, and authoritative. To achieve these goals, it uses sophisticated words and complex grammatical constructions that can disrupt reading comprehension and block learning. Students need help in learning academic vocabulary and how to process academic language if they are to become independent learners of science.

2   Literacy scholars and secondary teachers alike are puzzled by the frequency with which students who read words accurately and fluently have trouble comprehending text (1, 2). Such students have mastered what was traditionally considered the major obstacle to reading success: the depth and complexity of the English spelling system. But many middle- and high-school students are less able to convert their word-reading skills into comprehension when confronted with texts in science (or math or social studies) than they are when confronted with texts of fiction or discursive essays. The greater difficulty of science, math, and social studies texts than of texts encountered in English language arts (mostly narratives) suggests that the comprehension of "academic language" may be one source of the challenge. So what is academic language?

3   Academic language is one of the terms [others include language of education (3), language of schooling (4), scientific language (5), and academic English (6, 7)] used to refer to the form of language expected in contexts such as the exposition of topics in the school curriculum, making arguments, defending propositions, and synthesizing information. There is no exact boundary when defining academic language; it falls toward one end of a continuum (defined by formality of tone, complexity of content, and degree

of impersonality of stance), with informal, casual, conversational language at the other extreme. There is also no single academic language, just as there is no single variety of educated American English. Academic language features vary as a function of discipline, topic, and mode (written versus oral, for example), but there are certain common characteristics that distinguish highly academic from less academic or more conversational language and that make academic language—even well-written, carefully constructed, and professionally edited academic language—difficult to comprehend and even harder to produce (*8*).

4   Among the most commonly noted features of academic language are conciseness, achieved by avoiding redundancy; using a high density of information-bearing words, ensuring precision of expression; and relying on grammatical processes to compress complex ideas into few words (*8, 9*). Less academic language, on the other hand, such as that used in emails, resembles oral language forms more closely: Most sentences begin with pronouns or animate subjects; verbs refer to actions rather than relations; and long sentences are characterized by sequencing of information rather than embeddings. The two excerpts in Fig. 1, both about torque (a topic included in many state standards for seventh grade science), display the difference between a nonacademic text (from the website www.lowrider.com) and an academic text (from the website www.tutorvista.com).

5   A striking difference between more informal and more academic language exemplified in the Lowrider/TutorVista text comparison is the greater presence of expressive, involved, interpersonal stance markers in the first Lowrider posting (". . .guys get caught up. . .," "I frequently get asked. . .," "Most of us. . .,") and in the response ("Jason you are right on bro"). Though both the Lowrider authors are writing to inform, they are not assuming the impersonal authoritative voice that is characteristic of academic language. They claim their authority to provide information about the advantage of torque over horsepower adjustments on the basis of personal experience. The scientist's authoritative stance, on the other hand, derives from membership in a community committed to a shared epistemology; this stance is expressed through a reduction in the use of personal pronouns, a preference for epistemically warranted evaluations (such as "rigorous study" and "questionable analysis") over personally expressive evaluations (such as "great study" and "funky analysis"), and a focus on general rather than specific claims. Maintaining the impersonal authoritative stance creates a distanced tone that is often puzzling to adolescent readers and is extremely difficult for adolescents to emulate in writing.

6   Perhaps the simplest basis for comparing the Lowrider and TutorVista texts is to consider how rare in other contexts are the words they use most frequently. The rarest words used in the Lowrider text are the special term "lolo" and its alternative form "lowrider," "upgrade," "carb," "HP," "exhaust," "spin," and "torque." Only two words from the Academic Word List (*10*), a list of words used frequently across academic texts of different disciplines, appear in this passage. The TutorVista text rare words include "magnitude," "perpendicular," "lever," "pivot," "hinge," "fulcrum," and "torque," and it uses the academic words "task," "maximum," "significance," and "illustration." The difference in word selection reflects the convention in the more academic text of presenting precise information in a dense, concise manner.

7   Nominalizations are a grammatical process of converting entire sentences (such as "Gutenberg invented the printing press") into phrases that can then be embedded in other sentences (such as "Gutenberg's invention of the printing press revolutionized the dissemination of information"). Nominalizations are crucial to the conciseness expected in academic language. In the TutorVista sentence "We may increase the turning effect of the force by changing the point of application of force and by changing the direction of force," "application" and "direction" are nominalizations representing entire propositions. "Application" is shorthand for "where we apply," and "direction" is shorthand for "how we direct." Thus, although this sentence has the same apparent structure as "We can get a smile from a baby by changing his diaper and by patting his back," the processing load is much higher. "Increase" in the original sentence is a verb referring to a relation between two quantities, whereas "get" in the baby-sentence adaptation refers to an action or effect in the real

From www.lowrider.com/forums/10-Under-the-Hood/topics/183-HP-vs-torque/posts (spelling as in the original posting)

Often times guys get caught up in the hype of having a big HP motor in their lolo. I frequently get asked whats the best way to get big numbers out of their small block. The answer is not HP, but torque. "You sell HP, you feel torque" as the old saying goes. Most of us are running 155/80/13 tires on our lolo's. Even if you had big HP numbers, you will *never* get that power to the ground, at least off the line. I have a 64 Impala SS 409, that i built the motor in. While it is a completely restored original (I drive it rolling on 14" 72 spoke cross laced Zeniths), the motor internals are not. It now displaces 420 CI, with forged pistons and blalanced rotating assembly. The intake, carb and exhaust had to remain OEM for originality's sake, and that greatly reduces the motors potential. Anyway, even with the original 2 speed powerglide, it spins those tires with alarming ease, up to 50 miles per hour!

In my 62, I built a nice 383 out of an 86 Corvette. I built it for good bottom end pull, since it is a lowrider with 8 batteries. And since it rides on the obligitory 13's, torque is what that car needs. It pulls like an ox right from idle, all the way up to its modest 5500 redline. But I never take it that high, as all the best power is from 1100 to 2700 RPM.

So when considering an engine upgrade, look for modifications that improve torque. That is what your lolo needs!

Posted by Jason Dave, Sept 2009

Jason you are right on bro. I have always found an increase in torque placement has not only provided better top end performance but also improved gas mileage in this expensive gas times.

Posted by Gabriel Salazar, Nov 2009

FIGURE 1   EXAMPLES OF NONACADEMIC TEXT (LOWRIDER, ABOVE) AND ACADEMIC TEXT (TUTORVISTA, RIGHT).

world. "Diaper" and "back" are physical entities subjected to actions, whereas "application" and "direction" are themselves actions that have been turned into nouns. Part of the complexity of academic language derives from the fact that we use the syntactic structures acquired for talking about agents and actions to talk about entities and relations, without recognizing the challenge that that transition poses to the reader. In particular, in science classes we may expect students to process these sentences without explicit instruction in their structure.

8   Science teachers are not generally well prepared to help their students penetrate the linguistic puzzles that science texts present. They of course recognize that teaching vocabulary is key, but typically focus on the science vocabulary (the bolded words in the text), often without recognizing that those bolded words are defined with general-purpose academic words that students also do not know. Consider the TutorVista definition of torque: "Torque is the product of the magnitude of the force and the lever arm of the force." Many seventh graders are unfamiliar with the terms "magnitude" and "lever"; and some proportion will think they understand "product," "force," and "arm" without realizing that those terms are being used in technical, academic ways here, with meanings quite different from those of daily life. Yet this definition, with its sophisticated and unfamiliar word meanings, is the basis for all the rest of the TutorVista exposition: the trade-off between magnitude and direction of force.

9   Efforts to help students understand science cannot ignore their need to understand the words used to write and talk about science: the all-purpose

From www.tutorvista.com/content/physics/physics-iii/rigid-body/torque.php

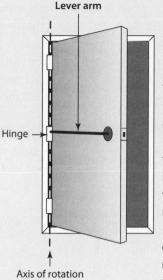

Lever arm

Hinge

Axis of rotation

Torque is the product of the magnitude of the force and the lever arm of the force.

What is the significance of this concept in our everyday life?

Dependence of torque on lever arm

To increase the turning effect of force, it is not necessary to increase the magnitude of the force itself. We may increase the turning effect of the force by changing the point of application of force and by changing the direction of force.

Let us take the case of a heavy door. If a force is applied at a point, which is close to the hinges of the door, we may find it quite difficult to open or close the door. However, if the same force is applied at a point, which is at the maximum distance from hinges, we can easily close or open the door. The task is made easier if the force is applied at right angles to the plane of the door.

When we apply the force the door turns on its hinges. Thus a turning effect is produced when we try to open the door. Have you ever tried to do so by applying the force near the hinge? In the first case, we are able to open the door with ease. In the second case, we have to apply much more force to cause the same turning effect. What is the reason?

The turning effect produced by a force on a rigid body about a point, pivot or fulcrum is called the moment of a force or torque. It is measured by the product of the force and the perpendicular distance of the pivot from the line of action of the force.

Moment of a force = Force x Perpendicular distance of the pivot from the force.

The unit of moment of force is newton metre (N m). In the above example, in the first case the perpendicular distance of the line of action of the force from the hinge is much more than that in the second case. Hence, in the second case to open the door, we have to apply greater force.

academic words as well as the discipline-specific ones. Of course some students acquire academic vocabulary on their own, if they read widely and if their comprehension skills are strong enough to support inferences about the meaning of unknown words (*11*). The fact that many adolescents prefer reading Web sites to books (*12*), however, somewhat decreases access to good models of academic language even for those interested in technical topics. Thus, they have few opportunities to learn the academic vocabulary that is crucial across their content-area learning. It is also possible to explicitly teach academic vocabulary to middle-school students. Word Generation is a middle-school program developed by the Strategic Education Research Partnership that embeds all-purpose academic words in interesting topics and provides activities for use in math, science, and social

studies as well as English language arts classes in which the target words are used (see the website for examples) (*13*). Among the academic words taught in Word Generation are those used to make, assess, and defend claims, such as "data," "hypothesis," "affirm," "convince," "disprove," and "interpret." We designed Word Generation to focus on dilemmas, because these promote discussion and debate and provide motivating contexts for students and teachers to use the target words. For example, one week is devoted to the topic of whether junk food should be banned from schools, and another to whether physician-assisted suicide should be legal. Discussion is in itself a key contributor to science learning (*14*) and to reading comprehension (*15, 16*).Words learned through explicit teaching are unlikely to be retained if they are taught in lists rather than embedded in meaningful texts and if opportunities to use them in discussion, debate, and writing are not provided.

10   It is unrealistic to expect all middle- or high-school students to become proficient producers of academic language. Many graduate students still struggle to manage the authoritative stance, and the self-presentation as an expert that justifies it, in their writing. And it is important to note that not all features associated with the academic writing style (such as the use of passive voice, impenetrability of prose constructions, and indifference to literary niceties) are desirable. But the central features of academic language—grammatical embeddings, sophisticated and abstract vocabulary, precision of word choice, and use of nominalizations to refer to complex processes—reflect the need to present complicated ideas in efficient ways. Students must be able to read texts that use these features if they are to become independent learners of science or social studies. They must have access to the all-purpose academic vocabulary that is used to talk about knowledge and that they will need to use in making their own arguments and evaluating others' arguments. Mechanisms for teaching those words and the ways that scientists use them should be a part of the science curriculum. Collaborations between designers of science curricula and literacy scholars are needed to develop and evaluate methods for helping students master the language of science at the undergraduate and high-school levels as well as at the middle-school level that Word Generation is currently serving.

Science. 2010. 328 (450).

References and Notes

1. Carnegie Council on Advancing Adolescent Literacy, *Time to Act: An Agenda for Advancing Adolescent Literacy for College and Career Success* (Carnegie Corporation of New York, New York, 2010); http://carnegie.org/fileadmin/Media/Publications/PDF/tta_Main.pdf.
2. J. Johnson, L. Martin-Hansen, Sci. Scope **28**, 12 (2005).
3. M.A.K. Halliday, paper presented at the Annual International Language in Education Conference, Hong Kong, December 1993.
4. M.J. Schleppegrell, *Linguist. Educ.* **12**, 431 (2001).
5. M.A.K. Halliday, J.R. Martin, *Writing Science: Literacy and Discursive Power* (Univ. of Pittsburgh Press, Pittsburgh, PA, 1993).
6. A. Bailey, *The Language Demands of School: Putting Academic English to the Test* (Yale Univ. Press, New Haven, CT, 2007).
7. R. Scarcella, *Academic English: A Conceptual Framework* (Technical Report 2003-1, Univ. of California Linguistic Minority Research Institute, Irvine, CA, 2003).
8. C. Snow, P. Uccelli, in *The Cambridge Handbook of Literacy*, D. Olson, N. Torrance, Eds. (Cambridge Univ. Press, New York, 2008), pp. 112–133.
9. Z. Fang, *Int. J. Sci. Educ.* **28**, 491 (2006).
10. A. Coxhead, *TESOL Q.* **34**, 213 (2000).
11. J. Lawrence, *Read. Psychol.* **30**, 445 (2009).
12. E.B. Moje, M. Overby, N. Tysvaer, K. Morris, *Harv. Educ. Rev.* **78**, 107 (2008).
13. C. Snow, J. Lawrence, C. White, *J. Res. Educ. Effectiveness* **2**, 325 (2009); www.wordgeneration.org.
14. J. Osborne, *Science* **328**, 463 (2010).
15. J. Lawrence, C. Snow, in *Handbook of Reading Research IV*, P.D. Pearson, M. Kamil., E. Moje, P. Afflerbach, Eds. (Routledge Education, London, 2010).
16. P.K. Murphy, I.A.G. Wilkinson, A.O. Soter, M.N. Hennessey, J.F. Alexander, *J. Educ. Psychol.* **62**, 387 (2009).
17. Preparation of this paper was made possible by collaborations supported by the Strategic Education Research Partnership and research funded by the Spencer Foundation, the William and Flora Hewlett Foundation, the Carnegie Corporation of New York, and the Institute for Education Sciences through the Council of Great City Schools. Thanks also to www.TutorVista.com for permission to reprint their lesson on torque.

KEY AND CHALLENGING WORDS

discursive, proposition, redundancy, animate (adj), epistemology, emulate, syntactic, proficient, impenetrability

QUESTIONS

1. In your own words, explain the problem discussed in paragraph 1.
2. a) Why do you think the author believes that narrative texts are less difficult for high school students to understand than those in the sciences or social studies ? b) Are narratives, such as novels, the only kinds of texts studied in English language arts?
3. How does academic language differ from non-academic (informal) language? Give two examples of everyday writing situations in which you would use non-academic language.
4. What is the function of the two excerpts in Fig. 1? How would you describe a typical reader of each excerpt? How could audience and purpose affect the way both excerpts are written?
5. Several phrases in this article demonstrate "a high density of information-bearing words" (paragraph 4). Using a dictionary, if necessary, explain in your own words the meaning of one of the following phrases from paragraph 5: "epistemically warranted evaluations"; "impersonal authoritative stance."
6. a) In your own words, define *nominalization* (paragraph 7); b) Change the following verbs into nouns that could be embedded in a sentence (e.g., *classify* (verb) → *classification* (noun: how we classify): associate, combine, observe.
7. Explain why putting all your effort into learning the meanings of bolded terms in textbooks might be of limited usefulness. What else can be done to make comprehension of academic language easier?
8. Why might it be particularly important to address the issue of academic language at the middle-school level?

POST-READING

1. Find an encyclopedia entry of at least 200 words on one topic and a comparable entry from the Internet, ensuring that the Internet entry is not from an educational or similar authoritative source. Using the same criteria as discussed in "Academic language and the challenge of reading for learning about science," compare the entries, noting the kinds of detail referred to in paragraphs 4–5.
2. Write a paragraph in informal (non-academic) prose that explains a topic you're knowledgeable about. Rewrite the paragraph in academic language. Use the guidelines given in paragraph 3. For example, you can use a "chatty" tone and 1st- and 2nd-person pronouns in the non-academic example but an impersonal tone and nouns originating as verbs (nominalizations) in the academic example.
3. The following are verbs from the Academic Word List (see paragraph 6). Change five verbs below into corresponding nouns and use each in a sentence on a topic you're interested in (e.g., identify → *identification*. The use of DNA identification to establish guilt in a criminal case has been subjected to recent legal challenges.).

    acquire
    assume
    compute
    conclude
    define
    estimate
    interpret
    regulate
    specify
    vary

RELATED WEBSITE OF INTEREST

Oxford Advanced Learner's Dictionary (Academic Word List):
www.oxfordadvancedlearnersdictionary.com/academic/

ADDITIONAL LIBRARY READING

Krajcik, J.S., & Sutherland, L.M. (2010). Supporting students in developing literacy in science. *Science, 328*, 456–459.

Osborne, J. (2010). Arguing to learn in science: The role of collaborative, critical discourse. *Science, 328*, 463–466.

Schleicher, A. (2010). Assessing literacy across a changing world. *Science, 328*, 433–434.

van den Broek, P. (2010). Using texts in science education: Cognitive process and knowledge representation. *Science, 328*, 453–456.

Examining student and instructor task perceptions in a complex engineering design task

Allyson F. Hadwin, Mika Oshige, Mariel Miller, and Peter Wild

(3,015 words)

Pre-reading

1. How much consideration do you give to the details of an assignment? Make a list of the questions you typically ask yourself (or the instructor) about an assignment and of common practices you follow before you begin your research or writing. (You could update your answer *after* you have studied "Examining student and instructor task perceptions in a complex engineering design task.")

2. a) Consider the stages in completing a challenging and complex assignment in your discipline. What different processes might be involved? What kinds of knowledge, concepts, or skills would you need to complete the task successfully? *OR* b) Choose a challenging assignment from this or a previous year in a discipline unrelated to English; in pairs, discuss your perceptions and the other student's perceptions of the assigned task, using questions like those in 2. a). This will likely work best if your partner is enrolled in a different discipline from you.

Abstract

Understanding assigned tasks is an important skill for academic success. However, few studies have examined task perceptions as they develop over the duration of a complex assignment. This study examined explicit, implicit, and socio-contextual aspects of task understanding. Specifically, this study examined: (1) the agreement between student and instructors task perceptions for the same complex engineering design task, and (2) changes in both instructor's and students' task perceptions from the beginning to the end of the task. Findings indicate that: (1) students' task perceptions were often incomplete regarding both explicit and implicit aspects of the task, (2) being well attuned in ratings of professor beliefs about knowledge and learning was related to higher course performance, (3) instructor task-perceptions evolved over time, and (4) socio-contextual aspects of task-understanding correlated with task and course performance.

1 Introduction

1   Understanding what you are being assigned to do (the assigned task) is an important component of academic success [1][2][3][4][5]. To understand assignments or tasks, students must consider what they are being asked to do, activate prior knowledge and experience that is relevant to the assignment, and construct a personal representation of an externally assigned task. Previous research suggests that students often fail to engage in cognitive processes to define and interpret the task, or they are ill-equipped from a strategic standpoint to effectively interpret the nature, scope, or purpose of the assigned task [6][4].

2   As tasks become less structured or require students to define or explore aspects of the task, students struggle even more in constructing complete and accurate representations of the task [7]. Yet ill-defined problems are the very kind that university programs, and professional programs in particular, strive to prepare students to be able to tackle in the field.

3   Differences in students' perceptions of task demands and their skills for carrying out activities to complete the task are mediated by, for example, what they perceive about instructional cues within the instructions for a task, or through reading text materials associated with the assignment. Instructional cues are designed to guide students' cognitive engagement in a task; however, students may misperceive these cues and elect tactics for studying that may not be effective for the present one while they may be effective in other contexts [1][4].

4   Self-regulated engagement in learning is important for academic success. Self-regulated learning (SRL) refers to how students strategically engage, evaluate, and regulate their own cognitive, motivational, and behavioural strategies to optimize learning in a given learning environment [11][12]. Winne and Hadwin's (1998) model of SRL identifies four phases to the process including: (a) developing task perceptions, (b) setting goals and making plans, (c) enacting the task and strategies, and (d) evaluating and adapting learning. Models of SRL suggest understanding the assigned task or developing task perceptions is central to the SRL process.

5   Task understanding is a key theoretical component in students' self-regulation and performance of academic tasks as it provides the foundation for effective and appropriate task engagement [1][4].

1.1 Definition of Task Understanding.

6   According to Doyle (1983), academic tasks are distinct units of academic work that consist of the products students are required to formulate, the processes necessary to produce these products and the resources available to students while they create the product [13]. Task understanding refers to students' construction of an internal representation of the externally assigned task [3]. Accurate and complete task understanding depends on students' engagement in a range of cognitive, metacognitive, and motivational processes to assess and interpret task information provided or implied by an instructor within a particular context [5][8]. Specifically, students must interpret the important procedures and parameters of the task while incorporating what they know about the task and task domain with self-knowledge and beliefs [3][5][6].

7   Hadwin's (2006) model of task understanding (figure 1) theorizes that at least three layers or spheres of information affect constructions of task understanding including, explicit, implicit, and socio-contextual information about tasks [9][10].

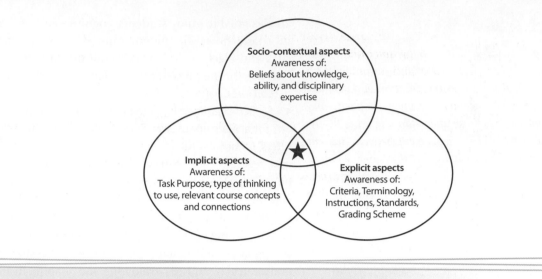

FIGURE 1   MODEL OF TASK UNDERSTANDING.

8   ***Explicit features*** of a task include information that is overtly presented in task descriptions and discussions such as key task criteria, steps or instructions to be followed, form and style of presentation, and specific standards for grading. Explicit aspects of tasks are often described in the assignment and are the aspects of the task that give it structure and some type of cohesiveness across students. We posit these are the aspects of tasks that are generally given the most attention in classroom discussion, written information, and student-teacher discussions about tasks since they most directly answer the questions "What am I supposed to do? Or What is this supposed to look like?"

9   ***Implicit features*** of a task include information students might be expected to extrapolate beyond the assignment description, such as the purpose for the task, connections to learning concepts, potential resources for completing the task, and key types of thinking and knowledge targeted by the task. Implicit features of tasks are the things that often seem obvious to course instructors and designers because they are the immediate context for tasks, but the connections may never be explicitly stated for students. For example, when a problem set is assigned in a course, students are often expected to recognize that the problem set draws on concepts covered in the last couple of chapters or lectures. In other words, we want students to put the pieces together such that:

Course objective + text chapters 3-4 + lectures 4-5 = ingredients for assignment

10   ***Socio-contextual*** features of a task include information about the broader course, program, and discipline context for the task. Socio-contextual factors tap into what is valued in the course and discipline such as beliefs about knowledge and expertise; discipline-specific expectations for presentation, writing, or argumentation; and beliefs about ability.

11   For example, in engineering, beliefs about the centrality of the design process and its importance in preparing professional engineers might contextualize tasks students encounter in a course. Importantly, beliefs may vary within a discipline not just across disciplines. An engineering student may participate in one course where particular procedures and solutions are emphasized and others where decisions and reasoning about solution paths are emphasized.

12   Despite the theoretical and practical importance of task understanding for student success, it has been under-researched, particularly in the context of complex and ill-structured task contexts.

1.2 Purpose

13   This study examined explicit, implicit, and socio-contextual aspects of task understanding and its relationship with academic success. We examined three questions: (1) How complete are students' task

perceptions in a complex engineering task? (2) How do student and teacher task perceptions change from task assignment to task completion? (3) Is the accuracy of student task perception (implicit, explicit, socio-contextual) related to academic performance?

2 Methods

14   Participants included 54 upper year undergraduate engineering students enrolled in a design-based engineering course (M= 23.33, sd=4.73 years old; M= 3.13, sd=.80 years in the program). At Time 1, when the task was assigned to students, there were 47 participants (Male=40, Female=5, undeclared=2). At Time 2, when the preliminary report was submitted to the instructor, there were 37 participants (Male=27, Female=3, Undeclared=7). At Time 3, when the final project report was submitted to the instructor, there were 25 participants (all male). Eighteen students participated across all data collection sessions.

2.1 Course and Task Context

15   The task was the major assignment in a required 13-week project-based mechanical engineering course. The assignment was a complex, problem-based collaborative design task completed by groups of three to four students. The task had historically posed challenges for students due to their unfamiliarity to this type of engineering design problem.

16   The objective of the task was to: *design or specify components for the gearbox of a 2.0 MW horizontal axis wind turbine in accordance with provided specifications. Components to be designed or specified included: the main or input shaft and its bearings; the output shaft and its bearings and; the final gear set.*

17   Deliverables included two reports. Both reports were graded, using a precise grading rubric. The preliminary report (Time 2–Week 4) consisted of report format, design load calculations, including reactions and free body diagrams, presentation of engineering calculations, and determination of lead on the turbine, and drawing/technical design, including shaft drawings and its formatting. The final report (Time 3–Week 10) consisted of engineering drawings for main shaft and output shaft, shaft design

calculations, fatigue calculations for main shaft and output shaft, gear calculations, and bearing selections. Each category was further divided into specific points that should be included in each report.

2.2 Data Collection Instruments

18   *Task-Analyzer (TA).* The task analyzer was designed to engage students in self-regulatory thinking about tasks and to elicit data about student task perceptions. Two parallel versions: one for students (administered on paper) and the other for the course instructor/teacher (administered through oral interview). Questions in both versions addressed three aspects of task understanding for the assigned task: explicit (3 questions), implicit (6 questions), and socio-contextual understanding (2 questions).

19   At the *explicit level*, students and teachers were asked to make a list the key things that need to be included in the assignment.

20   At the *implicit level*, students and the instructor were asked about the kind of thinking the assignment is intended to elicit (remember, understand, apply, evaluate, create), the kind of knowledge to be emphasized through the task (factual, conceptual, metacognitive, procedural), the purpose of the task, important resources for completing the task, course concepts or theories to be used to complete the task, and characteristics of a top quality assignment. Questions were open-ended, except questions about the kind of thinking and kind of knowledge emphasized in the task. Those questions required rating each term on the scale of 0 (Not Relevant to the project) to 10 (Extremely Relevant) identifying the most relevant term.

21   At a *socio-contextual level*, data were collected about the instructors' beliefs about knowledge (EBI-T) and students' perceptions about the instructor's beliefs (EBI-S) using a modified 28-item Epistemological Beliefs Inventory EBI[14]. Some of the examples for the EBI-T were "I believe what is true is a matter of opinion" and "I believe people who learn things quickly are the most successful." In the EBI-S, students were instructed to take the instructor's perspective about beliefs about learning so questions were reworded as follows "My professor believes what is true is a matter of opinion" and "My professor believes people who learn things quickly are the

most successful." Responses were on a 5-point Likert scale from 1 (strongly disagree) to 5 (strongly agree).

22   Data were collected at three points over the course: (a) when the task was assigned to students (Time 1, mid-September), (b) when the preliminary report was submitted to the instructor (Time 2, beginning of October), and (c) when the final project was submitted to the instructor (Time3, early December). Students completed the Task Analyzer in paper formant during class time. Instructor data were collected by interview and transcribed by the researchers.

23   Assignment grade and course grade were used as performance measures.

3 Findings

24   Open ended questions were coded as follows. First instructor data was analyzed to identify each idea unit per question for each semester separately. Instructor idea units (target responses) were used to create a comprehensive checklist for scoring student responses A subject matter expert examined instructor idea units to make sure they were accurately represented. Student answers were coded as 0 = idea unit not present in answer, or 1 = idea unit present in answer. Two coders coded and scored students' responses at Time 1, 2, and 3 respectively. The percentage of the students' answers that matched with the instructor's keys (percentage agreement) was calculated and used as the student's score. For each question, there were two coders.

25   The Likert scale items (kind of thinking and kind of knowledge emphasized in the task) were scored by calculating the absolute difference between the instructor and student rating of the item. We also calculated the percentage of students identifying each

type of thinking and each kind of knowledge as most relevant and compared that with the instructor response at time 1, 2, and 3 respectively.

26   For EBI measure of socio-contextual awareness of the task, inter-observer reliabilities between teacher and student item responses were used to examine how well attuned students were in their ratings of beliefs that were valued in the course. Pearson Moment Correlation was calculated across all the EBI items between the teacher's rating and each student's rating across all 28 items, yielding a correlation coefficient for each student. A high positive correlation indicates that the teacher and student responded similarly across items. We refer to this as high attunement in socio-contextual task awareness. While a student may not have rated items exactly the same as the teacher, there was a tendency to rate an item as high when the teacher rated it as high, and low when the teacher rated it as low. A high negative correlation indicates that students rated items low, when the teacher rated them as high. No correlation indicates there was little similarity across items in how students and the teacher responded. We refer to both high negative correlations and low correlations as being poorly attuned.

3.1 Students did not evidence complete understanding of the explicit aspects of the task

27   On average, students did not evidence complete understandings of the key things that should be included in the assignment (explicit aspects). Students most accurately identified the most key points at Time 2 (see Table 1).

28   This is particularly alarming considering: (a) students were given a very detailed assignment

TABLE 1   MEAN PERCENTAGE OF KEY INSTRUCTOR POINTS RELATED TO EXPLICIT TASK FEATURES IDENTIFIED BY STUDENTS

	Time 1 N=47		Time 2 N=34-37		Time 3 N=25	
	M %	sd	M %	sd	M %	sd
Explicit points	17.02	15.69	26.19	21.12	7.00	11.46
# points (teacher)	(9)		(6)		(4)	

description regarding explicit aspects of the task, and (b) over time, the professor identified fewer key points related to explicit task requirements. Therefore, at T3 it should have been easier to score high since students only needed to identify 4 key points to get 100 per cent compared to 9 key things at T1.

3.2 Evidence that understanding of implicit aspects of the task relates to performance.

29   The mean absolute difference between student and instructor Likert scale ratings of items related to the kind of thinking for this task was strongly negatively correlated with final course grades $r(25)= -.47$, $p<.05$ at T3 only. This suggests that students who were poorly attuned with the instructor in rating the importance of each type of thinking for the task at the time the final assignment was submitted, also performed poorly in the course. This finding warrants future investigation in courses and tasks where the final grade does not include a shared mark across team members. In this case, we correlated implicit aspects with final grade which included other individual measures instead of with group marks on the assignment.

3.3 Instructor versus student identification of thinking and knowledge emphasized in the task

30   The instructor identified *Evaluate* (T1&T3) & *Analyze* (T2) as most relevant for the task. *Analyze* was rated as most relevant by the highest percentage of students at T1, T2, &T3. Since analyze and evaluate are both higher levels of thinking with some related aspects, we suggest that students were reasonably accurate in identifying higher levels of thinking as being relevant for this course.

31   The instructor identified *Metacognitive* (T1) and *Procedural* (T2 & T3) as the most relevant kind of knowledge for this task. *Conceptual* was rated as most relevant by the highest percentage of students across all times.

32   This finding warrants further investigation. The instructor shift from metacognitive to procedural knowledge as being most relevant was not consistent with other questions. It is possible, that the definitions and examples we provided for each type of knowledge may have been confusing for participants who were not familiar with the underlying concepts. Nevertheless, we note that higher percentages of students recognized that this type of design based task is designed to emphasize knowledge other than factual knowledge. Past research with early undergraduate students suggests that they tend to misperceive tasks as focusing on factual knowledge. From that perspective, findings in this engineering course may be seen as promising.

3.4 The importance of socio-contextual task perception for academic performance

33   We used a median split to identify students with high versus low inter-observer reliability (correlation) scores on the EBI. Students who were

TABLE 2   Mean percentage of students identifying each type of thinking as most relevant

	Time 1 (T1)	Time 2 (T2)	Time 3 (T3)
Understand	6 %	3 %	8 %
Apply	17 %	17 %	28 %
Analyze	36 %	44 %	28 %
Evaluate	9 %	22 %	24 %
Create	2 %	6 %	12 %
No Answer	30 %	8 %	0 %

Underline denotes correspondence with instructor response

TABLE 3   MEAN PERCENTAGE OF STUDENTS IDENTIFYING EACH TYPE OF KNOWLEDGE AS MOST RELEVANT

	Time 1 (T1)	Time 2 (T2)	Time 3 (T3)
Procedural	21 %	<u>26 %</u>	<u>24 %</u>
Conceptual	30 %	38 %	40 %
Factual	15 %	18 %	28 %
Metacognitive	<u>2 %</u>	0 %	4 %
No Answer	32 %	18 %	4 %

Underline denotes correspondence with instructor response

well attuned with the instructor in estimating instructor beliefs about knowledge (at T1 only) performed better on the task and the course overall (see Table 4).

34   While findings point to the importance of accurate awareness of beliefs that underlie course instruction, they should be interpreted with some caution. Sample size was small for EBI reporting, and on average, students' responses to the EBI were not very consistent with the instructor's responses to the same items and there was a great deal of variability in attunement (see Table 5).

4 Discussion

35   Overall, findings indicate that students often had incomplete understandings of the explicit, implicit, and socio-contextual aspects of the task. Students who were better attuned with the professor in task perceptions tended to perform better in the course. Therefore, it may be important for students to develop broader perceptions of academic tasks, than just interpreting the explicit words, criteria, and instructions articulated in assignment descriptions. Students may also benefit from developing

TABLE 4   MEAN PERFORMANCE SCORES FOR STUDENTS WITH LOW VERSUS HIGH ATTUNEMENT WITH INSTRUCTOR BELIEFS

	Prelim. Report Grade		Final Report Grade		Final Course Grade	
	M sd	t-test	M sd	t-test	M sd	t-test
Low N=14	16.96 14.80		77.40 8.32		70.21 10.63	
High N=15	79.74 13.44	2.06*	85.81 8.75	2.67*	79.27 12.04	2.14*

TABLE 5   MEAN ATTUNEMENT CORRELATIONS BETWEEN STUDENT AND INSTRUCTOR RESPONSES TO EBI ITEMS

	Time 1	Time 2	Time 3
Mean r	.27	.24	.33
SD	.24	.22	.19

understandings of the kind of thinking or processing the instructor is trying to stimulate as well as the kinds of beliefs about knowledge and learning that precipitated course and task design and planning.

36   Importantly, findings indicated that tasks themselves are dynamic, not static; even the instructor's task representations changed over time. This implies that students and instructors co-construct expectations about tasks in situ. It may be important to re-align task perceptions as a course develops.

37   Findings lend support to Hadwin's model of task understanding. Explicit, implicit, and socio-contextual aspects provide different profiles about the accuracy and completeness of task perceptions. We posit that University courses should prepare students to successfully tackle poorly defined or ill-structured tasks that are common in the workplace. Our findings indicate that even upper year students may benefit from developing skills and strategies for improving accuracy and completeness of their task perceptions.

38   Findings warrant follow up investigation. Participation varied from time 1 to 3 making it difficult to compare task understanding over time. The impact of task perceptions on task performance was statistically difficult to examine on a task that was group based.

5 References

[1] Butler D.L., & Cartier, S.C. (2003). Promoting effective task interpretation as an important work habit: A key to successful teaching and learning. *The Teachers College Record, 106*, 1729–1758.

[2] Hadwin, A.F. (2000). *Building a case for self-regulating as a socially constructed phenomenon.* Unpublished doctoral dissertation, Simon Fraser University, Burnaby, BC, Canada.

[3] Hadwin, A.F. (2006). Do your students really understand your assignment? *LTC Currents Newsletter, II (3)*, 1–9.

[4] Jamieson-Noel, D. (2004). Exploring task definition as a facet of self-regulated learning. Unpublished Doctoral Dissertation, Simon Fraser University.

[5] Winne, P.H., & Hadwin, A.F. (1998). Studying as self-regulated engagement in learning. In D. Hacker, J. Dunlosky, & A. Graesser (Eds.), *Metacognition in educational theory and practice* (pp.277–304). Mahwah, NJ: Lawrence Erlbaum.

[6] Hadwin, A.F., Wozney, L., & Venkatesh, V. (2003). A narrative analysis of the dynamic interplay between two students' emerging task understanding and instructional scaffolds. In A.F. Hadwin (Coordinator). *What are students self-regulated about? Task features, context and understanding as conditions for self-regulated learning.* American Educational Research Association, Chicago.

[7] Oshige, M. (2009). *Task understanding and social aspects of self-regulated learning: Task understanding as a predictor of academic success for undergraduate students.* Unpublished Master's thesis. University of Victoria, BC.

[8] Winne, P.H., & Hadwin, A.F. (2008). The weave of motivation and self-regulated learning. In D.H. Schunk & B.J. Zimmerman (Eds.), *Motivation and Self-regulated learning: Theory, Research and Applications* (pp. 298–314). New York: Lawrence Erlbaum.

[9] Hadwin, A.F. (2006, August). Do your students really understand your assignments? *LTC Currents: Optimizing Learning Environments, Vol. II (3)*, 1, 6, 8–9. Victoria, British Columbia, Canada: University of Victoria.

[10] Hadwin, A.F. (2008, March). Do your students really understand your assignments? *Tomorrow's Professor Blog.* Massachusetts Institute of Technology and Stanford University. http://amps-tools.mit.edu/tomprofblog/archives/2008/03/857_do_your_stu.html

[11] Zimmerman, B.J. (2004). Sociocultural influence and students' development of academic self-regulation: A social-cognitive perspective. In D.M. McInerney & S. Van Etten (Eds.). *Big Theories Revisited* (Vol. 4, pp. 139–164). Greenwich, CT: Information Age Publishing.

[12] Zimmerman, B.J. (1989). A social cognitive view of self-regulated academic learning. *Journal of Educational Psychology, 81*, 329–339.

[13] Doyle, W. (1983) Academic work. *Review of Educational Research, 53*, 159–170.

[14] Schraw, G., Bendixen, L.D., & Dunkle, M.E. (2002). Development and validation of the Epistemic Belief Inventory (EBI). In B.K., Hofer & P.R. Pintrich, (Eds.), *Personal epistemology: The psychology of beliefs about knowledge and knowing* (pp. 261–275). Mahwah, NJ: Lawrence Erlbaum Associates

KEY AND CHALLENGING WORDS

mediate, optimize, metacognitive, contextual, cohesiveness, posit, extrapolate, elicit, epistemological, precipitate, in situ

QUESTIONS

1. Why might professional programs try to equip students with the skills to tackle "ill-defined" problems (paragraph 2) more than clearly defined or more structured tasks?

2. a) Paraphrase one of the definitions in the Introduction; b) In addition to definition, what other rhetorical pattern is used in section 1.1.? c) Why might both patterns be useful as strategies for coherence in this essay?

3. Explain why instructors and students might diverge in their understanding of the "explicit features" of a task. Why might they diverge in their understanding of the "implicit features" of a task?

4. a) What is the study's justification? b) Where are the answers to the three questions posed in 1.2 to be found? c) After you have read the essay, summarize the answers to these questions.

5. Explain the purpose of the task analyzer and its importance in the experiment.

6. a) Why might open-ended questions pose a particular challenge in an empirical study like this one? What steps did the researchers take to ensure the validity of their results with respect to open-ended questions? b) What is the function of paragraph 26?

7. Analyze the authors' explanation for the results summarized in Table 3. Are the results adequately accounted for? Why or why not?

8. In a couple of sentences, explain the results summarized in Table 1 or 4.

POST-READING

1. *Collaborative activity:* Brainstorm to come up with a list of suggestions that might improve students' understanding of a complex task, following up on some of the recommendations in the "Discussion" section and/or other suggestions that occur to you. The suggestions should be specific and practical, designed to focus the student on cognitive, conceptual, or perceptual tasks leading to self-reflection (see paragraph 3). One list should focus on what *instructors* can do to improve task perception; a separate list should focus on what *students* can do to improve task perception. Choose two or three items from each list and discuss them with members of other groups.

2. *Collaborative activity:* In groups composed of students from different disciplines, discuss "socio-contextual" features of your discipline, referring for general characteristics to the description of "socio-contextual" features in paragraphs 10–11. If you wish, you can use the examples in paragraph 10 as a starting point.

3. Identify two limitations of the study that are raised in the "Findings" or the "Discussion" section. Consider specific ways that *one* of these limitations could be addressed in a future study. If your instructor wishes, you can use the format of Hadwin et al. in section 1.2.

RELATED WEBSITES OF INTEREST

Many university websites and online writing centres/"labs" focus on understanding university-level assignments—for example, *Writing at the University of Toronto* [understanding topics]:

www.writing.utoronto.ca/advice/general/essay-topics

An exploratory study of cyberbullying with undergraduate university students

Carol M. Walker, Beth Rajan Sockman, and Steven Koehn

(3,843 words)

Pre-reading

1. Consider the following questions about cyberbullying (you could reflect on them, freewrite about them, or respond in question-answer format): What constitutes cyberbullying? How prevalent do you think cyberbullying is at the university level? Have you been a target of cyberbullying or do you know someone who has been? What effects could cyberbullying have on the student-victim?

Abstract

Understanding the covert events surrounding the undergraduate students' experience is essential to educators' and counselors' involvement in their success. Research into bullying behaviours has documented victims' feelings of anger, sadness, and poor concentration. Affordable technologies have propagated this concern into cyberspace. This exploratory study evaluated the instances of cyberbullying experienced by undergraduate students. Additionally, the forms of technology utilized in cyberbullying were queried. A 27-item survey was distributed to 120 undergraduate students in social science, technology, and education departments. The majority of all respondents (54 per cent) and 100 per cent of male respondents indicated they knew someone who had been cyberbullied. The perpetrators primarily used cell phones, Facebook, and instant messaging. The study results provide legitimate concerns regarding the undergraduate students' exposure to cyberbullying and numerous areas for future research.

Keywords: bullying, cyberbullying, cyberharrassment, technology and information systems, undergraduate university students

*

1   Growing up, most people have experienced bullying behaviour—often on the playground or on the school bus—resulting in negative memories. Consequently, it seems natural that bullying behaviour became a research topic, which has evolved with the advent of new technologies. The following section reviews research focused on traditional bullying and serves as a basis for understanding cyberbullying, where bullying takes a disturbing twist.

2   In the late 1970s Dan Olweus led social and psychological bullying research and provided an understanding of two primary forms: direct and relational, or indirect, bullying (Smith & Gross, 2006; Chapel et al., 2006). Much of this research focused on students who were either bullies or victims. Chapell, et al. (2004) explored bullying with a sample of 1,025 undergraduates and found that 24.6 per cent of respondents had been bullied.

3   Further work found a significant positive correlation between being a bully in university, high school and elementary school, with 21 per cent having been bullied (Chapell, et al., 2006). Chapell et al. (2006) evaluated 119 undergraduate students to determine the continuance of being a bully, victim, or bully-victim from elementary school through university. Over 70 per cent of students who were bullied in high school and elementary school bullied others in university. Forty to over 50 per cent of students who had been bully-victims or bullies (respectively) in elementary and high school repeated the pattern in university.

4   The victims of bullying reported feelings of anxiety, depression, and suicidal ideation. Ybarra and Mitchell (2004) reported an increase of psychosocial problems in those reporting cyberbully/victim behaviours including: problem behaviours, drinking alcohol, smoking, depression, and low commitment to academics. Somewhat alarming are the incidences of school shootings where the perpetrators report suffering from bullying behaviour. In addition, university counselling centres report increasing concerns of anxiety, depression, and suicidal ideation with the undergraduate student (Chapell et al., 2006). Research regarding incidents of bullying on campus is imperative to provide a pro-active approach for educating the twenty-first century student.

5   With the advent of affordable, user-friendly technology comes cyberbullying—bullying in cyberspace. Haber and Haber (2007) define cyberbullying as the following:

> The use of information and communication technologies such as email, cell phone and pager text messages, instant messaging, personal websites or blogs, and online personal polling websites. The technology is used to promote deliberate, repeated, and hurtful behaviour by an individual or group, with the intent to harm others. (p. 52)

6   This cyberbullying is Internet harassment taking the form of comments, information, or pictures posted online for others to see with the intent to harass or embarrass (Ybarra, Diener-West, & Leaf, 2007). User-friendly technology and the proliferation of social networking have initiated new avenues for research into how technology is being used on the college campus to bully or harass. The terms cyberbullying, cyberharassment, and cyber-stalking are often discussed in tandem. However, in popular culture, cyber-harassment is linked more closely with cyber-stalking. The focus of this study was cyberbullying in which the definition is broader and can encompass harassing behaviours.

7   Studies of cyberbullying have primarily focused on the adolescent years with emphasis on technologies used, reactions to cyberharassment, and the extent of the experience. Li (2007) investigated the nature and extent of adolescents' experience of cyberbullying. Li's study surveyed 177 students in grade seven of an urban city. The results showed over 25 per cent of students had been cyber-bullied and almost 15 per cent had cyber-bullied others.

8   Juvonen and Gross (2008) provided data from an anonymous web-based survey (http://bolt.com; conducted in 2005) to determine the extent of online bullying experienced by youth between 12- to 17-years-old (N = 1454, mean age = 15.5, SD = 1.47). Respondents indicated experiences of bullying described by the researchers as *"mean things,"* defined as "anything that someone does that upsets or offends someone else." There was no requirement of a repetitive nature to the *"mean thing."* Five forms of bullying were reported: insults (66 per cent), threats (27 per cent), sharing embarrassing pictures (18 per cent), privacy violation (25 per cent), and password theft (33 per cent). Almost one-fifth of respondents reported repeated experiences, and 72 per cent reported at least one online bullying encounter during the past year.

9   Two studies addressed aspects of cyberbullying on the university level. Finn (2004) documents 2002 survey results in which 10 to 15 per cent of 339 students at the University of New Hampshire reported experiencing repeated email or Instant Messenger messages that "threatened, insulted, or harassed" and more than half of the students received unwanted pornography.

10   Psychological need as a predictor of cyberbullying was also evaluated with surveys distributed to 666 students in the Faculty of Education at Selcuk University, Turkey. The primary focus of this research was to assess the psychological needs of the cyberbully. The results indicated that aggression ("engaging in behaviours which attack or hurt others") and succorance ("soliciting sympathy, affection, and emotional support from others") positively predicted cyberbullying,

whereas interception ("engaging in attempts to understand one's own behaviour or the behaviour of others") negatively predicted it (Dilmac, B., 2009, p. 1313). Additionally, 22.5 per cent of the students reported cyberbullying another at least once and 55.3 per cent reported being a victim of cyberbullying at least once in their lifetime (Dilmac, 2009).

11 The Social Dominance theory may be applied to better understand bullying. Pratto, Sidanius and Levin (2006) assessed fifteen years of research that evaluated this theory. Social groups are divided into three classifications: *age system*, adults have social power over children; *gender system*, men have disproportionate power compared to women; and *arbitrary-set system*, arbitrary groups have access to things of positive and negative social value. Arbitrary-set groups may be defined by social distinctions meaningfully related to power. Discrimination that favors dominant groups over subordinate groups is the primary dynamic that produces these group-based social hierarchies. It is the ideologies shared by society, or *legitimizing myths,* that permit discrimination (Pratto, Sidanius, & Levin, 2006).

12 Discrimination by individuals is also prevalent. *Social dominance orientation* (SDO) defines the psychological orientations that delineate dominant and subordinate group relations. Although these intergroup processes produce better outcomes for dominants than for subordinates, both groups justify their actions and relative positions with *legitimizing myths* (Pratto, Sidanius, & Levin, 2006).

13 Bullying may be the result of *legitimizing myths* that allow the *gender* and *arbitrary-set systems* to delineate this power struggle. Technology allows this struggle to exist surreptitiously away from the watchful eye of the educator.

14 As technology becomes more accessible to today's youth more questions arise. CTIA, International Association for the Wireless Telecommunications Industry (2010), indicated that wireless penetration in the US increased 78 per cent from 1995 to 2009, with 276.6 million subscribers and 1.36 trillion annualized SMS messages. Facebook (2010) has more than 350 million users with more than 3.5 billion pieces of content (web links, news stories, blog posts, notes, photo albums, etc.) shared each week.

15 Additional research is necessary to address the upsurge of technology, and its impact on the age-old events of bullying. Questions that are important to address include: What impact does the cell phone have on the interactions of undergraduate students as they maintain their status according to the Social Dominance theory?, How do social networking sites affect these students?, and Has the ability to reply instantly, without personal contact, augmented the bullying scene? This study explores the extent of cyberbullying on the university campus to address the questions:

1. What instances of cyberbullying do undergraduate students experience, and what role does gender play in cyberbullying at the undergraduate level?
2. What forms of technology do undergraduate students use to perpetrate or receive bullying, and how often does it occur?

Method

16 Four department chairs were contacted to obtain permission to distribute surveys in a US University with an undergraduate population of less than 10,000 students. The selection was designed to diversify the respondents in four divisions of study. Ultimately, surveys were distributed in three departments: social science, technology and education.

Participants

17 A total of 131 students (73 female and 57 male) were surveyed from seven undergraduate classes during the 2008 spring semester. Survey questionnaires were distributed to students in class. Students were informed that they were not obligated to complete the surveys, and they were instructed to check a box and not complete the packet if they had done so in another class. An Information Sheet was provided, with Haber and Haber's (2007) cyberbullying definition and the location and hours of operation for campus counseling and security. Anonymity was guaranteed with instructions not to record their names on the survey; packets were also returned face down in a box provided that was placed away from the surveyor.

Measures

18   The authors adapted surveys from Li (2006) and Spitzberg and Hoobler (2002) to develop a 27-item survey. Spitzberg and Hoobler's research evaluated incidences of "cyberstalking." During IRB review, concerns were expressed regarding the utilization of the term "cyberstalking" in college research. The ethical and moral dilemma of conducting an exploratory study to fully understand what college students are experiencing, combined with the legal implications of the term "stalking," led the authors to combine the information under the term "cyberbullying."

19   Closed questions addressed demographic data and asked about instances of hearing about and experiencing cyberbullying at the university. An open-ended question was included to allow respondents to offer other instances of cyberbullying experienced.

20   A pilot study was conducted with twelve undergraduate students ranging in age from 19 to 22. The participants reviewed the information sheets and completed the study privately. Then, a group forum was utilized to discuss the survey content. The authors obtained valuable input that was taken into consideration as the final 27-item survey was created. The questions from the cyberstalking survey were accepted as fitting the cyberbullying definition, and the additional question of "friending someone to get personal information" was recommended.

21   When the survey was finalized, participants received the six-page survey packet. Respondents were directed not to write their names on the survey papers and were directed to keep the information sheet.

22   The second page provided information to the participants regarding the researcher and the purpose of the research. Also included was a discussion of the risks, the voluntary nature of the study, and informed consent.

23   The survey contained a demographic questionnaire to determine gender, age, living arrangements, ethnicity, school grade average, and hours of technology use per day. Data were analyzed from 120 students (70 female and 50 male) ranging from age 18 to 24. Two percent classified themselves as Asian, two percent Hispanic, seven percent Black, one percent Indian, 85 percent White, and three percent Other. When queried about living environment, 16 per cent lived at home with parent/guardian; 53 per cent lived in campus housing; and 31 per cent lived off campus but not at home.

24   Academic grade averages were reported at 51 per cent in the A–B range, 47 per cent in the B–C range, and two percent reported grades in the C–D range. No respondents reported a lower than D range.

25   No respondent reported daily use of technology (computer, cell phone, PDA, etc.) below one hour. Fourteen percent of students use technology between one and two hours daily, 31 per cent between three and four hours, and 55 per cent of respondents use technology more than four hours daily.

26   Twenty-one questions were utilized to gather data. Respondents specified their knowledge of students being cyberbullied and technologies used. Their direct experience with cyberbullying was analyzed based on technologies used, who perpetrated the bullying, the frequency of cyberbullying, and whether they told a parent/guardian or other adult. The survey was concluded with fourteen specific instances of undesirable and obsessive communication via computer or other electronic means.

Results

27   Fifty-four percent of all respondents indicated knowing someone who had been cyberbullied (Table 1). One hundred percent of male respondents knew someone who was cyberbullied.

TABLE 1   NUMBER OF STUDENTS REPORTING KNOWING SOMEONE WHO HAS BEEN CYBERBULLIED.

Gender	n	per cent
Female	15	23
Male	50	100
Totals (N=120)	65	54

28   Specific examples of technologies used to cyber-bully were also delineated (Table 2). Of the items listed Facebook (56 per cent), cell phones (45 per cent), and AIM (43 per cent) were most frequently reported.

29   Eleven percent of the respondents indicated having experienced cyberbullying at the university (Table 3). Of those, Facebook (64 per cent), cell Phones (43 per cent), and AIM (43 per cent) were the

TABLE 2   Technology Students Report Hearing of Being Used to Bully / Harass (N = 120)

Item	Technology	n	per cent
A	Email	23	19
B	Cell Phones [text, pictures, video, or messages]	54	45
C	Video cameras, web cam	8	7
D	AOL Instant Messaging (AIM)	52	43
E	Facebook	67	56
F	My Space	37	31
G	Blogging	11	9
H	Twitter	1	1
I	Chat Rooms	5	4

TABLE 3   Number of Students Who Reported Experiencing Cyberbullying and the Technology Used (N = 14)

Item	Technology	n	per cent
A	Email	3	21
B	Cell Phones [text, pictures, video, or messages]	6	43
C	Video cameras, web cam	0	0
D	AOL Instant Messaging (AIM)	6	43
E	Facebook	9	64
F	My Space	4	29
G	Blogging	0	0
H	Twitter	0	0
I	Chat Rooms	0	0

Frequency of Experiencing Cyberbullying (N = 14)

Item	Frequency	n	per cent
1	Less than 4 times	8	57
2	4–10 times	4	29
3	Over 10 times	2	14

most frequent technologies used. Of the respondents who were cyberbullied, 57 per cent were bullied less than four times, 29 per cent were cyberbullied four to 10 times and 14 per cent over 10 times. Students indicated that 50 per cent of the cyberbullies were classmates, 57 per cent someone outside of university, and 43 per cent did not know who was cyberbullying them. Seventy-one percent of the students replied they had told a parent/guardian or other adult about the cyberbullying incident(s).

30   When participants were queried regarding the extent of undesirable and obsessive communication through computer or other electronic means (Table 4) four areas were reported at or above 30 per cent: sending tokens of affection (33 per cent); sending excessively 'needy' or demanding messages (30 per cent); pretending to be someone he or she wasn't (34 per cent); and 'friending' in order to obtain personal information (31 per cent). Several other areas of undesirable and obsessive communication ranged from 10 to 28 per cent. An independent- samples t-test was conducted to compare these categories. There was no significant difference in scores for males and females.

TABLE 4   NUMBER OF STUDENTS REPORTING BEING UNDESIRABLY AND OBSESSIVELY COMMUNICATED WITH VIA TECHNOLOGY (N = 120)

Item	Description	n	per cent
A	Sending tokens of affection (e.g. poetry, songs, electronic greetings, praise, etc.)	40	33
B	Sending exaggerated messages of affection (e.g. expressions of affections implying a more intimate relationship than you actually have, etc.)	33	28
C	Sending excessively explicit messages (e.g. inappropriately giving private information about his/her life, body, family hobbies, sexual experiences, etc.)	31	26
D	Sending excessively 'needy' or demanding messages (e.g. pressuring to see you, assertively requesting you to go out on a date, arguing with you to give him/her 'another chance', etc.)	36	30
E	Sending pornographic/obscene images or messages (e.g. photographs or cartoons of nude people, or people or animals engaging in sexual acts, etc.)	28	23
F	Sending threatening written messages (e.g. suggesting harming you, your property, family, friends, etc.)	15	13
G	Sending sexually harassing messages (e.g. describing hypothetical sexual acts between you, making sexually demeaning remarks, etc.)	14	12
H	Sending threatening pictures or images (e.g. images of actual or implied mutilation, blood, dismemberment, property destruction, etc.)	3	3
I	Exposing private information about you to others (e.g. sending email out to others regarding your secrets, embarrassing information, unlisted numbers, etc.)	14	12
J	Pretending to be someone he or she wasn't (e.g. falsely representing him/herself as a different person or gender, claiming a false identity, status or position, pretending to be you, etc.)	41	34
K	Sabotaging your private reputation (e.g. spreading rumours about you, your relationships or activities with friends, family, partner, etc.)	19	16
L	Sabotaging your work/school reputation (e.g. spreading rumours about you, your relationships or activities in organizational networks, electronic bulletin boards, etc.	8	7
M	'Friended' people you know to get personal information about you	37	31

31   A one-way, between groups analysis of variance (ANOVA) was conducted to explore the impact of living environment on whether respondents felt their private reputation had been 'sabotaged' via rumours spread with computers or other electronic means $F (2, 117) = 3.9, p = .02$; eta squared = .06). An ANOVA was also conducted to evaluate the effect of hours of technology use and being cyberbullied at college $F (2, 117) = 3.16, p = .05$; eta squared = .05). These tests were run to explore relationships between the various demographic and bullying responses. However, the sample size (N = 120) prohibits generalization of any nature. Future research with a larger, nationwide sample is recommended.

32   When students were given the opportunity to express individual experiences with being undesirably pursued through computer or other electronic means, three students responded. One recalled the following event:

> I have a friend who was dating a boy named Jim on my space for an entire year. She met Jim though a friend on the basketball team we will call LL. For a while it was going very well with my friend and Jim. Then he started getting obsessive. He was never home when she tried to see him. Finally, after a year and being in love with Jim she finds out that Jim and LL are the same person. She was heartbroken because LL created the perfect guy and is a girl. So, my friend was harassed by LL for a long while and then the cops were involved. LL sought help. In the end, my friend lost her senior year to false promises and hope.

33   Additionally, a respondent discussed a random person who signed in to a chat room and pretended to be the respondent to harass the respondent's friends. This occurred on several occasions before the person quit. A third participant stated they were "rick rolled," defined by Wikipedia (2010) as being directed to a web link for the Rick Astley music video, *"Never Gonna Give you Up."*

Discussion

34   This study explores a little-examined area of the undergraduate experience. The dearth of literature in this area left the authors with only two similar studies to evaluate. The preliminary analysis of the 120 participants indicated that the majority (54 per cent) of respondents knew someone who had been cyberbullied.

35   Eleven percent had personally experienced cyberbullying, with 57 per cent having been cyberbullied less than four times, 29 per cent four to 10 times, and 14 per cent over 10 times. Finn's (2004) findings support the results; 10–15 per cent of his respondents received email or instant messaging that "threatened, insulted, or harassed."

36   When specific examples of incidents of undesirable and obsessive communication through the computer or other electronic means were queried, 33 per cent of respondents had received unsolicited tokens of affection, 34 per cent had someone pretend to be someone he or she was not, and 30 per cent experienced excessively 'needy' or demanding messages. Twenty-three percent of respondents had received pornographic or obscene images. This is relatively lower than Finn's (2004) finding of 58.7 per cent. Finn did not query if the pornography was sent directly to respondent or via group messages.

37   The findings bring to light a discrepancy. Interestingly, 30 per cent or more students indicated they had experienced incidents of undesirable and obsessive communication. Based on the operational definition of cyberbullying given in the student survey, these incidents are *forms* of cyberbullying. One would expect that all of those who indicated that they had experienced these incidents would have also reported yes to cyberbullying. Instead, only 11 per cent reported "yes" to being cyberbullied. One questions why these undesirable incidents are higher than the 11 per cent that responded yes to being cyberbullied.

38   It is possible that students consider the undesirable and obsessive communication instances as accepted behaviours of harassment that occur within "online" social life. Therefore, the students may not consider them to be cyberbullying. In addition, if students consider the undesirable and obsessive communication acceptable acts, legitimizing myths may be active (Pratto, Sidanius, & Levin, 2006). This would need to be studied further since neither the research questions nor survey questions aimed to address legitimizing myths.

39   From the data, 71 per cent of the respondents indicated they had told a parent/guardian or other

adult about the cyberbullying experience. Upon reflection, the researchers question whether a respondent considers a university peer to be an "other adult."

40   To better understand who was doing the cyberbullying, question four queried if the respondent was cyberbullied by classmates (50 per cent), someone outside of university (57 per cent), or "I don't know" (43 per cent). The combined percentage of greater than 100 per cent raises the question of whether the victims were being bullied by more than one person.

41   When studying traditional bullying at the university level, the findings produce smaller results than this research. Chapell, et al. (2004) explored college bullying with a sample of 1,025 undergraduates and found that 24.6 per cent of respondents had been bullied. Other research conducted by Chapell, et al. (2006) found a significant positive correlation between being a bully in university, high school, and elementary school, with 21 per cent having been bullied. This exploratory research indicates an increase of bullying, via a cyberbullying format, to up to 34 per cent. The availability of affordable technology may contribute to this increase.

42   Students report feeling angry, sad, and hurt when cyberbullied. Poor concentration and low school achievement is also a concern (Beran & Li, 2005). Chapell et al. (2006) report on a number of studies that found that most school shooters had been bullied. This supports a concern that further campus violence is possible due to this relatively new form of bullying. University educators and counselling centres need to be aware of the ability of undergraduate students to surreptitiously bully victims via technology.

43   Pratto, Sidanius and Levin's (2006) evaluation of *arbitrary-set systems, gender systems,* and the *legitimizing myths* that permit such discrimination may provide a basis of understanding for the cyberbullying actions of the undergraduate student. In the stressful environment of a university, students may feel they must dominate to succeed. The relative ability to feel control of a situation as the dominant bully may allow the cyberbully to justify his or her actions. Dilmac (2009) supported this theory with the finding that aggression and succorance positively predict cyberbullying.

44   The authors faced several limitations. Data gathered from 120 participants inhibits the ability to generalize to either the entire university being studied, much less to a national level. The convenience sample format may not have provided a widely diversified study group. Finally, standardization of the surveying procedure was not possible; the researchers did not administer the survey to every group.

45   Further research is needed to expand our understanding of cyberbullying at the university level. More detailed gender data would be valuable to determine if the males who responded they knew someone that had been cyberbullied were referring to men or women. Are they more often the confidants of fellow female students? In addition, more information needs to be gathered to determine if one or more perpetrators are victimizing those being cyberbullied. When one considers the relatively high percentage of respondents who told a parent/guardian or other adult about being cyberbullied, it would be valuable to know if these respondents are considering university peers as the "other adult." Finally, a nation-wide survey of undergraduate students would provide valuable data.

Conclusion

46   This exploratory study examines the extent of cyberbullying that undergraduate students experience and provides a basis for future research in cyberbullying on the college campus. The ability of individuals to surreptitiously bully others via technology combined with results indicating 54 per cent of respondents knew someone who had been cyberbullied, and up to 34 per cent had been cyberbullied themselves, indicates a need for such research.

47   In addition, while the cyberbullying definition of Haber and Haber (2007) was utilized to initiate this research the authors feel the definition should evolve for future studies. Cyberbullying should be considered the use of interactive technologies such as social networking sites, cell phones (text, video, voice, or picture messaging), instant messaging, or other newly developed technology-based communication tools. These tools are used to deliberately and repeatedly deliver slanderous, harassing, obsessive, or obscene messages that *result* in harm to the recipient. It is only the individual

being harassed who can determine the extent of harm, whether the harasser intends to harm or not. This expanded definition may more readily provide counselors and other professionals the ability to intercede on behalf of the victim.

48   The academic college setting values the mature, eschewing the sophomoric behaviour of bullying,

but even the university is not safeguarded from cyberbullying in a technological age. Those concerned with the welfare of students need to keep abreast of their cyber troubles.

TechTrends. 2010. March/April 55 (2).

References

Beran, T., & Li, Q. (2005). Cyber-harassment: A study of a new method for an old behaviour [Electronic version]. *Journal of Educational Computing Research, 32*(3), 265–277.

Chapell, M., Casey, D., De la Cruz, C., Ferrell, J., Forman, J., Lipkin, R., Newsham, M., Sterling, M., & Whitaker, S. (2004) Bullying in university by students and teachers [Electronic Version]. *Adolescence, 39*, 53–64.

Chapell, M.S., Hasselman, S.L., Kitchin, T., Lomon, S.N., MacIver, K.W., & Sarullo, P.L. (2006) Bullying in elementary school, high school, and university [Electronic Version]. *Adolescence, 41* (164), 633–648.

CTIA (2009, June). *Wireless Quick Facts.* Retrieved from www.ctia.org/advocacy/research/index.cfm/ AID/10323

Dilmac, B. (2009). Psychological needs as a predictor of cyber bullying: A preliminary report on college students [Electronic Version]. *Educational Sciences: Theory & Practice, 9*(3), 1307–1325.

Facebook (2010). *Press Room.* Retrieved from www.facebook.com/press/info.php?statistics

Finn, J. (2004). A survey of online harassment at a university campus [Electronic Version]. *Journal of Interpersonal Violence, 19*(4), 468–481.

Haber, J.D. & Haber, S.B. (2007). Cyberbullying: A "virtual" camp nightmare? [Electronic Version]. *Camping Magazine, 80*, 52–57.

Juvonen, J. & Gross, E.F. (2008). Extending the school grounds? —Bullying experiences in cyberspace [Electronic Version]. *Journal of School Health, 78*(9), 496–505.

Li, Q. (2006). Cyberbullying in schools: A research of gender differences [Electronic Version]. *School Psychology International, 27*(2), 157–170.

Li, Q. (2007). New bottle but old wine: A research of cyberbullying in schools [Electronic Version]. *Computers In Human Behaviour, 23*, 1777–1791.

Pratto, F., Sidanius, J., & Levin, S. (2006) Social dominance theory and the dynamics of intergroup relations: Taking stock and looking forward [Electronic version]. *European Review of Social Psychology,* (17) 271–230.

Smith, R.G. & Gross, A.M. (2006). Bullying: Prevalence and the effect of age and gender [Electronic Version]. *Child & Family Behaviour, 28*, 13–37.

Spitzberg, B.H. & Hoobler, G. (2002) Cyberstalking and the technologies of interpersonal terrorism [Electronic Version]. *New Media & Society, 4*(1), 71–92.

Wikipedia (2010, January, 4). *Rickrolling.* Retrieved from http://en.wikipedia.org/wiki/Rickrolling

Ybarra, M.L., Diener-West, M., & Leaf, P.J. (2007). Examining the Overlap in Internet Harassment and School Bullying: Implications for School Intervention. *Journal of Adolescent Health, 41*, S42–S5.

Ybarra, M.L. & Mitchell, K.J. (2004). Online aggressor/targets, aggressors, targets: A comparison of associated youth characteristics [Electronic Version]. *Association for Child Psychology and Psychiatry, 45*(7), 1308–1.

KEY AND CHALLENGING WORDS

propagate, ideation, proliferation, delineate, surreptitious, dearth, eschew, sophomoric

QUESTIONS

1. Subdivide the introductory section (paragraphs 1–15) into three or four subdivisions with appropriate descriptive headings for each subsection.

2. In paragraphs 5–6, the authors attempt to define cyberbullying: a) Do you believe they successfully distinguish between cyberbullying, cyberharassment, and cyberstalking? b) Which of these is most relevant to their

study? c) Why is it important that the term is defined as precisely as possible?

3. Briefly summarize the two most relevant studies, including their purposes and results.

4. In your own words, define "legitimizing myths" (paragraphs 11–12). How could Social Dominance Theory and legitimizing myths be especially important in cyberbullying?

5. Why do you think the authors express their thesis in the form of questions rather than as hypotheses? (See paragraph 15.)

6. What can you infer about the importance of the IRB [Institutional Review Board] review? Why do you think such a review would be necessary before the experiment proceeded?

7. What was the purpose of the pilot study (paragraph 20)? Specifically, how did the pilot study affect the 27-item survey used in the study?

8. In the "Discussion" section of Type B essays, the authors often compare their results with those of other studies: a) Identify one study that yielded results consistent with those of the present study; b) Identity one study that yielded different results and explain in your own words how the authors account for the difference.

9. In paragraphs 41 and 46, the authors state that "up to 34 per cent" of undergraduates in the study have experienced cyberbullying. How can this figure be considered consistent with the results given in paragraph 29 and in Table 3? Discuss its possible significance for future research.

POST-READING

1. *Collaborative activity:* Using brainstorming, come up with a realistic and practical definition of "cyberbullying." You may use elements of the definitions mentioned in the essay, but it must be different from these and should not exceed 50 words. Groups could then exchange their definition with another group's or share with the class to come up with a consensus on what constitutes cyberbullying.

2. *Collaborative or individual activity:* How can cyberbullying best be addressed at the university level? Could intervention strategies be used? If so, which ones might be most useful? Write a 400–500-word proposal that outlines the need for such strategies. Your audience should be a university funding body, either a real or made-up one.

3. In the "Results" and, particularly, the "Discussion" sections, the authors suggest several directions for future research. Take one of these suggestions and come up with two central questions or hypotheses that could be used to extend the findings of the current study.

4. Access two Canadian anti-bullying websites and compare them, using at least two of the criteria mentioned on pp. 146–147 for evaluating websites. Your analysis should be 500–750 words.

RELATED WEBSITES OF INTEREST

Bullying Prevention: Nature and Extent of Bullying in Canada:
www.publicsafety.gc.ca/res/cp/res/2008-bp-01-eng.aspx
—includes links to related sites.

PrevNet:
www.prevnet.ca/Home/tabid/36/Default.aspx

BullyingCanada:
www.bullyingcanada.ca/

University wars: The corporate administration vs. the vocation of learning

John McMurtry

(2,561 words)

Pre-reading

1. Unlike most of the other readings in this textbook, this essay is from a periodical published by an independent research institute. After scanning the article, write a brief paragraph considering at least two ways it differs from other readings, such as the one before and after it. Go to the institute's home page and read the brief introduction at www.policyalternatives. ca/offices; then, summarize this information in a couple of sentences.

1   For over 20 years, the academy has undergone a cumulative subordination of the university to corporate-market methods and appropriation of educational funds by central administrations overriding academic standards. This "internal assault on academic freedom" warned of by the Canadian Association of University Teachers (CAUT) has deepened and widened in both visible and invisible ways.

2   The occupation of the academy by a corporate agenda forwarded by university central administrations themselves has been analyzed by Howard Woodhouse in his forthcoming book, *Selling Out: Academic Freedom and the Corporate Market.* Yet tracking of this corporate invasion of the academy leads back to what is not yet confronted: the unaccountable right of central administrations to spend public money on their own growth, privileges, and salaries instead of the constitutional objectives of the university: the advancement of learning and the dissemination of knowledge. University presidents who once received a faculty member's salary with a modest stipend now arrange with their business-dominated boards to have incomes exceeding the prime minister's, while raising tuition fees for students to unaffordable levels.

3   In historical fact, university presidents deliberately planned with corporate executives to defund the universities *"to provide a greater incentive in the university community to seek out corporate partners,"* as Howard Buchbinder and Janice Newson put it in their 1991 paper, "Social Knowledge and Market Knowledge." This early strategy was planned by the Corporate Higher Education Forum (CHEF), founded in 1983 to join 25 university presidents to 25 senior executives of major corporations in setting the "new direction" for universities. Most academics were and are so caught up in their career microworlds that they did not recognize what was going on.

4   "Bring your knowledge to market" is the master slogan of the corporate occupation. As one professor promoted to deputy minister of education, and then to head of a major national research granting council declared: "I contend that the one global object of education must be for the people of Ontario to develop new services which we can offer in trade in the world market." To this Paul Martin, our next

Prime Minister, added that "tripling of the commercialization of university research is not nearly fast enough."

5   The underlying contradiction in purpose and method between the market's private exchanges for money and the university's public commitment to advanced learning is not yet realized, even as low-paid sessional teachers replacing normal faculty carry more and more of university teaching loads and as salaries for corporate management escalate. University presidents now conceive themselves as corporate CEOs; research is increasingly only possible with outside money backing it; campuses are ever more pervasively occupied by corporate ads, brands and products; multinational corporations control the academic journal and textbook system across borders; and students are cumulatively made into debt-slaves to banks.

6   Few seem to observe that the ongoing financial marketization has led the rest of the world to ecological, social, and economic collapse; nor the coincidence of this profile with the academy as its knowledge servant. Even less do corporate administrations notice the contradiction of values between the academy's purpose of critical search for truth and the university's stripping down to a commercial venture. As Ursula Franklin has memorably said from her own experience of the 1930s era of Nazi Germany in Europe and the corporatizing academy today: "They had their collaborators, and we have ours."

*

7   The control of all knowledge that corporations can copyright or patent is a given of the global market, but it systematically contradicts the university's freedom of dissemination of knowledge. Consider how academic journals have become copyright-controlled by private corporations' buying up the journals, and then multiplying the prices for their purchase and use by university libraries, whose own faculties have created the material for no cost to the corporations. Indeed, there is a standard copyright form required to be signed by faculty authors whose work is produced and refereed free for these corporately-owned journals, which demand exclusive world copyright in perpetuity for no returns to the university or the author.

8   Thus the public, the students, and the universities pay for faculties to research and publish and for all the university resources to support them, while private corporations buy the vehicles of publication to sell them back to the university communities that have created them at staggering prices that beggar libraries themselves. The academy's freedom of knowledge dissemination is thus reversed, but university administrators and funders increasingly press for still more commercialization of university knowledge creation.

9   In the global market as a whole, the inner logic of value adding is to turn money into more money for money managers and possessors, appropriating ever more money command for themselves. Corporate university administrations have been an unidentified fifth column of imposing this meta-program on universities. They lead privatization of the knowledge commons, the casualization and low pay of teaching positions, escalation of student costs, commodification of university spaces and functions, and—in general—streaming ever more university income into their corporate hierarchy of pay, privileges and positions performing no teaching or research functions.

10   There are five properties by which we can recognize corporate administrations:

1. They have exclusive hierarchical signing control of all financial expenditures, their ultimate lever of control mystified as their "leadership."
2. They do not perform the constitutional goals and primary functions of the academy: to advance learning and disseminate knowledge.
3. They draw off ever more of the academy's financial and physical resources to multiply their positions and incomes.
4. They call themselves "the university" although they perform no function of advancing or disseminating learning.
5. They selectively gang-attack faculty members for anti-academic reasons (as Professor Ken Westhues valuably describes in his book, *The Envy of Excellence: Administrative Mobbing of High-achieving Professors*).

11   At present, we may most deeply understand the university wars of corporate administration versus the learning vocation by laying bare their opposite

structures of rationality, method, and purpose. Corporate administrators and their retinues follow the global market program of *i)* self-maximizing strategies in *ii)* conditions of scarcity, or conflict over *iii)* desired payoffs at *iv)* minimum costs for the self to *v)* appropriate ever more for the self with no productive contribution.

12   In direct opposition, those in the learning vocation follow an opposite inner value code: *i)* to maximize learning advancement and dissemination by *ii)* knowledge sharing without limit for *iii)* understanding and truth as ultimate value in itself at *iv)* any cost of difficulty to *v)* develop humanity's more inclusive comprehension of natural and human phenomena.

13   We can directly see corporate administrations warring against the learning vocation by an onslaught of anti-learning practices. Corporate research displaces independent science; knowledge sharing is prohibited by contract and specialty lock-in; research is made dependent on external money received by faculty; every decision is increasingly financialized with money gain the supreme value; and, to fortify the powers to impose marketization, those who follow the search for truth where it leads against the ruling value program are besieged by bureaucratic campaigns of anti-educative isolation and destruction of academic freedom—for example, inciting students to formal complaint, publishing personal attacks, closing off academic resources, and perhaps, as in the case of Professor Denis Rancourt of the University of Ottawa, CEO banning from campus, handcuffing and firing.

*

14   To get a sense of the academy's increasing submergence in corporate-market values, consider the words of the past Harvard President, Larry Summers, now chief economic adviser to the Obama administration. He was interviewed by the *Globe and Mail* in glowing admiration after a lecture in 2003 at University of Toronto. "The essential truth," he declared, is that all "basic value"—including "literacy"—is "linked to market growth."

15   We may formalize the equation of the paradigmatic corporate president as follows: More/less money-value sales = more/less market growth = more/less "basic values" for the world. No substantiation of the given equations is deemed necessary. No explanation of contra-indicative evidence is conceived. Yet mind-numbing implications follow. Whatever is without a market price is therefore without any value—the world's biodiversity of species, for example. Life itself is of no value except as it sells for a market price. So, too, research and knowledge. If they are not marketable, they do not exist.

16   *The New York Times* recently gave much page and blog space to Stanley Fish, an academic servant to money and power as Allan Bloom before him. In his tirade against academics following "the inner light," Fish defended the use of coercive force against them. Indeed, he said that coercion was required. Professors need to be reduced to a master–servant relationship with "their employer," the same as all other employees: that is, with university CEOs and designates who hire and fire by unilateral control of the purse-strings with no ultimate accountability to academic standards.

17   When it is believed that academics' work is at the leading edge of the "global knowledge economy," none ask what the criterion of "knowledge" is. There is none, except what reduces money costs and increases money revenues for money managers and possessors. That is what "accountability" means in this value system. Thus teaching comes to mean only what produces graduates who make more money in the global market than they would without their degree, with ever higher tuition fees as the cost of acquiring and selling their skills at a higher price. At the same time, selling campus grounds as marketing sites follows from the same money-value program: corporate ads, junk foods, and market franchises invading space and sightlines across university schools, buildings, lecture halls, and courses.

18   Consider corporate-partner research. Here university researchers must find projects that corporations are willing to fund. Independent research in the public interest that is most urgently required is thus silently selected out—for example, in the agricultural sciences, integrated pest management, organic farming for productive efficiency, management-intensive grazing, small-scale producer cooperatives, and alternatives to factory-processed livestock and avoidance of ecological contamination

by genetically-engineered commodities. According to organic farming research leader Professor Ann Clark, who has long been persecuted and ostracized by factory-farm colleagues and agribusiness administrators at the University of Guelph, "the end of the historical role of governments in supporting impartial agricultural science was brought about by corporate-partnerships [because] non-proprietary research of the sort that benefits everyone is of no interest to industry sponsors."

19   In the humanities, too, corporate administrations require that professors bring in money from outside the university to defray the costs of their student's graduate education, or they cannot have graduate students. Educational costs are thus downloaded onto faculty themselves, who are forced to become funding entrepreneurs. Those not competing successfully at getting grants have no graduate students, and may lose their jobs. Faculty are generally so wound up in getting the grant money that they do not think about the structural undermining of independent research and academic freedom in the university, as well as in their own work. The result is more effective than direct censorship control. Either faculty get money committed from private corporations which are structured to repel any finding against their interests, or they lose their lab space. Either they bring money into administrations' revenues from a government or private funding body, or their research and graduate students are shut off. A silent rule of gagging prevails. *Nothing that does not payoff in more money to administrations is supported within the corporate university.*

20   The ultimate assault on the university's vocation lies at the level of truth-seeking itself. The university is constitutionally committed to critically reasoned inquiry which goes wherever the quest for truth leads it. The truth is not an end state, but an open process in which partialities are continually exposed by thinking through deep assumptions, evidence, and connections. This thinking through is the nature of learning and knowledge. Reason's movement is always by a more inclusive taking into coherent account open to counterevidence and argument, the inner logic of all disciplines—from the problem of self and other in philosophy, to the nature of tropes in literature, to the hypotheses of subatomic waves and particles in physics. In one way or another,

the critical search for more comprehensively coherent understanding leads the academy in every domain and the human condition itself. Deprived of the freedom to pursue truth independent of external money added to administration funds, the academy's learning vocation is systematically blocked. Academic excellence now means what gets more money coming in.

21   The known standard of research to guard against conflict of interest and cooked results is straightforward. *Any research in which the funder has a financial stake in the outcome is a conflict of interest which must be ruled out.* Yet this standard of research independence and validity has been usurped by the centre. For example, when a "research integrity" clause was explicitly specified on two occasions by decision of the Medical Research Council of Canada, it was annulled with no justification. If universities are not to be so subordinated to such political control, a research integrity condition must be instituted on campuses to protect higher research from conflicts of interest and corporately cooked science. Just as research biased by conflict of interest must be stopped, so too must be making graduate student supervision dependent on external revenues captured by faculty. Faculty dependency on outside money determines the topics and direction of faculty research. Thus, solicitous grantmanship and academic fads supplant original and critical inquiry. This structural violation of academic freedom, however, is taboo to discuss for fear of offending the granting authorities. Yet one has to wonder: why have the most self-evident defences of the academy's research integrity been so easily overridden by corporate administrations? Why have faculty and faculty organizations submitted to these assaults on academic integrity and freedom? The answer is that a collective academic presence on campus has been lacking. This is why an independent Faculty Board of Academic Review (or Academic Freedom) needs to bring active scholars across disciplines into one independent body on every university campus to review all administrative decisions so as to ensure against financially-led distortions and depredations of research and teaching—including by arbitrary administrative cuts of courses to claw back money to inflated executive revenue siphons serving no academic function.

22   Cuts must begin at the top, and campus-based faculty associations and unions must in the end be willing to strike for protection of the university's learning objectives against their system-wide violations by corporate administrations. At the same time, such a faculty academic review body needs to institute policy-by-policy identification and ranking of the performance of local central administrations, including so-called academic senates and like bodies whose terms of reference are financially dictated from the centre and vote-loaded by ex-officio members.

23   A Faculty Board of Academic Review needs also to press hard specifically for ceilings on ballooned salaries as an item of faculty negotiations: for starter norms, no administrative salary higher than the provincial premier's, and no faculty salary more than $120,000 to bring balance back into the gross money-class divisions which have grown ever deeper in the corporate university. Once the facts on the systematic misallocation of public education funds on anti-educative salaries, privileges and offices are flushed into the open, they will not be accepted by the public. Those in the university who follow more money as their ruling goal are then free to leave the academy where they do not belong. The vocation of the academy is the advancement of higher learning by academic freedom, but the mission has been usurped.

CCPA Monitor. 2009. July/August 16 (3).

KEY AND CHALLENGING WORDS

fifth column, casualization, hierarchical, substantiation, unilateral, solicitous

QUESTIONS

1. Identify three words or phrases in the first paragraph that reveal the writer's argumentative tone. What audience is this essay written for?

2. Identify the thesis statement. What is the writer's argumentative purpose?

3. Although citations aren't given, as they are in scholarly journal articles, the essay does include specific names of professors, politicians, and writers. Choose one of the following names and use a reliable source to find out about the individual and his/her importance to the essay itself: Ursula Franklin (paragraph 6); Ken Westhues (paragraph 10); Stanley Fish (paragraph 16).

4. In paragraph 11, the writer outlines the "opposite structures of rationality, method, and purpose" that characterize "corporate administration versus the learning vocation." Paraphrase the sentences that contrast the two positions, according to McMurtry. (You could set it up in chart form in which two columns represent the two sides and the rows represent the corresponding points.)

5. McMurtry includes direct quotation from several people with whom he disagrees. In general, do you think this is an effective strategy? Using one such quotation, analyze its effectiveness.

6. Who does the author primarily blame for the situation he criticizes at universities? Does he believe others are also accountable to some degree? Refer to specific passages.

7. In a brief paragraph, explain what you consider the author's strongest, most effective point. In another brief paragraph, explain what you consider his least effective point.

POST-READING

1. *Collaborative activity:* a) In groups, discuss the accuracy or validity of McMurtry's thesis; b) Consider how corporate relationships between university administrators and business could affect or have affected you as a student.

2. Do you think the money for research derived through corporate sponsorship is essentially a bad thing or a good thing? Defend your point of view.

RELATED WEBSITE OF INTEREST

Higher Education Public Forum:
http://www.highereducationforum.net/

ADDITIONAL LIBRARY READING

Newsome, J. (1998). The corporate-linked university: From social project to market force. *Canadian Journal of Communication, 23*(1), 107–124.

Universities, governments and industry: Can the essential nature of universities survive the drive to commercialize?

Simon N. Young

(2,622 words)

Pre-reading

1.   Based on the essay's title, come up with a reading hypothesis of two sentences that includes a) the kind of essay to follow (i.e., argumentative or expository) and b) the author's thesis. Do not use any major words from the title.

---

1   Having spent 40 years in universities, I have had sufficient time to consider some of the idiosyncrasies, foibles, and problems of these academic institutions. The purpose of this editorial is to discuss the current state of university research and explain why I find some aspects of the current situation disturbing. Changes that started during the second half of the twentieth century and that have continued into the twenty-first threaten to bring about fundamental changes in the nature of universities. Some of the changes are commendable, for example, the large expansion in the proportion of the population

attending universities, at least in the richer nations. Other trends are disturbing, especially the increasing tendency of governments and industry to view universities as engines for short-term economic gain. While universities certainly cannot ignore the context in which they function and the needs of society, responding purely to short-term economic considerations threatens to subvert the very nature of universities and some of the benefits they provide to society.

2   So what exactly is a university, and what is its purpose? I much prefer the *Oxford English Dictionary* definition of the word "university" to some of the more utilitarian definitions in other dictionaries. The Oxford definition reads, in part, "whole body of teachers and scholars engaged in the higher branches of learning." Thus, it is the community of faculty and students that is the essence of a university. The higher branches of learning in which teachers and scholars engage have two important products: the educated minds that are essential for the well-being of society and new knowledge and ideas. Some of that new knowledge will enrich society by producing economic growth, directly or indirectly, but the benefits of new knowledge go far beyond economic gain.

3   Universities have always been subjected to outside influences. The oldest European university, the University of Bologna, has existed at least since the 1080s. Some time before 1222, about 1,000 students left Bologna and founded a new university in Padua because of "the grievous offence that was brought to bear on their academic liberties and the failure to acknowledge the privileges solemnly granted to teachers and students."[1] The outside interference came from the Roman Catholic Church, and for several centuries, Padua was home to the only university in Europe where non-Catholics could get a university education. Both Bologna and Padua were student-controlled universities with students electing the professors and fixing their salaries. However, in spite of marked differences, there are similarities between what happened then and what is happening today, with important outside influences—then the dogma of religion, now the dogma of business—threatening to change the activities of the community of teachers and scholars.

4   The seeds of what is happening now were sown in the years following World War II. Before the war, the most important influence on a faculty member was probably the departmental chair, who in those days had power to influence in an important way what went on in the department. Nonetheless, a faculty member would have had access to departmental resources and would not necessarily have required outside research funding (although such funding was sometimes available from private foundations). The mechanism of funding research, and the amount of money available for research, changed greatly in the postwar years. In 1945, Vannevar Bush's landmark report to President Harry Truman, *Science the endless frontier,*[2] had an important influence on university research. In this report, Bush stated, "The publicly and privately supported colleges, universities, and research institutes are the centres of basic research. They are the wellsprings of knowledge and understanding. As long as they are vigorous and healthy and their scientists are free to pursue the truth wherever it may lead, there will be a flow of new scientific knowledge to those who can apply it to practical problems in Government, in industry, or elsewhere." Bush supported the idea that the US government should provide strong financial support for university research but also supported the idea that the individual investigator should be the main determinant of the topics for investigation, with statements such as "Scientific progress on a broad front results from the free play of free intellects, working on subjects of their own choice, in the manner dictated by their curiosity for exploration of the unknown."[2]

5   In the latter half of the last century, many countries adopted the model of granting councils, which used a system based on peer review to distribute money for investigator-initiated research. This model has been a great success, but it has also contributed to important changes in universities. Much more money has been available to support medical research, basic science research, and engineering research than has been available for the social sciences or arts. Thus, decisions about support for different disciplines devolved from the universities to governments, who decided on the budgets of their various grant-giving bodies. Also, individual researchers who were successful in obtaining grants no longer depended as much on departmental facilities. In my opinion, this not only weakened the power of departmental chairs but also decreased collegiality within departments.

6   With increased enrolments, as a university education became accessible to a greater proportion of the population, and an increased need for infrastructure for the larger student population and for complex research equipment, administrators became more concerned about sources of funding and consequently more detached from the faculty. There is always a tendency for senior academic administrators to speak and behave as though they *were* the university (when of course they are there to serve the community of teachers and scholars). This is of course a normal human trait, no different from the tendency of politicians to forget that they are elected to serve the people. However, this increasing detachment of senior university administrators from the faculty has facilitated the erosion of collegiality within departments and universities. The individual personalities of university faculty probably also facilitated this change. I learned recently, when looking at the literature on personality, that an inverse correlation between intelligence and conscientiousness has been demonstrated in a number of studies (see, for example, Moutafi et al[3]). Thus, it might be more than just my paranoia leading me to believe that the small proportion of university faculty who lack conscientiousness and collegiality is larger than in some other walks of life. The erosion of collegiality is not a matter of great significance, except that it probably played a role in making researchers more open to the efforts of governments to transform them into entrepreneurs.

7   The most recent and possibly the most important change in university research resulted from the push by governments to commercialize the results of such research. In the United States, the Bayh-Dole Act of 1980 encouraged universities to license to private industry discoveries made with federal funds.[4] The push by governments for commercialization of new knowledge grew during the 1980s and 1990s and continues to have an important influence on universities. Recently, Lord Sainsbury, the science and innovation minister in the United Kingdom, boasted that there had been a cultural change in universities there, which has resulted in a substantial increase in university spin-offs.[5] In 2002 the Association of Universities and Colleges of Canada entered an agreement with the government to double the amount of research performed by these institutions and to triple their commercialization performance by 2010.[6] Although this agreement was reached in the absence of any broad consultation with the faculty who are supposed to commercialize their work, the universities seem to be well on track to achieve this objective, with a 126 per cent increase in revenues from licence royalties between 1999 and 2001.[7] Most major universities now have a technology transfer office, and at many universities success in commercialization is taken into account when faculty are considered for tenure. Will there come a time when success in commercialization carries the same weight as (or more weight than) teaching and research in the awarding of tenure?

8   The end result of all the changes discussed above is that individual faculty members have become much more like entrepreneurs whose main allegiance is to the maintenance or growth of their own research programs and not infrequently to the commercialization of their research. The researcher exploring Vannevar Bush's "endless frontier" could be considered the modern equivalent of the homesteader taming the seemingly endless frontier of the nineteenth-century American West.[8] This is not necessarily detrimental if a new generation of university research entrepreneurs provides the new knowledge that will benefit patients and society. However, the change in culture that made university faculty more like entrepreneurs also made them more open to the desire of governments to make them entrepreneurs in the economic sense. Although the nature of universities has been changing, there was no threat to the fundamental nature of universities until the drive for commercialization began.

9   A recent report of the Canadian Association of University Teachers[9] states that university administrators have been "building increasingly hierarchical management structures" that "place the future of academic medicine in danger." The report's main concern is that "incentives to create commercializable products push economic concerns, rather than scientific and ethical considerations, to the forefront."[9] In the fields of biologic psychiatry and behavioural neuroscience, the emphasis on commercial applications has already, to some extent, moved research priorities away from an emphasis on mental well-being to an emphasis on commercial products. There are many examples of this shift. For example, more research is being carried out

on antidepressant drugs than on psychotherapy, even though in mild to moderate depression (the majority of cases) drugs and psychotherapy are approximately equal in efficacy. There is increasing evidence for the efficacy of exercise[10,11] and fish oils[12,13] in the treatment and prevention of depression. However, these strategies receive much less attention than antidepressant drugs. Even an established antidepressant treatment such as S-adenosylmethionine (SAMe)[14] receives little attention. Searching the abstracts of the 2004 meeting of the Society for Neuroscience, I found 179 with the keyword "antidepressant" and only four with the keyword "S-adenosylmethionine," and none of those four was concerned with the antidepressant action of SAMe. SAMe is a major methyl donor and seems to work in a fundamentally different way from any product being investigated by drug companies. Surely we could expect that an antidepressant acting through a different mechanism would be a popular topic of investigation. However, SAMe is a natural product and not of commercial interest. Similarly, insights into what exercise or fish oils do to the brain may provide important insights into the pathophysiology of depression and its treatment, but these subjects receive little attention.

10   Many basic science researchers investigating the mechanisms of antidepressants produced by drug companies do not receive funding from those companies. However, enough are lured by drug company research funds into working on topics of interest to the companies to significantly influence what are fashionable topics of research. Laboratories with funding from industry can often afford more trainees, who may then adopt a more industry-centred approach in their own research. While the availability of funds from industry has certainly influenced research, the pressure on university faculty to commercialize the results of their research will undoubtedly cause even greater distortion in the areas of research that are most popular.

11   Granting agencies have increasingly tried to foster research in neglected areas by allocating funds to specific areas of research and requesting applications in those areas. Although this approach is certainly necessary, it has not done much to alter the effects of drug company money on research output. Also, in some ways it moves research even further

away from the ideal in Vannevar Bush's report that "Scientific progress on a broad front results from the free play of free intellects, working on subjects of their own choice, in the manner dictated by their curiosity for exploration of the unknown."[2] This model was notably successful in the last half of the twentieth century, but it may not survive the pressure to commercialize. While there is still much scope for curiosity-driven research, the curiosity of researchers is likely to be aligned increasingly with the interests of drug companies. As mentioned above, a cultural change has accompanied the increasing commercialization of university research. The pressure to commercialize has been critiqued in some quarters, but many university faculty have nonetheless embraced commercialization or at least remained unconcerned about it. Are we far from a time when a researcher without a patent that is being commercialized will be regarded in the same way as those who do not publish regularly in the top journals? And how long will it be before governments make commercialization a mandate of granting councils and a requirement for the majority of grants?

12   A fascination with the workings of the brain and how it can malfunction in mental illness is the usual motivator for researchers in neuroscience and psychiatry research. As a result, curiosity-driven research will always tend to serve the best interests of patients. Although research driven by commercial interests will certainly benefit psychiatric patients in some ways, it cannot serve their overall needs, as it is much too narrowly focused. The designation of funds by granting agencies for specific neglected topics will help but is unlikely to produce any large changes in the direction of research. Thus, the biggest losers from the pressure to commercialize will be psychiatric patients. In addition, I am concerned whether students who are trained to focus on the short-term commercial implications of their research will be able to maintain the breadth of vision that is a characteristic of the majority of creative researchers.

13   Changes due to pressure from governments to commercialize are not limited to researchers. The increased emphasis on commercialization in universities has in some ways distorted the perceptions of senior university administrators about the purpose of the institutions. For example, there seems to be a lack

of concern about some of the sources of funds that universities receive. Universities now hold patents on many life-saving drugs. These patents sometimes limit access to the drugs, particularly in low-income countries.[15] In Canada, one-quarter of the faculties of medicine receive funding from the tobacco industry.[16] Perhaps a suitable future definition of a university will be a "whole body of teachers and scholars engaged in turning ideas into profit."

14   In thirteenth-century Italy, the response to interference by the Roman Catholic Church in the work of scholars was a move to another location to escape the interference. In the twenty-first century, that option is not available even to the minority who are concerned about the drive to commercialize. However, the picture is not entirely bleak. Charitable foundations will remain immune to commercial interests. In addition, even though charitable foundations will probably remain relatively small players in the funding of research, there are promising signs. For example, the Bill and Melinda Gates Foundation, created in 2000, has an endowment of about US$27 billion and is striving to use its money for the benefit of humankind in areas neglected by governments. This foundation is not involved in psychiatric research, but its focus on preventive approaches may help to direct interest to that important area. Research on prevention in psychiatry is still in its infancy and will certainly remain that way if short-term commercial considerations stay paramount. However, charitable foundations cannot be expected to have any large effect on the change in university culture brought about by the drive to commercialize. Although I would like to be able to end this editorial on a more hopeful note, I am concerned about these cultural changes, and I do not see any solution. Still, one lesson from history is that the communities of teachers and scholars making up universities have adapted to many changes over the centuries without changing the fundamental nature of universities, and they will surely continue to do so. I am just not sure how.

Journal of Psychiatry & Neuroscience. 2005. 30 (3).

References

1. *History.* Padua (Italy): Università Degli Studi di Padova. Available: www.unipd.it/en/university/ history.htm (accessed 2004 Dec 13).
2. Bush V. *Science the endless frontier. A report to the President by Vannevar Bush, Director of the Office of Scientific Research and Development, July 1945.* Washington: US Government Printing Office; 1945. Available: www.nsf.gov/ od/lpa/ nsf50/vbush1945.htm (accessed 2004 Dec 13).
3. Moutafi J, Furnham A, Paltiel L. Why is conscientiousness negatively correlated with intelligence? *Pers Individ Differ* 2004;37:1013–22.
4. Thursby JG, Thursby MC. Intellectual property. University licensing and the Bayh-Dole Act. Science 2003;301:1052.
5. Sainsbury L. A cultural change in UK universities [editorial]. *Science* 2002;296:1929.
6. Allan Rock welcomes framework on federally funded university research [press release]. Toronto: Industry Canada; 2002 Nov 19[modified 2003 Jun 16]. Available: www.ic. gc.ca/cmb/welcomeic.nsf/558d6365909929 4285256488005215 5b/85256a220056c2a 485256c76004c7d44 (accessed 2004 Dec 13).
7. Berkowitz P. Spinning off research: AUCC sets new tool to measure universities' commercialization performance. *Univ Aff* [serial on-line] 2004;June/July. Available: www. universityaffairs.ca/issues/2004/junejuly/ print/spinning-off.html (accessed 2004 Dec 13).
8. Kennedy D. Enclosing the research commons [editorial]. *Science* 2001;294:2249.
9. Welch P, Cass CE, Guyatt G, Jackson AC, Smith D. *Defending medicine: clinical faculty and academic freedom.* Report of the Canadian Association of University Teachers (CAUT) Task Force on Academic Freedom for Faculty at University-Affiliated Health Care Institutions. Ottawa: Canadian Association of University Teachers; 2004 Nov. Available: www.caut.ca/en/issues/academic freedom/ DefendingMedicine.pdf (accessed 2004 Dec 21).
10. Salmon P. Effects of physical exercise on anxiety, depression, and sensitivity to stress: a unifying theory. *Clin Psychol Rev* 2001; 21:33–61.
11. *Depression: management of depression in primary and secondary care.* Clinical guideline 23. London (UK): National Institute for Clinical Excellence; 2004 Dec. Available: www.nice.org.uk/pdf/CG023NICEguideline.pdf (accessed 2005 Mar 8).
12. Nemets B, Stahl Z, Belmaker RH. Addition of omega-3 fatty acid to maintenance medication treatment for recurrent unipolar depressive disorder. *Am J Psychiatry* 2002; 159:477–9.
13. Su KP, Huang SY, Chiu CC, Shen WW. Omega-3 fatty acids in major depressive disorder. A preliminary double-blind, placebo controlled trial. Eur *Neuropsychopharmacol* 2003;13:267–71.
14. Papakostas GI, Alpert JE, Fava M. S-Adenosyl-methionine in depression: a comprehensive review of the literature. *Curr Psychiatry Rep* 2003;5:460–6.
15. Kapczynski A, Crone ET, Merson M. Global health and university patents [editorial]. *Science* 2003;301:1629.
16. Kaufman PE, Cohen JE, Ashley MJ, Ferrence R, Halyak AI, Turcotte F, et al. Tobacco industry links to faculties of medicine in Canada. *Can J Public Health* 2004; 95:205–8.

KEY AND CHALLENGING WORDS

dogma, collegiality, infrastructure

QUESTIONS

1. Explain why it is important for Young to define the common word "university" in paragraph 2.
2. Do you believe that the comparison in paragraph 3 between what happened at Italian universities before 1222 and what is occurring at today's universities is valid? Why or why not?
3. Name two negative consequences that resulted from adoption of the "model of granting councils" in the second half of the twentieth century.
4. Analyze paragraph 9. Among the factors you could consider are the method(s) of development (rhetorical patterns), the kinds of support, and the writer's credibility.
5. Who does Young believe will ultimately be most affected if research in neuroscience and psychiatry research continues to be "driven by commercial interests?"

6. Comment on the author's use of *two* argumentative strategies in the essay (see pp. 124–125): a) establishing common ground with the reader; b) making concessions to the other side; c) using an emotional appeal; or d) appealing to reader interests.
7. Could Young have ended his editorial more positively or assertively than he did? Does the concluding paragraph add or detract from the strength of the essay?
8. Would you say that Young's main purpose is (a) to expose a problem, (b) to change a situation, (c) to critique a position, or (d) to reach a compromise? How might his audience affect his purpose?

POST-READING

1. *Collaborative activity:* As students who may be going on to intensive undergraduate work or perhaps graduate school, are you concerned about the increasing ties of university research to commercial interests? How do you think it could affect you or students like you in the next few years?
2. *Collaborative activity:* It is well known that substantially more money is given today to research in science, engineering, and medicine than to research in the arts. Do you think this allocation is inevitable? Do you think it is fair? Do you believe that students, administrators, or society should be concerned about the possible consequences to arts programs throughout the country?

3. Reflect on the idea of a "student-controlled university" (see paragraph 3). Write up a one- to two-page proposal in which you urge your government to finance such a university. In your proposal, you should outline the need for the project, along with goals and objectives, and provide a few specific features of such a university.
4. Write a rhetorical analysis in which you compare this essay with John McMurtry, "University wars: The corporate administration vs. the vocation of learning," p. 191. Establish two or three bases of comparison (see p. 87), at least one of which pertains to the effectiveness of each author's argument.

Heavy drinking on Canadian campuses

Louis Gliksman, PhD, Edward M. Adlaf, PhD, Andrée Demers, PhD, and
Brenda Newton-Taylor, MA

(2,189 words)

Pre-reading

1. Scan the abstract and introduction in order to get more information about the study's approach and focus than what is available from the title.
2. Note that the authors acknowledge the Brewers Association of Canada for its partial funding. Why might this association be interested in the study's outcome? Do you believe that this funding could affect the study's credibility in any way?
3. Reflect on 1) the problem of drinking on your university campus. Does it affect you or people you know? Does your university have a policy on drinking? 2) possible solutions to the problem.

Abstract

Objective: To describe the prevalence and frequency of heavy drinking episodes among Canadian undergraduates.

Methods: Data are drawn from the Canadian Campus Survey, a national mail survey, conducted in the fall of 1998, with a random sample of 7,800 students from 16 universities.

Results: Overall, 62.7 per cent and 34.8 per cent of students reported consuming five or more drinks and eight or more drinks, respectively, on a single occasion at least once during the fall semester. On average, drinkers reported having five or more drinks almost five times during the fall semester, and having eight or more drinks almost twice during the same period. The groups reporting the highest rates of heavy drinking were males, those living in university residences, those with low academic orientation, and those with high recreational orientation.

Interpretation: Generally, this study has shown that heavy drinking is highly engrained in Canadian undergraduates' drinking patterns, and is related to a number of factors. These factors can be used to develop targeted prevention efforts.

*

1   One of the most salient public health issues confronting college campuses is the consequences of heavy drinking, traditionally defined as consuming five or more drinks in a single drinking occasion.[1] In addition to alcohol intoxication, these consequences include motor vehicle crashes, high-risk sexual behaviour, and poor academic performance.[2-6] In addition, heavy drinking on campus affects non-drinkers as well as drinkers.[7,8]

2   The epidemiological knowledge regarding heavy drinking in the US is longstanding, but the history of such studies in Canada is recent, sparse, and regionalized,[9-12] and no study has been conducted nationally. This paper will describe the prevalence and frequency of heavy drinking among a nationally representative sample of Canadian undergraduates and assess the character of subgroup differences related to key demographic and campus lifestyle factors.

Method

3   The 1998 Canadian Campus Survey (CCS) is the first Canadian survey conducted nationally to assess alcohol and other drug use among university

students.[13] The CCS employed a stratified two-stage cluster selection of undergraduates enrolled in full-time studies at accredited universities during the 1998–9 academic year. The sample was stratified equally according to five regions: British Columbia, Prairies, Ontario, Québec, and Atlantic provinces. Four universities per region were selected with probability-proportional to size (i.e., larger universities had a higher probability of selection than smaller universities) for all regions except BC, which sampled all four universities with certainty. In total, 23 universities (including three randomly selected replacements) were approached for their participation, of which 16 agreed to participate. Within each university, 1,000 students were randomly selected with equal probability. Sixteen thousand questionnaires were mailed, of which 15,188 were deemed eligible mailings. A total of 7,800 eligible and useable completions, representing about 442,000 Canadian undergraduates, were returned, for a 51 per cent student cooperation rate. Mean student cooperation rates varied from 42 per cent to 64 per cent by university and from 46 per cent (Ontario) to 59 per cent (Québec) by region. Table I, which displays the number of respondents and the weighted percentages, also indicates that the weighted distributions closely approximate the Canadian undergraduate population for key variables.

Measures

4   Our outcome variable, heavy drinking episode, is represented by the percentage and frequency of consuming five or more drinks (*5-plus*) and eight or more drinks (*8-plus*) on a single occasion "since September," an eight to 12-week period. This timeframe was intended to capture any drinking occasions occurring on or off campus since the student began the 1998–9 academic year.

5   These outcomes were examined relative to seven independent variables. Sex was represented by a binary measure (male=1). The five regional categories (BC, Prairies, Ontario, Québec, and Atlantic) were represented by four effect-coded dummy variables. Living arrangement was represented by two dummy variables (university residence and off campus without

parents or family) versus living at home with parents. The four categories of year of study were represented by three dummy variables (second through fourth years) versus first year. Year of study was chosen over age since it provides more campus-relevant risk factor information. Recreational orientation was based on the perceived importance of being involved in three activities (parties, athletics, and recreation), while academic orientation was based on the importance of involvement in five activities (arts, academics, student associations, political organizations, and cultural organizations).[14] What distinguishes these groups of activities is the intellectual aspect of one versus the other. Academic hours was based on the quartile distribution of the weekly sum of hours devoted to class attendance and studying.

6   We first present prevalence analyses based on the total sample of students (Table II) and then present multivariate logistic regression assessing the prevalence of heavy drinking among past-year drinkers (Table III) and OLS regression assessing the frequency of heavy drinking among drinkers (Table IV). This analysis was performed on both the raw and log-transformed data. The raw results are presented since the substantive results of the two analyses did not differ.

7   Because our sample design employs unequal probabilities of selection and heavy clustering, Taylor series methods were used to estimate variances and related statistical tests. (Design effects for heavy drinking variables, which varied between two and 12, averaged 6.3.)

Results

8   To provide some context to our results, we begin by describing the past-year drinking patterns by gender. As seen in Table II, 86.6 per cent of Canadian undergraduates report consuming alcohol in the past year, and 37 per cent drank weekly. On average, students reported consuming 5.6 drinks per week (6.48 among past-year drinkers). Gender differences are also evident, with men being more likely than women to drink at least twice per week (27.0 per cent vs 15.1 per cent) and to drink in greater quantities per week (8.8 vs 4.6 drinks among past-year drinkers). The

TABLE I   SAMPLE CHARACTERISTICS

	N (unweighted)	% (weighted)
Total	7800	
Gender		
Male	2884	45.6
Female	4916	54.5
Region		
British Columbia	1795	9.8
Prairies	1467	18.4
Ontario	1277	40.5
Québec	2306	22.5
Atlantic	955	8.8
Year of study		
First	1903	25.9
Second	1910	25.3
Third	2044	25.4
Fourth	1943	23.4
Living arrangement		
University residence	1254	15.3
Off campus with parents	3433	48.0
Off campus without parents	3072	36.7

percentage reporting a *5-plus* heavy drinking episode during the past 12 months was 62.4 per cent (72.1 per cent of drinkers) and varied significantly by gender.

9   More germane to the campus environment is the heavy drinking that occurs while students are enrolled in university, in our case the period since September. Table III shows the percentage of past-year drinkers consuming *5-plus* and *8-plus* drinks per occasion. In total, 62.7 per cent of the drinkers reported *5-plus* drinking, while 34.8 per cent reported *8-plus* drinking at least once. The adjusted odds ratios show that four variables—gender, residence, academic and recreational orientation—are significantly associated with both *5-plus* and *8-plus* drinking. Regarding gender, the odds of *5-plus* and *8-plus* drinking are respectively 1.75 and 2.5 times higher among men than women. Living arrangement also shows

sizeable variation, with students living in residence being more likely to consume *5-plus* (or=1.53) and *8-plus* (or=1.77) drinks than students living with their parents.

10   The logit regression shows that academic and recreational orientations, as well as time devoted to academic work, were significantly associated with both *5-plus* and *8-plus* drinking. Generally, heavy drinking declined with increasing academic orientation and academic hours and increased with increasing recreational orientation. Compared to those with low academic orientation, the likelihood of *5-plus* drinking was 29 per cent lower (or=0.71) among those with moderate academic orientation and 43 per cent lower among those with high academic orientation (or=0.57). As well, compared to those with low recreational orientation, the likelihood of *5-plus* drinking was 1.83 times higher among those with moderate

TABLE II   Frequency of drinking, mean weekly alcohol intake, and prevalence of heavy drinking (5-plus) during the past 12 months

	Total (n=7800)		Males (n=2884)		Females (n=4916)	
Drinking frequency						
Never	13.4	(11.1–16.1)	14.6	(12.4–17.2)	12.5	(9.7–15.8)
< Once/month	22.0	(18.9–25.4)	18.0	(14.8–21.6)	25.3	(21.9–29.1)
1–3 times/month	27.7	(25.7–29.8)	22.8	(20.7–25.1)	31.8	(29.3–34.5)
1/week	16.4	(15.0–17.8)	17.6	(16.0–19.3)	15.3	(13.5–17.3)
2–3 times/week	16.0	(13.5–18.9)	20.6	(18.2–23.2)	12.2	(9.8–15.1)
4+ times/week	4.4	(3.2–4.8)	5.6	(4.4–7.1)	2.6	(2.1–3.1)
Daily	0.5	(0.3–1.0)	0.8	(0.5–1.6)	0.3	(0.1–0.6)
Mean drinks weekly						
Total sample	5.60	(4.60–6.60)	7.51	(6.50–8.52)	3.99	(3.08–4.89)
Among drinkers	6.48	(5.41–7.55)	8.80	(7.62–9.98)	4.56	(3.63–5.49)
Prevalence of 5-plus						
Total sample	62.4	(56.4–68.1)	66.9	(61.2–72.2)	58.7	(52.2–65.0)
Among drinkers	72.1	(66.8–76.9)	78.4	(73.0–82.9)	67.1	(61.5–72.2)

Gender difference: Frequency of use, Wald $F_{(3,33)}=31.01$, $p < 0.001$; Mean drinks, total sample, Wald $F_{(1,11)}=32.09$, $p < 0.001$; Prevalence 5-plus, total sample, Wald $F_{(1,11)}=29.07$, $p < 0.001$; Drinkers, Wald $F_{(1,11)}=70.90$, $p < 0.001$.

recreational orientation and 4.33 times higher among those with high recreational orientation. Similar associations were also found for *8-plus* drinking. Academic hours are generally inversely associated with both *5-plus* and *8-plus* drinking. This is especially true for *8-plus* drinking, in which the odds ratios show a clear reduction in *8-plus* drinking with every quartile increase in number of academic hours.

11   The analysis also shows that region is significantly associated only with *8-plus* drinking. Students in Québec universities are significantly less likely to report *8-plus* drinking compared to the average student (or=0.65). This contrast is also noticeable for *5-plus* drinking, although the overall region effect is not significant at the p<0.05 level. The only variable unrelated to both *5-plus* and *8-plus* drinking is year of study.

12   While most students engaged in some heavy drinking while in university, more compelling is the frequency of heavy drinking. As seen in Table IV, on average, drinkers reported consuming *5-plus* drinks per occasion 4.7 times since September and *8-plus*

drinks 1.9 times. Generally, the same factors that predict prevalence of heavy drinking also predict the frequency of heavy drinking. Five variables are significantly related to the frequency of both *5-plus* and *8-plus* heavy drinking: gender, living arrangements, academic orientation, recreational orientation, and academic hours.

13   Males reported twice as many heavy episodic drinking occasions than did females (6.7 and 3.2 times for *5-plus* drinks and 3.0 and 1.0 times for *8-plus* drinks). For both *5-plus* and *8-plus* drinking, those living on campus reported significantly more heavy drinking than did those living with parents (6.7 vs 4.0 and 2.8 vs 1.5, respectively). As well, those living off campus without parents also reported slightly more *8-plus* drinking than did those living with parents (1.9 vs 1.5). Again, both heavy drinking measures were negatively associated with academic orientation and positively associated with recreational orientation. *Five-plus* and *8-plus* heavy drinking declined from 5.0 to 3.5 occasions and from 2.0 to

TABLE III   PERCENTAGE CONSUMING 5-PLUS AND 8-PLUS DRINKS ON A SINGLE OCCASION SINCE SEPTEMBER, PAST-YEAR DRINKERS

	% 5-plus since September (n=6359)			% 8-plus since September (n=6351)		
	%	(95% CI)	Adjusted odds ratio	%	(95% CI)	Adjusted odds ratio
Total sample	62.7	(55.9–69.4)	—	34.8	(29.7–39.9)	—
Gender	***		***	***		***
Female	56.1	(48.8–63.2)	—	25.2	(21.1–29.7)	—
Male	70.6	(64.0–76.5)	1.75***	46.5	(40.8–52.5)	2.50***
Region	NS		NS	NS		*
British Columbia	58.6	(49.7–67.0)	0.76	35.2	(29.1–41.8)	0.89
Prairies	69.5	(56.1–80.3)	1.26	44.6	(33.9–55.7)	1.49
Ontario	60.2	(43.5–74.8)	0.84	33.2	(22.7–45.7)	0.90
Québec	58.5	(56.3–60.7)	0.73*	27.9	(27.6–28.2)	0.65**
Atlantic	73.9	(57.1–85.8)	1.70	39.5	(26.4–54.3)	1.28
Living arrangements	*		***	**		***
University	70.3	(66.0–74.3)	1.53***	44.2	(39.8–48.8)	1.77***
Off campus with parents	59.7	(50.2–68.4)	—	32.3	(25.5–39.9)	—
Off campus no family	62.5	(55.8–68.7)	1.21	33.2	(27.7–39.3)	1.14
Year	NS		NS	NS		NS
First	65.0	(59.9–69.8)	—	35.9	(31.4–40.7)	—
Second	63.5	(56.7–69.8)	0.99	36.0	(31.1–41.1)	1.06
Third	62.0	(54.8–68.7)	0.93	33.9	(28.3–40.0)	0.97
Fourth	60.1	(49.2–70.1)	0.82	33.3	(26.5–40.8)	0.92
Academic orientation	NS		**	NS		**
Low	63.6	(55.9–70.7)	—	36.2	(29.9–43.0)	—
Medium	60.3	(55.0–65.4)	0.71**	32.3	(28.7–36.1)	0.74*
High	60.9	(50.6–70.3)	0.57**	27.3	(22.2–33.0)	0.49**
Recreational orientation	***		***	***		***
Low	54.2	(45.4–62.7)	—	27.4	(21.8–33.8)	—
Medium	67.7	(61.2–73.6)	1.83***	38.0	(33.3–42.9)	1.63***
High	83.0	(80.4–85.3)	4.33***	54.8	(50.9–58.7)	3.23***
Academic hours (weekly)	**		NS	***		***
1st quartile	66.0	(59.0–72.4)	—	40.6	(34.7–46.7)	—
2nd quartile	63.9	(55.3–71.6)	0.94	35.1	(27.2–43.9)	0.82
3rd quartile	60.9	(56.5–65.2)	0.84	31.1	(27.6–34.9)	0.71*
4th quartile	57.2	(47.9–65.9)	0.68**	27.2	(23.5–31.2)	0.53***

Notes: *$p < 0.05$; **$p < 0.01$; ***$p < 0.001$

TABLE IV FREQUENCY OF CONSUMING FIVE OR MORE DRINKS AND EIGHT OR MORE DRINKS ON A SINGLE
OCCASION SINCE SEPTEMBER, AMONG PAST-YEAR DRINKERS

	Mean 5-plus since September (n=6359)			Mean 8-plus since September (n=6351)		
	Mean	(95% CI)	b	Mean	(95% CI)	b
Total sample	4.7	(3.8–5.6)		1.9	(1.4–2.3)	
Gender			***			***
Female	3.2	(2.3–4.1)	—	1.0	(0.6–1.3)	—
Male	6.7	(5.7–7.6)	3.05***	3.0	(2.4–3.6)	1.79***
Region			0.06			0.57
British Columbia	5.2	(3.9–6.4)	−0.17	2.0	(1.3–2.8)	−0.22
Prairies	6.3	(3.7–8.8)	1.21	2.9	(1.3–4.5)	0.82
Ontario	4.4	(2.5–6.2)	−0.51	1.6	(0.8–2.4)	−0.41
Québec	3.6	(3.2–4.0)	−1.42**	1.3	(1.1–1.4)	−0.77**
Atlantic	5.7	(3.2–8.1)	0.89	2.5	(0.6–4.5)	0.59
Living arrangements			***			***
University	6.7	(5.6–7.8)	2.59***	2.8	(2.1–3.5)	1.3***
Off campus w parents	4.0	(3.0–5.0)	—	1.5	(1.1–2.0)	—
Off campus no family	4.7	(3.5–5.9)	1.01	1.9	(1.1–2.6)	0.46*
Year			NS			NS
First	5.0	(3.9–6.1)	—	1.9	(1.4–2.5)	—
Second	4.8	(3.9–5.7)	−0.01	1.9	(1.4–2.4)	−0.01
Third	4.4	(3.3–5.5)	−0.33	1.7	(1.1–2.3)	−0.16
Fourth	4.8	(3.5–6.1)	−0.08	2.0	(1.3–2.8)	0.08
Academic orientation			***			***
Low	5.0	(4.0–6.1)	—	2.0	(1.5–2.6)	—
Medium	4.2	(3.5–4.8)	−1.34**	1.6	(1.2–2.0)	−0.65**
High	3.5	(2.0–5.1)	−2.60**	1.0	(0.5–1.5)	−0.16***
Recreational orientation			***			***
Low	3.3	(2.6–4.0)	—	1.2	(0.9–1.5)	—
Medium	5.5	(4.1–6.9)	2.16***	2.2	(1.4–3.1)	1.02**
High	8.3	(7.1–9.4)	4.64***	3.7	(3.0–4.5)	2.36***
Academic hours (weekly)			***			***
1st quartile	5.9	(4.8–6.9)	—	2.5	(1.9–3.1)	—
2nd quartile	4.6	(2.8–6.4)	−1.07	1.8	(0.9–2.7)	−0.58**
3rd quartile	4.0	(3.3–4.7)	−1.50*	1.5	(1.1–1.8)	−0.84*
4th quartile	3.4	(2.9–3.9)	−2.34***	1.2	(1.0–1.4)	−1.20***

Notes: *$p < 0.05$; **$p < 0.01$; ***$p < 0.001$

1.0, respectively, among those with low vs high academic orientation and increased from 3.3 to 8.3 and from 1.2 to 3.7, respectively, among those with low vs high recreational orientation. Also evident is a significant inverse association between heavy drinking and academic hours. *Five-plus* drinking declined from 5.9 episodes among those in the lowest quartile hours to 3.4 among those in the highest quartile, and *8-plus* drinking declined from 2.5 to 1.2 episodes. Region and year of study did not show significant group effects, although the region contrasts again showed below-average frequencies among those attending Québec universities.

Discussion

14   Although all survey findings are bounded inherently by both sampling and non-sampling errors, we believe that our data reasonably represent Canadian undergraduates. First, although there were no means to compare respondents to non-respondents, an analysis of early versus late responders indicated no significant differences for the major demographic factors and for drinking patterns, with the exception that late responders, who had a longer exposure period, reported more heavy drinking episodes. Second, a comparison of undergraduates drawn from the 1996 National Population Health Survey revealed no significant differences for sex, age, and frequency of alcohol use. And third, the correlation between mean student completion rates by university and rates of heavy drinking was nominal and non-significant ($r=-0.14$; $p=0.61$).

15   This study has shown that heavy drinking is highly engrained in Canadian undergraduates' drinking patterns. Most students are drinkers, and roughly two-thirds of them reported at least one *5-plus* drinking episode and one third an *8-plus* drinking episode during the initial eight to 12-week period at school. On average, drinkers reported *5-plus* drinking roughly once every two weeks (4.7 times/8–12 weeks) and *8-plus* drinking once every month (1.9 times/8–12 weeks). Our results indicated that heavy drinking is more prevalent and more frequent among men and among students living in university residences and that heavy drinking increased with the importance attached to recreational activities and decreased when students reported being more academically oriented. However, no association between heavy drinking and year of study was evident. Finally, undergraduates in Québec were less likely to drink heavily than those in the rest of Canada.

16   The fact that men are more likely than women to be heavy drinkers and drink heavily more often is a recurring finding for the general population as well as for college students.[15,16] However, we must note that because our definition of heavy drinking was identical among both men and women, we might be underestimating the impact of female heavy drinking given some biological differences.[7] Thus, we should not conclude that heavy drinking among women is not a health issue worthy of concern by campus services.

17   Our results highlight the importance of individual experiences of university life on heavy drinking. Students who place more importance on recreational activities and those who reside in student residences are more likely to drink heavily than other students, whereas those attaching more importance to academic activities are less likely to do so. Consistent with previous results,[14,17,18] these findings suggest a pattern of social integration into university life associated with heavier alcohol intake. However, we cannot ignore the possibility of a self-selection bias in which heavy drinkers are attracted to events or locations that are heavy-drinking milieus. Longitudinal data would be needed to clarify the causal relationships of these data.

18   Finally, students attending university in Québec seem less likely to drink heavily, despite a higher drinking prevalence and greater availability of alcohol in Québec. This might reflect a different drinking culture or might be related to the different school system in Québec, which has cegep as an intermediate institution between high school and university.

19   The results suggest that universities may be in a position to affect the rates of heavy drinking by its students through targeted interventions. For example, by focusing on men, on students who live in residences, and by trying to get students more involved in the academic parts of the university community, heavy drinking may be decreased.

Canadian Journal of Public Health.
2003. January/February 94 (1).

References

1. Room R. Measuring alcohol consumption in the United States: Methods and rationales. In: Kozlowski LT, et al. (Eds.), *Research Advances in Alcohol and Drug Problems*, Vol 10. New York, NY: Plenum, 1990;39–80.
2. Butcher AH, Manning DT, O'Neal EC. hiv-related sexual behaviors of college students. *J Am College Health* 1991; 40,115–18.
3. Milgram GG. Adolescents, alcohol and aggression. *J Studies on Alcohol* 1993;54:53–61.
4. Wechsler H, Davenport A, Dowdall G, Moeykens B, Castillo S. Health and behavioral consequences of binge drinking in college: A national survey of students at 140 campuses. *JAMA* 1994;272:1672–77.
5. Johnston ID, O'Malley PM, Bachman JG. *Monitoring the Future. National Survey Results on Drug Use, 1975–1999: Volume II College Students and Adult Ages 19–40*. Washington, DC: National Institute on Drug Abuse, 2000.
6. Wechsler H, Lee JE, Kuo M, Lee H. College binge drinking in the 1990s: A continuing problem. *J Am College Health* 2000;48:199–210.
7. Wechsler H, Dowdall GW, Davenport A, Rimm EB. A gender-specific measure of binge drinking among college students. *Am J Public Health* 1995;85:982–85.
8. Wechsler H, Lee JE, Nelson TF, Lee H. Drinking levels, alcohol problems and second-hand effects in substance-free college residences: Results of a national study. *J Studies on Alcohol* 2001;62:23–31.
9. Campbell RL, Svenson LW. Drug use among university undergraduate students. *Psychological Reports* 1992; 70:1039–42.
10. Gliksman L, Newton-Taylor B, Adlaf E, Giesbrecht N. Alcohol and other drug use by Ontario university students: The roles of gender, age, year of study, academic grade, place of residence and program of study. *Drugs: Education, Prevention and Policy* 1997;4:117–29.
11. Hindmarsh KW, Gliksman L, Newton-Taylor B. Alcohol and other drug use by pharmacy students in Canadian universities. *Can Pharmaceutical J* 1993;126:358–59.
12. Spence JC, Gauvin L. Drug and alcohol use by Canadian university athletes: A national survey. *J Drug Education* 1996;26:275–87.
13. Gliksman L, Demers A, Adlaf EM, Newton-Taylor B, Schmidt K. Canadian Campus Survey 1998. Toronto, ON: Centre for Addiction and Mental Health, 2000.
14. Demers A, Kairouz S, Adlaf EM, Gliksman L, Newton-Taylor B, Marchand A. A multilevel analysis of situational drinking. *Soc Sci Med* In press.
15. Kellner F. Alcohol. In: MacNeil P, Webster I (Eds.), *Canada's Alcohol and Other Drugs Survey 1994: A Discussion of the Findings*. Ottawa: Minister of Public Works and Government Services, 1997;15–42.
16. Substance Abuse and Mental Health Services Administration: Summary of Findings from the 2000 National Household Survey on Drug Abuse. Office of Applied Statistics, NHSDA Series H-13, DHHS Publication No. (SMA) 01-3549, 2001.
17. Chaloupka FJ, Wechsler H. Binge drinking in college: The impact of price, availability and alcohol control policies. *Contemporary Economic Policy* 1996;14:112–24a.
18. Perkins HW, Wechsler H. Variation in perceived college drinking norms and its impact on alcohol abuse: A nationwide study. *J Drug Issues* 1996;26:961–74.

Acknowledgement: This study was partially funded by the Brewer's Association of Canada.

KEY AND CHALLENGING WORDS

epidemiological, prevalence, demographic, stratified, salient, quartile

QUESTIONS

1. What is the justification for the study?
2. Although the authors state that the "epidemiological knowledge regarding heavy drinking in the US is long-standing," they do not refer further to such knowledge, nor do they compare data between the two countries. Why do you think they do not do this?
3. a) Tables I and II: Table I does not present any data from the questionnaire itself. Why is it important for the study's credibility? Table II summarizes students' drinking frequencies during the previous 12 months. Why did the authors include it in the study? b) How is what is presented in Table III different from what is presented in Table IV (i.e., what is each intended to show)? Which table, in the words of the authors, is more "compelling" and why?
4. Which variables are significantly associated with the prevalence of 5-plus and 8-plus drinking? Which variables are significantly associated with the frequency of 5-plus and 8-plus drinking? (See Appendix A.)
5. How does the authors' analysis of early versus late respondents in the "Discussion" section contribute to the study's reliability?

6. Why might heavy drinking among female undergraduates be an important concern in spite of the study's findings relative to gender? Summarize in one or two sentences.

7. In the "Discussion" section, the authors propose two hypotheses to account for the lower rate of drinking among Quebec undergraduates. Paraphrase the paragraph in which this is discussed. Suggest a hypothesis that could account for each of the following: (a) heavier drinking among students living on campus compared to those living with parents; (b) heavier drinking among students with low academic orientation compared to those with high academic orientation; and (c) heavier drinking among students with high recreational orientation compared to those with low recreational orientation. (See "Measures" for the activities on which academic orientation and recreational orientation are based.)

POST-READING

1. *Collaborative activity:* In the last paragraph, the authors suggest an important use for their study: "targeted interventions" by university bodies to reduce heavy drinking. In discussion groups, brainstorm ideas to come up with an intervention strategy, specifically targeting male students, students who live on campus, students with a high recreational orientation, or students with a low academic orientation. After each group has decided on an effective strategy, a spokesperson could outline this strategy to the class for comments and feedback.

2. Write a letter to the editor of a campus student newspaper in which you draw the attention of its readers to the problem of heavy drinking on campus. Refer to the study "Heavy drinking on Canadian campuses" in your letter. *OR* Write a letter to the editor of a campus publication for faculty and administration in which you draw the attention of its readers to the problem of heavy drinking on campus. Refer to and provide a bibliographically correct citation for the study "Heavy drinking on Canadian campuses" in your letter.

ADDITIONAL LIBRARY READING

Flett, G., Goldstein, A., Wall, A., Hewitt, P., Wekerle, C., & Azzi, N. (2008). Perfectionism and binge drinking in Canadian students making the transition to university. *Journal of American College Health, 57*(2), 249–256.

Higdon, L.I. (2011). How to make students uncomfortable with drinking. *The Chronicle of Higher Education, 57*(37), A36-A37.

Kuo M., Adlaf E.M., Lee H., Gliksman L., Demers A., & Wechsler H. (2002). More Canadian students drink but American students drink more: Comparing college alcohol use in two countries. *Addiction, 97*, 1583–1592.

Perkins, H. (2007). Misperceptions of peer drinking norms in Canada: Another look at the "reign of error" and its consequences among college students. *Addictive Behaviors, 32*(11), 2645–2656. doi:10.1016/j.addbeh.2007.07.007

Tarmageddon: Dirty oil is turning Canada into a corrupt petro-state

Andrew Nikiforuk

(1,604 words)

1   Europeans once regarded Canada as a decent "do-gooder" democracy, celebrated for its vast forests, pristine waters, and pleasant cities. But the rapid development of the tar sands, the world's largest energy project, has not only blackened the country's environmental reputation, but also dramatically undermined its political and economic character.

2   Oil, a politically corrosive resource, has unsettled the nation. Ever since Canada supplanted Mexico and Saudi Arabia nearly a decade ago as the No. 1 oil supplier to the United States, the federal government has become an increasingly aggressive defender of hydrocarbons and little else.

3   The nation's dismal record on climate change, and minimal investments in green energy, simply reflect a growing dependence on oil revenue, oil volatility, and petroleum lobbyists. As a consequence, Canada now shares the same sort of unaccountability and lack of transparency that marks fellow petrostates such as Saudi Arabia. Nowadays, Canada is, as one *Toronto Star* columnist pointedly put it, "a nation that doesn't say much, doesn't do much, and doesn't seem to stand for much."

4   Canada's dramatic transformation began with the rapid exploitation of the tar sands in the mid-1990s. This resource, a true symbol of peak oil, is neither cheap nor light. Bitumen, an inferior and ultra-heavy hydrocarbon that resembles asphalt, is so thick that it can't move through a pipeline unless diluted with a solvent.

5   Bitumen also contains so much carbon (and so little hydrogen) that it must be upgraded into "synthetic crude," a product with a higher sulphur, acid, and heavy metal content than West Texas crude or North Sea oil. As a consequence, bitumen remains the world's most capital-intensive oil at $60–80 a barrel; in contrast, US domestic crude can be produced at $10 a barrel.

6   Although industry studies claim that bitumen production is only 15 per cent dirtier than light oil, the facts speak otherwise. The U.S. National Energy Technology Laboratory, for instance, recently calculated that jet fuel made from bitumen has a carbon footprint 244 per cent greater than fuel made from US domestic crude. While Statoil, Norway's state-owned company, reports greenhouse gas emissions of 8 to 19 kilograms per barrel in the North Sea, production emissions in the tar sands range from 22 to 417 kilograms or higher. In addition, scientists report a disturbing lack of public transparency on tar sands emissions reporting.

7   Nevertheless, every major global oil company has joined the bitumen boom. To date, the $200 billion scramble has directly industrialized 1.4 million hectares of forest—the equivalent of 40 Denvers or 17 Berlins.

8   The spectacle has not been pretty. Open pit mines the size of cities excavate shallow bitumen deposits in the forest, while steam plants inject deeper formations with as many as 12 barrels of steam to melt just one barrel of bitumen. Both recovery methods create enormous environmental messes.

9   The mines generate extraordinary volumes of toxic waste, which companies store in massive unlined dykes. These geologically unstable "tailing ponds" occupy 140 square kilometres of forest along the Athabasca River and contain a variety of fish-killers and cancer-makers, including arsenic, cyanide, naphthenic acids, and polycyclic aromatic hydrocarbons. Any breach of these impoundments would be catastrophic for the world's third-largest watershed, the Mackenzie River Basin.

10   Federal and provincial standards for reporting the volume of pollutants in these waste sites, and for reducing mining waste, didn't materialize until 2009. Even Boston-based Cambridge Energy Research Associates has decried the total lack of transparency on the reporting of tar ponds seepage into ground water or surface water.

11   The steam plants have equally impressive footprints. These heavily subsidized enterprises are fragmenting a forest the size of England with wells and pipelines. A fifth of Canada's natural gas demand goes into boiling the water to melt out the bitumen. This makes the energy intensity of steam plants so high that, at one joule of energy to make 1.4 joules of bitumen, there is little net gain in energy from the process.

12   The amount of groundwater pumped through these steam plants keeps growing, and threatens the hydrology of the entire region. Opti-Nexen, a large steam plant operator, initially calculated that it would take two barrels of steam to make one barrel of bitumen. Now the company boils up to six.

13   Due to its energy and water intensity, the tar sands has become its own carbon-making nation within Canada. It now accounts for 5 per cent of the nation's emissions and pollutes the global atmosphere with 40 megatonnes of greenhouse gases a year. That's nearly double the annual emissions of Estonia or Latvia. By 2020, the project will likely exceed the emissions of Belgium, a nation of 10 million people. (These industry calculations do not include the burning of the oil in cars or the destruction of peat-lands, forests, and grasslands by the mines and natural gas drillers.)

*

14   The most poisonous legacy of the tar sands project has been its impact on public policy. Canada, once a global leader on tackling ozone pollution and acid rain, now has no effective climate change policy. Canada is the only signatory to the Kyoto Protocol that has completely abandoned its targets. It now ranks 59th out of 60 countries on responsible climate action: only Saudi Arabia boasts a worse record.

15   At the failed Copenhagen talks last year, an almost invisible Canada, one of the world's top ten emitters, gave a mere three-and-a-half-minute presentation. Even Saudi Arabia managed a six-minute talk.

16   Canada's Prime Minister, Stephen Harper, the son of an Imperial Oil executive, hails from the tar sands-producing province of Alberta, where a third of the population conveniently does not believe in climate change. Like many of Saudi Arabia's elites, Harper remains a bona-fide climate change skeptic—if not an outright denier. He has also appointed climate change deniers to important scientific posts. One of his close associates, Ken Boessenkool, even works as an oil industry lobbyist. Many of his fishing buddies support the country's pro-oil, anti-climate-action lobby group, Friends of Science.

17   Given that corporate taxes on tar sands production yield the federal government nearly $5 billion a year, steady oil revenue has trumped the public interest. The country has opposed low carbon fuel standards in the US, while Canada's Foreign Affairs branch says it "will resist efforts to label one form of energy as appropriate, such as renewables." Canada's Environment Minister, Jim Prentice, openly criticizes provinces such as Quebec for implementing green policies that reduce fossil fuel consumption.

18   Like Saudi Arabia, Canada has increasingly relied on foreign temporary workers, whose numbers (250,000) now exceed permanent immigrants, to develop its oil fields. In 2008, Alberta actually had 20 times as many temporary foreign workers (from places as diverse as China, South Africa, and the Philippines) as the US in proportion to its population.

19   Abuses by brokers and employers abound. A 2009 report by the University of Sussex concluded that Canadian authorities, much like Saudi politicians, view temporary workers as "stocks that can be bought in or out as required." The Canadian and Alberta governments have also failed to consult local workers, unions, and the general public about their temporary foreign worker programs.

*

20   Although industry and government describe the tar sands as "Canada's new economic engine," the project has in reality given Canada a bad case of the Dutch Disease. This economic malaise, a form of deindustrialization, takes its name from a 1977 *Economist* article that detailed how a natural gas boom hollowed out the manufacturing base of the Netherlands. Gas exports inflated the value of the Dutch guilder, which in turn undermined the ability of its manufacturers to export their goods.

21   Thanks to rapidly growing tar sands exports (from 600,000 barrels a day in 2000 to 1.3 million barrels today), the loonie, as the Canadian dollar is known, has now reached parity with—and may soon surpass—the US dollar in value. But the high-priced loonie has made it particularly difficult for Canadian manufacturers to sell their goods. A 2009 study by Luxembourg's Centre for Research in Economic Analysis confirmed that Canada's oil-priced currency has indeed hammered industries as varied as textile mills, electronics, fabricated metal, and paper. It concluded that 54 per cent of the nation's manufacturing employment losses (nearly 5 per cent of the workforce) were due to the rapid tar sands development from 2002 to 2007.

22   Unlike Norway, the world's most transparent petro-state, Canada has also failed to exercise any fiscal accountability over its non-renewable oil wealth. The country has no sovereign fund and has saved no wealth to date, much to the consternation of the Organization for Economic Cooperation and Development (OECD), which concluded in a damning 2008 report that "other nations have shown much more restraint and foresight in managing their resource revenues to mitigate boom-and-bust cycles."

23   In addition, neither Canada nor Alberta charges much for the bitumen. Alberta has even described its royalty regime as a "give-it-away" scheme. Alberta's share from a $60 barrel of oil is a mere 30 cents, one of the lowest royalties in the world. The province also permits corporations to deduct royalties for federal corporate tax purposes.

24   Nevertheless, Alberta still garners nearly a third of its revenue from hydrocarbons. To date, much of it has been used to lower taxes, manipulate public sentiment, and recklessly build infrastructure to fuel more tar sands development. Ruled by one political party for an astounding 38 years, Alberta's government has been increasingly described as incompetent, authoritarian, and corrupt.

25   Canada has yet to have a national debate about the pace and scale of the tar sands development. Until it acknowledges the project's cancerous hold on national life, Canada will increasingly become an unstable petro-state marginalized by oil price volatility and global carbon politics.

CCPA Monitor. 2010. May 17 (1).

KEY AND CHALLENGING WORDS

corrosive, volatility, breach (n.), decry, hydrology, malaise, consternation, mitigate, authoritarian

QUESTIONS

1. Does Nikiforuk provide a successful introduction? Briefly analyze the first paragraph.

2. Using a reliable source, such as an encyclopedia, research bitumen, determining whether the description of this substance, along with the facts about its effects and extraction methods discussed in paragraphs 4–10, seems accurate.

3. Analyze Nikiforuk's use of compare and contrast in his essay: a) Identify two passages in which he uses a comparison, analyzing them for their effectiveness; b) Why does Nikiforuk often compare Canada to Saudi Arabia, and what are the effects of such comparisons?

4. How many main points does Nikiforuk's essay contain? Which point do you believe is the most important one for his argument? Why?

5. From paragraph 9, a) Define "'tailing ponds'" in your own words; b) What is the significance of the word "Even" in the last sentence of paragraph 10?

6. Does Nikiforuk present all his points fairly? Identify any examples of slanted language and of logical or ethical fallacies. Explain why you think they undermine (or do not undermine) his claim.

7. Explain what is meant by the "Dutch Disease" (paragraph 20) and how this "disease" could affect Canada's economy.

POST-READING

1. Find two reviews of Nikiforuk's book *Tar Sands: Dirty Oil and the Future of a Continent* (these could be in a journal, magazine, or newspaper, but not a personal website or blog). Compare and contrast the two reviews in approximately 500 words.

2. *Collaborative or individual activity:* Discuss or debate one of the following topics: a) How is the development of the Alberta Oil Sands project affecting Canada's reputation internationally or how do you think it will affect Canada's reputation? b) Do you believe Nikiforuk successfully defends the claim he makes in the title and introduction?

3. Do you believe the absence of cited sources reduces Nikiforuk's credibility? Do you believe it reduces his credibility for readers of the *CCPA Monitor*? (To answer the second question, you should access the home page of the publication in which this essay appeared in order to determine the kind of audience he is writing for.)

RELATED WEBSITES OF INTEREST

Friends of Science (mentioned in the essay, paragraph 15):
www.friendsofscience.org/

Alberta government "Oil Sands" website:
www.oilsands.alberta.ca/

The Tyee (an online magazine for which Andrew Nikiforuk has written many articles as its first "writer in residence"; browse by topic [energy] or search for Nikiforuk from the home page to access articles):
http://thetyee.ca/

The ugly Canadian

Amir Attaran

(4,297 words)

Pre-reading

1. Scanning the essay, note differences between this essay and scholarly essays you have encountered before (in this book or in other books or journals). What could account for these differences? How is this essay similar to scholarly essays you have encountered?
2. Does the simple title suggest the content of the essay? What about the headings? In one sentence, summarize what you think the essay will be about.

---

1   On April 22 of this year, a mysterious four-month-long nightmare ended for Robert Fowler and Louis Guay, the Canadian diplomats abducted in Niger by a shadowy group calling itself al Qaeda in the Islamic Maghreb. Fowler and Guay were on a secret mission for the secretary general of the United Nations, although when they were abducted they were on a private trip to a Canadian-run goldmine, travelling without a protective escort. The kidnappers ripped them from their UN-marked vehicle with such intensity of purpose that the engine was left idling and nothing was stolen. The village where it happened was named Karma.

2   The story had a happy ending, at least in terms of Fowler and Guay's physical health. Yet all kinds of questions hang in the air, beginning with what exactly did al Qaeda receive—and from whom—in exchange for the hostages. Prime Minister Stephen Harper adamantly denied that Canada pays ransoms or releases prisoners to satisfy kidnappers, but it is clear from news reports that a complex negotiation took place involving several countries and that money, prisoners, or both probably changed hands. But there are other questions as well: Why was there such a silence in Canada over those four months? Didn't we care that two of our top diplomats had been seized in this way? Officially the silence was said to be for their security, but it is also true that many in Ottawa's establishment disliked the reminder that to be Canadian no longer implies beneficence and safety from harm. In the face of a national mythology that everyone loves Canadians—a mythology that has resulted in innumerable maple leaves being stitched like amulets onto countless backpacks—the Fowler and Guay episode was a cold wind of reality.

3   When ill fate strikes one's country, it is awkward or even taboo to pose the question of whether it is deserved, for lack of a better word. In the wake of 9/11, Americans reacted ferociously to anyone who dared to hint that they shared in the blame. Yet many foreigners knew America had it coming and, after a dignified period of mourning, they said so. On the first anniversary of the Twin Towers attack Prime Minister Jean Chretien famously reminded Americans that "you cannot exercise your powers to the point of humiliation of the others." Canadians agreed with him, and in a 2002 poll by the *Globe and Mail*, 84 per cent believed that America bore partial or total responsibility for the attacks.

4   But the notion that there is karma for a country, which trips so easily off the tongue when tut-tutting about the United States, is surely not a notion

from which Canada is exempt. Canada too makes the mistake of exercising powers to the point of humiliation of the others, and it would be fanciful to imagine that Canada lacks the biblical sin of pride. Indeed, if one takes an unflinching look at Canadian conduct in the world, the evidence permits no conclusion other than that the country has lately been engaged in a liquidation of its internationalism. Canada has lost the outward gaze that the British Empire imposed, and that Prime Minister Lester Pearson cultivated. Today's Canadians, just 0.5 per cent of the world's population, are more insular than even their modest numbers suggest.

5   I do not make this criticism in the spirit of an unpatriotic hatchet job. Unlike Canadians born in this country, I carne to it by choice, faults and all. As a born Californian with a Berkeley and Oxford education, probably I could live elsewhere, but I was attracted to this very Pearsonian country in the 1990s. I settled in Vancouver, studied law at the University of British Columbia and became a Canadian. While I love this place, learning it through its laws has also shown me a dark side.

6   In a democracy where legislation is freely chosen, laws are a country's DNA: they are the code the country lives by, and if the code is ugly, by merciless logic so too will be the country. On that level, Canada's laws give objective evidence that Pearson's Canada is comatose, if not dead. Today's Canada would not please Pearson, and he would find the country's outlook on foreign people and international obligations oddly picayune and ignorant. He might even say that we are hazardously far down the road of becoming a country of diverse but ugly Canadians—and if we do not check this tendency, karma could pay us back.

Belonging

7   Lester Pearson was a great many things, but complex was not one of them. By a certain age, he bad a formula—be assiduous, be respectful, be canny, be humorous, be mindful of who is on the way up, be a dove and a hawk, be principled but not dogmatic— and it served him (and Canada) so well he rarely deviated from it. In Pearson's five years as a minority

prime minister, he enacted laws and policies for universal health care, official bilingualism, colour-blind immigration, crop insurance, student loans, and the national pension.

8   Yet nothing drove Pearson more than the will to find solutions short of war. He was hardly a pacifist: as a youth he enlisted in the Great War, and later in life he cut short a vacation to be at his diplomatic post in London during the Blitz. War taught him the value of its avoidance and the importance of countries honouring diplomatic commitments to live together harmoniously.

9   Pearson made it his business to slip velvet handcuffs on the exercise of state power. He did this as a diplomat long before being prime minister, by building international institutions and making Canada an early and eager joiner: the United Nations, the North Atlantic Treaty Organization, and the Food and Agriculture Organization were all largely shaped by Pearson at their creation. When international crises emerged—Palestine, or Suez, for example—it was to the international organizations that Pearson turned. He knew Canada would lose some sovereignty through its chronic reliance on internationalism, but as Canada had only just gained sovereignty from Empire, giving or taking a little sovereignty bothered Pearson less than it might politicians today. This flexibility was shared by Pearson's contemporaries, such as Eleanor Roosevelt with her human rights treaties, or Robert Schuman with his European Coal and Steel Community, which later became the European Union, and it was their vision that unlikely-sounding legal institutions could bind countries and cement the peace. Like so many Lilliputians, these great thinkers believed that bureaucrats, lawyers, and businesspeople could tie down generals, demagogues, and terrorists—and actually win.

10   Sixty years later, the internationalists' experiment must be judged a qualified success. The UN is warily regarded: it struggles against incoherent and wasteful complexity, but sometimes inspires by averting a war, epidemic, famine, or other nightmare. The EU is unimaginably successful: not only are Europeans richer and healthier than ever, but the decision to take dominion over the raw materials of war—coal and steel were chosen for a reason—has given Europe an antidote to the poisonous tribalism that for a

millennium made it the world's bloodiest continent. NATO has a celebrated past and uncertain future: as a bureaucratic organization it kept the peace during the Cold War, but forced to become a war-making organization in Afghanistan, it is struggling.

11   The lesson of these three cases is subtle: the Lilliputians of the international institutions can preserve the commonweal, but only if governments perpetuate their Pearsonian enchantment with building institutions (as with the EU), while at the same time discouraging bloat (the UN) and avoiding infirmity of purpose (NATO). Left–right politics has little to do with it. Simply put, internationalism is a pragmatic lesson in how collectively to make the world, and Canada, a safer and more prosperous place.

12   Of course, none of this is really new. Pearson did not invent any guiding ideas, so much as raise them to a functional place in statecraft. Centuries ago, Thomas Hobbes wrote of people's need for "a common power to keep them all in awe," else they revert to the "war of all against all." In the war-weary generation of Pearson, politicians had learned by blood that "if there be no power erected, or not great enough for our security, every man [or country] will and may lawfully rely on his own strength and art for caution against all other[s]," as Hobbes wrote. How remote those days seem now, as the Pearsonian belief in a larger common power has been throttled by Blairs and Bushes who believed foremost in the exceptionalism of their own countries and the dangerous conceit that they might become the common power. It has not ended well for Blair and Bush and their countries.

Backtracking

13   But just as exceptionalism is going back out of fashion, along comes Canada to dumbly clench it. Our recent history is embarrassingly rich in examples of joining institutions and then breaking the rules. Saddest of all, Canadian exceptionalism is frequently arbitrary, unexplained, or self-sabotaging, and the rest of the world is left baffled about the motivations for our country's behaviour. In this, Canadian exceptionalism often makes even less sense than American exceptionalism: at least when Washington thumbs its

nose at the international order, it does so with undeterred conviction and a raft of intellectually veneered (if often wrong) arguments. A look at Canada's laws across the board—in matters of economics, health, or human rights—shows how pointless Canadian exceptionalism has become.

14   *Global Trade Law.* Before the current global recession, the most prominent globalization debate, which nearly killed the Doha round of World Trade Organization negotiations, was whether free trade advanced developed and developing country interests alike. The debate is not new, and three decades ago it dogged the international trade system, until countries agreed on a principle of "differential and more favourable treatment." The thought was that if richer countries such as Canada opened their markets, for instance by discounting tariff rates preferentially for poorer exporting countries, the latter could gain a toehold on the free trade bandwagon. This lopsided deal would eventually pay itself back, as the poor countries grew, became rich and became new export markets; in the long run everyone would win. Nothing could be more internationally minded, and so as poorer countries fought their corner, Ottawa decided to be as accommodating as it could.

15   But since then, the way in which Canada applies differential and more favourable treatment is nothing short of bizarre.

16   In law, the Governor-in-Council decides which developing countries get the preference of exporting to Canada at a discounted tariff rate. While that is supposed to be a decision based on countries' poverty and need, politics plays a role too. Hence democratic Belize and Botswana get the preference, hut despotic Belarus and Burma do not. Neither, obviously, do developed Belgium and Bulgaria.

17   But how does one explain the Governor-in-Council's decision to give Vladimir Putin's Russia or Robert Mugabe's Zimbabwe the preference? Neither seems a democratic government. Why do Hong Kong, Israel, South Korea, and Singapore get the preference? Certainly none is poor or developing. The height of absurdity is Qatar: it gets the preference too, although per capita it is the world's richest country.

18   When we twist global trade rules so arbitrarily, imagine how it represents Canadian values. Foreigners might wonder: Are Canadians cruel or are they

fools? Cruel, because we give a preference intended for the poor to the rich, or fools, for handing rich countries unnaturally low tariffs to clobber our industries? Not only do Canada's random actions misrepresent Canadian values, whether among leftist bleeding hearts or rightist free traders, but they also damage our prosperity and economy.

19   *Corporations Law.* A more extreme example of exceptionalism departing from Canadian values is in the morally undisputed area of corruption. Corruption is bad. Countries that coddle corruption are bad. Yet Canada deliberately maintains the loosest corruption laws of any developed country.

20   A decade ago, the Organisation for Economic Co-operation and Development advanced a treaty, called the Anti-Bribery Convention, which aimed to criminalize the giving of bribes to foreign public officials. Canada signed on and passed a law to fulfil the Anti-Bribery Convention's purpose. A self-congratulatory press release at the time quotes justice minister Anne McLellan touting Canada as "a constant supporter of international anti-corruption efforts."

21   That was, and remains, deeply untrue. Far from targeting international corruption, Canada's law criminalizes only corruption in Canada. Injecting accuracy where its own minister would not, the Department of Justice writes that "Canada has jurisdiction over the bribery of foreign public officials when the offence is committed in whole or in part in its territory." Thus if a Canadian corporation passes cash-stuffed envelopes in Caracas and Harare, rather than Calgary and Halifax, it is allowed. None of the other 29 OECD countries has this loophole and, despite mighty complaints from abroad, Canada cravenly refuses to close it.

22   In fact, Canada is now arguably the "leading" advanced country in which to base a corrupt international business. In 2007, the same year that the United States prosecuted 67 violations of the Anti-Bribery Convention, Canada prosecuted only one. By giving Canadian firms a loophole in international bribery rules, Ottawa gives them an incentive to perfect skills in giving *baksheesh* rather than skills for real competitiveness. Neither the right nor the left can possibly consider this a long-run strategy for Canada's prosperity.

23   *Health Law.* While it is bad enough that Canadian exceptionalism costs this country money, taken a bit further, it can kill. When the SARS epidemic hit Toronto and claimed 44 lives in 2003, residents were stunned that the World Health Organization recommended not travelling to their city. Although SARS affected dozens of countries, only two drew WHO's wrath: China, because the apparatchiks in Beijing would not provide information on the epidemic's spread, and Canada, because the bureaucrats in Ottawa could not provide that information. When WHO asked about Toronto's epidemic, an epic cat fight erupted between federal and provincial officials over the answer. Left hanging, WHO had no option but to do the prudent thing and isolate Toronto—a decision that embarrassed Canada and cost it more than a billion dollars.

24   You might think that this humbling experience would have taught Ottawa a lesson about playing well with international organizations, but you would be wrong. WHO learned during SARS that it needed a stronger commitment from governments to disclose information on epidemics, before they become globally threatening. More than 190 countries agreed and, in 2007, WHO's revised International Health Regulations came into force. These regulations oblige national governments—meaning Ottawa, not the provinces—to share epidemiological information during outbreaks.

25   Yet Canada has done nothing to write WHO's new rules into Canadian law. Although the Harper government passed a law to establish the new Public Health Agency of Canada, it deliberately kept the agency toothless. Canada's auditor general complains that without mandatory powers, PHAC "relies on the goodwill of the provinces"—not law—to obtain epidemic information in emergencies. Goodwill, of course, is what failed during SARS. The auditor general also warns that PHAC is "not assured of receiving timely, accurate and complete information" in a future epidemic. Of the ten provinces, PHAC has reached formal agreement with only one (Ontario) to share information during an emergency—and even that agreement is a failure because it is secret and not legally binding. Thus even as listeria-contaminated meat was killing Canadians last year, Ottawa still refused to tell Ontario which stores and restaurants were affected.

26   More than any other example, epidemic preparedness shows how Canadian exceptionalism is a knife pointed outward and inward simultaneously. Senior WHO officials privately admit that Canada is a country of concern, because without a national agency having powers over epidemiological information, Canada could seed deadly infections in other countries before officials become aware. WHO's fears are well founded, because if Canada's governments are too secretive to share information on a comparatively minor listeriosis outbreak, it is fanciful to think that openness will characterize a larger emergency such as an influenza pandemic, during which PHAC expects "between 15 and 35 per cent of Canadians could become ill . . . and between 11,000 and 58,000 deaths could occur." With the H1N1 virus certain to reappear in the 2009 autumn influenza season, perhaps in deadlier form, and our laws still not conforming to WHO's wise direction, Canadians could pay with their lives.

27   *Human Rights Law*. Up to this point, I have stuck to politically neutral examples of Canadian exceptionalism. Everyone loves money, and nobody wants to die of a deadly pandemic, so these issues raise few ideological hackles. But not everyone loves humans, or rather, not every human is easy to love—there is Omar Khadr. Exceptionalism in this territory is harder to evaluate because it reflects ideological choices. Even so, there are clear examples that reveal the pointlessness of Canada's human rights exceptionalism.

28   Consider the violation known as the enforced disappearance of persons, which is basically state-orchestrated secret kidnapping. Security never demands it, as governments can engage in lawful preventive detention or deportation without shadowy disappearances. The only "advantage" in disappearing persons is to ward off pesky lawyers and to keep loved ones in confusion and terror—a handy trick if the government intends to torture or assassinate a person, as military dictatorships in Argentina, Brazil, and Chile did, and as the United States has done in undisclosed CIA "dark sites" in recent years.

29   You might think that Canada, which, under both left- and right-wing governments has nurtured a global reputation as a human rights defender, could not move quickly enough to sign a treaty against enforced disappearances. But again, you would be wrong. The UN's International Convention for the Protection of All Persons from Enforced Disappearance has been open for Signatures since 2007, and so far 81 countries have signed. The Harper government refuses to sign, although it assured the UN General Assembly that Canada was "pleased to support" the treaty. In short, our government lied and reneged.

30   Currently, a disturbingly possible reason for Canada not signing the enforced disappearance treaty is that Canada is committing enforced disappearances. In Afghanistan, the Canadian Forces detain persons secretly, without criminal charges, without notice to their families, and without recourse to Jaw. When lawyers asked General Rick Hillier for access to these detainees, he refused. A few hundred detainees—the exact number is classified—have been transferred by the Canadian Forces to the Afghan secret police this way, in full knowledge that those police torture. When a Canadian Foreign Affairs official visited some transferred detainees in the Afghan prison in November 2007, he found not only allegations of torture, but the torture implements themselves:

> When asked about his interrogation the detainee came forward with an allegation of abuse . . . He alleged that during the [censored] interrogation, [censored] individuals held him to the ground [censored] while the other [censored] beating him with electrical wires and rubber hose. He indicated a spot on the ground in the room we were interviewing in as the place where he was held down. He then pointed to a chair and stared the implements he bad been struck with were underneath it. Under the chair, we found a large piece of braided electrical wire as well as a rubber hose. He then showed us a bruise (approx. 4 inches long) on his back that could possibly be the result of a blow.

31   The federal court now notes several instances where detainees were apparently tortured or went "missing."

32   Seizing persons and disappearing them to the purveyors of torture is the sort of conduct one associates with the United States; no wonder Washington rejects the enforced disappearance treaty. But love or hate Washington's choices. America is more honest than Canada, because it never pretended to have a

great commitment to human rights law. For the US, rejection works—the world has low expectations, and American power makes for distinction in other ways— but for a country otherwise as unadorned as Canada, faith toward certain national ideals is its identity and branding. Stripped of its human rights reputation, Canada is like Switzerland without neutrality, Italy without fashion, or Tanzania without safaris.

Belonging Again

33   I have outlined four completely different examples of pointless Canadian refusal to go along with the global rules—so pointless that the outcome is actually to diminish Canadians' wealth, health, and standing in the world. I could outline more negative examples—Canada's directionless foreign aid, its contempt for global climate change initiatives, and its densely layered disincentives to foreign investment— or acknowledge some positive examples—the land-mines treaty, or certain aspects of Canada's mission in Afghanistan. There is no need, because they do not change this central point: Canada's foreign and trade policies are so irrational as to violate the global rules even when we are victims of the violation.

34   Fixing this situation—as is only wise—requires major improvements to the low quality of Canada's foreign and trade policy establishment.

35   Most importantly, Canada needs serious ministers in the foreign and trade portfolios. Pearson was secretary of state for external affairs for nine unbroken years—a tenure instrumental to his and Canada's success. Yet in the last decade, Canada has had five trade ministers and seven foreign ministers. You have to go back to 1989 in the United States to count a total of seven secretaries of state. Allies and enemies who see Canada swapping its top representatives even more often than Japan changes prime ministers can only conclude that Canadian diplomacy is not serious—and they will walk all over us.

36   Intellect and dedication also matter. Pearson was an Oxford-educated university professor with a hyperactive work ethic. If finding a comparable candidate requires the prime minister bypassing elected members of Parliament to appoint an outsider by way of the Senate, that is a lesser evil than entrusting a diffident poseur like Maxime Bernier with the job of picturing Canada to the world.

37   The Department of Foreign Affairs and International Trade also needs a near-complete makeover to make it less picayune and more insightful about the world. As the Maher Arar inquiry so pointedly illustrated, even the most senior and worldly-seeming Canadian diplomats can be ignorant of obvious realities. Recall Franco Pillarella, formerly DFAIT's human rights chief and ambassador to Syria during Arar's ordeal, answering no when asked if he was aware of "serious human rights abuses . . . being committed" in that country. His consul, Leo Martel, testified to doing *"le maximum et plus"* for Acar, but also admitted ignorance of public reports concerning Syria's human rights record. Many DFAIT officials lacked the insight to perceive and act on the foreign realities ensnaring Arar, Abdullah Almalki, Ahmad El Maati, Muayyed Nureddin—and now Abousfian Abdelrazik. (How odd that the same DFAIT bureaucracy which was so incapable of helping these Muslim men swung into high action when the victims were Brahmins such as Robert Fowler or Louis Guay.)

38   One wants not to ascribe this pattern to intentional racism in DFAIT, so one requires an alternative hypothesis. Mine is that DFAIT failed on these and unrelated challenges (so, not simply racism) because it is actually quite naive, and lacks a culture with empathic imagination for foreign persons or foreign realities—a *sine qua non* of good diplomacy. Currently, DFAIT's senior ranks are a monoculture of the scions of *pure laine* Canadian families of European descent, so how surprising is it that Canadian diplomacy is complaisant and Eurocentric in outlook?[1] Even the Canadian Space Agency now hires more "aliens," of the visible minority kind, than xenophobic DFAIT. A large-scale effort to employ more minorities or recent immigrants and to make DFAIT's culture more heterogeneous, as other outward-facing agencies have done (e.g., the Immigration and Refugee Board, Passport Canada), would go a long way toward giving it the imagination and flexible *Weltanschauung* it now lacks. Obviously, a diplomatic corps that can better understand foreigners and better explain Canadian actions to them will better advance Canada's political and economic interests abroad.

39   While it is a subtle point, Canada also needs a civil society that is less captured by government. Some of my fellow academics, particularly in schools of government or international affairs, fear criticizing the emperor's wardrobe too vigorously because support from government agencies might dry up. Self-censorship also stymies those Canadian non-governmental organizations whose core budgets depend on government grants; they should really be called GOs, but calling them so is to hint they are unnecessary. The practice, firmly established in DFAIT, of hand-picking scholars and NGOs for patronage is highly dangerous, for just when Canada's diplomatic or trade interests may call for *les vérités qui dérangent*, the temptation is greatest to solicit *les mensonges qui arrangent* from a sycophantic gallery. A wise federal government would recognize this fact and dispense academic funding only through the arm's-length research councils, would cap Ottawa's largesse to NGOs and would reform the tax laws so that a larger charitable sector financed by private benefactors could fill the void. These changes would favour neither the right nor the left, and would create a more vibrant brain trust of truly non-governmental analysts to impose accountability and, especially, purpose on Canada's lackluster foreign and trade policy.

40   If Canada is a magnificent country, which it is, then it should look itself in the mirror and fearlessly examine the evidence of its conduct in the world. Currently, that evidence teaches that the high-functioning diplomacy of Pearson's era is a thing of the past, to the shocking extent that Canada lets slip even those international obligations that economically and socially benefit Canadians. Self-neglect is our clearest warning that Canada's global outlook is misguided. We can take the warning and do what is best for ourselves and others, or we can wait for a meeting with karma to announce that Canada has chosen a wrong road.

Literary Review of Canada. 2009. June 17 (5).

Note

1. A glance at DFAIT's organizational chart, available on its website at <www.international.gc.ca> (under "About the Department"), shows an apparent dearth of non-European surnames among DFAIT's senior officials. Knowing most of those officials, I can confirm this is the case.

KEY AND CHALLENGING WORDS

amulet, unflinching, insular, picayune, assiduous, dogmatic, Lilliputian, commonweal, throttle (v.), conceit, undeterred, veneer, cravenly, renege, recourse, purveyor, diffident, scion, complaisant, stymie

QUESTIONS

1. Who are Robert Fowler and Louis Guay? Using reliable sources, like newspapers or magazines, answer this question. From your research, does it appear that the author's concerns about the government's actions and statements are valid? Why does Attaran begin with their story?
2. Why does the author refer to his own background in paragraph 5? Why does he declare he is not a Canadian by birth? Do his statements in this paragraph affect his credibility?
3. Who does Attaran believe is the key figure in creating Canada's positive international reputation? In a brief paragraph summarize this person's role.
4. Attaran characterizes the "internationalists' experiment" as "a qualified success" (paragraph 10). Does such a claim strengthen or weaken his argument? Explain.
5. What is the significance of the ideas of Thomas Hobbes to the essay (paragraph 12)? Using a reliable source, briefly explain Hobbes's ideas on statecraft and their importance to Attaran's argument.

6. What main rhetorical pattern does the author use to support his points? Choose one subsection under the heading "Backtracking" and discuss his strategies to increase reader comprehension. Could he have used other strategies to help? How does that subsection function within the larger section, contributing to its effectiveness?

7. Referring to paragraph 32 and at least one other paragraph in which the US is mentioned, explain the author's reasons for comparing the Canada to the US. How do the comparisons advance his argument?

8. Summarize paragraphs 35–37 in two or three sentences.

9. Analyze Attaran's argument as a whole. You could consider purpose and audience, order of points, use of appeals, and other argumentative strategies.

POST-READING

1. In about 500 words, analyze the role of a Canadian prime minister after Lester Pearson (for example, Pierre Elliott Trudeau) in promoting Pearson's ideals of internationalism, as described in Attaran's essay. Use at least two reliable sources.

2. *Collaborative or individual activity:* Do you agree with Attaran's assessment concerning Canada's international reputation? What evidence have you seen that convinces you that Canada's status is declining (or not declining)? Such evidence could be based on news reports, discussions with friends, observations, etc.

See also "Into Afghanistan: The transformation of Canada's international security policy since 9/11," Post-reading question #4, p. 233.

RELATED WEBSITES OF INTEREST

"The ugly Canadian" refers in passing to many Canadian and international organizations, whose pages can be searched for more specific information. For example, information on the Anti-Bribery Convention (see paragraph 20) can be found by performing a search at the Organisation for Economic Co-operation and Development (OECD) homepage.

Organisation for Economic Co-operation and Development:
www.oecd.org

World Health Organization:
www.who.int/en/

World Trade Organization/Tariffs:
www.wto.org/english/tratop_e/tariffs_e/tariffs_e.htm

International Convention for the Protection of All Persons from Enforced Disappearance:
www2.ohchr.org/english/law/disappearance-convention.htm

Into Afghanistan: The transformation of Canada's international security policy since 9/11

Paul H. Chapin

(4,730 words)

Pre-reading

1. After reading the abstract, along with scanning the titles of sources on the References pages, assess the writer's attitude to the war in Afghanistan and Canada's past and present role in the conflict. If you wish, you can also assess information about the author using a reliable source. Write a short paragraph explaining your assessment and including a reading hypothesis. (See Chapter 5, p. 52).

2. Do an Internet search to investigate Canada's past and present role in Afghanistan. You could use a reliable news report or a government site like the following: Foreign Affairs and International Trade Canada (NATO page with link to "Canada in Afghanistan" page): www.international.gc.ca/nato-otan/index.aspx

After 9/11, Canadians began to take the world seriously again and insisted that their government do so as well. Grudgingly, ministers and officials stopped talking about human security and effective multilateralism and got on with devising a national security strategy, defending the country, and fighting Islamist terrorism in Afghanistan. US interests benefited from the changes in Canada's outlook and abilities, and Washington was appreciative of the outstanding performance of the Canadian Forces in Kandahar. Support for the war is declining in Canada and it will take more than compliments from the White House and the Pentagon for Canada to retain a robust military presence in Afghanistan beyond 2011.

Keywords: Canada; international security policy; transformation; Afghanistan; post-9/11

Introduction

1   Canadians and Americans have enjoyed a measure of security unlike that of almost any other people. Protected by vast oceans and an impenetrable Arctic region, with little to fear from one another after the British army left Canada and the Union army was demobilized at the end of the Civil War, their wars have been foreign wars and largely ones of choice rather than necessity. Canada was still close enough to Britain to declare war on Germany almost immediately in 1914 and again in 1939, but in neither case was the decision automatic. The United States waited until 1917 and 1941, when attacks on US interests overseas demanded a response. In Korea, Vietnam, and Kuwait, it was the calculus of international peace and security, not defense of the

homeland, that drove the decision to fight rather than let aggression stand. In these and other wars of the twentieth century, the security interests of North Americans were certainly engaged. But not for generations had the folks at home in Toronto or Toledo had to worry about foreign armies the way they did—and still do—in Tallinn or Tel Aviv. Their soldiers fought many battles, but they fought them in Europe, the Middle East, and the Pacific. Some 100,000 Canadians and 125,000 Americans lie buried in military cemeteries overseas.

2   Where you live matters. Israelis, possessing a strip of territory less than 20 kilometres across at its waist and surrounded by hostile neighbours, have lived in fear of extinction since the founding of their state. Poles, with an expansion-minded Germany on one side and a Russian colossus on the other, have seen their state relocated, carved up, and three times disappear altogether. For centuries, Britons were secure only as long as they could prevent a hostile power from dominating the continent and suffocating their offshore island.

3   For North Americans, it was not until 2001 that foreigners assaulted their homeland and killed citizens in the streets. Canadian casualties were a fraction of the US total, but the trauma Canadians suffered approached that of Americans. They lived through the tragedy in real-time in the same time zones as Americans. The lessons of 9/11 were many, but the most important was that North America had become "an area of operations" like every other continent.

Responding to 9/11

4   Canada's response to the events of 9/11 is a study in contrasts. Shock and confusion were the first reactions, as people struggled to comprehend what they had seen but could not believe. The population, however, was hardier than the government. Before the day was over, Canadian airports received 142 airliners denied permission to land in the United States, and Canadian homes, schools, and community centres took in 24,000 people. By that evening, Canadian emergency crews were gearing up to go to New York. The following day, across

Canada there were spontaneous displays of support and affection for Americans—and growing pressure on the government to show some solidarity in the face of adversity.

5   For days, Canada's political leadership remained paralyzed. While the Canadian Forces assigned some 80 CF-18s to combat air patrol duty, while Canadian warships took up picket stations and linked to NORAD to detect air traffic not conforming to expected patterns, while army rapid response units were placed on alert, and while the security and intelligence community went into overdrive to uncover any planned strikes against Canada, the prime minister settled for keeping "in contact by phone" with his advisors (Chrétien 2007). There was no need for an emergency meeting of Cabinet, Jean Chrétien wrote in his memoirs, nor for the recall of Parliament. If the opposition wanted to ask questions, they could wait until Monday when the House of Commons returned from recess.

6   Nor did the prime minister want to "bother" George Bush by putting a call in to him; it was the president who called the next morning to thank Canadians for their sympathy and generosity. Chrétien knew that Tony Blair had called the president and would be traveling to the United States to underscore Britain's support, but Chrétien himself had no desire "to push myself forward." If Blair wanted to be seen at Bush's side "to strengthen his position in Europe as the United States' closest ally, that was his call" (Chrétien 2007, 299). By Friday, however, the prime minister had heard the voice of history: "There go my people. I must find out where they are going so I can lead them."[1] Agreeing to a national day of mourning, he arrived on Parliament Hill expecting 15,000 people and found ten times that number. "At moments like this," he pronounced, "what we feel and the gestures we make are all that matter." To Americans, he said: "You are not alone in this. We are with you" (Chrétien 2007, 297).[2]

7   The government mobilized slowly and grudgingly, taking steps it could not avoid and fretting about costs. Not until two years later, after Chrétien had left office, did the new Liberal administration of Prime Minister Paul Martin articulate a Canadian national security policy. By the time it did, the cumulative impact of the measures already taken was substantial. Not only had Canadian security-related

expenditures exceeded $10 billion, but new anti-terrorism laws had been enacted, new departments and agencies of government had been created, and stringent border management arrangements had put the lie to Churchill's observation that the long Canada–US frontier "guarded only by neighbourly respect and honourable obligations is an example to every country and a pattern for the future of the world."[3] A year later, the Canadian Forces established the first Canada Command responsible for the defense of the country.[4]

National security interests

8   The appearance in April 2004 of *Securing an Open Society: Canada's National Security Policy* (Government of Canada 2004) was notable for being the first comprehensive statement of national security policy ever issued by a Canadian government. The document, which discussed the security threats that confronted Canada, described the legal and administrative changes made since 9/11, and outlined plans for the future. A *Progress Report on the Implementation of Canada's National Security Policy* was issued in April 2005 (Government of Canada 2005a).

9   *National Security Policy* was particularly noteworthy for articulating core security interests. The first of these was "protecting Canada and the safety and security of Canadians at home and abroad." Unremarkable as it might sound to Americans and Europeans, the pursuit of such an interest in Canada required governments at every level to do something few had believed necessary since World War II: look to the physical security of their citizens, their institutions, and their critical infrastructure.

10   For generations before 9/11, Canadians had lived in what was often referred to as the "peaceable kingdom," going about their lives rarely giving a thought to their personal safety. They treated each other with such pronounced civility, it had become Canadians' defining characteristic—at least for American late-night television. Even their protests were usually peaceful. As Canada's most distinguished civil rights scholar Alan Borovoy once observed, "In Canada we don't ban demonstrations, we re-route them."[5] More importantly, acts of terrorism were so

rare there was little law or policy to deal with them. Canadians could walk into virtually any public building—including the Parliament buildings, National Defence Headquarters, and the Department of Foreign Affairs and International Trade—uninspected and often unchallenged. The role of the aged and unarmed corps of commissionaires was to direct you if you got lost and to phone the police in the event of a disturbance.

11   The second core interest identified in *National Security Policy* was "ensuring that Canada is not a base for threats to our allies." It is a longstanding principle of international law that states are responsible for controlling activities on their territory which could pose a threat to others, but it had been generations since Canadians and Americans had thought about their reciprocal security obligations. The last time these had been politically articulated was in 1938 as war loomed in Europe. The public exchange between President Roosevelt and Prime Minister Mackenzie King was diplomatic in tone but nonetheless had an edge to it:

> Roosevelt: I give to you assurance that the people of the United States will not stand idly by if domination of Canadian soil is threatened by any other Empire.

> King: We, too, have our obligations as a good friendly neighbour, and one of them is to see that, at our own instance, our country is made as immune from attack or possible invasion as we can reasonably be expected to make it, and that should the occasion ever arise, enemy forces should not be able to pursue their way, either by land, sea or air, to the United States across Canadian territory.[6]

12   In *National Security Policy*, the ally the government had in mind was again the United States—where the conventional wisdom held that some of the 9/11 hijackers had crossed over from Canada. None had, but governments on both sides of the border knew well how easily the charge could have been true. Virtually all the most notorious international terrorist organizations maintained a presence in Canada. Entering the United States using one of the 86 official points of entry and numerous unofficial crossings provided ample opportunity for operatives to penetrate US national security, and some jihadist

terrorists had already done so—including the hapless Ahmed Ressam, who had tried to cross the border in 1999 intending to blow up Los Angeles International Airport (Bell 2005).

13   The third security interest identified in *National Security Policy* was "contributing to international security." The paper was notable for characterizing the world as a rather more dangerous place than most Canadians had heard their government describe it, featuring international terrorism, weapons of mass destruction, failed and failing states, and intra- and interstate conflicts. There was little mention of peace-keeping; rather, Canada needed "armed forces that are flexible, responsive and combat-capable," enhanced capacity for "helping restore peace, order and good government" in war-torn societies, and greater effort to halt the proliferation of weapons of mass destruction.

14   It was also clear, however, that the government remained reluctant to fully confront the new security realities. The paper made scant reference to the fact that the Canadian Forces were fighting a war in Afghanistan, hardly mentioned al Qaeda or the Taliban, and did not once use the words *Islamist* or *jihadist* to describe the terrorism that *National Security Policy* was intended to deal with.

The new internationalism

15   As it happened, the real transformation post-9/11 was in the outlook of Canadians rather than that of their government, and it was little short of revolutionary.

16   For more than 30 years Canada had been drawing back from international engagement, the product of a succession of political leaders whose interests and abilities were largely confined to federal/provincial power struggles. When Pierre Trudeau came to office in 1968, he declared his priority to ensure the political survival of Canada as a federal and bilingual state, not "to go crusading abroad." Canada's foreign policy, he said, should be "the extension abroad of national policies," which he identified as social justice, quality of life, and economic growth (Hillmer and Granatstein 1994).

17   In office almost without interruption until 1984, Trudeau lowered the country's international expectations while attempting to position Canada somewhere between East and West. He sought to distance Canada from the United States; forged "alternative sources of influence, of trade, of friendship" with the USSR and China; and cultivated the leaders of the "non-aligned" movement in Latin America, Africa, and Asia. Not until the very end did Trudeau begin to appreciate that Canada's foreign policy should also reflect the country's security interests—at which point, with mere months to go before retirement, he undertook a highly publicized and embarrassingly fruitless self-described "peace mission." By then, however, the belief was deeply rooted in the minds of Canadians that they were above the fray, a superior people with an international vocation to point out others' failings and, through dispassionate peace-keeping, to keep them from killing each other. Few bothered to explore how other liberal democratic countries viewed Canada's international convictions or what their leaders thought of Trudeau.[7]

18   The Conservative government of Brian Mulroney, who practiced a brand of international *realpolitik* better suited to the times, demonstrated how to work more effectively with allies and adversaries alike, achieving remarkable results. The period from 1984 to 1993 was arguably one of the most successful in the history of Canadian foreign policy, with the Free Trade Agreement writing *finis* to 150 years of Canadian insecurity about trading with the Yankees and the prime minister engaging in high-level diplomacy to bring the Cold War to a peaceful conclusion—a performance as impressive as any in Canadian history.[8] The Mulroney government, however, was never able to convince Canadians that the world remained a dangerous place after the Cold War ended, that US policy was key to Canada's security, and that Canada could influence the United States if it had more to contribute than simply offering sermons about US shortcomings.

19   In 1993, when the Liberals returned to office under Jean Chrétien, Canadians found themselves back in the Trudeau era: a national government preoccupied with federal/provincial politics, catering to pacifist sentiment, fearful and disdainful of Canada's southern neighbour, and determined to keep Canada out of foreign entanglements. When these were inevitable, as in the Balkans and the Horn of Africa,

Canada followed rather than led, avoiding participation in the "contact groups" managing crises, holding that Canadian military deployments were for peacekeeping purposes, and not reporting casualties. Between 1992 and 2004, some 40,000 Canadian soldiers served in Bosnia-Herzegovina under either UN or NATO command, and 23 lost their lives. Few Canadians ever appreciated the magnitude of the role their forces played.

20   Meanwhile, Canadian foreign policy was diverted from protecting and promoting national interests into "new age" pursuits that stressed "values" (Government of Canada 1995). With a population conditioned to believe that the end of the Cold War meant that the international order was likely to be remain peaceful indefinitely, that multilateral institutions could manage any vexing problems that arose, and that the only problem state was the United States, foreign policy engagements were viewed as a discretionary activity. Issues could be selected for their psychic stimulus, not for their contribution to protecting and promoting the interests of the people.

21   The results were hardly benign:

- The pursuit of "human security" in remote regions of the world at the cost of misleading Canadians about real dangers closer to home, which one day would leave the population angry and unprepared for the changes they would have to make in their domestic laws and institutions to deal with external threats that few suspected even existed;

- A "global" ban on anti-personnel mines achieved through deceitful practices effectively denying the Canadian Army and international peacekeeping forces longstanding means of self-defense in combat zones, arguably compromising important security interests of key allies, and excluding countries essential to the ban's effectiveness—notably, the United States, Russia, China, India and Pakistan, Egypt and Israel, and the two Koreas;

- The establishment of an International Criminal Court (ICC) lacking the democratic accountability of every court in every democratic state across the globe. ICC advocates swore that the new court was intended for use only in failed states without functioning judicial systems and that it would never subject Canadians or Americans to frivolous or political prosecution.[9] These assurances have since proven empty.[10]

22   When Paul Martin wrested power from Jean Chrétien in December 2003, he was attuned to the concerns that had been mounting about the direction of Canadian international security policy, amply documented in parliamentary committee reports, think tank studies, and publications with titles such as *Borderline Insecurity* (Senate of Canada June 2005a), *Wounded: Canada's Military and the Legacy of Neglect* (Senate of Canada September 2005b), *Canada Without Armed Forces* (Bland 2003), *Cold Terror: How Canada Nurtures and Exports Terrorism Around the World* (Bell 2005), and *While Canada Slept* (Cohen 2003).

23   A finance minister of long standing and the son of a minister who had served in the St Laurent, Pearson, and Trudeau cabinets, Paul Martin was arguably one of the best-prepared prime ministers Canada ever had. As prime minister, however, his tenure was short: six months with a majority in Parliament, followed by 18 months in minority before going down to defeat in January 2006. But it was enough time to reorient Canadian security policy, beginning with the *National Security Policy* report of April 2004, followed by the government's *International Policy Statement* (IPS) tabled in Parliament in April 2005 proposing to restore Canada to "a role of pride and influence in the world" (Government of Canada 2005b).

24   Martin took a personal hand in writing the introduction to the IPS, returning security issues to a central place in Canada's international policy priorities. The key foreign policy priority, he wrote, was to "revitalize" the Canadian–American partnership, principally through enhancing security cooperation while maintaining the free flow of goods and services across the border. He also wanted Canada to "make a difference globally" on security, economic, and human rights issues, and to improve the functioning of vital multilateral institutions. But progress in relations with Washington was stalled by the government's decision in 2005—and how it announced it—not to participate in ballistic missile defense of

the continent. Nor, in the final analysis, was the Martin government sufficiently disciplined in its public comments on US trade and environmental policy to convince everyone in Washington that Ottawa was concerned enough about improving relations not to resort to anti-American rhetoric when there was political advantage to be gained.

Into Afghanistan

25   It was Afghanistan, however, that mattered most, and on that count Americans, Brits, and others were not reluctant to laud the fact that "Canada is back." Afghanistan represents Canada's largest international security undertaking since the Korean War, when 25,600 Canadian Forces personnel were sent to the Korean peninsula and casualties totaled 1,609, of whom 406 never returned home (Stairs 1974, 279). And it has been vastly more expensive.

26   Canada has participated in the Afghanistan war since the beginning, starting in October 2001 with the dispatch of a naval task group and aircraft to secure sea lanes and airspace in the region, followed by a detachment of special forces from the army's elite Joint Task Force 2 (JTF2). A battalion from the Princess Patricia's Canadian Light Infantry (3PPCLI) arrived in February 2002, first to help protect the American airfield in Kandahar and then to hunt for al Qaeda and the Taliban.

27   The Chrétien government undertook the operation in large part because it couldn't avoid doing so in the face of overwhelming support for participation from the public, Parliament, the media, allies, and the United Nations. In his memoir, Chrétien makes a virtue of necessity, but he is careful to explain that Afghanistan was "a multilateral undertaking in keeping with our commitment to NATO" (Chrétien 2007, 304). In a second phase of Canadian operations, he approved Canada assuming command of the NATO/ISAF force in Kabul in 2003 because he believed "we were going to get our soldiers in a more secure place where their assignment was closer to traditional peacekeeping" (Chrétien 2007, 305). Tellingly, he devotes not much more than a page in his 400-page memoir to the two years of his stewardship of Canada's military engagement in Afghanistan.

28   In fact, the government's decision in January 2003 to commit a large force to ISAF in Kabul had little to do with keeping Canadian soldiers out of harm's way in Afghanistan and almost everything to do with keeping them out of Iraq in March 2003—a subject to which Chrétien devotes a dozen pages in his memoirs.

29   Early in its first mandate, the Martin government declared its intention to maintain a Canadian military presence in Afghanistan when the existing ISAF commitment ended in August 2004, undertaking to send "a new rotation of ground troops and air personnel to support the NATO mission in Afghanistan." It was not until well into 2005, however, that government settled on the main elements of the next phase of Canada's engagement. Indecision is not an adequate explanation for the delay. Canada's unsettled political scene was a contributing factor, as were NATO's own deliberations on the next phases of its engagement in Afghanistan and the Canadian Forces requirement for an operational pause to allow them to train and re-equip for new engagements.

30   In any event, the decision was that Canada would return to Kandahar to take responsibility for a provincial reconstruction team (PRT) there in the fall of 2005 and deploy a battle group there in February 2006 to help train Afghan security forces and help secure the southern region of the country.

Out of Afghanistan

31   In the summer of 2006, the Taliban set out to win the war in Afghanistan. Marshalling their forces in the densely populated Panjwayi district of southern Afghanistan and transferring in fighters from other districts and from Pakistan, the Taliban had an army of some 12,000 mobilized to attack and take the city of Kandahar. Ten years earlier, Afghans recalled, the Taliban had raised an army in the same area, captured Kandahar, and eventually seized control of the whole country.

32   If Kandahar had fallen this time, the consequences might not have been much less dire. In the view of a former ISAF commander, Canada's Gen. Rick Hillier, "If Kandahar had been encircled, if Highway 1 had been shut down and if the Panjwayi had

been held by the Taliban, the government in Kabul would have fallen" (Horn 2009, 400). The ISAF commander of the day, British Gen. David Richards, had feared worse. Were Kandahar to have been lost, he recalled, it would not have mattered how well the British did in Helmand or the Dutch in Uruzgan, contiguous to Kandahar. "Their two provinces would also, as night followed day, have failed because we would have lost the consent of the Pashtun people because of the totemic importance of Kandahar" (Horn 2009, 400).

33   What stood in the way was the recently arrived Canadian battle group supported by elements of the Afghan National Army (ANA) and small contingents of British, Dutch, and US forces. In 16 weeks of intensive ground action, accorded the NATO code name Operation Medusa, the Canadian-led force under the command of Brig. Gen. David Fraser defeated the much larger Taliban force and saved Kandahar—and maybe also Afghanistan. The price was considerable. In their first four years in-theater, the Canadian Forces had sustained just eight casualties, four of them in a friendly-fire incident at the hands of the US Air Force. In 2006 alone, 38 Canadian soldiers lost their lives, along with the senior Canadian diplomat assigned to the PRT in Kandahar. Casualties would continue at comparable levels in the years that followed: 30 in 2007, 32 in 2008, and 27 in 2009.[11] As casualties mounted, Canadians at home began to worry.

34   Canadian opinion on Afghanistan had always been divided. From the very beginning, a significant minority opposed sending Canadian troops to Afghanistan just as they had opposed sending troops to every other war. But until the summer of 2006, more than half of those polled regularly voiced support for the mission. Canadians understood the mission: the Canadian Forces were providing critical assistance to Afghans, helping them create a peaceful and democratic society. And they understood the risks: their soldiers, diplomats, and aid workers might be killed or injured.

35   The picture changed, however, when IEDs and suicide bombings began to take a large toll. On television, the evening news regularly led with military ceremonies in which flag-draped caskets were loaded onto transport aircraft at Kandahar Airfield, were met by grieving families at Canadian Forces Base Trenton,

and escorted along Highway 401 (the "highway of heroes") to Toronto for autopsy—with onlookers, local police, and firefighters crowding the overpasses to pay quiet tribute. In the newspapers, an avalanche of breathless and tendentious "eye-witness" reports from city-beat reporters on single assignment in Afghanistan covered the ramp ceremonies and buried offsetting stories on Afghan political and economic successes. By the fall of 2006, polls regularly reported that more Canadians now opposed than supported the war effort.

36   By then a new Conservative government had taken office (in January 2006) led by Prime Minister Stephen Harper, more attuned to Canada's national security interests and in favour of the mission in Afghanistan. The Harper government, however, did not command a majority of seats in the House of Commons and thus required the support of at least some of the opposition parties to remain in office—as it still does after Canada's third successive inconclusive election in October 2008. With distemper rising in Parliament over the Afghanistan mission, the government resorted to the Bush administration's strategy of commissioning a high-level group to review options. Astutely, the government asked one of the Liberal Party's retired luminaries, John Manley—a nationally respected former deputy prime minister and foreign minister—to head up an Independent Panel on Canada's Future Role in Afghanistan.[12]

37   In January 2008, the Manley Panel reported back, endorsing a continuation of Canada's military mission provided NATO allies committed more troops to the Kandahar region (Independent Panel 2008). The panel also recommended boosting Canadian aid delivery with a special focus on job creation, signature projects to enhance the visibility of Canadian development programs, better coordination of the overall effort, and a full-scale multinational review of NATO's security, governance, and development efforts in 2011.

38   The panel's recommendations were well received and formed the basis for a government-sponsored resolution in Parliament (13 March 2008) which passed by a vote of 198 to 77, Conservatives and Liberals supporting the motion, the socialist New Democratic Party and the separatist Bloc Québécois party opposing. Canada would maintain its

military presence in Kandahar for the time being, training Afghan forces and providing security for reconstruction and development efforts. But the government would notify NATO that "Canada will end its presence in Kandahar as of July 2011," with the redeployment of Canadian troops out of Kandahar to be completed by December 2011.

39   As of January 2010, it remains to be seen what actually will transpire. The Harper government has given no indication that it is planning for anything other than a withdrawal of Canadian Forces as scheduled. But three years is a long time in international politics, and it is unlikely that a decision taken in 2008 will not be revisited in some form before it is to take effect in 2011. Some have suggested that the government reconvene a group similar to the Manley Panel to take stock and make recommendations for the future (Conference of Defence Associations 2009).

40   Selling Canadians on the idea of extending the military mission in Afghanistan would be difficult, but not impossible. In a recent poll for the Canadian Defence and Foreign Affairs Institute, a majority (53 per cent) believed that Canada should end its military mission in 2011 and concentrate exclusively on humanitarian work and reconstruction, while only 15 per cent wanted to see an ongoing role for the Canadian Forces past 2011 (Innovative Research Group 2009). But support for an ongoing military role increased to 40 per cent in that poll if the United States increased its own troop presence and "Obama asked Canada to stay as a part of a plan to provide military security to allow renewed international efforts to address Afghanistan's economic, political and social issues." The first condition has since been met; whether Obama will act on the second is anyone's guess. In the final analysis, much will depend on how the administration in Washington approaches its own deadline, announced by the president in his address at West Point in December 2009, "to begin the transfer of our forces out of Afghanistan in July of 2011" (Obama 2009).

American Review of Canadian Studies.
2010. June 40 (2).

Notes

1. Alexandre Ledru-Rollin (1807–1874).
2. September 11, 2002. A year later, on the anniversary, Chrétien would tell Peter Mansbridge of the CBC that the US was arrogant and greedy, used its power to humiliate others, and was itself partly to be blame for 9/11. "I said that in New York one day. I said, you know talking, it was Wall Street, and it was a crowd of capitalists, of course, and they were complaining because we have a normal relation with Cuba, and this and that, and, you know, we cannot do everything we want. And I said . . . if I recall, it was probably these words: 'When you're powerful like you are, you guys, is the time to be nice.' And it is one of the problems. You know, you cannot exercise your powers to the point of humiliation for the others. And that is what the Western world, not only the Americans, the Western world has to realize, because they are human beings too, and there are long term consequences if you don't look hard at the reality in 10 or 20, or 30 years from now. And I do think that the Western world is going to be too rich in relation to the poor world. And necessarily, you know, we look upon us being arrogant, self satisfying, greedy and with no limits. And the 11th of September is an occasion for me to realize that it's even more" (CBC News Online Staff 2002).
3. An observation made by Ronald Reagan in speaking to a joint session of the Canadian House of Commons and Senate in Ottawa, March 11, 1981.
4. The establishment of Canada Command was part of a major reorganization of the command structure of the Canadian Forces conceived some years earlier and rolled out in 2005. The transformation also saw the creation of a new Canadian Expeditionary Forces Command (CEFCOM) given responsibility for all operations outside North America, a Canadian Special Forces Command, and a Canadian Operational Support Command. The establishment of Canada Command helped to simplify *bilateral* cooperation with US Northern Command (USNORTHCOM) created in 2002. NORAD remained as a *bi-national* command in which Canadians and Americans served together in the same chain of command, providing aerospace warning and control of North America.
5. Quoted in Peter (1979).
6. Address of President Franklin D. Roosevelt at Queen's University, Kingston, Ontario, August 18, 1938; remarks by Prime Minister William Lyon Mackenzie King, Woodbridge, Ontario, August 20, 1938.
7. The British, among others, couldn't stand Trudeau. Margaret Thatcher quarrelled with him about most things, describing him in her memoir as a typical "liberal leftist" (1993, 321) unable to grasp the brutal realities of Soviet communism. Trudeau agreed: "It's well known that we disagreed on many things, including East–West relations and North–South relations. . . . She'd be very critical of me and I of her. What separated her and me were clear and wide ideological disputes, so wide that there was no point trying to convert each other" (1993, 222). In his diary, Ronald Reagan recounts an argument between the two: "I thought at one point Margaret was going to order Pierre

to go stand in a corner" (2007, 156). Courtesy of recently declassified documents, we also know what one British High Commissioner to Ottawa, Richard Moran (British High Commissioner, 1981–1984) thought of Trudeau. "He has not been greatly respected or trusted in London. He has never entirely shaken off his past as a well-to-do hippie and draft dodger. His views on East/West relations have been particularly suspect. Many of my colleagues here admire him. I cannot say I do. He is an odd fish and his own worst enemy, and on the whole I think his influence on Canada in the past sixteen years has been detrimental."

8. See, for instance, the numerous references to the role played by Brian Mulroney in *A World Transformed* (Bush and Scowcroft 1998) and in *Germany United and Europe Transformed* (Zelikow and Rice 1997).

9. A good example of the assurances offered that the ICC would not be politicized can be found in a speech given at the University of Toronto Law School on January 13, 2003, by Bill Graham, the Canadian Minister of Foreign Affairs and a former professor in the Faculty of Law at the University of Toronto: "I very much regret that the United States withdrew its support for the Court. While respecting the opinion of our US colleagues, I (along with our European allies) find the intensity of their present campaign against the Court mystifying. To suggest, as the President's spokesperson did recently, that the Court would subject 'Americans—civilians and military—to arbitrary standards of justice' ignores the efforts that were made to accommodate US concerns when drafting the treaty. Safeguards ensure that no American, or Canadian for that matter, could ever be subject to a frivolous or political prosecution. The principle of complementarity in Article 17 of the ICC Statute ensures that the International Criminal Court is not a threat to democratic states whose legal systems enshrine the rule of law. Rather it is a modern and necessary tool of international justice."

10. The Court's main function today seems to be to provide the political left with the means to criminalize the policies of the political right. In 2009, opposition MPs in the Canadian Parliament suggested government ministers, officials, and military officers were guilty of war crimes for ignoring "warnings" that Taliban fighters detained by the Canadian Forces were being "tortured" when transferred to Afghanistan authorities. Michael Byers, a professor at the University of British Columbia and an NDP candidate for Parliament, has written to ICC Prosecutor Luis Moreno-Ocampo requesting that the Court open an investigation into the detainee issue.

11. The single best source of up-to-date information on US, Canadian, and other nations' casualties in both Afghanistan and Iraq is the website of iCasualties.org, created in 2003 to track casualties, drawing on both official and news accounts. Good numbers on a variety of subjects related to both conflicts are also available from the Brookings Institution, which regularly updates and posts an *Afghanistan Index* and an *Iraq Index*.

12. Other members of the Panel were: Derek Burney, chief of staff to Prime Minister Mulroney and later Ambassador to Washington; Jake Epp, a federal Cabinet minister in the Conservative governments of Joe Clark and Brian Mulroney, later chairman of Ontario Power Generation; Paul Tellier, a past clerk of the Privy Council, president of CN Rail, and CEO of Bombardier; and Pamela Wallin, a noted CBC radio and television journalist and Canadian consul general in New York, appointed to the Canadian Senate in 2009. The Panel was supported by a Secretariat of senior officials and military officers, and by external advisors drawn from universities, think tanks, and business and communications interests.

References

Bell, Stewart. 2005. *Cold terror: How Canada nurtures and exports terrorism around the world.* Mississauga, ON: John Wiley.

Bland, Douglas L., ed. 2003. *Canada without armed forces?* Kingston, ON: Queen's University Press.

Bush, George, and Brent Scowcroft. 1998. *A world transformed.* New York: Alfred P. Knopf.

Byers-Schabas. 2009. Letter to ICC, 3 December. http://rideau institute.ca/file-library.

Chrétien, Jean. 2007. *My years as prime minister.* Toronto: Alfred A. Knopf.

CBC News Online Staff. 2002. Chretien interview on September 11. CBC, September 16. www.cbc.ca/news/features/chretien_interview.

Cohen, Andrew. 2003. *While Canada slept: How we lost our place in the world.* Toronto: McClelland & Stewart.

Conference of Defence Associations. 2009. *A Canadian military presence in Afghanistan post 2011: CDA position paper–December 2009.* Ottawa: Conference of Defence Associations.

Government of Canada. 2005b. *Canada's international policy statement: A role of pride and influence in the world.*

Government of Canada. 1995. *Canada in the world, government statement, 1995.*

Government of Canada. 2004. *Securing an open society: Canada's national security policy, April 2004.*

Government of Canada. 2005a. *Securing an open society: One year later. Progress report on the implementation of Canada's national security policy, April 2005.*

Hillmer, Norman, and J.L. Granatstein. 1994. *Empire to umpire.* Toronto: Irwin.

Horn, Bernd, ed. 2009. *Fortune favours the brave: Tales of courage and tenacity in Canadian military history.* Toronto: Dundurn.

Independent Panel on Canada's Future Role in Afghanistan. 2008. *Final Report.*

Innovative Research Group Inc. 2009. *Canadian Defence and Foreign Affairs Institute 2009 conference poll, October 2009.*

Moran, Richard. 1984. Last impressions of Canada, 12 June 1984. BBC Radio 4, *Parting shots.*

Obama, Barack. 2009. Remarks by the president in address to the nation on the way forward in Afghanistan and Pakistan, United States Military Academy at West Point, New York, December 1. www.whitehouse.gov/the-press-office.

Peter, Laurence J. 1979. *Peter's quotations: Ideas for our time.* Toronto: Bantam.

Reagan, Ronald. 2007. *The Reagan diaries.* New York: Harper-Collins.

Senate of Canada 2005a. *Borderline insecurity: Canada's land border crossings are key to Canada's security and prosperity.* Standing Senate Committee on national Security and Defence.

Senate of Canada. 2005b. *Wounded: Canada's military and the legacy of neglect.* Standing Senate Committee on National Security and Defence.

Thatcher, Margaret. 1993. *The Downing Street years.* New York: HarperCollins.

Trudeau, Pierre. 1993. *Memoirs.* Toronto: McClelland & Stewart.

Zelikow, Philip, and Condoleezza Rice. 1997. *Germany united and Europe transformed: A study in statecraft.* Cambridge, MA: Harvard University Press.

KEY AND CHALLENGING WORDS

colossus, cumulative, commissionaire, reciprocal, hapless, proliferation, dispassionate, multilateral, vexing, discretionary, contiguous, totemic, tendentious, astutely, luminary, redeployment, reconvene

QUESTIONS

1. Analyze the effectiveness of the Introduction. Consider whether it satisfies the general requirements of introductions and whether its claims appear reasonable.

2. Consider the purpose of the section "Responding to 9/11." Show how and why Chapin uses Jean Chrétien's own words against him.

3. a) According to the author, what is remarkable about *Canada's National Security Policy*? b) Summarize the three main aims of the document; c) Where does Chapin criticize the document?

4. Explain the use of direct quotations from the *National Security Policy* in paragraphs 10–13; how is this use different from the use of direction quotations in paragraphs 5–7?

5. a) What rhetorical pattern is used throughout "The New Internationalism"? b) After reading this section, summarize in 1–2 sentences Chapin's "new internationalism";

c) What Canadian prime ministers does Chapin associate with the "new internationalism"?

6. Show how Chapin's diction in paragraph 20 reveals his attitude toward Canada's foreign policy from 1995 to 2003.

7. How does Chapin undermine or qualify the significance of Chrétien's government's role in beginning Canada's commitment to the Afghanistan war?

8. Why does Chapin say the Conservative government of Stephen Harper was "astute" to ask John Manley to lead the panel looking into Canada's role in Afghanistan? Paraphrase the paragraph that discusses the Panel's recommendations.

9. Do you believe Chapin would have supported Canada's continuing military role in Afghanistan beyond 2011? Justify your answer by at least three references to his essay.

POST-READING

1. *Collaborative or individual activity:* Discuss or debate one of the following statements from the essay: a) "…[T]he trauma Canadians suffered [from the events of 9/11] approached that of Americans. They lived through the tragedy in real-time in the same time zones as Americans" (para. 3); b) ". . .[T]he real transformation post-9/11 was in the outlook of Canadians rather than that of their government, and it was little short of revolutionary" (paragraph 15).

2. *Collaborative or individual activity:* Discuss or debate the merits of the policies of "the new internationalism" as

outlined in the essay versus the international policies of Trudeau and Chrétien.

3. Using a reliable source, such as the Canadian government Afghanistan website (see "Related websites of interest"), provide a one to two paragraph update concerning Canada's role in Afghanistan post-2011.

4. Write a comparative analysis of about 750 words on this essay and "The ugly Canadian" (p. 215). You should consider both similarities and differences, making sure you have several bases for comparison.

RELATED WEBSITES OF INTEREST

International Campaign to Ban Landmines:
www.icbl.org/intro.php
(referred to in the second bullet in paragraph 21)

International Criminal Court:
www.icc-cpi.int/Menus/ICC/About+the+Court/
(referred to in the third bullet in paragraph 21)

Federal Government Afghanistan website:
www.afghanistan.gc.ca/canada-afghanistan/index.
aspx?lang=eng

Canadian cannabis: Marijuana as an irritant/problem in Canada–US relations

Paul Gecelovsky

(2,019 words)

Pre-reading

1. Search a government website, such as the federal Department of Justice, to determine the current laws and policies in Canada on marijuana possession and production. Consider the following questions: Under what circumstance, if any, are they legal? What are the penalties for possession and production? Do policies vary from province to province?
2. Define the following terms and briefly explain their differences: legalization, decriminalization, re-criminalization.

1   In a recent survey of the Canada–US relationship, Munroe Eagles noted that the "popular impression" for many Americans was that Canadians were "out of step with their more conservative neighbor to the south" (Eagles 2006, 821). John Herd Thompson made a similar claim in his review of the bilateral relationship over the 1994–2003 period, writing that Canadians are perceived by some Americans as being

"left wing wimps" (Thompson 2003, 17). One area in which Canada may be regarded as out of step with the United States, and Canadians as left wing wimps, is the issue of marijuana. There are real and noticeable differences between Canada and the US in the way each side deals with the issue of marijuana. The following pages examine the marijuana issue in terms of the growing volume of the drug being smuggled into the United States from Canada, the increased potency of the strains of marijuana grown in Canada, and the differences in judicial deterrents adopted to penalize possession and cultivation. This is followed by a look at a couple of possibilities that have the potential to transform the marijuana irritant into the marijuana problem in Canada–US relations.

2   The amount of marijuana being produced in Canada and then illegally exported to the United States is of increasing concern to all levels of American law enforcement. While British Columbia (BC), Ontario, and Quebec are all of concern to US officials, British Columbia presents the largest source of Canadian marijuana for the US market, so the discussion will focus primarily upon that province. The marijuana cultivation industry in BC is thriving, as demonstrated by the fact that the province accounted for almost 40 per cent of all growing operations found by law enforcement officials in Canada in 2003, the last year for which full data are available (CCJS 2004). During that year, the province also had the highest rate of cultivation "incidents" in Canada, at 79 per 100,000 people. What this means is that 79 marijuana cultivation operations were found for every 100,000 people in the province. This is nearly triple the national rate of 27 per 100,000 people, and 33 higher than second-place New Brunswick, at 46. More marijuana cultivation facilities were uncovered by Canadian law enforcement officials in BC (3274) than in all of the other provinces combined (2564), except Quebec (2939), in 2003 (CCJS 2004). In their study of the BC marijuana growing industry over the 1997–2003 period, Darryl Plecas, Aili Malm, and Bryan Kinney identified over 25,000 cultivation operations uncovered by police officers in the province (Plecas, Malm, and Kinney 2005). In terms of the monetary value of marijuana, it is estimated that the annual wholesale value of the provincial industry is approximately C\$6 billion, or what is equivalent to about 5 per cent of the annual provincial gross domestic product. To provide some perspective, the BC marijuana industry is relatively equal in dollar value to the province's public sector, and bigger than the legal exports of sawmill products (C\$4.6 billion) and oil and gas (C\$2.5 billion). In terms of employment, it is estimated that the provincial marijuana industry employs roughly 150,000 people (Mulgrew 2006, 109).

3   The size of the BC marijuana industry is of concern to US law officials, because upwards of 90 per cent of the crop is exported to the American market (Hamilton et al. 2004, 36). More disconcerting to American law enforcement is that there has been a "sharp rise" in the smuggling of marijuana into the United States from Canada and that this has resulted in a near tripling in both the *number* of seizures and the *volume* of marijuana seized over the 2001–2004 period, the last period for which data are available (US Department of Justice 2006).The 2006 International Narcotics Control Strategy Report (INCSR) prepared by the US Department of State indicated that marijuana cultivation is a "thriving industry in Canada" and that "large scale cross-border trafficking" is "a serious concern" of the American government (US Department of State 2006).

4   It is not just the volume of marijuana being smuggled from Canada to the United States that is of concern to Americans; it is also the potency of the marijuana. Of particular interest is the marijuana cultivated in British Columbia: the so-called BC Bud. The US Drug Enforcement Agency assessed BC Bud for its tetrahydrocannabinol (THC) content—the psychoactive drug in marijuana—and found that its THC content was 25 per cent. In comparison, the average THC content is 7 per cent for marijuana consumed in the United States today and only 2 per cent for marijuana smoked in the 1970s (Hamilton et al. 2004, 36). The result of this is that, as Ian Mulgrew has noted, British Columbia "is a marijuana Mecca" and BC Bud is "a globally recognized brand name" that stands "in a pantheon of pot beside such legends as Acapulco Gold or California Sinsemilla" and "is sought by cannabis cognoscenti and commands the highest price" (Mulgrew 2006, 21). The INCRS, in 2006, listed Canada as "a principal drug concern" due to the "continuing large-scale production of high-potency, indoor grown marijuana for export to the United States" (US Department

of State 2006). Moreover, John Walters, Director of the White House Office of National Drug Control Policy (the US drug czar), critically remarked that "Canada is exporting to [the United States] the crack of marijuana" (Hamilton et al. 2004, 36).

5   While the increasing volume of marijuana being smuggled into the United States from Canada and the high potency of the drug are of importance to Americans, the source of gravest concern is what is perceived by Americans to be lax Canadian laws regarding marijuana possession and cultivation. The reasoning goes that if Canada adopted more stern measures and penalties concerning marijuana, the flow to the United States would be abated somewhat. The first area in which Canada is seen as being out of step with the United States is in penalties for marijuana possession. This was demonstrated in the 2003–2006 period, wherein the Chretien and Martin governments in Canada proposed, wrote, and introduced legislation to decriminalize possession of marijuana of 15 grams or less. The American response to this was immediate and forceful. The US drug czar, John Walters, pledged to "respond to the threat" that this posed to the United States (Klein 2003, 12). One of the means proposed to deal with the threat was the "re-criminalizing" of marijuana possession at the American border. Christopher Sands has noted that some members of Congress and the media in the United States "advanced the notion that such possession could be 're-criminalized' by US border officials if it appeared on the criminal record of a Canadian requesting entry into the United States, even as a misdemeanor" (Sands 2006, 130). The American concerns over decriminalization of marijuana were allayed with the election, in January 2006, of the Conservative government led by Stephen Harper. The Harper government had campaigned on a promise to end the decriminalization initiative of the Martin government and, therefore, did not reintroduce the marijuana legislation after it died in committee at the end of the 38th Parliament.

6   While the decriminalization issue has been resolved for the duration of the present Conservative government, the laxity of Canadian laws pertaining to the production of marijuana is still troubling to many Americans. Of the 25,000 growing operations identified by BC law enforcement between 1997 and 2003 mentioned previously, less than 17,000 were investigated and less than one-half of those were prosecuted (Plecas, Malm, and Kinney 2005). Plecas, Malm, and Kinney found that charges were entered in less than one-half of all raids conducted on marijuana operations in British Columbia over the last seven years. Moreover, they noted that only about one in ten of those convicted were sentenced to a jail term, with the average sentence being five months (Plecas, Malm, and Kinney 2005, 50). The authors compared the sentences handed out in BC with what would have happened had these cases come to trial in Washington state, just south of the border. Under sentencing guidelines found in Washington state, one-half of the convictions would have resulted in mandatory jail sentences of at least five years and over two-thirds of those convicted would have served some time in prison (Plecas, Malm, and Kinney 2005, 56). In comparison, the sentences received in Canada appear lenient. Mulgrew has noted that marijuana cultivators in Canada view judicial punishments not as a deterrent but rather as "an operating cost" (Mulgrew 2006, 5). Marijuana cultivation "has been a relatively minimum-risk activity due to low sentences meted out by Canadian courts," as noted in the 2006 INC SR. The report further "encourage[d] Canada to take steps to improve its ability to expedite investigations and prosecutions" and to "strengthen judicial deterrents" (US Department of State 2006).

7   The result of all this is that Canada is regarded as being soft on marijuana use and cultivation. Evidence of this is provided by Canada being consistently mentioned in the annual Presidential Determination on Major Drug Transit or Major Illicit Drug Producing Countries. While Canada has thus far escaped being placed on the Majors List (i.e., those states listed as major drug transit or producing countries), it is the only state not on the list to have been mentioned in the reports over the last five years. For 2007, Canada and North Korea are the only two states not on the list but noted in the Presidential Determination (US Office of the President 2006).

8   The Canadian and American governments cooperate on a wide range of policy issues, and the bilateral relationship is mostly without major controversy or difficulty. The differences in the Canadian and American approaches to marijuana are regarded

primarily as an irritant in the relationship, but one of a number of policy areas on which Canada and the United States differ. There are, however, two ways in which the marijuana irritant could become the marijuana *problem* in the bilateral relationship. The first would be if the marijuana irritant were to become more directly linked with homeland security in the United States. Marijuana is still largely regarded as a law enforcement issue, not a national security problem. It is perceived more as a state-level concern than a national policy issue. This may change, however. For instance, if it is determined that groups in Canada on the US list of foreign terrorist organizations maintained by the State Department are using marijuana to generate revenue for their operations, including purchasing weaponry and planning attacks in the US, this could result in the marijuana issue being redefined as part of the war on terror and, therefore, a homeland security problem. A second, and related, manner in which the marijuana irritant could become more problematic for Canada is if the Bush administration, or the US Congress, began to link more closely the export to the US of marijuana from Canada with cocaine and other drugs from Mexico in the current American war on drugs. Thus far, Canadian officials have been relatively successful in persuading American government officials of the differences in the scale and nature of the drug threats emanating from Canada and from Mexico. The result of this has been to differentiate the northern border with Canada from the southern border with Mexico (Sokolsky and Legasse 2006).

9   If either of the two scenarios outlined above were to occur, and the marijuana irritant were to become the marijuana problem, this would have significant implications for Canada. Two main lines of potential American response may be outlined briefly. The first would entail a further intensification and militarization of the Canada–US border, or movement toward what Peter Andreas has referred to as a "Mexicanization of the Canadian border" (Andreas 2005). This, in turn, would cause a significant reduction in and delay of human and commercial cross-border traffic, thereby negatively impacting the bilateral commercial relationship for both countries. A second manner in which the United States might respond should marijuana become a problem in the Canada–US relationship is to increase pressure on Canada to more closely align Canadian marijuana policy with that of the United States.

The American Review of Canadian Studies.
2008. Summer 38 (2).

Sources

Andreas, Peter. 2005. "The Mexicanization of the US–Canada Border: Asymmetric Interdependence in a Changing Security Context." *International Journal*, 60: 449–62.

Canadian Centre for Justice Statistics. 2004. "Canadian Crime Statistics 2003." http://statscan.ca/english/freepub/85-205XIE/0000385-205-XIE.pdf. Accessed April 17, 2007.

Eagles, Munroe. 2006. "Canadian–American Relations in a Turbulent Era." *PS: Political Science and Politics* 39:821–24.

Hamilton, Anita, Ben Bergman, Laura Blue, Chris Daniels, Deborah Jones, and Elaine Shannon. 2004. "This Bud's for the US" *Time* 164:36–37.

Klein, Naomi. 2003. "Canada: Hippie Nation?" *The Nation* July 21/28:12.

Mulgrew, Ian. 2006. *Bud Inc.: Inside Canada's Marijuana Industry* (Toronto: Vintage).

Plecas, Darryl, Aili Maim, and Bryan Kinney. 2005. "Marihuana Growing Operations in British Columbia Revisited, 1997–2003." www.ucfV.ca/pages/Special/Marihuana_Grow_Ops_in_BC_Study.pdf. Accessed April 17, 2007.

Sands, Christopher. 2006. "The Rising Importance of Third-Country Issues in Canada's Relations with the United States." In Andrew E. Cooper and Dane Rowlands, eds., *Canada Among Nations 2006: Minorities and Priorities* (Montreal and Kingston: McGill-Queen's).

Sokolsky, Joel J., and Philippe Lagasse. 2006. "Suspenders and a Belt: Perimeter and Border Security in Canada–US Relations." *Canadian Foreign Policy* 12: 15–29.

Thompson, John Herd. 2003. "Playing by the New Washington Rules: The US–Canada Relationship, 1994–2003." *American Review of Canadian Studies* 33:5–26.

United States. Department of justice. 2006. "National Drug Threat Assessment 2006." http://usdoj.gov. Accessed March 7, 2007.

United States. Department of State. 2006. "International Narcotics Control Strategy Report." www.state.gov. Accessed March 7, 2007.

United States. Office of the President. 2006. "Presidential Determination on Major Drug Transit or Major Illicit Drug Producing Countries for the Fiscal Year 2007." http://state.gov/p/inl/rls/prsrllps172379.htm. Accessed March 7, 2007.

KEY AND CHALLENGING WORDS

deterrent, cognoscenti, abate, misdemeanour, bilateral, emanate, align

QUESTIONS

1. a) Identify the essay plan; b) Identify by paragraph number(s) the main points discussed in the essay.
2. a) How does the author support his main points in paragraphs 2–3? b) Identify one primary source and one secondary source in these paragraphs.
3. Using a reliable source, explain the roles of the Office of the National Drug Control Policy and its director (paragraph 4). Who is the current director?
4. Can you infer from the comments of Ian Mulgrew and John Walters in paragraph 4 their respective stances on the legalization or decriminalization of marijuana?

5. Explain why, at the time this article was written, the American concern with Canada's proposed decriminalization of marijuana was not a major issue.
6. What are the different meanings of "irritant" and "problem," as discussed in paragraph 8? Summarize the two potential problems raised in this paragraph.
7. Analyze paragraph 9, explaining whether it functions as an effective conclusion to the essay.

POST-READING

1. Construct a timeline that outlines the history of marijuana in Canada from a political/legal perspective, beginning with the results of the *Le Dain Commission* in 1972 to the present; include only the most significant developments.
2. *Collaborative activity:* Discuss or debate a) the pros and cons of legalizing marijuana in Canada, or b) the likelihood that marijuana will be decriminalized in the next five years.
3. a) A number of Canadian websites advocate or promote the use and/or legalization of marijuana in Canada.

Evaluate the credibility of one of these sites, focusing on the use of statistics, facts, and claims. In your evaluation, include at least one comparison between a topic (e.g., a statistical claim) that is also mentioned in Gecelovsky's essay. *OR* b) Many opinion pieces on legalizing marijuana have appeared in Canadian magazines and newspapers in the last five years. Find two that take opposite positions and analyze the effectiveness of their arguments.

RELATED WEBSITES OF INTEREST

Senate Special Committee on Illegal Drugs report:
www.parl.gc.ca/common/committee_senrep.asp?language=e&parl=37&Ses=1&comm_id=85

Centre for Addictions Research of BC:
www.carbc.ca

Listen to the North

John Ralston Saul

(4,115 words)

Pre-reading

1. After scanning the article, list five ways that it differs from the academic/scholarly essay as it is discussed in Chapter 2.
2. Come up with a one-sentence definition of "colonialism" or "colonial," using freewriting or another pre-writing technique, if you wish, to generate ideas. When you read the essay, note the uses of the term, beginning with paragraph 1. Are Saul's uses consistent with your definition?

1   Sometimes we understand events in our lives immediately. Sometimes it takes decades. I have gradually realized over the last year that my view of Canada, indeed my view of how my own life could or should be lived, was radically transformed late in the winter of 1976 on my first trip to the Arctic. I was 29, fresh from seven years in France, first writing my PhD, then running a small investment firm in Paris. Those are experiences that produce a southern, urban, European-oriented self-confidence, which could also be described as the attitude of a classic colonial Canadian.

2   I travelled north with Maurice Strong, the founding chair and CEO of Petro-Canada. It had begun operations on the first of January that year. Maurice was its first employee. As his assistant, I was the second and so doubled the size of the national oil company. It was a Crown corporation and had inherited the shares the government held in some of the private companies exploring for oil and gas in the High Arctic islands. The government had financed some of these risky ventures or rescued them. And so we were going north to look over our property; that is, the people's property.

3   On our way to the High Arctic islands, we flew into Inuvik—then an oil and gas boom town—on the delta of the Mackenzie River where it flowed into the Arctic Ocean. The first meeting Maurice had organized was with the local hunters and trappers associations. I believe they represented the Inuit, the Dene, and the Gwich'in. I went into the room filled with goodwill, thanks to my urban, southern, western views—in other words, I was out to lunch. An hour and a half later I walked out in a state of deep confusion. It seemed that there was another way of looking at society, another way of looking at the land, at human relationships, and the relationship between society and the land.

4   This other view was not necessarily to the left or the right, for or against oil exploration or other forms of development. This was a different philosophy, a Canadian philosophy, not derivative of the South or the West. It existed outside of those rational structures of thought that aim to separate humans from everything else in order to raise us to a privileged position in which our interests trump those of the place in which we exist. Whatever the advantages of this approach, we are now faced with unintended outcomes such as climate change. This other philosophy, when I first heard it applied in Inuvik, is just as interested in human well-being, but sees it in a context integrated with the place. And so these hunters

were asking tough questions about the broader, longer-term impacts of each narrow southern-style proposal for what we thought of as progress.

5   In those days, you could get through school and university, get a PhD, and live an intellectually active life in Canada without anyone mentioning this more integrated, in many ways more modern, way of thinking. Today this would not be so easily possible. And yet what people in the South do know today will still have been delivered to them in southern, western forms. You could say that northern ideas are still so deformed by southern intellectual and political systems that the situation is almost worse. There is now an assertion of understanding and sympathy so constructed on the western model that we are protected against deep confusion; in other words, we are protected from the possibility of listening and understanding.

6   Ever since 1976, I have gone north as often as I can. This year those of us who organize the LaFontaine-Baldwin Lecture with the Institute for Canadian Citizenship held it in Iqaluit. The Inuit leader Siila Watt-Cloutier spoke about the North and about Canada as a whole as seen from a northerner's point of view (a transcript is available on the ICC's website at www.icc-icc.ca). And that really is the point. The key to Canada as a northern or Arctic or circumpolar nation is the people of the North.

*

7   People like myself ought therefore to be happy with the place the North and the Arctic in particular are now playing in our news and sometimes in our daily conversations. I read. I listen. Yet what I hear is mainly the South talking to the South and sometimes to the outside world about the North. There are a few signs, but very few, of any attempt to see the North from the North's point of view.

8   Most of the sovereignty debate has been framed in old-fashioned western empire terms: *We have a distant frontier that must be defended. This frontier is ours, not theirs,* whoever they may be. It is only in this context that the people of the North are mentioned, as if the reason for their existence were to serve Canadian Sovereignty. There is little sense in all of this that the well-being and success of the people of the North is a purpose in and of itself. And they do not need to be the guarantors of our sovereignty—even though they

are—in order to deserve well-being and success. They deserve these exactly as any other Canadian citizen deserves them.

9   Besides, the whole idea of sovereignty is meaningless if we cannot sustain a long-term, solid northern policy. Today there is southern-style enthusiasm. Very little of this seems attached to such northern realities as housing shortages, ill-adapted school curricula, and difficult communications of every sort. And this raises the old fear that something else will soon catch our fancy and the North will retreat once again from the general public consciousness and that of the government.

10   This failure to build and maintain a strong, integrated northern policy and northern foreign policy is clearly laid out in *Arctic Front: Defending Canada in the Far North*, a book written by Ken Coates, Whitney Lackenbauer, William Morrison, and Greg Poelzer, four sensible northern experts. They argue that this is just a continuation of Canada's incapacity as a state to sustain any serious level of attention on the North. Northern success is all about continuity and maintenance, internally and internationally. Periodic enthusiasms do not do the trick.

*

11   This essay focuses on the Arctic. But the larger context is that we are a northern nation. Two thirds of our country lies in what is normally categorized as North lands. One third of our gross domestic product comes out of the three territories and the equally isolated northern parts of our provinces. And that one third is what makes us a rich, not a poor, country. Our cities, our high-tech service-based lives are built upon the foundation provided by that one third of riches. And now the South believes that the percentage of the GDP coming from the Arctic section of the North will grow. We ought to be a central player in the northern world in general and in particular in the circumpolar world. But first we all need to see ourselves as part of it and, at the moment, we do not.

12   The current Arctic enthusiasm instead resembles an updated manifestation of George Brown's old rep by pop argument, in which the shape and direction of Canada are supposed to be controlled simply by those who have the most votes. We act as if the second largest country in the world is only real in a

handful of southern cities. That is why our current approach to Arctic sovereignty has such a Toronto-Montreal-Ottawa-Calgary-Vancouver feel to it. And that is why there is little sign of the balance between people and place that has always been and remains central to Canada's success. In this atmosphere, the point of view of northerners is treated as if it weighed three House of Commons seats, which is what a strict geographical definition of the region allots them: three territories, one seat apiece. And so, throughout our history, when the moment comes to spend the money or talk about the issues, ministers tend to become distracted by a bridge in their riding or in a swing riding, and the northern monies evaporate.

13   Our contemporary northern history therefore looks like this. In the early 1970s, there was little southern interest in things northern. Then came the oil crisis and with it a southern passion for energy sources under the ice. The Berger Commission revealed, even to the half-asleep majority, that northerners had a point of view and enough power to impose themselves. Then the South slipped back into disinterest. Suddenly a US ship—the *Manhattan*—made its way through the Northwest Passage. This produced a sovereignty panic in the 1980s. A flood of ardent reactive policies followed. These quickly evaporated and the South fell back asleep. But northerners and a small number of committed southerners worked hard through the 1990s to produce real action—not reaction, but something healthy, with roots. The result was a series of northern land settlements, the growth of Nunavik, the creation of Nunavut, the Arctic Council, a serious northern foreign policy in 2000 and so on. The twenty first century brought a brutal political reaction against these initiatives, as if our infatuation with economic integration with the United States meant that we were an urban people for whom the northern nature of our country was an embarrassment. In effect, the South once again forgot the North. There was, however, a strong enough northern and pro-North institutional base for quiet work to continue. The Makivik Corporation in Nunavik expanded. Leaders such as Paul Okalik, Nellie Cournoyea, Mary Simon, Siila Watt-Cloutier and others worked ceaselessly; northern studies expanded in the universities. All of this was happening below the political radar.

14   And then the most recent sovereignty panic began, largely spurred by the rapider-than-expected effects of climate change. With the northern icefields turning into navigable ocean passages, other countries began viewing "our" North as an international highway. Overnight, urgent reactive promises were again being made in Ottawa by the very people who five years before had denigrated northern policies. People have the right to change their minds. And the difference this time is that northerners are far better organized and are prepared to navigate the political waters. And yet the new promises and policies continue to resemble old-fashioned southern views of the North.

15   Northerners keep pointing this out. But in order to be heard, ideas and arguments must pass through the national communications systems. And these systems, whether political or journalistic are run through a reconceptualization process in three southern cities.

*

16   Take a very simple example. Among all the new military promises, only one directly involves northerners. The Rangers are a highly successful part-time force of 4,000 spread throughout the northern two thirds of Canada. They play both a military and a search and rescue role, as well as an important social function for youth with the Junior Rangers. For example, hunters are traditionally men. Through the Junior Rangers, teenage girls are becoming good shots and then hunters, which can give them great self-confidence.

17   Throughout the North, the Rangers are the most important presence of the Canadian state. They have great experience on the land. And yet there are virtually no regular force officers involved. And there are virtually no northerners serving in command positions above their particular communities. The Ranger Patrols—as they are called—are trained by very good regular force warrant officers who, from what I have seen, love working outside the normal army system and being in the community.

18   The costs of all of this are minimal. On parade the Rangers wear a red sweatshirt and baseball cap, although this is now changing. Their rifles are basic, but good. Almost everything else is their own.

19   The new national policy is to expand the Rangers to 5,000, and that is a good thing. But there is no public debate about the existing model and whether it should change. For example, the Rangers could be structured into a formal regiment, to put them on the same level as the rest of the regular and militia forces. Their regions could be structured as battalions and integrated on an east-west northern basis. Under the current system each Ranger area is tributary to the southern commands immediately below them—a perfectly colonial structure.

20   One of the other new promises is for an Arctic training centre. Again a good idea, but for what purpose? It could be used to bring northerners into the full-time regular army at all rank levels so that the new regiment would be led increasingly by northerners, just as all our other regiments are led largely by people from the part of Canada in which they are based. This process could be sped up by the new Aboriginal Leadership Opportunity Year (ALOY) program, which is run out of the Royal Military College in Kingston and aims to draw aboriginal youth into the officer corps. In other words, the Rangers could become a regiment with a core of regular force, largely northern leaders and a majority remaining in the militia.

21   But let's go back to the conceptualization process. If this is a northern unit, why are the Rangers dressed in baseball caps and sweatshirts? You can't wear this outfit outside ten months of the year. Of course, this is more or less a dress uniform, but why a dress uniform that has to be worn inside? The whole idea and reality of the Rangers is that they are outside and on the land. Their outfit is symbolic of a southern view, symbolic of a generalized southern failure to support the development of northern equipment.

22   For example, we do not produce snowmobiles appropriate to the Arctic. Each time I am with Rangers, they point out the weaknesses of what is available. The best machines are made by Bombardier in Finland. The explanation no doubt is that our Arctic market is not big enough for such specific-use machines. Why, then, are those machines made in Finland (population five million)?

23   When you are out on the land in full winter most of the machines Canadians use freeze up so badly overnight that the common way to get them going is to turn the machine on its side (even the block is placed according to southern logic). Then all the men stand in a circle and pee on the block. This is just the beginning of a 30-minute start-up process—not very helpful in a crisis. I have thought, while standing in these circles, that basic details often reveal how Canada's practical imagination has not focused on the North; and how the practical imagination of northerners has been prevented form shaping what is done.

24   When you look at the heavy hand of the South on northern architecture or power systems or education methods or food supply systems, you begin to realize how difficult it has been and remains for the new Arctic leadership in particular to put a northern perspective in place. Not always, but very often, the insistent and unimaginative ideas coming from the South have solved immediate specific difficulties while creating systemic problems.

*

25   If southern Canadians are now seriously concerned about the status of the North, then this is an ideal moment to listen to what northerners are saying. They are continuing to suggest a myriad of approaches, practical and philosophical. The latter, among the Inuit, is often called IQ—Inuit Qaujimajatuqangit. This is often translated as traditional ways or culture. But as Peter Irniq and Frank Tester point out in the December 2008 issue of *Arctic*, that suggests something anthropological, something locked in the past. Or it is seen as "a 'holistic' concept that includes spiritual as well as factual knowledge." This western interpretation suggests that "understanding the whole can be achieved by understanding the parts."

26   This is just the sort of interpretation that comforts southern-style science in the North. It involves endlessly collecting information that is meant one day to add up to something. That's fine. By all means keep collecting. The results are fascinating and no doubt useful. But it is this approach that has comforted two decades of inaction. For example, the science of glaciers is fascinating. There is more to learn. But precise pictures have been taken of them for a half-century. Anyone can hold those pictures in their hands and fly low over the glaciers and compare. The glaciers are melting. The next step is action. Or as Watt-Cloutier put it in her LaFontaine-Baldwin

Lecture: "Slowing down climate change would be the best long-term solution to enforcing Canada's Arctic sovereignty." After all, that sovereignty is only in question because the ice is melting.

27   The point of IQ, or, more broadly, northern philosophies, is that they provide a completely different approach to the Arctic reality—a non-western, non-silo, non-sum-of-the-parts approach. Irniq and Tester call this a seamless approach. It is one in which the human is seen as an integrated part of the place. And so IQ relates to the Cree idea of Witaskewin—*living together in the land*—and the West Coast Nuu-chah-nulth world-view of Tsawalk—*everything is one.*[1]

28   These are philosophies of harmony and balance. They are indeed seamless and appropriate evocations of our physical reality. They remove the separation of the human from the place—that separation that has brought us many wonderful things, more recently along with global warming and an incapacity to act when what we think of as scientific progress seems to contradict the stability of our physical reality. The southern idea is that progress is an uncontroversial reality that solves problems. Anyone sitting on the outside of western philosophy simply responds: What do you mean by progress?

29   No one in the North is saying that southern science or its concepts of progress should simply go away. What northerners are perhaps saying is that the philosophical concepts that shape most southern ideas are undermining the advantages and promoting destructive side effects. And these side effects are now becoming their principal outcome. Northern architecture, for example, continues to evolve largely from southern assumptions. Technical problems, such as dealing with cold, are solved on a one-off basis. But there is no debate about what Arctic buildings should look like and what their relationship to each other should be. What should the underlying principles of those shapes be? Do southern assumptions and solutions about housing cause family and even broad social problems while concentrating on heating systems?

30   The stubbornness of the western intellectual approach and the relentless self-promotion of its silo structures make it very difficult for northern leaders to inject their own philosophical approaches into the heart of their own policy making. The southern, western system insinuates itself everywhere with religious fervor.

31   And yet there are breakthroughs. Nunavut is now building a cultural school, called Piqqusilirivvik, and is doing so with interesting architecture. It will be in Clyde River, up the east coast of Baffin Island. The school will promote the reality of a fundamentally northern and non-western philosophy. And Nunavut is working hard to get itself out from under the Alberta school curriculum, which shapes Arctic schools in a way that undermines Inuktituk and an integrated northern life. The recent *Nunavut Education Act* is making another stab at correcting this problem.

32   Perhaps most problematic is that there is still no university in the Canadian North. We remain the only circumpolar country without northern or Arctic universities.

33   We have hundreds, perhaps thousands, of northern experts. Almost all of them are based in southern universities. All our Arctic study centres are in southern universities. Millions of public dollars are invested every year in these southern universities to work on the North. And most of this money stays in the south. Doctorates on the North are organized and written in the South, with periodic trips up to check things out. MAs on the North are done in the South, perhaps with one or two research visits to the distant frontier. Lecturers are hired in the South. Tenure track is in the South.

34   Yes, there are worthwhile programs aimed at producing northern lawyers, nurses, and so on. These contractual arrangements with southern universities are delivered by excellent northern colleges, but the intellectual form, the conceptualization, the real control remain largely in the South.

35   What this means is that there are no intellectual centres based in the North at which students can gather and then make their way. Why? Because they are all in the South. And public money—federal and provincial—keeps it this way.

36   This is a fundamental Canadian failure. It is a failure of our intellectual class. What we have is a colonial structure.

37   Four other circumpolar countries, each with populations a fraction of ours, have healthy northern universities, as does Alaska, as does Russia. Canada alone continues to treat northern higher education in a colonial manner.

38   Among the new policies coming out of Ottawa is the promise of an Arctic research centre. Another good idea. But without universities in the North, this will simply comfort our southern institutions in their "live south, work south, invest south, think south, visit north" structure. Norway—population four million—has leapt far ahead of Canada—population 33 million—with their Arctic research centre. Theirs is served by a very good northern university. Ours will serve universities in the South.

39   What is our excuse? Usually that we don't have the concentration of population or the infrastructure necessary to justify such universities. No other circumpolar country says this. Why? Because they believe that part of being a northern country is that you must create the intellectual and physical infrastructure in the North from which everything can grow. Imagine five federal research chairs in each of three northern universities. The reality of centres of excellence would rush north overnight.

40   In the meantime southern Canada, with the national government, the universities and businesses, continues to act as if northerners were not full Canadians and the North not an integrated part of who we are. Above all, the south still has not absorbed the reality that northerners have modern leadership views—both philosophical and practical—on how their part of the country could function.

41   Three universities in the North (or one with three different campuses) matter because they are the key to building fully rounded northern communities. These are institutions northerners could attach themselves to, places young southerners would be attracted to. They would immediately become a reason for young northerners to finish high school, as they are continually admonished to do in an old-fashioned southern way—*Get an education and get a job.* But what sort of education? Will it relate to the North? Will it help young people to build their north or cut them off from it, and make them insecure because it only makes sense in the South? And what kind of job? Where?

42   These simple questions could be partially answered in a positive way if there were northern-imagined centres of excellence in the North. Which raises the strategic point in conceptualizing these universities, one that relates to IQ and northern approaches to learning.

43   There are already good colleges in the three northern capitals. They need to be strengthened and expanded to fully cover the essential areas of utilitarian training. But there is no need for universities that are basically fancy training centres, or for imitation southern universities in the North.

44   This is what an increasing number of northerners who have made their way through the southern system are saying. One group of young lawyers and public administrators in Iqaluit—Sandra Inutiq, Elisapi Davidee-Aningmiuq, Kirt Ejesiak, Hugh Lloyd, and Aaju Peter—has created the Ilitturvik University Society to advance the idea of programs "politically, economically, culturally and socially relevant to the Arctic and Inuit."[2] Another group, in the Northwest Territories, has created a project called Dechinta, aimed at a field school approach toward post-secondary education.[3]

45   These young people have all more than proved themselves in the southern university system. They are a small part of a growing critical mass of young northern leaders.[4] What they are saying is that those southern systems are not appropriate to the North. So there is now a remarkable opportunity to break away from the disease of the silo education and utilitarian approaches, which have so damaged our southern universities. We have the opportunity to recognize that this approach is central to our incapacity to act when faced by crises such as climate change.

46   We have seen that model fail when faced with the reality of the North, the needs of the North. There is every reason to embrace the seamless model being put forward by an increasing number of northerners.

Literary Review of Canada.
2009. October 17 (8).

Notes

1. See, for example, Harold Cardinal and Walter Hilde-brandt's *Treaty Elders of Saskatchewan* (University of Calgary Press, 2000) or Umeek-E Richard Atleo's *Tsawalk, A Nuu-chah-nulth Worldview* (University of British Columbia Press, 2004).
2. See <www.ilitturvik.org>

3. See <www.dechintabushuniversity.ca>
4. For example, see those who have spoken out in *Northern Exposure: Peoples, Powers and Prospects in Canada's North*, edited by Frances Abele, Thomas Courchene, Leslie Seidle and France St.-Hilaire and produced by the Institute for Research on Public Policy in 2009.

KEY AND CHALLENGING WORDS

derivative, guarantor, ardent, reactive, denigrate, utilitarian

QUESTIONS

1. a) Identify Saul's thesis; b) Provide descriptive headings for the different sections in the essay; c) In which section does Saul provide the most direct support for his thesis?
2. a) In paragraph 4, what does Saul suggest is to blame for climate change? b) Summarize the two different philosophies referred to in the opening paragraphs and their aims.
3. What two main rhetorical patterns does Saul use in the consecutive paragraphs 12 and 13? In paragraph 13, identify the sentence that announces this pattern.
4. Explain the problems Saul finds with the way the Canadian Rangers are being used.
5. Demonstrate the way Saul uses the example of snow-mobiles (paragraphs 22–23) to support his point in paragraph 21; analyze his argument in these paragraphs for its logic and effectiveness.

6. What is IQ (paragraphs 25–27) and how does it differ from the traditional use of the concept by western/southern societies?
7. Discuss Saul's use of comparisons in the last section of his essay, showing how they contribute to this section as a whole.
8. Using a reliable reference source, define the term "centres of excellence" (first mentioned in paragraph 39) and explain how they are connected to other institutions or organizations mentioned in the essay.
9. Analyze Saul's use of personal experience in his essay, referring to specific passages. Does it affect his credibility and help support his argument?

POST-READING

1. Find a recent news item about Canada's north and analyze the author's point of view about the north or the views of those mentioned in the article. Would you consider the views that inform the article "southern" or "northern," according to Saul's distinction?
2. Write a one-paragraph mission statement for a prospective university in the Canadian north; to get an idea of what such statements look like, you could consult the one for your own university or check another university's statement, such as that of the University of Northern British Columbia: www.unbc.ca/about/
3. *Collaborative or individual activity:* What is "Arctic sovereignty"? Consider the following questions, among others of your choosing: How might the definition of "Arctic sovereignty" be different for Canada compared to that of other circumpolar countries? How might it be different for a non-Arctic country? Do you believe this is an issue that will affect future generations? Why or why not?

RELATED WEBSITES OF INTEREST

Canadian Rangers:
www.army.forces.gc.ca/land-terre/cr-rc/index-eng.asp

Canada's Northern Strategy:
http://northernstrategy.gc.ca

DEFINING CANADIANS: IDENTITY AND CITIZENSHIP

Which "Native" history? By whom? For whom?

J.R. (Jim) Miller

(2,267 words)

Pre-reading

1. Using a dictionary of usage or a reliable online source, define the terms "First Nations," "Inuit," and "Métis." Then, look up "aboriginal," "native," and "indigenous" to determine distinctions among them. Scan "Which 'Native' history?" for these words. Does their usage seem to conform to the definitions you have looked up?

Abstract

Although "Native" history is often discussed as though it were a single type of scholarship, in reality it takes many forms. Different rules apply to the different varieties, and some research methods are more applicable to one type than to others. In most cases, the approach known as Native-newcomer history, which focuses on the evolving relationship between indigenous and immigrant peoples, is the most useful.

*

1   During the last twenty years, controversies have occasionally erupted over "Native" history. Who should write it? For whom is it intended? Greater illumination and less heat would be achieved if authors were clear about what they mean when they say they are writing "Native" history. The indiscriminate use of the term to cover several distinct, though related, historical approaches has resulted in a great deal of confusion and not a little acrimony. The fact of the matter is that "Native" and "Native history" are not simple or unproblematic terms. Authors and speakers have used "Native" history when addressing one of several genres that exist under the term, with the result that gate-keepers have sometimes got up in arms when there was no necessity for them to do so. Particularly in the 1990s, and still sometimes in the twenty-first century, non-Aboriginal scholars writing on indigenous subjects have been accused of "appropriating the voice" of Native people. Usually, however, the charge is unjustified because what is being considered is not something that pertains specifically or exclusively to Native peoples. It is helpful to be clear about what sort of history is under consideration before worrying about appropriation.

2   Certainly, there are topics involving Native people to which they alone have a proprietary right.

In general, these are matters that involve personal or family property, or things that have great spiritual significance to Aboriginal people. So, for example, a Potlatch song or a dance might belong to a family; others have no right to sing or perform it without the family's permission. To ignore this property right is akin to violating copyright or a trademark. Other cases involve ceremonies of great spiritual significance, or rituals that are associated with certain seasons of the year among particular indigenous people. To perform the ceremonies indiscriminately is rude and disrespectful; to tell stories at the wrong season of the year is inappropriate, and might be considered threatening by the people to whom they matter a great deal. In these areas, simple courtesy requires scrupulous observation of the norms that prevail among the peoples whose ceremonies, stories, or dances are being considered. It is worth noting, though, that such indigenous practices rarely figure directly in what we usually think of as "Native" history.

3   The study of the distinctive role of the First Nations, Métis, or Inuit in historical events since contact with Europeans is a second genre of what is said to be "Native" history. A clear example can be found in the Northwest Rebellion of 1885, a topic that has attracted a great deal of attention. Until comparatively recently, most of the writing on this confrontation was the work of non-Native scholars and journalists. This writing tended to range widely over the motives and actions of the non-Native settlers and government, Métis, and First Nations in the events in the Saskatchewan country and the consequences for them. In the 1990s, however, a pair of historians, one First Nations and the other non-Native, decided that it was time that the particular role of First Nations in the Rebellion be studied carefully and in detail. Blair Stonechild of the First Nations University of Canada and Bill Waiser of the University of Saskatchewan joined forces to study the actions of the First Nations in 1885 and their consequences. They first consulted a number of First Nations Elders and chiefs to ensure that their inquiries would not be considered offensive. Reassured that their project was welcome and would receive support, they plunged into the research.

4   Stonechild and Waiser conducted their research in a thoroughly bicultural manner. Both were intimately involved in the research, as they were later in the writing of the resulting book based on both documentary and interview evidence. With the cooperation and guidance of Elders and political leaders on individual reserves, they hired First Nations interviewers, who worked with Elders to identify and interview members of the communities with the necessary historical knowledge. First Nations protocol was observed at all meetings, including those attended by Stonechild and Waiser, by presenting tobacco and cloth before asking an individual to speak. The result of this bicultural project was *Loyal Till Death: Indians and the Northwest Rebellion* (Fifth House, 1997), which substantially revised understanding of the forces involved in the events of 1885. These scholars and their informants showed convincingly that First Nations involvement was minimal and usually the result of individual motives rather than community will. *Loyal Till Death* refuted the sixty year-old view, first promulgated by G.F.G. Stanley in *The Birth of Western Canada: A History of the Riel Rebellions* (Longmans, Green, and Co, 1936) that Louis Riel had been at the head of an alliance of Métis and First Nations. Stonechild and Waiser showed convincingly that the 1885 rising in Saskatchewan was not a Métis movement. As a result, they provided a fuller and more rounded version of the 1885 events than earlier works.

5   A bicultural approach can also be found in the work of a single scholar. The Anicinabe of what is now southern Ontario have been prominent practitioners of this style of history. In the first half of the nineteenth century, Ojibwa historians such as Peter Jones (Kahkewaquonaby) and George Copway (Kahgegagahbowh) produced histories of their own people. These writers were the beneficiaries of substantial Euro-Canadian education, which they combined with their understanding of their Aboriginal heritage to interpret and explain their people's history. Their twentieth-century intellectual descendant is John Borrows, a Chippewa of Newash, who has enjoyed a distinguished academic career. Educated first in history and then in law, Borrows became an academic lawyer and is now based at the University of Victoria. His legal analyses are grounded both in history and law, employing Anicinabe and Euro-Canadian ways of knowing. His many articles and his recent book, *Recovering Canada: The Resurgence of*

Indigenous Law (University of Toronto Press, 2002), skillfully combine evidence from both intellectual traditions. For example, he frequently employs wampum and government documents, or Anicinabe stories and Euro-Canadians' letters to support his arguments. Borrows, Copway, and Jones are prime examples of a bicultural approach to history executed by a single, broadly educated, and especially well-informed person.

6   The work of these three has sometimes been exclusively about Native peoples and sometimes about Native-newcomer relations. The latter, which is increasingly being noticed as a distinct genre called Native-newcomer history, is in fact what most of the work on "Native" history is actually about. Native-newcomer history is the story of the change over time in the relationship between indigenous and immigrant peoples, usually in the western hemisphere, and most commonly in what is now Canada. For example, it examines the shift in relations that began with commercial interactions in the fur trade and imperial rivalries, and continued into the era of agricultural settlement, mining and other resource-extractive industries, and urban-industrial society. This style of inquiry always focuses in the first instance on the interaction between the immigrant and indigenous people.

7   Native-newcomer history also studies the impact that the successive changes in the relationship had on both parties. For example, in the fur trade, Aboriginal people were affected by positive influences, such as European technology, as well as negative forces, such as epidemic disease and distilled alcohol. For their part, the newcomers found that local knowledge and indigenous technology, particularly in transportation, brought them great wealth. A similar pattern of beneficial and detrimental forces flowing from contact was also found in later eras.

8   Native-newcomer history requires a special set of skills that is not the exclusive preserve of either Aboriginal or non-Aboriginal researchers. Of course, the historian's standard tool kit of investigation, analysis, synthesis, and exposition are essential, but more is required. Researchers need some awareness of the techniques of other disciplines, including art, literature, law, political studies, and, above all, oral research and cultural anthropology. Why is such a diverse range of skills needed? Changes in the native-newcomer relationship were reflected in literature and art, or in political attitudes and behaviour. A great deal of Native-newcomer history was inspired by the need to prepare claims, especially land claims, and a good deal of that history is embodied in court rulings. The evolution of the courts' attitudes and treatment of indigenous people, as in the case of the complex issue of Aboriginal title, both reflects societal changes and stimulates further development of the native-newcomer relationship.

9   Why is some familiarity with anthropology a major asset to working in Native-newcomer history? The answer can be summarized in one word: ethnohistory. Ethnohistory, which was invented in the 1930s by Canadian historian Alfred G. Bailey (*The Conflict of European and Eastern Algonkian Cultures, 1504-1700: A Study in Canadian Civilization*, New Brunswick Museum, 1937), became prominent in North America in the 1950s, as American anthropologists became involved in claims research for cases going to the US Indian Claims Commission. To put it simply, anthropologists had to learn to work with historical documents to back their claims with longitudinal analysis. The blend of anthropology and history that resulted from their innovative research became known as ethnohistory. Ethnohistory involves the analysis of documents that historians have used for some time, though now European and Euro-American documents are interpreted in light of the additional cultural knowledge that anthropologists bring to their examination. With knowledge of kin-based indigenous societies, researchers could read accounts of Natives' speeches in which they referred to themselves as "children" and the French or English governor as "father," and understand that the familial language conveyed not notions of dependence on the part of Natives, but mutuality and reciprocal obligation. For example, it is impossible to study the history of treaty-making between the Crown and Native peoples, without an appreciation of the significance of the kinship terminology that was used in negotiations. Historians and ethnohistorians have been learning about kinship from anthropology.

10   Similarly, anthropology was the main source of oral research that historians have begun to employ in their research concerning the Native-newcomer

relationship. Aboriginal peoples were not initially literate in European languages, although they often had other ways to record important events, such as wampum in the northeast woodlands or winter counts on the plains. Sometimes oral accounts were written down and could be interpreted from the documents following the guidelines of ethnohistorical practice. In other cases, oral history had to be collected for research because memories of the question being investigated had not yet been gathered. Treaty-making is an example of the former situation, with residential schooling being an example of the latter. In both cases, oral history research permits a fuller understanding of the process and results.

11   It should be obvious that Native-newcomer history has the advantage of inclusiveness. When it comes to researching and writing this style of history, it is a field for both Aboriginal and non-Aboriginal students and scholars. Native-newcomer history is for all or it is for none, because it deals with past events and processes in which people from both societies were involved. If non-Native researchers should refrain from studying Native-newcomer history, then so should Native investigators. Who, then, will research the history of the Beothuk, the Newfoundland First Nation that became extinct in 1829? At the consumption end of Native-newcomer historical production, the benefits flow broadly as well. Because so much of Canadian history is the story of the interactions of indigenous peoples and immigrants, the study of changes in their relationship over time is relevant to Canadians today.

12   A Native-newcomer approach to history also produces more rounded informative accounts of events from our past. It is possible to study treaty-making from a predominantly Euro-American point of view, but this does not take into account the rich contribution of First Nations to the process. It is possible as well to study the history of treaty-making by concentrating on the Native role, as American legal scholar Robert Williams did in *Linking Arms Together: American Indian Treaty Visions of Law and Peace, 1600–1800* (Oxford University Press, 1997). However, the author completely neglected the Royal Proclamation of 1763, the single most important document in the history of treaty-making, as well as the emergence of territorial treaties, the predominant form of treaty in North American history. While *Linking Arms Together* is a valuable work in many ways, it is not the comprehensive treatment that a question like treaties between indigenous and immigrant peoples in North America requires. A better model is found in the historiography of the Northwest Rebellion of 1885. Blair Stonechild and Bill Waiser's *Loyal Till Death* explains the insurrection more fully and accurately than G.F.G. Stanley's *Birth of Western Canada*.

13   The most useful answer to the question "Which "Native" history?" is "Native-newcomer history". Historical study of the relationship enriches our understanding of the past by focusing on intercultural processes and their results. It provides a fuller and more comprehensive understanding of the history of Canada over the past four hundred years than more parochial approaches. It is a historical genre that requires the application of methods and insights from many disciplines, but it is also a field of inquiry to which all are welcome as both producers and consumers of research.

14   Which "Native" history? Native-newcomer history. By whom? Any and all students who are qualified and willing to carry out its methods. For whom? All Canadians.

Canadian Issues. 2008. Fall 33-35.

KEY AND CHALLENGING WORDS

acrimony, proprietary, scrupulous, longitudinal, reciprocal, parochial

QUESTIONS

1. How could you describe the author's tone in paragraph 1? From the tone, what can you infer about the purpose of the essay? What does it suggest about Miller's audience?

2. What primary organizational method (rhetorical pattern) is used in the essay? Identify a different pattern that Miller uses to develop one of his paragraphs.

3. Explain why the Northwest Rebellion of 1885 provides a good example of a historical event to analyze for Miller's purposes. How does the approach of non-Native historians differ from that of Stonechild and Waiser?

4. Find two reviews of the book *Loyal Till Death: Indians and the Northwest Rebellion* from an academic journal, a historical society website, or another reliable source. Do the reviewers' conclusions about the book differ from those of Miller? Write a 500–750 word analysis of one of the reviews, comparing the reviewers' comments with those of Miller.

5. In one or two sentences, explain the distinction between the second and third genres of Native history discussed in the essay.

6. What term is are used in paragraphs 6–7 to identify non-Aboriginal peoples? Do you believe it is an appropriate term?

7. a) What are the advantages that Native-newcomer history offers over other kinds of Native history? b) Why does Miller state, "If non-Native researchers should refrain from studying Native-newcomer history, then so should Native investigators" (paragraph 11)?

8. Analyze the rhetorical effectiveness of the concluding two paragraphs.

POST-READING

1. *Collaborative activity:* Discuss the significance of names, labels, and titles as they have been applied to cultural groups in the past; how could a label affect the identity of a group or individual in the group? You could consider, for example, stereotypes associated with the word "Indian."

RELATED WEBSITES OF INTEREST

Aboriginal Canada Portal (links to various Canadian aboriginal organizations):
www.aboriginalcanada.gc.ca/acp/site.nsf/eng/ao20001.html

Media—Magazines:
www.ammsa.com/publications/windspeaker
www.theturtleislandnews.com/

ADDITIONAL LIBRARY READING

King, Thomas. "Godzilla vs. Post-colonial." *Journal of Post-colonial Writing* 30.2 (1990): 10–16. Print.

Miller, J.R. *Skyscrapers Hide the Heavens. A History of Indian-White Relations in Canada.* 3rd ed. Toronto: University of Toronto Press, 2000. Print.

Retzlaff, Steffi. "What's in a Name? The Politics of Labelling and Native Identity Constructions." *The Canadian Journal of Native Studies* 25.2 (2005): 609–26. Print.

Response to Canada's apology to residential school survivors

Beverley Jacobs

(1,874 words)

Pre-reading

1. Who is Beverley Jacobs? Using a reliable source, write a one-paragraph profile that summarizes her background and major achievements.

2. Read the complete text of Canadian Prime Minister Stephen Harper's apology to former students of residential schools in order to prepare for Jacobs's response (the text is accessible through several media sources).

---

1   On June 11, 2008, Prime Minister Stephen Harper, on behalf of the Canadian government, made a Statement of Apology to former students of residential schools. All Opposition leaders, Stephane Dion, Jack Layton, and Gilles Duceppe, also made statements of apology. All Aboriginal leaders of the National Aboriginal Organizations responded to the Statement of Apology. All of the National Aboriginal leaders who met with the Prime Minister fifteen minutes prior to the Statement made in the House of Commons were provided with a copy of the Statement to review and were advised at that time that we would be providing responses on the floor of the House of Commons.

2   As the National President of the Native Women's Association of Canada, I was given a responsibility that day to make a statement that the rest of the world would hear. I was honoured to represent Aboriginal women in Canada and speak from the heart regarding the impacts of the residential school system, specifically on Aboriginal women in Canada. It was one of the most powerful experiences that I have ever had not only personally but professionally as well. The following is the statement that I made in response to the Prime Minister's Statement of Apology. After I reviewed the written statement, the effect was not the same, so I have made a few minor additions to provide further context to my statement.

*

3   [I began an introduction of myself by speaking in my language.] What I said in my Mohawk language is, "Greetings of peace to you." My nation is Mohawk of the Haudenosaunee Confederacy, Bear Clan. And my real name is Gowehgyuseh, which means "She is Visiting."

4   I am here to represent the Native Women's Association of Canada and the women that we represent have a statement. It is about the respect of Aboriginal women in this country.

5   Prior to the residential schools system, prior to colonization, the women in our communities were very well respected and honoured for the role that they have in our communities. Women are the life givers, being the caretakers of the spirit that we bring [in] to this world, Our Mother earth. We [were] given those responsibilities [by the Creator to bring that spirit into this physical world and to love, take care of and nurture our children].

6   [The government and churches' genocidal policies of the] residential schools caused so much harm to that respect for women and to the way women were honoured in our communities. There were ceremonies for young men and for young women that [taught them how to respect themselves and each other. These ceremonies] were [stolen from them] for generations.

7   Despite the hardships, we have our language still. We have our ceremonies. We have our elders. And now we have to revitalize those ceremonies and the respect for our people not only within Canadian society but even within our own peoples.

8   I want to say that I come here speaking from my heart, because two generations ago, my grandmother, being a Mohawk woman, was beaten in residential school, sexually beaten and physically beaten, for being a Mohawk woman. She did not pass on her traditions. She did not pass it on to my mother and her siblings. That matriarchal system that we have was directly affected. Luckily, I was raised in a community where our knowledge and our ceremonies have been [kept] by all of our mothers.

9   I want to say that as mothers, we teach our boys and our girls, equally. That is what I am here to say, that although I represent the Native Women's Association, we also represent men and women because that is our traditional responsibility. It is not just about women's issues. It is about making sure that we have strong nations again. That is what I am here to say.

10   We have given thanks to you for your apology. I have to also give you credit for standing up and starting to tell the truth. I did not see any other governments before today come forward and apologize, so I do thank you for that. But in return, the Native Women's Association wants respect.

11   I have just one last thing to say. To all of the leaders of the Liberals, the Bloc, and NDP, thank you as well. I thank you for your words. But it is now about our responsibilities today. Words must turn into action. The decisions that we make today will affect seven generations from now. My ancestors did the same seven generations ago. While they tried hard to fight against you, they knew what was happening. They knew what was coming.

12   We have had so much impact from colonization and that is what we are dealing with today. Women have taken the brunt of it all. In the end it must be about more than what happened in the residential schools. For women, the truth telling must continue.

13   Thank you for the opportunity to be here, at this moment in time, to talk about those realities that we are dealing with today. But at the end of it, I am left with questions. What is it that this government is going to do in the future to help our people? Because we are dealing with major human rights violations that have occurred to many generations. These violations have impacted on my language, my culture, and my spirituality. I know that I want to transfer those to my children and my grandchildren, and their children, and so on. What is going to be provided? That is my question. I know that is the question from all of us. That is what we would like to continue to work on, in partnership.

14   *Nia:wen.* Thank you.

*

15   I had to prepare emotionally, mentally, physically, and spiritually to make this statement. I first began to realize the impacts of the residential school system 14 years ago when I made a decision in law school to write a major research paper about the residential school system. It was one of those papers where I read story after story of the most horrific abuses against Aboriginal children. It was a time when residential school survivors were just beginning to open up and to disclose the various forms of abuses.

16   I then had to reflect on my own personal upbringing and heard about the horrendous abuses that my own grandmother and her siblings had to endure while they attended the "Mush Hole," the Mohawk Institute in Brantford, Ontario. I also reflected and reviewed my matrilineal family and the effects that these abuses had on my mother, her siblings, and their families. My grandmother and mother had already passed away when I began to realize the intergenerational impacts, so I wasn't able to have direct conversations with them about

this issue. I am not sure my grandmother would have wanted to talk about it anyway. I was, however, able to sit with my uncle, my grandmother's brother, and he told me many horrible stories. I began to understand how much was stolen from my matriarchal family as a result of my grandmother attending the Mush Hole. It became a reality that our traditional form of educating our children through language and traditional teachings that were supposed to be taught to us by our grandmothers was stolen from her; her language was sexually beaten from her and her spirit was beaten by a system designed to destroy her. She was a Mohawk girl who was taken from us by genocidal policies of the Canadian government and religious denominations of churches.

17   The most detrimental effect is that this systemic form of assimilation occurred to thousands and thousands of families throughout at least six generations, a hundred years, a century. As you can imagine, the transference of traditional knowledge and languages was directly impacted and replaced with a violent cycle of abuse. Every Aboriginal person has been affected whether a family member attended residential school or not. When a systemic process is created to destroy a people by erasing a language, a culture, and a spirit, every single person is affected. When this system attacked children, the heart of our Nations, the heart of our Mothers and Grandmothers, it attacked every single person. Despite the blatant attacks on our people to try to erase our existence, the process didn't work. As noted in my Response to the Apology, I believe that we have to celebrate the fact that we still have our grandmothers, grandfathers, mothers and fathers, aunties and uncles, who have been able to keep the traditional values, beliefs and language. Although most Indigenous languages in Canada are becoming extinct, the processes to revitalize has begun. Our people have survived cultural genocide through their resilience and the strength of those people who have ensured that the language and culture continue. We have done this because of our belief in our spirituality, and it has been through the strength of spirit that our culture and tradition is alive.

18   Damage has been done, though. Many generations of families have been affected. Languages are becoming extinct. It is now up to the federal government to provide the resources needed to Aboriginal peoples today and in the future. It is ironic that the Conservative minority government apologized for its wrongdoing in the creation of the residential school system; but yet, it eliminated language revitalization programs. It would seem to me that what is needed now, as noted in my response, is action. This government must provide direct resources to Aboriginal communities to continue programs and services that will enable the continued transference of Indigenous traditional knowledges and languages.

19   Most Canadians became a little educated on June 11, 2008 about the assimilationist policy of the Canadian government. Being that this is one of the most troubling "black marks" against Canada, every Canadian person should be knowledgeable that the human rights violations that occurred against Aboriginal children were as a result of Canada's genocidal policies. Every Canadian person should know its impacts on Aboriginal peoples, and more specifically on Aboriginal women. Everyone should know that the negative issues of the poverty, alcoholism, drug addiction, and the cycle of violence can be traced back to Canada's policies. We can even trace the issue of missing and murdered Aboriginal women to the residential school system. All of this must be mandatorily taught in all Canadian schools. It shouldn't have taken until the year 2008 for most Canadians to be educated about the residential school system.

20   When such action is taken by the Canadian government to not only apologize, but to create a process in which it actually acknowledges the harm it's done, then we can accept the Apology. A process needs to ensure that the financial resources are in place to deal with all of the impacts we are dealing with today. When our languages are fully revitalized, then we will know that change has occurred. When Aboriginal women are no longer targets of violence, then we know that change has occurred. When our Nations are flourishing and no longer living in poverty, then we know that change has occurred. I look forward to the day when we are no longer fighting for equality because we have reclaimed our way of being.

Canadian Woman Studies. 2008.
Winter/Spring 26 (3/4).

KEY AND CHALLENGING WORDS

matriarchal, genocidal, detrimental, systemic, assimilationist

QUESTIONS

1. What is the purpose of the first two paragraphs? How does this section differ from other essay introductions you have studied?

2. What is the function of the brackets in the first few paragraphs of the spoken text? Does Jacobs identify her main point early in her speech? If so, what is it?

3. Paragraphs 3–14 include the text of Jacobs's 11 June 2008 response to Harper's apology. Discuss with specific examples how this example of oral discourse differs from written discourse; for example, you could consider organization, language, style, rhetorical strategies, and other differences.

4. Paraphrase paragraph 13, which discusses the wide-ranging consequences of residential schooling.

5. Explain the relationship between Jacobs's oral response (paragraphs 3–14) and the paragraphs that follow. How do these paragraphs reiterate, qualify, or expand on the response itself? What rhetorical purpose do they serve?

6. What specific action(s) does Jacobs advocate in order to remedy the effects of residential schooling and the "assimilationist policy"?

7. Analyzing the essay as a whole, do you think Jacobs responds positively or negatively to the Harper apology? Refer to specific points in your answer.

POST-READING

1. a) Access one of the other Aboriginal leaders' response to Harper's 11 June apology (see paragraph 1) and summarize the main points; b) Compare the spoken text of Jacob's response with that of the other Aboriginal leader.

2. *Collaborative or individual activity:* Do think Harper's apology was adequate? Was there anything missing that should have been there? Consider the effects of language, tone, and similar stylistic features on the intended audience.

RELATED WEBSITES OF INTEREST

Truth and Reconciliation Commission of Canada:
www.trc.ca

CBC News (timeline for residential schools and related issues):
www.cbc.ca/canada/story/2008/05/16/f-timeline-residential-schools.html

Native Women's Association of Canada:
www.nwac.ca/home

Inuit Tapiriit Kanatami (national Inuit organization in Canada):
www.itk.ca/media-centre/speeches/speeches-response-apology-residential-school-survivors

ADDITIONAL LIBRARY READING

Many essays in newspapers, magazines, and journals exist on issues related to residential schooling and can be accessed through your library's databases. For example, see the special issue on "Aboriginal redress" in *English Studies in Canada* 35.1

(2009). Canadian Aboriginal media that have covered the apology and related issues include *Alberta Sweetgrass, Indian Life, Saskatchewan Sage,* and *Windspeaker.*

The Senate and the fight against the 1885 Chinese Immigration Act

Christopher G. Anderson

(4,254 words)

Pre-reading

1. Anderson's essay is occasioned by the apology of Prime Minister Stephen Harper to Chinese Canadians for the Head Tax of 1885 and other discriminatory policies of the late nineteenth- and early twentieth centuries in Canada. a) Using a reliable source, such as an encyclopedia or recent government document, research the history of Chinese immigration to Canada from 1885 to 1923, including the laws enacted to limit or exclude Chinese immigration; b) Using a reliable dictionary, find a definition for "racism" or "racial discrimination."

---

1   *On June 22, 2006, the Prime Minister rose in the House of Commons to "offer a full apology to Chinese Canadians for the head tax and express our deepest sorrow for the subsequent exclusion of Chinese immigrants." After recalling the fundamental role that Chinese Canadians had played in the nation-building construction of the Canadian Pacific Railway (CPR), the Prime Minister observed how—once the line was completed—"Canada turned its back on these men" as it imposed a $50 Head Tax on Chinese migrants in 1885, increased this to $100 in 1900 and then to $500 in 1905, and finally expanded the scope of its exclusionary measures in 1923 to make it all but impossible for Chinese immigrants to resettle legally in Canada through into the post–Second World War period. Although the various race-based measures instituted to exclude Chinese migrants were deemed to be legal at the time, they were, according to the Prime Minister, "inconsistent with the values that Canadians hold today." This article argues that at the time of the 1885 legislation, and for some time after, there were voices that spoke out against these discriminatory policies. Most specifically, this sentiment dominated debates on the question in the Canadian Senate between 1885 and 1887, and it did so to such an extent that government supporters had to resort to some clever procedural maneuvers to see the law passed and* amended against the will of the majority of Senators. In an important sense, then, these restrictive measures are not only "inconsistent with the values that Canadians hold today," but also conflict with values held by Canadians in the late nineteenth century, values that can be traced to a set of liberal beliefs on the rights of non-citizens inherited from Britain. The debates that took place in the Senate are, therefore, both interesting and important because they provide greater depth to our understanding of the historical record of race relations in Canada. They also speak to the more general issue of the role of the Senate in Canadian politics.*

2   Although Chinese migrants had lived in Canada since as early as 1858, it was not really until the 1880s that their numbers began to rise appreciably. Thus, while 4,383 were identified in the 1881 Canadian census, the population is then thought to have grown to around 10,550 by September 1884 as the construction of the Canadian Pacific Railway picked up steam. More generally, some 16,000 to 17,000 Chinese migrants probably came to Canada during the early 1880s to work on the rail line.[1] For economic and geographic reasons, Chinese migrants generally arrived and lived in British Columbia, and it is from there that the most persistent and vocal

cries were heard for greater control from the late nineteenth century onward.

3   At first, the reception of the Chinese was relatively cordial: "Colonial British Columbians were initially remarkably tolerant of the thousands of Chinese who came. British officials refused to countenance any discrimination, and whites, rather than pressing for hostile action, boasted of the British justice enjoyed by the Chinese."[2] Although there were certainly incidents of racism, including violence, against the Chinese, British liberalism formed the basis of the government's response to their presence in the colony. While Britain itself had had very limited experience with receiving Chinese migrants, the country's official position on the presence of non-citizens was primarily defined at this time by a recognition of the right of foreigners to enter and remain, which precluded any wholesale restriction.[3] However, after British Columbia joined Confederation in 1871, local politicians (first at the provincial level and then at the federal level) began to pressure Ottawa to pass legislation to restrict the ability of the Chinese to immigrate to or—for those who had already arrived—find work in Canada.[4]

4   The first major effort in the House of Commons was undertaken by Arthur Bunster (Vancouver Island), who sought and failed to convince his fellow MPs in 1878 to make it illegal to hire people to work on the construction of the CPR if their hair was greater than 5.5 inches in length—an obvious attack on the Chinese, whose hair was generally worn in long queues.[5] In words that recalled those famously used by Lord Palmerston some 20 years earlier in the defence of the rights of foreigners in Britain,[6] Prime Minister Alexander Mackenzie stated that the motion "was one unprecedented in its character and altogether unprecedented in its spirit, and at variance with those tolerant laws which afforded employment and an asylum to all who came within our country, irrespective of colour, hair, or anything else."[7] Mackenzie did not "think it would become us, as a British community, to legislate against any class of people who might be imported into, or might emigrate to, this country."[8]

5   Although calls for "repressive measures" against the Chinese—including their forced removal from the country—were made time and again in Parliament through into the 1880s, Prime Minister John

A. Macdonald, while he personally opposed such immigration, appointed two separate commissions of inquiry to investigate the situation in 1879 and 1884. Once the CPR was completed, however, the government introduced changes in May 1885 to the proposed *Electoral Franchise Act* before Parliament to deny any person of Chinese origin the right to vote in federal elections.

6   John A. Macdonald justified this action on the grounds that the Chinese migrant "is a stranger, a sojourner in a strange land . . . [H]e has no common interest with us . . . [H]e has no British instincts or British feelings or aspirations, and therefore ought not to have a vote."[9] Moreover, if given the vote, he warned, the Chinese would likely elect a sufficient number of Chinese-origin MPs in British Columbia to force the rest of the country to adhere to their "eccentricities" and "immorality."[10] The Prime Minister's move received strong support from a number of MPs (especially those from British Columbia), but it also sparked some vocal opposition. For example, L.H. Davies (Queen's) argued that "If a Chinaman becomes a British subject it is not right that a brand should be placed on his forehead, so that other men may avoid him."[11] For his part, Arthur H. Gillmor (Charlotte), while he did "not think they are a desirable class of persons," argued all the same that "as British subjects, we ought to show them fair play."[12] Despite such protests, however, the motion was carried. For reasons that are not clear, such voices became mute when the House turned to consider the government's legislation to restrict Chinese immigration two months later.

7   It was left to Secretary of State Joseph A. Chapleau to explain Bill 125 (later renumbered Bill 156) "to restrict and regulate Chinese Immigration into the Dominion of Canada" to the House, and he did so with such an expression of regret as to lead one MP to comment that "one would almost imagine [that he] were in opposition to the Bill rather than in favour of it."[13] Chapleau began by declaring that he had been surprised when

a demand was made for legislation to provide that one of the first principles which have always guided the English people in the enactment of their laws and regulations for the maintenance of the peace and prosperity of the country, should be violated in excluding from the shores of this great country, which is a part of the British Empire, members of the human family.[14]

8   Although he agreed that it was a good thing to ensure the continuance of a "white" British Columbia, he took issue with the way in which the Chinese had been demonized. As co-chair of the 1884 commission, he had found little evidence to support the uniformly negative image put forward by those who wanted to prevent their arrival; moreover, he had concluded that such migration had had a generally positive impact on the regional economy. Chapleau had come to see, however, that when it came to the Chinese people Canadians were "naturally disposed, through inconscient prejudices, to turn into defects even their virtues."[15]

9   The law would not only impose a $50 "Head Tax" (or "Capitation Tax") on Chinese migrants before they could be landed, but would also put in place several other restrictions. For example, only one Chinese passenger was to be allowed per each 50 tons weight of the arriving vessel (s.5), and a system of certificates was to be put in place to control those who desired to leave and return without paying the Head Tax again (s.14). Those most in favour of restriction were not wholly satisfied by these proposals but saw in them "the thin end of the edge" in the creation of a more extensive system of control.[16] Indeed, amidst concerns over the administration of the legislation, the only opposition came from those who wanted to make it more restrictive, although these critics supported Bill 156 all the same as it passed easily through the House.

10   Subsequently, amendments were introduced to the *1885 Chinese Immigration Act* during the next two years. In 1886, the government sought to enforce compulsory registration of those already in Canada (with penalties for non-compliance), expand the scope of the law to cover trains as well as ships, and remove merchants from the list of those exempt from paying the Head Tax. Although the bill was passed in the Lower Chamber with little dissent, it was ultimately held up in the Senate by the opponents of restriction. In 1887, the government introduced new amendments that were notable for the absence of any further restrictions, save a change to allow the Chinese only three months leave from the country before having to repay the Head Tax.[17] Even these proposals, however, barely made it through the Upper Chamber, and that lone restrictive feature was ultimately removed.

11   There was an intimation of the level of support that the Chinese might receive in the Senate during its debate on the 1885 *Electoral Franchise Act*. "I cannot myself see the propriety," Alexander Vidal commented, "of excluding the Mongolians, who have shown themselves to be patient, industrious and law-abiding, from privileges which are given to every other member of the human family in this country."[18] For his part, Lawrence G. Power did not think "the Parliament of Canada should make any distinction of race at all; that the Chinese, Negroes, Indians and Whites should be on the same footing; that no exceptions should be made in favour of one or against another race."[19] Striking a position that would be repeated by a number of his colleagues when Bill 156 arrived not long thereafter, Richard W. Scott observed that having sought to open up China to the world, Canada should not "set up a Chinese wall on our side," for to do so would be "entirely contrary to the principles of the Empire."[20] Despite such objections, however, the franchise legislation was passed. The protests that were made over denying the Chinese the right to vote paled, however, in comparison to the outrage expressed by the many Senators who spoke against the restriction of Chinese migration.

The Senate in Defence of the Chinese (1885–87)

12   Early on in the debate, Alexander Vidal set the tone for the majority in the Senate when he declared: "I think it is entirely inconsistent with the very fundamental principle of the British constitution that legislation of this kind should find a place on the statute book."[21] To pursue such a course as that proposed in Bill 156, observed James Dever, would tarnish the reputation of the country:

We, who pride ourselves on the freedom of our institutions, and the abolition of slavery in the United States, and who fancy we are going over the world with our lamp in our hand shedding light and lustre wherever we go—that we should become slave-drivers, and prohibit strangers from coming to our hospitable shore because they are of a different colour and have a different language and habits from ourselves, in deference to the feelings of a few people from British Columbia, is a thing I cannot understand.[22]

13   To the extent to which the law would discriminate against a particular group, concluded William Almon, it remained "contrary to the genius of the nineteenth century."[23] Moreover, it was suggested that if the Chinese did not seem to adapt well to Canadian society, then this was in part the fault of Canadians themselves when they instituted such barriers as disenfranchisement and the prevention of family reunification. Indeed, it was observed that the Chinese became further excluded from European Canadian society by the stereotypes that the latter employed.

14   Although the opponents of restriction were unable to prevent the passage of the bill, the way in which it was returned to the House is worth noting, for it was only on account of some fancy procedural footwork on the part of the government side that it happened with so little disturbance. William Almon had "given notice that [he] would oppose it at the third reading, and that [he] would move that it be read the third time three months hence"—thereby making it impossible for the legislation to pass that session.[24] The Senator, however, apparently committed a procedural error that allowed the legislation to emerge from the committee stage unscathed and pass through Third Reading without any discussion. Not only did Almon not give notice in writing, but he also wrongly assumed that debate could not pass through two stages on the same day. As a result, his efforts to scuttle the bill were sidestepped and it was returned to the House of Commons without a word altered, despite the considerable opposition to the very principles on which it was based that had been expressed. Almon's frustration comes through quite clearly, as does his firm conviction that it was a fundamentally illiberal piece of legislation:

I think such legislation is a disgrace to humanity. I think it is rolling back civilization from the end to the beginning of the nineteenth century. The early part of this century did away with the Slave trade, with the *Test Act*, and gave Catholic emancipation and abolished slavery in the West Indies. We now enact a law which is as vile as any of those to the repeal of which I have just alluded, and I think it will impress an indelible disgrace on this House and on the Dominion.[25]

15   The chances that Almon's effort might otherwise have succeeded would seem to be slim—after all, it was fairly rare for a government bill to be turned back in the Senate, especially when the same party controlled both chambers—but the fate of the government's attempt to amend the 1885 *Chinese Immigration Act* by passing Bill 106 the following year makes it difficult to claim that there were none. As noted above, the proposed amendments in 1886 were mostly restrictionist in nature, but rather than simply debate these measures, opponents attacked the law itself. While much of the criticism trod upon familiar ground (e.g., "It is so repugnant to all that is English, and honourable or right that one can hardly discuss it in a proper frame of mind"),[26] there were important developments as well.

16   For example, Alexander Vidal raised the question of Canadian sovereignty and the country's right to restrict entry at its borders, and he suggested that this should not be held to be absolute but rather ought to conform to the principles on which the land had come to be settled. He began by inquiring as to the foundations of Britain's occupation of North America:

By what royal right have we and our fathers crossed the ocean and taken possession of this western continent? What right had we to come here and dispossess the Indians, native proprietors of this country, and take possession of their lands? . . . [Do we] not only consider that we have a better right to it than they have, but to consider it so exclusively our own as to shut out from sharing in the advantages of this country others of God's people who have as much right to it as we have?[27]

17   The land was taken not by right, he claimed, but "because we believed that where our civilization and enlightenment have been introduced we have carried with us the blessings of Christianity to the people amongst whom we have settled."[28] To restrict other people now from coming to live in the country on the basis of race, he concluded, was so "utterly inconsistent with our professions as Christians and with the vaunted freedom we profess to cherish as a British people" that it undermined the basis on which the land had been occupied—the superiority of "the Anglo-Saxon race."[29] Thus, while Senators often still viewed the issue from a race-based and even missionary perspective, they also operated within a rights-based framework, with potentially quite important policy implications for Chinese Canadians.

18   Even George W. Allan, who introduced the amendments in the Senate for the government, said that he had "no special leaning towards this Chinese legislation."[30] Given the level of agreement against the proposals, it would be, Richard W. Scott averred, "a service to the empire if we allow this question to stand over another year."[31] By that time, he hoped, passions in British Columbia might have calmed somewhat and a more reasonable examination of the question might be assayed. Thus, the same Senate that had seemed to sanction the *1885 Chinese Immigration Act* now let the debate on its amendment stand for six months, thereby signaling an unwillingness to allow the law to be changed in a more restrictive manner.

19   The government's second attempt to amend the law, Bill 54, responded to some of the criticisms that had been expressed in the Senate by removing the restrictive elements included in the previous bill. Moreover, the one aspect of the new bill that would have made it more difficult for Chinese migrants— the three-month return clause—was first extended to six months and then dropped altogether. Nonetheless, the legislation received extended criticism ("a diabolical Bill . . . [that] has not a shadow of justice or right on its side"),[32] out of which emerged—amidst the old complaints—other lines of argumentation. For example, Almon asked: "How will it be now if we pass [this] Act to say that there is a dividing line between Canada and the United States? . . . Can we any longer point with pride to our flag and say that

under that emblem all men, be they Mongolian, Circassian or Caucasian, are equally free?"[33]

20   The Senator who sponsored the bill on the government's behalf, future Prime Minister John J.C. Abbott, agreed that the principle that lay behind the 1885 *Chinese Immigration Act* was offensive to the chamber, but he argued all the same that the amendments on the floor might help to temper the harshness of the law. If too many alterations to the proposed bill were presented to the House, he cautioned, then it would reject them, with the result that the modest positive alterations that could be made would not come into effect, leaving the Chinese worse off than they might otherwise have been. This line of reasoning found some sympathy but little support, as "the sentiment of the Senate seemed to be that the Act should be wiped off the Statute Book."[34] Indeed, Vidal introduced Bill P to do just that, and he had such backing that Abbott himself admitted that it would likely pass on a vote. The justification for repeal was succinctly expressed by Robert Haythorne, who declared that "it is a difficult thing to amend a Bill based upon a wrong principle, and the principle upon which [the 1885 *Chinese Immigration Act* is] based is a bad and cruel one."[35] Even if the House would not accept it, Vidal argued, passage of Bill P would "show that we have proper views of British freedom and the responsibilities that are attached to our professions as Christians."[36]

21   The government side, however, was once again able—through procedural means—to steer its legislation through the chamber. It argued successfully before the Speaker that since the law involved the collection of revenue—the Head Tax—the Senate could not seek to repeal it. The Speaker based his ruling on s.53 of the 1867 *BNA Act* ("Bills for appropriating any Part of the Public Revenue, or for imposing any Tax or Impost, shall originate in the House of Commons") and on the 47th Rule of the Senate according to *Bourinot* ("The Senate will not proceed upon a Bill appropriating public money that shall not within the knowledge of the Senate have been recommended by the Queen's representative"). The question of the Senate's authority to amend money bills would long trouble Parliament and was eventually the subject of a Special Committee of the Senate in 1917. In response to this decision, Vidal argued: "I can easily

understand that if we found the word 'Chinese' between cheese and cigars in the tariff bill that we could not touch it, but it is an extraordinary thing that we cannot amend a public Bill simply because there is a penalty attached for which the Government derives a revenue."[37] Although the purpose behind the Head Tax was clearly one of policy (that is, to restrict the entry of Chinese migrants) rather than one of generating revenue, the Speaker supported the government's line of reasoning. Thus, not only was Vidal's initiative ruled out of order but any chance of pursuing meaningful change to the bill seemed to have been thwarted. With the wind so completely and effectively taken out of the opposition's sails, Third Reading was speedily accomplished. It would be some years before the Senate would again exhibit such a rights-based outlook on the issue of migration control, even as the government expanded the scope of its restrictions towards Chinese migration as well as all other non-white, non-Christian, and non-British groups.

22   After coming into effect in January 1886, the 1885 *Chinese Immigration Act* doubtless contributed to the low levels of Chinese migration to Canada that occurred during the remainder of the 1880s. It is difficult, however, to assess the effect of the new law as there was an anticipated reduction in arrivals due to the completion of the CPR, which led many to leave the country, either to return to China or to try their fortunes in the United States. However, throughout the 1890s the number of entries recorded each year grew, if somewhat erratically, sparking a new wave of restrictive measures towards Chinese migration that culminated in the extremely effective 1923 *Chinese Immigration Act*. Indeed, according to official tallies, only eight Chinese immigrants were landed in Canada between 1924–25 and 1938–39—less than one every two years.

Conclusions

23   This examination of the response in the Senate to the government's first attempts to control Chinese immigration between 1885 and 1887 is instructive in at least two major respects. First, it uncovers an important feature of the history of Canadian state relations with Chinese migrants that has too long been overlooked. While it is certainly true that the Chinese had few friends willing to support them in Canada, they could count a large number of Senators amongst them. Thus, Senator William J. Macdonald, himself a representative of British Columbia, took note of the role that many of his colleagues were playing:

> I wish to express my satisfaction at the fact that a people who have been treated so rigorously and ungenerously, who are unrepresented, and who have been hunted to the death, should have found representatives to stand up on the floor of this House and speak on their behalf.[38]

24   Of course, rights-based British liberalism was not the sole motivation for opposition to the 1885 *Chinese Immigration Act*. Indeed, there were traces of distrust of organized labour, alongside a desire that business should have access to such—as one Senator would put it a few years later—"good labour-saving machines."[39] Moreover, an opposition to discrimination did not necessitate admiration for the Chinese either as individuals or as a group (although it often was joined to such sentiments).[40] It also was at times connected to an opinion that "whites" were superior to the Chinese,[41] and for some Senators accepting such migrants in Canada was an important means by which the Chinese might be converted to Christianity.[42] Nonetheless, there is a clearly expressed respect for the individual rights of the Chinese that comes through in these debates, one that found widespread support amongst the opponents of restriction. Their racism, in short, did not fully displace their belief in equality, and they were able to support, as a result, radically different policy options from those that were being pursued by the government, and that would ultimately be transformed into a source of national shame.

25   As well as recalling an important piece of Canadian history, one that has been completely ignored or overlooked in the literature, the relevance of these Senate debates today can also be seen in the extent to which members of that institution sought to institute a policy position that is much more in keeping with what we understand to be modern

values held by Canadians. This not only suggests that Canadians possess a much richer and more complex political history than is often recognized, but it also underlines the potential role for the Senate in broadening our political ideas and language, of providing the sort of sober second thought that was supposed to be one of its central functions in the Canadian political system.

Canadian Parliamentary Review.
2007. Summer 30 (2).

Notes

1. Patricia E. Roy, *A White Man's Province: British Columbia Politicians and Chinese and Japanese Immigrants, 1858–1914* (Vancouver: University of British Columbia Press, 1989), x–xi.
2. *Ibid.*, 4. See also W. Peter Ward, *White Canada Forever: Popular Attitudes and Public Policy Toward Orientals in British Columbia* [Second Edition] (Montreal and Kingston: McGill-Queen's University Press, 1990), 24–29.
3. See Colin Holmes, *John Bull's Island: Immigration and British Society,* 1871–1971 (London: Macmillan Education Ltd., 1988).
4. See Bruce Ryder, "Racism and the Constitution: The Constitutional Fate of British Columbia Anti-Asian Immigration Legislation, 1884–1909," *Osgoode Hall Law Journal,* Volume 29, Number 3 (1991), 619–76.
5. 1207. See also James Morton, *In the Sea of Sterile Mountains: The Chinese in British Columbia* (Vancouver: J.J. Douglas Ltd., 1973),43–44.
6. "Any foreigner, whatever his nation, whatever his political creed, whatever his political offences against his own Government may, under this Bill, as he does today, find in these realms a safe and secure asylum so long as he obeys the law of the land." Quoted in T.W.E. Roche, *The Key In The Lock: A History of Immigration Control in England from 1066 to the Present Day* (London: John Murray, 1969), 58.
7. Canada, House of Commons, *Debates,* March 18, 1878, p. 1209.
8. *Ibid.*
9. *Ibid.*, May 4, 1885, p. 1582.
10. *Ibid.*, p. 1588.
11. *Ibid.*, p. 1583.
12. *Ibid.*, p. 1585.
13. *Ibid.*, Edgar C. Baker (Victoria), July 2, 1885, p. 3013.
14. *Ibid.*, p. 3003.
15. *Ibid.*, p. 3006.
16. *Ibid.*, Noah Shakespeare (Victoria), July 2,1885, p. 3011.
17. The new bill kept a provision to allow Chinese travelers in transit to pass through Canada without paying the Head Tax, while it added a clause to allow the Chinese wife of a white man to enter without paying the Head Tax, and another that would ensure that a portion of the Head Tax was sent to provincial coffers in Victoria.
18. Canada, Senate *Debates,* July 13, 1885, p. 1276.
19. *Ibid.*, p. 1280.
20. *Ibid.*
21. *Ibid.*, p. 1297.
22. *Ibid.*, p. 1298.
23. *Ibid.*, p. 1295.
24. *Ibid.*, July 18, 1885, p. 1411.
25. *Ibid.*
26. *Ibid.*, Richard W. Scott, January 30,1886, p. 692.
27. *Ibid.*, May 21, 1886, p. 687.
28. *Ibid.*
29. *Ibid.*
30. *Ibid.*
31. *Ibid.*, May 26, 1886, p. 747.
32. *Ibid.*, William J. Macdonald, June 10, 1887, pp. 311–12.
33. *Ibid.*, p. 299.
34. *Ibid.*, Richard W. Scott, June 13, 1887, p. 349.
35. *Ibid.*, June 10, 1887, p. 313.
36. *Ibid.*, p. 307.
37. *Ibid.*, June 14, 1887, p. 396.
38. *Ibid.*, June 10, 1887, p. 311.
39. *Ibid.*, Henry A.N. Kaulbach, July 8, 1892, p. 497.
40. See W. Peter Ward, *White Canada Forever: Popular Attitudes and Public Policy Toward Orientals in British Columbia* [Second Edition] (Montreal and Kingston: McGill-Queen's University Press, 1990), Chapter 1.
41. According to Vidal, for example, the "superior civilization" of the "Anglo-Saxon race" meant that whites should have no fear of being overpowered by the Chinese; see Canada, Senate, *Debates,* July 13, 1885, p. 1297.
42. See *ibid.*, William Almon, p. 1296.

KEY AND CHALLENGING WORDS

exclusionary, cordial, demonize, intimation, propriety, disenfranchisement, illiberal, indelible, restrictionist, aver, succinctly, appropriate, culminate

QUESTIONS

1. Identify in Anderson's introduction the justification for his essay and his thesis; paraphrase the thesis.
2. Construct a timeline for the most significant events referred to in the essay from 1878 to 1887.
3. a) Identify a primary source used in the first three paragraphs of the essay; b) Select a primary source that is set up in the block format and show its importance to the passage in which it occurs and the essay as a whole.
4. Briefly discuss the function of paragraph 11, which focuses on a time before Bill 125 (156) was introduced.

5. Explain in your own words the basis of the government manoeuvre that prevented Bill 54 from being repealed. How was faulty reasoning involved?
6. Explain how the views expressed by the senators who opposed the Head Tax exemplified a "rights-based" outlook (paragraphs 17 and 21) that characterized British thought in the nineteenth century.
7. According to the author in his conclusion, what can be learned from the debate in the Senate from 1885–7?

POST-READING

1. *Collaborative or individual activity:* After coming up with a working definition of "racism" or "racial discrimination," consider whether the views expressed by the senators who opposed the Chinese Head Tax were, in fact, racist or discriminatory. Defend your point of view, making specific references to the senators' speeches.

2. Essays in the humanities often put forward a new interpretation of primary source material, arguing that the new interpretation is more valid than older interpretations or represents a significant perspective that is worthy of consideration. In 500 words, analyze the effectiveness of Anderson's argument; what made it convincing or not?

RELATED WEBSITES OF INTEREST

Address by the Prime Minister on the Chinese Head Tax Redress, 22 June 2006:

http://pm.gc.ca/eng/media.asp?id=1220

CBC Archives:

http://archives.cbc.ca/society/immigration/topics/1433/

Citizenship and Immigration Canada: Chinese Head Tax Redress:

www.cic.gc.ca/english/multiculturalism/programs/redress.asp

Enhancing democratic citizenship

Elisabeth Gidengil, André Blais, Richard Nadeau, and Neil Nevitte

(4,648 words)

Pre-reading

1. This essay is an excerpt from a book chapter. Read the first paragraph in order to determine the purpose and structure of the excerpt as well as the authors' methodology. Scan the rest of the essay to confirm the answers to these questions.

---

1   The challenges [for enhancing] democratic citizenship are clear. One is to find ways of reengaging young citizens. A second is how to create a more informed citizenry, and a third concerns how to narrow the existing democratic divides. Identifying the challenges is easier than setting out solutions to such complex problems. But it is possible to scan the horizons to see solutions others have turned to and with what effect.

Re-Engaging Young Canadians

2   Turnout in federal elections has declined massively among young Canadians since 1988. A recent study in the United States is suggestive; it points to the importance of getting young citizens to vote for the first time. Once young people have paid the "start-up costs of voting," they are likely to keep on voting (Plutzer 2002). So, what can be done to reduce the start-up costs for young Canadians? First, political parties have a role to play. Political parties are representative institutions, and if they make little effort to mobilize the citizenry, then citizens are less likely to vote. Regardless of which party they heard from, people who reported being contacted by a political party or a candidate during the 2000 campaign were more likely to vote. As the data in Chapter 5 demonstrated, young Canadians were much less likely than

others to report being contacted. The clear implication is that a concerted get-out-the-vote effort by the political parties could well help to reverse the downward trend in voting among the young.

3   Second, the problems with the permanent voters list need to be resolved (see Courtney 2004). In 2000 young Canadians were the segment of the population least likely to have received a voter information card and the most likely to have found it difficult to get their names on the permanent voters list. Part of the problem is that young people are much more mobile; they are likely to be tenants rather than homeowners. They are also less likely to file tax returns (which is one way that the list is updated). So they are either not on the list or listed under the wrong address. If these flaws in the system can be addressed, young people will find it easier to vote.

4   In addition to these short-term solutions, various long-term solutions should be considered. Early experiences can lay the foundation for a lifetime of democratic engagement. In this regard, research on volunteering may hold broader lessons for civic engagement. Michael Hall and his colleagues (Hall, McKeown, and Roberts 2001, 39) found that there was a clear, albeit weakening, connection between volunteering and people's experiences early in life. Volunteering rates were higher, for example, among people who had been active in student government, who had a parent who spent time volunteering, or

who belonged to a youth group. Having been helped by others in early life was also a motivating factor. If volunteering in adulthood is encouraged by experiences during people's formative years, the trend toward mandatory community service in high school could have effects that persist into later life. And as the evidence presented in Chapter 6 indicated, volunteering tends to go hand in hand with civic engagement.

5 In addition, a large US survey of students in Grades 9 to 12 and their parents indicates that community service enhances students' knowledge of politics. It also encourages more discussion of politics with their parents and fosters a sense of political competence (Niemi, Hepburn, and Chapman 2000). However, these benefits only seem to accrue if the amount of service is substantial. Moreover, the authors of this study sound an important cautionary note: students who were involved in few other activities, who had lower grades, and whose parents did not perform any community service were much less likely to be involved in community service themselves. In other words, unless community service is universal, it risks deepening the democratic divides. For this reason, Benjamin Barber (1992) argues forcefully that service in the community should be made mandatory rather than voluntary. But as Hepburn and her colleagues (Hepburn, Niemi, and Chapman 2000, 621) ask, "If service is required, will the students forced to participate learn from it?"

6 Community service seems to be most beneficial when it takes the form of "service learning." This term denotes service that is actually incorporated into high school courses in ways that encourage both awareness of the related social and political issues and reflection upon the experience (Hepburn, Niemi, and Chapman 2000; Galston 2001). The rationale for service learning is found in John Dewey's (1916; 1938) argument that schooling must be linked to real-world experience. Some educators have raised concerns, though, about the possible partisan and ideological connotations of training for citizenship.

7 What about civic education classes? Many see civics courses as a way of enhancing democratic engagement, and the province of Ontario actually introduced a mandatory civics course for Grade 10 students in fall 2000 (Myers 2000). But some critical questions remain unanswered:

When should students receive civics/government instruction? . . . What classroom and extra-classroom methods are best suited to teaching about government? How much training should there be in research methods? Are the skills needed for citizenship the same as the skills needed for political analysis? What kind of instruction, if any, will make young people less cynical about (yet appropriately skeptical of) politicians? (Niemi and Smith 2001, 286)

8 For all the interest in revitalizing civic education, surprisingly little research systematically evaluates its benefits, especially over the long term (Niemi and Smith 2001). This is partly because conventional wisdom has long held that civics courses are ineffective. Most of the evidence about the effectiveness of civics education comes from the United States, where the experience has been mixed. The proportion of US high school students taking American government courses has risen steadily since 1980. According to a recent study (Niemi and Smith 2001), nearly 80 per cent of graduating seniors have had a government class at some stage of their high school education. And yet knowledge of politics remains low, and concern about political disengagement on the part of young adults has continued to grow. Indeed, the 1998 Civics Assessment, conducted as part of the National Assessment of Educational Progress mandated by the US Congress, found that only a quarter of high school seniors met or exceeded the standard of proficiency, while over a third tested below basic, "indicating near-total civic ignorance" (Galston 2001, 221). Evidently, civics education can fail.

9 Others believe that civics education can be effective, but much depends on the content (Niemi and Junn 1998; Galston 2001). Ken Osborne (1988, 228), for example, suggests that what is needed is "a genuinely political education, if the schools are to produce informed, participating citizens," and that this means bringing real-world political issues into the classroom (see also Osborne 2000). In a similar vein, Richard Niemi and Jane Junn (1998, 150) have been critical of "the Pollyannaish view of politics" that is encouraged when civics education is devoid of any serious discussion of partisan politics and interest groups. "If students can be taught to understand that political parties and interest groups form to

promote and protect legitimate differences in points of view," they argue, "they would be in a much better position to understand, appreciate, and participate in the political process." It is not just a matter of *what* is taught in civics classes but *how* it is taught (Osborne 1988). Context matters, and a number of commentators have pointed to the importance of fostering a democratic classroom climate so that students are not just learning about democratic skills and dispositions but actually practicing them (Levin 2000; Sears and Perry 2000). Timing also appears to be important: high school government courses seem to be most effective when they are taken in Grade 12 rather than earlier in a student's career (Niemi and Junn 1998).

10   The intractable problem with solutions like mandatory service learning and required civics courses is that they cannot reach those who are no longer in school. Indeed, for the long term, the key to democratic engagement may simply be to keep more young people in school. As William Galston (2001, 219) observes, "all education is civic education in the sense that individuals' level of general educational attainment significantly affects their level of political knowledge as well as the quantity and character of their political participation." Indeed, the one group of young people that has been immune to the trend toward disengagement is university graduates. It is hardly surprising that university graduates are typically the most engaged citizens, because becoming a well-informed citizen requires considerable cognitive capacity. Consider one public opinion expert's advice:

> Whenever you read or see political material, exercise skepticism. Figure out motivations and ideologies in the newspaper, magazine, or television show you are looking at; watch for its editorial thrust and for slants in the news or information it presents. What stories are made prominent? Why? What is ignored? Who is quoted, and why? What evaluative material is slipped in? Try to read between the lines, spotting what the reporter did not say, and try to dig out obscure but important bits that contradict the main story line (Page 1996, 125–6).

11   These tasks will be quite beyond the capabilities of people who do not even possess basic literacy skills, which are precisely what many of Canada's high school dropouts lack (Applied Research Branch 2000). Canada's dropout rates appear to be more or less in line with other OECD (Organisation for Economic Co-operation and Development) countries, but Canadian dropouts typically have much lower levels of literacy. This is because "a large proportion of those who drop out do so at an early age and at low levels of education. . . . Almost one third drop out with Grade 9 education or less and almost two thirds drop out with Grade 10 or less. . . . The earlier that students drop out, the less knowledge and fewer skills that they will have accumulated" (Applied Research Branch 2000, 13–14). And, we could add, the less likely they are to have any interest in politics or to be acquainted with the sorts of political information required for meaningful engagement in democratic politics.

Creating a More Informed Citizenry

12   There is a lively debate about whether citizens really need to know "textbook facts" about their political world to make adequately informed decisions about how to vote. Yet one of the clearest messages to emerge from this audit of democratic citizenship is that information matters. Indeed, information is the essential prerequisite of responsive and responsible government: governments cannot be held accountable if citizens do not know what those in power have been doing. Knowing who the key political actors are may not be that consequential in itself, but differences in knowledge of several such 'minor' facts are diagnostic of more profound differences in the amount and accuracy of contextual information voters bring to their judgments" (Converse 2000, 333; see also Neuman 1986; Delli Carpini and Keeter 1996).

13   Having a store of contextual information is important because it helps people to make sense of and to impart meaning to new pieces of information. This is the so-called Matthew principle: "to them that hath shall be given" or, as Converse (2000, 335) puts it more colloquially, "them what has, gets." This principle clearly applies to campaign learning. Election campaigns actually widen the knowledge gap: those who know the most about politics in general end up learning the most, while those who know little to

begin with learn the least. And information shortcuts often end up helping those who need them least, because those who need these shortcuts the most often lack the contextual information required to take advantage of them.

14   More important, opinion on some significant policy issues would very likely be different if Canadians were better informed about politics. This is especially true when people are misinformed about policy-relevant facts. Informed opinion on social policy questions is typically more liberal than actual opinion. The same holds for opinions about some fiscal matters and some issues concerning the role of the state versus the market. Because information can affect policy preferences and political attitudes, people who share similar background characteristics may hold very different opinions, depending on how well informed they are. This finding implies that people who are poorly informed are more likely to get it "wrong" when it comes to translating their preferences into appropriate political choices.

15   The extent to which citizens are informed is not a function of their own abilities and motivation alone: "Voters are not fools. . . . The electorate behaves about as rationally and responsibly as we should expect, given the clarity of the alternatives presented to it and the character of the information available to it" (Key 1966, 7). The main sources of information for citizens are the media and political actors, neither of which necessarily have a vested interest in disseminating the objective facts. Politicians and other political factors may be tempted to deploy facts in self serving ways to build support for their preferred positions. If politicians obfuscate and political parties fail to articulate clear alternatives, is there reason to be surprised if many citizens end up with only a vague or confused sense of what the politicians stand for?

16   However, even when politicians and political parties take clear stands, their messages do not necessarily reach the voters. Economic incentives encourage the media to put the emphasis on entertaining first and informing only second (Zaller 1999). Whether publicly or privately owned, broadcasters have to be concerned about audience share, just as the print media are preoccupied with circulation figures. Consequently, a party's issue positions may receive only token coverage if what the party is saying

or doing is not deemed newsworthy, and newsworthiness is often determined by standings in the polls. When an issue position does receive extensive coverage, even poorly informed voters have the opportunity to learn about it.

17   A striking finding from recent election data is that even otherwise relatively well-informed voters had difficulty matching the parties with their promises or classifying the parties in terms of left and right. Providing more coverage of the issues and being more even-handed in the amount of coverage provided to the various political parties would help to raise the mean level of knowledge about the parties and their stands.

Narrowing the Democratic Divides

18   When it comes to inclusiveness and responsiveness, diminishing the variance in political knowledge is at least as important as raising the mean. Proposals to increase the amount of information available to voters by regulating the nature and amount of coverage that broadcasters provide are going to benefit only those who are following politics to begin with. The same objection applies to another suggested solution, namely, having longer campaigns (Moore 1987). The idea is that longer election campaigns would give people more time to learn about the issues. In theory, election campaigns represent an unparalleled opportunity to engage voters (Cappella and Jamieson 1997, 241). Indeed, Popkin (1991) has likened elections to civics education, with political parties as the teachers. In practice, though, the least informed typically also learn the least during a campaign.

19   Eveland and Scheufele (2000, 216) actually go so far as to argue that increasing the amount of political information (and participation) "among some groups but not others . . . could be worse for democracy than no overall increase at all." This is especially true "when the group increasing in knowledge or participation is already politically advantaged and has interests at odds with the disadvantaged group." At issue is not just the low level of knowledge per se but the uneven *social* distribution of knowledge. Older Canadians know more than younger Canadians,

affluent Canadians know more than poor Canadians, and men know more than women. The worry is that the needs and wants of affluent, older men are the most likely to be reflected in collective expressions of opinion. Differences would be larger on important questions of public policy if the young, the poor, and women were better informed. To the extent that this is so, public policy may well be less responsive to their needs and interests. Communications scholars put the point bluntly: "When there are disparities across social groups in political knowledge and participation, democracy is at least a little less democratic, regardless of the underlying reasons for these inequities" (Eveland and Scheufele 2000, 216).

20   The observation that information shortfalls are associated with democratic divides points to a deeper issue: why are some Canadians not better informed about politics? There is no shortage of potential answers to that question, and many of them take us back to the more basic question of why interest in politics is not higher. The preeminent point to acknowledge is that the costs of acquiring information are higher for some citizens than for others. The cost of subscribing to a daily newspaper, cable television, or an Internet access service may be beyond the reach of poor families. However, the effects of structural inequalities run deeper than differences in the costs of becoming informed. As Page and Shapiro (1992, 164) note, when it comes to the dissemination of political information, economic inequality tends to win out over political equality: "A large corporation has a much better chance of learning how a tax bill will affect it than do many unorganized taxpayers with small, diffuse interests." The challenge, then, is to narrow the information gap by "lifting the bottom." Information presumes interest. If people have little or no interest in political affairs, they are unlikely to invest time and energy in seeking out political information. This is why John Zaller (1999, 2) argues that the problem is not lack of informational content in the media. On the contrary, he maintains, large numbers of citizens are being turned off by a style of politics and political communication that is "stilted, overly rationalistic, and just plain dull." Zaller takes intellectuals to task for bemoaning the rise of "infotainment" journalism when they should be seeing it as a way of reengaging citizens' interest in politics. His point is that "infotainment" journalism offers citizens a way to fulfill "the informational obligations of citizenship . . . with less effort and more pleasure" (p. 3). Zaller supports this seemingly heretical suggestion by pointing to the disappointing experience with the free television-time experiment in the 1996 US presidential election. The provision of large blocks of free television time on the three major networks was greeted with a singular lack of enthusiasm on the part of the candidates, the networks, and the electorate alike.

21   Rather than "fact-packed and informationally turgid" media content, Zaller argues, what is required are more stories that truly engage people. Dan Quayle's attack on the television character Murphy Brown is one case in point. The former US vice-president took the fictional character to task for having a child outside marriage. By focusing so much coverage on this seemingly trivial incident, the media succeeded in making "the family values debate accessible to Americans in a way that traditional political rhetoric did not" (Zaller 1999, 16). The 2000 federal election provided a Canadian analogue to the Murphy Brown story in the form of the Doris Day petition. The CBC comedy program *This Hour Has 22 Minutes* satirized the Alliance party's stand on direct democracy by inviting Canadians to add their names to a petition requesting that the party's leader, Stockwell Day, be required to change his name to Doris Day. Over one million people signed the petition through the show's website. There was a serious point: to demonstrate how easy it was to gather the requisite number of signatures required to initiate a binding referendum. And that point supports Zaller's contribution that some attention to politics is better than no attention at all, especially when viewers are being informed as well as entertained. A recent study by Matthew Baum (2002) also lends some support to this argument. He found that "due to selective political coverage by the entertainment-oriented soft news media, many otherwise politically inattentive individuals are exposed to information about high-profile political issues, most prominently foreign policy crises, as an incidental byproduct of seeking entertainment" (91).

22   Zaller also takes a sanguine view of "horserace journalism." This is coverage that focuses on "who is

ahead, who is behind, who is gaining, who is losing, what campaign strategy is being followed, and what the impact of campaign activities is on the candidate's chances of winning" (Joslyn 1984, 133). In Canada, as elsewhere, television news coverage seems preoccupied with the horserace in general and with the leaders' abilities as campaigners in particular, to the neglect of serious coverage of the issues (Mendelsohn 1993; 1996; Mendelsohn and Nadeau 1999). In Zaller's view, the unanimous condemning of the prevalence of this type of coverage is wrong. Horserace coverage, he argues, is not devoid of substantive content but can provide citizens with "a palatable mix of entertainment, information, debate, and politically useful cues," especially about the opinions of relevant groups (Zaller 1999, 19). Above all, though, this style of coverage appeals to millions of voters by making politics a spectator sport. If making politics seem like a game gets people to pay attention, Zaller maintains, then this is all to the good.

23   But does the prevalence of the "game frame" get viewers to tune in, or does it simply turn them off? There is evidence, for example, that some people are less active politically because they want to avoid conflict (Mansbridge 1980; Ulbig and Funk 1999; Mutz 2002). If media coverage reinforces the perception that politics is all about confrontation and competition, it may discourage such people from being politically active. We also need to ask what sort of people typically "spend many leisure hours" (Zaller 1999, 18) watching sports events on television. The audience for the sporting events that typically dominate the airwaves is still predominantly male, and politics may be just another game watched by men. After all, the players are still mostly men. We know that women are less likely than men to follow politics closely. It is not clear whether this is related to the way politics is covered, but there is certainly cause to wonder. These are the sorts of questions, in our view, that need to be answered before Zaller's enthusiasm for horserace journalism can be readily embraced. But Zaller is surely right to encourage us to think outside the box when it comes to ways of stimulating greater political awareness.

24   Political interest is likely to be higher to the extent that citizens see a link between political affairs and their own lives. If politics is perceived to be remote and abstract or, worse yet, corrupt and

self-serving, citizens will simply tune out. Globalization and market rhetoric encourage the view that governments are not only relatively powerless in the face of global economic forces but govern best when they govern least. That view is certainly open to challenge, but it should come as little surprise to discover that many citizens seem to have internalized the message that politics just does not matter very much.

25   This message has perhaps been encouraged by changes in the way that the media cover politics. Over the past two decades, media coverage in Canada (as in the United States) has taken on an increasingly negative tone; straight reporting of the facts has become subordinate to interpretation and evaluation, and the framing of stories too often highlights partisan calculation, conflict, and personal motives. The result, Richard Nadeau and Thierry Giasson (2003, 9) suggest, is a "devalued concept of politics" that discredits the electoral process "by reducing the broad debates of society to simple partisan issues." They go on to advocate a shift to "public journalism," or "civic journalism," as an antidote. This is a type of political reporting that puts citizens and their needs at the forefront of coverage: "From this angle, electoral news must principally focus on citizens' questions about issues they consider to be priorities and on party positions concerning these precise issues. The reporting in public journalism must cover campaigns by uncovering ordinary citizens' experiences" (18). The task of the journalist is to contextualize social issues and to foster debate with citizens about the proffered solutions. While admittedly somewhat idealistic, this approach has been practised in parts of the United States for the past dozen years; it has also been associated with significant gains in citizens' political knowledge. Changing media practices is no easy task, though, given the constraints under which journalists work, be they organizational, technical, financial, or the constraints of the genre itself (see Nadeau and Giasson 2003).

26   The single most important step that can be taken to narrow the democratic divides is to increase the number of Canadians who complete high school and go on to post-secondary education. One of the central findings to emerge from this audit of democratic citizenship is just how well education serves democracy. The more education people have, the more interested they are in politics, the more

attention they pay to news about politics, and the more they know about politics. And the more education people have, the more likely they are to vote, to belong to a political party or an interest group, to sign petitions and join in boycotts, and to be active in their communities. Education does not just provide citizens with better tools for democratic citizenship, it also provides them with the inclination for it.

27   A recent report by the Applied Research Branch of Human Resources Development Canada (2000, 58) outlines some of the policy options for encouraging more Canadians to complete their high school education: "awareness campaigns, raising the legal age at which youth can leave school, improving literacy, modifying programs for those who have difficulties with academic programs, developing alternative pathways to the workplace, policies directed to families, schools and the community, lowering the minimum wage, and developing non-accreditation learning options."

28   The HRDC report makes the point that lowering the dropout rate is good economic sense. The report estimates that the total monetary rate of return to society for completing high school as opposed to stopping at Grade 10 is 17 per cent. But a lower dropout rate is not only good for the Canadian economy; it is also good for Canadian democracy. More Canadians would be equipped with the cognitive skills and the motivation needed to be active and engaged citizens. Keeping students in school would also help to address the other root cause of democratic disengagement, namely poverty. The same study makes the relationship between socioeconomic factors and dropping out clear. Poor children are at greater risk of dropping out, and dropping out makes a lifetime of poverty more likely.

Citizenship Today

29   The picture of democratic citizenship in Canada is mixed. A core of highly engaged citizens pays close attention to politics and takes an active part in civic life. At the same time, a very significant minority of Canadians knows little about politics and cares less. Most disturbing, perhaps, is the evidence of deep pockets of political ignorance within certain groups in Canadian society. These democratic deficits diminish the inclusiveness and impair the responsiveness of Canadian democracy. And the most striking deficits are those defined by material circumstances, age, and gender. Of course there are poor young women who are highly engaged in civic life, just as there are affluent older men who are not. But the association between democratic engagement and social background is indisputable.

30   The systematic nature of this association should make us look to its deeper causes. The numerical under-representation of certain groups in Canada's political institutions is one factor. And patterns of media coverage and the conduct of election campaigns are implicated. But the roots of democratic disengagement also lie deep in the structural inequalities that characterize Canadian society. To the extent that they do, only by tackling those inequalities can democratic citizenship in Canada become truly inclusive.

In Gidengil et al., *Citizens*. 2004. Seattle: University of Washington Press.

References

Applied Research Branch. 2000. *Dropping out of high school: Definitions and costs*. R-01-1E. Ottawa: Human Resources Development Canada.

Baum, Matthew A. 2002. Sex, lies, and war: How soft news brings foreign policy to the inattentive public. *American Political Science Review* 96: 91–109.

Cappella, Joseph N., and Kathleen Hall Jamieson. 1997. *Spiral of cynicism: The press and the public good*. Oxford: Oxford University Press.

Converse, Philip E. 2000. Assessing the capacity of mass electorates. *Annual Review of Political Science* 3: 331–53.

Courtney, John C. 2004. *Elections*. Canadian Democratic Audit. Vancouver: UBC Press.

Delli Carpini, Michael X., and Scott Keeter. 1996. *What Americans know about politics and why it matters*. New Haven, CT: Yale University Press.

Dewey, John. 1916. *Education and democracy*. New York: Macmillan.

———. 1938. *Experience and education*. London: Collier Macmillan.

Eveland, William P., Jr., and Dietram A. Scheufele. 2000. Connecting news media use with gaps in knowledge and participation. *Political Communication* 17: 215–37.

Galston, William A. 2001. Political knowledge, political engagement, and civic education. *Annual Review of Political Science* 4: 217–34.

Hall, Michael, Larry McKeown, and Karen Roberts. 2001. *Caring Canadians, involved Canadians: Highlights from the 2000 National Survey of Giving, Volunteering and Participating*. Catalogue no. 71-542-XIE. Ottawa: Statistics Canada.

Joslyn, Richard. 1984. *Mass media and elections*. New York: Random House.

Key, Vladimir O. 1966. *The responsible electorate: Rationality in presidential voting 1936–1960*. Cambridge, MA: Belknap Press of Harvard University Press.

Levin, Ben. 2000. Democracy and schools: Educating for citizenship. *Education Canada* 40: 4–7.

Mansbridge, Jane. 1980. *Beyond adversary democracy*. New York: Basic Books.

Mendelsohn, Matthew. 1993. Television's frames in the 1988 Canadian election. *Canadian Journal of Political Science* 18: 149–71.

——, and Richard Nadeau. 1999. The rise and fall of candidates in Canadian election campaigns. *Harvard International Journal of Press/Politics* 4(2): 63–76.

Moore, David W. 1987. Political campaigns and the knowledge-gap hypothesis. *Public Opinion Quarterly* 51: 186–200.

Mutz, Diana C. 2002. The consequences of crosscutting networks for political participation. *American Journal of Political Science* 46: 838–55.

Myers, John. 2000. Ontario's new civics course: Where's it going? Paper presented at the conference Citizenship 2000: Assuming Responsibility for Our Future, McGill Institute for the Study of Canada, Montreal, 20–1 October. <www.misc-iecm.mcgill.ca/citizen/myers2.htm>. 8 February 2004.

Nadeau, Richard, and Thierry Giasson. 2003. Canada's democratic malaise: Are the media to blame? *Choices: Strengthening Canadian democracy*, vol. 9. Montreal: Institute for Research on Public Policy.

Neuman, W. Russell. 1986. *The paradox of mass politics: Knowledge and opinion in the American electorate*. Cambridge, MA: Harvard University Press.

Niemi, Richard G., Mary A. Hepburn, and Chris Chapman. 2000. Community service by high school students: A cure for civic ills? *Political Behavior* 22: 45–69.

——, and Jane Junn. 1998. *Civic education: What makes students learn*. New Haven, CT: Yale University Press.

——, and Julia Smith. 2001. Enrolments in high school government classes: Are we short-changing both citizenship and political science training? *PS: Political Science and Politics* 34(2): 281–7.

Osborne, Ken. 1988. Political education for participant citizenship: Implications for the schools. In *Political education in Canada*, ed. Jon H. Pammett and Jean-Luc Pepin, 227–34. Halifax: Institute for Research on Public Policy.

——. 2000. Public schooling and citizenship education in Canada. *Canadian Ethnic Studies* 32: 8–37.

Page, Benjamin I. 1996. *Who deliberates? Mass media in modern democracy*. Chicago: University of Chicago Press.

——, and Robert Y. Shapiro. 1992. *The rational public: Fifty years of trends in Americans' policy preferences*. Chicago: University of Chicago Press.

Plutzer, Eric. 2002. Becoming a habitual voter: Inertia, resources, and growth in young adulthood. *American Political Science Review* 96: 41–56.

Popkin, Samuel L. 1991. *The reasoning voter: Communication and persuasion in presidential campaigns*. Chicago: University of Chicago Press.

Sears, Alan, and Mark Perry. 2000. Paying attention to the contexts of citizenship education. *Education Canada* 40: 28–31.

Ulbig, Stacy G., and Carolyn L. Funk. 1999. Conflict avoidance and political participation. *Political Behavior* 21: 265–82.

Zaller, John. 1999. A theory of media politics: How the interests of politicians, journalists, and citizens shape the news. Unpublished typescript, UCLA. <www.uky.edu/AS/PoliSci/ Peffley/pdf/ZallerTheoryofMediaPolitics(10-99). pdf>. 9 February 2004.

KEY AND CHALLENGING WORDS

partisan, intractable, contextual(ize), disseminate, obfuscate

QUESTIONS

1. In the first section of the chapter, the authors refer to many US studies in their attempt to propose solutions to the problem of "re-engaging young Canadians." Are the findings relevant to Canada, in your view?

2. What is a possible reason that civics education courses work more effectively in Grade 12 than they do in the earlier grades (see paragraph 9)?

3. How is the dropout rate in Canada related to the number of politically engaged citizens? What kinds of skills,

according to Page (cited in paragraph 10), must be developed in order to produce knowledgeable citizens?

4. Summarize the ways that (a) political parties and (b) the media are often served through inaccurate or distorted reporting of the "facts."

5. a) In the section "Re-engaging Young Canadians," consider strategies the writers use to make the section clear and easy to read; for example, you could analyze the authors' style, their organization, their use of transitions

or rhetorical patterns; b) In the section "Creating a More Informed Citizenry," identify two paragraphs where the topic sentence is *not* the first sentence of the paragraph; c) Paraphrase the first sentence in "Narrowing the democratic divides."

6. The authors devote a lot of space to summarizing and evaluating the views of Zaller and other critics of "'fact-packed'" media (see "Narrowing the democratic divides"). Why? Do you think that they are basically supportive or dismissive of these views? What shows you this?

7. What do the authors believe is the single best way to bridge the disparity between citizens in terms of their political knowledge and interest? Do you agree with them?

8. Is this chapter just about the problem of low voter turnout? After reading it completely at least once, consider the nature of the concept referred to in the title, and in two to three sentences, provide a complete definition of "democratic citizenship."

POST-READING

1. *Collaborative activity:* Some students may have taken civics classes at school or performed community service for school credits. Based on your direct experience or indirect knowledge of them (perhaps through friends), assess their value. Do they in fact make participants more informed about or interested in politics and citizenship? Discuss or debate this issue.

2. Reflect on one of the following proposals to increase democratic citizenship referred to in the essay: (a) "fostering a democratic classroom climate" (paragraph 9); *OR* (b) encouraging the media to adopt a practice of "public journalism," (paragraph 25). Adopting the role of (1) a school consultant or (2) a media consultant, begin by justifying the need for the proposal; then outline at least four to five specific and realistic recommendations that would make the proposal viable.

3. What do you believe is the major cause of voter apathy? How can it be overcome? Give yourself five to 10 minutes to freewrite, using one of the questions as your starting point.

RELATED WEBSITE OF INTEREST

The following website includes the complete report, report highlights, and "Ten Ideas for Positive Change" based on several sections of the report for download.

Canadian Institute of Well Being. (2010). *Democratic engagement.* Retrieved from www.ciw.ca/en/TheCanadianIndexOfWellbeing/Domains OfWellbeing/DemocraticEngagement.aspx

Imagining a Canadian identity through sport: A historical interpretation of lacrosse and hockey

Michael A. Robidoux

(6,772 words)

Sport in Canada during the late nineteenth century was intended to promote physical excellence, emotional restraint, fair play, and discipline; yet these ideological principles were consistently undermined by the manner in which Canadians played the game of hockey. This article explores the genesis of violence in hockey by focusing on its vernacular origins and discusses the relevance of violence as an expression of Canadian national identity in terms of First Nations and French-Canadian expressions of sport.

Pre-reading

1. How important is hockey to the concept of a Canadian identity? Using a pre-writing technique, explore your beliefs and opinions on the connections between hockey and national identity.

---

*

1   In *Imagined communities*, Benedict Anderson convincingly reduces the concept of nationalism to an imagining—imagined "because members of even the smallest nation will never know most of their fellow-members, meet them, or even hear of them, yet in the minds of each lives the image of their communion" (1991:6). It is this notion of communion that motivates nations to define and articulate their amorphous existence. If Anderson is correct—which I believe to be the case—the task of defining a national identity is a creative process that requires constructing a shared history and mythology(ies) that best suit the identity *imagined* by those few responsible for responding to

this task. For a nation as young as Canada (confederated in 1867), this constructive process is somewhat recent and largely incomplete, which is disconcerting for Canadians who have twice witnessed the threat of national separation.[1] As a result, what it means to be Canadian is often scrutinized, lamented, and at times even celebrated (most recently through a Molson Canadian beer advertisement).[2] Yet through all of this there has been one expression of nationalism that has remained constant since Confederation, that being the game of ice hockey.[3]

2   Since World War II, Canadians have been internationally perceived more as peacekeepers and, perhaps, even as being unreasonably polite—both political constructions in themselves—which makes it difficult to comprehend why a game such as hockey, known for its ferocity, speed, and violence, would come to serve as Canada's primary national symbol. The mystery intensifies if we consider that the game of hockey was born out of a period of social reform in Canada, where popular pastimes that involved violence, gambling, and rowdiness were being replaced by more "civilized" leisure pursuits imported from Europe. For instance, cricket, as Richard Gruneau states, was

especially palatable to Canada's colonial merchants and aristocrats because it combined an excellent and enjoyable forum for learning discipline, civility, and the principles of fair play with a body of traditions and rules offering a ritual dramatization of the traditional power of the colonial metropolis and the class interests associated with it. [1983:104]

3   The question becomes, then, how did a game such as hockey not only take shape in Canada but become "frequently cited as evidence that a Canadian culture exists" (Laba 1992:333)? Furthermore, to what extent does the game of hockey embody a Canadian collective sensibility, or is this *imagining* of Canadian identity without justification even at a symbolic level? In order to respond to these questions, it is necessary to explore early vernacular forms of sport in this nation and consider how these sensibilities have maintained themselves in a contemporary sporting context.

The Process of Modernization

4   Sport historians and sociologists have documented extensively the development of physical activity from a traditional folk (vernacular) pastime to a modern organized event.[4] Much of this discourse, however, concerns itself with the impact of modernization on traditional physical activities without taking into account the influences of traditional sporting behaviour and its role in shaping (at least from a Canadian perspective) a national sport identity. Colin Howell is critical of these prejudicial tendencies and writes:

> Modernization theory views history as a linear continuum in which any given circumstance or idea can be labeled "pre-modern" or traditional, and thus, can safely be ignored as something that the seemingly neutral process of "modernization" has rendered anachronistic. [1995:184][5]

5   What needs to be understood is that the process of modernization is not, in fact, a linear progression but rather a series of contested stages that maintain certain aspects of the past, while housing them in an entirely different framework. Before further discussing the relationship between traditional and modern sport, a brief explanation of these terms is necessary.

6   In sport theory, loosely organized, periodic, and self-governed sporting contests fit under the rubric of *traditional* sport (Metcalfe 1987:11). This form of physical activity is devoid of field or participant specifications and "was closely interwoven with established conventions of ritual . . . as well as the daily and seasonal rhythms of domestic and agrarian production, entertainment and religious festivals" (Gruneau 1988:12–13). There is a tendency to refer to traditional sport as rural, tribal, and in the past tense; in truth, however, this manner of participation continues to exist in a variety of forms. An example would be road/ball/pond hockey in which people engage in variations of the game of hockey in unspecified locales, with unspecified participants in terms of age, number, gender, and skill; these spontaneous games are performed around daily routines, whether these routines be dictated by work, school, personal, or familial responsibilities. For this reason, I have substituted the term *traditional* with *vernacular*, as it connotes similar meanings but remains viable in a contemporary context and is, in fact, clearer.

7   The significance of the term *modern* sport is twofold in that it relates not only to the changes that have taken place in the way people engage in play, but *modern* also implies the political motivations that dictated these changes. To begin, modern sport is not a random pursuit but rather a highly organized event played within specific boundaries and performed with uniform rules maintained by leagues and organizations. In time, equipment becomes standardized, and play becomes recorded and measured. The result is greater uniformity over time and space, reducing the "localized forms of individual and community-based expressions of pleasure, entertainment, physical prowess, and ritual display" (Gruneau 1988:13). Importantly, the consequence of this reductive process was not simply the limiting of specific expressions of sport, but behaviour itself has been reduced to satisfy a limited and highly specific social order. Pierre Bourdieu explains that "it would be a mistake to forget that the modern definition of sport is an integral part of a 'moral ideal,' that is, an ethos which is that of the dominant fractions of the dominant class" (1993:344), notions that were

instilled and maintained by religious and education institutions (Wheeler 1978:192). It is through the standardization of sport that undesirable qualities of vernacular play could be eliminated—behaviours such as violence, public disorder, and mass rowdiness—thus controlling behaviour to ensure a compliant and nonvolatile populace. However, it must be stressed that while levels of control were successfully manufactured through sport, and play was indeed standardized, "undesirable" vernacular elements were not, in fact, entirely reduced but actually remain critical features of specific sports such as lacrosse and hockey.

8   The political motivations behind the modernization of sport cannot be separated from the actual changes that occurred in expressions of physical activity. In Canada, these motivations stemmed from a British Victorian sensibility. By the turn of the eighteenth century, sport in Britain was being realized as an excellent means of social control and conditioning (Jarvie and Maguire 1994:109). The successes that church and school officials had enjoyed by providing the ever-increasing urban working class with productive non-threatening activities, such as cricket and (a "refined" version of) football, were soon being implemented in the colonies as a means of "correcting" the rougher, more vulgar vernacular pastimes. Perhaps even more importantly, there was symbolic value in having newly colonized peoples engaging in these uniquely British activities; thus, regulated sport quickly became a vehicle for cultural imperialism. Metcalfe speaks to the imperialistic role of cricket by stating that it "illustrated the powerful forces of tradition and the way in which dominant social groups perpetuated their way of life in the face of massive social change" (1987:17).

9   In early nineteenth-century Canada, attempts were well underway to introduce imported European games such as cricket and curling to a nation only beginning to take shape. However, in its earliest stages, organized sport was something suitable only for "gentlemen" and not worthy of the working class or ethnic minorities. Howell points out that while "middle-class reformers advocated a more disciplined and rational approach to leisure, seeking to replace irrational and often turbulent popular or working-class recreations with more genteel and improving leisure activities," these "bourgeois sportsmen" primarily "concentrated their attention on the improvement of middle-class youth" (1995:14). It was not until later in the century that schools and churches began to take a more active role in introducing structured forms of physical activity to Canadians of various class and ethnic backgrounds. The intent of making sport and physical activity more socially democratic was threefold: to acquire levels of control over increased amounts of leisure time made possible by industrialization and a shorter workweek; to reduce class conflict by enabling male participants of various backgrounds to compete on an equal playing field; and to build a physically fit yet subordinate workforce, ensuring maximum levels of industrial production. In short, advocating for institutionalized sport served as an important means of reproducing a Victorian social order in Canada, where young men learned to be honourable and genteel gentlemen. As with any hegemonic process,[6] however, control was never absolute, and almost immediately emergent and residual cultures affected the desired outcome in unexpected ways.

Resisting an Imported Canadian Identity

10   The development of "controlled" sport took an important turn by the middle of the nineteenth century with a new emergent class—led by Montreal-born dentist, George Beers—responding to impositions of British nationalism in Canada. Beers's role in Canadian sport history was that of a romantic nationalist, as his politics were comparable to Herder's romantic nationalism of eighteenth-century Germany. Like Herder, Beers understood that to construct a national identity, two things needed to occur. First, foreign influence needed to be eliminated—Herder contended with French influence; Beers contended with English imperialism. And second, a national history/mythology needed to be consciously constructed. Instead of turning to indigenous poetry and language as Herder did, Beers turned to indigenous sport as a means of portraying the soul of a nation. What better place to look, he surmised, than Canada's First Peoples whose game of *baggataway*—filled with speed, violence, and skill—appeared to best embody

the harsh and gruelling existence of Canadian natives as well as the trials of early Canadian settlers in this new and untamed land.

11   The game *baggataway*, renamed lacrosse by French settlers,[7] was played by many First Nations (Native Canadians) across North America prior to European contact, and it proved to be a game that both fascinated and repulsed early settlers (Eisen 1994:2). Some English Europeans were least sympathetic to First Nations' leisurely activities largely because of puritanical sensibilities that tended to perceive all forms of play as wasteful and unproductive. It is not surprising that English observations of lacrosse disparaged the violence; yet negative comments were often countered with admiration for First Nations players who exuded remarkable sportsmanship and respect for their opponents. One late eighteenth-century account reads:

> The Chippewas play with so much vehemence that they frequently wound each other, and sometimes a bone is broken; but notwithstanding these accidents there never appears to be any spite or wanton exertions of strength to affect them, nor do any disputes ever happen between the parties. [Carver 1956:237]

12   More detailed accounts of lacrosse come from French missionaries and settlers, who, unlike the English, lived with First Nations peoples and made efforts to learn their language, customs, and social practices. One of the earliest accounts comes from Nicolas Perrot, who encountered the game while living as a *coureur de bois*[8] between 1665 and 1684:

> Il y a parmy eux un certain jeu de crosse qui a beaucoup de raport avec celuy de nostre longue paume. Leur coustume en joüant est de se mettre nation contre nation, et, s'il y en a une plus nombreuse que l'autre, ils en tirent des hommes pour rendre égale celle qui ne l'est pas. Vous les voyez tous armez d'une crosse, c'est à dire d'un baston qui a un gros bout au bas, lacé comme une raquette; la boule qui leur sert à joüer est de bois et à peu près de la figure d'un oeuf de dinde. [1973:43–44][9]

> [Among them there is a certain game of crosse that compares to our tennis. Their custom is to play nation (tribe) against nation (tribe), and if one side has more players than the other, more players are brought forth

to ensure a fair game. Each has a stick, called a crosse, that has a big curve at the end that is laced like a racket; the ball that they play with is made of wood and looks a little bit like a turkey's egg.]

13   He continues by describing the violent nature of the sport:

> Vous entendez le bruit qu'ils font en se frapant les uns contre les autres, dans le temps qu'ils veulent parer les coups pour envoyer cette boule du costé favorable. Quand quelqu'un la garde entre les pieds sans la vouloir lascher, c'est à luy d'eviter les coups que ses adversaires luy portent sans discontinuer sur les pieds; et s'il arrive dans cette conjuncture qu'il soit blessé, c'est pour son compte. Il s'en est veü, qui ont eü les jambs cassées, d'autres les bras, et quelques uns ont estez mesme tüez. Il est fort ordinaire d'en voir d'estropiez pour le reste de leurs jours, et qui ne l'ont esté qu'à ces sortes de jeu par un effect de leur opiniâtreté. [1973:45]

> [One can hear the noise they make when they hit one another, while they attempt to avoid receiving blows in order to throw the ball to a favourable location. If one secures the ball in his feet without letting it go, he must fend off blows from his opponents who continually strike his feet; and if in this situation he is injured, it is his own concern. Some are seen with broken legs or arms, or are even killed as a result. It is common to see players maimed permanently, yet this does not change the way they play the game on account of their obstinacy.]

14   For many young French males, the rough nature of the sport was appealing, and as a result, these men became enamoured with not only the game of lacrosse but with its participants as well.

15   The radical impositions of European colonization on North American indigenous peoples has been taken to task in recent academic and popular discourse; clearly, arguments that perceive this relationship to be unidirectional are often overstated. In *The skyscrapers hide the heavens*, Miller offers some balance to this historical analysis by revisiting early Euro-Indian relations and discussing them in terms of cultural change, both "non-directed" and "directed" (2000:95). In other words, Miller understands these relations as being far more equitable than is often portrayed. Not only did First Nations

peoples often *willingly* take advantage of such things as European technology to benefit their own situations, but Miller documents, as well, the gross reliance of European settlers on First Nations knowledge and technologies. In fact, he states that European survival in Canada would not have been possible without First Nations assistance and charity. Furthermore, and more importantly for our purposes, is the knowledge concerning the extensive cultural borrowings of European settlers (in this case French) from First Nations peoples.

16   For a certain sector of French Canadian males—later known as *les Canadiens*—the First Nations male provided an alternative model of masculinity to what they had known in France, one where physicality, stoicism, and bravado were valued and celebrated, not repressed, as was the typical Christian model of masculinity:

> The young voyageurs struggled to copy the Indians' stoicism in the face of adversity and their endurance when confronted with hardship, deprivation, and pain. They also copied, to the extent that their employers and governors could not prevent, the autonomy that Indian society inculcated in its young. French males found the liberated sexual attitudes of young Indian women before matrimony as attractive as the missionaries found them repugnant. [Miller 2000:54]

17   Early French settlers began emulating First Nations males and, in doing so, began sharing in their cultural practices. Occupational and survival-related pursuits such as canoeing, snowshoeing, and hunting were some of the obvious activities that were learned and performed. Native team sports such as lacrosse also proved to be of tremendous interest to *les Canadiens*, as these games gave both First Nations and French males the opportunity to prove their worth to one another as men. According to Joseph Oxendine, these white settlers did not fare very well, however, "because of the Indian's clear superiority of the game. Indians were frequently reported to have used fewer players in an effort to equalize the competition" (1988:48). First Nations proficiency at lacrosse was highly regarded by early sport enthusiasts, but these skills were also perceived by others to be violent and dangerous, a perception that began generating its own folklore among the early North American settlers.

18   Perhaps the most popularly known lacrosse event was a legendary contest between two First Nations tribes at Fort Michilimackinac in 1763—an ambush disguised as a sporting contest. According to Alexander Henry's account of the "contest," the tribes used lacrosse as a means of staging an attack on the British fort during the Pontiac Rebellion (Henry 1901). Francis Parkman supports this in his account, which states:

> Suddenly, from the midst of the multitude, the ball soared into the air and . . . fell near the pickets of the fort. This was no chance stroke. It was part of a preconcerted stratagem to insure the surprise and destruction of the garrison. . . . The shrill cries of the ballplayers were changed to the ferocious warwhoop. The warriors snatched from the squaws the hatchets, which the latter . . . had concealed beneath their blankets. Some of the Indians assailed the spectators without, while others rushed into the fort, and all was carnage and confusion. [1962:254]

19   It was the legendary status the sport commanded that made it the perfect vehicle for George Beers's nationalist agenda. The game ran counter to British bourgeois sensibilities that understood sport to be refined and gentlemanly, one that could ultimately serve as a breeding ground for proper British mores and values. Instead, lacrosse was a display of rugged, brutal, and aggressive behaviours that were said to embody what it meant to be a Canadian settler in this unforgiving northern territory. Thus, Beers called on Canadians to refrain from engaging in the imperial pursuit of cricket and take up lacrosse as the new national game, in effect ridding Canada of foreign influences and acquainting the new populations with the soul of the nation.

20   In order to make this fictious proposal possible, the native game needed to be claimed by the male settlers and then incorporated into a modern sporting climate. *Baggataway*, as First Nations peoples played it, was not merely a sport but a spiritual and religious occasion, often having healing or prophetic significance.[10] The game also had regional and tribal idiosyncrasies, which meant that there was no standard form of play, making Euro-Canadian adoption difficult. Thus, *baggataway* as a native vernacular entity needed to be transformed into lacrosse, which

meant claiming the game and eliminating traits that were linked to First Nations culture. To achieve this transformation, it was necessary to standardize the rules to create a sense of uniformity. An important step was made, in fact, by George Beers, who published the first rules of lacrosse under the name "Goal-keeper" in a series of advertisements in the *Montreal Gazette* in 1860 (Cosentino 1998:15). These rules were later adopted by the Montreal Lacrosse Club and became the "official" rules of lacrosse, later republished in the *Montreal Gazette* in July of 1867 (Morrow 1989:47). Efforts to standardize the game not only eliminated regional variation but also seemed to dictate how the game of lacrosse was to be played. All that was left, then, was to attract people to the game, and, again, in this Beers was instrumental.

21   Through various print forms (magazines and newspapers), Beers began to promote lacrosse as Canada's national game and in the process deride cricket as foreign and irrelevant to Canadians. In an article that appeared in the *Montreal Gazette* in August of 1867, suitably entitled, "The national game," Beers writes:

> As cricket, wherever played by Britons, is a link of loyalty to bind them to their home so may lacrosse be to Canadians. We may yet find it will do as much for our young Dominion as the Olympian games did for Greece or cricket for our Motherland. [1867]

22   Of course, Beers makes no apologies for appropriating an Aboriginal game and promoting it as the national pastime. Instead, he sees appropriation as an accurate depiction of European presence in Canada and argues, "just as we claim as Canadian the rivers and lakes and land once owned exclusively by Indians, so we now claim their field game as the national field game of our dominion" (1867). Beer's proselytizing was enormously effective, to the extent that a National Lacrosse Association was formed—the first national sporting body in Canada—and lacrosse was being touted by many as Canada's official national game.[11]

23   These developments, which documented how a vernacular sporting pastime was transformed into a modern sport, were not as complete as scholars have suggested. Sports historian Don Morrow claims: "At first heralded in adoption, then transformed in nature, the Indian origins of the game were finally

shunned by nineteenth-century white promoters and players" (1989:46). While ritual/sacred components and regional variations were erased from modern lacrosse competitions, there were native/vernacular elements of the game that remained, largely to the chagrin of elite sporting officials who were governing these developments. To begin, the popularization of lacrosse did not arise merely because of Beers's ideological ravings. It is incorrect to claim, as Morrow does, that the new national affinity of lacrosse was achieved through the word of George Beers. Crediting only one person simply does not allow for human agency, and while public consciousness can be influenced, it is not something that can be dictated. In other words, there needed to be some preexisting value in lacrosse that allowed it to be so willingly adopted by Canadian sport enthusiasts. It is here, then, that we can begin examining the cultural value of lacrosse (and later hockey) and its relationship to Canadian identity.

Sport Sensibilities in Conflict

24   One of the primary reasons lacrosse served as a viable alternative to imported British sports such as cricket was its emphasis on physical aggression, volatility, and danger. The game appealed to males who identified with a more physically aggressive notion of masculinity rather than the reserved and civil expressions of masculinity exemplified in cricket. In essence, the attraction to lacrosse was an extension of early French Canadians' infatuation with First Nations masculinity, where the emphasis was on physical superiority, bodily awareness, and perseverance. Lacrosse provided males the opportunity to display these heralded qualities and challenge themselves through formal competitions. However, in the attempt to modernize lacrosse and market it to a broader audience, the game needed to become less violent and needed to be played in a manner more suitable for "gentlemen"; otherwise the game would not enter dominant sport culture. Efforts were in place to sanitize the game, but they were not entirely successful. In fact, those who were most successful at the sport were First Nations and working-class players who played the game as it was originally

designed—aggressively and intensely. Attempts to turn the game into something else merely put those who engaged in it as "gentlemen" at a clear disadvantage to those who maintained its aggressive style of play. One team renowned for its aggressive play was the Montreal Shamrocks, who "were, without question, the most successful team prior to 1885. . . . The Shamrocks were out of place both socially and athletically. Social misfits on the middle-class playing fields, the Shamrocks were Irish, Roman Catholic, and working-class" (Metcalfe 1987:196).

25   What is critical here is that the ideological and political value of lacrosse as advocated by those in power paled in relation to the actual meanings early participants experienced through playing it. Colin Howell, also a sports historian, correctly observes that lacrosse was "a relatively minor sport" that "was suddenly elevated to prominence because of the symbolic role that was associated with it at the time of Confederation" (Howell 1995:103). However, those elite officials who helped elevate the status of lacrosse understood the sport symbolically, not according to its literal value as a meaningful expression of Canadian consciousness. I do not wish to imply that this is a singular phenomenon, but there is evidence that lacrosse did have value for certain Canadian males as an identifiable articulation of who they were as men. In essence, lacrosse did signify class, gender, and ethnic values, but these values were generally unacknowledged by elite sporting officials who were suddenly threatened by their own ideological manoeuvrings. The official recourse was to prohibit the "people" from playing the game and to attempt to make it instead the game of an exclusive minority:

> The logical conclusion for lacrossists was that the incidence of disputes, violence, and undesirable conduct on the field of play could mean only one thing—some players were not gentlemen. The truth of this observation was given substance by the presence of Indians, who always played for money and, by race alone, could not be gentlemen, and of the working-class Shamrock team. [Metcalfe 1987:195]

26   This prohibition of undesirable participants eventually led to the introduction of amateurism.

27   Amateur athletics in Canada did not merely function as a means of ensuring that athletes engage in sport in a gentlemanly manner[12] but served as a discriminatory system that prevented "undesirable" players from playing. Prior to 1909, the year when a national amateur athletic union was formed in Canada, national sporting bodies used the concept of amateurism to best suit their sport's needs. In the case of the National Lacrosse Association, league officials decided to make it an "amateur" association restricted to those players who fit under the definition of amateur. An amateur was conveniently defined by the Amateur Athletic Union of Canada as someone who had "never competed for a money prize, or staked bet with or against any professional for any prize" or one who had "never taught, pursued, or assisted in the practice of athletic exercises as a means of obtaining a livelihood" (Metcalfe 1987:105–106). The stipulations were highly restrictive and deliberate in design.

28   First, the new requirements made working-class participation virtually impossible in that wage earners were no longer able to receive financial compensation for taking time off from work to play. Keeping in mind that it was illegal to play sports on Sunday and that the workweek ran from Monday to Saturday, working-class participation in sport was restricted generally to Saturday afternoons. As a result, players were not only prevented from receiving payment for time lost at work, but those players who at one time received compensation for their services were no longer eligible to play. The second aspect of the restrictions was equally effective because it denied access to individuals who at one time gambled on sport. During this period in Canadian history, gambling and sport were virtually inextricable: gambling made up part of the fabric of vernacular sporting pastimes. For First Nations cultures in particular, gambling in sport (by spectators and participants) was deeply ingrained in their traditions and at times even played a role in their overall economies (Oxendine 1988:31). Therefore, by these first two stipulations alone, most ethnic minorities and working-class players were considered ineligible and could no longer play amateur athletics. The final stipulation reinforced economic divisiveness further by making it clear that sport was not the property of the people but, rather, of men who "had the leisure, economic resources and social approval to explore intensive athletic training in a financially disinterested manner" (Burstyn 1999:224).

29   The restrictive measures imposed by the National Lacrosse Association did not go unchallenged, however. Teams tried to circumvent the rules by covertly using "professional" players to become more competitive and in certain cases even paid players for their services. In response, the National Lacrosse Association was compelled to enforce disciplinary measures to contend with these dissident organizations. Teams caught cheating were brought before the Canadian Amateur Athletic Union to face arbitration and potential censuring.[13] As these arbitration cases grew in number, tremendous pressures were being placed on the National Lacrosse Association to retract its strictly amateur policy and permit both professionals and amateurs into the league. Despite this, the National Lacrosse Association remained steadfast in its position to prohibit professional players and was ultimately successful in maintaining itself as an amateur association; this success, however, proved to be its inevitable downfall.

30   By maintaining its exclusive membership, the National Lacrosse Association forced potential lacrosse players to pursue alternative sporting options. Other team-sport leagues (i.e., baseball, football, and hockey) were not as resistive to the influences of professionalism, and thus, they provided working-class and ethnic minority players alternatives to play in these sports and be financially compensated at the same time. While baseball and football did attract many of the players, these sports did not possess the symbolic and literal value found in lacrosse. Instead, it was hockey that early Canadian sport enthusiasts embraced by the turn of century, for the same reasons they were attracted to lacrosse 20 years earlier. Unlike baseball or football, hockey was seen as uniquely Canadian in origin and character. An amalgam of modern and vernacular sporting pastimes, hockey resembled lacrosse in design and in the manner it was played. Play was aggressive and often violent, providing men the opportunity to display this emergent notion of masculinity. At a symbolic level, it was played on a frozen landscape, perfectly embodying what life as a Canadian colonialist was supposed to be like. Thus, hockey provided all that lacrosse entailed but without the restrictions of amateurism. By the 1920s, hockey had succeeded in becoming Canada's national sport pastime.

Violence, Masculinity, and Canadian Identity

31   It is here, then, that we return to the politics of identity and the manner in which hockey, a game notoriously aggressive and violent, serves as a potential symbol for national expression. Along with other social scientists,[14] I have been critical of popular discourse that tends to mythologize hockey and locate it as a unifying force in this nation. Gruneau and Whitson astutely observe:

> The myth of hockey as a "natural" adaptation to ice, snow, and open space is a particularly graphic example of what Barthes is alerting us to—about how history can be confused with nature. . . . This discourse of nature creates a kind of cultural amnesia about the social *struggles* and vested interests—between men and women, social classes, regions, races, and ethnic groups—that have always been part of hockey's history. [1993:132]

32   While these sentiments are certainly valid, it would be incorrect to say that hockey is without cultural or historical relevance in Canada. In fact, it is my contention that hockey is more than a mythological construct; it is a legitimate expression of Canadian national history and identity. Hockey *does* speak to issues of gender, race, ethnicity, and region in this nation, albeit not in an entirely positive manner. For this reason, hockey moves beyond symbol and becomes more of a metaphoric representation of Canadian identity.

33   First, hockey was born out of post-Confederation Canada,[15] in a period of political uncertainty and unrest. Canada was a disparate nation, divided in terms of language, region, and ethnicity—lacking in identity and national unity. Thus, while hockey was used ideologically to express national sentiment, its value as a vernacular entity was equal to, if not greater than, its symbolic value. From the outset, hockey's violent and aggressive style separated itself from other bourgeois (European) pastimes, including the increasingly popular game of baseball that was entering Canada from the United States. Early games often appalled certain sport writers and sport officials who saw the violence on the ice and in the stands as unfit for gentlemen.

ODDS AND ENDS AT THE HOCKEY STRUGGLE

FIGURE 1   Odds and Ends at the Hockey Struggle

J.W. Fitsell provides two accounts of the first recorded game of hockey, which took place in 1875. The first, from *The Daily British Whig*, states that "Shins and heads were battered, benches smashed and the lady spectators fled in confusion" (Fitsell 1987:36). The other report from *The Montreal Witness* claimed that:

> Owing to some boys skating about during play an unfortunate disagreement arose: one little boy was struck across the head, and the man who did so was afterwards called to account, a regular fight taking place in which a bench was broken and other damages caused. [Fitsell 1987:36]

34   These accounts of violence are undoubtedly extreme, yet what is significant is that even in its earliest stages hockey was a sport perceived as excessively aggressive and violent within a modern European context.

35   It was largely because of this excessive violence that hockey became a sport Canadians could call their own, and they quickly began to showcase it in international contexts. By the mid-1890s, competitions were being staged between Canadian hockey teams and American ice-polo teams. The Canadian teams dominated these early competitions and revelled in the press they received. Newspapers did applaud their skill, but at the same time reports were critical of their rough play. *The Daily Mining Gazette* of Houghton, Michigan, described one game as "rush, slash and check continually. . . . Calumet were knocked off the puck by Portage Lakes 'any old way.' Many a man had to be carried to the dressing room" (Fitsell 1987:120). In a game in Sault Ste. Marie,

THEY CALL FOOTBALL BRUTAL SPORT!

FIGURE 2   AMERICAN CARTOONISTS TOOK TO THE SLASH AND CRASH OF CANADIAN PLAYERS IN PITTSBURGH.

Michigan, an incident occurred where "Stuart [an American player] was laid out by a board check from Jack Laviolette. He recovered and tangled with the same player, fans rushed on the ice and as Stuart bled from the facial cuts, police were called in" (Fitsell 1987:120). These accounts illustrate that within 20 years of organized existence, hockey was internationally known as being first, Canadian, and second, notoriously violent. Further evidence of this is found in two American cartoons depicting Canadians playing hockey in Pittsburgh in 1904.[16]

36   The distinction hockey received as being a rough sport also served as a means for Canadians to display their proficiency in the clearly demarcated context of a sporting event, making hockey a valuable vehicle for expressing national identity. But it was not simply proficiency on the ice, it was physical proficiency within the masculinist tradition that was earlier identified in relation to lacrosse. Hockey displayed men who were perceived to be stoic, courageous, and physically dominant: precisely the same images of masculinity valued in First Nations culture and later

by early Canadian settlers. These historically pertinent attitudes attracted Canadians to hockey, as the game provided Canadian males with an identifiable image outside of a British Victorian framework. Moreover, through hockey competitions, Canadians could exude superiority over Americans, illustrating for many a "victory for the industrious Canadian beaver over the mighty U.S. eagle" (Fitsell 1987:106). In essence, hockey became a vehicle of resistance against British and American hegemony, something that Canadians continue to call on in periods of political or national uncertainty.

37   The political implications went beyond resistance to British and American rivalries. One such occasion was the 1972 Summit Series in which Canadian professional hockey players engaged in an eight-game series against the Soviet Union national hockey team. The event was a debacle, yet it is considered by many to be the greatest Canadian story ever told. The series was described as East meets West—communism versus capitalism. So as the players rightfully admitted, it was no longer just about hockey. Reflecting on the series, Team Canada member Phil Esposito stated: "It wasn't a game anymore; it was society against society . . . it wasn't fun. It was not fun" (*September 1972* 1997). The series was filled with incidents of extreme violence: one Canadian player (Bobby Clarke), following instructions from a coach, broke a Soviet player's ankle with his stick. Other incidents involved a Soviet referee nearly being attacked by a Canadian player; throat-slitting gestures; kicking (with skates); fighting; and a *melee* with NHL Players Association executive director Alan Eagleson, the Soviet Guard, and the Canadian hockey team. The event, which was advertised as an expression of goodwill between nations, turned sour when the favoured Canadians were defeated in the initial games and obviously outclassed in terms of skill and sportsmanship. Canadian players were simply unaware of the tremendous abilities of the Soviets and were, hence, humiliated both on the ice by the Soviets and off the ice by an unforgiving Canadian public who lambasted them with jeers.

38   In response to their dire predicament, Canadian players resorted to bullying and intimidation tactics and literally fought their way back into contention. In a miraculous comeback, overcoming real and imagined barriers, the Canadian team proved victorious, winning the final game and the series. Their "heroism" became permanently etched into the memory of Canadians, despite actions that have recently been described by two American journalists as "hacking and clubbing the Soviet players like seal pups and bullying their way to a thrilling, remarkable comeback" (Klein and Reif 1998:31). While there have been critics of the series, the games in the Canadian collective consciousness remain as "an orgy of self-congratulation about the triumph of 'Canadian virtues'—individualism, flair, and most of all, character" (Gruneau and Whitson 1993:263). Historically speaking, these seemingly appalling behaviours are compatible with Canadian hockey in general and for this reason are embraced, not denounced. The players performed in a manner consistent with Canadian play, illustrating a Canadian character that has yet to be defined in more concrete fashion. Therefore, despite Canadian behaviour that was an assault on international hockey, and on international competition in general, this assault was distinctly Canadian, something that is invaluable for the construction of a national identity.

Conclusion

39   The connection I have made between hockey and Canadian nationalism is very real.

40   I do not make the claim that Canadians are predisposed to violence or that they condone violent behaviour. Rather, I argue that hockey enabled Canadians to display qualities that have been valued in patriarchal relations: stoicism, courage, perseverance, and proficiency. The singularity of the game and the manner in which it was played were critical for a young and disparate nation to have as its own as it faced encroaching social, political, and cultural interests from Europe and the United States. At a more pedestrian level, hockey was accessible to men of various ethnic and class backgrounds, and thus, to a greater degree than lacrosse, it became a game of the people. The fact that "people" here is specific only to males established hockey as a male preserve, making

it a popular site for males to define their worth as men, drawing on notions of masculinity that date back to seventeenth-century Canada. In this sense, understanding hockey beyond its mythological rhetoric acknowledges the "social *struggles* and vested interests—between men and women, social classes, regions, races, and ethnic groups" and confirms that hockey was, as Gruneau and Whitson state, "all of these" (1993:132).

41   Finally, by linking hockey to Canadian nationalism I am not situating either as being positive. In fact, the Canadian penchant to understand itself through hockey repeats masculinist formulas of identification that reflect poorly the lives of Canadians. The physically dominant, heterosexist, and capitalist associations of this specific identity are certainly exclusionary, but for that matter, all nationalist expressions cannot suitably speak for the polyphony of a nation. Despite the obvious fallibility of nationalistic representation, the legitimacy of nationalistic expression remains. Canada's history is located firmly in patriarchy, heterosexism, and capitalism; thus, the use of hockey to promote national pride and unity was not random then, nor is it today. Playing hockey is a means of constructing an image of a nation in the manner in which dominant forces within it wish to be seen. With this, hockey does not merely symbolize the need to define a national identity, it offers insight into the actual imaginings of what this identity entails. Hockey provides Canada a means by which to be distinguished. As Benedict Anderson astutely observes, such distinction ought not to be characterized by the dichotomy of "falsity/genuineness, but by the style in which it is 'imagined'" (1991:6).

Journal of American Folklore.
2002. 115 (45).

Notes

1. The province of Quebec has twice voted to separate from Canada (1980 and 1995). The most recent referendum saw only 51 per cent of Quebecers voting "no" to separation.
2. The television commercial gained national notoriety because of its pro-Canadian stance. It depicts an ordinary "Joe" pronouncing his Canadian identity in contrast to perceived stereotypes of Canadians.
3. From this point forward ice hockey will be referred to as hockey.
4. See Gruneau 1983, 1988; Gruneau and Whitson 1993; Dunning 1975; Hargreaves 1986; Burstyn 1999; Metcalfe 1987; Morrow et al. 1989; Guttmann 1994; and Guay 1981.
5. Richard Gruneau in "Modernization and hegemony" similarly recognizes the shortcomings of "overlooking, or misconstruing, the importance of social and cultural continuities in sport" (1988:19).
6. Guttmann expresses his dissatisfaction with the term *cultural imperialism* to describe sport diffusion. Instead, he prefers the term *cultural hegemony*, which better communicates the lively "contestation that has accompanied ludic diffusion" (1994:178).
7. It has been argued that the term *la crosse* was applied to the game because the sticks used by the participants resembled a bishop's crozier (Thwaites 1959:326). Maurice Jetté argues, however, that the name comes from "an old French game called 'la soule' which was played with a 'crosse' very similar to the Indian implement" that was also cross-like in shape (1975:14).
8. Literally means, "runner of the woods." More specifically, *coureurs de bois* were French male fur traders and trappers who lived as the indigenous population did during the

seventeenth century. J. R. Miller writes that these young males were "neither French peasants nor Indian braves, they were a bit of both" (2000:56).
9. All translations provided by Robidoux unless otherwise stated.
10. Jean de Brébeuf, a Jesuit priest, writes in 1636: "There is a poor sick man, fevered of body and almost dying, and a miserable Sorcerer [Shaman] will order for him, as a cooling remedy, a game of crosse. Or the sick man himself, sometimes, will have dreamed that he must die unless the whole country shall play crosse for his health" (Thwaites 1959:185).
11. Despite claims made in *The story of nineteenth-century Canadian sport* (1966) and the 1894 edition of the *Dictionnaire canadien-français* that lacrosse was the national game of Canada, there are no official records that substantiate this claim (Morrow 1989:52–53).
12. Varda Burstyn writes, "For many of the founding sport associations of the late-nineteenth century, 'amateur' athletics meant 'gentlemen' athletics" (1999:49).
13. The Amateur Athletic Association of Canada changed its name in 1898 to the Canadian Amateur Athletic Union in an attempt to strengthen its position as a national sport governing body (Metcalfe 1987:110).
14. See Robidoux (2001); Gruneau and Whitson (1993); and Laba (1992).
15. Canada became a confederation in 1867, and the first recorded game of hockey took place in 1875.
16. The figures and caption are taken from J.W. Fitsell's *Hockey's captains, colonels and kings* (1987:119). The cartoons depict games that took place in Pittsburgh in 1904. No information is provided to indicate where they were originally published.

References

Anderson, Benedict. 1991 [1983]. Imagined Communities: Reflections on the Origin and Spread of Nationalism. New York: Verso.

Beers, W.G. 1867. National Game. Montreal Gazette, August 8.

Bourdieu, Pierre. 1993. "How Can One Be a Sports Fan?" *In* The Cultural Studies Reader. Simon During, ed. Pp. 339–358. London: Routledge.

Burstyn, Varda. 1999. The Rites of Men: Manhood, Politics, and the Culture of Sport. Toronto: University of Toronto Press.

Carver, J. 1956 [1796]. Travels through the Interior Parts of North America. Minneapolis: Ross and Haines, Inc.

Cosentino, Frank. 1998. Afros, Aboriginals and Amateur Sport in Pre-World War One Canada. Ottawa: Canadian Historical Association.

Dunning, Eric. 1975. Industrialization and the Incipient Modernization of Football. Stadion 1(1):103–139.

Eisen, George. 1994. Early European Attitudes toward Native American Sports and Pastimes. *In* Ethnicity and Sport in North American History and Culture. George Eisen and David K. Wiggins, eds. Pp. 1–18. Westport, CT: Greenwood Press.

Fitsell, J. Williams. 1987. Hockey's Captains, Colonels, and Kings. Erin, Ontario: The Boston Mills Press.

Gruneau, Richard. 1983. Class, Sports, and Social Development. Amherst: University of Massachusetts Press.

———. 1988. Modernization or Hegemony: Two Views on Sport and Social Development. *In* Not Just a Game: Essays in Canadian Sport Sociology. Jean Harvey and Hart Cantelion, eds. Pp. 9–32. Ottawa: University of Ottawa Press.

———, and David Whitson. 1993. Hockey Night in Canada: Sport, Identities and Cultural Politics. Culture and Communication Series. Toronto: Garamond Press.

Guay, D. 1981. L'Histoire de l'Éducation Physique au Québec: Conceptions et Évènements (1830–1980). Chicoutimi: Gaetan Morin.

Guttman, Allen. 1994. Games and Empires: Modern Sports and Cultural Imperialism. New York: Columbia University Press.

Hargreaves, John. 1986. Sport, Power and Culture: A Social and Historical Analysis of Popular Sports in Britain. New York: St. Martin's Press.

Henry, Alexander. 1901 [1809]. Travels and Adventures in Canada and the Indian Territories between the Years 1760 and 1776. James Bain, ed. Toronto: G.N. Morang.

Howell, Colin D. 1995. Northern Sandlots: A Social History of Maritime Baseball. Toronto: University of Toronto Press.

Jarvie, Grant, and Joseph Maguire. 1994. Sport and Leisure in Social Thought. London: Routledge.

Jetté, Maurice. 1975. Primitive Indian Lacrosse: Skill or Slaughter? Anthropological Journal of Canada. 13(1):14–19.

Klein, Jeff Z., and Karl-Eric Reif. 1998. Our Tarnished Past. Saturday Night Magazine 113(10):30–33.

Laba, Martin. 1992. Myths and Markets: Hockey as Popular Culture in Canada. *In* Seeing Ourselves: Media Power and Policy in Canada. Helen Holmes and David Taras, eds. Pp. 333–444. Toronto: Harcourt Brace Jovanovich Canada.

Metcalfe, Alan. 1987. Canada Learns to Play: The Emergence of Organized Sport, 1807–1914. Toronto: McClelland and Stewart.

Miller, J.R. 2000 [1989]. Skyscrapers Hide the Heavens: A History of Indian-White Relations in Canada. 3rd edition. Toronto: University of Toronto Press.

Morrow, Don. 1989. Lacrosse as the National Game. *In* A Concise History of Sport in Canada. Don Morrow, Mary Keyes, Wayne Simpson, Frank Cosentino, R. Lappage, eds. Pp. 45–68. Toronto: Oxford University Press.

———, M. Keyes, W. Simpson, F. Cosentino, and R. Lappage, eds. 1989. A Concise History of Sport in Canada. 3rd edition. Toronto: Oxford University Press.

Oxendine, Joseph B. 1988. American Indian Sports Heritage. Champaign, IL: Human Kinetic Books.

Parkman, Francis. 1962. The Conspiracy of Pontiac. 10th edition. New York: Collier Books.

Perrot, Nicolas. 1973 [1864]. Mémoire sur les Moeurs, Coustumes, et Relligion des Sauvages de l'Amérique Septentrionale. Publié pour la première fois par J. Tailhan. Montréal: Éditions Élysée.

Robidoux, Michael A. 2001. Men at Play: A Working Understanding of Professional Hockey. Montreal: McGill-Queen's University Press.

September 1972. 1997. By Ian Davey. August Schellenberg, narrator. Robert MacAskill, dir. Ian Davey and Robert MacAskill, producers. CTV.

Thwaites, Reuben G., ed. 1959. The Jesuit Relations and Allied Documents: Travels and Explorations of the Jesuit Missionaries in New France, 1610–1791, vol. 10. New York: Pageant Book Company.

Wheeler, Robert F. 1978. Organized Sport and Organized Labour: The Workers' Sports Movement. Journal of Contemporary History 13:191–210.

KEY AND CHALLENGING WORDS

amorphous, disconcerting, connote, hegemonic, enamour, proselytize, resistive, amalgam, disparate, debacle, pedestrian (adj.), masculinist, dichotomy, polyphony

QUESTIONS

1. Identify Robidoux's thesis statement and comment on the form it takes. The author does not include a literature review early in the body of his essay, but he does refer to the work of sports historians in note 4. Why do you think he does not include a full literature review?

2. Briefly consider why it is beneficial for the author to define the following concepts before proceeding to the body, or main part, of his essay: a) nationalism (paragraph 1); b) modernization (paragraph 4).

3. What is the function of the first main section, "The process of modernization," in terms of the overall essay?

4. The author uses several primary sources in his essay. Referring to one example of a primary source, briefly explain its purpose and effectiveness. Note: You can consider any original source in this essay as a primary source even if Robidoux cites it from a secondary source.

5. Why is it important for Robidoux's purposes that he draws attention to the "often overstated" perception that European colonization imposed only negative effects on the indigenous population (paragraph 15)?

6. Does Robidoux consider the role of George Beers an important one in the rise of the popularity of lacrosse as a national game (paragraphs 10, 19–23)? Explain his reliance (or lack of reliance) on Beers in his essay.

7. Summarize Robidoux's point concerning the regulations imposed by the National Lacrosse Association and the way they worked to exclude participation in the sport by the working-class and First Nations peoples.

8. Identify the paragraph in which the author makes the transition from discussing lacrosse to discussing hockey. Why is this an important paragraph?

9. In the final two paragraphs preceding his conclusion, Robidoux uses a relatively familiar (1972) example of hockey operating within a political/nationalistic framework. What does this detailed example contribute to the author's thesis and to the effectiveness of the essay as a whole? What is the author's tone in this passage, and how is it conveyed?

10. What do the two cartoons (figures 1 and 2) contribute to the essay?

POST-READING

1. *Collaborative activity:* Do you think that Robidoux would subscribe to the common perception that sports builds character? Why or why not? *OR* Do you believe that participation in sports builds character? Discuss or debate one of these questions.

2. Write a critical analysis of the final two paragraphs. Support your analysis by specific references to the text. *OR* Write a critical response to the author's critique of the 1972 "Summit Series" (the final two paragraphs before the conclusion).

ADDITIONAL LIBRARY READING

Allain, K.A. (2011). Kid Crosby or golden boy: Sidney Crosby, Canadian national identity, and the policing of hockey masculinity. *International Review for the Sociology of Sport, 46,* 3–22. doi:10.1177/1012690210376294

GENDER AND SEXUALITY

Women in politics: Still searching for an equal voice

Ann Wicks and Raylene Lang-Dion

(2,364 words)

Pre-reading

1. Do you believe it is important in a successful democracy to have equal representation? How many women do you think hold federal seats in Canada today: a) approximately 50 per cent; b) 30–40 per cent; c) 20–30 per cent; d) under 20 per cent?

2. Access *Equal Voice*, an organization in which the authors hold or have held executive positions (www.equalvoice.ca/). Evaluate the website, determining its credibility. Does the purpose of the website affect its reliability? Explain.

In the United States, Hillary Clinton's presidential campaign is cause for hope and reflection on the status of women's leadership in world politics. The prospect of a woman occupying the oval office represents an exciting turning point in history that is in need of further attention, particularly as it affects current Canadian political discourse. This article looks at recent developments in some other countries and considers the prospects for more women in Canada's Parliament following the next election.

*

1   Women have rarely held positions of political leadership. In 2006, only 11 or 5.7 per cent of the world's 191 nations were led by women.[1] Similar patterns of inequity can be observed in the world's national parliaments. Only three nations come close to boasting gender balance; Rwanda ranks first in the world with 48.8 per cent female legislators, Sweden has 47.3 per cent women parliamentarians, and Finland ranks third with 42 per cent women elected.

2   While Hillary Clinton's campaign is exciting for many women, it also serves as a reminder of the challenges women encounter when seeking elected office. Despite the small gains women may have made in politics over the past two decades, political leadership remains defined on masculine terms. Political Scientists Linda Trimble and Jane Arscott note there is a "persistent observation that women leaders just do not fit," and women politicians are repeatedly evaluated by their "looks, clothing, relationships, and the tone of their voices—anything but their political skills and acumen."[2]

3   Hillary Clinton is no exception. Recently, a Fox news commentator proclaimed Hillary Clinton was losing the male vote because of her nagging tone of voice stating, "When Barack Obama speaks, men hear, 'Take off for the future'. And when Hillary Clinton speaks, men hear, 'Take out the garbage'." In Canada, a *Globe and Mail* article criticized Clinton's "dumpy pantsuit" advising the

presidential candidate that her "bee-hind looks like a tree-ruck in those boxy, double-breasted nightmare pantsuits."[3]

4   Female politicians in Canada are not exempt from similar treatment. While at a conference, a female cabinet minister from Ontario was introduced by a male cabinet colleague with the statement, "She's got better legs, what can I say?"[4] The *Ottawa Citizen* recently reported that a female Member of Parliament "looked stunning in a black gown with a plunging neckline,"[5] while failing to mention the attire or appearance of other politicians in attendance.

5   Media reports occasionally discuss the appearances of male politicians, yet the greater frequency of this type of coverage on female politicians has been well documented. Joanna Everitt, who studies media and gender in Canada, notes male leaders have "fewer sex-typed images applied to them."[6] Given politics is still a male dominated field, it is not surprising that newsrooms covering politics are, generally, male dominated as well. Everitt says political reporting, generally, "employs a masculine narrative that reinforces conceptions of politics as a male preserve and treats male as normative . . . reinforcing the image that politics is something that men do."

6   The sentiment that politics is something "men do" still exists. A study conducted by Jennifer Lawless and Richard Fox uncovered a significant gender gap in how women perceive themselves as potential candidates for office. Even when men and women possessed similar qualifications, women were more than twice as likely as men to believe they were not qualified to run for office.[7] Christy Clark, British Columbia's former Deputy Premier, observed this gender gap first hand. Ms. Clark, who was responsible for candidate recruitment, said, "Ask a woman to run for office and she'll say, 'Why are you asking me?' Ask a man, and he'll say, 'I can't believe it took you so long to ask.'"[8]

7   Lawless and Fox suggest political actors are less likely to see women as political leaders.[9] Women occupying the same professional spheres as men were only half as likely as men to receive encouragement to run for office from political parties. The gender gap was also evident in the different levels of information men and women possessed on how to launch a campaign and raise money.

8   Kim Campbell, Canada's first and only female Prime Minister, suggests perceptions of leadership can change when women occupy high profile leadership positions: "In other words, if women are never in certain roles, then we think it's almost unnatural for them to be in those roles. That's why in most cultures leadership is gendered masculine. And the only way to change that is when people, particularly enlightened male leaders, use their positions to put women in these portfolios and give them these opportunities. . . ."[10]

9   Societal definitions of leadership are only one piece of the gender gap puzzle. Studies have shown other factors influence women's political opportunities, including electoral systems, parliamentary systems, political culture, political party nomination processes, societal divisions of domestic labour, and the influence of women's movements.[11]

TABLE 1   THE CANADA CHALLENGE: TRACKING FEDERAL NOMINATIONS

Party	Candidates Nominated 2008	Men Nominated 2008	Women Nominated 2008	Women Nominated 2006 Election	Women MPs Elected 2006
NDP	163/308 (52%)	101 (61.9%)	62 (38%)	35%	41%
Liberal	203/308* (65.9%)	129 (63.5%)	74 (36.4%)	25.6%	21%
Bloc Québécois	40/75 (53.3%)	30 (75%)	10 (25%)	30.6%	11%
Conservative	238/308 (77.2%)	199 (83.6%)	39 (16.3%)	12.3%	11%

*Data collected by Equal Voice Researchers, updated January 25, 2008

10   What can be done? What are other countries doing to elect more women? Why are 47.3 per cent of national legislators in Sweden female and compared with only 21.7 per cent in Canada? How did the numbers of women elected to Iceland's national parliament increase from 25 per cent to 35 per cent in one election?

Sweden: A World Leader in Electing Women

11   Sweden has enjoyed gender balanced parliaments for over a decade. Gains in women's representation began in the 1970 s and by 1985, women made up 31 per cent of the Swedish Riksdag.[12] Political opportunities for women in Sweden are shaped by its electoral system, a conciliatory political culture, the activity of women within political parties, and societal divisions of domestic labour.

12   Sweden uses a list system of proportional representation (PR) to elect members of the Riksdag. Political parties nominate 9 candidates per district and seats are allocated based on the party's proportion of the vote.[13] With a list PR system, positioning on the party list is important. Political will and commitments from the party leaders are still needed to ensure women candidates are placed in "winnable" positions on party lists.

13   Political scientist Lisa Young concludes this structure provides more opportunities for women candidates because it "affects the behaviour of the political parties in terms of who they choose to represent them in the electoral process."[14] With 9 seats open for every district, candidate turnover, and a centralized party nomination process, political parties in Sweden literally have more opportunities to nominate female candidates. The First Past the Post System used in Canada and the United States, however, elects one representative per district. In the United States, where 90 per cent of incumbents get re-elected, there are fewer chances to modernize the demographic composition of Congress. This is one of many reasons cited for the lack of gender and racial diversity in Congress. Financial barriers for candidates in the United States are also much higher than most democracies. With only 16 per cent of women elected to Congress

and the Senate, the United States is near the bottom of the pack, ranking 65th in the world on women's representation. Typically, countries using some form of a list system of proportional representation elect the most female representatives. Olivia Chow, NDP Member of Parliament for Trinity–Spadina recently noted, "Remember that in the democratic world, there are three or four countries that do it the way we do. The rest of them have had proportional representation for years. . . . And on top of it they have economic vibrancy, more women elected and greater representation of different voices."[15]

14   Sweden's political culture and family friendly working conditions may be another factor facilitating the recruitment and retention of female politicians. Sweden is often referred to as a "consensual democracy," with a parliamentary system structured to support the resolution of conflict. This is reflected in its seating plan, where members of the Riksdag, sit in a semi-circle facing the speaker's chair. Whereas the Westminster model of parliament pits the governing party against the opposition, two and half sword lengths apart, members of the Riksdag have a regional seating plan. Members from the same region are seated together, regardless of political party affiliation. This may be one reason for the Riksdag's conciliatory political culture where debates are both passionate and respectful. Ingrid Iremark Sweden's Ambassador to Canada, notes, "There is no heckling in the Riksdag."

15   The Riksdag's parliamentary schedule is also structured to provide balance between work, family, and political activity. The parliamentary calendar is prepared one year in advance with sittings scheduled Tuesdays, Wednesdays, and Thursdays, commencing in October and ending in June. Norway's national parliament adopted a similar schedule in the early 1990s. Kirsti Kolle Grondahl, who served as Norway's first female president of parliament, was instrumental in bringing about family friendly changes to the parliamentary calendar and the addition of on-site child care facilities. With 37.9 per cent women elected, Norway ranks 6th in the world on women's political representation.

16   Women in Ontario's provincial legislature are looking for similar changes. "The truth, regardless of political party—is the legislature does not recognize a basic reality: women bear children," said Progressive

Conservative MPP Lisa MacLeod: "Women are often primary care-givers and if we want more women in the legislature we need to respect and address our unique challenges . . . We have the opportunity to address some very real and systemic barriers facing parents at Queen's Park through changes to sitting hours and providing daycare options for a more family friendly Queen's Park."[16]

Sweden: Women's Participation in Political Parties

17   In the 1970s, Sweden's political parties voluntarily began facilitating women's participation in party politics. Women's movements within party structures successfully advocated for the aggressive recruitment and training of female candidates. In 1979, women from all political parties joined forces and worked together to pressure political parties to nominate more women candidates.

18   Multi-party cooperation continued into the 1980s, when a high profile report was released recommending political parties nominate 50 per cent female candidates. The report served to increase awareness on the under- representation of women in politics and rallied public support for change. Political parties responded and generally "adhere to the 60/40 principle: neither sex is to have more than 60 per cent nor less than 40 per cent of representation within party ranks." The target is not mandatory, legislated or even formally imposed on political parties. Rather, political parties have voluntarily taken action because the public expects it; running women candidates is now seen as a necessary ingredient for electoral success.

19   Swedish political scientist Orude Oahlerup says, "In Sweden, it would be unthinkable to form a government or appoint government committees with fewer than 40 per cent women. It is no longer democratically legitimate to have political assemblies with an overwhelming male majority."[17]

20   Ingrid Iremark, Sweden's Ambassador to Canada notes, "In Sweden, the presence of women in politics is very normal. Political parties would have a tough time getting elected if they did not run equal numbers of female and male candidates."

Iceland: Multi-party Awareness Campaign

21   Iceland's parliament, the Althingi, launched a unique multi-partisan awareness campaign in 1997. Members of the Althingi worked together across party lines to pass a motion instructing the government to form a parliamentary committee responsible for increasing the representation of women. The committee included male and female representatives from each political party, the Ministry responsible for Gender Equality and women's organizations. The product of the committee was a well-funded, five year awareness campaign which included a humorous, attention-getting advertising program, training courses, education, communications networks, public meetings, and mentoring programs. The campaign successfully rallied public support and increased public awareness about the need for gender balanced government. Women's political representation increased from 25 per cent to 35 per cent after the campaign had been in operation for one year.

Equal Voice: Delivering Results in Canada

22   The under-representation of women in Canadian politics has been documented time and time again. There have been two Royal Commissions devoted to the topic (the 1970 Royal Commission on the Status of Women and the 1992 Royal Commission on Electoral Reform and Party Financing) and enough publications to fill the lobby on Parliament Hill.

23   Equality in decision-making is essential to the empowerment of women. Canada agreed when we signed on to the United Nations 1995 Beijing Action Plan for Women, committing to "take measures to ensure women's equal access to and full participation in power structures, decision-making and leadership." The United Nations notes a critical mass of at least 30 to 35 per cent women is needed before legislatures produce public policy reflecting women's priorities and before changes in "management style, group dynamic and organization culture" take place.[18]

24 Equal Voice is taking action. On International Women's Day, March 8, 2007, Equal Voice launched the multi-partisan Canada Challenge, asking the four party leaders—Stephen Harper, Stéphane Dion, Jack Layton, and Gilles Duceppe—to nominate more women candidates in the next federal election. On April 17, 2007 the political parties accepted the *Canada Challenge* by making statements in the House of Commons. This is the first federal multi-partisan commitment to electing more women in Canadian history. It follows on the success of Equal Voice's *Ontario Challenge* campaign, where in 2007, the number of women elected to Queen's Park reached a historic milestone of 27 per cent.

25 Equal Voice is pleased to report that the *Canada Challenge* is yielding results. Newly released data tracking federal party nominations shows the numbers of women nominated reaching historic levels (see Table 1). Since 2004, Equal Voice has monitored federal election results, via Equal Voice Researcher Vicky Smallman, providing data for Canadians, political parties, and the press. Equal Voice data shows that when women run, they win. Political parties need to be pro-active recruiting and training women candidates. To level the playing field, parliaments around the world are implementing well-funded national action plans, providing family friendly working environments, launching electoral and financial campaign reforms, constitutional reforms, education, and mentoring.

26 All political parties need to make the decision on how to increase women's representation, and all parties have to identify processes that work for them.

27 It is all of us—men and women—who must take responsibility for achieving this goal. The efforts of those who came before us cannot be in vain. Women must have an equal voice if Canada is to have a flourishing and prosperous democracy.

Canadian Parliamentary Review.
2008. Spring 31 (1).

Notes

1. Inter-Parliamentary Union, "Women in Politics: 60 Years in Retrospect", 2006, p. 16.
2. Jane Arscott and Linda Trimble. *Still Counting,* Broadview: 2003. p. 98.
3. Leanne Delap. "Women Only", *Globe and Mail,* March 3, 2007.
4 Chinta Puxley. "Finance minister under fire for 'sexist' comments." *The Canadian Press,* November 21, 2007.
5. William Lin and Tony Atherton. "Press Gallery undeterred by PM's snub; Five Tory MPs attend annual dinner," *Ottawa Citizen,* October 28, 2007, p. A3.
6. Joanna Everitt. "Uncovering the Coverage: Gender Biases in Canadian Political Reporting", Presentation to the Canadian Federation for the Humanities and Social Sciences, November 17, 2005. p. 3.
7. Jennifer Lawless and Richard L. Fox. *It Takes a Candidate,* Cambridge: 2005, p. 98.
8. Christy Clark. "I've changed my mind—we need quotas to get women into politics", *Vancouver Province,* March II, 2007.
9. Jennifer Lawless and Richard L. Fox. p 85 and 46.
10. Jennifer Ditchburn. "Women in power not a priority for Tories: ex PM Campbell," *The Canadian Press,* January 10, 2008.
11. Jill Vickers. *Reinventing Political Science,* Fernwood, 1997, p. 130.
12. Joyce Web, *Feminism and Politics: A Comparative Perspective,* University of California Press: 1989, p. 155.
13. Equal Voice interview with Ingrid Iremark Sweden's Ambassador to Canada, December 4, 2007.
14. Vickers, p. 139.
15. Vit Wagner. "Electoral Reform: Chow envisions greater voice for women," *Toronto Star,* September 09, 2007.
16. News Release, "Equal Voice Calls for the Speaker to Implement Family Friendly Reforms at Queen's Park." November 21, 2007. Available at: www.equalvoice.ca/uploads/363374450a75ea2d.pdf
17. Karin Alfredsson. *Equal Opportunities: Sweden Paves the Way,* Swedish Institute: 2005, p.19.
18. United Nations, "Women and Decision Making," 2000. Available at: www.un.org/womenwatch/daw/public/w20ct97/Partlen.htrn

KEY AND CHALLENGING WORDS

inequity, acumen, normative, conciliatory, vibrancy

QUESTIONS

1. What use do the authors make of direct quotations from the popular media in paragraphs 3–4? In the authors' view, why do the media represent women politicians in a sexist and stereotypical fashion?

2. Summarize Lawless and Fox's findings about the "gender gap" in politics today.

3. Do the authors believe that the social perception of female leaders is the major contributor to the "gender gap"? Discuss, referring to the essay as a whole.

4. What inference(s) can be made about the four main national political parties in Canada from the percentages of women that each party nominated in the 2006 and 2008 elections (see Table 1)?

5. The use of precedent, a kind of example (see p. 120), is effective if the example can be realistically applied to the topic being argued (i.e., increasing the percentage of women politicians in Canada). Do you believe the precedents of Sweden and Iceland can be applied to Canada? Why or why not?

6. What electoral system is used in Canada and the United States? What system is the most common among democratic nations?

7. Using a reliable source, such as an encyclopedia, dictionary, or government website, in one paragraph explain "proportional representation," citing your source. Why might this system facilitate the election of more women politicians?

8. Analyze the final section, "Equal Voice: Delivering Results in Canada," considering the use and effectiveness of specific argumentative strategies.

POST-READING

1. Investigate the role of advocacy groups in affecting Canadian political life: a) Analyze the role of *Equal Voice* (www.equalvoice.ca/) in improving women's representation in Canadian politics; *OR* b) Analyze the role of *Fair Vote Canada* (www.fairvote.ca/) in changing the current electoral system. You can also analyze the role of another advocacy group that seeks to change an aspect of Canadian politics.

2. *Collaborative activity:* a) Is the issue of women in government primarily a "women's" issue or does it transcend gender discourse? Discuss or debate the importance of this issue; *OR* b) What do you consider the main contributor to the "gender gap" in politics and what do you see as the best way to overcome this gap? Discuss or debate these questions.

3. a) Write an informational or analytical report on Agnes MacPhail, the first Canadian woman member of parliament, summarizing/analyzing her achievements and contribution to Canadian political and social issues; *OR* b) Write an informational or analytical report on the "women's suffrage" movement in Canada, summarizing/analyzing its major developments throughout Canadian history.

4. Provide an update on the number of women currently in Canadian parliament. Do you believe that the concerns expressed in "Women in Politics" are as pressing today as when this article was published? Explain your reasoning.

RELATED WEBSITE OF INTEREST

CBC map showing women in federal and provincial politics:

www.cbc.ca/news/interactives/map-cda-womenpolitics/

Listening to the voices of *hijab*

Tabassum F. Ruby

(9,405 words)

Pre-reading

1. What are your perceptions of the *hijab*? Where do these perceptions come from (e.g., sociology/women's studies classes, newspaper articles)? How much do you know about the origins of the *hijab*? What about the practices, values, and beliefs of its wearers?

Synopsis: This article illustrates the ways in which immigrant Muslim women in Canada perceive the *hijab* and associate it with diverse meanings. The article reveals a gap between dominant understandings of the *hijab* as a symbol of Muslim women's oppression, and the self-expressed sense of women participating in the study that the wearing of the *hijab* is a positive experience in their lives. Through focus groups, the participants stated that the *hijab* confirms their Muslim identities, provides them a chance to take control of their lives, and offers them the status of "respectable person." The meaning of the *hijab*, nonetheless in this study, is not limited to attire and most participants described modesty as being an important dimension of the *hijab*. The concept and deeper meanings of the *hijab* as expressed by the participants of the study, however, are not woven into larger Canadian society, and this article argues that the *hijab* in the form of Muslim woman's clothing emerges as a device to negotiate spaces within the Muslim community, as well as in the dominant western culture.

*

The question is not simply what do clothes mean or not mean. Rather, how do we use them to negotiate border—spaces we need to conceptualize as tenuous, fragile, barbed, or elastic, rather than as fixed and dichotomous? (Freitas et al., 1997: 334).

1   With the increasing number of *muhajibh*[1] around the globe, the issue of the *hijab* has become a topic of debate among Muslim and non-Muslim scholars. Researchers such as Nasser (1999) have pointed out that the "new *hijab* phenomenon" initially began two decades ago in countries such as Egypt, and the practice has since been embraced by Muslim women around the globe. In Canada, the *hijab* is often seen as a symbol of Muslim women's oppression and a restriction to their mobility, particularly in the media.[2] Many Muslim women, however, claim that the *hijab* empowers them in numerous ways: making their identities[3] distinct; taking control of their bodies; and giving them a sense of belonging to a wider Muslim world. Thus, the discussion on the *hijab* is contentious, revealing the complexity of the issue.

2   The intricacy of the issue of *hijab*, nonetheless, is not limited to whether the *hijab* oppresses a Muslim woman or liberates her. Most often the Muslim community and the dominant culture recognize the *hijab* as clothing that is used to cover the female body, i.e., a headscarf and/or long coat. This research, however, indicates that immigrant Muslim women[4] perceive the *hijab* in a variety of ways and associate it with diverse meanings that range from covering of the head to modest behaviour. As a result, the participants often negotiate their places in the larger community as well as in the Muslim community,

because they feel pressure whether wearing or not wearing the *hijab*.

Methodology and sampling

3   There is a small population of immigrant Muslim women in Saskatoon (the geographical location of my research), and most of them know each other. I have personal contact with many of these Muslim women, and through the use of the "snowball technique," I was able to identify participants. The "snowball" or "chain" method occurs when "sampling identifies cases of interest from people who know other people with relevant cases" (Bradshaw & Straford, 2000: 44). In recruiting the sample, the Islamic Association of Saskatchewan played a particularly important role. Along with Friday prayers, weekly gatherings in the mosque facilitated meetings with diverse groups of women and provided opportunities to talk with them about my research project.[5]

4   The focus group, a qualitative research tool that has been widely utilized in the social sciences, could be defined as an interactional interview involving at least 3, but ideally no more than ten, participants.[6] Utilizing this technique, researchers who act as moderators strive to learn through discussion about psychological and sociocultural characteristics and process among various groups (Berg, 1998, citing Basch, 1987 and Lengua et al., 1992). Using focus groups, I interviewed 14 women who came from 12 different countries. I conducted three interview sessions and divided my participants into two groups of five based on whether or not they wore a headscarf. I conducted one interview session with participants who did not wear a headscarf and one with those who did. Each interview session was 1.5 h long. My third group consisted of a mix of participants, some of whom wore the headscarf and some who did not. The session with the mixed group, which had four participants, lasted 1 h and 50 min. With the participants' permission, the interviews were audiotaped.

5   The focus group was a particularly useful method for conducting this research. This technique brought together many cultural groups among immigrant Muslim women and enabled exploration of the range amongst them of cultural differences and similarities in reference to the *hijab*. Berg (1998) states that the focus group is an effective method of observing group dynamics. Rich data were collected by recording conversations that were not necessarily directed at the researcher, but took place between participants who often talked among themselves. Thus, group energy and interaction nurtured considerable stimulation, and provided an opportunity to explore diverse meanings of the *hijab*.

6   In addition to taking cultural diversity into account, language was also a big consideration in selecting the participants. Even though immigrant Muslim women speak various languages, I conducted the focus groups in English so that the group (including myself) had a common language. Conducting the interviews in English, however, also meant limiting the research to participants who spoke and understood the language. It may also have affected the data: ideas about the practice of the *hijab* expressed by the women through metaphors in their mother tongue could have different meanings when articulated in English.

7   In order to protect the anonymity of my participants, personal details such as place of birth, age, and occupation cannot be fully described here, but general characteristics are as follows. The participants' countries of origin include Afghanistan, Bangladesh, Brunei, Burma, Egypt, Guyana, India, Iran, Jordan, Kuwait, Pakistan, and Turkey. The women's ages range from just under 20 to 60. The participants' occupations vary from physician to accountant, writer to insurance officer, and students. Their immigrant experiences range from arrival in Canada within the last few years to immigration more than two decades ago. Some informants have lived in other cities such as Toronto and Edmonton; others have resided in Saskatoon since they emigrated. Six participants did not wear the *hijab*, and eight were *muhajibh*. As the overall number of participants is quite small, the results of this study may best serve as a "case study."

Etymology of the *hijab*

8   The term *hijab* has various meanings in the dictionary[7] and in the Qur'an. According to Lane (1984),

the meanings of the word *hijab* are: a thing that prevents, hinders, debars, or precludes; a thing that veils, conceals, hides, covers, or protects, because it prevents seeing, or beholding. The *hijab* also means a partition, a bar, a barrier, or an obstacle. In the Qur'an, the word *hijab* appears seven times, in five instances as *hijab* (noun) and twice as *hijaban* (noun). Neither *hijab* nor *hijaban* is used in the Qur'an in reference to what Muslims (and non-Muslims) today call the *hijab*, that is, a Muslim women's dress code. In most cases, the Qur'an uses the word *hijab* in a metaphysical sense, meaning illusion or referring to the illusory aspect of creation (Ibrahim, 1999). For instance, the Qur'an states ". . .Until (the sun) was hidden in the *hijab* (of Night)" (38:32).[8] In this context, the word *hijab* is used symbolically: the sun is concealed due to the darkness.

9   The *hijab*, in the Qur'an, is a concept that has double meanings: not only something that protects, but also something that can hinder. For example, the Qur'an states, "They say: Our hearts are under veils, (concealed) from that to which thou dost invite us, and in our ears is a deafness, and between us and thee is a *hijab*" (41:5). In this verse, the *hijab*, which is not a physical object, is an obstacle or a hindrance, keeping non-believers from understanding the message of God. In another verse, the Qur'an states, "Between them shall be a veil, and on the heights will be men who would know every one by his marks: they will call out to the Companions of the Garden, "peace on you": they will not have entered, but they will have an assurance (thereof)" (7:46). In this verse, the *hijab* is used to indicate separation between different groups of people who would be waiting to enter heaven. These Qur'anic examples show that the *hijab* has positive as well as negative connotations, depending on the situation in which the term is used; however, as mentioned earlier, it is not used in the Qur'an to denote or refer to a Muslim women's dress code.

10   Verse 33:53 is known as the *a'yah* (verse) of the *hijab*, in which God says, "And when ye ask [the Prophet's wives] for anything ye want, ask them from before a *hijab*: that makes for greater purity for your hearts and for theirs." Many scholars see this as a rule not only for the Prophet's wives, but also for ordinary women, the former being role models for

the latter. Some scholars, however, disagree with this approach. The Qur'an clearly sates that the Prophet's wives are not ordinary women, and that God has commanded them to abide by certain rules which do not apply to other Muslim women, such as not marrying after the death of the Prophet, and getting double reward for good deeds and double punishment for bad deeds. Since this verse clearly addresses only the Prophet's wives, I argue that this restriction of *hijab* is just for them, and not for other Muslim women.

Does the veil equal the *hijab*?

11   One complexity regarding the subject of *hijab* is that the term veil is often used synonymously, or interchangeably, with the word *hijab*. However, El Guindi (1999) points out that in Arabic, which is the language of the Qur'an—the spoken and written language of 250 million people and the religious language of more than 1 billion people around the globe—the word *hijab* has no single equivalent such as "veiling." Therefore, the distinction between the words veil and *hijab* is important, as the latter has Islamic association that differentiates it from the former term.

12   In addition, researchers such as Fernea and Fernea (1979) and Roald (2001) have indicated that regional and global terms differ in classifying the diverse articles of women's clothing, and the word *hijab* varies from culture to culture. El Guindi (1999) states that *The Encyclopedia of Islam* identifies over 100 terms as pieces of clothing, many of which, such as *burqu'*, *'abayah*, *jilbab*, *jellabah*, *niqab*, and *izar*, are used for the covering of a female body. Thus, while a Saudi woman may wear a *niqab* and call it *hijab*, a Canadian Muslim woman could use a headscarf and also identify it as a *hijab*. The concept of the *hijab*, hence, emerges in multiple ways. The veil, which is often interpreted in Western[9] traditions as a covering of the head, does not illuminate the complexity of the practice in the Muslim context. For this reason, I have used the word *hijab*, but for the sake of better flow, I have not changed the word veil when the writers cited, or the study's participants, used this word.

The *hijab* in the Muslim context

13   Before illustrating the participants' views about the *hijab*, I would like to outline some of the basic concepts of the *hijab* in the Muslim context, because many participants referred to them. The Qur'anic verses that are traditionally cited to describe women's dress code are as follows:

1. And say to the believing women that they should lower their gaze and guard their modesty; that they should not display their beauty and ornaments except what (must ordinarily) appear thereof; that they should draw their veils over their bosoms and not display their beauty. . . And that they should not strike their feet in order to draw attention to their hidden ornaments. (24: 31)

2. O Prophet! Tell thy wives and daughters, and the believing women, that they should cast their outer garments over their persons (when abroad): this is most convenient, that they should be known (as such) and not molested. And God is oft forgiving, most merciful. (33: 59)

14   In the first verse, the Qur'an uses the word *khomoore henna* (from *khimar*), which means veiled, covered, or cancelled. Asad (1980, 1900–1992) states that *khimar* was worn more or less as an ornament in pre-Islamic times and was let down loosely over the wearer's back. In accordance with the fashion prevalent at the time, the upper part of a woman's tunic had a wide opening in the front, and her breasts were left bare. Thus, the *khimar* as an ornament was very familiar to the contemporaries of the prophet, and Asad writes that the Qur'an uses the word *khimar* to make it clear that a woman's breasts are not included in the concept of "what (must ordinarily) appear" of her body and should not therefore be displayed.[10] In the second verse, the Qur'an uses the word *jalabib* (from *jilbab*), which means an outer garment, a long gown covering the whole body, or a cloak covering the neck and bosom. *Khimar* and *jilbab*, then, are the basic words which often lead scholars to conclude that the Qur'an requires that Muslim women should

wear specific types of clothing, which nowadays is called the *hijab*.

15   Other scholars, however, have interpreted the words *khimar* and *jlbab* in numerous ways. Ibn Kathir (1981, 1300–1372), for example, argues that *khimar* and *jilbab* signify that women should cover their whole bodies, except one eye. al-Tabari (1994, 1839–1923), on the contrary, cites several scholars who see the first verse as implying that women's faces and hands can be exposed. Commenting on the second verse, nonetheless, he cites a number of scholars who interpret the verse as requiring the covering of the whole female body except for one eye. Most often, scholars' commentaries on the Qur'an link similar contexts and interpret them in light of each other. al-Tabari, however, highlights the fact that not only do many classical commentators understand the first verse differently from the second, but also have diverse opinions as to the extent to which Muslim women need to cover up.

16   The scholars' explanation that women should cover their bodies is not only based on the interpretation of the cited verses, but also on *hadith*[11] literature. However, many *hadiths* that are often cited as justification for women's covering have been challenged, with researchers arguing that these *hadiths* are not authentic[12] (*sahih*). Ibe-al-Jawzi (d. 1201), as cited in Roald (2001), argues that women should stay at home and, if they need to go out, should wear the *hijab* because they can cause *fitnah* (temptation).[13] Ibe-al-Jawzi bases his argument on a *hadith* that reads: the Prophet says that "the best mosque for woman is her home." Contrary to Ibe-al-Jawzi, however, Al-Ghazzali (1989, 1054–1111) argues that there are many *hadiths* that provide evidence that women used to pray at the mosque during the Prophet's time and that those *hadiths* are stronger than the one cited (Roald, 2001).

17   Khaled (2001) argues that the debate on the *hijab* among classical and contemporary scholars is fundamentally rooted in the previously mentioned idea of *fitnah*[14] (temptation). He states that the Qur'an uses the word *fitnah* for non-sexual temptations, such as "money and severe trials and tribulations" (Khaled, 2001: 233). Nonetheless, scholars often associate the notion of *fitnah* with women's

sexuality, which is signalled, in part, by an uncovered appearance in public. Khaled writes that women are prohibited from attending mosques or driving cars, and that "every item and colour of clothing is analyzed under the doctrine of *fitnah*" (Khaled, 2001: 235). He argues, however, that these restrictions are misplaced, and that *fitnah* reflects men's fantasies of uncontrollable lust which they have associated with women's sexuality:

> It does not seem to occur to the jurists who make these determinations that this presumed *fitnah* that accompanies women in whatever they do or wherever they go is not an inherent quality of womanhood, but is a projection of male promiscuities. . . Instead of turning the gaze away[15] from the physical attributes of women, they obsessively turn the gaze of attention to women as a mere physicality. In essence, these jurists objectify women into items for male consumption, and in that, is the height of immodesty. (Khaled, 2001: 235–6)

18   Khaled (2001) further argues that the injunction that women need to cover their bodies to avoid bringing on *fitnah* is not in harmony with Islam's message; the Qur'an does not use the word to imply women's temptation, and does not view women's bodies as *fitnah*. Moreover, Islam requires lowering of the gaze and guarding modesty for both men and women; thus, a covered female body will not lead to a modest society (the essence of the *hijab*) until men behave in a similar manner.

What is the *hijab*? The discussion among the participants

That is a question that I ask myself. (Almas)[16]

19   The extent to which Muslim women should cover their bodies is not only a controversial issue among scholars, but also emerged as a contentious matter among the participants in this study, where the meanings of the *hijab* are interpreted in a variety of ways. The *hijab* in the form of physical garments signifies headscarves (as worn by some of the women interviewed), but also modest clothing that

does not include the covering of the head. Equally important, the *hijab* in this research also refers to modest behaviour.

20   Some participants indicated that although the Qur'an requires head covering, "the instructions are not clear, and people have diverse views about the *hijab*." Scholars such as Asad (1980, 1900–1992) have pointed out that there are sound reasons for not stating precise rules regarding the covering of women's bodies. He argues that human circumstances vary over time, and that the verses are moral guidelines that could be observed against the ever-changing background of time and social environment. Similarly, Dilshad', one of the participants, recognized the purpose of the vague regulations of Islam, and stated that the religion accommodates people's cultural differences. She remarked:

> Islam defines certain [rules] very strictly, because you have to follow them throughout your life. Even till the end of the world. . . these rules will remain the same. But some things are [a] little flexible, because you have to adjust with time, culture, and country.

21   Dilshad' is aware that human beings cannot free themselves from the bondage of time and space, and need to adjust their lives frequently. People's dress codes differ not only from culture to culture, but even within a culture, and patterns and styles indeed change over time. Drawing on the concept of "flexibility" and "adjustment," Dilshad' argues that Islamic rules about women's clothing can be modified according to their needs.

22   The idea of the *hijab* with reference to headscarves or covering of the body, however, is only one element of the *hijab*. Most participants reported that physical articles such as clothing would not serve the purpose of the *hijab* unless women believe in the practice. Islam requires lowering the gaze, avoiding seeing what is forbidden, and not inviting the male gaze. For these reasons, many participants mentioned that whether a woman wears a headscarf or not, modest behaviour is a fundamental aspect of the *hijab*. Raheelah, for example, remarked that the *hijab* is not limited to head covering: conducting life unpretentiously is also significant in fulfilling the requirements of the *hijab*. "To me," she stated, "the

hijab is not just covering of your head. . . it is your life, your portrayal of yourself as a person. As long as you dress decently, and you do not draw attention to yourself, that to me is the *hijab*." Raheelah does not wear a headscarf, but her concept of the *hijab* dictates modesty of dress, such as not wearing miniskirts or tight dresses that could be seen as bringing attention to oneself. She also believes that moral behaviour is part of the *hijab*. This indicates that she sees the *hijab* not as a material garment, but as an ethical belief. Raheelah then, while not wearing the headscarf, feels that she is maintaining the boundaries of the *hijab*.

Why or why not wear the *hijab*?

It keeps the society pure in many, many ways. (Dilshad')

23   Following the discussion of the concept of the *hijab*, some participants mentioned the rationale of the Qur'an requiring the *hijab*. For example, Farza'nah' argues that the *hijab*[17] sets a boundary between men and women that helps them avoid premarital relationships, which are not permissible in Islam. She commented that a woman's beauty needs to be concealed, because "beauty brings a lot of other things. . . freedom, the kind that we see here." Farza'nah' identifies the *hijab* as a means of minimizing easy interaction between men and women, which in turn promotes chastity. However, according to Farza'nah's views, chastity is not restricted to women's behaviour, but it is extended to society, where women's modesty grants chaste society.

24   Contrary to Farza'nah's opinion, Dilshad' did not think that women's bodies should be covered simply because they are eye-catching. She believes that the *hijab* is a tool that diminishes sexual appeal and as a result promotes a virtuous public domain. She stated that women need to wear the *hijab* because "it keeps the society pure in many, many ways." Despite the seeming differences about the attractiveness of women's bodies, both Farza'nah' and Dilshad' linked the *hijab* with women's sexuality. Underlying their views is a concept of women's bodies as either

tempting (their beauty will seduce men) or polluting (their immodest behaviour can corrupt society). The status of women's bodies, in turn, is seen as a sign of the moral status of the nation, because women are perceived as the cultural carriers of their society (Yuval-Davis, 1994). Thus, a chaste, moral, or pure society is dependent upon the condition of women's bodies according to Farza'nah' and Dilshad'.

25   Farza'nah's and Dilshad's reasoning also indicates that because they see women's bodies as *fitna*, their views contradict the Qur'an as discussed earlier. In verse 33:59, already mentioned, the Qur'an states that women should cover themselves so as not to be "molested." The context of the verse indicates that at the time this verse was revealed, men treated slave women very disrespectfully, and there were incidents in Medina[18] when the men assaulted Muslim women. The offenders' excuse was that they did not know that these were Muslim women. In order to protect Muslim women, it was stated that they should dress modestly so that they could be recognized. Implied in the Qur'an is the idea that men are the aggressors and women the victims, whereas according to these participants, women are the actors and men the victims (Roald, 2001). Thus, as Roald (2001) points out, many Muslims have turned the Qur'anic view around to suggest that women are responsible for a corrupted and unchaste society.

26   While some women wear the *hijab* because they feel responsible for a moral society, others wear it because it offers them respect, dignity, and protection. Almas, for example, is just under 20 and away from her country of origin, as well as her family, for the first time. She reported that because she is living by herself, the *hijab* has become a security measure, that men are respectful towards *muhajibh* and do not treat them like sexual objects. She remarked that "to me now it's like protection. . . I wear the *hijab* and people do not treat you the way they treat other girls here. They are more respectful." Although she had difficulty explaining why men respect *muhajibh*, for Almas the *hijab*, as it desexualizes her body, is a device for earning respect and ensuring her safety from potential male viewers. Many studies, such as Read and Bartkowski (2000) have found that many women wear the *hijab* because they think men will respect them. These researchers did not discuss why men

respect *muhajibh*, and it was difficult for me to specu-late about the reason(s). Nonetheless, Almas's remarks indicate that she feels that the *hijab* gives her the status of a respectable person, which shows that the *hijab* has a significant impact on its wearer regarding her social relationships and her perception of her "self."

27   Moghadam (1994: 21) states that women "find value, purpose, and identity in religious practice", and in this study, the practice of the *hijab* emerges as a significant religious symbol. Many of the wearers of the headscarves felt that wearing the *hijab* indicated commitment to the religion and to self-discipline, because it covers the hair sign of women's beauty and sexuality. Sima, for example, remarked that when women want to look beautiful, they show off their hair, but women who cover their hair "do not do it just for the sake of Allah [God]. . . It is a sacrifice that you do not [expose hair]. . . You just submit your-self." Sima considers wearing the *hijab* a part of her religious obligation, which is expressed by denying her (sexual) desires and pleasures as symbolized by her hair.

28   Since people often recognize the *hijab*[19] as a religious sign that offers its wearers respect and dig-nity, many Muslims look negatively upon women who do not wear it, and non-wearers often feel com-munity pressure to conform. Despite the dominant view that the *hijab* is a symbol of religious commit-ment, non-wearers of headscarves[20] argue that a woman not wearing a headscarf still could be a dedi-cated *muslimah*.[21] Bilqis', for instance, remarked:

> Within the Muslim community, if you are not wearing the *hijab*, then you know you are not Muslim or you are not Muslim enough, when . . . it's a totally personal choice, you know. My relationship as a Muslim and my spiritual development is between me and God, and that's it.

29   Arthur (1999: 1) states that "while a person's level of religiosity cannot be objectively perceived, symbols such as clothing are used as evidence that s/he is on the 'right and true path.'" Similarly, Bilqis' points out that her devotion to the religion is judged by her dress codes, and since she does not wear the *hijab*, the Muslim community in Saskatoon does not recognize her as a committed *muslimah*. Although for

Bilqis' her relationship with her God is a personal matter that is not connected with the visible marker of a headscarf, the community's attitude is that the *hijab* signifies a pervasive identity symbol of a devoted *muslimah*.

30   The participants who did not wear headscarves perceived the *hijab* as a cultural dress code rather than as a religious symbol. These women indicated that wearing the *hijab* is a new cultural phenomenon locally and globally, and that it does not have a reli-gious connotation. Ati'yah, for example, remarked, "I think it's more like a culture that is the way they are raised there ["back home"]. . . I do not think it is taken as a religion when they started." According to Ati'yah, women are taught traditionally to cover their bodies with the *hijab*, and they do not wear it because of religious requirement.

31   The non-wearers of the headscarves, in addi-tion to perceiving the *hijab* as a cultural marker, also reported the irregularity of many of the *muhajibh*'s clothing. These participants mentioned that many women who wear the *hijab* often dress in tight and transparent garments at home and/or in women's gatherings, whereas they could not "imagine" putting on a tight, revealing outfit. These women thought that because of some "immodest" clothing practices, *muhajibh* usually needed to cover their bodies with the *hijab* when they went out. Moreover, non-wearers reported that they adopted a consistent wardrobe whether they were at home or outside.

32   Although non-wearers of the headscarves ascribed different reasons for wearing the *hijab* from those who did wear it, both group categories felt that the *hijab* was a way of demonstrating the difference between Muslim and Western values. Mali'hah, for instance, commented that morality is declining in Canadian society, and wearing the *hijab* shows people that its wearers do not subscribe to immoral values; also, she added, *muhajibh* are afraid, because they do not have control over these undesired values. Mali'hah reported that:

> The sense of morals has gone way over the other end. . . permissiveness has gone to its utter extreme. Even if you go to the library now, which was a safe place for kids to go to, they have access to the most, um, horrific pornographic literature. . . . It is really scary.

There is complete lack of morals and I think it's a swing in the opposite direction. . . . People are afraid and so they are sort of running to cover themselves, literally speaking and metaphorically.

33   Most people will concur with Mali'hah that access to pornographic[22] material has become easy for young people. The fact that Mali'hah singled out the library as a site of access for pornography is particularly symbolic since, as a writer, she holds the library in some esteem—denoted by the term "even"—as if one could expect to find pornography at "other" places but never at the library, because she sees it as "a safe place for children." The availability of pornographic material at the library—an important cultural source for seeking knowledge—represents the defilement of something previously regarded by Mali'hah as "pure." Even though she does not wear the *hijab*, she sees a link between the *hijab* and pornographic literature, the former standing as a reaction to the latter, with *muhajibh* using the *hijab* to oppose immoral values. In addition, as I demonstrated in the preceding section, some of the participants perceived the *hijab* as a protector of their cultures, as they think that women are responsible for chaste societies. Likewise, Mali'hah believes that covering women's bodies, and hence Muslim society, shields Muslims from immorality.

The *hijab* as an identity symbol

In the global context, if I see a woman in the *hijab* I know she is a Muslim and it creates sense of community in that respect, which is a nice feeling, I think. (Bilqis')

34   The reasons for wearing it can be diverse, but the *hijab* has become a very powerful, pervasive symbol of Muslim women's identity, particularly in the West. Ibrahim (1999) states that it is a growing feeling on the part of Muslim women that they no longer wish to identify with the West, and that reaffirmation of their identities as Muslims requires the kind of visible sign that the adoption of traditional clothing implies. For these women, the issue is not that they have to dress traditionally, but that they choose to embrace the *hijab* as a marker of their Muslim identities.

35   Similarly, many participants who wear the *hijab*[23] claimed that it was a mark of their Muslim identities, ensuring that people immediately recognize them as Muslim women. Sima, for example, who wears a headscarf, commented that her distinct clothing symbolizes Muslim identities, and that the *hijab* makes her visible in a non-Muslim society. Being visible as a Muslim, however, also means encountering the negative stereotypes that are linked with Muslims, and Sima is aware of that. She remarked:

Nothing else tells them that I am a Muslim, just my *hijab*. And. . . if they have the idea, oh, Muslims are terrorists, they might look at me like [that], and if they have the idea that, oh, Muslims are good people, they might look at me [with] respect But still it gives me. . . identity.

36   Nasser (1999: 409) writes that adoption of the *hijab* "conveys a public message/statement, both about the wearer and about the relationship between the wearer and potential viewers". Accordingly, Sima's response shows that she recognizes her *hijab* as a public statement. However, whether she would be identified as a "terrorist" or a "good" person in Canada is a secondary consideration for her. The significant element to her is that she will be known as a Muslim in a non-Muslim country. Sima thus uses her *hijab* as a tool for declaring her Muslim identities.

37   The concept of the *hijab* is not limited to personal identity; it has also become the symbol of the Muslim *ummah*, or community. An immigrant Muslim woman's attempt to identify herself as a Muslim by wearing a headscarf is an acknowledgement of general support for the attitudes, values, and beliefs of Islam and her culture that links her to the broader community of believers (Daly, 1999; Read & Bartkowski, 2000). Some participants in this study also saw the *hijab* as representative of the Muslim community, and argued that the *hijab* helped them to stay away from un-Islamic practices. Farza'nah' stated that the practice of the *hijab* defined boundaries for her, and that she would not do anything that could portray the religion negatively:

The *hijab* limits me from doing certain things. When I have the *hijab* on. . . as a Muslim woman, I consider myself basically representative of the whole Muslim community. So, I do not go to bars with my *hijab* on. I do not go to strips clubs with my *hijab* on because I know [that] by wearing the *hijab*, I am not representing only myself. . . it's the whole Muslim community, basically.

38   Farza'nah' believes that the *hijab* symbolizes both individual and collective Muslim identities. For her, the *hijab*, as a visible sign of Muslim identities, is a public statement for potential viewers. It is also a reminder for the wearer to conduct her life in accordance with the Muslim belief system by not going to bars and/or strips clubs–places where sexuality is on display–as doing so contradicts the Qur'an's demand for modesty.

39   The *hijab* not only links the wearers with a larger community, but it is also a symbol of rites of passage. In Iran, reported Pervin', when a young woman begins to wear the *hijab*, the family celebrates it. It is a "memorable" event and "part of the life of a girl as a graduation party." According to Sima,[24] it signifies that a young woman is now a responsible person, and family and friends rejoice in her honour. In this cultural context, the *hijab* appears as a sign of adulthood and offers the wearer prestige and appreciation from friends and family members.

40   The participants in this study who have maintained the practice of wearing headscarves in Canada indicated that they are stricter in the use of their *hijab* in Canada than are those "back home." Shaffir (1978) states that usually people become more loyal to their traditions and customs if their identities are threatened by the larger society:

A feature common to groups that perceive the outside world as a threat is the belief that they must resist the assimilative influence of the larger society. . . [This helps the] group members to feel more committed and increases their awareness of their separate identity. (Shaffir, 1978: 41)

41   Confirming Shaffir's observations, a number of informants in this study reported that they have embraced the *hijab* in Canada more enthusiastically

than have people in their country of origin. Pervin', for instance, stated, "I find that our *hijab* here is better than people are wearing in Iran. . . and I think the reason is [that] . . . somehow we need more to do this here than there." The *hijab* helps Pervin' keep her distinct identities in a non-Muslim country, and it appears as a sign of resistance to the assimilative influence of the larger society.

42   In comparing the practice of wearing the *hijab* in Canada to its usage "back home," the wearers of headscarves are crafting their Muslim identities not only in relation to the dominant values of their residing country, but also to the values of their country of origin. Many informants held a static view of their places of birth, and on their occasional visits they were surprised that the societies had changed. They argued that there is now a tendency "back home" for women to dress in tight clothes and not to wear "proper" *hijab*. The contrast of two different places allows these informants to notice differences in the *hijab*, and "improper" *hijab* emerges as a symbol of the loss of Islamic values. Thus, the *hijab* for these participants stands as a guardian of Muslim standards, and they thought that "back home" people were careless in not maintaining it.

The *hijab*, body, and gaze

The study of dress as situated practice requires moving between, on the one hand, the discursive and representational aspects of dress, and the way the body/dress is caught up in relations of power, and on the other, the embodied experience of dress and the use of dress as a means by which individuals orientate themselves to the social world. (Entwistle, 2000: 39)

43   Many prominent scholars, such as El Saadawi (1980) and Mernissi (1987; 1991) have situated the practice of *veiling* as an act of controlling women both physically and psychologically. These writers argue that *veiling* represents, and is a result of, oppressive social hierarchies and male domination (Read & Bartkowski, 2000; Roald, 2001); therefore, it should be condemned. Mernissi (1991), for instance, states that "all debates on democracy get tied up in the woman question and that piece of cloth [the *hijab*] that opponents of human rights today claim to be the very essence of Muslim identity" (188). Mernissi views the *hijab* as a hindrance to accessing human rights and, consequently, inherently oppressive. Equally important, she denies the lived experiences of many of those women who recognize the *hijab* as a positive experience that empowers them and grants them Muslim identities.

44   For the wearers of the headscarves in this study, the *hijab* is a tool that confers power and, contrary to the above writers' opinions, helps many of them to take control of their bodies. Many of the participants seem to be utilizing the *hijab* to set boundaries between themselves and the outside world. Di'ba, for example, commented that she likes keeping her curtains closed when she has the lights on, because otherwise people walking down the street can see her. One of Di'ba's friends, however, finds her precautions odd, and argues that Islam is not that strict, that she can relax without the *hijab* while she is in her home. For Di'ba, putting a barrier between herself and potential viewers is not due to Islamic restrictions; rather, she wants to create a space where she feels free from the male gaze. Di'ba reported her friend's reaction:

> What's the big deal? Like, you are in your house. . . Allah is not going to punish you for what you are doing in your own house, you know. And I am, like, but it is not about being punished. . . I do not know how Allah is going to view this, but I do not want people, like [some] guy, [looking in]. . . that's the thing.

45   Secor (2002) writes that veiling as a form of dress is a spatial practice embedded in relations of power and resistance. Accordingly, extending the idea of the *hijab* from headscarf to the creation of "safe" space, Di'ba uses her curtains to assert power and resistance, her freedom from the undesired gaze.

46   The notion that the *hijab* liberates women from the male gaze and helps them to be in charge of their own bodies is a very prominent claim by those Muslim women who wear it. They argue that the *hijab* is not a mark of oppression; rather, it is a sign of liberation that protects them from a sexist society. The *hijab* allows Muslim women physical mobility because they feel free from the male gaze. Consequently, they move in the public sphere more comfortably (Hoodfar,

1993; Khan, 1995; Odeh, 1993). Noreen's story of being released from the gaze by wearing the *hijab* is particularly significant, because she suffered heavily from the "inspecting gaze." Noreen was 18 years old when she got married and came to Canada. When her husband did not let her wear the *hijab*, she reports, "it got [her] into real trouble." She and her husband ran a store where she often worked there by herself. After being harassed in her workplace by some non-Muslim men, her husband consented to allowing her to wear the *hijab*. Noreen's distress due to the harassment can be heard in the following passage:

> The first thing that made my husband let me wear it was because I have four guys [following] behind me and I was married. Imagine what that [would do]. . . especially if your husband. . . [is] think[ing]. . . how [will] she. . . react to all those people who are asking for her. It was terrible for four months, the first four months, because I had to work. . . It was very hard, but now I like the work and I am way freer than before. . . So, yeah, it's the protection, the main thing.

47   From the conversation in other parts of my interview with Noreen about her experience of harassment, and as the emotional tone of her narrative indicates, she was not only the victim of harassment, but her response to the harassers was also inspected by her husband. The behaviour of Noreen's spouse indicates that he blamed the victim, as if Noreen were responsible for the harassment. The *hijab*, however, elevated her position from the "observed" to the "observer," as she felt free from the male gaze. This granted Noreen the protection that otherwise might not have been possible for her.

48   Contrary to the opinions of those women who perceive the *hijab* as protection, the non-wearers of the headscarves argued that the *hijab* is not an appropriate dress in Canada. These participants stated that while the basic purpose of the *hijab* is not to draw attention to oneself, in Canada, where it is not customary dress, people often scrutinize women who wear the *hijab*. Citing the example of her daughters who wear the *hijab*, Ati'yah reported that whenever she goes out with her daughters, she notices that people stare at them, which "is the opposite of what the *hijab* is supposed to be." Ati'yah's observation indicates that the *hijab* is a marker of difference in

Canada, as people find it "strange." Equally import-ant, since it draws attention to the wearer, Ati'yah sees it as contrary to the teachings of the Qur'an.

49   While some women in this study retain their distinct Muslim identities by wearing the *hijab*, Ati'yah, in order to be more anonymous in main-stream society, did not wear the *hijab*. Both wearers and non-wearers are crafting their identities and negotiating a place as Muslim women immigrants in a Western society. As noted earlier, the sample of this study is very small and the results cannot be general-ized to the larger population of Muslim women in Saskatoon. Nonetheless, the results indicate that the reasons for wearing or not wearing the *hijab* are var-ied and complex, and cannot be reduced simply to religious or cultural reasons.

Western perception of the *hijab*

Veiling—to Western eyes, the most visible marker of the differentness and inferiority of Islamic societies—became the symbol now of both the oppression of women (or, in the language of the day, Islam's deg-radation of women) and the backwardness of Islam, and it became the open target of colonial attack and the spearhead of the assault on Muslim societies. (Ahmed, 1992: 152)

50   The formation of identities is not only restricted to the ways in which we relate and present ourselves to others; it also depends on how others perceive us. One avenue for understanding the ways in which a society views different people or cultures is to study media representations, because the media often play a powerful role in suggesting and shaping national and personal identities. Studies such as Bullock and Jafri (2000), Jafri (1998), and Kutty (1997) show that mainstream North American media have consistently portrayed an image of "the Muslim woman" as an oppressed and passive *hijab* wearer. Bullock and Jafri (2000) argue that Muslim women are presented by the media as "others," members of a religion that does not promote "Canadian" values but, rather, anti-Canadian values such as indiscriminate violence and gender oppression.

51   In the media, wearing the *hijab* is seen as a powerful signifier of Muslim women's oppression, and the majority of articles in print about the *hijab* suggests that this practice is a sign of Muslim women's subjugation, and therefore to be condemned. The print media's negative stereotypes of the *hijab* are demonstrated in the following headlines: "Wearing a uniform of oppression" (*The Globe and Mail* 1993), "Women's legacy of pain" (*Toronto Star* 1997) June 26: (5–6), "The new law: Wear the veil and stay alive" (*The Globe and Mail* 1994) April 11:B3, "Lifting the veil of ignorance" (*Toronto Star* 1996) July 30: E1, E3 (Bullock & Jafri, 2000; Jafri, 1998). These headlines illustrate that the popular media not only see the *hijab* as a mark of Muslim women's subjugation, but that the media perpetuate this image. The media do not, however, draw attention to the banning of the practice. Bullock and Jafri (2000) argue that when Tunisian and Turkish governments banned the *hijab* and many women refused to go to work or attend the universities, the media did not report these events. Thus, the media contribute only to the negative stereotypes of Muslim women.

52   While there is a general intolerance about the *hijab* in the media, there are some specific incidents in Canada which further support the idea that mainstream society does not perceive the *hijab* as acceptable clothing. In Montreal, in 1994, students were sent home by school officials for wearing the *hijab*, and the young women were told that unless they "removed their *hijab* they could not attend school" (Shakeri, 2000: 130). Similarly, in May, 1995, in Quebec, "the largest teacher's union in the province, the Centrale de l'enseignment du Quebec (CEQ) voted to ban the *hijab* in school" (Shakeri, 2000: 130).

53   Discrimination against *muhajibh* students was not limited to Montreal and Quebec schools. Partici-pants in the case study who attended schools in Sas-katoon also reported experiences of racism in the classrooms. Di'ba', for instance, commented that when she began to wear the *hijab* in high school, one of her teachers started to ignore her as if she was not part of the class, which deeply disturbed Di'ba'. "It was art class," she recalled, "we were sitting all around the classroom and he just, like, totally skipped me. He would be handing out something or whatever. . .

and I guess at that time it was bad. . . I took it hard." The teacher's approach shows the negative attitude toward the *hijab* by some Canadians. More importantly, it highlights the impact of such discrimination on Di'ba's self-esteem.

54   In mainstream society, the negative stereotypes of Muslim women have become more visible since the attacks in New York on September 11, 2001, and the *hijab* has become a sign of a "terrorist" woman. There are a number of incidents in Canada where *muhajibh* were harassed after September 11,[25] and some participants mentioned that they also had encountered racist harassment. Pervin', for instance, who has also experienced racism in Canada, reported that someone has since called her a "terrorist," and she inferred that it was because she wore the *hijab*. "Some guy said 'Terrorist,' because I wear the *hijab*," she remarked. ". . . Some people stare at me. They think that if you have the *hijab*, you are a 'terrorist'. . . really, some of them think so." Pervin's experience reveals the powerful and negative stereotypes that have linked the *hijab*—the sign of Muslim identity—with terrorism, resulting in verbal, racial, and ethnic assaults like the one cited above. These racist incidents demonstrate that Muslim women (and men) are often seen as "other" in Canadian society and, despite claims that it is a multicultural country, many Muslims face difficulties living in Canada.

55   Price and Shildrick (1999) point out that the negative portrayal of the *hijab* in the West stretches back to the nineteenth and earlier-twentieth century. "Removing the veil, both real and metaphorical, was the prime concern of the missionaries" and "the prevailing discourse was that women needed to be rescued" (Price & Shildrick, 1999: 392). The most recent example of the West as "rescuer" of Muslim women is the "liberation" of Afghan women from the *burqa*. While I do not support the Taliban's compulsory enforcement of the wearing of *burqas*, I recognize that as attire, the *burqa*, as well as some kind of *hijab*, such as a *chadar*, is a centuries-old tradition in Afghanistan; the Taliban did not invent the practice. Moreover, Afghan women are still wearing *burqas* even though the Taliban regime is no longer in power, which illustrates the fact that the custom has not died.

56   The "liberation" of Afghan women from the *burqa*, nonetheless, is portrayed in mainstream North American society as if the covering of women is inherently oppressive, and the participants in this study mentioned that people often have the view that Muslim women are forced to wear the *hijab*. I interviewed two Afghan women who wore the *hijab*, and one of them said that people often told her that she could remove her scarf in Canada as her family would not know that she was not wearing it. The participant argues that "it's not for [my parents], but [people] thought I am scared of my parents and. . . I am doing this just for them. I said, 'No, it's different.'" During the interview, the same woman expressed very strong feelings about wearing the *hijab*, and spoke very enthusiastically about it; however, she reported that she often encountered negative views of the *hijab*, based on the assumption that she was forced to wear it.

57   The participants not only mentioned the negative stereotype of the *hijab*, but they also recognized that many Western-style clothes could be construed as oppressive. Bilqis', for example, remarked that many North American women wear short dresses and expose their bodies, but this is not perceived as an act of oppression in Canada, whereas covering the body is interpreted as a sign of subjugation. She commented:

> Western women, when they see a Muslim woman in the *hijab*, they think, ah, oppression. But you know, ten-inch heels and a miniskirt is not seen as oppressive. To me it is more oppressive than a putting a scarf on your head.

58   Wolf (1991) has demonstrated that the "beauty myth" has often resulted in the objectification of women, and the expenditure of large amounts of money to achieve the ideal body. Wolf (1991: 13) writes that there is no justification for the beauty myth: "What it is doing to women today is a result of nothing more exalted than the need of today's power structure, economy, and culture to mount a counter-offensive against women". Similarly, Bilqis' argues that the Western style of wearing scanty outfits is a form of women's oppression.

59   The representation of the *hijab* is intimately related to issues of voice in the West, which has been expressed through the colonial relationship between the "Occident" and the "Orient" explored by Said (1978). He argues that the link between Occident and Orient is a relationship of power, of domination, and of varying degrees of complex hegemony, where the Occident spoke for and represented the Orient. As a result, there are many myths about Muslim women created by the "Occident." One of the fairy tales is that Muslim women are passive victims of their societies and their religion, and the example of *hijab* is often cited as a sign of their submissiveness. In the present study, however, some of the participants did not see the *hijab* as a mark of subordination. Moreover, they consciously chose to wear the *hijab*, undercutting the myth of the submissive Muslim woman. For example, Di'ba' reported that she always wanted to wear the *hijab*, but she thought that it would hinder her participation in sports activities, and so she did not wear it. She decided, however, to put it on when she realized that it would not hamper such activities:

> It was a weekend and I saw one girl who was a year younger than me at the mosque the night before and, uh, she was wearing the *hijab* and playing basketball, and I mean that's the whole thing, you know. So, I [thought], well, it is not preventing her from doing all those things. She is still having fun, she is still enjoying herself, so why not? So that night, actually, it was snowing and I made *dua* [supplication]. . . The next morning, *Alhumdulliah* [praise be to God], I woke up and I was like, I am ready. I am just going to do it and, *Alhumdulliah*, I put on [the *hijab*] since then.

60   This decision was a significant act in Di'ba's life. Several years later, she still vividly remembers the details of the event: it was a weekend. . . "it was snowing." Thus, the *hijab* stands for her asserting her own agency and demonstrates that she is not a passive victim of a Muslim society whose life is ruled by male relatives.

Conclusion

61   This article discussed the concept of the *hijab* and its meanings to immigrant Muslim women.

Wearing the *hijab* in the last two decades has become a popular phenomenon, locally and globally; however, to what extent Muslim women need to cover is a debatable question among scholars as well as among the participants. The idea of the *hijab* ranges from wearing headscarves to demonstrating modest behaviour, depending on one's understanding of religious precepts. The participants described the *hijab* in a variety of ways; some linked it with the moral Muslim society and others thought that it was a sign of opposing immoral values. For those informants who wear the *hijab*, it is a religious obligation. The non-wearers of the headscarves view it as a cultural symbol. The *hijab* as a mark of identity is a persistent theme and the *muhajibh* use the *hijab* to assert agency, which in turn confers status and dignity to its wearers. At the same time, however, the *hijab* disempowers non-wearers, because the Muslim community does not perceive them as "good" *muslimah*.

62   While the *hijab* holds multiple meanings for Muslim women, mainstream North American society's perception of the *hijab* is usually negative, and the practice is often is presented in the Canadian media without proper cultural and historical reference. Unlike the participants' views, the depiction of the *hijab* in Canada suggests that there is only one form of the *hijab*, that is, as a symbol of the oppression of Muslim women. Canadian attitudes towards the *hijab* suggest that Westerners "know the Orient better than the Orient can know itself" (Khan, 1995: 149).

63   In some situations the *hijab* may indeed be imposed on Muslim women, but in this study many of the participants chose to wear it. Living in Canada, where the connotation of the *hijab* is often negative, has a strong impact on those immigrant Muslim women who wear it, as they consequently face negative stereotypes of Muslim women such as being labelled "terrorists." In spite of these racist acts, the *muhajibh* wear the *hijab* as a sign of their Muslim identities and in opposition to "immodest" Western values. Those who do not identify with the visible marker recognize that the *hijab* is not an acceptable dress code in Canada. In fact, their refusal to wear the *hijab* could be read as a symbol of assimilation, but in not drawing attention to themselves and by

wearing modest clothes (without the headscarf) these women, nonetheless, maintain the practice of the *hijab*. Thus, the non-wearers of the headscarves may not confront the racism that wearing the *hijab* can prompt; however, they usually encounter criticism within the Muslim community. The *hijab*, therefore, in the form of Muslim woman's clothing, emerges as a device to negotiate spaces within the Muslim community, as well as in the dominant western culture.

Acknowledgement

I would like to acknowledge the financial support of Community-University-Institute for Social Research (CUISR) for this project.

Women's Studies International Forum.
2006. 29.

Endnotes

1. A woman who wears a *hijab*, such as a headscarf, is called *muhajibh*.
2. Media is defined here as any form of written text, i.e., books, magazines, journal articles, reports or articles in newspapers, and audio or visual productions, i.e., radio, television shows, and documentary films.
3. The use of the word "identities" in plural form is more appropriate here because a person's identity is multi-faceted. For instance, a Muslim woman living in Saskatoon is not only viewed as a woman, but also as a woman of colour, an immigrant, and a member of an ethnic, as well as a religious, group.
4. The term refers here to any Muslim woman born outside Canada, but currently is residing in Canada with any kind of official documents, such as a Canadian passport or student visa.
5. Please note that men's and women's gatherings are held separately in the mosque.
6. Though different researchers have different opinions about the size of groups, for instance Morgan (1988) states that "use 'moderate sized' groups, which is somewhere between 6 and 10" (43). However, he also indicates that the currently favored range in marketing is 6 to 8, and several years ago it was 8–10.
7. Lane's (1984) Arabic–English lexicon, is a classical dictionary, which originally appeared in 1863. The meanings of all the Arabic words discussed here are taken from this source.
8. The meanings of all the Qur'anic verses are taken from Ali (trans) (1946).
9. By using the term "Western and/or the West," I do not intend to homogenize the Western world. "The West is as diverse as any other part of the World" (Mojab, 1998: 25); consequently, Western people are heterogeneous. However, the purpose here is to indicate the assumed superiority of the West. Western discourses often profoundly mould the majority of people's lives, because they have managed to impress an ideology of white supremacy over the last few centuries (Jhappan, 1996). Western views that often underscore their superiority in reference to the *hijab* are discussed later in this article.
10. Many classical and contemporary commentators, for instance, al-Tabari (1994, 1839–1923), Ibn Kathir (1981, 1300–1372), and Ali (1946), agree that at the Prophet's time, Arabian women used to wear clothing that left the breasts uncovered; the Qur'an required covering of the bosom.
11. A collection of the Prophet's sayings and actions is called *hadiths*.
12. There is a science of knowledge that studies the authenticity of *hadiths*.
13. I will discuss this issue below. The idea of *fitnah* is also found in the Judeo-Christian veiling tradition, where it was thought that an uncovered female head aroused sexual desire in men (Bronner, 1993; D'Angelo, 1995).
14. Please note that he discusses the *hadith* literature in reference to the *fitnah*, and argues that they are not authentic *hadiths*.
15. A reference to the Qur'anic verse 24:30, where it states that men should lower their gaze and guard their modesty.
16. Please note that all participants have been given pseudonyms.
17. The *hijab* here signifies a headscarf.
18. Geographical location where the Prophet was residing.
19. Here the *hijab* is identified by the form of headscarf and/or long coat.
20. I used the word headscarf here to make a distinction between those whose concept of the *hijab* includes the physical article, such as a headscarf, and those who view the *hijab* as modest clothing (without the head covering) and modest behaviour.
21. *Muslimah* is the feminine for a Muslim woman.
22. *Mali'hah* defines pornographic material as explicit sexual images.
23. The *hijab* here particularly refers to the material article; nonetheless, modest behaviour is not excluded.
24. As stated earlier, please note that as I conducted focus groups, the participants talked among themselves and commented on each others' views.
25. See for instance, *The Globe and Mail*, October 15, 2001, and Jain (2001) www.rediff.com/us/2001/oct/12ny31.htm.

References

Ahmed, Leila (1992). *Women and gender in Islam: Historical roots of a modern debate*. New Haven: Yale University Press.

Al-Ghazzali, Muhammad (1989). *as-sunna an-anbawiya bayna ahl al-fiqh wa ahl al-hadith*. Cairo: Dar ash-Shuruq.

al-Tabari, Abu Ja'far Muhammad Ibne Jarir (1994). tafsir al-Tabari. Beirut: al Mu'assasa r-Risala.

Arthur, B. Linda (1999). Introduction: Dress and the social control of the body. In Linda Arthur (Ed.), *Religion, dress and the body* (pp. 1–7). Oxford: Berg.

Asad, Muhammad (trans.) (1980). *The message of The Qur'an*. Gibraltar: Dar Al-Andalus.

Berg, Bruce (1998). *Qualitative research methods for social sciences*. Toronto: Allyn and Bacon.

Bradshaw, Matt, & Straford, Elaine (2000). Qualitative research design and rigour. In Iain Hay (Ed.), *Qualitative research methods in human geography* (pp. 37–49). South Melbourne, Vic.7 Oxford University Press.

Bronner, Leah Leila (1993). From veil to wig: Jewish women's hair covering. *Judaism*, 42(4), 465–477.

Bullock, Katherine, & Jafri, Joua (2000, Summer). Media (mis) representations: Muslim women in the Canadian nation. *Canadian Woman Studies*, 20(2), 35–40.

Daly, C. M. (1999). The paarda' expression of hejaab among Afghan women in a non-Muslim community. In Linda Arthur (Ed.), *Religion, dress and the body* (pp. 147–161). Oxford: Berg.

D'Angelo, Rose Marry (1995). Veils, virgins, and the tongues of men and angles: Women's heads in early Christianity. In Howard Eilberg-Schwartz, & Wendy Doniger (Eds.), *Off with her head! The denial of women's identity in myth, religion, and culture* (pp. 131–164). Berkeley: University of California Press.

El Guindi, Fadwa (1999). *Veil: Modesty, privacy and resistance*. Oxford: Berg.

El Saadawi, Nawal (1980). *The hidden face of Eve: Women in the Arab world* (Hetata, Trans.). London: Zed Press.

Entwistle, Joanne. (2000). *The fashioned body: Fashion, dress, and modern social theory*. Cambridge: Polity Press; Malden, MA: Blackwell.

Fernea, Elizabeth, & Fernea, Robert A. (1979). A look behind the veil. *Human Nature*, 2(2), 68–77.

Freitas, Anthony, Hall, Carol, Kim, Jung-Won, Kaiser, Susan, Chandler, Joan, & Hammidi, Tania (1997, Summer). Appearance management as border construction: Least favorite clothing, group distancing, and identity. . .Not!. *Sociological Inquiry*, 67(3), 323–335.

Hoodfar, Homa (1993). The veil in their minds and on our heads: The persistence of colonial images of Muslim women. *Resources for Feminist Research*, 22(3/4), 5–18.

Ibn Kathir, Imad ad-Din (1981). *Mukhtasir Tafsir ibn Kathir*. I–III. Beirut: Dar al-Qur'an al-Karim.

Ibrahim, B. Syed (1999). Women in Islam: Hijab. Aalim: Islamic Research Foundation (IRF).

Jafri, Gul Joya. (1998). The portrayal of Muslim women in Canadian mainstream media: A community based analysis. Online Afghan women's organization. Project report. http://www.fmw.org/political_activities.htm

Jain, Ajit. (2001). Complaints of harassment of Muslims riding in Montreal. www.rediff.com/us/2001/oct/12ny31.htm

Jhappan, Radha (1996, Fall). Post-Modern race and gender essentialism or a post-mortem of scholarship. *Studies of Political Economy*, 51, 15–63.

Khaled, Abou El Fadl (2001). Speaking in god's name: Islamic law, authority and women. Oxford: Oneworld.

Khan, Shahnaz (1995). The veil as a site of struggle: The Hejab in Quebec. *Canadian Woman Studies*, 15(2/3), 146–152.

Kutty, Sajidah. (1997). Speaking for her: The representation of the Muslim woman in popular culture. *Canadian Muslim civil liberties association. Pamphlet*.

Lane, W. Edward (1984). *Arabic–English lexicon*. Cambridge, England: The Islamic Texts Society.

Mernissi, Fatima (1987). *Beyond the veil: Male–female dynamics in modern Muslim society*. London: Al Saqi Books.

Mernissi, Fatima (1991). *Women and Islam: A historical and theological enquiry* (M.J. Lakeland, Trans.). Oxford: B. Blackwell. Basil.

Moghadam, M. Valentine (1994). Introduction: Women and identity politics in theoretical and comparative perspective. In Valentine Moghadam (Ed.), *Identity politics and women: Cultural reassertions and feminism in international perspective* (pp. 3–26). Boulder: Westview Press.

Mojab, Shahrzad (1998, December). Muslim women and western feminists: The debate on particulars and universals. *Monthly Review*, 50(7), 19–30.

Morgan, David (1988). *Focus groups as qualitative research*. Newbury Park, CA7 Sage Publications.

Nasser, Mervat (1999). The new veiling phenomenon—is it an anorexic equivalent? A polemic. *Journal of Community & Applied Social Psychology*, 9, 407–412.

Odeh, Lama Abou (1993, Spring). Post-colonial feminism and the veil: Thinking the difference. *Feminist Review*, 43, 26–37.

Price, Janet, & Shildrick, Margrit (1999). Mapping the colonial body: Sexual economies and the state in colonial India. In Janet Price, & Margrit Shildrick (Eds.), *Feminist theory and the body: A reader* (pp. 388–398). New York: Routledge.

Read, G. Jen'nan, & Bartkowski, P. John (June 2000). To veil or not to veil? A case study of identity negotiation among Muslim women in Austin, Texas. *Gender and Society*, 14(3), 395–417.

Roald, S. Anne (2001). Women in Islam: The Western experience. London: Routledge.

Said, Edward (1978). *Orientalism*. New York: Pantheon Books.

Secor, Anna (2002). The veil and urban space in Istanbul: Women's dress, mobility and Islamic knowledge. *Gender, Place and Culture*, 9(1), 5–22.

Shaffir, William (1978). Canada: Witnessing as identity consolidation: The case of the Lubavitcher Chassidim. In Hans Mol (Ed.), *Identity and religion: International, cross-cultural approaches* (pp. 39–57). Beverly Hills, CA: Sage Publications.

Shakeri, Esmail (2000). Muslim women in Canada: Their role and status as revealed in the *hijab* controversy. In Yvonne Haddad, & John Esposito (Eds.), *Muslims on the Americanization path?* New York: Oxford University Press.

The holy Qur'an. Ali, A. Yusuf (trans.) (1946). Durban: Islamic Propagation Center International.

Wolf, Naomi (1991). *The beauty myth*. Toronto: Vintage Books.

Yuval-Davis, Nira (1994). Identity politics and women's ethnicity. In Valentine Moghadam (Ed.), *Identity politics and women: Cultural reassertions and feminism in international perspective* (pp. 408–424). Boulder: Westview Press.

KEY AND CHALLENGING WORDS

contentious, intricacy, etymology, differentiate, injunction, rationale, religiosity, pervasive, ascribe, defilement, assimilative, discursive, confer, scrutinize, indiscriminate

QUESTIONS

1. What are the functions of the epigraphs (quotations) that precede the essay and many of the sections? Discuss the functions of the first epigraph (preceding paragraph 1) and one other epigraph.

2. Define the term "focus group" in your own words (paragraph 4). Why was it an effective research tool to use in this study, according to the author?

3. Since the word "*hijab*" does not occur in the Qur'an in reference to a Muslim woman's clothing, why does Ruby discuss its significance (paragraphs 8–10)?

4. In the section "The *hijab* in the Muslim context," explain the role of classic commentators on the Qur'an (15–16) and that of the modern scholar Abou El Fadl Khaled (paragraphs 17–18).

5. In the section "Why or why not wear the *hijab*?" a) identify one example in which the writer successfully synthesizes the views of two participants (i.e., primary sources); b) identify one example in which she synthesizes a primary source and a secondary source; c) identify a passage in which she integrates a paraphrase and a direct quotation; d) identify a passage in which she uses the words of a participant to support a point made by an Islamic scholar (i.e., a secondary source).

6. Explain the differences between using the *hijab* as a personal identity symbol and as a collective identity symbol, as discussed in "The *hijab* as an identity symbol."

7. Summarize paragraph 43, which discusses the views of scholars on veiling as a loss of women's control.

8. Discuss the author's decision to use direct quotations extensively. Focusing on the two direct quotations of participants in the section "The *hijab*, body, and gaze" and their contexts, explain whether they add or detract from the points Ruby is making.

9. How is the focus of the section "Western perception of the hijab" different from that of previous sections? Analyze the rhetorical effectiveness of this section in two or three paragraphs; you could refer specifically to elements like structure, argument, evidence, tone, or other relevant strategies or techniques.

POST-READING

1. *Group discussion:* Laws have been proposed—and, in some places, enacted—to ban articles of clothing often worn by Muslim women in public. Discuss or debate the merits of such bans. If you believe there should be a ban in place, what articles should be banned—for example, the *burqa* (traditional veil), headscarf, body covering?—and under what circumstances?

2. *Group discussion or individual activity:* Respond to one of the following passages from the essay, evaluating the validity of the claim, and using your knowledge, observation, and/or experience to support your claims.

"[T]he media contribute only to the negative stereotypes of Muslim women" (paragraph 51).

"'Western women, when they see a Muslim woman in the *hijab*, they think, ah, oppression. But you know, ten-inch heels and a miniskirt is not seen as oppressive. To me it is more oppressive than putting a scarf on your head'" (paragraph 57).

ADDITIONAL LIBRARY READING

Hamdan, A. (2007). Arab Muslim women in Canada: The untold narratives. *Journal of Muslim Minority Affairs, 27*(1), 133–154.

Rana, A. (2007). On being a Muslim woman. *Intercultural Education, 18*(2), 169–175.

Post-princess models of gender: The new man in Disney/Pixar

Ken Gillam and Shannon R. Wooden

(4,993 words)

Pre-reading

1. Are you aware that Disney animated films have long been criticized for their stereotypical and sexist portrayals of their main characters? Consider one Disney animated film you have seen or for which you know the plot, focusing on its male and/or female stereotypes.

2. Scan the abstract and first paragraph of the essay: a) Identify two examples of *jargon* in the abstract (i.e., words/phrases used within the discipline that a knowledgeable reader would be expected to understand but that a non-specialist might not understand); b) Why do you think the authors chose to begin their essay with a brief personal narrative?

Abstract

Unlike most Disney animated films, which have been criticized for decades for their stereotypical female leads and traditional representations of gender, all the major features released by Disney's Pixar studios since 1990 have featured masculine protagonists. These male plots are remarkably alike, and together, we argue, they indicate a rather progressive post-feminist model of gender. Beginning with alpha-male traits in common, from emotional inaccessibility to keen competitiveness, the stars of these stories follow similar *Bildungsroman* plots. In this article, we chart the pattern of masculine development in three of these films—*Cars, Toy Story,* and *The Incredibles*—noting that Pixar consistently promotes a new model of masculinity. From the revelation of the alpha male's flaws, including acute loneliness and vulnerability, to figurative emasculation through even the slightest disempowerment, each character travels through a significant homosocial relationship and ultimately matures into an acceptance of his more traditionally "feminine" aspects.

Keywords: animated film, *Bildungsroman,* Disney, gender studies, homosociality, masculinity, Pixar, Eve Sedgwick

*

1   Lisping over the Steve McQueen allusion in Pixar's *Cars* (2006), our two-year-old son, Oscar, inadvertently directed us to the definition(s) of masculinity that might be embedded in a children's animated film about NASCAR. The film overtly praises the "good woman" proverbially behind every successful man: the champion car, voiced by Richard Petty, tells his wife, "I wouldn't be nothin' without you, honey." But gender in this twenty-first-century *Bildungsroman* is rather more complex, and Oscar's mispronunciation held the first clue. To him, a member of the film's target audience, the character closing in on the title long held by "The King" is not "Lightning McQueen" but "Lightning the queen"; his chief rival, the always-a-bridesmaid runner-up "Chick" Hicks.

2   Does this nominal feminizing of male also-rans (and the simultaneous gendering of success) constitute a meaningful pattern? Piqued, we began examining the construction of masculinity in major feature films released by Disney's Pixar studios over the past thirteen years. Indeed, as we argue here, Pixar consistently promotes a new model of masculinity, one that matures into acceptance of its more traditionally "feminine" aspects. Cultural critics have long been interested in Disney's cinematic products, but the gender critics examining the texts most enthusiastically gobbled up by the under-six set have so far generally focused on their retrograde representations of women. As Elizabeth Bell argues, the animated Disney features through *Beauty and the Beast* feature a "teenaged heroine at the idealized

height of puberty's graceful promenade. . ., [f]emale wickedness. . . rendered as middle-aged beauty at its peak of sexuality and authority [. . ., and] [f]eminine sacrifice and nurturing. . . drawn in pear-shaped, old women past menopause" (108). Some have noted the models of masculinity in the classic animated films, primarily the contrast between the ubermacho Gaston and the sensitive, misunderstood Beast in *Beauty and the Beast,*[1] but the male protagonist of the animated classics, at least through *The Little Mermaid,* remains largely uninterrogated.[2] For most of the early films, this critical omission seems generally appropriate, the various versions of Prince Charming being often too two-dimensional to do more than inadvertently shape the definition of the protagonists' femininity. But if the feminist thought that has shaped our cultural texts for three decades now has been somewhat disappointing in its ability to actually rewrite the princess trope (the spunkiest of the "princesses," Ariel, Belle, Jasmine, and, arguably, even Mulan, remain thin, beautiful, kind, obedient or punished for disobedience, and headed for the altar), it has been surprisingly effective in rewriting the type of masculine power promoted by Disney's products.[3]

3   Disney's new face, Pixar studios, has released nine films—*Toy Story* (1995) and *Toy Story 2* (1999); *A Bug's Life* (1998); *Finding Nemo* (2003); *Monsters, Inc.* (2001); *The Incredibles* (2004); *Cars* (2006); *Ratatouille* (2007); and now *WALL•E* (2008)—all of which feature interesting male figures in leading positions. Unlike many of the princesses, who remain relatively static even through their own adventures, these male leads are actual protagonists; their characters develop and change over the course of the film, rendering the plot. Ultimately these various developing characters—particularly Buzz and Woody from *Toy Story,* Mr. Incredible from *The Incredibles,* and Lightning McQueen from *Cars*—experience a common narrative trajectory, culminating in a common "New Man" model[4]: they all strive for an alpha-male identity; they face emasculating failures; they find themselves, in large part, through what Eve Sedgwick refers to as "homosocial desire" and a triangulation of this desire with a feminized object (and/or a set of "feminine" values); and, finally, they achieve (and teach) a kinder, gentler understanding of what it means to be a man.

Emasculation of the Alpha Male

4   A working definition of *alpha male* may be unnecessary; although more traditionally associated with the animal kingdom than the Magic Kingdom, it familiarly evokes ideas of dominance, leadership, and power in human social organizations as well. The phrase "alpha male" may stand for all things stereotypically patriarchal: unquestioned authority, physical power and social dominance, competitiveness for positions of status and leadership, lack of visible or shared emotion, social isolation. An alpha male, like Vann in *Cars*, does not ask for directions; like Doc Hudson in the same film, he does not talk about his feelings. The alpha male's stresses, like Buzz Lightyear's, come from his need to save the galaxy; his strength comes from faith in his ability to do so. These models have worked in Disney for decades. The worst storm at sea is no match for *The Little Mermaid's* uncomplicated Prince Eric—indeed, any charming prince need only ride in on his steed to save his respective princess. But the post-feminist world is a different place for men, and the post-princess Pixar is a different place for male protagonists.

5   *Newsweek* recently described the alpha male's new cinematic and television rival, the "beta male": "The testosterone-pumped, muscle-bound Hollywood hero is rapidly deflating . . . . Taking his place is a new kind of leading man, the kind who's just as happy following as leading, or never getting off the sofa" (Yabroff 64). Indeed, as Susan Jeffords points out, at least since *Beauty and the Beast*, Disney has resisted (even ridiculed) the machismo once de rigueur for leading men (170). Disney cinema, one of the most effective teaching tools America offers its children, is not yet converting its model male protagonist all the way into a slacker, but the New Man model is quite clearly emerging.

6   *Cars, Toy Story,* and *The Incredibles* present their protagonists as unambiguously alpha in the opening moments of the films. Although Lightning McQueen may be an as-yet incompletely realized alpha when *Cars* begins, not having yet achieved the "King" status of his most successful rival, his ambition and fierce competitiveness still clearly valorize the alpha-male model: "Speed. I am speed . . . . I eat losers for breakfast," he chants as a prerace mantra.

He heroically comes from behind to tie the championship race, distinguishing himself by his physical power and ability, characteristics that catapult him toward the exclusively male culture of sports superstars. The fantasies of his life he indulges after winning the coveted Piston Cup even include flocks of female cars forming a worshipful harem around him. But the film soon diminishes the appeal of this alpha model. Within a few moments of the race's conclusion, we see some of Lightning's less positive macho traits; his inability to name any friends, for example, reveals both his isolation and attempts at emotional stoicism. Lightning McQueen is hardly an unemotional character, as can be seen when he prematurely jumps onto the stage to accept what he assumes to be his victory. For this happy emotional outburst, however, he is immediately disciplined by a snide comment from Chick. From this point until much later in the film, the only emotions he displays are those of frustration and anger.

7   *Toy Story's* Buzz Lightyear and Sheriff Woody similarly base their worth on a masculine model of competition and power, desiring not only to be the "favourite toy" of their owner, Andy, but to possess the admiration of and authority over the other toys in the playroom. Woody is a natural leader, and his position represents both paternalistic care and patriarchal dominance. In an opening scene, he calls and conducts a "staff meeting" that highlights his unambiguously dominant position in the toy community. Encouraging the toys to pair up so that no one will be lost in the family's impending move, he commands: "A moving buddy. If you don't have one, GET ONE." Buzz's alpha identity comes from a more exalted source than social governance—namely, his belief that he is the one "space ranger" with the power and knowledge needed to save the galaxy; it seems merely natural, then, that the other toys would look up to him, admire his strength, and follow his orders. But as with Lightning McQueen, these depictions of masculine power are soon undercut. Buzz's mere presence exposes Woody's strength as fragile, artificial, even arbitrary, and his "friends," apparently having been drawn to his authority rather than his character, are fair-weather at best. Buzz's authority rings hollow from the very beginning, and his refusal to believe in his own "toyness" is at best silly and at

worst dangerous. Like Lightning, Buzz's and Woody's most commonly expressed emotions are anger and frustration, not sadness (Woody's, at having been "replaced") or fear (Buzz's, at having "crash-landed on a strange planet") or even wistful fondness (Woody's, at the loss of Slink's, Bo Peep's, and Rex's loyalty). Once again, the alpha-male position is depicted as fraudulent, precarious, lonely, and devoid of emotional depth.

8   An old-school superhero, Mr. Incredible opens *The Incredibles* by displaying the tremendous physical strength that enables him to stop speeding trains, crash through buildings, and keep the city safe from criminals. But he too suffers from the emotional isolation of the alpha male. Stopping on the way to his own wedding to interrupt a crime in progress, he is very nearly late to the service, showing up only to say the "I dos." Like his car and toy counterparts, he communicates primarily through verbal assertions of power—angrily dismissing Buddy, his meddlesome aspiring sidekick; bantering with Elastigirl over who gets the pickpocket—and limits to anger and frustration the emotions apparently available to men.

9   Fraught as it may seem, the alpha position is even more fleeting: in none of these Pixar films does the male protagonist's dominance last long. After Lightning ties, rather than wins, the race and ignores the King's friendly advice to find and trust a good team with which to work, he browbeats his faithful semi, Mack, and ends up lost in "hillbilly hell," a small town off the beaten path of the interstate. His uncontrolled physical might destroys the road, and the resultant legal responsibility—community service—keeps him far from his Piston Cup goals. When Buzz appears as a gift for Andy's birthday, he easily unseats Woody both as Andy's favourite and as the toy community's leader. When Buzz becomes broken, failing to save himself from the clutches of the evil neighbour, Sid, he too must learn a hard lesson about his limited power, his diminished status, and his own relative insignificance in the universe. Mr. Incredible is perhaps most obviously disempowered: despite his superheroic feats, Mr. Incredible has been unable to keep the city safe from his own clumsy brute force. After a series of lawsuits against "the Supers," who accidentally leave various types of small-time mayhem in their wake, they are

all driven underground, into a sort of witness protection program. To add insult to injury, Mr. Incredible's diminutive boss fires him from his job handling insurance claims, and his wife, the former Elastigirl, assumes the "pants" of the family.

10   Most of these events occur within the first few minutes of the characters' respective films. Only Buzz's downfall happens in the second half. The alpha-male model is thus not only present and challenged in the films but also is, in fact, the very structure on which the plots unfold. Each of these films is about being a man, and they begin with an outdated, two-dimensional alpha prototype to expose its failings and to ridicule its logical extensions: the devastation and humiliation of being defeated in competition, the wrath generated by power unchecked, the paralyzing alienation and fear inherent in being lonely at the top. As these characters begin the film in (or seeking) the tenuous alpha position among fellow characters, each of them is also stripped of this identity—dramatically emasculated—so that he may learn, reform, and emerge again with a different, and arguably more feminine, self-concept.

11   "Emasculated" is not too strong a term for what happens to these male protagonists; the decline of the alpha-male model is gender coded in all the films. For his community service punishment, Lightning is chained to the giant, snorting, tar-spitting "Bessie" and ordered to repair the damage he has wrought. His own "horsepower" (as Sally cheerfully points out) is used against him when literally put in the service of a nominally feminized figure valued for the more "feminine" orientation of service to the community. If being under the thumb of this humongous "woman" is not emasculating enough, Mater, who sees such subordination to Bessie as a potentially pleasurable thing, names the price, saying, "I'd give my left two lug nuts for something like that!"

12   Mr. Incredible's downfall is most clearly marked as gendered by his responses to it. As his wife's domestic power and enthusiasm grow increasingly unbearable, and his children's behaviour more and more out of his control, he surreptitiously turns to the mysterious, gorgeous "Mirage," who gives him what he needs to feel like a man: superhero work. Overtly depicting her as the "other woman," the film requires Elastigirl to intercept a suggestive-sounding phone call, and to

trap her husband in a lie, to be able to work toward healing his decimated masculinity.

13   In *Toy Story*, the emasculation of the alpha male is the most overt, and arguably the most comic. From the beginning, power is constructed in terms conspicuously gender coded, at least for adult viewers: as they watch the incoming birthday presents, the toys agonize at their sheer size, the longest and most phallic-shaped one striking true fear (and admiration?) into the hearts of the spectators. When Buzz threatens Woody, one toy explains to another that he has "laser envy." Buzz's moment of truth, after seeing himself on Sid's father's television, is the most clearly gendered of all. Realizing for the first time that Woody is right, he is a "toy," he defiantly attempts to fly anyway, landing sprawled on the floor with a broken arm. Sid's little sister promptly finds him, dresses him in a pink apron and hat, and installs him as "Mrs. Nesbit" at her tea party. When Woody tries to wrest him from his despair, Buzz wails, "Don't you get it? I AM MRS. NESBIT. But does the hat look good? Oh, tell me the hat looks good!" Woody's "rock bottom" moment finds him trapped under an overturned milk crate, forcing him to ask Buzz for help and to admit that he "doesn't stand a chance" against Buzz in the contest for Andy's affection, which constitutes "everything that is important to me." He is not figured into a woman, like Buzz is, or subordinated to a woman, like Lightning is, or forced to seek a woman's affirmation of his macho self, like Mr. Incredible is, but he does have to acknowledge his own feminine values, from his need for communal support to his deep, abiding (and, later, maternal) love of a boy. This "feminine" stamp is characteristic of the New Man model toward which these characters narratively journey.

Homosociality, Intimacy, and Emotion

14   Regarding the "love of a boy," the "mistress" tempting Mr. Incredible away from his wife and family is not Mirage at all but Buddy, the boy he jilted in the opening scenes of the film (whose last name, Pine, further conveys the unrequited nature of their relationship). Privileging his alpha-male emotional

isolation, but adored by his wannabe sidekick, Mr. Incredible vehemently protects his desire to "work alone." After spending the next years nursing his rejection and refining his arsenal, Buddy eventually retaliates against Mr. Incredible for rebuffing his advances. Such a model of homosocial tutelage as Buddy proposes at the beginning of the film certainly evokes an ancient (and homosexual) model of masculine identity; Mr. Incredible's rejection quickly and decisively replaces it with a heteronormative one, further supported by Elastigirl's marrying and Mirage's attracting the macho superhero.[5] But it is equally true that the recovery of Mr. Incredible's masculine identity happens primarily through his (albeit antagonistic) relationship with Buddy, suggesting that Eve Sedgwick's notion of a homosocial continuum is more appropriate to an analysis of the film's gender attitudes than speculations about its reactionary heteronormativity, even homophobia.

15   Same-sex (male) bonds—to temporarily avoid the more loaded term *desire*—are obviously important to each of these films. In fact, in all three, male/male relationships emerge that move the fallen alphas forward in their journeys toward a new masculinity. In each case, the male lead's first and/or primary intimacy—his most immediate transformative relationship—is with one or more male characters. Even before discovering Buddy as his nemesis, Mr. Incredible secretly pairs up with his old pal Frozone, and the two step out on their wives to continue superheroing on the sly; Buddy and Frozone are each, in their ways, more influential on Mr. Incredible's sense of self than his wife or children are. Although Lightning falls in love with Sally and her future vision of Radiator Springs, his almost accidentally having befriended the hapless, warm Mater catalyzes more foundational lessons about the responsibilities of friendship—demanding honesty, sensitivity, and care—than the smell-the-roses lesson Sally represents. He also ends up being mentored and taught a comparable lesson about caring for others by Doc Hudson, who even more explicitly encourages him to resist the alpha path of the Piston Cup world by relating his experiences of being used and then rejected. Woody and Buzz, as rivals-cum-allies, discover the necessary truths about their masculine strength only as they discover how much they need one another.

Sedgwick further describes the ways in which the homosocial bond is negotiated through a triangulation of desire; that is, the intimacy emerging "between men" is constructed through an overt and shared desire for a feminized object. Unlike homosocial relationships between women—that is, "the continuum between 'women loving women' and 'women promoting the interests of women'"—male homosocial identity is necessarily homophobic in patriarchal systems, which are structurally homophobic (3). This means the same-sex relationship demands social opportunities for a man to insist on, or prove, his heterosexuality. Citing Rene Girard's *Deceit, Desire, and the Novel*, Sedgwick argues that "in any erotic rivalry, the bond that links the two rivals is as intense and potent as the bond that links either of the rivals to the beloved" (21); women are ultimately symbolically exchangeable "for the primary purpose of cementing the bonds of men with men" (26).

16   This triangulation of male desire can be seen in *Cars* and *Toy Story* particularly, where the homosocial relationship rather obviously shares a desire for a feminized third. Buzz and Woody compete first, momentarily, for the affection of Bo Peep, who is surprisingly sexualized for a children's movie (purring to Woody an offer to "get someone else to watch the sheep tonight," then rapidly choosing Buzz as her "moving buddy" after his "flying" display). More importantly, they battle for the affection of Andy—a male child alternately depicted as maternal (it is his responsibility to get his baby sister out of her crib) and in need of male protection (Woody exhorts Buzz to "take care of Andy for me!").[6] *Cars* also features a sexualized romantic heroine; less coquettish than Bo Peep, Sally still fumbles over an invitation to spend the night "not with me, but . . ." in the motel she owns. One of Lightning and Mater's moments of "bonding" happens when Mater confronts Lightning, stating his affection for Sally and sharing a parallel story of heterosexual desire. The more principal objects of desire in *Cars*, however, are the (arguably) feminized "Piston Cup" and the Dinoco sponsorship. The sponsor itself is established in romantic terms: with Lightning stuck in Radiator Springs, his agent says Dinoco has had to "woo" Chick instead. Tia and Mia, Lightning's "biggest fans," who transfer their affection to Chick during his absence, offer viewers an even less subtly gendered goal, and Chick uses this to taunt Lightning. It is in the pursuit of these objects, and in competition with Chick and the King, that Lightning first defines himself as a man; the Piston Cup also becomes the object around which he and Doc discover their relationship to one another.

The New Man

17   With the strength afforded by these homosocial intimacies, the male characters triumph over their respective plots, demonstrating the desirable modifications that Pixar makes to the alpha-male model. To emerge victorious (and in one piece) over the tyrannical neighbour boy, Sid, Buzz and Woody have to cooperate not only with each other but also with the cannibalized toys lurking in the dark places of Sid's bedroom. Incidentally learning a valuable lesson about discrimination based on physical difference (the toys are not monsters at all, despite their frightening appearance), they begin to show sympathy, rather than violence born of their fear, to the victims of Sid's experimentation. They learn how to humble themselves to ask for help from the community. Until Woody's grand plan to escape Sid unfolds, Sid could be an object lesson in the unredeemed alpha-male type: cruelly almighty over the toy community, he wins at arcade games, bullies his sister, and, with strategically placed fireworks, exerts militaristic might over any toys he can find. Woody's newfound ability to give and receive care empowers him to teach Sid a lesson of caring and sharing that might be microcosmic to the movie as a whole. Sid, of course, screams (like a girl) when confronted with the evidence of his past cruelties, and when viewers last see him, his younger sister is chasing him up the stairs with her doll.

18   Even with the unceremonious exit of Sid, the adventure is not quite over for Buzz and Woody. Unable to catch up to the moving van as Sid's dog chases him, Woody achieves the pinnacle of the New Man narrative: armed with a new masculine identity, one that expresses feelings and acknowledges community as a site of power, Woody is able to sacrifice the competition with Buzz for his object of desire.

Letting go of the van strap, sacrificing himself (he thinks) to Sid's dog, he plainly expresses a caretaking, nurturing love, and a surrender to the good of the beloved: "Take care of Andy for me," he pleads. Buzz's own moment of truth comes from seizing his power as a toy: holding Woody, he glides into the family's car and back into Andy's care, correcting Woody by proudly repeating his earlier, critical words back to him: "This isn't flying; it's falling with style." Buzz has found the value of being a "toy," the self-fulfillment that comes from being owned and loved. "Being a toy is a lot better than being a space ranger," Woody explains. "You're *his toy*" (emphasis in original).

19   Mr. Incredible likewise must embrace his own dependence, both physical and emotional. Trapped on the island of Chronos, at the mercy of Syndrome (Buddy's new super-persona), Mr. Incredible needs women—his wife's superpowers and Mirage's guilty intervention—to escape. To overpower the monster Syndrome has unleashed on the city, and to achieve the pinnacle of the New Man model, he must also admit to his emotional dependence on his wife and children. Initially confining them to the safety of a bus, he confesses to Elastigirl that his need to fight the monster alone is not a typically alpha ("I work alone") sort of need but a loving one: "I can't lose you again," he tells her. The robot/monster is defeated, along with any vestiges of the alpha model, as the combined forces of the Incredible family locate a new model of post-feminist strength in the family as a whole. This communal strength is not simply physical but marked by cooperation, selflessness, and intelligence. The children learn that their best contributions protect the others; Mr. Incredible figures out the robot/monster's vulnerability and cleverly uses this against it.

20   In a parallel motif to Mr. Incredible's inability to control his strength, Buddy/Syndrome finally cannot control his robot/monster; in the defeat, he becomes the newly emasculated alpha male. But like his robot, he learns quickly. His last attempt to injure Mr. Incredible, kidnapping his baby Jack-Jack, strikes at Mr. Incredible's new source of strength and value, his family. The strength of the cooperative family unit is even more clearly displayed in this final rescue: for the shared, parental goal of saving Jack-Jack, Mr. Incredible uses his physical strength and, with her

consent, the shape-shifting body of his super-wife. He throws Elastigirl into the air, where she catches their baby and, flattening her body into a parachute, sails gently back to her husband and older children.

21   Through Lightning McQueen's many relationships with men, as well as his burgeoning romance with Sally, he also learns how to care about others, to focus on the well-being of the community, and to privilege nurture and kindness. It is Doc, not Sally, who explicitly challenges the race car with his selfishness ("When was the last time you cared about something except yourself, hot rod?"). His reformed behaviour begins with his generous contributions to the Radiator Springs community. Not only does he provide much-needed cash for the local economy, but he also listens to, praises, and values the residents for their unique offerings to Radiator Springs. He is the chosen auditor for Lizzy's reminiscing about her late husband, contrasting the comic relief typically offered by the senile and deaf Model T with poignancy, if not quite sadness. Repairing the town's neon, he creates a romantic dreamscape from the past, a setting for both courting Sally ("cruising") and, more importantly, winning her respect with his ability to share in her value system. For this role, he is even physically transformed: he hires the body shop proprietor, Ramone, to paint over his sponsors' stickers and his large race number, as if to remove himself almost completely from the Piston Cup world, even as he anticipates being released from his community service and thus being able to return to racing.

22   Perhaps even more than Buzz, Woody, and Mr. Incredible do, the New Man McQueen shuns the remaining trappings of the alpha role, actually refusing the Piston Cup. If the first three protagonists are ultimately qualified heroes—that is, they still retain their authority and accomplish their various tasks, but with new values and perspectives acquired along the way—Lightning completely and publicly refuses his former object of desire. Early in the final race, he seems to somewhat devalue racing; his daydreams of Sally distract him, tempting him to give up rather than to compete. The plot, however, needs him to dominate the race so his decision at the end will be entirely his own. His friends show up and encourage him to succeed. This is where the other films end: the

values of caring, sharing, nurturing, and community being clearly present, the hero is at last able to achieve, improved by having embraced those values. But Lightning, seeing the wrecked King and remembering the words of Doc Hudson, screeches to a stop inches before the finish line. Reversing, he approaches the King, pushes him back on the track, and acknowledges the relative insignificance of the Piston Cup in comparison to his new and improved self. He then declines the Dinoco corporate offer in favor of remaining faithful to his loyal Rust-eze sponsors. Chick Hicks, the only unredeemed alpha male at the end, celebrates his ill-gotten victory and is publicly rejected at the end by both his fans, "the twins," and, in a sense, by the Piston Cup itself, which slides onto the stage and hits him rudely in the side.

Conclusion

23   The trend of the New Man seems neither insidious nor nefarious, nor is it out of step with the larger cultural movement. It is good, we believe, for our son to be aware of the many sides of human existence, regardless of traditional gender stereotypes. However, maintaining a critical consciousness of the many lessons taught by the cultural monolith of Disney remains imperative. These lessons—their pedagogical aims or results—become most immediately obvious to us as parents when we watch our son ingest and express them, when he misunderstands and makes his own sense of them, and when we can see ways in which his perception of reality is shaped by them, before our eyes. Without assuming that the values of the films are inherently evil or representative of an evil "conspiracy to undermine American youth" (Giroux 4), we are still compelled to critically examine the texts on which our son bases many of his attitudes, behaviours, and preferences.

24   Moreover, the impact of Disney, as Henry Giroux has effectively argued, is tremendously more widespread than our household. Citing Michael Eisner's 1995 "Planetized Entertainment," Giroux claims that 200 million people a year watch Disney videos or films, and in a week, 395 million watch a Disney TV show, 3.8 million subscribe to the Disney Channel, and 810,000 make a purchase at a Disney store (19). As Benjamin Barber argued in 1995, "[T]he true tutors of our children are not schoolteachers or university professors but filmmakers, advertising executives and pop culture purveyors" (qtd. in Giroux 63). Thus we perform our "pedagogical intervention[s]" of examining Disney's power to "shap[e] national identity, gender roles, and childhood values" (Giroux 10). It remains a necessary and ongoing task, not just for concerned parents, but for all conscientious cultural critics.

Journal of Popular Film and Television. 2008. 36 (1).

Notes

1. See Susan Jeffords, "The Curse of Masculinity: Disney's *Beauty and the Beast*," for an excellent analysis of that plot's developing the cruel Beast into a man who can love and be loved in return: "Will he be able to overcome his beastly temper and terrorizing attitude in order to learn to love?" (168). But even in this film, she argues, the Beast's development is dependent on "other people, especially women," whose job it is to tutor him into the new model of masculinity, the "New Man" (169, 170).

2. Two articles demand that we qualify this claim. Indirectly, they support the point of this essay by demonstrating a midcentury Disney model of what we call "alpha" masculinity. David Payne's "Bambi" parallels that film's coming-of-age plot, ostensibly representing a "natural" world, with the military mindset of the 1940s against which the film was drawn. Similarly, Claudia Card, in "Pinocchio," claims that the Disneyfied version of the nineteenth-century Carlo Collodi tale replaces the original's model of bravery and honesty with "a macho exercise in heroism [. . . and] avoid[ing] humiliation" (66–67).

3. Outside the animated classics, critics have noted a trend toward a post-feminist masculinity—one characterized by emotional wellness, sensitivity to family, and a conscious rejection of the most alpha male values—in Disney-produced films of the 1980s and 1990s. Jeffords gives a sensible account of the changing male lead in films ranging from *Kindergarten Cop* to *Terminator 2*.

4. In Disney criticism, the phrase "New Man" seems to belong to Susan Jeffords's 1995 essay on *Beauty and the Beast*, but it is slowly coming into vogue for describing other post-feminist trends in masculine identity. In popular culture, see Richard Collier's "The New Man: Fact or Fad?" online in *Achilles Heel: The Radical Men's Magazine* 14 (Winter 1992/1993). www.achillesheel.freeuk.com/article14_9.html. For a literary-historical account, see *Writing Men: Literary Masculinities from Frankenstein to the*

New Man by Berthold Schoene-Harwood (Columbia UP, 2000).

5. Critics have described the superhero within some framework of queer theory since the 1950s, when Dr. Fredric Wertham's *Seduction of the Innocent* claimed that Batman and Robin were gay (Ameron Ltd, 1954). See Rob Lendrum's "Queering Super-Manhood: Superhero Masculinity, Camp, and Public Relations as a Textual Framework" (*International Journal of Comic Art* 7.1 [2005]: 287–303) and Valerie Palmer-Mehtan and Kellie Hay's "A Superhero for Gays? Gay Masculinity and Green Lantern" (*Journal of*

American Culture 28.4 [2005]: 390–404), among myriad nonscholarly pop-cultural sources.

6. Interestingly, Andy and *Toy Story* in general are apparently without (human) male role models. The only father present in the film at all is Sid's, sleeping in front of the television in the middle of the day. Andy's is absent at a dinner out, during a move, and on the following Christmas morning. Andy himself, at play, imagines splintering a nuclear family: when he makes Sheriff Woody catch One-Eyed Black Bart in a criminal act, he says, "Say goodbye to the wife and tater tots . . . you're going to jail."

Works Cited

Bell, Elizabeth. "Somatexts at the Disney Shop: Constructing the Pentimentos of Women's Animated Bodies." Bell, *From Mouse to Mermaid* 107–24.

Bell, Elizabeth, Lynda Haas, and Laura Sells, eds. *From Mouse to Mermaid: the Politics of Film, Gender, and Culture.* Bloomington: Indiana UP, 1995.

Card, Claudia. "Pinocchio." Bell, *From Mouse to Mermaid* 62–71.

Cars. Dir. John Lasseter. Walt Disney Pictures/Pixar Animation Studios, 2006.

Collier, Richard. "The New Man: Fact or Fad?" *Achilles Heel: The Radical Men's Magazine* 14 (1992–93). <www.achillesheel.freeuk.com/article14_9.html>.

Eisner, Michael. "Planetized Entertainment." *New Perspectives Quarterly* 12.4 (1995): 8.

Giroux, Henry. *The Mouse that Roared: Disney and the End of Innocence.* Oxford, Eng.: Rowman, 1999.

The Incredibles. Dir. Brad Bird. Walt Disney Pictures/Pixar Animation Studios, 2004.

Jeffords, Susan. "The Curse of Masculinity: Disney's *Beauty and the Beast.*" Bell, *From Mouse to Mermaid* 161–72.

Lendrum, Rob. "Queering Super-Manhood: Superhero Masculinity, Camp, and Public Relations as a Textual Framework." *International Journal of Comic Art* 7.1 (2005): 287–303.

Palmer-Mehtan, Valerie, and Kellie Hay. "A Superhero for Gays? Gay Masculinity and Green Lantern." *Journal of American Culture* 28.4 (2005): 390–404.

Payne, David. "Bambi." Bell, *From Mouse to Mermaid* 137–47.

Schoene-Harwood, Berthold. *Writing Men: Literary Masculinities from Frankenstein to the New Man.* Columbia: Columbia UP, 2000.

Sedgwick, Eve Kosofsky. *Between Men: English Literature and Male Homosocial Desire.* New York: Columbia UP, 1985.

Toy Story. Dir. John Lasseter. Walt Disney Pictures/Pixar Animation Studios, 1995.

Wertham, Fredric. *Seduction of the Innocent.* New York: Reinhart, 1954.

Yabroff, Jennie. "Betas Rule." *Newsweek* 4 June 2007: 64–65.

KEY AND CHALLENGING WORDS

nominal, retrograde, trope, trajectory, valorize, stoicism, paternalistic, precarious, diminutive, emasculate, gendered (adj.), decimate, arsenal, tutelage, coquettish, insidious, nefarious, pedagogical, purveyor

QUESTIONS

1. In the Introduction, identify a) the justification for the study; b) the thesis statement and the type of thesis (i.e., simple or expanded).

2. Scholarly studies in the humanities often utilize a theoretical perspective, interpreting primary sources in light of that perspective. Is it clear from the introduction that the authors will be using theory? What theorist will they be using and what is her discipline/field of study? (You may have to do some research to answer the second part

of the last question.)

3. In paragraph 5, the authors use a direct quotation from the magazine *Newsweek*. What purpose does it serve? Why might it be appropriate for the authors to use a variety of non-academic sources in this essay (see "Works Cited")?

4. In analyzing literature, students are often told to avoid simple plot summary. Why is plot summary necessary in this essay, and what are its main functions? Refer to specific passages in your answer.

5.   From their contexts, define in one or two sentences "homosocial continuum" (paragraph 14) and "triangulation of desire" (paragraphs 15 and 16).

6.   Name the three primary sources analyzed in the essay. Which one do the authors believe provides the best or strongest support for their claim about the new man? Why?

7.   As is typical in humanities essays, the authors synthesize primary sources to support their points. Analyze the use of synthesis in paragraph 9, 15, or 16 (these paragraphs use at least two primary sources).

8.   Analyze the rhetorical effectiveness of the Conclusion; in what way(s) does it broaden, expand on, or universalize the thesis?

POST-READING

1.   *Collaborative activity:* a) Discuss the concept of the "alpha male," finding examples from literature and history, or from your observation or knowledge of Western society; *OR* b) Discuss the concept of the "new man" as analyzed in the essay, finding other examples.

2.   *Collaborative or individual activity:* Consider the validity or truth of the following direct quotation, exploring its significance to our society: "'[T]he true tutors of our children are not school teachers or university professors but filmmakers, advertising executives and pop culture purveyors'" (paragraph 24).

ADDITIONAL LIBRARY READING

Wohlwend, Karen E. "Damsels in Discourse: Girls Consuming and Producing Identity Texts through Disney Princess Play. *Reading Research Quarterly* 44. 1 (2009): 57–83. Print.

Zarranz, Libe Garcia. "Diswomen Strike Back? The Evolution of Disney's Femmes in the 1990s." *Atenea* 27.2 (2007): 55–67. Print.

Sexuality and sexual health of Canadian adolescents: Yesterday, today, and tomorrow

Eleanor Maticka-Tyndale

(4,973 words)

Pre-reading

1.   Scan the title, abstract, headings, and subheadings to help determine the essay's content and organization. Why is organization so important in a review essay?

2.   Review essays usually synthesize many sources. What can you tell from the "References" pages about the kinds of sources used in the essay? Are there a large number? A wide variety of kinds of sources (e.g., not all scholarly articles)? Does the name of the essay's author appear among the references? Why might this be important?

Abstract

A profile of the sexual health and behaviours of contemporary Canadian adolescents is developed based on current research and compared to adolescents in the latter half of the twentieth century. While notable changes occurred in the sexual lives of youth between the late 1950s and the early 1990s, the patterns of behaviour established in the latter part of the twentieth century have continued into recent years. There is strong evidence that today's youth are experiencing better sexual health and taking more measures to protect their sexual health than prior generations of youth did. However, problems remain. Canadian teens and young adults continue to be challenged by STIs; many GLBTQ youth continue to face homonegativity and discrimination in their schools and communities; youth living in poverty, in rural areas, and aboriginal youth carry the greatest burdens of poor sexual health and are the most poorly served by sexuality education and sexual health care. Recommendations are made to strengthen both sexuality education and sexual health services to meet the needs of all Canadian youth.

Introduction

1   Those who rely on media reports to keep them up to date about the sexual health of Canadian adolescents may well have come to the conclusion that we live in particularly troubling times. Over the past few years we have been told that pregnancies are sought after with little thought of the long-term needs of a child (Gulli, 2008; Lunau, 2008); there is a widening repertoire of sexual acts such as masturbatory displays for others via webcams and oral sex "games" that are believed to have become part of what teenagers regularly do in their sexual lives (Stepp, 1999; Wilson, 2004); teens are easy victims for adult predators who have ready access to them, especially via the Internet (CBC News, 2008b); and dramatic increases in sexually transmitted infections are a growing threat to the sexual and reproductive health of our youth (Pearce, 2008). There is also a persistent interest in age of first intercourse among teens and the sense that this is happening much earlier than in the recent

past. In these and other such cases, we, the professionals and organizations who are the sources for the stories, are at times insufficiently careful in the way we present and explain our findings. When we turn to the actual research, we find that the impressions created by most of these claims arise from misunderstanding or misinformation reinforced by an underlying expectation that the news about adolescent sexuality and sexual health has to be bad. What the research evidence suggests is that although there remains room for improvement, the picture of the sexual health and well-being of today's Canadian teens is, in many ways, more positive than in previous generations. The picture is also far more complex and context laden than is often portrayed. This article reviews the evidence, considers the context, and suggests possible future directions for supporting the sexual health of youth in Canada.

Adolescent sexuality and sexual health: Yesterday and today

2   Comparing adolescents in the most recent 10 years to earlier generations we find that the major changes in what adolescents 'do' sexually occurred between the 1950s and late 1960s. There have been few changes in the patterns of teenage sexuality since the time when many of today's adults were teens (1970s), and many aspects of adolescent sexual health have improved since then. Using data for recent adolescents from the *National Longitudinal Survey of Children and Youth* (NLSCY) and for adolescents in earlier generations from the *National Population Health Survey* (NPHS) (Statistics Canada, 1998)—two national surveys using comparable research methodologies—and comparing these data to findings from various other large-scale studies conducted nationally or regionally (Boyce, 2004; Boyce, Doherty, Fortin, & MacKinnon, 2003; McCreary Centre Society, 2004; Rotermann, 2008; Saewyc, Taylor, Homma, & Ogilvie, 2008; Tonkin, Murphy, Lee, Saewyc, and the McCreary Centre Society, 2005), we find that since the 1970s the age of first sexual intercourse has remained relatively stable. For the large majority, first sexual intercourse occurs at

16 to 18 years of age. Also relatively consistent throughout this period has been that around 15–22 per cent have first intercourse before 16 years of age, with this percentage being lower for the most recent cohort than for earlier ones. Clearly, teens are not initiating sexual intercourse earlier, but rather slightly later than their parents' generation did.

3   What about claims of a more "casual" approach to sex, of oral sex becoming a common and early activity, and of teens engaging in virtual (or display) sex over the Internet? The best we can do in assessing the "casualness" of adolescent sexual encounters is to consider the number of partners they have. Comparing results from the *Canada Youth and AIDS Study* conducted in the late 1980s (King et al., 1988) to its sequel, the *Canadian Youth Sexual Health and HIV/AIDS Study* conducted after 2000 (Boyce et al., 2003) we find youth currently in-school reporting slightly fewer lifetime sexual intercourse partners in the more recent than in the earlier study. If we assume that more partners suggests more "casualness" about sex, these results suggest that we are seeing somewhat less "casualness" among current adolescents than we were 10–15 years ago.

4   With respect to oral sex, it is important to remember that over the last 30 to 40 years oral sex has become a normative aspect of the adult sexual script and this trend has been followed by youth. Studies conducted on adolescent populations in the United States and Canada during and since the 1970s consistently show that oral sex is about as common as sexual intercourse, is most typically initiated at about the same time as intercourse, but precedes first coital activity for 15–25 per cent of adolescents (for US see: DeLamater & MacCorquadale, 1979; Lindberg, Jones & Santelli, 2007; Newcomer & Udry, 1985; for Canada see: Boyce et al., 2003; Gillis, 2005; Herold & Way, 1985; Warren & King, 1994).

5   Something that is new with the most recent generations of teens is the role played by communications technologies such as cell phones and the Internet. Here we have very little research other than basic counts that confirm what we already know, i.e., that adolescents and young adults are using cell phones and the Internet to an increasing extent and more than those who are older. An entirely new language and culture of communication has developed for text messaging and chat rooms. In her doctoral research, Smylie (2008) found that younger teens, who had more limited access to transportation or lived in peri-urban or rural areas, relied heavily on cell phones to connect with each other and maintain relationships while older, more urban adolescents relied more on face-to-face contact. Levine (2002), in interviewing adolescents in the United States about their sexual experiences quoted one 13-year-old girl as saying that she prefers experimenting sexually on-line because face-to-face is too "gropey" whereas on-line there is more talk. With every new technology—the printing press, movie theatres, telephones, automobiles, drive-in-theatres—youth have found ways to incorporate the technology into their rituals of "connecting" and adults have expressed dismay over what the implications are for morality and safety. What we can conclude about the sexual behaviours of contemporary Canadian teens is that they are maintaining patterns established in the late 1960s and early 1970s.

Sexual health trends

Pregnancy and parenting

6   The majority of Canadian adolescents are taking responsibility for their own sexual health by accessing contraception, using condoms, and seeking out abortion when necessary far more than any previous Canadian generation (compare, for example, trend data reported in Maticka-Tyndale, McKay and Barrett, 2000, to that in more recent reports on youth, e.g., Boyce, 2004; Boyce et al., 2003; McKay, 2006; Saewyc et al., 2008). In preventing pregnancies and postponing parenthood, teens today benefit from changes that were just beginning to be realized in the 1970s and '80s such as legal access to contraception and abortion as well as more recent changes such as the availability of emergency contraception (Pancham & Dunn, 2007). Legal access does not, however, guarantee access to all. Rural and very young teens remain poorly served by sexual and reproductive health services (e.g., Langille, Flowerdew & Andreou, 2004; Shoveller et al., 2007) and access to abortion remains limited or

non-existent in some provinces and all territories. The continuing declines in pregnancy and birth rates (see McKay, 2006) speak not only to the greater availability of contraception and abortion today, but also to the ability of the vast majority of today's teens to take the necessary actions to prevent pregnancy and postpone parenthood.

Sexually transmitted infections

7   In comparison to pregnancy prevention, the picture for sexually transmitted infections (STI) is not as positive. Following a steady decline in reported rates for chlamydia among youth into the mid-1990s, rates rose steadily among 15- to 19- and 20- to 24-year olds from 1997–2004. Paradoxically this increase in teen chlamydia rates occurred concurrently with a decline in teenage pregnancy rates and an increase in teen condom use over the same time period (compare teen condom use data from repeated surveys conducted among British Columbia youth in 1992, 1998, and 2003 as reported in Saewyc et al., 2008). These trends seem inconsistent with the increase in reported rates of chlamydia among teens and raise the question of whether increasing rates necessarily reflect an increase in prevalence of infection. Rising rates would also occur with introduction of more sensitive testing methods and more frequent testing, both of which would detect more cases but would not necessarily indicate a rise in the percentage infected (McKay & Barrett, 2008). However, regardless of whether the prevalence of chlamydia among youth has or has not increased, the present levels of infection are still grounds for concern. Many STI carry long-term consequences for health and reproductive potential (MacDonald & Brunham, 1997; PHAC, 2007) and efforts to raise the low levels of chlamydia screening of all sexually active 15- to 24-year-old youth by physicians (Hardwick, McKay & Ashem, 2007; Moses & Elliott, 2002) are thus an important health promotion priority. Indeed, a range of STI (in particular, human papilloma virus, HPV, and herpes simplex virus, HSV, as well as chlamydia) are common in the teen population and require a sustained prevention effort from the education and health care systems.

Sexual abuse

8   While data on pregnancies and STI, and policies and programs designed to address them are within the domain of public health, sexual abuse, which is also a component of sexual health, is within the domain of the criminal justice system. Data on the actual prevalence of sexual abuse are not readily available, since only cases that are reported to the police are recorded and research suggests that this is a minority of cases. Several small-scale and regional studies conducted in Canada provide some insight into the extent of this threat to sexual health. Sexual harassment and unwanted sexual comments are experienced by the majority of female and gay adolescents of varying ages and this is the most prevalent form of sexual abuse (Berman, McKenna, Arnold, Taylor, & MacQuarrie, 2000; BC Ministry of Children and Family Development, 2002; Egale, 2008). As the severity of the sexual abuse increases, fewer adolescents are affected. However, various forms of unwanted sexual contact (being verbally, physically, or forcefully coerced into sex play or sexual intercourse) are reported by up to 35 per cent of adolescent women and approximately 15 per cent of adolescent men (Bagley, Bolitho, & Bertrand, 1997; Bagley, Wood & Young, 1994; Murray & Henjem, 1993; Newton-Taylor, DeWit, & Giiksman, 1998; Rhynard & Krebs, 1997; Saewyc et al., 2008). Women are consistently more likely to be victims of all forms of sexual abuse (from unwanted comments and harassment to forced sex) than are men, and reports of sexual abuse increase as teens get older. Multivariate analyses conducted on data collected from youth across British Columbia show that experiencing sexual abuse is a precursor for other threats to sexual health such as very early sexual intercourse (before age 14), experiencing or causing a pregnancy, and lower likelihood of using condoms (Saewyc, Magee & Pettingell, 2004; Saewyc et al., 2008). A persistent finding across all studies is that sexual harassment, coercion, and violence are perpetrated most often by someone known to the victim. This extends from classmates, co-workers, and neighbours, to friends and family members. Despite the "truism" that the danger most often originates within our circle of

acquaintances, media attention and public fear focus on the danger posed by strangers, often identifying them as sexual predators.

Internet concerns

9   As Internet chat rooms and social networking sites have become more popular among teens, fears have mounted about sexual predators who make contact with teens via the Internet and lure them into sexual liaisons. Parents are advised to monitor Internet use and teens are cautioned against providing personal information or arranging face-to-face meetings with those met on-line. Police and service providers tell us that, as with all forms of sexual violence or abuse, the majority of cases are not reported, but that the dangers abound. Researchers from the Crimes Against Children Research Center and Family Research Laboratory at the University of New Hampshire recently published the first study of online predators and victims (Wolak, Finkelhor, Mitchell, & Ybarra, 2008). Based on their research, they conclude that social networking, posting personal information, and engaging in conversations with 'strangers' over the Internet are not associated with any elevated danger for teenagers. While there are adults who solicit sex from adolescents via the Internet, this is rarely done surreptitiously such as by feigning friendship or pretending to be a teenager. Rather, adults and adolescents searching for partners (of any age) for sexual conversation or sex in virtual or real time tend to be open about their interest and age. Most adolescents do not report distress over these encounters and "click off" when they encounter such communications, especially from adults. Wolak and her colleagues found that teenagers who engaged in Internet communication with adults about sex or met these adults did not display naivety about the Internet or about these encounters. They were fully aware and willingly engaged in sexual liaisons in the virtual and/or the real world. Wolak et al.'s study suggests that with encounters initiated via the Internet, there is considerably less danger than we have assumed and adolescents are generally able to, and do, effectively protect themselves. These findings are less inflammatory than some police and media reports but are unlikely to dispel fears about safety surrounding Internet use by adolescents.

10   Concern over the safety of younger adolescents from older sexual predators, especially those encountered over the Internet, was voiced as a primary motivator for recent changes in age-of-consent laws in Canada (CBC News, 2008a). Bill C-22 , which received Royal assent on May 1, 2008, raised the age of consent from 14 to 16 years with a "close in age" (five or less years) exemption. Critics of the change have questioned its necessity and raised concerns about its consequences including the concern that it may discourage youth under 16 from seeking preventive or therapeutic health care (for discussion see Wong, 2007). What is criminalized in age-of-consent laws is consensual sex based on age categories. Under the law's premise of providing new protection for 14- and 15-year-olds, the age of their chosen partner is regulated. While 12- to 15-year-olds are considered capable of consenting to sexual intercourse, they are not considered capable of consenting to sexual intercourse with partners who are more than five years older than they are. Under the new law, adolescents and youth of 18 (or even 17), 19, 20, and 21 years (as well as older youth and adults) are charged as felons if they engage in consensual sex with partners who are 12, 13, 14, or 15 years respectively. Such a charge carries a lifelong designation as a sex offender, exclusion from various occupations, prohibition on travel to some countries (e.g., the United States), and community ostracization. The way the new law will be implemented and its implications for Canadian youth remain to be determined.

Sexual health inequities

11   The picture of adolescent sexual health, as indicated by pregnancies, STI, and sexual aggression or violence is not the same for all Canadian adolescents. The burden of poor sexual health is unevenly distributed across the adolescent population. Within Canada, teens who experience the poorest sexual health live in regions where families with particularly low incomes and tenuous connections to the labour force are concentrated (Hardwick & Patychuk, 1999; Langille et al., 2004), in more isolated and rural areas (Shoveller et al., 2007), and in provinces

and territories with greater concentrations of rural and aboriginal populations (Canadian Federation for Sexual Health, 2007). In these regions, geographical, social, and economic forces interact to create environments that increase the likelihood that youth will become sexually active early in their teens, will experience early pregnancies, will be victims of sexual abuse, and will be more susceptible to STI. Social and health policies, programs, and services are critical to improving the sexual health and well-being of youth living in these circumstances.

12   Another group of adolescents whose sexual health is particularly threatened is teens who are gay, lesbian, bisexual, transgender, or questioning (GLBTQ). Because of the heterosexist bias and homonegativity that permeate our social institutions and even the personal thinking of many Canadians, GLBTQ teens often struggle in isolation to make sense of their feelings and experiences and to develop a sexual identity in relation to their other identities (e.g., ethnic, familial, religious). Research in the United States has consistently shown that when youth are identified as GLBTQ they run the risk of psychological and physical assault and rejection by fellow students, co-workers, and even teachers, "friends" and family (Savin-Williams, 1999). Although Canadians are considered more accepting of diversity in sexual orientation and more supportive of equal rights than are Americans (Alderson, 2002), research has consistently demonstrated that GLBTQ students face psychological and physical harassment and violence in their schools precisely because they are GLBTQ (Bortolin, Adam, Brooke, & McCauley, unpublished; Bortolin, 2008; Egale, 2008; Saewyc et al., 2006; Sims, 2000; Youthquest, 2002). Preliminary findings from 1,200 respondents drawn from all provinces, territories, and sexual orientations to an on-line survey about school climate launched in December 2007 by Egale together with University of Winnipeg faculty (www.climate survey.ca) show that sexual minority youth are far less likely to feel safe in their schools and are far more likely to have been verbally and physically harassed, or to have skipped school for safety reasons than majority youth (www.egale.ca/extra/1393-Homo phobiaBackgrounder.pdf). The consequences of the sexual violence perpetrated on GLBTQ youth include higher school drop-out rates (Saewyc et al., 2006) as

well as higher rates of depression and other forms of psychological distress, substance use, and suicide than experienced by "straight" youth (Savin-Williams 1999). Homonegativity and heterosexism also pose barriers to access to social and health services. In both American and Canadian studies, GLBTQ youth report high levels of distrust of health and social service providers and feel they need to hide their identities to ensure better quality care (Barbara, Quandt, & Anderson, 2001; Travers & Schneider, 1996). Clearly, despite legal advances for gay and lesbian adults, GLBTQ adolescents continue to face serious impediments to their sexual health primarily as a result of the homonegativity and homophobia that continue to permeate many Canadian institutions.

Changing contexts

13   The changed biological and social contexts within which today's adolescents experience their sexuality present new challenges for their sexual and reproductive health. Teens today are looking towards more years as sexually mature singles than did previous generations. The age of sexual maturation has continued to dip below the teenage years while the median age of first marriage and childbearing remains at 29–34 years (Statistics Canada, 2006), leaving the majority of Canadian youth with many years from sexual maturation to first marriage. If the trend toward delayed childbearing continues, many of today's adolescents will be trying to become pregnant during years when the fertility of women is naturally declining. Given the negative impact of STI on sexual and reproductive health of both men and women, couples are more likely to face difficulties in becoming pregnant or maintaining a pregnancy (MacDonald & Brunham, 1997; PHAC, 2007). Increasing numbers are likely to seek fertility assistance or adoption, while others will not have children.

14   Relationship and family forms are also undergoing profound changes. With each succeeding census (Statistics Canada, 2006), there are increasing numbers of Canadians living in relationships and family forms other than the traditional form of two parents with biological children. Increasing numbers of today's adolescents are likely to find themselves living in such situations as common-law couples, gay

and lesbian marriages and families, singles, childless couples, divorced parents, blended families, and long-distance or geographically separated families. What do we know about the implications of these diverse forms of family and relationship for sexual health and well-being? Research, public health programs, sexual health education, and popular discourse have focused considerable attention on sexuality and sexual health during the adolescent years, most often with a focus on the burden of STI and their sequelae and the issues of unintended pregnancy and early parenthood faced by some teens. Less attention has been paid to the pervasive discrimination and threats faced by adolescents who are gay, lesbian, questioning, or transgender (Egale, 2008), to the effects of legislation on the sexual well-being of adolescents, or to the challenges accompanying the changing social fabric of Canada. Yet, it is long-term changes in the social fabric that are likely to have the most profound effects on adolescent sexual health and well-being in the future.

Facing the challenges

15   A central challenge for policy makers and programmers is deciding how to promote and develop educational and health services and environments that enhance sexual health and well-being for all Canadian adolescents not only today, but throughout their lives. We are strongly influenced when setting policy and programs by the discourse of risky, irresponsible youth and sexual danger that permeates both media and public policy, much of it imported from our close neighbour, the United States (US). Our media report events, evidence, and the ideological discourse from the US as if they were our own. This is so despite the distinct differences between Canada and the US in terms of demography, attitudes toward adolescent sexuality, adolescent sexual health outcomes (e.g., teen pregnancy and STI rates), and provision of sexuality education and health care. Perhaps more importantly, if we wish to set a course to improve adolescent sexual health and well-being we should look to countries with strong records of sexual health among their adolescents. For such examples, we are best to turn to western Europe (Singh & Darroch, 2001).

16   International cross-country comparative studies of developed countries conducted under the direction of the Alan Guttmacher Institute (Darroch, Frost, Singh & The Study Team, 2001) and by Advocates for Youth (2000) identified some of the environmental contributors to better sexual health among adolescents. Sex education and sexual health services for adolescents in North America are influenced by a pervasive concern about when, and in what type of relationship, it is desirable for youth to become sexually active. In the United States this is evidenced in a focus on promoting abstinence-until-marriage in sex education programs, as well as on the reduction of sexual health services available to adolescents, and increased requirements of parental notification and approval to receive services or participate in education programs. Even the more "comprehensive" sexuality education programs have been increasingly labelled as "abstinence-plus" programs. This contrasts with sex education programs in western European countries which are more often based on the assumption, and acceptance, that adolescents and young adults will engage in sexual activity prior to marriage or without it. Programs are founded on and teach values of responsibility, integrity, respect for self and others, together with techniques that contribute to safety and pleasure (Advocates for Youth, 2000; Darroch et al., 2001; Levine, 2002; Schalet, 2004). Freely available health care, accessible to adolescents without requiring parental approval, accompanies quality sex education in most western European countries. Contrary to concerns voiced by some in Canada (and more generally in the United States) that such permissiveness and openness to adolescent sexual activity will lead to earlier sexual activity and elevate the dangers to sexual health, the timing and forms of sexual activity among western European adolescents and young adults closely parallel those in Canada and indicators of sexual health point to better sexual health for western European youth (Darroch et al., 2001; Singh & Darroch, 2001). The example of western Europe, together with evaluations of sex education programs delivered in diverse countries, is clear. The focus on abstinence that permeates sex education and the shift toward greater external regulation and control of the sexual lives and activities of adolescents evidenced in the United States do not contribute to an

environment conducive to sexual health (Bruckner & Bearman, 2005; Darroch et al., 2001). Instead, the approach that Canada has already begun to take in the development of the *Canadian Guidelines for Sexual Health Education* (Health Canada, 1994, 2003) and in setting a framework for improving sexual and reproductive health (Health Canada, 2002) offers a far more promising direction.

17   There are, however, gaps to be filled and improvements to be made. With respect to professional education, a national study of sexual health-related residency training of physicians (Barrett & McKay, 1998) found considerable variability between programs with a sizeable degree of under-coverage of key field-specific topics. McKay and Barrett (1999) found decided limitations in the extent and content of sexual health pre-service training of teachers which they described as a missed opportunity to prepare educators to deliver sexuality education early in their training (thus placing greater pressure on in-service training thereafter). Canadian physicians do the sexual health assessments and routine chlamydia screening of all sexually active 15- to 24-year-old female patients

18   (Hardwick et al., 2007; Moses & Elliott, 2002) at a frequency considerably below that recommended by the *Canadian Guidelines on Sexually Transmitted Infections* (Public Health Agency of Canada, 2006). Although the reasons for the low screening rates are complex, Hardwick et al. (2007) suggest a number of interventions to increase testing frequency given the time pressures of busy practices. A first essential step to filling the gaps in these and other areas of sexual health training and service is to prioritize the kind of training that will best prepare teachers to deliver broadly-based sexual health education and physicians to counsel and provide sexual health preventive, diagnostic, and treatment services to all Canadians. Broadly-based sexual health education as conceptualized in the *Canadian Guidelines for Sexual Health Education* (2003) that is accessible to all students in all schools is a must.

19   While we may well look to western Europe for examples of approaches that produce an environment conducive to sexual health and well-being among adolescents, Canadians must also consider several unique circumstances in Canada which are unlike those found in western European countries.

Distinct subgroups of Canadian adolescents carry the very highest burden of poor sexual health. These include, first and foremost, aboriginal youth (Canadian Federation for Sexual Health, 2007; Devries, Free, Morison, & Saewyc, 2007) and also poor and rural youth (Hardwick & Patychuk, 1999; Langille et al., 2004; Shoveller et al., 2007). Broadly-based sexual health education and provision of better sexual health services suited to the environments in which these youth live are essential. But they are only a first step in relieving this burden. Policy and program initiatives that address the poverty, isolation, and lack of future opportunity are also necessary to improve sexual health and prepare these adolescents for the challenges of the future.

20   Canada also has a unique multicultural profile. We are second only to Australia in receiving immigrants, with increasing numbers of new Canadians coming from regions of the globe where sexuality is grounded in different social and cultural roots than those that dominate in Canada. These new immigrants and their children face unique challenges in adapting to the "sexual scene" they experience in Canada (e.g., Shirpak, Maticka-Tyndale & Chinichian, 2007) and to accessing sexual health care (e.g., Maticka-Tyndale, Shirpak, & Chinichian; 2007). Our official policy of multiculturalism provides an ideological guide for development of policies and programs that respect the integrity and address the needs of diverse cultural groups. Unfortunately, our ability and commitment to working out ideological disagreements about the delivery of sexuality education and sexual health services has considerable room for improvement. All too often we respond to disagreements by allowing parents to restrict their children's access to education and services. This reinforces divisions between groups and detracts from the weaving of a cohesive social fabric by creating two classes of adolescents (and future adults): those who have had education and access to care and those who did not. Canada needs to lead the way in developing models of sexuality education and health care that respect and weave together diversities and differences whether they are differences in ethnicity, attitudes toward sexual orientation, or religion.

21   The sexual health and well-being of Canadian adolescents has fared relatively well compared to earlier

generations. Challenges remain, including unwanted pregnancies; the sequelae of STI; psychological and physical violence perpetrated against primarily women and GLBTQ teens; changing social, sexual and relationship structures; inequities in health and well-being based on geographical region, economic status, and sexual orientation; and ideological differences that restrict the access of some adolescents to the education and services they deserve. These are the realities that should stir news commentators and motivate public policy, educational programming, and improvements in health care services. Much can be learned by looking to the examples set by countries in Western Europe where the sexual health of adolescents is better than in Canada (see Maticka-Tyndale, 2001). However, there are also situations unique to Canada where we need to find our own solutions.

The Canadian Journal of Human Sexuality.
2008. 17 (3).

References

Advocates for Youth. (2000). *Adolescent Sexual Health in Europe and the US - Why the difference?* 2nd ed. Washington, DC: Advocates for Youth.

Alderson, K. (2002). Reflecting on shattered glass: Some thoughts about gay youth in schools. *The Alberta Counsellor, 27,* 3–11.

Bagley, C, Bolitho, F., & Bertrand, I. (1997). Sexual assault in school, mental health and suicidal behaviors in adolescent women in Canada. *Adolescence, 32,* 341–366.

Bagley, C, Wood, M., & Young, I. (1994). Victim to abuser: Mental health and behavioral sequels of child sexual abuse in a community survey of young adult males. *Child Abuse and Neglect, 18,* 683–97.

Barbara, A.M., Quandt, S.A., & Anderson, R.T. (2001). Experiences of lesbians in the health care environment. *Women and Health, 14,* 45–61.

Barrett, M., & McKay, A. (1998). Training in sexual health and STD prevention in Canadian medical schools. *The Canadian Journal of Human Sexuality, 7,* 305–320.

Berman, H., McKenna, K., Arnold, C, Taylor, G., & MacQuarrie, B. (2000) Sexual harassment: Everyday violence in the lives of girls and women. *Advances in Nursing Science, 22,* 32–46.

British Columbia Ministry of Children and Family Development. (2002). *The health and well-being of Aboriginal children and youth in British Columbia.* Vancouver, BC: BC Ministry of Children and Family Development.

Bortolin, S., Adam, B.D., Brooke, C, & McCauley, J. (unpublished ms) Gay, lesbian and bisexual youth's experiences of school climate. University of Windsor.

Bortolin, S. (2008). Exploring the interplay of masculinities and homophobia in the high school climate. MA thesis. University of Windsor.

Boyce, W. (2004). *Young People in Canada, Their Health and Well-Being.* Ottawa, ON: Health Canada.

Boyce, W, Doherty, M., Fortin, C, & MacKinnon, D. (2003). *Canadian Youth, Sexual Health and HIV/AIDS Study: Factors influencing knowledge, attitudes and behaviours.* Toronto, ON: Council of Ministers of Education, Canada.

Bruckner, H., & Bearman, P. (2005). After the promise: The STD consequences of adolescent virginity pledges. *Journal of Adolescent Health, 36,* 271–278.

Canadian Federation for Sexual Health. (2007). *Sexual Health in Canada: Baseline 2007.* Ottawa, ON: Canadian Federation for Sexual Health.

CBC News. (April 29, 2008b). Internet predator stalking Surrey teens: RCMP. Retrieved June 20, 2008, from www.cbc.ca/canada/british-columbia/story/2008/04/29/bc-sun-ey-predator.html.

CBC News. (May 1, 2008a). Canada's age of consent raised by 2 years. Retrieved May 15, 2008, from www.cbc.ca/canada/story/2008/05/01/crime-bill.html.

Darroch, J.R., Frost, J.J., Singh, S., & The Study Team. (2001). *Teenage Sexual and Reproductive Behavior in Developed Countries: Can more progress be made.* Occasional Report No. 3. New York, NY: Alan Guttmacher Institute.

DeLamater, J., & MacCorquodale, P. (1979). *Premarital Sexuality.* Madison, WI.: University of Wisconsin Press.

Devries, K.M., Free, C.J., Morison, L. & Saewyc, E. (2007) Factors associated with the sexual behavior of Canadian aboriginal young people and their implications for health promotion. *AJPH,*

Dryburgh, H. (2000). Teenage pregnancy. *Health Reports,* 72(1), Statistics Canada, Catalogue 82-003.

Equality for Gays and Lesbians Everywhere Canada (EGALE). (2007). *The First National School Climate Survey on Homophobia in Canadian Schools* in conjunction with the University of Winnipeg. Retrieved January 12, 2008, from www.climatesurvey.ca.

Equality for Gays and Lesbians Everywhere Canada (EGALE). (2008). *Preliminary Results of the First National School Climate Survey.* Retrieved June 15, 2008, from www.egale.ca/extra/1393-Homophobia-Backgrounder.pdf.

Gay, Lesbian and Straight Education Network (GLSEN). (2005). *The 2005 National School Climate Survey: The experiences of lesbian, gay, bisexual and transgender youth in our nation's school* (2005). New York, NY: GLSEN National.

Gillis, R. (2005) Examining the *National Longitudinal Survey of Children and Youth:* A profile of Canadian adolescent sexuality. MA thesis. Windsor, ON: University of Windsor.

Gulli, C. (2008). Suddenly teen pregnancy is cool? For the first time in years, more kids are having kids—and not just in the movies. *Maclean's,* 17 January 2008.

Hardwick, D., McKay, A., & Ashem, M. (2007) Chlamydia screening of adolescent and young adult women by general practice physicians in Toronto, Canada: Baseline survey data from a physician education campaign. *The Canadian Journal of Human Sexuality, 16,* 63–76.

Hardwick, D., & Patychuk, D. (1999). Geographic mapping demonstrates the association between social inequality, teen births and STDs among youth. *The Canadian Journal of Human Sexuality. 8*, 77–90.

Health Canada. (1994). *Canadian Guidelines for Sexual Health Education.* First edition. Ottawa, ON: Minister of National Health and Welfare. Division of STD Control, Health Protection Branch and Health Services Systems Division, Health Programs and Services Branch, Health Canada.

Health Canada. (2003). *Canadian Guidelines for Sexual Health Education.* (Second edition). Ottawa, ON: Minister of Health. Community Acquired Infections Division, Population and Public Health Branch, Health Canada.

Health Canada. (1999). *A Report from Consultations on a Framework for Sexual and Reproductive Health.* Ottawa, Government of Canada. Health Canada. (2002). Reported *genital chlamydia/gonnorhea cases and rates in Canada by age group and sex.* Division of Sexual Health Promotion and STD Prevention and Control, Bureau of HIV/AIDS, STD and TB. Ottawa, Government of Canada, www.hc-sc.gc.ca/pphb-dgspsp.

Herold, E., & Way, L. (1985). Oral–genital sexual behavior in a sample of university females. *The Journal of Sex Research. 19*, 327–338.

King, A.J.C., Beazley, R.P, Warren, W.K., Hankins, CA., Robertson, A.S., & Radford, J.L. (1988). *Canada Youth and AIDS Study.* Ottawa, ON: Health and Welfare Canada.

Langille, D., Flowerdew, G, & Andreou, P (2004). Teenage pregnancy in Nova Scotia communities: Association with contextual factors. *The Canadian Journal of Human Sexuality, 13*, 83–94.

Lindberg, L.D., Jones, R., & Santelli, J.S. (2007). Noncoital sexual activities among adolescents. *Journal of Adolescent Health, 42*, S44–S45.

Levine, J. (2002). *Harmful to Minors.* Madison, WI: University of Wisconsin Press.

Lunau, K. (2008). Babies are the new handbag. *Maclean's.* January 17, 2008.

MacDonald, N.E., & Brunham, R. (1997). The effects of undetected and untreated sexually transmitted diseases: Pelvic inflammatory disease and ectopic pregnancy in Canada. *The Canadian Journal of Human Sexuality, 6*, 161–170.

Maticka-Tyndale, E. (2001). Sexual health and Canadian youth: How do we measure up? *The Canadian Journal of Human Sexuality, 10*, 1–17.

Maticka-Tyndale, E., Barrett, M., & McKay, A. (2000). Adolescent sexual and reproductive health in Canada: A review of national data sources and their limitations. *The Canadian Journal of Human Sexuality, 9*, 41–65.

Maticka-Tyndale, E., McKay, A., & Barrett, M. (2001). *Teenage Sexual and Reproductive Behavior in Developed Countries: Country Report for Canada.* Occasional Report No. 4. New York, NY: Alan Guttmacher Institute.

Maticka-Tyndale, E., Shirpak, K.R., & Chinichian, M. (2007). Providing for the sexual health needs of Canadian immigrants: The experience of immigrants from Iran. *Canadian Journal of Public Health. 98*, 183–186.

McCreary Centre Society. (2004). *Healthy Youth Development: Highlights from the 2003 Adolescent Health Survey III.* Vancouver, BC: McCreary Centre Society.

McKay, A. (2006). Trends in teen pregnancy in Canada with comparisons to USA. and England/Wales. *The Canadian Journal of Human Sexuality, 15*,157–161.

McKay, A., & Barrett, M. (2008). Rising reported rates of chlamydia among young women in Canada: What do they tell us about trends in the actual prevalence of the infection? *The Canadian Journal of Human Sexuality, 17*, 61–69.

McKay, A., & Barrett, M. (1999). Pre-service sexual health education training of elementary, secondary, and physical education teachers in Canadian faculties of education. *The Canadian Journal of Human Sexuality, 8*, 91–101.

Moses, S., & Elliott, L. (2002). Sexually transmitted diseases in Manitoba: Evaluation of physician treatment practices, STD drug utilization, and compliance with screening and treatment guidelines. *Sexually Transmitted Diseases, 29*, 840–846.

Murray, J., & Henjum, R. (1993). Analysis of sexual abuse in dating. *Guidance & Counseling, 8*, 181–202.

National Longitudinal Survey of Children and Youth (NLSCY); Human Resources Development Canada and Statistics Canada, www.statcan.ca/english/sdds/4450.htm.

Newcomer, S.Q, & Udry, R.J. (1985). Oral sex in an adolescent population. *Archives of Sexual Behavior, 14*, 41–46.

Newton-Taylor, B., DeWit, D., & Giiksman, I. (1998). Prevalence and factors associated with physical and sexual assault of female university students in Ontario. *Health Care for Women International, 19*, 155–165.

Pancham, A., & Dunn, S. (2007). Emergency contraception in Canada: An overview and recent developments. *The Canadian Journal of Human Sexuality, 16*,129–133.

Pearce, T. (2008). Chlamydia in teens jumps 50%. *Globe and Mail.* February 13, 2008.

Public Health Agency of Canada. (2007). *Supplement: 2004 Canadian Sexually Transmitted Infections Surveillance Report.* CCDR 2007, 33S1, 1–69.

Public Health Agency of Canada (PHAC). (2006) *Canadian Guidelines on Sexually Transmitted Infections.* Ottawa, ON: Public Health Agency of Canada.

Rhynard, J., & Krebs, M. (1997). Sexual assault in dating relationships. *Journal of School Health, 67*, 89–93.

Rotermann, M. (2008) Trends in teen sexual behaviour and condom use. *Health Reports, 19(3).* Statistics Canada, Catalogue no. 82-003-XPE.

Saewyc, E.M., Magee, L.L., & Pettingell, S.E. (2004). Teenage pregnancy and associated risk behaviors among sexually abused adolescents. *Perspectives on Sexual and Reproductive Health, 36*, 98–105.

Saewyc, E.M., Skay, C.L., Pettingell, S.L., Reis, E.A., Bearinger, L., Resnick, M., Murphy, A., & Combs, L. (2006). Hazards of stigma: The sexual and physical abuse of gay, lesbian, and bisexual adolescents in the United States and Canada. *Child Welfare, 85*,195–213.

Saewyc, E., Taylor, D., Homma, Y, & Ogilvie, G (2008). Trends in sexual health and risk behaviours among adolescent students in British Columbia. *The Canadian Journal of Human Sexuality, 17*, 1–13.

Savin-Williams, R.C. (1999). Matthew Shepard's death: A professional awakening. *Applied Developmental Science, 3*, 150–154.

Schalet, A. (2004). Must we fear adolescent sexuality? *Medscape General Medicine, 6.* 22 pages. Retrieved March 3, 2006, from www.medscape.com/viewarticle/494933_print.

Shirpak, K.R., Maticka-Tyndale, E., & Chinichian, M. (2007). Iranian immigrants' perceptions of sexuality in Canada:

A symbolic interactionist approach. *The Canadian Journal of Human Sexuality, 16,* 113–128.

Shoveller, J., Johnson, J., Prkachin, M., & Patrick, D. (2007). "Around here, they roll up the sidewalks at Night": A qualitative study of youth living in a rural Canadian community. *Health and Place, 13,* 826–838.

Shoveller, J., Johnson, J., Langille, D.B., & Mitchell, T. (2004). Socio-cultural influences on young people's sexual development. *Social Science and Medicine, 59,* 473–487.

Warren, W.K., & King, A.S. (1994). Development and evaluation of an AIDS/STD/sexuality program for grade 9 students. Kingston, Ontario. Social Programs Evaluation Unit, Queen's University.

Wilson, S. (2004). Good girls do. *Globe and Mail.* 1 February 2004.

Wolak, J., Finkelhor, D., Mitchell, K.J., & Ybarra, M. (2008). Online "predators" and their victims. *American Psychologist, 63,* 111–128.

Youthquest. (2002). Youthquest! Low-cost, high impact: Programs for lesbian, gay, bisexual and transgender youth. *Youthquest! 2002 Strategic Services Plan.* Retrieved from www.youthquest.bc.ca/servplan2002/needassessment.htm#ftnref2.

Sims, M.W. (2000). Gay/straight alliance clubs—understanding our differences. Retrieved from sss.bchrs.gov.bc.ca/PressRelease2000.asp.

Singh, S., & Darroch, J. (2001). Adolescent pregnancy and childbearing: Levels and trends in the developed countries. *Family Planning Perspectives, 32,* 14–23.

Smylie, L. (2008). The influence of social capital on the timing of first sexual intercourse among Canadian youth. Doctoral dissertation. University of Windsor.

Statistics Canada. (1998). *National Population Health Survey (NPHS),* 1996-1997. Ottawa, Canada.

Statistics Canada. (2006). Family portrait: Continuity and change in Canadian families and households in 2006: Highlights. Retrieved June 20, 2008, from www12.statcan.ca/english/census06/analysis/famhouse/highlights.cfm.

Stepp, L.S. (July 8,1999). Unsettling new fad alarms parents: Middle school oral sex. *Washington Post.* July 8,1999.

Tonkin, R.S., Murphy, A., Lee, Z., Saewyc, E., and The McCreary Centre Society. (2005). *British Columbia Youth Health Trends: A Retrospective, 1992–2003.* Vancouver, BC; McCreary Centre Society.

Travers, R., & Schneider, M. (1996). Barriers to accessibility for lesbian and gay youth needing addictions services. *Youth & Society, 27,* 356–378.

KEY AND CHALLENGING WORDS

coercion, precursor, surreptitious, feign, inflammatory, consensual, homonegativity, permeate, sequela, pervasive

QUESTIONS

1. Consult the "References" list for the works referenced in paragraph 1. Which titles seem to most clearly support the author's point about media "misunderstanding or misinformation" (paragraph 1)? Does she solely blame the media for misleading stories?

2. What specific bases of comparison does Maticka-Tyndale use for comparing this generation's sexuality and sexual health to that of previous generations?

3. Does the author seem to feel that the role played by new technologies in sexuality represents a threat to adolescent safety or morality? Why or why not?

4. Using one of the first three subheadings in the section "Sexual health trends," analyze in one paragraph the subsection, showing how Maticka-Tyndale's presentation of the information assists with clarity and coherence; if appropriate, you could consider what she could have done to improve ease of reading.

5. Why does the author devote so much space to Wolak et al. in the subsection "Internet concerns"? Why might these findings be significant?

6. Does the author appear to have concerns about Bill C-22? What can be inferred about her opinion of the bill? In your answer, refer to specific features (such as language) of the paragraph.

7. In the subsection "Sexual health inequities," a) summarize paragraph 11; b) in paragraph 12, explain why the author has put "friends" and "straight" in quotation marks; c) paraphrase the last sentence of paragraph 12.

8. How do the sex education and sexual health education objectives and services differ in the US as compared to many Western European nations? According to the author, how has the media affected policy making in Canada in the past and how is it likely to affect policies in the future?

9. What specific challenges to adolescent sexual health confront Canadian policy makers as distinct from those of other nations? How can these challenges be overcome?

POST-READING

1. "Abstinence-plus" programs, prominent in the US, are mentioned in paragraph 16. Using a reliable source, such as a scholarly review article, newspaper/magazine article, or health-related website, define "abstinence-plus" education and summarize the effectiveness of such programs, according to researchers or other experts.

2. *Collaborative activity:* Discuss or debate approaches to health/sex education received in high school (of course, this could differ considerably among high schools). Consider such factors as resources available, access to resources, health/sex education classes or classes that include a health-sex education component, teaching methods, and attitude toward health/sex education. What is the need or value of such classes? How could they be improved?

3. Identify central issues or problems in sexual health education today in Canadian high schools and suggest ways they could be addressed. This could take the form of an informal report in which you begin with an introduction that states the problem; follow with paragraphs that summarize the most relevant information, such as the findings of studies and/or current statistics; and conclude with a list of recommendations. Include references to "Sexuality and sexual health of Canadian adolescents: Yesterday, today and tomorrow" in your report; if your instructor permits, you may use additional sources.

RELATED WEBSITE OF INTEREST

Canadian Guidelines for Sexual Health Education (2008): www.phac-aspc.gc.ca/ publicat/cgshe-ldnemss/pdf/ guidelines-eng.pdf

Moral panic and the Nasty Girl

Christie Barron and Dany Lacombe

(7,494 words)

Pre-reading

1. Scan the essay and subject the first two paragraphs to a focused reading in order to determine what type of essay Barron and LaCombe have written (i.e., Type A, B, or C).

Abstract

We examine why, despite evidence to the contrary, recent incidents of female violence have been interpreted as a sign that today's girls are increasingly nasty. We argue that the Nasty Girl phenomenon is the product of a moral panic. We show that while girl violence always existed, today's discussion is dominated by the concept of risk. Reform initiatives resulting from the panic consist of disciplinary mechanisms acting on the body of the individual delinquent and techniques that regulate individuals through the fostering of a culture of risk management and security consciousness. Finally, we situate the panic in the current backlash against feminism.

*

1   Female violence became a topic of much discussion in the mid-1990s in the wake of the gruesome sexual murders of teenagers by the infamous Ontario couple Paul Bernardo and Karla Homolka. But it was the murder of Reena Virk by a group of mostly female teens, in a suburb of Victoria in November 1997, that led Canadians to believe that something had gone terribly wrong with teenage girls. The belief that girl violence is rampant is a social construction. According to Statistics Canada, the annual youth charge rate for violent crime dropped 5 per cent in 1999, signalling a decline for the fourth year in a row (Statistics Canada, 2000). Moreover, Doob and Sprott (1998) have shown that the severity of youth violence did not change in the first half of the 1990s. Questioning the federal government's concern about the increase in girls' participation in violent and gang-related activities, Reitsma-Street (1999: 350) indicates that the number of girls charged for murder and attempted murder has been constant for the past 20 years and that such charges are infrequent. Although statistics indicate a phenomenal increase in the number of young women charged with minor or moderate assault over the past 10 years (from 710 charged under the Juvenile Delinquents Act in 1980 to 4,434 under the Young Offenders Act in 1995–96), several researchers indicate that the increase is more a reflection of the youth justice system's change in policy and charging practices than a "real" change in behaviour (Doob and Sprott, 1998; Reitsma-Street, 1999). Yet the public continues to believe that youth violence, particularly girl violence, is increasing at an alarming rate and necessitates immediate attention (Chesney-Lind and Brown, 1999: 171). This perception begs the important question: Why, despite evidence to the contrary, are recent isolated incidents of female violence interpreted as a sign that today's girls have become increasingly "nasty"?

2   We argue that the recent alarm over girl violence is the product of a moral panic that has had a significant impact on social, educational, and legal policy-making. Drawing on the moral panic and risk society literature, as well as the work of Michel Foucault, this paper examines how the recent concern with girl violence emerged; what effects that concern has had on policy-making in particular and on society in general; and why the panic over young females is occurring today.

How the Nasty Girl Emerged

3   In this paper, we refer to the anxiety over girl violence as the Nasty Girl phenomenon. The expression, Nasty Girl, is not often used in journalistic or academic discourse on young female violence. It was, however, the title of a 1997 CBC documentary (*Nasty girls*, 5 March 1997) that examined high school girls' experience of violence and incarceration (Barron, 2000: 81–85). In our brief review of the documentary, we highlight how it reflected an overall sensation that we have entered the age of the Nasty Girl. The documentary begins with old black-and-white film footage of two charming little girls playing with dolls. "Some things are at the heart of every little girl," claims the voice-over. The next scene, a little girl ironing with her mom, is accompanied by the comment: "mother's little helper is learning to become a homemaker." This reassuring 1950s view of girls as essentially maternal and domestic is, however, shattered in the next scene. The screen goes black, and a female voice authoritatively announces the dawn of a new age: "things have changed in the 1990s." In the following scenes, we learn just how bad things have become:

> In the late 1990s, almost everything your mother taught you about polite society has disappeared from popular culture, and nowhere is this more apparent than in what is happening to our teenage girls. Once the repository of sugar and spice and everything nice, today young women celebrate materialism, aggressive sexuality, and nasty behaviour. . . . Canada's teenage girls are committing more violent crimes than ever before, and girl crime is growing at an even faster rate than boy crime.

4   The documentary proceeds to show how this metamorphosis from sweet to Nasty Girl is activated

by a liking for gangsta rap music, rock videos, and teen magazines filled with scantily dressed fashion models. The disastrous effects of popular culture are illustrated by a succession of scenes of high-school girls pushing, kicking, and fighting each other, followed by scenes of incarcerated girls being searched by guards or walking behind jail fences. This imagery is interspersed with shocking newspaper headlines announcing the increase in girl violence.[1] Popular culture, the force behind the destruction of polite society, becomes the source of social decline in the 1990s. By disrupting social norms, popular culture has displaced the ideal role model of little girls—the mother/housewife—and thus produced a new species, the Nasty Girl, whose threat to the stability of our present and future society is only becoming apparent. The Nasty Girl, therefore, has become a folk devil in the 1990s.

5   All moral panics identify and denounce a personal agent responsible for the condition that is generating widespread public concern. As Schissel explains, "folk devils are inherently deviant and are presumed to be self-seeking, out of control and in danger of undermining the stability of society. . . ." (1997: 30). Hence, during the "warning phase" of a panic, there are, as in the documentary *Nasty girls*, predictions of impending doom, sensitization to cues of danger, frequent overreactions, and rumours speculating about what is happening or what will happen (Cohen, 1980: 144–48). Subsequently, a large part of the public becomes sensitized to the threat, and, as in the case of the Nasty Girl, when confronted with an actual act of girl violence, their perception of danger and risk solidifies.

6   It is not surprising, therefore, that the beating and murder of 14-year-old Reena Virk by a group of seven girls and one boy would become the event that provided evidence that girl violence had become a significant problem in Canada. On 14 November 1997, Virk, "a pudgy East Indian girl trying desperately to fit in," (Cernetig, Laghi, Matas and McInnes, 1997: A1) was on her way back to her foster home when friends asked her to join them under the bridge, a popular hangout. According to trial testimony, an argument broke out, and accusations were directed at Virk for spreading rumours about one of the girls, talking to another's boyfriend, and rifling through the address book of another (Tafler, 1998: 20). The news that Virk was beaten to death by a youth group part of "a teen subculture where girls pretending to be members of L.A. street gangs fight each other" shocked the country. According to *The Globe and Mail*, Reena's death became: "a national tragedy" (Cernetig et al., 1997: A1).

7   As is often the case in a moral panic, the media distorted and exaggerated the extent of isolated acts of girl violence following Virk's death. For example, newspaper and magazine headlines associated the case with a larger trend in girl violence: "Bad girls: A brutal B.C. murder sounds an alarm about teenage violence" (Chisholm, 1997), "Spare the rod and run for cover: When students hold the cards, school violence grows, especially among the girls" (McLean, 1999), "Virk's death triggers painful questions: Girls' involvement 'exacerbates rage'" (Mitchell, 1997), and "In Reena's world, being a 'slut' can get you killed" (Anon., 1997).

8   Also typical of a moral panic was the media claim that girl violence today is a "new" phenomenon, stemming from an altogether different "type" of girl (e.g., Sillars, 1998; McGovern, 1999; McLean, 1999). "The girl who is charged with second-degree murder," we are told, "could be the babysitter who minds your children" (Martin, 1998: 75). This presentation of an aggressive and murderous "girl next door" with a Jekyll-and-Hyde nature is more akin to science fiction than reality. Yet it serves to amplify an already heightened fear of crime.

9   Girl violence is not a new phenomenon. A glimpse at newspaper articles in 1977 reveals that acts of girl violence are not new; rather, the attention paid to them is novel. For example, one article reports a violent confrontation between a group of teenage girls who had been feuding for a week. The confrontation began after one girl told friends that two other girls had ganged up on her in a fight. "Amid the kicking and screaming, a pierced ear-ring was ripped from the lobe of one of the youthful combatants . . . the small jack-knife was plunged into the chest of another

---

[1] The headlines read: "Girl violence reported on rise," "Girls in gang," "Girl-gang violence alarms expert," "Girl-gang members more violent than boys, experts agree," and "Girl, 13, beaten by gang girls."

[13-year-old] girl [who] fell to the street, gasping and moaning" (Wilkes, 1977: A7). Despite a rich description of violent details, the tone of the article is non-threatening. The title, "Teenager girl in knife feud says: 'We're friends again,'" certainly prepares the reader for an account of violence but it also emphasizes the fact that the dispute has been resolved amicably. Presenting the stabbing as an act of innocent girlhood play-fighting, the author further deflates the fight by pointing out that it "wasn't a battle between warring gangs, but an argument among friends." Whereas any type of remorse is rarely documented in current accounts of girl violence, one girl in the 1977 article is quoted as saying, "everyone started crying and telling each other we were sorry." The article ends with the assurance that this violent incident is not typical of girl behaviour, a conclusion justified by the knowledge that the weapon used in the girl feud did, after all, belong to a boy. In the wake of fear created by Virk's murder, the relationship between girls and violence is presented differently.

10   Also central to the creation of a climate of fear is statistical manipulation of crime data to establish the amplitude of girl violence. As journalist Nolan astutely recognizes in her analysis of the media reporting of the Virk case: "'experts' and authors were appearing on TV and radio talk shows trumpeting—with the solemn self-importance that always accompanies adult laments about the various wickedness of youth—the shocking fact that, according to the Canadian Centre for Justice Statistics, crime by young girls had increased 200 per cent since 1986" (1998: 32). However, most articles failed to recognize that the increase was in reference to minor assaults, such as pushing or slapping, which did not cause serious injury. Doob and Sprott explain, "[o]ne would, we believe, have more confidence that this increase reflected a change in girls' behaviour if it were to have shown up in the 'most serious' category of assaults" (1998: 192).[2] At the time of Virk's murder, girls were still far less involved than boys in all levels of assault,

and only 4.5 per cent of youths charged with a homicide offence were female (ibid.). Moreover, according to more recent official statistics, the rate of male youth crime is almost three times higher than the female rate, and in 1999 the violent crime rate dropped (-6.5 per cent) for female youths (Statistics Canada, 2000). Yet inflated statistics about girl violence are usually assumed to be factual because, as Cohen (1980) explains, they are voiced by "socially accredited experts" whose expertise alone serves to legitimize the moral panic.

11   It is also the experts who construct the identity of the unruly girl and establish her as a real concern for panic. Historically, as Klein (1995) details, female offenders were described by experts as masculinized monsters (Lombroso, 1920), insensitive and lacking moral values (Thomas, 1907), envious of men due to lack of a penis (Freud, 1933), psychologically maladjusted (Pollack, 1950), and promiscuous (Davis, 1961) (Madriz, 1997: 26). Moreover, conceptions of morality increasingly became central to the identification and supervision of "dangerous" females. As the legitimate guardians of the moral sphere, middle-class women, in particular, participated in social purity movements that succeeded in criminalizing females who used their sexuality to survive. The reformers' efforts to rescue "fallen women" and "delinquent girls" from the harmful effects of industrial capitalism indicate how the bourgeois preoccupation with uplifting moral standards became central to the supervision of working-class girls.

12   Such reform movements also led to the establishment of child welfare agencies and the creation of juvenile justice systems. The youth criminal court evolved as a judicial parent or "parens patriae" that signalled the increasing involvement of the state in regulating and rehabilitating adolescent behaviour (Geller, 1987: 116). Girls, in particular, were deemed vulnerable and were incarcerated for status offences for their own protection, both from themselves and others. In the mid-twentieth century, the

---

[2] Doob and Sprott bring to our attention the problems associated with statistics on minor offences among youth by revealing how their increase is more related to institutional changes in reporting policies than in an actual increase in violence. For example, the Ontario Ministry of Education requested that education boards develop violence-prevention policies and implementation plans for reporting and recording violent incidents by September 1994. Increasingly, policies of "zero tolerance" of violence in the schools mandate that all cases of violence be brought to court. According to Doob and Sprott, "such policies can be expected to result in increased numbers of minor cases of violence—these are the cases that are likely to have been ignored in the past" (1998: 188).

popularization of psychology helped foster a shift in the understanding of unruly girls and women: from being inherently bad or immoral they became inherently mad (Faith and Jiwani, 2002: 87). As Myers and Sangster uncovered in their study of Canadian reform schools for girls from 1930–60, the "girl problem" was constructed by "psychologists, penal workers, administrators and nuns whose preconceived expert knowledge about the nature of young women shaped their reconstructions of delinquent girls' rebellions within a language of irrationality, incredulity and pathology" (2001: 669).

13   Overall, the dominant idea throughout most of the twentieth century was that females who offend are rejecting their feminine role and are emulating their male counterpart. Consequently, many criminologists feared the impact of the 1960s women's movement on the feminine role. While Thomas indicated that promiscuity among girls was increasing with women's greater participation in the workforce and Pollack anticipated that, with emancipation, female crime would become masculinized and lose its masked character (Boritch, 1997: 61), it was the media interpretation of Freda Adler's book, *Sisters in crime* (1975), that cemented the notion that the women's movement for equality had a darker side.

14   Adler's "emancipation hypothesis" appealed to some contemporary analysts of girl violence. In *When she was bad* (1997b), journalist Patricia Pearson mocks politically correct society by reminding us that women's equality comes at a price:

> If we concede that women are ambitious, like men, and possess a will to power as men do, then we need to concede that women, like men, are capable of injuring others who thwart them. We cannot insist on the strength and competence of women in all the traditional masculine arenas yet continue to exonerate ourselves from the consequences of power by arguing that, where the course of it runs more darkly, we are actually power*less*. (Pearson, 1997b: 32)

15   Female aggression, the will to power, seems a fact of nature for Pearson. And yet she links it to the social when she argues that if they commit crimes today, it is because "Girls don't *want* to be endlessly told that they're nothing but sex objects with low self-esteem. . . ; they are rejecting victimhood" (Pearson,

1997a: D3). In the process of resisting sexism, girls have unfortunately "gotten hip" (ibid.) to their capacity for violence. In a critique of Pearson's book, Chesney-Lind (1999) notes:

> Every one of [Pearson's] discussions of women's aggression and violence, in fact, erases patriarchy as the context within which the behavior occurs. . . . She minimizes and dismisses women's victimization and its clear connection to women's violence, and then argues that such violence should be punished without regard to gender. (1999: 117–18)

Pearson's journalistic musings about the darker side of female power is appealing in the current climate of feminist backlash, but it is simplistic.

16   Also appealing for current media accounts of girl violence are expert opinions from professionals who tend to comprehend the issue in psychosocial terms. For example, in a draft document she prepared for the Ontario Ministry of Training and Education, Debra Pepler, a psychology professor and expert on school bullying and girl relationships, cautions the reader on the complexity of girl aggression. However, she decontextualizes the phenomenon through her emphasis on bio-psychological traits and psychosocial circumstances relating to peers, the family, and the school:

> The development of aggressive behaviour is a function of individual characteristics, and social interactions with families, peers, and romantic relationships. Individual factors contributing to the development of aggression in girls include: temperament, hyperactivity, early pubertal timing, and deficits in social cognitive processing. Family factors contributing to the development of aggression include: poor attachment to a parent; poor parental monitoring of children's behaviours; many conflicts within the family; harsh parenting practices; aggressive siblings; and marital problems. Low school achievement, frequent truancy, and negative school experiences may contribute to the development of aggressive behaviour in girls. (1998: 10)

17   In a published document she and a colleague prepared for the Canadian government, Pepler reaffirms her position by discussing aggressive girls as suffering from problems "in the biological, family context, peer context, and psychosocial domains" (Pepler and Sedighdeilami, 1998: iii). Explanations

that focus on individual circumstances—self-esteem, family life, and personal relationships—are complex, significant, and valuable, but they tend to marginalize the impact of structural factors on the life of young female offenders. The media use such explanations to reduce the complexity of the violent girl to her dysfunctional, bio-psychological self. In the Virk case, the media often presented female violence as irrational, the product of an individual pathology capable of rearing its ugly head over petty reasons, such as slights about appearance, likeability, and intelligence.

18   One leading authority who underscores structures of power when discussing girl violence is Sybille Artz, director of the School of Child and Youth Care at the University of Victoria. In her book, *Sex, power, and the violent school girl* (1998), Artz clearly locates girl aggression in a culture characterized by sexism, abuse, and inequality. However, she also emphasizes psychosocial problems, such as dysfunctional families, internalization of sexist gender roles, and lack of anger management skills, as explanatory factors. For example, Artz explains that the six girls she studied:

> All come from families with many generations of experience with violence, alcohol misuse, and a generalized dysfunction that has left them with a less than helpful way of constructing self and world. All have internalized notions of being female that assign low general worth to women, hold that women achieve their greatest importance when they command the attention of males, and support the entrenchment of the sexual double standard. . . . In their immediate families, and in their social circle . . . [they] have been exposed to no forms of conflict resolution other than those that settle disputes through threat, intimidation, and violence. They have internalized a way of perceiving those who displease them that shifts moral and causal responsibility for their own displeasure onto those with whom they are displeased. . . . [T]hey are quick to anger, and quick to assume that others have it in for them. (Artz, 1998: 195–96)

19   Those individualizing factors figure highly in the media discussion of girl crime. According to Faith and Jiwani, the media "colluded with [Artz's] emphasis of girl-on-girl violence as signifying a rising trend, with the attendant theme of family dysfunction" (2002: 90).

20   Lacking from media analyses of female violence is the considerable impact of structural factors, including institutional racism, and economic and social inequality in the life of young female offenders and their victims. As Faith and Jiwani contend: "Significantly absent in the range of explanations put forward by the media was Reena Virk's marginalized positioning vis-à-vis those who had beaten and killed her. The issue of race and racism was either absent from the media discourse or presented in terms of her inability to fit in" (2002: 101–02). In a re-examination of her research data, Artz (2004) draws on social interdependence theory to acknowledge the importance of social structures in girls' use of violence because they "provide us with clues as to how people may be interpreting self and world and how they may be morally positioned with regard to their actions" (Artz, 2004: 104).

21   In summary, we have drawn on the moral panic literature to examine the recent preoccupation with the violent girl. We argued that through distortion, exaggeration, and statistical manipulation of data, as well as expert evidence, the media was able to construct a new breed of female, the Nasty Girl, who has become one of our current folk devils. This construction is not without consequences: "We want assurances that what happened to Reena couldn't happen to anybody else," asserts the popular magazine *Chatelaine*, because "after all, next time it might be my daughter or yours who is the victim" (Martin, 1998: 71). In a climate of fear, Schissel (1997: 30) reminds us, it is easier "for average citizens to become embroiled in the alarm over [folk devils] and to call for harsh justice." Unfortunately, the reforms resorted to in a time of panic often fail to address the real source of public anxiety. It is to those reforms that we now turn.

The Effects of the Moral Panic on Policy-Making

22   The panic over the Nasty Girl has had a significant impact on legal, educational, and social policy in Canada. The result has been an increase in both formal and informal mechanisms of control. While proposals for legal reform mostly consist of repressive

measures targeted at delinquent youths, social and educational programs contain informal mechanisms of control targeting society more generally. As we show in this section, proposals for reform are not only disciplinary mechanisms of power acting on the body of the individual delinquent, they are also part of the more recent governmental techniques of power that regulate and manage free individuals through the fostering of a culture of risk management, public safety, and security consciousness (Foucault, 1982; Cohen, 1985; O'Malley, 1996; Garland, 1997).

23   Following the Virk case and other high-profile youth crimes, state policies on violent youth have become punitive. The Youth Criminal Justice Act (YCJA) came into effect on 1 April 2003, and although it offers positive measures to reduce the number of youths being incarcerated, its clear distinction between "non-violent," "violent" and "serious violent" offences reflects public desire to deal harshly with violent youth. This process of labelling, as expressed by Quebec youth justice officials, ensures that "the nature of the charge, rather than the circumstances and prognosis of the youth, becomes the major governing factor in how the youth is dealt with under the Act" (Green and Healy, 2003: 191). The YCJA (sections 61 and 62) also allows for youths as young as 14 years old to be sentenced as adults, and it expands the list of offences for which these presumptive transfers apply. Public support for such branding reforms, including provisions in the YCJA that allow for publishing the names of young offenders, was echoed in the sensational media coverage one of the accused received while on trial for Virk's murder (Hall, 2000: A1). Kelly Marie Ellard, who was 15 at the time of the incident, was initially found guilty on 20 April 2000 of second-degree murder in adult court. The final outcome of her third trial is pending.

24   Of even more concern for girls specifically is the passage of the Secure Care Act (Bill 25) in British Columbia. Following the lead of Alberta's Protection of Children Involved in Prostitution Act (PCHIP), the Secure Care Act is intended "to provide, when other less intrusive means are unavailable or inadequate, a means of assessing and assisting children who have an emotional or behavioral condition that presents a high risk of serious harm or injury to themselves and

are unable to reduce the risk. . . . These conditions may [include] severe substance misuse or addiction or the sexual exploitation of a child" (section 2 (1), cited in Busby, 2001). In essence, this legislation meant to protect children ultimately blames victims of sexual exploitation and permits the apprehension and incarceration of girls—who will be targeted more than boys due to their differential involvement in prostitution—for up to 100 days when the time for the assessment, hearing, and renewal of certificates is combined (*Justice for Girls*, 2001: 1–2). Reminiscent of the controversial nineteenth-century English Contagious Diseases Acts, which enacted a double standard into law by allowing for the forced examination and treatment of diseased prostitutes (Walkowitz, 1980), the Secure Care Act is an affront to the bodily integrity of young people (mostly girls) that authorizes medical examinations and disclosure of the results (sections 16 (1)(*b*) and 40 [Busby, 2001]). *Justice for Girls*, a Vancouver-based, nonprofit organization that promotes justice and equality for street-involved or low-income girls, opposes the Secure Care Act for its lack of accountability on the part of the professionals involved and for violations of Charter rights around issues of consent and confidentiality. Moreover, they see the Act as:

. . . a mechanism to further marginalize and institutionalize young women. Rather than addressing poverty, male violence, colonial devastation of First Nations communities, or shamefully inadequate and inappropriate voluntary services for young women, the *Secure Care Act* instead criminalizes and pathologizes young women. Ironically, young women who have actually committed a crime are entitled to greater protections under the *Charter of Rights and Freedoms* and *Young Offenders Act* than those who will be jailed under the *Secure Care Act* in the name of child protection. (*Justice for Girls*, 2001: 1)

Similar bills have been introduced in other Canadian provinces.

25   While harsh legal policy is aimed at incapacitating both violent boys and girls, informal mechanisms of control targeting young girls in particular have also resulted from the panic over girl violence. These mechanisms, however, did not emerge from within the centre of the criminal justice apparatus;

rather, they evolved at the margins of society, through the work of social agencies, activists, and experts who helped create a consensus about the problem of girl violence. This groundwork has produced new definitions of violence and new methods of controlling both young females and society in general.

26   The expansion in definitions of violence is most obvious in relation to what goes on at school, a site where the threat of the violent girl is most apparent. Pepler, who was commissioned by the Ontario and Canadian governments to prepare strategies for aggressive girls, helped foster a new rationality of bullying—teasing, gossiping, and quarrelling—as an intolerable act of aggression. The new definition of aggression, which "has been expanded to include the behaviours that typically comprise girls' attacks including indirect and verbal aggression . . . , aggression directed at peer relationships . . . , and aggression directed at damaging self-esteem and/or social status . . ." is said to pose "a challenge to schools as it is difficult to observe and deal with" (Pepler, 1998: 5). Early identification of girls at risk, however, is imperative, because, as Pepler and Sedighdeilami claim, "data on the development of aggressive girls into adulthood suggests that girls who are aggressive may also constitute a significant social concern in Canada" (1998: iii). To help school officials detect girls at risk, they identify "biological and social risk" and "psychosocial difficulties" (ibid.). As Pepler's work was part of a movement to develop antibullying handbooks across Canada (Galt, 1998), we can only surmise how the expansive definition of aggression and call for early detection could potentially increase the surveillance of teenage girls in schoolyards and at home.

27   The new rationality and concern over bullying is not only targeting the aggressive girl. It also actively seeks the participation of school authorities in the informal control of girls. For example, Pepler and Sedighdeilami's caution that "[g]irls in families with violence, ineffective parenting, and high levels of conflict should be identified for supportive interventions" (ibid.) encourages school staff to observe and detect signs of risk in girls. The popular magazine *Today's Parent*, in an article entitled "When the tough get going . . . the going gets tough: How to deal with bullies," promotes parents becoming detectives through continuous observation of their children, since bullying is an "underground activity." Stuart Auty, president of the Canadian Safe School Network, is known to give parents his expert advice on how to steer children away from violence, including basic strategies such as "knowing your kid, staying connected and providing them with opportunities to develop their self-esteem, as well as establishing limits and consequences when rules are broken" (cited in Martin, 1998: 77). While it is ironic that mainstream parental and educational advice is now repackaged as state-of-the-art technology to prevent bullying, we see in this strategy a sign of the current shift in crime control policy that Foucauldian scholars have identified as "government-at-a-distance" (Rose and Miller, 1992; Garland, 1997).

28   As we know from Foucault's studies of the asylum, the prison, and sexuality, power—which he also refers to as "governmentality"—is better understood as a rationality evolving from the margins of society than as one concentrated exclusively in its centre, the state. It is in the interstice between the state and the individual, that is to say, in the social field occupied by the school, the hospital, the juvenile court, and social workers' and psychologists' offices, that different forms of rationality emerge and produce their disciplinary and regulatory effects onto the social body. Diverse professionals and agencies come together to govern the behaviour and mentality of both those who pose problems, such as the violent girl, and those they can enlist in the management of the violent girl. While the strategies of power produced in those "centres of governance" (Garland, 1997: 179–80) have disciplinary effects meant to break and tame those at the receiving end, some act through the subjects for the purpose of creating a "responsibilized autonomy" in them. For example, since Virk's death, expert advice encourages parents, teachers, and youth to change their behaviour and self-image to bring them into line with socially approved desires and identities and, in the process, ensure the good functioning of the family and the school. The participation of these individuals in the management of the violent girl does not rely on force but rests instead upon an alliance with expert authorities, which is grounded in what Garland perceives as "the willingness of individuals—whether as family

members, or workers, or citizens—to exercise a 'responsibilized' autonomy, and to pursue their interests and desires in ways which are socially approved and legally sanctioned" (1997: 180). This strategy of governmental power, Garland continues, characterizes most current crime control policy:

> State authorities . . . seek to enlist other agencies and individuals to form a chain of coordinated action that reaches into criminogenic situations, prompting crime-control conduct on the part of 'responsibilized' actors (see Garland, 1996). Central to this strategy is the attempt to ensure that all the agencies and individuals who are in a position to contribute to these crime-reducing ends come to see it as being in their interests to do so. "Government" is thus extended and enhanced by the creation of "governors" and "guardians" in the space between the state and the offender. (Garland, 1997: 188)

29   Youths are particularly targeted by this strategy of power grounded in a "responsibilized" autonomy. For example, as part of its "Taking a Stand" program, the BC government made available a toll-free, province-wide phone number to "prevent crime and violence and to offer youth a safe, confidential means to obtain information and help." The "Youth against Violence Line" wallet card distributed to schools invites young people to phone in and report incidents where they feel "scared," "threatened," or "don't know what to do." Similarly, the police force of a suburb of Victoria, BC, launched a program named "Solid Rock" in which police officers or actors perform skits to convince young people that teenagers who go to the authorities rather than putting up with bullies are not rats but exemplary, responsible citizens (McInnes, 1998: A4). We see in these well-intentioned government programs an attempt to help youth become not only law-abiding citizens but *homo prudens* (O'Malley, 1996) too, thus enticing them in the creation of a culture of risk management in which they learn to fear youth and think of themselves as potential victims (Ericson and Haggerty, 1997). These programs illustrate the profound change in current crime control policy Garland foresaw: "the new programmes of action are directed not towards individual offenders, but towards the conduct of potential victims, to vulnerable situations,

and to those routines of everyday life which create criminal opportunities as an unintended byproduct" (Garland, 1996: 451). Hence, we need to understand the moral panic about the violent girl or youth in general as a process that leads not only to the containment and transformation of violent girls and boys but also to the increased self-discipline and regulation of all youths, who learn to think of themselves as potential victims of bullying.

30   To summarize, the policies and programs stemming from the moral panic about violent girls include repressive measures towards violent youth that are deployed by the crime-control apparatus. They also include more informal mechanisms of crime control directed at society, which are deployed by a "government-at-a-distance." While repressive measures stem from traditional crime-control agencies, such as the police or prisons, informal control operates rather indirectly or "at a distance" by fostering the cooperation of non-state organizations and private individuals (Garland, 1997: 188). Through the actions of various experts involved in the fight against bullies, parents, teachers, young people, and, specifically, girls are encouraged to become responsible and prudent individuals. To this effect, policies and programs seek to make them recognize their responsibility in reducing crime and persuade them to change their behaviour to reduce criminal opportunities (Garland, 1996: 453).

Why Is the Panic Happening Today?

31   Why did the reaction to girl violence take the particular form and intensity it did during the late 1990s? The moral panic literature emphasizes that, during a panic, the anxieties the public experiences are real, but their reaction is often misplaced. Hence, the object of the panic, the violent girl, is not always the source of people's anxiety. In psychoanalytical terms, she is more likely to be the object of a projection rather than the source of concern and fear. As one media article stated, the murder of Virk resulted in "a profound self-examination and fear among Canadians that society's rules are undergoing unsettling change" (Mitchell, 1997: A1). This section attempts

to situate the moral panic about girl violence in its larger social and political context in order to uncover some of the anxieties that propelled it to become symbolically attached to aggressive girls. We follow this discussion with a brief examination of the way policies aimed at violent girls could better attempt to address the problems young girls face today.

32   We start our attempt at contextualizing the moral panic over the violent girl by examining the larger structural forces characterizing our present. According to Young (1999), the transition from modernity (the "Golden Age" of the postwar period) to the present late modernity (late 1960s and onwards) resulted in significant structural and psychological changes that produced social anxieties. The shift primarily entailed a movement from an inclusive to an exclusive society: from a society that incorporated its members and enjoyed full (male) employment, rising affluence, stable families, and conformity to an exclusive society arising from changes in the labour force. These changes included a shift from a more social-based, communitarian labour force to one of individualism stemming from the new knowledge-based, technology society. As late-modern society became increasingly characterized by a plurality of values, self-reflexivity, multiculturalism, and scientific and political relativism, the solid foundation of modernity began to melt. Material certainty and shared values shattered, leaving us with a heightened sense of risk and uncertainties. In such a precarious climate, crime acquires a powerful symbolic value. If we could only control crime better, we would bring safety into one aspect of our disrupted lives. It is not surprising that our quest for security often translates into a projection of our fears onto specific scapegoats, who are made responsible for our feelings of insecurity.

33   What social anxieties are projected onto the violent girl today? What threat to societal values has she come to represent? Acland provides direction when he argues that the fear stemming from the Virk case suggests "we are failing in the ability to reproduce our social order in the exact manner we think it ought to be done" (cited in Mitchell, 1997: A1). In our attempt to examine what transformations might account for the panic over girl violence, we are drawn back to the documentary *Nasty girls*, described at the beginning of this article, which related the problem of girl violence to the disappearance of the familial and domestic ideology of the 1950s, an ideology feminists have fought hard to challenge. Our culture associates young female offenders with feminism. As Schissel (1997) states: "[t]he 'sugar and spice' understanding of femaleness is often the standard upon which young female offenders are judged, and, in effect, the images of 'bad girls' are presented as . . . sinister products of the feminist movement" (1997: 107). Similarly, we argue that what troubles society most about the violent girl is that she has come to represent the excesses of the changed social, political, and economic status women have gained through their struggles for equality since the 1960s. The moral panic over the Nasty Girl is part of a backlash against feminism (Faludi, 1991).

34   In the wake of the Virk case, it was not difficult to find newspaper articles emphasizing the dangers of the rise in "Girl Power." A pullout section of the *Vancouver Province*, for example, had a picture of the petite head of the popular sitcom star Ally McBeal superimposed on the body of Rambo. While she smiles innocently at the camera, her muscular arms are holding a machine gun. The caption reads: "It's a girrrl's world: Yikes! It's only a matter of time before women take over" (Bacchus, 1998). Although Bacchus writes in a tongue-in-cheek manner, he outlines "evidence" of a shift from patriarchy to matriarchy: the Spice Girls, Buffy the Vampire Slayer, angry chanteuses like Alanis Morissette and Xena, Lilith Fair, WNBA, Martha Stewart, Rosie, and the Women's Television Network. While Bacchus quickly clarifies that women have not achieved superiority or even equality in the workplace, the evidence of the shift to matriarchy he posits is in the form of a change "in spirit." The mantra of this spirit, Bacchus claims, is "Go girl!" (ibid.).

35   The media sensationalized the spirit of girl power by positing it as the cause of girl violence. Showing insightful reflexivity, journalist Nolan suggests that "[f]ollowing long-standing misogynist traditions, they've made the assumption that the behaviour of a few reveals the brutality of all girls and that increased freedom for women—brought about specifically by feminism—is responsible for the supposed rise in young women's violence" (Nolan, 1998: 32). Girl power, the source of social anxieties, is the

real nasty here; the moral panic over the statistically insignificant Nasty Girl is a projection of a desire to retrieve a patriarchal social order characterized by gender conformity.

36   While a segment of our society is increasingly worried about the ill effect of the spirit of girl power and engrossed in attacking popular culture and in developing policies to transform all girls into good girls, another segment is capitalizing on girl power to turn a profit. "Bad girls = big bucks," claims the *Vancouver Sun* (Todd, 2001: A17). It is not the first time folk devils become prey to commercial exploitation and are given a greater ethos than they originally possessed (Cohen, 1980: 140, 176). Today, young girls are implored by marketers and the media to dress like adults and to express sexual, aggressive confidence (Clark, 1999: 47). Under the headline "Hollywood discovers girl power," *USA Today* acknowledges that "where the girls are is where Hollywood wants to be" (Bacchus, 1998: B1). And whereas girls were previously sex symbols in the background of beverage advertisements, they are now staring down the camera lens as they "growl": "This is our beer" (Bacchus, 1998: B3).

37   The spirit of girl power is paradoxically what policies and programming for violent girls aim at transforming through the adoption of anger management skills based on a cognitive behavioural model. Programs that encourage control, empathy, self-esteem, communication, and social skills are important, yet they do little in addressing the wider social context in which girl power takes place, as well as the desire for autonomy and the consumerism it creates. These techniques assume individual pathology and are based on a punishment-correction model that has failed repeatedly to reform (Foucault, 1979). Moreover, while most current programs to curb girl violence are founded on cognitive skills training and risk technologies, we also believe there has been insufficient critical evaluation of actuarial practices with youth. As Lupton (1999: 2) argues, the technico-scientific approach to risk ignores how "risk" can be a socio-cultural phenomenon in its own right. In a study on girls incarcerated for violent offences in Saskatchewan, one of us questions if actuarial techniques depoliticize the process of social control by assisting in the efficient management of the offender

rather than addressing social conditions requiring reform (Barron, forthcoming).

38   An alternative approach to address violence would be to focus on gender, race, and class-specific initiatives that appeal to the realities of young females. Chesney-Lind and Brown (1999) argue that because girl violence differs from boy violence in magnitude and quality, the traditional approaches to treatment and models of law enforcement are inappropriate for girls. They, and others, call for programs that recognize factors that marginalize girls, including the extensiveness of girl victimization and the complicating factors of culture, racism, and social and economic inequality, which may contribute to violent behaviour (ibid., 194; Jiwani, 1998; Jackson, 2004).

Conclusion

39   Although the moral panic framework has much utility in understanding the recent concerns about girl violence, it also has the potential to dismiss them. The framework can be used simply to deconstruct the sources of fear for the purpose of demonstrating that the societal concern is unfounded. We think, however, it should be used to uncover how the configuration of ideas surrounding a phenomenon has come into being and has moulded our life, customs, and science (Doyle and Lacombe, 2000). In this way, we would be in a better position to resist the insidious effects of a moral panic.

40   Secondly, it is apparent that the moral panic framework may not go far enough in addressing the effect of the panic on the "folk devils" themselves. We believe that the media caricatures of the Nasty Girl for marketing and consumer purposes provide an appealing identity. Far from implying that popular culture causes the Nasty Girl, we suggest that the media is one venue among others that supply girls with a variety of models. What girls do with those models is a complex affair. As Young explains, "the actors can embrace these essences in order to compensate for [their marginalized position] and lack of identity. . . . We have seen how such a process of embracing the essence bestowed upon the deviant can be taken up ironically, mockingly and transformatively. But even

so, it still shapes individuals' notions of themselves" (1999: 118).

41   Despite its potential shortcomings, the moral panic framework is useful to uncover the social construction of the violent girl and the subsequent inclusion of this construction in policymaking. Punitive proposals to contain violent youths partly resulted from the panic, as well as policies that aim at enlisting the cooperation of the general public into supporting the objectives of state authorities to create a safe and security-conscious culture. The irony is that while we conscientiously join the effort to eradicate the Nasty Girl out of a sense of responsibility, we shamelessly continue to capitalize on the marketability of the power she has come to embody.

42   Discussing the construction of the Nasty Girl as a moral panic should not negate a search for positive reforms or undermine the devastation resulting from rare acts of female aggression and violence. Although

it can be argued that the call for gender-based programs would confirm the amplitude of girl violence, it cannot be denied that young females are incarcerated for violent acts and have different life experience and needs from those of males. Perhaps the most promising recommendations for female programming include giving girls a voice in program design, implementation, and evaluation in order to address the wider context in which violence takes place. We maintain that in addition to gender, the interlocking systems of oppression in young women's lives must be considered. Acknowledging and responding to the connections between racism, sexism, ableism, homophobia, and economic inequality is a challenge to the philosophical underpinnings of the criminal justice and education systems.

Canadian Review of Sociology and Anthropology.
2005. February 42 (1).

References

Acland, C.R. 1995. *Youth, Murder, Spectacle: The Cultural Politics of "Youth in Crisis."* San Francisco: Westview Press.

Alder, F. 1975. *Sisters in Crime: The Rise of the New Female Criminal.* New York: McGraw-Hill.

Anon. 1978. "16-year-old girl charged in death of taxi driver, 61." *The Globe and Mail.* 11 April, p. 5.

Anon. 1996. "When the tough get going . . . the going gets tough: How to deal with bullies." *Today's Parent,* Vol. 13, No. 7, pp. 66–70.

Anon. 1997. "In Reena's world, being a 'slut' can get you killed." *Toronto Star.* 6 December, pp. E1, E4.

Artz, S. 1998. *Sex, Power, and the Violent School Girl.* Toronto: Trifolium Books.

Artz, S. 2004. "Revisiting the moral domain: Using social interdependence theory to understand adolescent girls' perspectives on the use of violence." In *Girls and Aggression: Contributing Factors and Intervention Principles.* M. Moretti, C. Odgers and J. Jackson (eds.). New York: Kluwer Academic/Plenum Publishers, pp. 101–13.

Bacchus, C.L. 1998. "It's a girrrl's world." *Vancouver Province.* 2 August, pp. B1–B3.

Barron, C.L. 2000. *Giving Youth a Voice: A Basis for Rethinking Adolescent Violence.* Halifax: Fernwood Publishing.

Barron, C. (forthcoming). "Nasty girl: The impact of the risk society on female young offenders." Ph.D. dissertation, Burnaby, B.C.: Simon Fraser University, School of Criminology.

Boritch, H. 1997. *Fallen Women: Female Crime and Criminal Justice in Canada.* Toronto: Nelson.

Busby, K. 2001. "Protective confinement of children involved in prostitution: Compassionate response or neo-criminalization?" Notes for a presentation at the Women behind Bars Conference. University of New Brunswick, Fredericton, 9 February.

Canadian Broadcasting Corporation. 1997. *Nasty Girls.* Videotape. Broadcast 5 March.

Cernetig, M., B. Laghi, R. Matas and C. McInnes. 1997. "Reena Virk's short life and lonely death: Swept away: A 14 year-old girl beaten by the very teens she wanted as friends was left to the cold salt-water." *The Globe and Mail.* 27 November, p. A1.

Chesney-Lind, M. 1999. "When she was bad: Violent women and the myth of innocence." Book review. *Women and Criminal Justice,* Vol. 10, No. 4, pp. 113–18.

Chesney-Lind, M. and M. Brown. 1999. "Girls and violence: An overview." In *Youth Violence: Prevention, Intervention and Social Policy.* D. Flannery and C.R. Huff (eds.). Washington, DC: American Psychiatric Press.

Chisholm, P. 1997. "Bad girls: A brutal B.C. murder sounds an alarm about teenage violence." *Maclean's,* 8 December, p. 12.Clark, A. 1999. "How teens got the power: Gen Y has the cash, the cool—and a burgeoning consumer culture." *Maclean's,* 22 March, pp. 42–49.

Cohen, S. 1980. *Folk Devils and Moral panics: The Creation of the Mods and Rockers.* New York: St. Martin's Press.

Cohen, S. 1985. *Visions of Social Control.* New York: Oxford University Press.

Doob, A. and J.B. Sprott. 1998. "Is the 'quality' of youth violence becoming more serious?" *Canadian Journal of Criminology and Criminal Justice,* Vol. 40, No. 2, pp. 185–94.

Doyle, K. and D. Lacombe. 2000. "Scapegoat in risk society: The case of pedophile/child pornographer Robin Sharpe." *Studies in Law, Politics and Society,* Vol. 20, pp. 183–206.

Ericson, R. and K. Haggerty. 1997. *Policing the Risk Society.* Toronto: University of Toronto Press.

Faith, K. and Y. Jiwani. 2002. "The social construction of 'dangerous' girls and women." In *Marginality and*

Condemnation: An Introduction to Critical Criminology. B. Schissel and C. Brooks (eds.). Halifax: Fernwood Publishing, pp. 83–107.

Faludi, S. 1991. *Backlash: The Undeclared War against American Women*. New York: Crown.

Foucault, M. 1979. *Discipline and Punish: The Birth of the Prison*. New York: Vintage Books.

Foucault, M. 1982. *The Subject and Power*. 2nd ed. H.L. Dreyfus and P. Rabinow (eds.). Chicago: Chicago University Press.

Galt, V. 1998. "Handbook to address bullying by girls: Recent attacks lend urgency to project." *The Globe and Mail*. 31 January, p. A3.

Garland, D. 1996. "The limits of the sovereign state: Strategies of crime control in contemporary society." *British Journal of Criminology*, Vol. 36, No. 4, pp. 445–71.

Garland, D. 1997. "'Governmentality' and the problem of crime: Foucault, criminology, sociology." *Theoretical Criminology*, Vol. 1, No. 2, pp. 173–214.

Geller, G. 1987. "Young women in conflict with the law." In *Too Few to Count: Canadian Women in Conflict with the Law*. E. Adelberg and C. Currie (eds.). Vancouver: Press Gang Publishers, pp. 113–26.

Green, R.G. and K.F. Healy. 2003. *Tough on Kids: Rethinking Approaches to Youth Justice*. Saskatoon: Purich Publishing.

Hall, N. 2000. "Slain teen's grandparents in court for 'last chapter.'" *The Vancouver Sun*. 7 March, p. A1.

Jackson, M.A. 2004. "Race, gender, and aggression: The impact of sociocultural factors on girls." In *Girls and Aggression: Contributing Factors and Intervention Principles*. M. Moretti, C. Odgers and J. Jackson (eds.). New York: Kluwer Academic/Plenum Publishers, pp. 82–99.

Jiwani, Y. 1998. *Violence against Marginalized Girls: A Review of the Current Literature*. Vancouver: The Feminist Research, Education, Development and Action Centre.

Justice for Girls. 2001. "Statement of opposition to the *Secure Care Act*." www.moib.com/ jfg/publications/p_sca.htm.

Lupton, D. 1999. *Risk and Sociocultural Theory: New Directions and Perspectives*. Cambridge, UK: Cambridge University Press.

Madriz, E. 1997. *Nothing Bad Happens to Good Girls*. Berkeley: University of California Press.

Martin, S. 1998. "Murder in Victoria: Why did Reena Virk die?" *Chatelaine*, May, pp. 70–77.

McGovern, C. 1999. "No feelings: Teens at the Virk trial demonstrate a chilling lack of humanity." *British Columbia Report*, Vol. 10, No. 13, pp. 42–43.

McInnes, C. 1998. "Police probe gang assault of Nanaimo teen." *The Globe and Mail*. 12 March, p. A4.

McLean, C. 1999. "Spare the rod and run for cover: When students hold the cards, school violence grows, especially among the girls." *British Columbia Report*, Vol. 10, No. 9, pp. 52–54.

Mitchell, A. 1997. "Virk's death triggers painful questions: Girls' involvement 'exacerbates rage.'" *The Globe and Mail*. 28 November, pp. A1, A8.

Myers, T. and J. Sangster. 2001. "Retorts, runaways and riots: Patterns of resistance in Canadian reform schools for girls, 1930–60." *Journal of Social History*, Vol. 34, No. 3, pp. 669–97.

Nolan, N. 1998. "Girl crazy: After the brutal murder of Reena Virk, the media whipped the country into a frenzy over a supposed 'girl crime wave.'" *This Magazine*, March/April, Vol. 31, No. 5, pp. 30–35.

O'Malley, P. 1996. "Risk and responsibility." In *Foucault and Political Reason*. A. Barry, T. Osborne and N. Rose (eds.). Chicago: University of Chicago Press, pp. 189–208.

Pearson, P. 1997a. "You're so cute when you're mad." *The Globe and Mail*. 29 November, p. D3.

Pearson, P. 1997b. *When She Was Bad: Violent Women and the Myth of Innocence*. New York: Viking.

Pepler, D.J. 1998. "Girls' aggression in schools: Scenarios and strategies." Unpublished paper. The Ministry of Training and Education, Government of Ontario.

Pepler, D.J. and F. Sedighdeilami. 1998. *Aggressive Girls in Canada*. Working Papers. Hull: Applied Research Branch, Strategic Policy, Human Resources Development Canada.

Reitsma-Street, M. 1999. "Justice for Canadian girls: A 1990s update." *Canadian Journal of Criminology and Criminal Justice*, Vol. 41, No. 3, pp. 335–64.

Rose, N. and P. Miller. 1992. "Political power beyond the state: Problematics of government." *British Journal of Sociology*, Vol. 43, No. 2, pp. 173–205.

Schissel, B. 1997. *Blaming Children: Youth Crime, Moral Panics and the Politics of Hate*. Halifax: Fernwood Publishing.

Sillars, L. 1998. "Youth murders multiply, Ottawa ponders: Five brutal teen homicides have provincial ministers demanding a tougher YOA." *Alberta Report*, Vol. 25, No. 7, pp. 45–47.

Statistics Canada. 2000. "Crime statistics." *The Daily*. 18 July. www.statcan/Daily/English/000718/d00718a.htm.

Tafler, S. 1998. "Who was Reena Virk?" *Saturday Night*, Vol. 113, No. 3, pp. 15–22.

Todd, D. 2001. "Bad girls = big bucks." *The Vancouver Sun*. 26 January, p. A17.

Walkowitz, J.R. 1980. *Prostitution and Victorian Society: Women, Class, and the State*. Cambridge and New York: Cambridge University Press.

Wilkes, J. 1977. "Teenage girl in knife feud says: 'We're friends again.'" *Toronto Sun*. 17 September, p. A7.

Young, J. 1999. *The Exclusive Society*. London: Sage.

KEY AND CHALLENGING WORDS

amicable, incredulity, contextualize, exonerate, pubertal, punitive, presumptive, differential, interstice, deploy, posit, misogynist, actuarial, deconstruct, configuration

QUESTIONS

1. Determine by context the meaning of the following phrases, all of which are important in comprehending the essay: "moral panic," "folk devil," "risk management" (each occurs at least once in the first few pages). Provide a one-sentence definition of each, using your own words.

2. What common public perception of female violence do the authors challenge? Identify the essay plan in the introduction and any other markers throughout the essay designed to help with comprehension.

3. Name three general characteristics of moral panic.

4. What do the authors mean when they refer to "structural factors" (paragraphs 17–20) in girl violence? What factors, other than "structural" ones, has girl violence been attributed to?

5. Of the many researchers that the authors refer to in their discussion of the moral panic literature, they particularly stress the work of Debra Pepler and Sybille Artz. What makes them important sources for this essay? Summarize the authors' criticism of Pepler's work (paragraphs 26–27) and of the Secure Care Act (paragraph 24).

6. What is "government-at-a-distance" (first mentioned in paragraph 27), and what is its major failing, according to the authors?

7. In the final section of the essay ("Why is the Panic Happening Today?"), the authors contrast the postwar period with the period beginning in the late 1960s. What is their purpose in doing so? Under two headings, "postwar" and "late 1960s," list as many contrastive terms as you can (words or phrases) that define these two periods, according to the authors. Use your own words.

8. Why do the authors refer again to the CBC documentary discussed in detail in the first section ("How the Nasty Girl Emerged")? Has its significance or importance to the authors' argument changed?

9. Identify one example each of a popular (newspaper or magazine) source and an academic (journal article or book) source, and show how the authors use the sources as support.

POST-READING

1. *Collaborative activity:* To what extent do the authors blame the media for the misrepresentations discussed in the essay? Do you think this blame is fair? Do you believe that the "nasty girl" exists as a relatively recent phenomenon? Discuss or debate these questions.

2. Locate at least one newspaper or magazine article dealing with the death of Reena Virk (see "References"), showing how the authors' claims about the media reporting of the occurrence are supported or not supported by the article.

3. In their conclusion, Barron and Lacombe call attention to "[t]he irony . . . that, while we conscientiously join the effort to eradicate the Nasty Girl out of a sense of responsibility, we shamelessly continue to capitalize on the marketability of the power she has come to embody." Do you agree with this assessment? Would you characterize this dual behaviour as inconsistent, paradoxical, or an example of hypocrisy? Write a 300- to 500-word response to the authors' charge in which you use either a fact-based or argument-based claim.

ADDITIONAL LIBRARY READING

Batacharya, Sheila. "A Fair Trial: Race and the Retrial of Kelly Ellard." *Canadian Woman Studies* 25.1/2 (2006): 181–89. Print.

Luke, Katherine P. "Are Girls Really Becoming More Violent? A Critical Analysis." *Affilia* 23.1 (2008): 38–50. Print.

Sippola, Laurie K, Jaime Paget, and Carie M. Buchanan. "Praising Cordelia: Social Aggression and Social Dominance among Adolescent School Girls." *Aggression and Adaptation: The Bright Side to Bad Behavior*. Ed. Patricia H. Hawley, Todd D. Little, and Philip C. Rodkin. Mahwah: Lawrence Erlbaum, 2007. Print.

Sex, charades, and census records: Locating female sex trade workers in a Victorian city

Patrick A. Dunae

(9,428 words)

Pre-reading

1. What information does the title give you about the article? Based on the title and the headings, construct a reading hypothesis that summarizes what you believe the article will be about.
2. In the article abstract, the author mentions that he is using Victoria, BC, as a "case study." What is a case study? How can a case study be used to expand a knowledge base?
3. Scan notes 1–5. What kind of information do they provide? What is their function?

Prostitution was a prominent issue in Canada during the late nineteenth century. In many Canadian cities, female sex-trade workers resided in brothels located in so-called red-light districts. Although they were enumerated in every decennial census, sex-trade workers have been overlooked by historical demographers, urban geographers, and census historians because they used euphemisms such as dressmaker to disguise their occupation. Using Victoria (British Columbia) as a case study, this essay shows how female brothel keepers and brothel prostitutes can be identified on manuscript census schedules from 1891 and 1901 and how the records can delineate the geography of sexual commerce in a Victorian city. In the process, questions arise about the prima facie value of aggregate census data.

1   Alice Seymour was a well-known madam in Victoria, British Columbia. She operated a brothel at No. 11 Kane Street from the late 1880s to the early 1900s, during which time she provided accommodation for many female prostitutes. Regrettably, Seymour did not leave any record of her establishment. No account books, diaries, payroll ledgers, or staff photographs survive. But Seymour and some of the women who lived in her brothel were enumerated in 1891 and again ten years later, in 1901. On both occasions they provided their names and a great deal of personal information to the enumerators who interviewed them.[1] The information was recorded on nominal census schedules that, fortunately for social historians, have been preserved on microfilm.

---

[1] The nominal census schedule, with information on Seymour and her household in 1891, is available on microfilm from Library and Archives Canada [hereafter LAC]. See microfilm reel T6292, Victoria City, District 4, sub-district 4 c–1, p. 25, family #108. The nominal schedule for 1901 is also available on microfilm from LAC, microfilm reel T6429, Victoria City, District 4, sub-district 6, p. 27 for Seymour's household. A somewhat fanciful description of Seymour appears in Valerie Green, *Upstarts and Outcasts. Victoria's Not-so-Proper Past* (Victoria: Hordsdal & Schubart, 2000), pp. 107–108, 116.

2   Census records have provided the foundation for many important studies relating to women, work, and the urban milieu in nineteenth-century Canada.[2] Very few of those studies, however, have mentioned the sex trade. In fact, the term "prostitution" is almost entirely absent in historical demography in Canada.[3] The omission is curious. We know that some working-class women were involved in the sex trade during the late nineteenth century and that prostitution was a major concern for moral reformers in Canada during the period.[4] We also know that red-light districts were a distinctive feature in many communities, especially in Western Canada.[5]

3   Why, then, have sex-trade workers been overlooked by historical demographers, urban geographers, and census historians? Several explanations might be suggested, but the most likely reason involves an apparent dearth of evidence. Prostitutes were rarely described as such when they were enumerated. When prostitutes were recorded on nominal census schedules, the space beside their names for "occupation, trade or calling" was left blank, or some innocuous term or euphemism—such as dressmaker—was entered in the space. Either way, key information is missing, and, as a result, sex-trade workers have been camouflaged in census schedules.

4   Sex-trade workers may be camouflaged, but they are not invisible. It is possible to identify them on nominal census schedules if we read the records carefully, consider them in context, and are cognizant of certain code words. In this case study of Victoria, British Columbia, using records from the 1891 census and the 1901 census, I show how brothel-keepers and brothel prostitutes can be identified in manuscript census schedules, how the records might be used to construct a prosopographical profile of these sex-trade workers, and how the records can assist in mapping the geography of sexual commerce in a nineteenth-century city. In the process, I raise questions about the *prima facie* value of census records.

The Nature of Census Records

5   Census records are problematic. Census-making is a political process, and census-taking an imprecise exercise, as Bruce Curtis has shown in his landmark study *The Politics of Population*, and as

---

[2] Census-based studies relating to gender and labour include Suzanne Cross, "The Neglected Majority: The Changing Role of Women in Nineteenth-Century Montreal," *Histoire sociale / Social History*, vol. 6, no. 12 (November 1973), pp. 202–233; Bettina Bradbury, "Pigs, Cows and Boarders: Non-Wage Forms of Survival among Montreal Families, 1861–1891," *Labour / Le travail*, vol. 14 (Fall 1984), pp. 9–46; Eric W. Sager and Peter Baskerville, "Locating the Unemployed in Urban British Columbia: Evidence from the 1891 Census," *Journal of Canadian Studies*, vol. 25 (Fall 1990), pp. 38–54; D. A. Muise, "The Industrial Context of Inequality: Female Participation in Nova Scotia's Paid Labour Force, 1871–1921," *Acadiensis*, vol. 20 (Spring 1991), pp. 3–31; Peter Baskerville, "She Has Already Hinted at Board: Enterprising Urban Women in British Columbia, 1863–1896," *Histoire sociale / Social History*, vol. 26 (1993), pp. 205–283; Kris Inwood and Richard Reid, "Gender and Occupational Identity in a Canadian Census," *Historical Methods*, vol. 34, no. 2 (Spring 2001), pp. 57–70.

[3] Michael B. Katz acknowledged the existence of the sex trade in his pioneering work, *The People of Hamilton, Canada West. Family and Class in a Mid-Nineteenth-Century City* (Cambridge, MA: Harvard University Press, 1975), pp. 55–57. Katz identified two brothel-owners in his study, which is built on census records from 1851 and 1861. Bettina Bradbury acknowledged that working-class widows and their daughters in Montreal sometimes engaged in the sex trade as a survival strategy. See Bradbury, *Working Families: Age, Gender, and Daily Survival in Industrializing Montreal* (Toronto: McClelland & Stewart, 1993), pp. 198, 205, 208. However, the sex trade is not mentioned anywhere in the detailed and exhaustive study by Marjorie Griffin Cohen, *Women's Work, Markets and Economic Development in Nineteenth-Century Ontario* (Toronto: University of Toronto Press, 1988).

[4] See Lori Rotenberg, "The Wayward Worker: Toronto's Prostitute at the Turn of the Century" in Janice Acton, Penny Goldsmith, and Bonnie Sheppard, eds., *Women at Work: Ontario, 1850–1930* (Toronto: Canadian Women's Educational Press, 1974), pp. 33–69; Mariana Valverde, *The Age of Light, Soap, and Water. Moral Reform in English Canada, 1885–1925* (Toronto: McClelland & Stewart, 1991); Carolyn Strange, *Toronto's Girl Problem: The Perils and Pleasures of the City, 1880–1930* (Toronto: University of Toronto Press, 1995).

[5] James H. Gray, *Red Lights on the Prairies* (Saskatoon: Fifth House, 1995). This popular work was first published in 1971. See also Alan Artibise, *Winnipeg: A Social History of Urban Growth, 1874–1914* (Montreal and Kingston: McGill-Queen's University Press, 1975), especially the chapter entitled "Red Lights in Winnipeg: Segregated Vice, Moral Reformers, and Civic Politics," pp. 246–264; Judy Bedford, "Prostitution in Calgary, 1905–1914," *Alberta History*, vol. 29, no. 2 (Spring 1981), pp. 1–11; Deborah Nilson, "The Social Evil: Prostitution in Vancouver 1900–1920," in Barbara Latham and Cathy Kess, eds., *In Her Own Right* (Victoria: Camosun College, 1980), pp. 205–228; Charleen P. Smith, "Boomtown Brothels in the Kootenays, 1895–1905" in Jonathan Swainger and Constance Backhouse, eds., *People and Place: Historical Influences on Legal Culture* (Vancouver: University of British Columbia Press, 2003), pp. 120–152; Rhonda L. Hinther, "The Oldest Profession in Winnipeg: The Culture of Prostitution in the Point Douglas Segregated District, 1909–1912," *Manitoba History*, no. 41 (Spring/Summer 2001), pp. 2–13.

Eric Sager and Peter Baskerville have noted in their introduction to a recent work on the 1901 Canadian census, *Household Counts*.[6] Census records relating to women are especially problematic because women's economic contributions were not always recognized by enumerators and because national censuses have tended to "construct social reality in the interests of a male-dominated political and economic elite."[7]

6 Census records relating to female sex-trade workers are even more challenging to the historian. The records are contentious for several reasons. First of all, although prostitution itself was not illegal, nearly every activity associated with prostitution was illegal in late-nineteenth-century Canada. As Constance Backhouse has noted, between 1869 and 1892, legislation relating to the "evils of prostitution" burgeoned; by the end of the century, virtually "every aspect of prostitution except the actual and specific act of commercial exchange for sexual services" was prohibited.[8] This meant that "keepers of bawdy houses or houses of ill-fame," "inmates [residents] of bawdy houses," and anyone who supported themselves "by the avails of prostitution" could be prosecuted under the Criminal Code.[9] In many communities, including Victoria, "common prostitutes or street-walkers" and anyone who acted in a "lewd" manner in a public place could also be prosecuted under local by-laws.[10] Accordingly, brothel prostitutes and brothel-keepers had to be circumspect when describing their work to census-takers, even though enumerators were sworn to maintain the confidentiality of any information disclosed to them.[11]

7 Census records relating to female sex-trade workers are also difficult to decipher because of the casual and uncertain nature of prostitution. Prostitutes often drifted in and out of the sex trade, depending on their economic circumstances.[12] Similarly, many prostitutes derived a portion of their incomes from occupations outside the sex trade.[13]

---

[6] Bruce Curtis, *The Politics of Population. State Formation, Statistics, and the Census of Canada, 1840–1875* (Toronto: University of Toronto Press, 2001); Eric W. Sager and Peter Baskerville, eds., *Household Counts: Canadian Households and Families in 1901* (Toronto: University of Toronto Press, 2007).

[7] Peter Baskerville and Eric W. Sager, *Unwilling Idlers: The Urban Unemployed and their Families in Late Victorian Canada* (Toronto: University of Toronto Press, 1998), p. 196. The challenge of using census records to examine women's labour has also engaged British and American historians. See, for example, Eilidh M. Garrett, "The Dawning of a New Era? Women's Work in England and Wales at the Turn of the Twentieth Century," *Histoire sociale / Social History*, vol. 28, no. 56 (November 1995), pp. 421–465; Elizabeth Herr, "The Census, Estimation Biases, and Female Labor-Force Participation Rates in 1880 Colorado," *Historical Methods*, vol. 28, no. 4 (Fall 1995), pp. 167–181.

[8] See Constance B. Backhouse, "Nineteenth-Century Canadian Prostitution Law: Reflection of a Discriminatory Society," *Histoire sociale / Social History*, vol. 18, no. 36 (November 1985), pp. 387–423. Backhouse summarizes the impact of late-nineteenth-century legislation on pp. 394–395. See also Backhouse, *Petticoats and Prejudice: Women and Law in Nineteenth Century Canada* (Toronto: Women's Press, published for the Osgoode Society, 1991), chap. 8, "Prostitution."

[9] Prostitution was also an offence under the 1907 Immigration Act: "No immigrant shall be permitted to land in Canada who has been convicted of a crime involving moral turpitude, or who is a prostitute, or who procures, or brings or attempts to bring into Canada prostitutes or women for purposes of prostitution." *Statutes of Canada*. 6 Edw. VII, chap. 19, s. 29.

[10] See John McLaren, "Chasing the Social Evil: the Evolution of Canada's Prostitution Laws, 1867–1917," *Canadian Journal of Law and Society*, vol. 1 (1986), pp. 125–166. In Victoria, prosecutions could be laid under the Public Morals By-Law (1888). Under this ordinance, authorities could prosecute persons who used "profane, obscene, blasphemous or grossly insulting language" and persons who committed "any other immorality or indecency in the City of Victoria." Corporation of the City of Victoria, *Revised, Amended and Consolidated By-Laws* (Victoria: T. R. Cusack, 1901), p. 255.

[11] Beginning in 1881, enumerators were sworn to maintain the confidentiality of any information they received during the course of the census. The administration and logistics of the census are described in Patrick A. Dunae, "Making the 1891 Census in British Columbia," *Histoire sociale / Social History*, vol. 31, no. 62 (November 1998), pp. 223–239.

[12] The fluid and transient nature of the sex trade is described in Smith, "Boomtown Brothels in the Kootenays," pp. 120–152. See also Ruth A. Frager and Carmel Patrias, *Discounted Labour: Women Workers in Canada, 1870–1939* (Toronto: University of Toronto Press, 2005). Frager and Patrias note that some women "who turned to prostitution in desperation did so on a temporary basis, depending on the availability of other jobs, while others resorted to prostitution on the side to supplement their earnings from 'respectable' jobs that did not pay a living wage." The authors add that "some women workers apparently became prostitutes because they believed that work in the sex trade was easier and more lucrative than toiling away at a 'legitimate' job such as domestic service or garment work" (pp. 50–51).

[13] Charlene Porsild provides a good description of survival strategies and occupational patterns of women in the red-light districts of Dawson City during this period. See Porsild, *Gamblers and Dreamers: Women, Men, and Community in the Klondike* (Vancouver: University of British Columbia Press, 1999). The author notes that many women in the Dawson City demi-monde "combined incomes drawn as laundresses, dressmakers, waitresses, performers, and prostitutes" (p. 126).

Thus a sometime waitress who happened to be working as a prostitute at the time of the census would likely have described herself as a waitress when she was interviewed by an enumerator. The situation was obfuscated further when enumerators entered misleading information on the nominal census schedules. Alice Seymour's household at 11 Kane Street is a case in point. In the 1901 census, Seymour was described as a "lodging house keeper." Her household included several young women who were recorded as "lodgers" and identified with various occupations, including "dressmaker." The census official who enumerated Seymour's establishment likely knew he was visiting a brothel, not a respectable boarding house, but it was not his place to challenge the information provided. The process of enumeration was precise, and enumerators were required to adhere strictly to a set of rules when they recorded information on the nominal census schedules. We can be relatively confident, therefore, that, when the enumerator described Alice Seymour as a "lodging house keeper" and some of her lodgers as "dressmakers," he was simply recording information provided to him. Likewise, it was not the enumerator's place to infer information *not* specifically provided. In such cases, the column reserved on the census schedule for a person's "occupation, trade or calling" was left blank.

8   By following these procedures to the letter —that is, by completing the forms carefully, by recording occupations verbatim, and by omitting information not explicitly provided—the enumerator was executing his duties diligently. He was honouring the promise he made when he was enrolled as an enumerator and swore an oath under the *Census Act*. In affirming his oath, the enumerator promised "solemnly and sincerely" to "faithfully and exactly" discharge all of his duties "to the utmost of [his] skill and ability."[14] Most enumerators, including the one who recorded Alice Seymour's household, acquitted themselves well. Nevertheless, they provided a disguise for posterity for Seymour and some of the other women who comprised the *demi-monde* of Victoria. Indeed, census enumerators and the government officials who supervised them were part of charade in which agents of the state and deviant members of society played a role. Although not generally understood by historians, the charade becomes clear when we examine census records in conjunction with other records that relate to social deviancy and urban space from the same period. Victoria is a good place to examine the charade because the city's population is well documented in terms of its size, location, and character.

9   For Victoria, we can draw upon all nominal census records from the third (1891) and the fourth (1901) decennial census of Canada. The records have been transcribed, coded, and integrated in an extensive database. The data is available online at an authoritative, scholarly website called *viHistory.ca*.[15] As the *viHistory* website was constructed, the manuscript census schedules were scrutinized closely to eliminate or clarify as many transcription errors and ambiguities as possible. For the city of Victoria, therefore, we are working with a large and exceptionally clean data set.[16] Moreover—and of no little importance in this study—the search engine for the online database was designed to enable researchers to reconstitute census households.[17] As a result, we can clearly see social and spatial relationships between individuals within a census household.

10   Social deviancy for the period is documented in records generated by the Victoria City Police Department. Police charge books dating from the late 1880s are particularly revealing, providing the names, ages, origins, occupations, and physical descriptions

---

[14] Dunae, "Making the 1891 Census in British Columbia," p. 238, citing the official *Statistical Year-Book of Canada* (1895), p. 156.

[15] The website is located at www.*viHistory*.ca. All of the nominal records used in this study can be accessed at this site.

[16] Manuscript census data for the City of Victoria, 1891, were transcribed and coded by the Public History Group at the University of Victoria. Census records from 1901 were transcribed and coded at the University of Victoria as part of the Canadian Family History Project. The two data sets, along with data from the 1881 census, were integrated into the *viHistory* online database. Launched in 2003, the *viHistory* website is a joint venture of the University of Victoria and Vancouver Island University.

[17] Alex Dunae designed the search query for *viHistory* in 2003. The query is unique in machine-readable databases derived from historical census records. In 2006 the *viHistory* website was rebuilt using open source tools by David Badke in the Humanities Computing and Media Centre at the University of Victoria. The integrated database comprises over 100,000 census and directory records.

of everyone arrested for any type of offence, from loitering to murder.[18] As might be expected, women identified as "prostitutes" appear in the charge books, and most were brothel prostitutes rather than streetwalkers. They appear in the record books on charges of "keeping a bawdy house or house of ill fame" or with being an "inmate of a house of ill fame."[19] The charge books also link them with other offences, such as larceny, destruction of property, and receiving stolen goods, but these are incidental to this study. For our purposes, the charge books are useful because they identify brothel-keepers and brothel prostitutes. By locating those women in manuscript census schedules, we can start to reconstruct their census households, and at that point we can interrogate the records closely.

11   We can situate census households within the larger community by consulting contemporary directories; in the process, we can determine the geography of sexual commerce in Victoria. Directories—also called business or commercial directories and gazetteers—were compiled for towns and cities across Canada during the nineteenth century. Typically, directories included the names and addresses of employers and householders in a community.[20] The gazetteers were not definitive, because the names of casual labourers, Aboriginal residents, and members of ethnic minorities were often omitted. Nevertheless, as George Young and John Lutz note in a research guide to nineteenth-century British Columbia directories, these publications "hold much valuable and under used information."[21] Directories compiled by R.T. Williams & Company and the Henderson Directory Company were particularly valuable for this study. *Williams' Illustrated Official British Columbia Directory* (1892) included an alphabetical directory and a street directory for the city of Victoria. *Williams' Directory* was compiled in September 1891, four months after the Dominion census was taken; as a result, there is considerable overlap between names on the census and names in the directory. The ninth edition of *Henderson's City of Victoria Directory* (1902) was compiled in October 1901 and so augments the 1901 census, which got underway in March that year.[22] The two directories are remarkably inclusive, insofar as they include the names of brothel operators and brothel prostitutes, although they did not identify them as such. The directories also provide street addresses for many of the brothels. With this information, we can map the geography of Victoria's sex trade during the census years of 1891 and 1901.[23]

12   Records generated by a check census were also helpful in establishing the geography of sexual commerce in Victoria. The check census was initiated in

---

[18] This study has utilized information from the police charge books, Series CB 1 (1889–1902), held by the Victoria Police Department. I appreciate the cooperation of the Victoria Police Department and especially the assistance of Jonathan P. R. Sheldan, of the Victoria Police Department's Forensic Identification Service, in making these records available to me. In compiling this study, I also consulted a related series of records (Victoria Magistrates Charge Books/Police Court, Series 114) available in the City of Victoria Archives.

[19] During the period examined in this study, local authorities accepted brothels but were intolerant of street prostitution. Street prostitutes were harassed and so constituted a relatively small segment of the sex trade in Victoria. This study focuses on brothel prostitution rather than street prostitution.

[20] Gareth Shaw, "Nineteenth Century Directories as Sources in Canadian Social History," *Archivaria*, no. 14 (Summer 1982), pp. 107–122; LAC, *Canadian Directories*, www.collectionscanada.ca/ canadiandirectories/index-e.html (accessed June 27, 2007).

[21] George Young and John S. Lutz, *The Researcher's Guide to British Columbia Nineteenth Century Directories: A Bibliography and Index* (Victoria.: Public History Group, University of Victoria, 1988). The authors note, "Used with the same degree of care and caution that researchers should take to any of their sources, directories hold much valuable and under used information" (p. 9).

[22] See R. T. Williams, ed., *Williams' illustrated official British Columbia directory, 1892; under the patronage of the Dominion and provincial governments, as well as the various municipalities throughout the province, containing general information and directories of all the cities and settlements in British Columbia, with a classified business directory* (Victoria: Colonist Printers, 1892); and Henderson's *British Columbia Gazetteer and Directory . . . Comprising Complete Alphabetical Directories of the Cities and Complete Business Directory* (Victoria and Vancouver: Henderson Publishing Company, 1902).

[23] Several American scholars have used city directories to help identify and locate brothels in the American West. I have utilized the directories in the same way in this study. See Joel Best, *Controlling Vice: Regulating Brothel Prostitution in St. Paul, 1865–1883* (Columbus: Ohio University Press, 1986); Anne M. Butler, *Daughters of Joy, Sisters of Misery: Prostitutes in the American West, 1865–1890* (Chicago: University of Illinois Press, 1985); Marion S. Goldman, *Gold Diggers & Silver Miners. Prostitution and Social Life on the Comstock Lode* (Ann Arbor: University of Michigan Press, 1981); Jan MacKell, Brothels, *Bordellos, & Bad Girls: Prostitution in Colorado, 1860–1930* (Albuquerque: University of New Mexico Press, 2004).

September 1891, soon after the official census returns were published by the federal government. The city's leading newspaper, the *Daily Colonist*, members of the local Board of Trade, and Victoria city council believed that Victoria had been under-counted and so contracted the firm of R.T. Williams & Company to carry out a check census. The check census is useful because it includes the street addresses of persons who were enumerated, which the 1891 Dominion census did not. By referencing names on the Victoria check census to names on the Victoria portion of the Dominion census, we were able to connect nominal data from the official 1891 census to specific locations in the city.[24]

Taking the Census

13   Before locating the sex trade in Victoria, it may be helpful to recall the characteristics of the census and the process of enumeration. Historically, Canada has used a *de jure* rather than a *de facto* type of census. In the *de jure* system, persons are enumerated according to their permanent abode rather than where they are actually located at the time the census is taken. Therefore, we can assume that persons whose names were recorded by enumerators in a particular community—in this case, Victoria—were deemed to be permanent residents of that community. In the *de jure* system, a target date is set as a reference point for the count, and the population is enumerated as it would have existed on that particular date. In Canada's third decennial census, the target date was Monday, April 6, 1891. For the fourth decennial census, the target date was Monday, March 31, 1901.

14   Enumeration units in Canada were based on federal electoral districts and polling divisions, and in larger cities census sub-divisions corresponded to municipal wards and precincts.[25] In all cases, census tracts were clearly delineated, and enumerators were expected to be familiar with them before the census got underway. As the official *Manual containing the 'Census Act' and Instructions to Officers employed in the taking the third census of Canada* (1891) declared, in the convoluted prose of the bureaucracy: "An intelligent and well-trained enumerator will, in fact, generally speaking, know beforehand what are, as a whole, the conditions of every family in his sub-district."[26] In practice, this meant that a red-light district would not be *terra incognita* to an astute census taker.

15   Enumerators were required to visit and describe every occupied habitation within their district. In 1891, enumerators were supposed to record structural details for every dwelling, indicating whether it was constructed of wood, brick, or stone and how many floors and rooms it contained. In 1901, enumerators were required to note the location or street address of each household they visited. Since enumerators were required to register and record the built environment, they could not have failed to notice the moral environment of a neighbourhood.

16   Ultimately, the enumerator's task was to describe accurately every "census family" within his district. The "census family" was a fundamental unit. In the official *Manual containing Instructions to Officers* (1891) the term was defined as follows: "*A Family*, as understood for the purposes of the census, may consist of one person living alone or of any number of persons living together under one roof and having their food provided together."[27] Thus a "census

---

[24] A copy of the 1891 Victoria check census was forwarded through the British Columbia Provincial Secretary's office to the Dominion Statistician in the federal Department of Agriculture. At some point in the 1950s, the manuscript was microfilmed and a copy sent to the British Columbia Archives in Victoria, where it is accessioned as: Census of Victoria [1891], Add. MSS 1908, microfilm reel A–1356. For more information about the check census, see Dunae, "Making the 1891 Census in British Columbia," p. 235.

[25] In the city of Victoria, electoral wards were used as enumeration units in the 1891 and 1901 censuses. Ward boundaries were described in Victoria city by-laws, which have been transcribed and posted on the *viHistory*.ca website. In other cities, where the boundaries of wards and census sub-districts are not available, researchers may be able to reconstruct enumeration units from contemporary maps, directories, and nominal census schedules. The process is described in Ian Buck, David Jordan, Shaun Mannella, and Larry McCann, "Reconstructing the Geographical Framework of the 1901 Census of Canada," *Historical Methods*, vol. 33, no. 4 (Fall 2000), pp. 199–205.

[26] Canada. Department of Agriculture (Census Branch), *Manual containing "The Census Act," and the Instructions to Officers employed in the taking of the third census of Canada, 1891* (Ottawa: Queen's Printer, 1891), p. 7. Hereafter noted as Census Manual (1891).

[27] *Census Manual* (1891), p. 5.

family" might comprise a traditional nuclear family or persons who were not blood relatives but were living in the same place, as in a boarding house or a brothel. Census families were numbered consecutively within each census sub-division. In urban centres like Victoria, this usually meant that census family No. 2 was in close proximity to census family No. 1 and so on. It is relatively easy to reconstruct an enumerator's walk within an enumeration area in 1891 and to place census households in relation to each other within a neighbourhood.[28] The process is even easier for 1901, when enumerators recorded the street address for each household.

17   The Canadian census was patterned on the British census, but there were notable differences in how populations in the Dominion and the United Kingdom were recorded. In Britain, enumerators distributed blank census forms to householders. The forms were completed by householders and retrieved by enumerators a few days later.[29] In Canada, the process was more rigorous. Enumerators were supposed to interview personally every adult in every census household. The information was entered on a form called *Schedule One: Nominal Return of the Living.*

18   The nominal schedule in 1891 consisted of 24 questions dealing with age, nativity, civil condition, religion, and occupation. The schedule was designed so that one person would be identified as the head of the household and others would be assigned relative positions such as wife of head, son of head, lodger, and so forth. In some census families, particularly nuclear family units, the head of household may have supplied information about everyone in the household, but in extended census family households individual members probably answered themselves. This was likely the case in 1901. The nominal

schedule in the fourth decennial census, which consisted of 34 questions, was more comprehensive than previous schedules. In addition to basic questions concerning nativity, occupation, marital status, and religious affiliation, the 1901 schedule required detailed information on a wide range of topics. People were asked not simply to state their ages, but to give the day, month, and year of birth. They were asked about racial origin and mother tongue. Residents born in Canada were asked whether they had been born in a rural or urban community; residents born outside the country were required to indicate when they had arrived in Canada and whether they were naturalized citizens. Respondents were asked if they were employers or employees, whether they received a salary or wage, or whether they supported themselves by "their own means" from other sources of income.[30]

19   The actual process involved an enumerator asking the questions in sequence and recording the answers on large (30 cm by 38 cm) folio sheets. The information could not have been entered hastily or haphazardly. It must have taken close to an hour to complete schedules for an average census household, especially if enumerators followed to the letter instructions provided by the census office in Ottawa. Enumerators were told to be "painstaking" and "scrupulous" when completing the schedules. "Never insert anything which is not stated or distinctly acknowledged by the person giving the information," they were told. Moreover, they were supposed to confirm and clarify personal information at the end of the census interview. "In every case [the enumerator] must read over the facts he has taken to the person from whom he has obtained them, for checking the correctness of his entries."[31]

---

[28] Spatial locators, such as street addresses and property lot numbers, were not included on the census until 1901, but, from 1889 onwards, street names and house numbers were printed in Victoria city directories. This information has been helpful in placing households within census sub-districts in 1891.

[29] The logistics of the British census are described in Michael Drake, "The Census, 1801–1891" in E.A. Wrigley, ed., *Nineteenth Century Society: Essays in the Use of Quantitative Methods for the Study of Social Data* (London: Cambridge University Press, 1977); Richard Lawton, ed, *The Census and Social Structure: An Interpretive Guide to Nineteenth Century Censuses for England and Wales* (London: Frank Cass, 1978); Edward Higgs, Life, *Death and Statistics: Civil Registration, Censuses and the Work of the General Register Office, 1836–1952. A Local Population Studies Supplement* (Hatfield, UK: Local Population Studies, 2004).

[30] For a complete list and detailed descriptions of questions on the 1901 nominal schedule, see Eric W. Sager, ed., *The National Sample of the 1901 Census of Canada User's Guide* (Victoria: Canadian Families Project, University of Victoria, 2002). The guide includes the 1901 *Instructions to [Census] Officers.*

[31] *Census Manual* (1891), p. 6.

20   Enumerators were enjoined to be precise when recording occupations. "You cannot be too explicit in stating occupations," the official census *Manual* declared in 1891.[32] Five pages in the *Manual* were devoted to this issue, and dozens of examples were provided to illustrate the level of detail required.[33] Despite these instructions, ambiguous or misleading occupational descriptions were recorded for prostitutes or "public women," as they were primly called by some census officials. George Sargison, the chief census officer of British Columbia in 1891, remarked that "public women" often used the term "dressmaker" as an occupational disguise,[34] and so they did. Terms like "dressmaker" and "seamstress" were so widely deployed in the sex trade that "plain sewing" was used "as a euphemism for prostitution" in some places.[35] As will be seen presently, however, prostitutes in Victoria were recorded with other occupations on the census: as milliners, hairdressers, florists, musicians, actresses, dancers, and typewriters (typists), to name some of the occupations. Sex-trade workers in other parts of Canada were probably enumerated with similar substitute occupations or disguises. The challenge for historians is to see behind the disguises. It is easier to discern occupational camouflage if we have some local knowledge about the sex trade, and in Victoria the sites of sexual commerce are relatively well documented.

The Sex Trade in Victoria

21   Victoria was founded as an outpost for the Hudson's Bay Company in 1843. The community of a few hundred non-Native settlers languished until the late 1850s, when it was inundated with thousands of miners en route to the Fraser River gold fields on the mainland of British Columbia. Incorporated as a city in 1862, Victoria experienced another boom during the Cariboo gold rush. The Royal Navy base at nearby Esquimalt, and the hundreds of sailors stationed there, contributed to Victoria's reputation as a roisterous seaport.[36] Not surprisingly, prostitution was part of the scene. During the colonial period, sexual commerce involved Aboriginal women who consorted with non-Native men in local dance halls. Government documents, missionary reports, and newspaper editorials contain many references to dance halls and prostitution involving Aboriginal women.[37] First Nations women were still involved in the sex trade in 1871, when British Columbia joined Confederation and Victoria became a provincial capital, but Aboriginal participation in the sex trade abated steadily over the next decade as a result of a complex series of circumstances whereby Aboriginal women were "deterred from relationships with white men."[38] The characteristics of the sex trade changed in response to

---

[32] *Ibid.*,p.14.

[33] For example, the term "mason" was not sufficiently precise. Enumerators were supposed to use more precise terms such as "brick mason" or "stone mason." Similarly, the term "author" was too vague. Enumerators were supposed to indicate whether an author was an "editor, reporter, journalist, magazine writer, novelist or historian." *Census Manual* (1891), pp. 14, 16.

[34] British Columbia Archives, Add. MSS. 2454, George A. Sargison letter-book. Sargison to J. S. Bennett, June 10, 1891, p. 176.

[35] Joel Best, "Careers in Brothel Prostitution: St. Paul, 1865–1883," *Journal of Interdisciplinary History*, vol. 12, no. 4 (Spring 1982), p. 600. Many prostitutes from the United States worked in Victoria, and they may have brought the euphemism "dressmaker" with them. During this period, dressmakers and seamstresses were also associated with prostitution in England. See Christina Walkley, *The Ghost in the Looking Glass: The Victorian Seamstress* (London: Peter Owen, 1981), pp. 48–49, 81–90.

[36] On the economic history of Victoria, see Charles N. Forward, "The Evolution of Victoria's Functional Character" in Alan F.J. Artibise, ed., *Town and City: Aspects of Western Canadian Urban Development* (Regina: Canadian Plains Research Center, University of Regina Press, 1981); Peter A. Baskerville, *Beyond the Island: An Illustrated History of Victoria* (Burlington, ON: Windsor Publications, 1986).

[37] Jean Barman, "Taming Aboriginal Sexuality: Gender, Power, and Race in British Columbia, 1850–1900," *BC Studies*, no. 115/116 (1997/1998), pp. 243–244; Adele Perry, *On the Edge of Empire. Gender, Race, and the Making of British Columbia, 1849–1871* (Toronto: University of Toronto Press, 2001), pp. 110–123. The topic is also explored further by Perry in "Metropolitan Knowledge, Colonial Practice, and Indigenous Womanhood: Missions in Nineteenth-Century British Columbia" in Katie Pickles and Myra Rutherdale, eds., *Contact Zones: Aboriginal & Settler Women in Canada's Colonial Past* (Vancouver: University of British Columbia Press, 2005), pp. 109–130.

[38] Jay Nelson, "'A Strange Revolution in the Manners of the Country': Aboriginal-Settler Intermarriage in Nineteenth Century British Columbia" in John McLaren, Robert Menzies, and Dorthoy E. Chunn, eds., *Regulating Lives: Historical Essays on the State, Society, the Individual, and the Law* (Vancouver: University of British Columbia Press, 2002). As Nelson notes, in the closing decades of the nineteenth century "Aboriginal women were increasingly deterred from relationships with white men by policies implemented by a shifting alliance of missionaries, local Aboriginal men, and Indian agents" (p. 46). See also Jean Barman, "Aboriginal Women on the Streets of Victoria: Rethinking Transgressive Sexuality during the Colonial Encounter" in Pickles and Rutherdale, eds., *Contact Zones*, pp. 205–227; Renisa Mawani, "Legal Geographies of Aboriginal Segregation in British Columbia: The Making and Unmaking of the Songhees Reserve, 1850–1911" in Carolyn Strange and Alison Basher, eds., *Isolation. Places and Practices of Exclusion* (London: Routledge, 2003), pp. 173–90.

the changing character of the city. By 1891, Victoria had discarded vestiges of its frontier, fur-trade-post origins and emerged as a prosperous, modern North American city. The sex trade also shed its frontier character, as Aboriginal women were supplanted by non-Aboriginal women and as brothels, rather than dance halls, became sites of sexual commerce.

22   Sexual commerce in Victoria was located principally, but not exclusively, in three areas: around Broad Street in the commercial centre of the city; around the lower (western) end of Herald Street and Chatham Street in an industrial part of the city; and on Fisguard Street in Chinatown.[39] Prostitution on Fisguard Street was confined almost exclusively to the Chinese community, which was virtually closed to outsiders, including moral regulators like the police.[40] Since Fisguard Street was outside the mainstream of sexual commerce, it is not considered here. Instead, we focus on the denizens of Victoria's better-known and more accessible red-light districts, starting with Broad Street.

23   Broad Street is only a few blocks long. In the late 1800s, it appeared to be a respectable thoroughfare: a Methodist Church anchored one end of the street and Victoria's most prestigious hotel, The Driard, anchored the other. The exclusive Union Club, social headquarters of Victoria's patriarchy, was located nearby, and City Hall was just around the corner. The tax assessments on properties along Broad Street were among the

highest in the city.[41] Amidst the prosperous and respectable properties of Broad Street, however, were disreputable sites: in 1886, Victoria's chief of police identified seven brothels on Broad Street.[42] By 1891, the sex trade in this part of the city had expanded, as brothels were then operating on nearby Broughton Street, Kane Street (now an extension of Broughton Street), Courtenay Street, and View Street. Although the area was well established as a centre of sexual commerce, this was a *sub rosa* community: We know very little about the sex workers who lived here, but occasionally we catch a glimpse of the women from police registers, court records, newspaper reports, and city directories. When these documentary fragments can be connected, and when they intersect with census records, a picture of the *demi-monde* begins to emerge. Fortunately for the historian, several instances of documentary congruence occur in 1891. One such occurrence involves Helen Dewsup, listed at 47 Broad Street in the 1891 Victoria check census and the 1892 directory. In the 1891 Dominion census, she was enumerated as a "boarding house keeper." A few months after the census was taken, Dewsup (also spelled Dessup) was charged and convicted for "keeping a bawdy house or house of ill fame."[43] Hattie Spaulding, who lived at 49 Broad Street according to the directory, was also charged in 1891 for "keeping a bawdy house or house of ill fame." Spaulding had

---

[39] C.L. Hansen-Brett, "Ladies in Scarlet: An Historical Overview of Prostitution in Victoria, British Columbia, 1870–1939," *British Columbia Historical News*, vol. 19 (1986), p. 22; Harry Gregson, *A History of Victoria, 1842–1970* (Victoria: Observer Publishing, 1970), p. 126.

[40] Although Victoria city police occasionally raided gambling dens in the city's Chinese quarter, rarely did they arrest anyone on charges connected with the sex trade. John McLaren has concluded that "Chinese sexual vice does not appear to have been a police concern or priority" in Victoria during this period. See John McLaren, "Race and the Criminal Justice System in British Columbia, 1892–1920: Constructing Chinese Crimes" in G. Blaine Baker and Jim Phillips, eds., *Essays in the History of Canadian Law, Volume III, in Honour of R. C. B. Risk* (Toronto: University of Toronto Press, for The Osgoode Society for Canadian Legal History, 1999), p. 422. On the history and character of this community, see David Chueyan *Lai, Chinatowns: Towns within Cities in Canada* (Vancouver: University of British Columbia Press, 1988). Prostitution in Victoria's Chinatown is discussed in Tamara Adilman, "A Preliminary Sketch of Chinese Women and Work in British Columbia, 1858–1950" in Gillian Creese and Veronica Strong-Boag, eds., *British Columbia Reconsidered: Essays on Women* (Vancouver: Press Gang Publishers, 1992).

[41] P. D. Floyd, "The Human Geography of Southeastern Vancouver Island, 1842–1891" (MA thesis, Geography, University of Victoria, 1969), p. 172. Using city tax records, Floyd determined that the assessed value of properties on Broad Street was the second highest in the city. Only properties fronting Government Street were more valuable.

[42] City of Victoria Archives [hereafter CVA], Report of Charles Bloomfield, Chief of Police, to D. W. Higgins, chair, Victoria Police Committee, April 7, 1886.

[43] Victoria Police Archives [hereafter VPA]. Police Charge Book (1889–1902), August 4, 1891, p. 269. Years later, Helen Dessup was fined for keeping "a house of prostitution" in Nanaimo, 90 kilometers north of Victoria. ("City Police Court," Nanaimo Free Press, August 18, 1898).

a long record of morals-related offences in Victoria.[44] In the 1891 census, she was identified as a "seamstress." At 56 Broad Street, the enumerator recorded a household headed by Bertha Baker, a "florist." This was also a brothel.[45] Alice Seymour's house at 11 Kane Street was located nearby. A few weeks prior to the census, Seymour had been convicted for "keeping a bawdy house."[46]

24   In 1891, this part of Victoria lay within census sub-district No. 5, Yates Street Ward. Had the enumerator followed instructions in the official 1891 census Manual to the letter, he would have been familiar beforehand with "the conditions of every family in his sub-district."[47] Maybe he did not reconnoitre the district before the census got underway. Maybe he was not a worldly man. Even so, he must have been aware that he was dealing with the *demi-monde* when he visited the households of Mesdames Baker, Dewsup, Seymour, Spaulding, and others. First of all, he might have been struck by the size of their premises. Most of these places contained half a dozen separate rooms or apartments.[48] He might also have been struck by the age of the female residents and their origins. Most of the women were relatively young, and nearly all had been born in the United States.

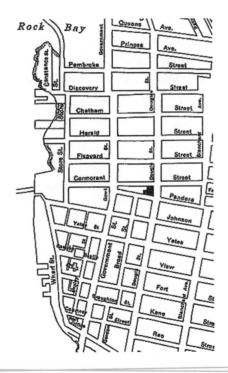

FIGURE 1   VICTORIA, BRITISH COLUMBIA, C. 1901, SHOWING THE DOWNTOWN CORE AND CITY HALL

Source as printed in article: LAC, Fourth Census of Canada, 1901, microfilm reel T6429, Victoria City, District 4, sub-district 6, p. 22, and sub-distict 7, p. 30.

[44] In 1889, Spaulding's Broad Street residence was raided by police, and she was charged with keeping a common bawdy house. See Victoria Daily Colonist, January 1, 1889 and Victoria Daily Colonist, January 12, 1889.

[45] Bertha Baker was well established in the sex trade when she was enumerated in 1891. She had been charged with keeping a bawdy house five years earlier, in 1886. The following year, she was charged with keeping a house of ill fame. See *Victoria Daily Colonist*, December 2, 1886 and *Victoria Daily Colonist*, December 9, 1887.

[46] VPA. *Police Charge Book* (1889–1902), pp. 53–55.

[47] *Census Manual* (1891), p. 7.

[48] The size of the brothels is evident from columns 3 and 4 on Schedule 1 of the manuscript census. For example, Fay Williams (census family #64) occupied a two-storey brick structure containing eight rooms; Bertha Baker (census family #92) occupied a one-storey wooden structure containing seven rooms; Alice Seymour (census family #108) occupied a two-storey wooden structure containing eleven rooms. LAC, microfilm reel T6292, Victoria City, Division 5 (Yates Street Ward), pp. 13–25.

25   Ten years later, Broad Street was still the nexus of Victoria's sex trade. In fact, by 1901 Broad Street had become a prestigious address for brothel owners who occupied the upper echelons of the sex trade. One of the city's most flamboyant madams, Stella Carroll, was located here.[49] Other brothels were located close by. These included 14 Courtney Street, run by Jenny Morris (also called Jennie Mores); Fay Williams' brothel at 14 Broughton Street; and Fay Watson's brothel house at 14 Douglas Street.[50]

26   In the 1901 census this area lay within the city's Central Ward and was part of census district 4, subdivisions 6, 7, and 8. Again, we cannot know whether the enumerators had reconnoitred their census subdistricts beforehand or whether they were men of the world. However, they must have known they were dealing with the *demi-monde* when they enumerated households like the one headed by Stella Carroll at 60½ Broad Street. The residents of the sumptuously furnished, lavishly decorated apartments were all American-born women between the ages of 18 and 32 years. Carroll identified herself as a landlady; her lodgers identified themselves as dressmakers, typewriters, singers, milliners, and actresses.[51]

27   Traditionally, sex trade workers—along with gamblers, bookies, and other marginal members of the labour force—are associated with the so-called invisible or non-market economy.[52] However, if we use the nominal census schedules as a lens, the sex trade looks very much like other activities associated with the formal economy. For example, on the 1891 census Broad Street brothel-keeper Helen Dewsup identified herself as an employer and indicated she employed two hired "hands" in her workplace. Likewise, Alice Seymour identified herself as an employer and indicated she paid the wages of two "hands" in her establishment on Kane Street.[53]

28   A decade later, Seymour was again identified as an employer who relied on her "own means" for her income. In the 1901 census, the term "own means" was entered for "persons who do not carry on any remunerative calling and live on their own means, as from incomes, superannuations, annuities, pensions, etc."[54] Seymour did not reveal her income to the enumerator. However, several of her lodgers obligingly declared earnings from their "occupation or trade" on the census.[55] If the information they provided was accurate, their earnings were substantial. A couple of her lodgers—a 25-year-old "dressmaker" and a 21-year-old "actress"—claimed annual earnings of $1,000 each. Women in other brothels reported comparable earnings. A "dressmaker" enumerated in Stella Carroll's household reported an annual income of $800, while her housemate, a 23-year-old "milliner," declared annual earnings of $1,000.[56]

29   To put these claims in perspective, on average women employed in nonprofessional, nonmanagerial positions in Canada only earned about $200 a year in 1901.[57] Wages in British Columbia were generally higher than the national average, but

---

[49] On Carroll's career, see Linda J. Eversole, *Stella: Unrepentant Madam* (Victoria: Touchwood Editions, 2005).

[50] Brothel operators Seymour, Morris, and Watson are mentioned in Valerie Green's gossip history, *Upstarts and Outcasts*, p. 116.

[51] Photographs showing the interior of Carroll's brothel are included in Eversole, *Stella: Unrepentant Madam*, p. 70.

[52] The issue of women's non-market work is discussed in Elizabeth Herr, "The Census, Estimation Biases, and Female Labor-Force Participation Rates in 1880 Colorado," *Historical Methods*, vol. 28, no. 4 (Fall 1995), pp. 167–181. The author includes prostitutes in her discussion.

[53] Dewsup and Seymour were probably referring to the cooks and domestic servants they employed in their brothels, not to the prostitutes who worked on their premises, when they reported the number of "hands" they employed. The prostitutes who lived on their premises may have paid a portion of their earnings as rent and so were classified as "lodgers" rather than "employees." Stella Carroll operated her brothel in this way, on "a boarding house basis." According to her biographer, "the girls would rent a room in the brothel and keep their earnings while Stella would make money from food and liquor sales and rent" (Eversole, *Stella: Unrepentant Madam*, p. 71).

[54] Canada, Department of Agriculture. Instructions to Officers [for] the Fourth Census of the Dominion (1901), p. xix, item 59, reprinted in Sager, ed., *National Sample of the 1901 Census of Canada*, p. 27.

[55] In the 1901 census, the enumerators' manual stated: "For census purposes the terms salary and wages have a common meaning, being the amount or sum of money which one person employed by another receives for his service, whether the work done be professional, literary or handicraft" (Instructions to Officers, p. xx, reprinted in Sager, ed., *National Sample of the 1901 Census of Canada*, p. 195).

[56] LAC, *Fourth Census of Canada*, 1901, microfilm reel T6429, Victoria City, District 4, sub-district 6, p. 22, and sub-district 7, p. 30.

[57] Baskerville and Sager, *Unwilling Idlers*, pp. 130, 205.

not substantially so. According to a provincial government handbook prepared in 1902, white domestic servants in Victoria earned between $180 and $240 a year; white women employed in merchant tailoring establishments received an average wage of $288 per year, while typists and stenographers earned about $300 a year.[58] Professional women such as school principals earned more than clerical workers, but they still earned less than the young women who lived with Seymour and Carroll.[59]

30   Women in the Kane Street and Broad Street brothels might have exaggerated their earnings to inflate their status, but undoubtedly they earned more than most female workers, including the female sex-trade workers who lived half a mile away on Herald Street, close to the harbour. The lower end of Herald Street was very different from Broad Street. It was separated from the commercial and ostensibly respectable part of Victoria by the city's Chinatown. It was located in an area dominated by a gas works, breweries, iron foundries, lumber mills, and warehouses. Whaling boats, sealing schooners, and clipper ships docked here. Hotels that provided inexpensive lodging for sailors and transient labourers were located in this part of town.

31   The lower end of Herald Street lay within census sub-district No. 2, Johnson Street Ward, in 1891. A couple of brothels were operating here when the census was taken in April that year. They were located in a newly built, two-storey brick building at 25–27 Herald Street.[60] This part of Victoria underwent a dramatic transformation during the Klondike gold rush (1898–1900) when thousands of men passed through the city en route to Dawson City and the gold fields. When the city's inexpensive hotels and rooming houses were filled to capacity, gold-seekers established temporary encampments on wastelands close to the harbour. Not surprisingly, the sex trade

burgeoned, as scores of prostitutes moved into the area. The newcomers did not reside in substantial brick structures; rather, the prostitutes who came to this corner of Victoria during the Klondike gold rush worked and lived in hastily built, one-room wooden cabins known as cribs. The lower end of Chatham Street, located one block to the north of Herald Street, was soon crowded with cribs.

32   In 1901, this part of Victoria was located within census sub-district No. 14, North Ward. The nominal census records for residents in this part of the city are revealing in several respects. Nearly every female resident on the lower end of Chatham Street was identified as a "head of household" on the census schedule. From this information we can infer that most of these women occupied a physical space (a crib) by themselves, unlike the brothel prostitutes who resided in larger census households. The records also invite comment because of information they do not provide. Unlike residents in city centre brothels, women in this part of town did not identify themselves as dressmakers, milliners, or actresses. No information was entered in the column devoted to "profession, occupation, trade or means of living" beside their names on the nominal census schedules. Moreover, none of the women on Chatham Street offered any information about their income. Rather, the enumerator has noted simply that the respondents supported themselves by their "own means" or on their "own account." Those terms were used by the enumerators to denote "persons employed in gainful work, doing their own work."[61] When they were visited by the enumerator, many of these women were probably doing their own work as part of the sex trade. As ever, some of the evidence is circumstantial, but some is compelling. According to Victoria City police records covering the period December 1900 to September 1901, nearly a dozen of the women enumerated in

---

[58] R. E. Gosnell, *The Year Book of British Columbia and Manual of Provincial Information* (Victoria: Government Printer, 1903), p 335.

[59] In Victoria, the most highly-qualified female school teachers earned about $600 per year. Victoria School Board, *Annual Report of the Public Schools of the City of Victoria* (Victoria: Board of School Trustees, 1899), pp. 20–21. See also Eric W. Sager, "Women Teachers in Canada, 1881–1901: Revisiting the 'Feminization' of an Occupation," *Canadian Historical Review*, vol. 88, no. 2 (June 2007), pp. 228–231.

[60] The brothels included apartments occupied by 26-year-old Ada Gault and 22-year-old Annie Howard (census sub-division 4–B, families 225 and 226). The enumerator for this district, B.W. Ward, has not been located on the census.

[61] Sager, ed., *National Sample of the 1901 Census of Canada*, p. 28.

sub-district 14 had been, or would be, charged with offences relating to prostitution.[62]

33   Women who worked in the cribs on Chatham Street were considered to be socially inferior to women who worked in the so-called "carriage trade" houses around Broad Street.[63] Police records and newspaper reports indicate that women on Chatham Street were more likely to be involved in affrays and altercations involving alcohol and violence.[64] In many respects, this was a precarious place, and on a hot summer day in 1907 the entire area was destroyed by fire.[65] Fortunately, there were no deaths or injuries in the conflagration. However, the sex trade in Victoria was never the same after the fire of 1907.

34   The fire alone did not affect the character of the sex trade. The change was partly due to the social purity movement, which made inroads in many North American cities during the Edwardian years.[66] By 1906 the social purity crusade had gained considerable momentum in Victoria, as organizations like the Woman's Christian Temperance Union and reform-minded city councillors embarked on a campaign to curtail the sex trade. Ultimately, they wanted to eradicate the trade, but in the interim they sought to eliminate brothels from the city centre and restrict the red-light district to the western end of Chatham Street and a single block on Herald Street.[67] In 1907, the Victoria Police Commission proscribed those two city blocks as a restricted district. Most of the brothels outside the district were compelled to close. Further restrictions were introduced in 1910, when Herald Street was removed from the restricted zone and efforts were made to confine brothels and cribs to the 500 block of Chatham Street. Moreover, during this period civic officials and members of the local chamber of commerce were making a concerted effort to promote Victoria as a genteel haven for retirees and an attractive destination for tourists.[68] Sex-trade workers came to be seen as nettles in the city of gardens. Thus, while the fire of 1907 and new regulations facilitated the social purity crusade in Victoria, the moral and economic climate of the city was already changing in ways not conducive to the sex trade.

Documentation and Charade

35   The nominal census records examined in this study coincide with the apogee of the sex trade in Victoria. The records are compelling because they provide traces of transient and marginalized workers who are not well documented elsewhere, and because they provide details of a community that had largely disappeared by the end of the Edwardian era. True, we are only seeing a portion of the community through the lens of census records. Because the census of Canada was conducted on *de jure* principles, persons who were not deemed to be permanent residents of Victoria in accordance with the *Census Act* were not enumerated. The precise number of

---

[62] The following women, who were enumerated in North Ward, sub district 14, were fined $50 each for being inmates of bawdy houses on various occasions between December 1900 and September 1901: Marie Dupont, Isabelle Rafichard, Minnie Williams, Susan Roberts, Marie Burman, Nellie Wood, and Georgee Scudder. During the same period, Nellie Earle and Eva Showers were fined $90 for "keeping" bawdy houses (CVA, *Victoria Police Magistrates' record book,* CB 16B5, vol. 2, passim). All of these women were enumerated in the 1901 census.

[63] Hansen Brett, "Ladies in Scarlet," p. 22.

[64] Police charge books frequently noted affrays in this part of Victoria. For example, on October 25, 1901, two "French" prostitutes, Jenny LeRoy and Virginie Dauzo, were arrested for "fighting." The police records also note that many of the women who were arrested were "immoderate" in their consumption of alcohol (VPA, *Police charge book,* 1889–1902, p. 209; VCA, *Victoria Police Magistrates' record book,* CB 16B5, vol. 2, p. 90).

[65] *Victoria Daily Colonist,* July 23, 1907.

[66] See Carolyn Strange and Tina Loo, *Law and Moral Regulation in Canada, 1867–1939* (Toronto: University of Toronto Press, 1997); Valverde, *The Age of Light, Soap and Water.*

[67] Evidence of the social purity campaign in Victoria can be seen in local newspapers and reports of city council debates. See the *Victoria Daily Colonist,* July 25, 1907 and *Victoria Daily Times,* April 15, 1908.

[68] Kenneth Lines, "A Bit of Old England: The Selling of Tourist Victoria" (MA thesis, History, University of Victoria, 1972); Michael Dawson, *Selling British Columbia. Tourism and Consumer Culture, 1890–1970* (Vancouver: University of British Columbia Press, 2004), pp. 15–37.

sojourner sex-trade workers is difficult to determine, but in 1900 Victoria's chief of police estimated that over 200 "known prostitutes" were working in the city.[69] Only a portion of them are identifiable on the census. Nevertheless, our case count is significant. For 1891, we have information on two dozen sex-trade workers; we can identify nearly 70 sex-trade workers on the 1901 census. The case count is large enough to suggest a prosopographical profile of female sex workers and shed some light on the *demi-monde* in Victoria during this period.

36   One of the most striking things about the tenderloin of Victoria is the prominence of American-born women. In 1891, over 80 per cent of sex-trade workers identified on the census reported the United States as their place of birth, a figure congruent with police department statistics.[70] This figure might be compared with the American component in the larger cohort of Victoria's female population between 20 and 30 years of age. In that cohort, only 12 per cent were born in the United States.[71] A decade later, American-born women still dominated the *demi-monde*. Among the sex-trade workers identified in Victoria brothels on the 1901 census, 80 per cent were from the United States. In the larger cohort of women between the ages of 20 and 30 years in Victoria in 1901, American-born residents comprised only 13 per cent of the population.[72]

37   The mean age of brothel prostitutes in 1891 was 24 years; the median age was 25 years. Brothel-keepers were slightly older, with a mean age of 29. Ten years later, the age difference between brothel prostitutes and brothel-keepers was greater. In 1901, the median age of brothel prostitutes was 21 while the median age of brothel keepers was 31. The increase in the age difference is due to the fact that brothel prostitutes in 1901 included some very young females, while there were no teenagers in the sorority of 1891. The age difference also reflects the fact that brothel owners like Alice Seymour were ten years older.

38   Demographic data from the census raise some interesting questions about the marital status of sex-trade workers. The data contradict the traditional view that prostitutes were societal rebels who disdained the conventional ties of marriage. In 1891, among the cohort of women who managed and worked in Victoria brothels, nearly two-thirds (15 out of 24) reported that they were married. The other women in the cohort were single. The ratio of married to unmarried female sex-trade workers in Victoria is relatively high compared to data from other communities. In her study of prostitution in Nevada in the 1880s, Marion Goldman found that less than half of Comstock prostitutes had been married. However, as Goldman suggests, in many cases the marital status of sex-trade workers was not indicative of conjugal conditions. "Most of those who were married no longer lived with their husbands, and they had simply ignored complicated divorce procedures."[73] None of the married women who resided in Victoria brothels in 1891 were living with their husbands. Indeed, males are notably absent from the nominal records of census households that functioned as brothels in 1891. Similarly, with the exception of male Chinese cooks and servants, males do not appear in the census returns of Victoria brothels in 1901.[74] The marital profile of female residents, however, had changed. Among the cohort of women who operated and worked in brothels, nearly 80 per cent (29 out of 37) were single. Three women were divorced, and three women were widows; only two women were married.

---

[69] British Columbia Archives. GR 784, British Columbia. Commission on Victoria Police Commissioners (1910), p. 12.

[70] During this period, over 80 per cent of the women recorded as prostitutes in Victoria police department charge books gave the United States as their place of birth. VPA, *Police Charge Book* (1889–1902).

[71] Information on the larger cohort is derived from statistical queries on 1891 census data. In 1891, N ¼ 1,860 (females between 20 and 30 years of age in Victoria). Of that number, 230 (12 per cent) were born in the United States.

[72] Information on the proportion of American-born women is derived from statistical queries on 1901 census data. In 1901, N ¼ 2,719 (females between 20 and 30 years of age in Victoria). Of that number, 344 (13 per cent) were born in the United States.

[73] Goldman, Gold Diggers & Silver Miners, p. 71.

[74] In 1901, Hattie Wickwire employed a 22-year-old Chinese cook, identified as Jim, in her brothel at 60 Broad Street. According to the census, he earned $300 a year. Alexina Ballinger, who ran a brothel at 54 Broad Street, employed a 36-year-old male Chinese domestic servant, Fun Lee. He earned $250 a year.

39   The demography of the cribs on Chatham Street in 1901 was different again. The women who occupied the cribs were generally older than the women who resided in brothels. Although the mean age was 24, the median age was 28. Over one-third of crib prostitutes (38 per cent) were 30 years of age and older. With regard to their marital status, all of the women indicated that they were single. Forty per cent of the crib prostitutes had been born in the United States, but 45 per cent had been born in France and the French-speaking region of Belgium. With women from Germany and Russia, this was a very cosmopolitan corner of Victoria. Its cosmopolitan character was also evident in the American-born contingent, which included African American women.[75]

40   The women enumerated in cribs on lower Chatham Street may have been part of a larger community described by Ronald Hyam in his book *Empire and Sexuality*. He discusses an international sorority of sex-trade workers who "moved around the globe to take advantage of labour opportunities caused by gold rushes and similar phenomenon" in the late Victorian and Edwardian years. Hyam describes these sojourner sex trade workers as "peripatetic prostitutes."[76] Some of the sex-trade workers enumerated in Victoria may once have been part of that group, since most were newly arrived when the census was taken. In fact, all of the women identified as sex-trade workers on Chatham Street arrived in Canada between 1899 and 1901, according to the census.[77] Some of the women may have worked previously in the mining towns in the Kootenay district of British Columbia; the cities of Nelson and Rossland both had well-defined red-light districts that offered opportunities to "transient prostitutes."[78] Undoubtedly some of the women may have worked in the Yukon before coming to Victoria, because their demographic profile fits that of sex-trade workers in Dawson City during the Klondike Gold Rush. In her study of community in the Klondike, Charlene Porsild found that over half of the prostitutes in Dawson City were European born, nearly one-third of them in France or Belgium.[79]

41   As Mary Murphy noted in a study of the sex trade in *fin-de-siècle* Butte, Montana: "Prostitution [was] a highly stratified occupation. Each woman's status was determined by a combination of race, ethnicity, education, sociability, and sexual skill and was reflected in the place she worked."[80] It would be helpful to know more about the dynamics of the *demimonde* in Victoria. How was it constructed and stratified? Who gained entry to the upper echelons, and who was consigned to the lower echelons of the sex trade in the city? These interesting questions must await another study, as ours concerns the character of census records relating to sex-trade workers, not the character of the trade itself.

42   What are we to make of these records? Are they reliable, are they veracious? If brothel-keepers and prostitutes in Victoria were enumerated with misleading or fanciful occupations, can we trust any of the information they provided? Can we be sure about their names, ages, places of birth? It is impossible to provide an unequivocal answer to these questions, but some general remarks might be offered. On the matter of names, it is likely that some women—especially women called Kitty, Flossie, Trixie, and Loo—offered nicknames or pet names to the enumerator.

---

[75] LAC, *Fourth Census of Canada*, 1901, microfilm reel T6430, Victoria City, District 4, sub-district 14, pp. 16–18.

[76] Ronald Hyam, *Empire and Sexuality: The British Experience* (Manchester: Manchester University Press), p. 148.

[77] LAC, *Fourth Census of Canada*, 1901, microfilm reel T6429, Victoria City, District 4, sub-district 14, p. 16.

[78] Charleen Smith provides a remarkably detailed account of the sex trade in the Kootenay in her essay, "Boomtown Brothels in the Kootenays, 1895–1905." The largest group of sex-trade workers in that region, she notes, were "transient prostitutes." These women are "also the most difficult to discuss with any degree of certainty because of the very nature of their movement in and out of towns throughout British Columbia. Frequently appearing in police records only once or twice and then dropping out of sight altogether, we can only speculate about their lives on the road" (pp. 136–137).

[79] Charlene Porsild, *Gamblers and Dreamers: Women, Men, and Community in the Klondike* (Vancouver: University of British Columbia Press, 1998), p. 124. For another study that has utilized census data and court records, see Bay Riley, *Gold Diggers of the Klondike: Prostitution in Dawson City, Yukon, 1891–1908* (Winnipeg: Watson & Dwyer, 1997).

[80] Mary Murphy, "The Private Lives of Public Women: Prostitution in Butte, Montana, 1878–1917" in Susan Armitage and Elizabeth Jameson, eds., The *Women's West* (Norman: University of Oklahoma Press, 1987), p. 194.

Some women may have used aliases. It is also likely that some women provided misleading information about their ages or dates of birth. The allure of youth was an important part of their trade, and we might expect women to have represented themselves as being younger than they actually were.[81] We might also expect them to exoticize their backgrounds by claiming to be from France. In the American West, French prostitutes "had a special reputation for mysterious fast living that added to their allure."[82] Some of the prostitutes on Chatham Street may have been trading on that reputation.

43   That being said, many indicators suggest that personal information was in the main accurate. Police charge books and newspaper reports often refer to "French prostitutes" on Chatham Street, and there is good reason to suppose that women who said they were from France had in fact been born there.[83] Since several women in the Chatham Street quarter indicated that French was their mother tongue, we can assume that they were telling the truth about their origins. Likewise, women who claimed to be from the United States appear to be genuine. Stella Carroll's biographer has corroborated personal information that the well-known, American-born madam provided to the enumerator in 1901. Carroll's place and

date of birth, her family background, and other information recorded in the census are accurate.[84] The data are consistent for other women identified with the sex trade, who appear in both the 1891 and the 1901 census. Alice Seymour was noted as 29 years old in the 1891 census and 39 in the 1901 census. Her religion (Roman Catholic), place of birth (US), and family origins (Germany) are consistent in both censuses. Personal information for another brothel-keeper, Jennie Morris, is similarly consistent across the two censuses. She was recorded as 25 years old in the 1891 census and as 35 years old in the 1901 census.[85] Police records also corroborate census records, albeit with minor discrepancies. Thus we find Matty Smith in the 1891 census and Mattie Smith in police charge books; Hattie Spaulding in the census and Hettie Spaulding in the police blotter.[86]

44   It would appear, then, that sex-trade workers in Victoria cooperated with enumerators; there is no evidence in the records of census officials to indicate otherwise.[87] Of course, it was expedient for sex-trade workers to be cooperative, simply because individuals who refused to participate in the census could be prosecuted and fined under the provisions of the *Census Act*. On the other hand, some of the women may have participated in the census as a means of

---

[81] Butler has noted that, in the American West, prostitutes sometimes gave "sketchy responses to census enumerators" when asked for their age. "Age was a particularly sensitive manner in a profession where physical appeal supposedly counted for everything" (Butler, *Daughters of Joy, Sisters of Misery*, p. 15).

[82] Goldman, *Gold Diggers & Silver Miners*, p. 67. Jacqueline Baker Barnhart concurs with this assessment in *The Fair But Frail: Prostitution in San Francisco, 1849–1900* (Reno: University of Nevada Press, 1986). In California, she says, "French prostitutes demanded and received greater respect, admiration, and fees" than any other sex-trade workers. "French prostitutes maintained this position throughout the nineteenth century. The most derogatory adjective ascribed to a French prostitute was that she was notorious" (Barnhart, *The Fair But Frail*, pp. 50–53).

[83] See, for example, *Victoria Daily Colonist*, February 21, 1903, which reported on a complex case involving three French prostitutes who had been working in a house on Herald Street. Because the house was disorderly, the women were ordered to leave Victoria. They went to Seattle, but were subsequently deported back to Victoria, on the grounds that they had entered the United States for immoral purposes. See also note 64, above, for additional references to "French" prostitutes in this part of Victoria.

[84] Stella Carroll's actual name was Estella Carroll, but she was universally known as Stella. I am grateful to Linda Eversole for allowing me to read a pre-publication copy of her biography, *Stella: Unrepentant Madam*, and for confirming details about some of the women in Stella's sorority.

[85] LAC, *Third Census of Canada*, microfilm reel T6292, Victoria City, District 4, sub-district 4 c–1, pp. 25, 30; Fourth Census of Canada, microfilm reel T6429, Victoria City, District 4, sub-district 6, pp. 27–28.

[86] LAC, *Third Census of Canada*, microfilm reel T6292, Victoria City, District 4, sub-district 4 c–1, p. 25; VCA, Police Magistrate's Book, 1888–1891, p. 269.

[87] In 1891, the chief census officer noted that some of Victoria's Chinese residents were not forthcoming. Since the government had recently introduced a head tax on Chinese immigrants, this is not surprising. In some parts of the province, census officials struggled to win the trust of Aboriginal people. But there is no evidence that sex-trade workers were obdurate (Dunae, "Making the 1891 Census in British Columbia," p. 232).

affirming their place in the community. This may help to explain why sex-trade workers came forward when the Victoria *Daily Colonist* asked for the names of householders who had been overlooked in the official census of 1891. When the newspaper declared that residents had a civic duty to participate in the check census, members of the *demi-monde* responded to the call. Civic-minded madams taking part in the Victoria check census included Della Wentworth, who operated a brothel at 14 Broughton Street, and Therese Bernstein, who owned a brothel at 19 Courtney Street.[88]

45   The unabashed nature of prostitution in Victoria and the general acceptance of the sex workers may explain their presence in local directories. As noted earlier, the directories printed the names and addresses of many women who were engaged in the sex trade. The directories did not assign any occupation to these women; to some degree, then, even these texts were encoded. Presumably, though, contemporaries knew how to read the code. Members of the so-called sporting set would how to interpret a listing in the 1892 directory that read simply: "Miss Dewsup, 47 Broad Street." Similarly, the *cognoscenti* could draw inferences from a seemingly nondescript entry in the 1902 city directory that read: "Flossie Raymond, 9 Chatham Street."[89] The men enrolled as enumerators probably knew how to interpret these entries and decipher their codes, especially after they had called on the addresses and interviewed the occupants.

46   Who were these men? Ostensibly, any adult male who was a British subject could be hired as an enumerator, although in practice census-making often involved a degree of patronage. Applicants who were recommended by local officials or community leaders, such as magistrates or city councillors, were invariably appointed over applicants who did not have such mentors. In many jurisdictions, men of a

"clerkly disposition" were regarded as being ideally suited for census field work.[90] In Victoria, several enumerators were in fact clerks. Frank Stannard, a 23-year-old office clerk, enumerated Victoria's downtown brothels in 1891. Stannard was a bachelor who roomed with a widow and her family in the respectable neighbourhood of James Bay. In 1901, the brothels identified in this study were enumerated by three men: Irving Lemm, who was responsible for census sub-division 6; Louis Watson, the enumerator for census sub-division 7; and Herbert Winsby, the census-taker for sub-division 8. Lemm was a 46-year-old salesman; he was married and lived with his wife and eight children in a large house on the eastern (residential) end of Johnson Street. Watson was a 49-year-old goods agent; he was married, had recently emigrated from England, and lived in the Clarence Hotel in the city centre. Winsby was a 23-year-old clerk employed by the Dominion Express Company. He was unmarried and lived with his family on Stanley Avenue, near Victoria High School. Since his father was the city tax collector and his brothers were bank clerks, Winsby may well have had a "clerkly disposition." Robert Houston, a 45-year-old journalist, enumerated the crib prostitutes on Chatham Street. A bachelor, Houston lived in "Roccabella," the city's premier boarding house, on Victoria Crescent, close to the Anglican cathedral.[91]

47   These enumerators did not leave diaries or journals, and we can only imagine how they felt when they interviewed women in brothels and cribs. The Dominion government placed great confidence in these men and expected them to maintain high moral standards when they carried out their solemn inquest of the nation."[92] Enumerators were supposed to be purposeful but tactful when they interviewed residents, and accurate and painstaking in their record-keeping. They were also supposed to be vigilant

---

[88] British Columbia Archives, Add. MSS 1908, *Census of Victoria* [1891], microfilm reel A–1356.

[89] The entry for Dewsup appears on p. 434 of *Williams' Victoria Directory* (1892). As noted earlier, the directory was compiled in September 1891 and published in December that year. The entry for Flossie Raymond appears on p. 810 of *Henderson's City of Victoria Directory* (1902). The directories are available in a searchable PDF format at the *viHistory*.ca

[90] Dunae, "Making the 1891 Census in British Columbia," p. 230.

[91] Enumerators are identified on manuscript census schedules. Information about the enumerators is derived from the census schedules and Victoria city directories.

[92] This lofty phrase was used by the Dominion government to describe the 1891 census (*Statistical Year-Book of Canada* for 1895, p. 156).

and astute. The official *Manual* for the 1891 census described the ideal enumerator as "an intelligent and conscientious officer, not a mere machine," whose primary duty was "to guard himself and all concerned against errors and frauds."[93] Clearly, though, there was a fraudulent aspect to their work; despite the high moral tone sounded in the official manuals, the census of the *demi-monde*—at least in Victoria—was a charade. How else can we characterize a process whereby enumerators knowingly described brothel operators as boarding house keepers and prostitutes as dressmakers, nurses, and florists?

48   The enumerators were not the only persons complicit in the charade. Having completed their census schedules, enumerators were required to submit their portfolios to a census commissioner. These officials coordinated and supervised the work of enumerators in the field. The census commissioner was supposed to review the enumerators' returns and check the nominal schedules, line by line, for accuracy. In 1891, the census commissioner for the city of Victoria was John B. Lovell, a longtime resident and alderman who represented Yates Street Ward on Victoria City Council. Lovell would have been very familiar with residents in his ward, including residents in census households around Broad Street. Lovell's superior was George Sargison, the chief census officer for the province of British Columbia. He, too, would have been familiar with the denizens of this part of town. An accountant by profession, Sargison worked in an office on Langley Street, literally around the corner from some of Victoria's most prominent brothels.

49   Likewise, the senior officials who oversaw the 1901 census of Victoria must have been aware of the charade. William Dalby, a long-established real estate agent, served as Victoria's census commissioner for the fourth decennial census. From his office on Yates Street in the centre of the city, he reviewed and approved schedules submitted by his enumerators. Dalby then passed the schedules on to his superior, Robert Drury, the chief census officer for the province of British Columbia. Drury was a prominent insurance agent in Victoria. His office was located on Broad Street, only a few doors away from some of Victoria's best-known brothels.[94]

50   Clearly, everyone—from enumerators in the field to census commissioners and chief census officers—knew that some of the information they had recorded, notably information relating to the occupations of sex-trade workers, was inaccurate and misleading. Why, then, did they agree to the charade? Local census officials may have been diffident or circumspect. Possibly they were too embarrassed to challenge the veracity of information they received from, say, Stella Carroll's female lodgers on Broad Street. Possibly they were too prudish to ask women on Chatham Street to elaborate on their work. As Bettina Bradbury has noted, enumerators sometimes found themselves in awkward circumstances in which they were reluctant to probe into the personal relations of the people they were enumerating. "Some questions were better not asked, some answers better not given."[95]

51   There may be other reasons why enumerators agreed to the charade, some of which are suggested by the characteristics of the term in question. Charade is a word that has many connotations, that can be defined and construed in different ways. However, one of the definitions provided by the *Oxford Dictionary* offers a good description of the kind of charade documented in this study. A "charade," according to this definition, is "an absurd pretense designed to create a pleasant or respectable appearance."[96] In the case of Victoria, census officials were obviously determined to maintain an edifice of respectability. The census commissioners appointed for Victoria were prominent members of the community: Lovell, the commissioner in 1891,

---

[93] Census Manual (1891), p. 7.

[94] The names of census officers in British Columbia are published in the (Canadian government) Auditor General's Report for 1901–1902. See Canada. *Sessional Papers*, I (1903), vol. 37, pp. D114–D120, D279. The 1901 *Henderson's British Columbia Gazetteer and Directory* indicates that William Dalby's office was located at 64 Yates Street near the corner of Broad Street. Robert Drury's office was located at 34 Broad Street.

[95] Bettina Bradbury, "Canadian Children Who Lived with One Parent in 1901" in Sager and Baskerville, eds., *Household Counts*, p. 257.

[96] *Oxford Pocket Dictionary* (Oxford: Oxford University Press, 2007).

was an alderman; Dalby, the commissioner in 1901, was a realtor. Neither of them would have wanted to represent the Queen City, as Victoria was styled in contemporary promotional literature, in a negative way. Certainly there was nothing to be gained by revealing large numbers of sex-trade workers on local census returns. The census commissioners may have conveyed this attitude to their enumerators who, it would seem, were agreeable to the pretense.

52   Alternatively, the charade might be understood by considering the role and responsibilities of enumerators. Having been sworn in as census officers, enumerators were supposed to carry out their work diligently. They were instructed to record verbatim information provided to them and not to insert any information that was not "explicitly stated or distinctly acknowledged to them." It was not their duty to challenge, edit, or annotate any information. Rather, their task was to conduct themselves with discretion and tact to win the confidence and secure the cooperation of the public. In most cases, at least in Victoria, they played their part in the solemn inquest of the nation by the book and to the letter. Social historians can be grateful that they did so. Thanks to the efforts of these conscientious and, we might suppose, conventional men—who otherwise worked as clerks, salesmen, accountants, and insurance agents—we have records of some rather unconventional women.

Interpreting the Records

53   As our understanding of these records increases, we can utilize them more efficiently as research tools that may shed light on the *demi-monde*, but we must handle the records with care. As British historian

Edward Higgs remarked, nineteenth-century census records pertaining to women and women's occupations must always be treated with "caution," and historians using these records need to be "circumspect."[97] These are useful *caveats* and might be applied to nominal census records in general, not only to those relating to women. Higgs's caveats remind us of the nuanced nature of census data, and social historians need to be cautious in using aggregate data to assert larger themes. Complex social entities and relationships may be embedded in aggregate data. The occupation of dressmaker is an exemplar in this respect. According to official returns from the 1891 census of Canada, 343 women in British Columbia were employed as dressmakers.[98] As we now know, not all of those women supported themselves using their skills with needle and thread. In all likelihood, some of the young, unmarried women who were identified as dressmakers in other Canadian cities were probably involved with the sex trade.[99] Dressmaker, however, is not the only signifier. We might be equally cautious in approaching aggregate data relating to seamstresses or lodging house keepers. In fact, we may feel hesitant in taking any occupation—including actresses, milliners, nurses, and music teachers—at face value. This is not to say that we should distrust and disregard the data entirely. However, we need to be mindful of the ambiguous character of nineteenth-century nominal census schedules. Although these records offer a cornucopia of evidence about late Victorian society, the records can be problematic, and some of the *prima facie* evidence they offer is misleading. Sometimes the problems are due to "misreporting," a term Richard Steckel used to explain certain anomalies in nineteenth-century American census records.[100] Sometimes, however, as

---

[97] Edward Higgs, "Women, Occupation and Work in Nineteenth Century Censuses," *History Workshop Journal*, vol. 23 (1987), p. 76. Higgs expands on his approach to historical census data in his monograph, *The Information State in England: The Central Collection of Information on Citizens since 1500* (Basingstoke, UK: Palgrave Macmillan, 2004).

[98] Canada. *Census of Canada 1890–91/Recensement du Canada*, vol. II (Ottawa: S.E. Dawson, Queen's Printer, 1893), p. 141.

[99] An analysis of the 1871 census of Ontario by Kris Inwood and Richard Reid suggests that sex-trade workers may be hidden within aggregate data for dressmakers. The authors note: "Among dressmakers (but not weavers), female proprietors lived in smaller and more urban households with a lower ratio of children to adults." Brothels in Victoria, which were headed by dressmakers like Bertha Baker, would fit this profile. See Inwood and Reid, "Gender and Occupational Identity in a Canadian Census," p. 67.

[100] Richard H. Steckel, "The Quality of Census Data for Historical Inquiry: A Research Agenda," *Social Science History*, vol. 15, no. 4 (Winter 1991), p. 594. Steckel suggested that "misreporting" was the cause of discrepancies in the ages and illiteracy rates of certain groups across decennial censuses. He did not consider the problem of misinformation.

in the cases described here, the problems are due to misinformation.

54   As historians, we might reasonably expect to encounter misinformation, especially when we probe a milieu defined by sex, money, and artifice. Still, we need some means of determining the character of the records. Perhaps the best way of assessing the reliability of information recorded on nominal census schedules and detecting misinformation is to consider the records in context. Ideally, researchers should try to situate the records spatially; that is, researchers should endeavour to associate information about a person within the context of the person's census family and community. Of course, we also need to be alert for occupational codes. Dressmaker was a popular disguise in the city of Victoria, but in other communities other disguises may have been used. In Dawson City, for example, brothel-keepers were enumerated as tobacconists and cigar dealers.[101]

55   With these *caveats* in mind, researchers might follow the methodology utilized in this study to explore the *demi-monde* in different parts of Canada. For example, social historians interested in the sex trade in Halifax might have a close look at census households on Barrack Street and Albemarle Street.[102] For Winnipeg, researchers might look at census households on Thomas Street, Annabella Street, and the Point Douglas district, while historians interested in prostitution in Vancouver might focus on census households along Dupont Street.[103] Eventually, we may be able to construct and compare prosopographical profiles of sex-trade workers in different parts of Canada. As well, these data may enable historians to map moral geographies in urban places and examine the cartography of sexual commerce in different cities. With these data, we may see more clearly how prostitutional space was constructed and regulated in Canada in the Victorian era.[104] Not only might we examine historical aspects of the sex trade across Canada; we might also compare the Canadian experience with sexual commerce in the United States, Great Britain, and elsewhere.[105]

56   The historical census in Canada has been described as "a text that encodes a three-way relationship between the government, the enumerators, and the enumerated."[106] As this study has shown, the relationship was complex, and the code is not always apparent. Indeed, the process of enumeration examined here might be characterized as a kind of performance. Record-takers (census commissioners and enumerators) and respondents (female sex-trade workers) both played a part and understood their respective roles in the performance. In this charade, the respondents were disguised, and because of their disguises they are not readily visible to historians. We can discern brothel-keepers, brothel prostitutes, and crib prostitutes in Victoria thanks to a large pool of digital data and the query interface available on the *viHistory* website. Having a large pool of machine-readable data and an application that links census records to directory listings and individuals to census households was invaluable in carrying out this

---

101 Porsild, *Dreamers and Gamblers*, pp. 122, 125.

102 Judith Fingard, *Jack in Port. Sailortowns of Eastern Canada.* (Toronto: University of Toronto Press, 1982), pp. 134–137, and *The Dark Side of Life in Victorian Halifax* (Porter's Lake, NS: Pottersfield Press, 1989), pp. 95–125.

103 Gray, *Red Lights on the Prairies*, pp. 37–55; Hinther, "The Oldest Profession in Winnipeg," *passim*; Nilson, "The Social Evil: Prostitution in Vancouver," *passim*.

104 For a spatial and theoretical analysis, see Patrick A. Dunae, "Geographies of Sexual Commerce and the Production of Prostitutional Space, Victoria, British Columbia, 1860–1914," *Journal of the Canadian Historical Association*, new series, vol. 19, no. 1 (2008), pp. 115–142.

105 Joel Best's study of prostitution in St. Paul, Minnesota (1982) and Marion Goldman's study of prostitution in Nevada (1981) may provide useful reference points for a comparative study, since they draw on census records and situate brothels spatially within their respective communities. See also Neil Larry Shumsky and Larry M. Spring, "San Francisco's Zone of Prostitution, 1880–1934," *Journal of Historical Geography*, vol. 7, no. 1 (1981), pp. 71–89; Philip Howell, "A Private Contagious Diseases Act: Prostitution and Public Space in Victorian Cambridge," *Journal of Historical Geography*, vol. 26, no. 3 (2000), pp. 376–402; Mark Wild, "Red Light Kaleidoscope: Prostitution and Ethnoracial Relations in Los Angeles, 1880–1940," *Journal of Urban Geography*, vol. 28, no. 6 (September 2002), pp. 720–742.

106 Cynthia Comacchio, "'The History of Us': Social Science, History, and the Relations of Family in Canada," *Labour / Le Travail*, vol. 46 (Fall 2000), p. 183.

project. However, researchers do not require digital tools for this kind of study. Rather, and as noted at the start, it is possible to identify urban sex-trade workers in late Victorian cities if we have some knowledge about local sites of sexual commerce and if we relate those areas to enumeration units. The next step is to read nominal census schedules closely, by considering the records in context and being cognizant of certain code words, especially the descriptors that female sex-trade workers offered when the enumerator enquired about their occupation, trade, or calling. Locating these women, who have been concealed and camouflaged on nominal census schedules for over a century, is a challenging task, but the reward may lie in opportunities for further research and understanding. If we look carefully, we may be able to find these women; once we can see them, we may be able to hear what they have to say.

Histoire sociale/Social History.
2009. November 42 (84).

KEY AND CHALLENGING WORDS

innocuous, euphemism, cognizant, prima facie, contentious, burgeon, circumspect, obfuscate, nominal, delineate, astute, roisterous, sub rosa, congruence, nexus, echelon, flamboyant, ostensibly, transient, affray, eradicate, interim, apogee, disdain (v.), veracious, unequivocal, allure, expedient, unabashed, vigilant, complicit, diffident, cornucopia, anomaly

QUESTIONS

1. What is the justification for this study? Identify the thesis or essay plan.
2. What are the differences between "historical demographers, urban geographers, and census historians" (paragraph 3)? Using a dictionary, if necessary, write one-sentence definitions of each term. Then, in one or two sentences, show how the three vocations are interrelated.
3. What two main reasons explain the "problematic" or "challenging" nature of census records of sex trade workers?
4. Identify three primary sources mentioned in paragraphs 10–12 and discuss how they are used to contribute to the emerging profile of sex trade workers in Victoria in 1891 and 1901.
5. Referring to specific points in "Taking the Census," explain how the requirements of Canada's census form and of BC enumerators made it possible to retrieve detailed information about those enumerated.
6. Choose two notes from the section "The Sex Trade in Victoria" and a) show how each relates to the paragraph of text that contains the note; b) explain why it was not included in the text.
7. Compare and contrast the nature and environment of sex trade workers in Broad Street with those in Herald Street, according to Dunae's reading of the information provided in the 1891 and 1901 censuses.
8. In light of Dunae's claim that census data "contradict the traditional view that prostitutes were social rebels who disdained the conventional ties of marriage" (paragraph 38), explain the evidence in paragraphs 39–40 about marital status; does this evidence contradict the earlier claim?
9. Explain the importance of the questions in paragraph 42. Does Dunae successfully establish his credibility as an historian in paragraphs 42–44? Refer to specific passages from the text in your answer.
10. Analyze the section "Interpreting the Records." To what extent does it function as an effective conclusion? What does the final paragraph contribute to the section as a whole?

POST-READING

1. *Collaborative or individual activity:* Discuss or analyze the following: What is the meaning of the term "demi-monde," referred to several times in Dunae's article and why, from a historical perspective, is it important to be aware of its existence and that of its inhabitants? What other "demi-mondes" have been or could be investigated by social historians?

2. *Collaborative or individual activity:* After defining the word "charade," Dunae gives two reasons why enumerators might have been complicit in the census deceptions. Which do you consider the most probable? Why? What other reasons could account for the charade?

3. a) Referring specifically to passages in the article, demonstrate how it exemplifies the need for critical thinking and the importance of making inferences in the reading process; b) Discuss the importance of inference making to the historical method in particular, again referring specifically to the text.

See also Post-reading question 4, Turcotte, "Life in metropolitan areas: Dependence of cars in urban neighbourhoods," p. 421.

RELATED WEBSITES OF INTEREST

viHistory (Vancouver Island census records):
www.vihistory.ca/

Statistics Canada (origins of census and history of census in Canada):
www12.statcan.gc.ca/census-recensement/2006/ref/dict/overview-apercu/pop1-eng.cfm

2001 Census of Canada in Beyond 20/20 format: Documentation (includes definitions of several terms used in Dunae's article):
www.library.mcgill.ca/edrs/data/dli/statcan/census/census2001/docs.html

ADDITIONAL LIBRARY READING

Thomas, D. (2010). The census and the evolution of gender roles in early 20th century Canada. *Canadian Social Trends, 89,* 20–30.

MEDIA AND IMAGE

Wikipedia grows up

Peter Binkley

(1,480 words)

Pre-reading

1. Scan the essay to determine the writer's stance towards his topic. Does the writer have an identifiable thesis? Why or why not?

1   The most common title for an encyclopedia in the Middle Ages (when the genre was formalized, at least in the Western tradition) was Speculum, or "Mirror." Such a work was intended to reflect the entirety of nature, history, and doctrine. The pre-eminent example, Vincent of Beauvais's monumental *Speculum maius,* ran to nearly 1,400 large double-column pages in a seventeenth-century edition of its history volume alone. Don't believe me? Look it up in Wikipedia: I just inserted that (true) figure in the article on Vincent.

2   The controversy over Wikipedia in library circles has died down over the last few months, as our attention has moved on to other representations of the new "Web 2.0" environment: social bookmarking services, blogs, etc. Nothing, of course, illuminates a complex question like a good buzzword—such as "Library 2.0"—but we should not let the new emphasis prevent us from following the development of one of the forerunners of Web 2.0. Wikipedia is entering its adolescence, at least in web terms: it passed its fifth birthday in January.

3   To review: Wikipedia aims to be a "multilingual free encyclopedia of the highest possible quality." Its English edition is closing in on one million articles. Anyone can create an account for himself or herself and create or edit articles; even without an account anyone can edit. Every article has a discussion page, where contentious changes can be discussed before they are implemented in the main article. Every article also has a history page where all past changes can be reviewed and reversed. It takes four clicks to restore any earlier version. Changes are ascribed to the user who made them; users have their own wiki pages with the Wikipedia site where they can list their interests, store work in progress, and receive and respond to comments from readers and other users.

Problems

4   Can such a process produce an authoritative encyclopedia? Common sense says no. Even when a knowledgeable author writes something worthwhile, any ignoramus can replace it with whatever nonsense he or she cares to paste into the edit form. Those of us who work in the information professions may well ask why we should involve ourselves in a forum where amateurism rules. Why should you go to the trouble to write a good and correct entry, only to see it defaced?

5   The openness of the Wikipedia model irritates its critics beyond endurance. The Parents for the Online Safety of Children have found the answer to the question of who edits it: "there is an underground cabal of pedophiles who edit Wikipedia" [sic].[1] Their evidence is in the discussion page for the article on pedophilia, where advocates for "childlove" argue for a more lenient attitude toward those who are sexually attracted to children. Perhaps you were unaware of this movement (I certainly was). It is difficult to imagine a more sensitive topic. But the article itself, in its present form, reports the existence and aims of the "childlove" movement without undermining its coverage of the medical and legal aspects of pedophilia. The "cabal" has certainly failed in its attempt to use Wikipedia to infect the world's youth.

6   Recently a series of minor scandals have drawn public attention to the dangers of Wikipedia's open editing model. A practical joke let a preposterous statement about a Tennessee journalist's involvement in the assassination of John F. Kennedy stand on the record for months. Congressional staff tidied up their senators' entries, in one case consigning an inconvenient campaign promise to the memory hole. Other celebrities were found to have taken a less than neutral approach to their own entries. Even IP addresses traceable to Canada's House of Commons have been found on Wikipedia history pages.

8   If you are outraged at the way that Wikipedia considers itself above the law, and you feel you have been personally maligned, you might care to join the budding class action suit and claim your share of the "substantial monetary damages" the organizers hope to recover. Wikipedia's problems, the anonymous proponents of the suit claim, "are intentional in design and purposeful in their intent; to cause harm, to permit and encourage a system of anonymous libel."[2] Even if you haven't been libelled yourself, you can still support their cause by clicking on one of the Google ads on their site.

Wikipedia vs. Britannica

8   There are a thousand reasons why Wikipedia should have been stillborn. And yet it moves, as Galileo said. A recent study published in the journal *Nature* found that Wikipedia compared well to the *Encyclopedia Britannica* in a side-by-side blind comparison of 42 articles conducted by experts.[3] The two encyclopedias were tied in major errors at four apiece; Wikipedia led in minor errors 162 to 123.

9   The sample articles were from the hard sciences. Where Wikipedia really excels is in the areas that you might expect to attract a demographic willing to sit in front of a browser and show off his or her knowledge: popular culture and current technology. If your question concerns a current indie band, an anime character, a class of monster in a particular role-playing game, wireless routers, or even OpenURLs, Wikipedia will often be an excellent source. Jon Udell made this point well last year with his screencast "documentary" on the Wikipedia article "Heavy metal umlaut."[4] This article traces the history of the extravagant use of umlauts by bands such as Mötley Crüe—a field of inquiry that Britannica, so far as I know, has yet to address.

10   Even in the realm of politics, Wikipedia has much to offer. Dip into the article on the Swift Boat Veterans for Truth, who were so prominent in the US election in 2004. You'll find a detailed chronology of the ads and descriptions of their contents and a reasonably balanced account of the issues at stake. The "neutral point of view" (NPOV) so prized at Wikipedia was not achieved in this case without controversy bordering on bloodshed: just look into the discussion page. This, I submit, is one of the most remarkable documents to emerge from the 2004 campaign. If you need a guide to the issues and the passions they provoked, reading this discussion among fierce partisans for both sides is as good as scanning a thousand political blogs. And what is most remarkable is that the two sides actually engaged each other and negotiated a version of the article that both can more or less live with. This is a rare sight indeed in today's polarized political atmosphere, where most on-line forums are echo chambers for one side or the other.

11   Such negotiations are never easy, and in fact Wikipedia has more institutional structure than at first appears. Some 800 experienced users are designated as administrators, with special powers of binding and loosing: they can protect and unprotect, delete and undelete and revert articles, and block and unblock users. They are expected to use their powers

in a neutral way, forming and implementing the consensus of the community. The effect of their intervention shows in the discussion pages of most contentious articles. Wikipedia has survived this long because it is easier to reverse vandalism than it is to commit it; but it still requires an enormous amount of volunteer monitoring to keep the ship afloat.

Ideal Patrons

12   To get a sense of the scale of activity in the Wikipedia community, dip a toe. Click the "Random page" link in the navigation menu a few times, until you find a typo to fix (it won't take long). Fix it, and save the perfected version. Admire your work, and click the "History" page to see your IP address immortalized in the annals of Wikipedia. Now click the "Recent changes" link in the navigation menu. You'll typically find that in the seconds since you saved your change, dozens of other pages have been modified. If you moved too slowly, your change may have scrolled off the list.

13   What is most striking about this community from the perspective of libraries is that it is made up of ideal library patrons. These are people who are passionate about acquiring and sharing information. Many of them are graduates enjoying an opportunity to maintain contact with their academic discipline and to make use of their scholarly skills. If you enter their community, you may be exposed to ideas that are unsavoury or worse. You will certainly encounter claims that are palpably inaccurate. But I believe it is incumbent on libraries to engage with them.

14   If an encyclopedia is a mirror, what does Wikipedia reflect? Its community of passionate amateurs—and beyond them the web, in all its variety, like a city described by Whitman. Wikipedia is a glorious experiment and a challenge to us to live up to our ideals. How can we devote ourselves to making information accessible to all and then scorn these devoted amateurs who delight in building with the bricks we give them?

Canadian Library Association. *Feliciter.*
2006. 52 (2).

Notes

1. http://news.baou.com/main.php?action=recent&rid=20679.
2. http://wikipediaclassaction.org.
3. www.nature.com/news/2005/051212/full/438900a.html.
4. http://weblog.infoworld.com/udell/gems/umlaut.html.

KEY AND CHALLENGING WORDS

pre-eminent, contentious, ascribe, cabal, proponent, palpable, incumbent (adj.)

QUESTIONS

1. How does the author attempt to generate interest in his introduction? Is he successful?

2. What is the author's purpose in writing the essay? Where and how does he indicate this? Who is his audience? Where and how does he indicate this?

3. How could you describe the author's tone in the sentence: "The 'cabal' has certainly failed in its attempt to use Wikipedia to infect the world's youth" (paragraph 5). Cite another place where he uses the same tone.

4. What does the author find "remarkable" about Wikipedia's article on the Swift Boat Veterans for Truth? Summarize the paragraph in which this reference occurs.

5. Who are the "ideal patrons" that Binkley refers to in the final section of his essay? Why does he call them this?

6. a) On the basis of reading this article, list two strengths and two weaknesses of Wikipedia; b) Do you think Binkley would recommend that students use this encyclopedia for their research essays? Why or why not?

POST-READING

1. *Collaborative activity:* Do you think that the "consensus" method for determining the content of an encyclopedia entry is as valid as the method of assigning experts/authorities in their field to write entries? Debate this issue.

2. Using at least two current and reliable sources published since December 2005, summarize in 300 to 400 words the controversy that arose when the academic journal *Nature* compared articles in Wikipedia with articles in the *Encyclopedia Britannica.*

3. Write an informational or evaluative report based on one entry from two different encyclopedias, one of which is Wikipedia. Ensure that the subject is one that you are familiar with so that you are qualified to compare and contrast the sources in their treatment of the subject.

ADDITIONAL LIBRARY READING

Baytiyeh, H., & Pfaffman, J. (2010). Volunteers in Wikipedia: Why the community matters. *Journal of Educational Technology & Society, 13*(2), 128–140.

Lim, S. (2009). How and why do college students use Wikipedia?. *Journal of the American Society for Information Science & Technology, 60*(11), 2189–2202.

Schweitzer, N.J. (2008). Wikipedia and psychology: Coverage of concepts and its use by undergraduate students. *Teaching of Psychology, 35*(2), 81–85.

The following is an online resource that includes 25 essays on Wikipedia by academics and media specialists:

Lovink, G., & Tkacz, N. (Eds.). (2011). *Critical points of view: A Wikipedia reader.* Retrieved from www.networkcultures.org/publications

Intended and unintended effects of an eating disorder educational program: Impact of presenter identity

Marlene B. Schwartz, PhD, Jennifer J. Thomas, MS, Kristin M. Bohan, PhD, and Lenny R. Vartanian, PhD

(3,861 words)

Pre-reading

1. From what you have read, heard, or observed about eating disorders, reflect on a) the prevalence of this problem in Canadian society today; b) the ways the problem can be alleviated or reduced, including any obstacles in society that must be overcome before solutions can be found.

2. Based on the essay's title, come up with a reading hypothesis of two sentences for the essay that follows. Do not use any major words from the title.

Abstract

Objective: This study examines the impact of presenter identity on the intended and unintended effects of an eating disorder educational program.

Method: High school students viewed one of two identical videotaped discussions about eating disorders. In one condition, the presenter was identified as an "eating disorder specialist"; in the other condition, she was identified as a "recovered patient." Before and after watching the video, participants reported on their awareness of various eating disorder symptoms, their beliefs about individuals with eating disorders, and their opinion of the presenter.

Results: At Time 2, both groups reported increased knowledge about eating disorders.

There was also evidence of increased endorsement of a number of implicit messages, particularly among those in the "recovered patient" group (e.g., "Girls with eating disorders are very pretty"; "It would be nice to look like" the presenter).

Conclusion: The unintended effects of eating disorder educational programs should be investigated before implementation because of their potential to undermine program efficacy.

Keywords: eating disorder educational programs; implicit messages; intended effects; unintended effects

Introduction

1   The US House of Representatives has deliberated the Eating Disorders Awareness, Education, and Prevention Act[1] in several successive congressional sessions from 2000 to the present. If passed, this legislation would promulgate the use of federal education funds to increase the awareness of eating disorders among parents and students, as well as to train educators in eating disorder prevention techniques. The prospect of implementing a nationwide prevention curriculum underscores the importance of identifying empirically supported strategies. A recent meta-analysis of research on eating disorder prevention programs indicated that 53 per cent of interventions resulted in

the reduction of at least one eating-disorder risk factor (e.g., body dissatisfaction) and 25 per cent led to the reduction of eating pathology (e.g., reduced frequency of binge eating and purging).[2] Importantly, a number of moderators of intervention effects were identified. For example, larger effect sizes were observed among programs that targeted high-risk populations (compared with those presented to a more general audience), and interactive programs were more effective than didactic programs.

2   One factor that has been relatively neglected in the empirical literature on eating disorder intervention and prevention programs is the impact of the characteristics of the presenter herself or himself. Clinicians and other specialists who work in the area of eating disorders are often recruited by various community groups (e.g., schools) to give educational talks about eating disorders. Their expertise is desirable as a means of effectively communicating information about eating disorders to audience members. Another common approach is to have presentations delivered by individuals who have themselves recovered from an eating disorder. The notion that listening to the personal story of a recovered individual would be preventative or therapeutic for vulnerable audiences is intuitively appealing. Twelve-step self-help programs, which are widely implemented in treating drug and alcohol addiction, feature personal recovery stories within a group format.[3] In the context of educational programs for eating disorders, not only can recovered individuals provide information about the etiology, symptoms, and treatment of eating disorders in general, but they are also uniquely disposed to provide descriptions of their own personal experiences with the illness, which the audience members might find particularly moving. These types of activities appear to be commonplace at colleges and universities; in one study, 13 of 18 randomly selected campuses with eating disorder prevention programs reported using recovered students as presenters.[4]

3   Despite the intuitive appeal of having individuals who have experienced and recovered from an eating disorder deliver educational materials, the effectiveness of these prevention efforts has been debated in the literature.[4,5] Several theorists have suggested that such interventions might be problematic in that they risk unintended iatrogenic outcomes by providing suggestive information about unhealthy weight control techniques or even normalizing and glamorizing eating disorder symptoms,[6] particularly among at-risk individuals. In particular, Garner[7] proposed that personal stories, especially those of celebrities, may inspire vicarious learning and emulation of disordered behaviours. The finding that some individuals have reported attempting self-induced vomiting after learning of the behaviour via magazine articles about eating disorders[8,9] lends credibility to these concerns. More recently, investigators have expressed growing apprehension over pro-eating disorder websites, which promote anorexia nervosa and bulimia nervosa as lifestyle choices rather than psychiatric conditions by featuring weight loss and purging tips, chat rooms, and "thinspiration" photos of ultra-slim models. In a study of eating disorder patients, Wilson et al.[10] found that 61 per cent of those who had visited pro eating disorder websites reported learning and implementing new weight loss or purging techniques as a result.

4   To our knowledge, only two studies[4,11] have investigated the impact of recovered patients on prevention program participants' eating attitudes and behaviours. First, Mann et al.[4] conducted a controlled study of small group panel discussions with two "poised, self-assured, attractive and personable" (p. 217) campus leaders who had recovered from anorexia and bulimia nervosa. The presenters provided educational information on etiology and treatment as well as personal accounts of their struggles. Eating disorder symptoms were assessed before the intervention, as well as four and 12 weeks after the intervention. When the researchers conducted a within-subjects analysis that included participants who completed the survey at all three time points, they found no effect of the intervention on eating disorder symptoms. In contrast, using a "more exploratory assessment" (p. 220) that included between-subjects comparisons of all participants who completed the survey at any time point, the researchers reported that at the four-week follow-up, the intervention group had significantly higher eating disorder symptoms than were found in the control group. This latter finding was interpreted as indicating an iatrogenic effect of the intervention. However, the appropriateness of the exploratory analyses and subsequent conclusions have been challenged.[2]

5   In another study, Heinze et al.[11] presented 7th-graders and 10th-graders with an educational video in which the presenter, an actress who had previously recovered from anorexia nervosa, differentially identified herself as a recovered anorexic, a peer, an expert, or did not provide a specific identity. After viewing these videos, participants expressed decreased drive for thinness and intentions to diet regardless of alleged presenter identity. In their study, the recovered-anorexic presenter did not provide any personal details related to her ill state or recovery, and this might have been a critical difference between the Heinze et al.[11] study and the Mann et al.[4] study.

6   The issue of presenter identity and disclosure of personal experiences in primary prevention for eating disorders remains a contentious one. The purpose of the present study was to explore one potential mechanism through which presenter identity could impact audience members. In particular, we focused on the explicit messages (intended effects) and on some possible implicit messages (unintended effects) of educational programs. We predicted that an eating disorder specialist and a recovered patient would be equally effective in communicating key information about the symptoms of eating disorders and the seriousness of those conditions. We also predicted, however, that the specialist and recovered patient would diverge with respect to the unintended or implicit messages that they conveyed. Based on previous theorizing regarding the normalization and glamorization of eating disorders, we hypothesized that an educational program delivered by a recovered patient would result in more positive views of women with eating disorders in general and of the recovered-patient presenter in particular.

Method

Participants

7   Participants were 376 students who were present at their all-female, predominantly Caucasian, parochial high school on the day the data were collected. Participants ranged in age from 12 to 18 years (M = 15.50, SD = 1.16); 25.3 per cent (n = 95) were in 9th grade, 23.7 per cent (n = 89) were in 10th grade, 26.3 per cent (n = 99) were in 11th grade, 20.7 per cent (n = 78) were in 12th grade, and 4.0 per cent (n = 15) did not report their grade level. The protocol for this study was approved by the Yale School of Medicine Human Investigation Committee.

Materials

8   *Educational videotape.* We produced two professional quality 12-minute videotapes depicting a clinical psychologist interviewing the third author (KMB) about eating disorders. The two videotapes were identical except that the 29-year-old female presenter was introduced by the interviewer as "Dr. Kristin Siebrecht, eating disorders specialist" in the first tape and as "Kristin, a recovered eating disorder patient" in the second. This information also appeared on the screen periodically throughout the video. The presenter was of normal weight, was well groomed and conservatively dressed, and wore light makeup. The first minute and a half of the interview described the personal story of a woman with an eating disorder who began dieting, binge-eating, and purging after being teased by her peers. In the specialist condition, the story was described as that of a typical patient, whereas in the recovered-patient condition, it was represented as the presenter's own experience. Each of the videotaped interviews then presented identical information regarding the symptoms, prevalence, etiology, health consequences, and treatment of anorexia nervosa and bulimia nervosa.

Eating disorders awareness questionnaire.

9   The Eating Disorders Awareness Questionnaire (EDAQ) was constructed for the present study to assess the educational impact (intended effects) of the video. The scale contained 14 items addressing material that was explicitly discussed in the video presentation, including basic knowledge about eating disorders and the perceived seriousness of eating disorders. To simplify wording, most items were phrased referring to "girls" because the participants were enrolled in an all-female high school and most of those who develop eating disorders are female. Sample items include: "Girls who have anorexia nervosa are very afraid of

becoming fat," "Girls who lose a lot of weight can stop getting their periods," and "People can die from eating disorders." Participants rated their agreement with these statements on a five-point scale ranging from 1 (*strongly disagree*) to 5 (*strongly agree*). After some items were reversed scored, responses were summed and averaged, with higher scores indicating greater knowledge (Cronbach's χ= .70).

10   *Implicit message items.* Interspersed throughout the EDAQ were an additional eight items regarding the personal characteristics of individuals with eating disorders, how difficult it is to recover from an eating disorder, and whether recovered individuals can lead normal lives. These items were designed to measure the implicit messages (unintended effects) that might be communicated by the video and were based on previous theorizing regarding the normalization and glamorization of eating disorders. The eight implicit message (IM) items were as follows: "Having an eating disorder would not be that bad if it meant you could look like a model," "Girls with eating disorders are usually very smart," "Girls with eating disorders are usually very pretty," "Girls with eating disorders are very strong (their personalities)," "Girls with eating disorders are especially in control of their lives," "It's not that hard to recover from an eating disorder if you get one," "People who recover from eating disorders can go on to lead normal lives," and "Having an eating disorder is a good way to lose weight." Participants rated their agreement with IM items on the same five-point EDAQ scale ranging from 1 (*strongly disagree*) to 5 (*strongly agree*). The internal consistency for these items was low (Cronbach's χ= .38); therefore, each item was treated separately in the analyses described below. Two additional IM items regarding the presenter herself were assessed only after participants viewed the video: "Kristin [Dr. Siebrecht], the woman being interviewed in the video, is a good role model for girls my age" and "It would be nice to look like Kristin [Dr. Siebrecht], the woman being interviewed in the video."

Procedure

11   Participants were divided into two conditions by the first letter of their last names (A–L and M–Z) and led to separate rooms where they would complete

the study; both groups participated simultaneously. Participants first completed the EDAQ, including the eight IM items. Participants then watched one of the two 12-minute videotaped interviews. After watching their assigned video, participants again completed the EDAQ, the IM items, and the two additional items about the presenter being "a good role model" and "nice to look like." Participants were then debriefed as to the study purpose and were informed that the presenter in both videos was actually an eating disorder specialist. The presenters then led a media literacy discussion of the idealized body shapes depicted in television and magazine images.

Results

12   Of the 376 initial participants, 17 had missing data, leaving 359 participants with complete data available for the following analyses. Of these 359, 127 were assigned to the specialist condition, and 232 were assigned to the recovered-patient condition.

EDAQ

13   A time x condition analysis of variance (ANOVA) on EDAQ scores revealed a significant main effect of time, $F(1,357) = 252.80$, $p < .001$, p2 = .42, indicating that participants' overall understanding of basic facts about eating disorders and the relative seriousness of those disorders increased after watching the educational video (see Table 1). As predicted, there was no significant time x condition interaction.

Implicit messages

14   The unintended effects of the education programs were examined using a 2 x 2 (time x condition) multivariate analysis of variance (MANOVA) on the IM items, which revealed a significant main effect for time, $F(8,347) = 5.13$, $p < .001$, p2 = .11, as well as a significant time x condition interaction, $F(8,347) = 2.70$, $p = .01$, p2 = .06. Each IM item was then examined in separate univariate analyses (see Table 1).

15   There was a main effect of time for the item "Having an eating disorder would not be that bad if

TABLE 1   MEANS (SD) FOR THE EATING DISORDERS AWARENESS QUESTIONNAIRE (EDAQ) AND IMPLICIT MESSAGE (IM) ITEMS

	Specialist		Recovered Patient	
	Time 1	Time 2	Time 1	Time 2
EDAQ	47.57ᵃ (5.58)	51.28ᵇ (5.75)	47.00ᶜ (5.39)	51.54ᵈ (4.48)
IM items				
Model	1.50ᵃ (0.97)	1.39ᵇ (0.98)	1.53ᶜ (0.98)	1.39ᵈ (0.90)
Strong	2.18ᵃ (1.09)	2.28ᵇ (1.07)	1.94ᶜ (0.99)	2.19ᵈ (1.05)
Not hard to recover	1.39ᵃ (0.80)	1.69ᵇ (1.00)	1.68ᶜ (1.14)	1.92ᵈ (1.15)
Smart	3.02ᵃ (0.77)	3.07ᵃ (0.78)	2.79ᶜ (0.89)	2.92ᵈ (0.87)
Normal lives	3.65ᵃ (1.24)	3.58ᵃ (1.14)	3.62ᶜ (1.16)	4.00ᵈ (0.99)
Pretty	2.54ᵃ (0.93)	2.60ᵃ (0.92)	2.39ᶜ (0.96)	2.61ᵈ (0.91)
In control	1.82ᵃ (1.00)	1.67ᵃ (0.94)	1.59ᶜ (0.95)	1.76ᵈ (1.17)
Lose weight	1.39ᵃ (0.82)	1.26ᵃ (0.74)	1.40ᶜ (0.84)	1.37ᶜ (0.87)
IM post-test only				
Role model	—	3.59ᵉ (1.03)	—	3.90ᶠ (1.06)
Nice to look like	—	2.45ᵉ (1.16)	—	3.04ᶠ (1.21)

Note: Superscripts a, b, c, d, e, and f denote group differences at $p < .05$.

it meant you could look like a model," with ratings decreasing after the interventions ($p = .01$, p2 = .02). There was also a main effect of time for the items "Girls with eating disorders are very strong (their personalities)" ($p = .01$, p2 = .02) and "It's not that hard to recover from an eating disorder if you get one" ($p < .001$, p2 = .04), indicating that ratings increased after watching the video. A trend was found for a main effect of time for the item "Girls with eating disorders are usually very smart" ($p = .06$, p2 = .01).

16   For the item "People who recover from eating disorders can go on to lead normal lives," there was a main effect of time, $F(1,354) = 6.55$, $p = .01$, p2 = .02, qualified by a significant time x condition interaction, $F(1,354) = 12.70$, $p < .001$, p2 = .04. Simple-effects analysis revealed that participants in the recovered-patient group significantly increased their ratings ($p < .001$), whereas participants in the specialist condition did not ($p = .53$). For the item "Girls with eating disorders are usually very pretty," there was a main effect of time, $F(1,354) = 8.61$, $p = .004$,

p2 = .02, qualified by a marginally significant time x condition interaction, $F(1,354) = 3.00$, $p = .08$, p2 = .01. Simple-effects analysis revealed that participants in the recovered-patient condition significantly increased their ratings ($p < .001$), whereas those in the specialist condition did not ($p = .45$). For the item "Girls with eating disorders are especially in control of their lives," there was only a significant time x condition interaction, $F(1,354) = 5.35$, $p = .02$, p2 = .02. Simple-effects analysis again revealed that ratings increased in the recovered-patient condition ($p = .04$) but not in the specialist condition ($p = .19$). Finally, there was no main effect or interaction for the item "Having an eating disorder is a good way to lose weight."

17   A one-way MANOVA on the two post-test items ("good role model" and "nice to look like") yielded a significant effect of condition, $F(2,350) = 10.98$, $p < .001$, p2 = .06. In both cases, ratings were higher in the recovered-patient condition than in the specialist condition (good role model: $p = .01$, p2 = .02; nice to look like: $p < .001$, p2 = .05).

Conclusion

18   The aim of the present study was to determine whether an educational program designed to increase awareness about eating disorders would have a differential impact, particularly in terms of some possible implicit messages, when delivered by an eating disorder specialist, as compared with someone who herself had purportedly recovered from an eating disorder. As hypothesized, the educational video successfully increased knowledge about the specific symptoms of eating disorders and the seriousness of those conditions (the intended effects). Also as hypothesized, the presenter's purported identity did not differentially impact knowledge acquisition. The observed increase in knowledge about eating disorders is consistent with the findings of Stice and Shaw's[2] meta-analysis that most prevention programs were successful in increasing such knowledge. The finding is also consistent with previous research in showing that presenter identity does not differentially influence knowledge acquisition.[11,13] Perhaps it is the case that both types of presenters were viewed as being "experts" on eating disorders, one because of professional training and the other because of personal experience.

19   In addition to the intended effects of the educational videos on knowledge about eating disorders, we also found preliminary evidence of some unintended effects, or implicit messages, associated with the educational videos. Several of these unintended effects emerged irrespective of presenter identity. After watching the video, participants in both the specialist and recovered-patient conditions were less likely to indicate that having an eating disorder would be "not that bad if it meant you could look like a model," were less likely to indicate that it is difficult to recover from an eating disorder, and were more likely to agree that girls with eating disorders have strong personalities. Other IM items, however, were differentially affected by the presenter's identity. Participants who saw the recovered-patient video (but not the specialist video) were more likely to indicate that girls with eating disorders were pretty, were in control of their lives, and could go on to lead normal lives when they recover. In addition, those who saw the recovered-patient video were more likely to perceive the presenter as a "good role model" and as "nice to look like" than were participants who saw the specialist video. It should be noted that, in general, the ratings for each of the IM items were fairly low and mostly below the midpoint of the scale. This might (1) reflect a general reluctance to strongly agree with what might be considered socially undesirable statements (e.g., "Having an eating disorder is a good way to lose weight") or (2) suggest that our measures were not sensitive enough to fully capture the implicit messages that were conveyed through the videos. Nonetheless, the observed effects were statistically reliable and in the small-to-moderate range. The fact that even these modest changes emerged after watching a single 12-minute video is remarkable.

20   Although we have attributed the unintended effects observed in the present study to implicit messages contained in the educational video, it is also possible that having participants complete the same questionnaire pre- and post-video may have created demand characteristics for participants to change their item ratings when completing the questionnaire the second time. The fact that impact of the videos varied across items and across conditions, however, suggests that such demand characteristics cannot fully account for the data. Future studies including a control group viewing a video on a topic unrelated to eating disorders would be useful to further rule out demand characteristics as an alternative explanation for the results of the present study.

21   Taken as a whole, our findings suggest that educational programs designed to increase awareness about eating disorders communicate not only the intended educational information but also implicit messages about the characteristics of individuals with eating disorders and the prospects of recovery. This might be particularly true when the program is delivered by someone who is believed to have herself recovered from an eating disorder. Theoretically, the implicit messages observed in the current study could be viewed as being positive or negative. On the one hand, eating disorders are to some extent socially stigmatized.[14,15] This stigmatization was in part reflected in the present study in that baseline ratings of some of the personal characteristics of individuals with eating disorders, such as smart and pretty, were fairly low. One possible effect of these implicit messages, therefore, is that they could serve to partially reduce the stigma of eating disorders and could in

turn promote self-disclosure of symptoms, which is associated with a higher likelihood of subsequent treatment seeking.[16] Similarly, promoting the belief that recovery is attainable and that individuals can go on to lead normal lives after recovery may also be beneficial; one study found that messages emphasizing the efficacy of current treatments as well as the medical seriousness of eating disorder symptoms were the most effective in prompting individuals with bulimia nervosa to seek professional help.[17]

22   In contrast, it is also possible that some of these implicit messages could contribute to the glamorization of eating disorders, which might in turn have negative consequences. Several theorists have expressed concern over the potential effects of the glamorization of eating disorders on people's eating attitudes and behaviours,[6,7,18] and these concerns are particularly salient in the context of media presentations of eating disorders. A recent cross-sectional study found that individuals with higher levels of eating disorder symptoms exhibited greater implicit associations between anorexia and glamour than did low-symptom participants.[19] In the present study, we found preliminary evidence that participants perceived people with eating disorders more positively after watching the educational program, particularly when it was delivered by a recovered patient. It is possible that some implicit messages might have iatrogenic effects on at-risk individuals' eating attitudes and behaviours. A worthwhile endeavour for future research would be to determine whether, and to what extent, existing eating disorder prevention programs convey implicit messages that glamorize eating disorders. Some limitations to the present study are worth

noting. First, the sample was drawn from a single all-female high school. It is possible that students at all-female schools might differ from students at co-educational schools on certain characteristics (e.g., socioeconomic status, achievement orientation) that could potentially influence the study results and limit their generalizability. A second limitation is that, although the measures that we created for the present study showed adequate internal consistency, other indices of reliability and validity remain unknown.

23   A final limitation of the present study is that we did not assess the impact of the implicit messages on recipients' eating attitudes and behaviours, so the broader implications of our findings remain unknown. We suggested earlier that one explanation for the difference between the findings of Mann et al.[4] and Heinze et al.[11] was that in the former study, the presenter provided a personal account of her struggles, whereas in the later study, the presenter did not. Insofar as implicit messages might emerge from personal accounts of eating disorders in particular, it is possible that the differential effects observed in those two studies are related in part to the implicit messages that were conveyed. An important consideration for future research, therefore, would be to examine the extent to which these implicit messages impact people's eating attitudes and behaviour in the longer term. Developing a better understanding of the implicit messages communicated in prevention programs, as well as the impact of these implicit messages on attitudes and behaviour, could ultimately lead to the development of more efficacious programs.

International Journal of Eating Disorders.
2007. 40 (2).

References

1. Eating Disorders Awareness, Prevention, and Education Act of 2005.
2. Stice E, Shaw H. Eating disorder prevention programs: a meta-analytic review. Psychol Bull 2004;130:206–227.
3. Kelly JF. Self-help for substance-use disorders: history, effectiveness, knowledge gaps, and research opportunities. Clin Psychol Rev 2003;23:639–663.
4. Mann T, Nolen-Hoeksema S, Huang K, Burgard D, Wright A, Hanson K. Are two interventions worse than none? Joint primary and secondary prevention of eating disorders in college females. Health Psychol 1997;16: 215–225.
5. Cohn L, Maine M. More harm than good. Eat Disord 1998;6:93–95.
6. O'Dea JA. School-based interventions to prevent eating disorders: first, do no harm. Eat Disord 2000;8:123–130.
7. Garner D. Iatrogenesis in anorexia nervosa and bulimia nervosa. Int J Eat Disord 1985; 4:701–726.
8. Murray S, Touyz S, Beumont P. Knowledge about eating disorders in the community. Int J Eat Disord 1990; 9:87–93.
9. Thomsen SR, McCoy JK, Williams M. Internalizing the impossible: anorexic outpatients' experiences with women's beauty and fashion magazines. Eat Disord 2001; 9:49–64.

10. Wilson JL, Peeble R, Hardy KK, Mulivhill LC, Kretzschmar AY, Litt I. Pro-eating disorder website usage and health outcomes in an eating disordered population. Presented at the Pediatric Academic Society, Washington, DC, May 14–17, 2005.

11. Heinze V, Werthein EH, Kashima Y. An evaluation of the importance of message source and age of recipient in a primary prevention program for eating disorders. Eat Disord 2000;8:131–145.

12. Phelps L, Sapia J, Nathanson D, Nelson L. An empirically supported eating disorder prevention program. Psychol Schools 2000; 37:443–452.

13. Moreno AB, Thelen MH. A preliminary prevention program for eating disorders in a junior high school population. J Youth Adolesc 1993;22:109–124.

14. Crisp AH, Gelder MG, Rix S, Meltzer HI, Rowlands OJ. Stigmatisation of people with mental illnesses.Br J Psychiatry 2000; 177:4–7.

15. Fleming J, Szmukler GI. Attitudes of medical professionals towards patients with eating disorders. Aust NZ J Psychiatry 1992; 26:436–443.

16. Becker AE, Thomas JJ, Franko DL, Herzog DB. Disclosure patterns of eating and weight concerns to clinicians, educational professionals, family, and peers. Int J Eat Disord 2005;38:18–23.

17. Smalec JL, Klingle RS. Bulimia interventions via interpersonal influence: the role of threat and efficacy in persuading bulimics to seek help. J Behav Med 2000;23:37–57.

18. Schulze E, Gray J. The effects of popular and textbook presentations of bulimia nervosa on attitudes toward bulimia nervosa and individuals with bulimia nervosa. Br Rev Bulimia Anorexia Nervosa 1990;4:83–91.

19. Thomas JJ, Judge AM, Brownell KD, Vartanian LR. Evaluating the effects of eating disorder memoirs on readers' eating attitudes and behaviors. Int J Eat Disord 2006; 39:418–425.

KEY AND CHALLENGING WORDS

implicit, didactic, etiology, iatrogenic, vicarious, contentious, prevalence, differential, efficacious

QUESTIONS

1. Using your own words, explain the justification for the study, its specific purpose, and the hypotheses.

2. Why do the authors choose to include such an extensive review of the literature in their introduction? (You could compare its length with that of "Heavy drinking on Canadian campuses," p. 202.)

3. Why do the authors question the findings of the two studies discussed in paragraphs 4 and 5? In a brief paragraph, summarize the importance of these studies to their own work.

4. What is the reason for adding two IM items to the EDAQ after the participants viewed the video?

5. Returning to the introduction, determine a) whether the first hypothesis was proved and b) whether the second one was proved. In b), you will have to be specific in your answer.

6. What are "demand characteristics" (paragraph 20), and what role could they have played in the results?

7. Explain the use of synthesis in the conclusion section of the study (see especially paragraphs 21 and 22).

8. A common practice in the conclusion/discussion section of Type B academic essays is for the researcher(s) to suggest directions for future research—particularly studies that might validate, broaden, or make more relevant the study's findings. Referring to two such suggestions for future research, a) briefly explain how each study would validate, extend, or make the present study more relevant, and b) come up with a prediction ("hypothesis") for each.

POST-READING

1. *Collaborative activity:* "Theoretically, the implicit messages observed in the current study could be viewed as being positive or negative" (paragraph 21). In discussion groups of three or four, consider the interpretations offered in this paragraph. How valid do you believe they are?

2. *Collaborative activity:* In their introduction, the authors refer to research into the effects that "pro eating disorder websites" (see paragraph 3) could have on site visitors. Do you believe that such websites could fulfill a useful purpose? Do you believe that governments should be able to take lawful action against them, such

as shutting them down? Discuss these or related questions.

3. *Collaborative activity:* This study investigates the possible effects of one form of media used as part of an educational program. To what extent are the media to blame for the prevalence of eating disorders today?

4. This study appeared in the *International Journal of Eating Disorders* (volume 40, issue 2). Consulting three other articles from the same issue, write an informal report or short essay (600–750 words) that summarizes content.

For each, write briefly on the study's objective, methodology (for example, questionnaires, interviews, psychological assessment), participants, and findings. The purpose of the report is to demonstrate the variety of approaches of researchers to eating disorders. Note: Most of this information can be obtained from the individual abstracts. If your library does not allow you access to this journal, find three other recent articles on eating disorders in other journals.

RELATED WEBSITES OF INTEREST:

Eating Disorders Foundation of Canada:
www.edfofcanada.com/

National Eating Disorder Information Centre:
www.nedic.ca/

Reality TV gives back: On the civic functions of reality entertainment

Laurie Ouellette

(3,029 words)

Pre-reading

1. Consider the documentaries you have watched. What were their names? What was their purpose? Their main features? Do they fit the description of the "documentary tradition" outlined in paragraph 1?

2. This essay has no descriptive (content) headings. Determine where the introduction ends and the body paragraphs begin. Read the first sentences of the first few paragraphs. Does it appear that they are topic sentences that can help you determine the essay's content?

Abstract

Reality TV is more than a trivial diversion. Civic aims historically associated with documentaries (particularly citizenship training) have been radically reinterpreted and integrated into current popular reality formats.

Keywords: citizenship, civic experiment, documentary, public service, reality TV.

*

1   In his influential 2002 essay "Performing the Real: Documentary Diversions," John Corner identified a *lack of civic purpose* as reality TV's defining attribute. His point of reference was the documentary tradition, from which the surge of "unscripted" entertainment since the late-1990s has selectively borrowed. Reflecting on the early stages of this development, Corner worried that if television programs like *Big Brother* drew from the look and style of serious documentary, they eclipsed its historical "civic functions," defined as official citizenship training, journalistic inquiry and exposition, and (from the margins) radical interrogation (48–50). Designed "entirely in relation to its capacity to deliver entertainment" and achieve "competitive strength" in a changing marketplace, reality TV repurposed "documentary as diversion," Corner argued (52). Serious techniques of observation, documentation, investigation, and analytic assessment were fused to the pleasure principles of soap opera and gaming—and focused inward. Cameras and microphones captured the performance of selfhood and everyday life within artificial settings and contrived formulas. For Corner, this interior play with the discourse of the real was symptomatic of a larger trend with troubling implications. Changing the whole point of documentary since the late-1800s, the new reality programming addressed TV viewers as consumers of entertainment instead of citizens. Would purposeful factual forms of television—and democracy itself—survive?

2   The broader institutional context for such concerns was—and is—the waning public service tradition. Public broadcasters such as the British Broadcasting Corporation (BBC) in the United Kingdom and to a lesser extent the Public Broadcasting Service (PBS) in the United States have played a major role in defining and developing television's civic potentialities (Scannell; Ouellette). Envisioning the medium as an instrument of education, not a mover of merchandise, public broadcasters embraced documentary and other nonfiction formats as a dimension of their broader mission to serve and reform citizens so they might better fulfill their national "duties and obligations" (Ang 29). Factual programming high in civic legitimacy but low in "exchange value" (Corner 52) was faithfully circulated as a "cultural resource for citizenship" as well as an instrument for enlightening and guiding national populations (Murdock 186). Since the 1990s, however, this commitment has been subject to reinterpretation and flux. As BBC scholar Georgina Born points out, the "concept and practice" of public broadcasting has been "radically transformed" across Western capitalist democracies by market liberalization, deregulation, digital technologies, and the post-welfare impetus to reform and downsize the public sector in general (Born, "Digitalising" 102; see also *Uncertain Vision*). Faced with budget cuts, entrepreneurial mandates, and heightened competition from commercial channels and new media platforms, many public broadcasters have backed away from traditional public service–inflected programming with limited audience appeal. At a juncture when citizens are increasingly hailed as enterprising subjects and consumers of do-it-yourself lifestyle resources, major European public broadcasters have embraced many of the popular reality conventions critiqued by Corner. The BBC, for example, helped pioneer the hybridization of documentary and entertainment, and is how a major player in the global circulation of unscripted formats. With fewer resources, PBS has also experimented with the popular reality show in an attempt to bolster ratings. With the market logic responsible for "documentary as diversion" operating across public and private channels, the conditions for fostering documentary as a civic project would appear to be closing down.

3   Although the further decline of journalistic and investigative documentary material on television is difficult to dispute, I want to suggest that the medium has not entirely withdrawn from civic engagement since Corner's essay was published—far from it. Many of the functions ascribed to the documentary and the public service tradition in general—particularly

citizenship training—have been radically reinterpreted and integrated into popular reality formats. While the specific aims and techniques have changed, reality TV continues to be mobilized as a resource for educating and guiding individuals and populations. If the civic functions of reality entertainment are more difficult to recognize, it is partly because they now operate *within* market imperatives and entertainment formats, but also because prescriptions for what counts as "good citizenship" have changed. Unlike the cultural resources for citizenship provided by the (partly) tax-funded public service tradition, reality TV's civic aims are also diffuse, dispersed, commercial (especially in the United States), and far removed from any direct association with official government policies or agendas.

4   In *Better Living through Reality TV: Television and Post-Welfare Citizenship*, James Hay and I argue that, particularly in the United States, reality TV does not "divert" passive audiences from the serious operations of democracy and public life, as much as it translates broader sociopolitical currents and circulates instructions, resources, and scripts for the navigating the changing expectations and demands of citizenship. Many reality programs explicitly address TV viewers as subjects of capacity who exercise freedom and civic agency within (not against) entertainment and consumer culture. This is not particularly surprising, to the extent that reality TV took shape alongside the neoliberal policies and reforms of the 1990s, including the downsizing of the public sector, welfare reform, the outsourcing of state powers and services, the emphasis on consumer choice, and heightened expectations of personal responsibility. Within this context, we suggest, the application of documentary techniques to the demonstration, performance, and testing of self and everyday life makes reality entertainment potentially useful to new strategies of "governing at a distance" that deemphasize public oversight and require enterprising individuals to manage their own health, prosperity, and well being (Rose). From *The Apprentice* to *The Biggest Loser*, reality games command an indirect and unofficial role in constituting, normalizing, educating, and training the self-empowering the citizens beckoned by political authorities. However artificial and staged these programs appear on the surface, they help to constitute powerful truths concerning

appropriate forms of civic conduct and problem-solving. To the extent that reality TV's civic functions are also marketable, affective, entertaining, and executed through dispersed partnerships among the television industry, sponsors, nonprofit agencies, celebrities, and TV viewers, they parallel with (and have helped to constitute) the "reinvention of government" in the United States (under Clinton and Bush) as a series of decentralized public-private partnerships on one hand, and self-enterprising citizens on the other (Ouellette and Hay 18–24).

5   Cultural studies scholar Toby Miller once theorized citizenship as an ongoing pull between the "selfish demands" of the consumer economy and the "selfless requirements" of the political order (136). This tension takes on an even greater degree of intensity as the line between consumerism and public politics further collapses, and the requirements of citizenship come to include the actualization of the self through consumer culture and the execution of compassion and ethical responsibility to others. We are expected to actualize and maximize ourselves in a world of goods and perform as virtuous subjects whose voluntary activities in the public world are, as George W. Bush explained during his inaugural address, "just as important as anything government does." In addition to calling on nonprofits, charities, and faith-based organizations to temper gaps left by the downsized welfare state, both the Bush and Clinton administrations promoted volunteerism as a preferred mode of privatized civic empowerment. Reality TV's contributions to what might be called post-welfare civic responsibility manifested within this milieu and are particularly evident in the "do-good" experiments that have flooded the airwaves since the millennium.

6   From *American Idol Gives Back* to *Oprah's Big Give*, a stream of high-profile helping ventures has appeared to redeem reality TV's scandalous associations with bug eating, navel gazing, and bed swapping. These programs (and the marketing discourses that surround them) make explicit claims about reality TV's civic importance. Do-good programs can take on a variety of for-mats—from the audience participation show to the competition to the make-over—but all reject the earlier notion of public service as education and preparation for participation in the official political processes. Reality entertainment

instead intervenes directly in social life, enacting "can do" solutions to largely personalized problems within emotional and often suspenseful formats. The template was established by *Extreme Makeover Home Edition* (2002–present), a successful ABC program that mobilizes private resources (sponsors, experts, nonprofits, volunteers) in a "race against time" to revamp the run-down houses of needy families (see Ouellette and Hay 42–56). The participants are selected by casting agents who find the most "deserving" and marketable stories of hardship from tens of thousands of applications weekly. Products and brand names are woven into the melodramatic interventions, and as many critics have noted, complex issues and socioeconomic inequalities are simplified and downplayed. Still, to dismiss these ventures as trivial or somehow less than "real" would be to overlook their constitutive role as technologies of citizenship, private aid, and volunteerism.

7   On *Home Edition*, for example, TV viewers are "activated" to practice compassionate citizenship by volunteering for nonprofit partners such as Habitat for Humanity and Home Aid. The ABC website provides direct links, publicity on sponsors and partners, advice on getting involved, and tips from volunteer agencies, thus further stitching the production and active consumption of reality TV into privatized networks of assistance and self-care. While often endorsed by public officials, do-good programs circulate as alternatives to the various ills (inefficiency bureaucracy, dependency, centralized control) ascribed to the welfare state. Needy subjects and their problems provide the raw material for the manufacture of entertainment commodities and circulation of advertising that cannot be zapped. The best and only solution to unmet needs and human hardships (private charity) is offloaded onto the private sector and TV viewers. More explicitly than other reality subgenres, the helping trend acknowledges the limitations of self-maximization and pure market logic—and capitalizes on the result.[1]

8   Do-good television is especially common on commercial channels in the United States. Although European public broadcasters offer reality-based lessons on living, most lack the resources to intervene directly in reality on a philanthropic scale. Why would the television industry take on such projects, given its historical avoidance of public service obligations? For

one thing, do-good experiments are fully expected to be profitable. More importantly, they also allow media outlets to cash in on marketing trends such as "citizen branding" and corporate social responsibility (CSR). Because networks are offered as branded interfaces to suggested civic practices, good citizenship—and the ethical surplus it is assumed to generate—can be harnessed to build consumer loyalty. This makes it possible to differentiate brands of television in a cluttered environment and exploit what business historian David Vogel calls the burgeoning "market for virtue." For example, ABC (home to many do-good ventures) brands itself as a Better Community, while the reality-based cable channel Planet Green provides a branded interface to green citizenship and environmental problem-solving. Recently, MTV (owned by Viacom) announced its intention to replace trivial reality entertainment with issue-oriented and civic-minded material. Last year, the wealthy debutantes of *My Sweet Sixteen* were sent to impoverished global locations to improve their character and ethics in a program called *Exiled*. The contestants on the third season of sister channel VH1's *Charm School* are currently being instructed on the importance and procedures of volunteering and performing community service. The change is part of MTV and VH1's efforts to re-brand their programming—and their images—in the wake of young people's overwhelming support of Barack Obama. Tellingly, *Charm School*'s off-screen male narrator not only sounds a lot like Obama, he also punctuates the ongoing question of whether the show can transform party girls into "model citizens" with the slogan, "Yes, we can." As this example attests, the spirit of accountability public sector renewal ushered in by the election can easily be evoked as a new justification for the enactment of philanthropy and self-help—in part because of television's commercial investments in these solutions as branding devices and marketing strategies.

9   If CSR is becoming the new public service, we need critical frameworks for assessing its cultural output. My aim here is not to fault Corner's early evaluation of mainly British reality TV but to begin to unravel the complexities of reality entertainment in its current forms. I have been arguing that any attempt to theorize the civic functions and consequences of popular reality will need to also address

its constitutive relationship to changing and colluding dynamics of commerce and governance. It also seems crucial to recognize the residual, emergent, and sometimes contradictory logics operating within the genre. For example, however market-driven and stitched into the circuitry of privatization, do-good reality programming does provide all-too-rare visibility on US television for the poor, the sick, the unemployed, the homeless, and the uninsured. As Anna McCarthy convincingly argues, it bears witness to the "trauma" of everyday life under neoliberal conditions, even as it deflects the causes and commodifies the consequences. Reality TV's helping interventions disrupt the calculated rationality of today's enterprise culture, encouraging visceral and affective reactions to poverty not unlike the industrial slum photographs of Jacob Riis or the gas company–funded social problem documentaries of John Grierson (see Winston). In the wake of the current financial crisis and recession, these dimensions of reality TV may be intensifying—as suggested by the recent Fox program *Secret Millionaire* (2008–09).

10   Developed by the UK company RDF Media, *Secret Millionaire* originated in 2006 on Channel 4, a publicly owned but commercially funded British channel. RDF developed the format for Fox Television last year, using US participants and locations but keeping the generic template and the series name intact. Conceived and marketed as reality entertainment, *Secret Millionaire* combines the techniques of the documentary, the social experiment, and the melodrama. Each week, a designated millionaire goes "undercover" into impoverished communities to observe hardship firsthand and give away one hundred thousand dollars of his money (tellingly, the millionaire is almost always white and male) while the cameras roll. The benefactors are required to give up their mansions, fancy cars, expensive restaurants, electronic gadgets, and other taken-for-granted consumer privileges and subsist on "welfare wages" like the struggling individuals and families they encounter. They perform hard labour, eat cheap food, live in substandard housing, and interact socially with have-nots, often for the first time in their lives. Along the way, they scout around for people and projects to donate a chunk of their fortune to. Eventually, the expected "reveal" occurs: The millionaire unmasks

his true identity and surprises the deserving recipients with a spectacular cash donation.

11   In the debut episode of the US version, a wealthy California lawyer who is also a successful business owner goes to live among the poor with his teenaged son. They perform temporary construction work, reside in a cheap motel, and quickly discover how much they have to learn about the "real world." What is innovative and potentially disruptive about the program is not its authenticity per se (the artificial conditions and staged aspects of other reality shows are readily apparent) but the alternative manner through which the intervention unfolds. In many respects, the formula draws from and exploits dominant representations of socioeconomic inequality: wealth is individualized, and only those "others" who are judged deserving on the basis of uncontrollable circumstances and/or exemplary character are candidates for assistance. Yet, unlike other do-good television programs, the *Secret Millionaire*'s purpose is ultimately *not* to evaluate or make over the poor. Nor is it to shower them with branded consumer goods (courtesy of sponsors) or to enact enterprising solutions to their complex social problems. Its point is to evaluate, educate, guide, enlighten, and transform the richest people in North America. Throughout the debut episode, father and son learn about routine dimensions of socioeconomic difficulties not from experts, but from the experiences and commiserations of people who mistakenly believe they share something in common with the main characters. A middle-aged, uninsured woman who became homeless for a time when she suffered a major back injury provides them breakfast and encouragement. She had subsequently found work at the same construction site and—unaware of their true identity (the cameras are ascribed to a documentary filming)—tries to help the best she can. Another family with a chronically ill child and no health coverage explains the everyday stresses and difficulties of making ends meet and their eventual slide into bankruptcy. While this constitution of the worthy poor is characteristic of other do-good reality experiments, *Secret Millionaire* also identifies the undernourished and collapsing public sector as a structural factor in their situations. TV viewers are allowed to identify with shared problems and difficulties that no television program can fix.

12   The millionaires perform extreme empathy and shock on hearing the hardship stories. As with all reality entertainment, their reactions are shaped and accentuated by casting, editing, camera work, and music. Yet, this artifice does not prevent the series from contributing in potentially useful ways to the "truth" about class and wealth in the current era. In the premiere, father and son undergo a process of self-recognition in which they become increasingly aware of their privilege. They come to see themselves as thoughtless and selfish and are unable to rationalize their "luxury spending" in the midst of unmet human needs and chronic suffering. While this recurring lesson can be easily dismissed as a cultural tempering of growing resentment against the business elites responsible for the current economic crisis, it also reworks the civic logic orienting of much of reality TV by reversing the process and subjects of transformation. Within this context, the millionaire's cash donation can be interpreted as a technology of private aid, but it can also be seen as enacting a reevaluation (if not quite a redistribution) of the allotment of resources and wealth in the United States. The lack of product placements in *Secret Millionaire* reinforces this possibility—not only because a consumer address is contained in the commercial breaks, but because the problem of uneven wealth cannot be resolved by a trip to Disney World or the installation of a free washing machine. Alas, this lack of marketability will undoubtedly keep the civic possibilities opened up by programs such as *Secret Millionaire* in check. Such are the limits of reality TV in its current form.

Journal of Popular Film and Television.
2010. April–June 38 (2).

Note

1.   For a more detailed analysis of the governmental dimensions of do-good TV (from which this article draws), see Ouellette and Hay ch. 1, "Charity TV: Privatizing Care, Mobilizing Compassion."

Works Cited

Ang, Ien. *Desperately Seeking the Audience*. London: Routledge, 2001. Print.

Born, Georgina. "Digitalising Democracy." *What Can Be Done? Making the Media and Politics Better*. Ed. J. Lloyd and J. Seaton. Oxford: Blackwell, 2006. 102–23. Print.

———. *Uncertain Vision: Birt, Dyke and the Reinvention of the BBC*. London: Secker and Warburg, 2004. Print.

Bush, George W. "Inaugural Address." *American Rhetoric Online Speech Bank* 20 Jan. 2001. Web. 11 May 2009. <www.americanrhetoric.com/speeches/ gwbfirstinaugural.htm.>

Corner, John. "Performing the Real: Documentary Diversions." *Television and New Media* 3 (2002): 255–69. Rpt. in *Reality TV: Remaking Television Culture*. Ed. Susan Murray and Laurie Ouellette. New York: NYU Press, 2009. 44–64. Print.

McCarthy, Anna. "Reality Television: A Neoliberal Theater of Suffering." *Social Text* 25.4 (2007): 17–41. Print.

Miller, Toby. *The Well-Tempered Self: Citizenship, Culture and the Postmodern Subject*. Baltimore: Johns Hopkins UP, 1993. Print.

Murdock, Graham. "Public Broadcasting and Democratic Culture: Consumers, Citizens and Communards." *A Companion to Television*. Ed. Janet Wasco. Malden: Blackwell, 2005. 174–98. Print.

Ouellette, Laurie. *Viewers Like You? How Public Television Failed the People*. New York: Columbia UP, 2002. Print.

Ouellette, Laurie, and James Hay. *Better Living through Reality TV: Television and Post-Welfare Citizenship*. Malden: Blackwell, 2008. Print.

Rose, Nikolas. "Governing 'Advanced' Liberal Democracies." *Foucault and Political Reason: Liberalism, Neoliberalism and Rationalities of Government*. Ed. Andrew Barry, Thomas Osbourne, and Nikolas Rose. Chicago and London: University of Chicago Press, 1996. 37–64.

Scannell, Paddy. "Public Service Broadcasting and Modern Public Life." *Media Culture Society* 11 (1989): 135–66. Print.

Vogel, David. *The Market for Virtue: The Potential and Limits of Corporate Social Responsibility*. Washington, DC: Brookings Institute Press, 2005. Print.

Winston, Brian. *Claiming the Real: Documentary, Grierson and Beyond*. New York: Palgrave Macmillian, 2008. Print.

KEY AND CHALLENGING WORDS

contrived, symptomatic, entrepreneurial, juncture, bolster, milieu, mobilize, constitutive, philanthropic, burgeoning, attest, collude, residual, visceral, benefactor, commiseration

QUESTIONS

1. a) In two sentences, summarize the views of John Corner as expressed in paragraph 1; *OR* b) In two sentences, summarize the abstract of John Corner's article "Performing the Real: Documentary Diversions" (*Television and New Media* 3.3 [2002]: 255–69).

2. Explain the different uses for quotation marks around the following words in paragraph 1: "unscripted," "civic functions," and "entirely in relation to its capacity to deliver entertainment."

3. Explain how the view of public broadcasting today differs from the traditional view. What accounts for these differences?

4. Type A essays often make connections between forms of art or entertainment and the "real" world, claiming universal relevance for such art. Show how Ouellette connects reality TV in the 1990s to political, social, or economic forces at play during that time (see paragraph 4).

5. a) Analyze Ouellette's use of synonyms, rephrasing, repetition, and sentence transitions to contribute to coherence in paragraph 5; b) Analyze the effectiveness of paragraph transitions by looking at two of the following, considering how the last sentence of the earlier paragraph is connected to the first sentence of the following one: paragraphs 5–6, 6–7, 7–8, 8–9, or 9–10.

6. What is *branding* (paragraph 8)? Explain how branding can be applied to "do-good television" and why it is important, according to the author.

7. a) In one paragraph, explain why *Secret Millionaire* (paragraphs 10–12) is a good illustration of what Ouellette discusses in the previous paragraphs; b) Compare *Secret Millionaire* with other "do-good" reality shows discussed in the article, noting at least one similarity and difference.

8. Analyze the conclusion of the essay for its effectiveness.

POST-READING

1. *Collaborative activity:* a) Discuss or debate the validity of Ouellette's main points about reality TV today. Refer to specific reality shows you have watched or are familiar with; *OR* b) Discuss or debate the concept of "reality" TV. How real is reality TV?

2. Access the home page of one of the TV shows mentioned in the article, such as *Charm School* or *Secret Millionaire,* or another "do-good" reality TV show. Is there a summary of the show itself (rather than episode summaries)? Does the description of the show stress what Ouellette considers its citizenship function? Summarize the website's description of the show and its function or purpose.

3. Find an argumentative essay on some aspect of reality TV in a popular (non-academic) source, like a magazine or a blog. Analyze the argument, first summarizing its thesis and main points, and then evaluating the effectiveness of the argument.

ADDITIONAL LIBRARY READING

Many studies on reality programming have been published in the last ten years and can be accessed through your library's databases. The first and third articles below are empirical studies of reality TV; the second focuses on the reality TV show *Charm School*, which is discussed in Laurie Ouellette's essay.

Barton, Kristin M. "Reality Television Programming and Diverging Gratifications: The Influence of Content on Gratifications Obtained." *Journal of Broadcasting & Electronic Media* 53.3 (2009): 460–76. Print.

Papacharissi, Zizi, and Andrew L. Mendelson. "An Exploratory Study of Reality Appeal: Uses and Gratifications of Reality TV Shows." *Journal of Broadcasting & Electronic Media* 51.2 (2007): 355–70. Print.

Holbrook, Alice, and Amy E. Singer. "When Bad Girls Go Good." *Journal of Popular Film & Television* 37.1 (2009): 34–43. Print.

Online video gaming: What should educational psychologists know?

Mark Griffiths

(2,191 words)

Pre-reading

1. What do you know about MMORPGs? Have you or friends played *World of Warcraft, EverQuest,* or another of the dozens of MMORPGs available for free or by subscription? Scan the home page of a MMORPG to orient yourself to the features of the game, including the object of the game, levels of play, terminology, and the like. In one paragraph, summarize the game's objective and salient features.
2. Read the abstract to determine the essay's purpose and audience. Formulate a reading hypothesis in which you consider how these factors could affect your reading of this essay.
3. Scan the References page. How many entries are written or co-written by Mark Griffiths? Identify one empirical study (Type B) and one critical review essay (Type C). From their titles, how many appear to be focused specifically on video game addiction?

Based on a significant increase in correspondence to the author from parents, teachers and psychologists concerning "addiction" to online video games like *World of Warcraft,* this paper provides a brief overview of the main issues surrounding excessive video game playing among adolescents. As an aid to educational psychologists, and based on two decades of the author's own research in this area, this paper briefly overviews: (i) online gaming addictions, (ii) the differences between online and offline video gaming, and (iii) video gaming benefits. The paper ends with some practical advice that educational psychologists can give to parents about the safe playing of video games.

Keywords: online video gaming; educational psychologists; addiction; adolescents

Introduction

1   Over the past year, this author received a noticeable increase in the number of emails and telephone calls from parents, teachers, and (educational and clinical) psychologists concerning children and adolescents excessively playing online games like *World of Warcraft* and *Everquest.* The most typical emails this author receives are along the lines of "Can children become addicted to an online game?", "Are online video games more addictive than offline games?", and "What advice can I give to a parent who appears to have a child who is addicted to online gaming?" In this article an attempt is made to answer these questions based on this author's two decades of research in the area ranging from research examining offline video games (Chumbley & Griffiths, 2006; Griffiths, 1991, 1993, 1997; Griffiths & Dancaster, 1995; Griffiths & Hunt, 1995, 1998; Phillips, Rolls, Rouse, & Griffiths, 1995; Wood & Griffiths, 2007) to more recent research examining online video games (Chappell, Eatough, Davies, & Griffiths, 2006; Cole & Griffiths, 2007; Griffiths, Davies, & Chappell, 2003, 2004a, 2004b; Hussain & Griffiths, 2008; Wood, Griffiths, & Parke, 2007).

Online gaming addiction

2   All addictions (whether chemical or behavioural) are essentially about constant rewards and reinforcement (Griffiths, 2005a, 2005b, 2005c). For many years, this author has operationally defined addictive behaviour as any behaviour that features all the core components of addiction (salience, mood modification, tolerance, withdrawal, conflict, and relapse) (Griffiths, 1996, 2002, 2005a, 2005b, 2005c, 2008a). Furthermore, it is this author's contention that any behaviour (for example, video game playing) that fulfils the six criteria below can be operationally defined as an addiction. In the case of video game addiction this would be:

(1) *Salience* – This occurs when video game play becomes the most important activity in the person's life and dominates his or her thinking (pre-occupations and cognitive distortions), feelings (cravings), and behaviour (deterioration of socialized behaviour). For instance, even if the person is not actually playing on a video game he or she will be thinking about the next time.

(2) *Mood modification* – This refers to the subjective experiences that people report as a consequence of engaging in video game play and can be seen as a coping strategy (e.g., they experience an arousing "buzz" or a "high" or, paradoxically, a tranquillizing feel of "escape" or "numbing").

(3) *Tolerance* – This is the process whereby increasing amounts of video game play are required to achieve the former mood modifying effects. This basically means that for someone engaged in video game playing, he or she gradually builds up the amount of time spent online engaged in the behaviour.

(4) *Withdrawal symptoms* – These are the unpleasant feeling states and/or physical effects that occur when video game play is discontinued or suddenly reduced, for example, the shakes, moodiness, and irritability.

(5) *Conflict* – This refers to the conflicts between video game players and those around them (interpersonal conflict), conflicts with other activities (job, schoolwork, social life, hobbies and interests), or from within the individuals themselves (intrapsychic conflict and/ or subjective feelings of loss of control) which are concerned with spending too much time engaged in video game play.

(6) *Relapse* – This is the tendency for repeated reversions to earlier patterns of video game play to recur and for even the most extreme patterns typical at the height of excessive video game play to be quickly restored after periods of abstinence or control.

3   Adolescents cannot become addicted to something unless they are constantly rewarded for the behaviour they are engaged in. Online gaming is potentially addictive although the number of people who are truly addicted, by the criteria outlined earlier, may be small in number (Griffiths, 2008a, 2008b). However, such individuals may play over 80 hours a week on games like *World of Warcraft* and *Everquest*, although playing excessively does not necessarily mean someone is addicted. If there are no negative detrimental effects as a result of excessive playing, the behaviour cannot really be classed as a genuine addiction (Griffiths, 2008a, 2008b).

4   Online gaming addiction is partly explained by the partial reinforcement effect (PRE) (Griffiths, 2008a). This is a critical psychological ingredient of gaming addiction whereby the reinforcement is intermittent (people keep responding in the absence of reinforcement hoping that another reward is just around the corner). Knowledge about the PRE gives the game designer an edge in designing appealing games. Magnitude of reinforcement (such as high points score for doing something in-game) is also important. Large rewards lead to fast responding and greater resistance to extinction—in short to increased "addiction" (Griffiths, 2008a). Instant reinforcement is also satisfying.

5   As with all addictions, there is a potential for long-term damage, but the good news is that very few people appear to have developed such problems, although there is research suggesting that, in extreme cases, online gamers can experience all the core signs and symptoms of more traditional addictions such as withdrawal symptoms, conflict with other activities,

mood modifying effects, and relapse (Chappell et al., 2006; Grüsser, Thalemann, & Griffiths, 2007). Healthy enthusiasms add to life; addictions take away from it. The vast majority of excessive gamers will say their activity has positive effects for them. There are many people who play excessively without it having any negative impact on their life at all, although many players experience some signs of addiction without necessarily being addicted (Grüsser et al., 2007).

Online versus offline gaming

6   Online gaming involves multiple reinforcements in that different features might be differently rewarding to different people (what could be called "the kitchen sink approach" where designers include a diverse range of gaming rewards in the hope that at least some of them will appeal to players). In video games more generally, the rewards might be intrinsic (for example, improving your highest score, beating your friend's high score, getting your name on the "hall of fame," mastering the machine) or extrinsic (such as peer admiration) (Griffiths, 2008a). In online gaming, there is no end to the game, and there is the potential for teenagers to play endlessly against (and with) other real people. This can be immensely rewarding and psychologically engrossing. For a small minority of people, this may lead to an addiction where online gaming becomes the single most important thing in that person's life and which compromises all other activities. Currently there is little research indicating how the addiction establishes itself and what people are actually addicted to (Griffiths, 2008b).

Gaming benefits

7   Despite this rather negative side of video games, there is much evidence suggesting that gaming can have very positive effects on people's lives. Online gaming can make people feel psychologically better and help raise their self-esteem (Griffiths, 2005b, 2005c). The immersive and disassociative experience of gaming may also be very therapeutic

and help people deal with everyday stresses and strains. Research has shown that many gamers love the fact that playing games leads to time loss (Wood & Griffiths, 2007; Wood et al., 2007). Many would argue that this is more positive than drug use, drinking alcohol, or other activities like gambling. Simulated environments also allow players to experiment with other parts of their personality, for example, gender swapping, that would be difficult to do offline (Hussain & Griffiths, 2008).

8   Accusations of "pointlessness" can be levelled at almost any leisure activity in life, not just online gaming. As more people engage in some kind of video gaming, so the number of people negatively commenting on such activities is likely to decrease over time. People are also becoming more digitally literate. The demographics of online gaming are also expanding (Griffiths et al., 2004a). The average age of a gamer is steadily increasing, and more females are starting to play (Cole & Griffiths, 2007). People only usually engage in leisure activities that are psychologically and socially rewarding for them. Recent research has also shown that around one-third of online gamers make good friends in the game (Cole & Griffiths, 2007).

Practical advice to help parents

9   Finally, based on research evidence outlined, practical advice that educational psychologists can give to parents in relation to child and adolescent video gaming (Griffiths, 2003) includes:

- Advise parents to check the content of the gaming activity. Encourage parents to give children and adolescents games that are educational rather than violent. Parents usually have control over what their child watches on television—gaming should not be any different.
- Advise parents to encourage their children to play video games as part of a group rather than as a solitary activity. This will lead to children and adolescents talking and working together. Also, remind parents that many online games

are based on social activity and working together. Research has consistently shown that the main reason for playing online games is for the social element (Griffiths et al., 2003, 2004b; Cole & Griffiths, 2007).

- Advise parents to set time limits on their child's playing time. It is fine for children and adolescents to play for a couple of hours after they have done their homework or their chores. Early research showed that those children who played video games for a couple of hours a day were more likely than those children who did not play video games at all to (a) have a wider circle of friends, (b) engage in physical activities, and (c) do their homework (Phillips et al., 1995).
- Advise parents to follow the recommendations by the game manufacturers and/ or the service providers (for example, sit at least two feet from the screen, play games in a well-lit room, never have the screen at maximum brightness, and never engage in gaming when feeling tired).
- Finally, if all else fails, advise parents to temporarily prohibit gaming and then allow the child to play again on a part-time basis when appropriate.

Conclusions

10   In over two decades of examining both the possible dangers and the potential benefits of video game playing, evidence suggests that in the right context playing video games can have positive health and educational benefits for a large range of different subgroups, such as those with autism and impulsive disorders (Griffiths, 2005a, 2008b). There are also recent reviews showing that online gaming can be used in an educationally beneficial context such as teaching topics like history and economics (de Freitas & Griffiths, 2007, 2008). If care is taken in the design, and if they are put into the right context, video games both online and offline have the potential to be used as training aids in classrooms and therapeutic settings, and to provide skills in psychomotor coordination, and in simulations of real life events (such as driving a car and flying a plane).

11   Countries such as China have introduced laws to limit the amount of time that adolescents and adults can spend playing online games, and other countries such as Holland and South Korea have seen the opening of dedicated treatment clinics for gaming addiction (Griffiths, 2008b). Whether such activity needs to be legislated for is arguable. Any activity when taken to excess can cause problems in a person's life, but it is unlikely that there would be legislation against, for example, people excessively reading or exercising. There is no argument that online gaming should be treated any differently. This author has only come across a handful of genuine gaming addicts in over two decades. However, it is evident that online gaming can be problematic to some individuals. As mentioned earlier, one of the main reasons why online gaming may be more problematic than "stand alone" (offline) gaming is that online games are potentially never ending and can be played all day every day (unlike "stand alone" games which can be paused and returned to some time later). In some cases, the Internet may be providing a potentially ever-present addictive medium for those with a predisposition for excessive game playing.

12   To date, the empirical evidence appears to indicate that, for the vast majority of individuals, online gaming is an enjoyable and harmless activity. It is possible that future empirical research may show increasing online gaming addiction and/or will show cultural differences (suggesting different policies in different countries). Real life problems need applied solutions and alternatives, and until there is an established body of literature on the psychological, sociological, and physiological effects of online gaming and online gaming addiction, then directions for education, prevention, intervention, treatment, and legislative policy will remain limited in scope. Evidently, more research is needed to help and inform educational psychologists, educators, and other stakeholders to give practical help to those who need it and for policy-makers to make evidence-based policy decisions.

Educational Psychology in Practice.
2010. March 26 (1).

References

Chappell, D., Eatough, V.E., Davies, M.N.O., & Griffiths, M.D. (2006). *EverQuest* – It's just a computer game right? An interpretative phenomenological analysis of online gaming addiction. *International Journal of Mental Health and Addiction, 4,* 205–216.

Chumbley, J., & Griffiths, M.D. (2006). Affect and the computer game player: The effect of gender, personality, and game reinforcement structure on affective responses to computer game-play. *CyberPsychology and Behaviour, 9,* 308–316.

Cole, H., & Griffiths, M.D. (2007). Social interactions in massively multiplayer online roleplaying gamers. *CyberPsychology and Behavior, 10,* 575–583.

De Freitas, S., & Griffiths, M.D. (2007). Online gaming as an educational tool in learning and training. *British Journal of Educational Technology, 38,* 536–538.

De Freitas, S., & Griffiths, M.D. (2008). The convergence of gaming practices with other media forms: What potential for learning? A review of the literature. *Learning, Media and Technology, 33,* 11–20.

Griffiths, M.D. (1991). Amusement machine playing in childhood and adolescence: A comparative analysis of video games and fruit machines. *Journal of Adolescence, 14,* 53–73.

Griffiths, M.D. (1993). Are computer games bad for children? *The Psychologist: Bulletin of the British Psychological Society, 6,* 401–407.

Griffiths, M.D. (1996). Behavioural addictions: An issue for everybody? *Journal of Workplace Learning, 8*(3), 19–25.

Griffiths, M.D. (1997). Computer game playing in early adolescence. *Youth and Society, 29,* 223–237.

Griffiths, M.D. (2000). Does internet and computer "addiction" exist? Some case study evidence. *CyberPsychology and Behaviour, 3,* 211–218.

Griffiths, M.D. (2002). *Gambling and gaming addictions in adolescence.* Leicester: British Psychological Society/Blackwells.

Griffiths, M.D. (2003). Video games: Advice for teachers and parents. *Education and Health, 21,* 48–49.

Griffiths, M.D. (2005a). A "components" model of addiction within a biopsychosocial framework. *Journal of Substance Use, 10,* 191–197.

Griffiths, M.D. (2005b). Video games and health. *British Medical Journal, 331,* 122–123.

Griffiths, M.D. (2005c). The therapeutic value of video games. In J. Goldstein & J. Raessens (Eds.), *Handbook of computer game studies* (pp. 161–171). Boston, MA: MIT Press.

Griffiths, M.D. (2008a). Video game addiction: Fact or fiction? In T. Willoughby & E. Wood (Eds.), *Children's learning in a digital world* (pp. 85–103). Oxford: Blackwell Publishing.

Griffiths, M.D. (2008b). Diagnosis and management of video game addiction. *New Directions in Addiction Treatment and Prevention, 12,* 27–41.

Griffiths, M.D., & Dancaster, I. (1995). The effect of Type A personality on physiological arousal while playing computer games. *Addictive Behaviors, 20,* 543–548.

Griffiths, M.D., Davies, M.N.O., & Chappell, D. (2003). Breaking the stereotype: The case of online gaming. *CyberPsychology and Behavior, 6,* 81–91.

Griffiths, M.D., Davies, M.N.O., & Chappell, D. (2004a). Online computer gaming: A comparison of adolescent and adult gamers. *Journal of Adolescence, 27,* 87–96.

Griffiths, M.D., Davies, M.N.O., & Chappell, D. (2004b). Demographic factors and playing variables in online computer gaming. *CyberPsychology and Behavior, 7,* 479–487.

Griffiths, M.D., & Hunt, N. (1995). Computer game playing in adolescence: Prevalence and demographic indicators. *Journal of Community and Applied Social Psychology, 5,* 189–193.

Griffiths, M.D., & Hunt, N. (1998). Dependence on computer games by adolescents. *Psychological Reports, 82,* 475–480.

Grüsser, S.M., Thalemann, R., & Griffiths, M.D. (2007). Excessive computer game playing: Evidence for addiction and aggression? *Cyberpsychology and Behavior, 10,* 290–292.

Hussain, Z., & Griffiths, M.D. (2008). Gender swapping and socialising in cyberspace: An exploratory study. *CyberPsychology and Behaviour, 11,* 47–53.

Phillips, C.A., Rolls, S., Rouse, A., & Griffiths, M.D. (1995). Home video game playing in schoolchildren: A study of incidence and pattern of play. *Journal of Adolescence, 18,* 687–691.

Wood, R.T.A., & Griffiths, M.D. (2007). Time loss whilst playing video games: Is there a relationship to addictive behaviours? *International Journal of Mental Health and Addiction, 5,* 141–149

Wood, R.T.A., Griffiths, M.D., & Parke, A. (2007). Experiences of time loss among video game players: An empirical study. *CyberPsychology and Behaviour, 10,* 45–56.

KEY AND CHALLENGING WORDS

deterioration, detrimental, intrinsic, extrinsic, immersive

QUESTIONS

1. What information about purpose and audience is revealed in the introduction? How do these factors affect a) the essay's structure, b) its content, c) its language, d) the author's credibility?
2. Paraphrase one of the numbered criteria applicable to video game addiction on page 383; summarize the paragraph that follows.
3. Explain the difference between "excessively playing" video games and addiction to video games.
4. What is the topic of paragraph 4? Explain how it is related to the topic of the essay itself; why is the word "addiction" in quotation marks?
5. What are the two bases of comparison used in "Online versus Offline Gaming"?
6. Review essays sometimes include recommendations at the end of the review. Choose one of the suggestions in "Practical Advice to Help Parents" and discuss its practicality and applicability for parents.
7. What can you infer about Griffiths's beliefs concerning the value of video games? Does he believe the costs outweigh the benefits or vice versa? Support your answer by specific passages in the "Conclusions" as well as at least one other section of the essay.

POST-READING

1. A student essay on a similar topic is on p. 161. Write a 500-word comparison of the two essays, using two or three bases of comparison for your analysis (see p. 87 for compare and contrast essay formats).
2. *Collaborative activity:* Divide the class into three "focus groups"* of 3–5 members each: 1) those who regularly play online games; 2) those who do not play online games regularly; 3) a mixed group composed of players and non-players. (Of course, depending on the make-up of the class, all these groupings may not be feasible.) One member should record comments. The topic for discussion is the same: What is the value of online video games? At the end of 20–30 minutes, each group should identify "themes" that emerged from the discussion. If your instructor requires it, each focus group could take one theme and collaborate on a report to be presented to the class or handed in as a written assignment.

   *small interactive groups formed to discuss, express opinions, feelings, etc. about a specific topic. See paragraph 4, p. 292, "Listening to the voices of *hijab*," for an extended definition of focus groups.
3. Write a critical response in which you agree or disagree with one of the article's main points, supporting your claims by logic and your observations/experiences with the topic of gaming addiction.

RELATED WEBSITES OF INTEREST

Canadian Games Studies Association:
http://playces.edu.yorku.ca/index.php

Digital games Research Association:
www.digra.org/

Centre for Addiction and Mental Health Library and Archives:
www.camh.net/About_Addiction_Mental_Health/CAMH_Library/index.html

Terror on Facebook, Twitter, and Youtube

Gabriel Weimann

(3,566 words)

Pre-reading

1. Who is Gabriel Weimann? Do an online or library search on the author to determine his qualifications for writing this article, professional background, publications, etc.
2. Using a current, reliable source, such as a recent edition of an encyclopedia or a yearbook, look up the following political organizations mentioned in the article: al-Qaeda, Hamas, Hezbollah. In a one-paragraph summary of each, include the country of origin, ideology, and aims.
3. Write a one-sentence definition of the word *jihad*. Check your definition with that of a reliable source, revising or adding to your definition, if necessary.

---

1   "My dear brothers in Jihad," wrote a man who identified himself as Abu Jendal, "I have a kilo of Acetone Peroxide. I want to know how to make a bomb from it in order to blow up an army jeep; I await your quick response." About an hour later the answer came: "My dear brother Abu Jendal," answered a Hamas supporter who called himself Abu Hadafa, "I understand that you have 1,000 grams of *Om El Abad*. Well done! There are several ways to change it into a bomb." *Om El Abad*—the mother of Abad—is the Hamas nickname for the improvised explosive TATP—triacetone triperoxide. Abu Hadafa then explained, in detail, how to change the homemade explosive into a deadly roadside bomb, and even attached a file that teaches how to make detonators for the bomb.[1] Abu Jendal and Abu Hadafa are two anonymous Palestinians who, it seems, never met one another. The exchange was not encoded or concealed, but was published completely openly on the website of the *Izz al din al Kassam* Brigades, the military faction of the Hamas.

2   This online form of exchanging of guidance, advice, and instructions has become commonplace in various terrorist chat rooms and online forums. Post-modern terrorists are taking advantage of the fruits of globalization and modern technology—especially advanced online communication technologies that are used to plan, coordinate, and execute their deadly campaigns. No longer geographically constrained within a particular territory, or politically or financially dependent on a particular state, they rely on technologically modern forms of communication—including the Internet. The Internet has long been a favorite tool for terrorists.[2] Decentralized and providing almost perfect anonymity, it cannot be subjected to controls or restrictions, and can be accessed by anyone. The Internet has enabled terrorist organizations to research and coordinate attacks; to expand the reach of their propaganda to a global audience; to recruit adherents; to communicate with international supporters and ethnic diasporas; to solicit donations; and to foster public awareness and sympathy for their causes. The Internet also allows terrorists to convey their messages to international and distant audiences with whom it would otherwise be difficult to communicate. The Internet provides a

means for terrorist groups to feed the mass media with information and videos that explain their mission and vision. By these means, the group's message can reach a greater audience and more easily influence the public agenda.[3]

3   In addition to launching their own websites, terrorists can harness the interactive capabilities of chat rooms, instant messenger, blogs, video-sharing websites, self-determined online communities, and social networks. As Noguchi and Kholmann found, "90 per cent of terrorist activity on the Internet takes place using social networking tools, be it independent bulletin boards, Paltalk, or Yahoo! eGroups. These forums act as a virtual firewall to help safeguard the identities of those who participate, and they offer subscribers a chance to make direct contact with terrorist representatives, to ask questions, and even to contribute and help out the cyber-jihad."[4]

4   By now, all active terrorist groups have established at least one form of presence on the Internet and most of them are using all formats of modern online platforms, including email, chatrooms, e-groups, forums, virtual message boards, and resources like You-Tube, Facebook, Twitter, and Google Earth. This essay examines the use of interactive online communication by terrorists and their supporters—from chatrooms to Twitter and Facebook.

Terrorist Chatrooms

5   Chatrooms and electronic forums enable terrorist groups to communicate with members and supporters all over the world, to recruit new followers and to share information at little risk of identification by authorities. The free chatroom service PalTalk, which includes voice and video capabilities, has become particularly popular with terrorist cells. In one PalTalk chat room, British Islamic militants were found to have set up support forums for the killed leader of the insurgents in Iraq, Abu Musab al-Zarqawi. In another chatroom, Arabic-speaking users shared personal experiences of fighting Arab-Afghans. In another, relatives of Iraqi insurgents praised the "martyrdom" of the terrorists.[5] On the alneda.com forum, al-Qaeda members posted comments praising Osama Bin Laden, such as "Oh Allah! Support

your fighting slave Osama bin Laden." Other message boards included threats against global security and reference to the 2005 London bombings. The website and forum were infiltrated and closed down by an American hacker, but that did not stop al-Qaeda members, who simply started a new forum.

6   In addition to generating support, terrorist groups use chatrooms to share tactical information. Jihadist message boards and chatrooms have been known to have "experts" directly answer questions about how to mix poisons for chemical attacks, how to ambush soldiers, how to carry out suicide attacks and how to hack into computer systems. One chatroom on the PalTalk index, with a name that is slightly altered each time but still identifiable, has been routinely advertised on Jihadi web forums and has been used on a daily basis to post links to al-Qaeda propaganda videos and terrorist instruction manuals.[6] The forums Qalah, Al-Shamikh, Majahden, and Al-Faloja are especially popular among terrorist cells, and new recruits are encouraged to refer to the sites to read the jihadist literature. These chatrooms also aim to convince prospective members to join or to stage personal suicide attacks.

7   According to SITE's special report on Western Jihadist Forums, during 2009 several notable technical changes occurred in many of the jihadist forums.[7] For example, the long offline, prominent English-language jihadist forum, al-Firdaws English, returned on 24 May 2009 in a form that is open to the public, rather than password-protected. Permitting non-members to view discussion and content on the forum is a significant departure for al-Firdaws style, as previous iterations of the forum have been both completely password-protected and not open to new membership. The forum administration's decision to open the forum to public observation suggests that they may envision the forum containing less sensitive information in the future. Despite allowing forum visitors to access threads and read content, al-Firdaws English remains closed to new and prospective members.

8   The case of Younes Tsouli is especially demonstrative of the resourceful uses of the Internet by terrorists. As one journalist put it, Tsouli, more commonly known by his pseudonym "Irhabi 007," "illustrated perfectly how terrorists are using the Internet not

just to spread propaganda, but to organize attacks."[8] Between 2003 and the time of his arrest in December 2007, Irhabi 007 engaged in several instrumental activities on the Internet. In 2003, he began joining various terrorist Internet forums, where he uploaded and published pictures, videos, and instruction manuals on computer hacking. Shortly thereafter his skills were sought out by al-Qaeda leaders who wanted him to provide logistical support for their online operations, and in 2005 Tsouli became the administrator of the extremist Internet forum al-Ansar, where he began publishing bomb making instruction manuals and details related to suicide bombing operations. He helped Zarqawi's al-Qaeda faction in Iraq and became a central figure in enabling Zarqawi to reestablish the links between al-Qaeda affiliated groups after the fall of the Taliban. Irhabi 007 eventually hacked his way into an unprotected file directory on an Arkansas state government website. He then posted propaganda and beheading videos. Cybertracking intelligence immediately noticed Irhabi 007's perfect English and questioned the cybercriminal's nationality. Younis Tsouli was caught in 2006. On his home computer, British investigators found photos of locations in Washington D.C. that had been emailed to him by colleagues which suggested that he was helping to organize a terrorist attack on Capitol Hill. Of course, after Tsouli was caught, other cyberterrorists learned from his mistake.

When Terrorists "Tweet"

9   An intelligence report released in October of 2008 by the US Army's 304th Military Intelligence Battalion included a chapter entitled the "Potential for Terrorist Use of Twitter," which expressed the Army's concern over the use of the blogging service.[9] The report says that Twitter could become an effective coordination tool for terrorists trying to launch militant attacks. The Army report includes references to several pro-Hezbollah tweets. The report also highlights three possible scenarios of terrorist use of Twitter. The first scenario is that terrorists can send and receive near real-time updates on the logistics of troop movements in order to conduct more successful ambushes. In the second, one operative with an

explosive device or suicide belt could use his mobile phone to send images of his or her location to a second operative who can use the near real-time imagery to time the precise moment to detonate the explosive device. The third is that a cyberterrorist operative could find and compromise a soldier's account and communicate with other soldiers under the stolen identity.[10] Although the last two options seem a bit far-fetched and difficult for terrorists to carry out successfully, the first option is a very viable threat. The instantaneous update capabilities could help the terrorists organize more precise and detrimental ambushes.

10   According to the SITE report, despite the potential utility of Twitter, members of terrorist groups continue to be wary of networking sites such as Facebook. In response to a forum member's suggestion to become friends on Facebook, some Ansar al-Mujahideen posters envisioned that such a network of friends could be a danger to Western jihadists. In a thread begun on 4 May 2009, Ansar al-Mujahideen members attempted to dissuade a member (called "islamic jihad union") from connecting with other jihad supporters on Facebook. Soon, other Ansar al-Mujahideen participants were warning against using Facebook. Several forum members opined that the risks of having their real identity tied to their online personas outweighed the potential gains from networking with other jihad supporters.

Social Networking

11   Popular social networking websites are another means of attracting potential members and followers. These types of virtual communities are growing increasingly popular all over the world, especially among younger demographics. Jihadist terrorist groups especially target youth for propaganda, incitement, and recruitment purposes. Terrorist groups and their sympathizers are using predominately Western online communities like Facebook, MySpace, Second Life, and their Arabic equivalents more frequently. Counter-terrorism expert Anthony Bergin says that terrorists use these youth-dominated websites as recruitment tools, "in the same way a pedophile might look at those sites to potentially groom would-be victims."[11]

12   Social networking websites allow terrorists to disseminate propaganda to an impressionable age bracket that might empathize with their cause and possibly agree to join. Many users join interest groups that may help terrorists target users they might be able to manipulate. Many social network users accept people as friends whether or not they know them, thereby giving perfect strangers access to personal information and photos. Some people even communicate with the strangers and establish virtual friendships. Terrorists apply the narrowcasting strategy to social networking sites as well. The name, accompanying default image, and information on a group message board are all tailored to fit the profile of a particular social group. The groups also provide terrorists with a list of predisposed recruits or sympathizers. In the same way that marketing groups can view a member's information to decide which products to target to a webpage, terrorist groups can view people's profiles to decide whom they are going to target and how they should configure the message. Yet, terrorists are well aware of the risks involved. A member of a Jihadi forum in English issued a warning, reminding readers that a Facebook network would allow security agencies to trace entire groups of jihadists, arguing:

> Don't make a network in Facebook . . . Then Kuffar will know every friend you have or had in the past. They will know location, how you look, what you like, they will know everything! Join Facebook if you want and use it to keep in touch with friends and brothers far away but not as a network.[12]

13   As a strategy to distribute jihadist propaganda to a wide range of Muslims and overcome countermeasures, a posting on the al-Fallujah jihadist forum on 16 March 2009 suggested that administrators of similar forums and media organizations create email groups. This mailing group is patterned after the Ansar Mailing Group, an inactive jihadist media distributor that dispatched news of the mujahideen to users via email. He suggested that other jihadists, too, create such groups to reach the largest possible number of users, and that they should remove any obstacle in the registration process that hinders distribution. To this end, the jihadist, in a later posting, provided instructions for creating groups on Google. Another forum

participant, pleased with the suggestion, gave instructions on how to create a user account on Yahoo, and added that groups may be created on that service.

You have a Friend Request: Facebook

14   Membership within the international Facebook community has boomed in recent years. Facebook is currently the world's most popular social networking website with an estimated 222 million users world wide, which includes a 66 per cent membership increase within the Middle East and a 23 per cent increase in Asia.[13] Terrorists have taken note of the trend and have set up profiles as well. There are numerous Facebook groups declaring support for paramilitary and nationalist groups that the US government has designated as terrorist organizations, such as Hezbollah, Hamas, the Turkish Revolutionary People's Liberation Army, and the Liberation Tigers of Tamil Eelam (LTTE). The majority of these groups have open pages and anyone interested can read the information, look at the discussion boards, clink on links to propaganda videos, and join the group.

15   Deputy Director for Intelligence at the National Counterterrorism Center Andrew Liepman recently reported to Congress that the Federal Bureau of Investigations is tracking a few Somali-Americans from the Minneapolis area that were reportedly recruited for the purpose of starting a US terrorist cell of the Al-Shabaab faction through Facebook.[14] The FBI is keeping a close eye on one Facebook user who posted a photo of a man wearing a black mask over his face and holding what appears to be the Koran in one hand and a grenade launcher in the other. Although some might argue that the aforementioned posting is probably in violation of Facebook's terms of use, which bans posting "threatening," "harassing," or "hateful" messages, the FBI is finding it difficult to regulate terrorist activity on the Internet because of First Amendment right issues. It is also nearly impossible to track down individuals involved in these sorts of instances because of the international nature of the websites. Social networking websites do not always have identifiable information about users; all that is needed to register for the websites in an email

address and users often set up their accounts under false names and details.

16   Terrorists can use these social networking sites to monitor military personnel. In 2008, the Canadian Defense Department and the British Secret Service M15 requested that troops remove personal details from social networking sites because of alleged monitoring by al-Qaeda operatives. US personnel are also warned against posting certain details or photos on their profile pages. Even if the information does not give details about the logistics of troop movements, it could potentially endanger the friends and relatives of military and security personnel. Many soldiers unwittingly post detailed information about themselves, their careers, family members, date of birth, present locations, and photos of colleagues and weaponry. Canadian troops have been asked to exclude any information from their profiles that might even link them with the military. A report from the Lebanese capital of Beirut later that year stated that Hezbollah had been monitoring Facebook to find potentially sensitive information about Israeli military movements and intelligence that could be harmful to the national security of Israel. The report quoted an Israeli intelligence official saying that "Facebook is a major resource for terrorists, seeking to gather information on soldiers and IDF [Israel Defense Forces] units and the fear is soldiers might even unknowingly arrange to meet an Internet companion who in reality is a terrorist."[15]

17   According to a posting on al-Ekhlaas, a password-protected al-Qaeda affiliated forum dated 21 August 2008, a group for supporters of the Islamic State of Iraq (ISI) and al-Qaeda is also using Facebook.[16] The post briefly describes the pictures found in this Facebook group, which include shots of Osama bin Laden, Ayman al-Zawahiri, and ISI mujahedeen. One of the members commented on the utility of such a group: "these sites can be exploited to post our ideas and what we owe Allah to those who do not carry our ideology."

YouTube and "TheyTube"

18   YouTube was established in February 2005 as an online repository facilitating the sharing of video content. YouTube claims to be the "the world's most popular online video community." A 2007 report from the Pew Internet and American Life Project put the percentage of US online video viewers using YouTube at 27 per cent, ahead of all other video sharing sites. In the 18 to 29 year-old age demographics, YouTube's leadership is even more pronounced, with 49 per cent of US online video viewers. In fact, *CNNMoney* reported that in January 2008 alone, nearly 79 million users worldwide viewed more than three billion YouTube videos.

19   Terrorist groups realized the potential of this easily accessed platform for the dissemination of their propaganda and radicalization videos. Terrorists themselves have praised the usefulness of this new online apparatus: "A lot of the funding that the brothers are getting is coming because of the videos. Imagine how many have gone after seeing the videos. Imagine how many have become shahid [martyrs]," convicted terrorist Younis Tsouli (so-called "Ithabi007") testified. In 2008, jihadists suggested a "YouTube Invasion" to support jihadist media and the administrators of al-Fajr-affiliated forums.[17] This suggestion was posted on al-Faloja, a password-protected jihadist forum, on 25 November 2008. The posting provides a synopsis of the YouTube site and its founding, and notes its use by, among others, President Barack Obama during his presidential campaign. YouTube is argued to be an alternative to television as a medium that allows for jihadists to reach massive, global audiences. This particular message even instructs jihadists to cut mujahedeen videos into ten-minute chunks, as per YouTube's requirements, and upload them sequentially to the site. "I ask you, by Allah, as soon as you read this subject, to start recording on YouTube, and to start cutting and uploading and posting clips on the jihadist, Islamic, and general forums," said the poster. "Shame the Crusaders by publishing videos showing their losses, which they hid for a long time."

20   Hezbollah, Hamas, the LTTE and the Shining Path of Peru all have propaganda videos on YouTube. One LTTE YouTube user has posted over 100 videos in 2009 alone.[18] In 2008, Hamas allegedly launched its own video-sharing website, although the group denied ownership of the site. AqsaTube, in addition to choosing a similar name, was designed to look just like YouTube and even copied its logo. Once certain Internet providers refused to host the website, Hamas

launched a PaluTube and TubeZik.[19] The LTTE has also launched TamilTube.[20] These videos are not just aimed at Middle Eastern Muslim youths. More recent videos posted on these video-sharing websites are dubbed in English or have English subtitles.

21   A recent study conducted by Conway and McInerney analyzed the online supporters of jihad-promoting video content on YouTube, focusing on those posting and commenting upon martyr-promoting material from Iraq.[21] The findings suggest that a majority are less than 35 years of age and reside outside the region of the Middle East and North Africa with the largest percentage of supporters located in the United States. As the researchers concluded: "What is clearly evident however is that jihadist content is spreading far beyond traditional jihadist websites or even dedicated forums to embrace, in particular, video sharing and social networking—both hallmarks of Web 2.0—and thus extending their reach far beyond what may be conceived as their core support base in the Middle East and North Africa region to Diaspora populations, converts, and political sympathizers."

Conclusion

22   Much of the original online terrorist content was one-directional and text-based, either in the form of traditional websites with a heavy reliance on text or as messages posted on forums. However, technological advances, particularly the increased availability of sophisticated, but cheap and user-friendly video capturing hardware (e.g., hand-held digital video cameras, mobile telephones, etc.) and interactive online networking platforms (e.g., Facebook) have changed terrorist online communications. The global community created by social networks and interactive forums on the Internet is advancing cultural awareness and reconciliation efforts, but it is also advancing terrorists' goals to share their extremist messages to global audiences. By using these online communities to their advantage, not only can terrorists promote global paranoia, share their messages with sympathizers, and obtain donations, but they can also create more terrorists. The Internet has provided terrorists with a whole new virtual realm to conduct their sinister back-alley transactions. Terrorist groups are no longer confined to specific regional boundaries—now terrorist networks can recruit and members located in any part of the globe.[22] A person in the United States can literally take a terrorist training course within the privacy of their bedroom.

23   The interactive capabilities of the Internet, like chatrooms, social networking sites, video-sharing sites and online communities, allow terrorists to assume an offensive position. Instead of waiting for web-surfers to come across their websites and propaganda materials, terrorists can now lure targeted individuals to the sites. Paradoxically, the most innovative network of communication developed by the West with its numerous online networking platforms now serves the interests of the greatest foe of the West, international terrorism.

The Brown Journal of World Affairs.
2010. Spring/Summer 14 (2).

Notes

1. This exchange was reported by Amit Cohen, "Hamas Dot Com", in *Maariv Online,* 7 February 2003.
2. Gabriel Weimann, "How Modern Terrorism Uses the Internet," United States Institute of Peace Special Report 116 (2004), www.usip.org/pubs/specialreports/sr116.pdf; Gabriel Weimann, *Terror on the Internet: The New Arena, The New Challenges.* (Washington, DC.: USIP Press Books, 2006a); Gabriel Weimann, "Virtual Training Camps: Terrorist Use of the Internet," in ed. James Forest *Teaching Terror: Strategic and Tactical Learning in the Terrorist World* (Boulder: Rowman & Littlefield Publishers, 2006b): 110-132.
3. David H. Gray, and Albon Head. "The Importance of the Internet to the Post- Modern Terrorist and its Role as a Form of Safe Haven." *European Journal of Scientific Research* 25 (2009): 396-404.
4. Yuki Noguchi, and Evan Kholmann. "Tracking Terrorists Online." Washingtonpost.com video report. 19 April 2006. *The Washington Post,* www.washingtonpost.com/wp-dyn/content/discussion/2006/04/11/DI2006041100626.html>, accessed 11 March 2009 .
5. Evan Kholmann, "Al Qaeda and the Internet." *Washingtonpost.com* video report. The Washington Post, accessed 2 August 2005.

6. Elizabeth Montalbano, "Social networks link terrorists." *Computer World,* 7 January 2009, accessed 13 March 2009.

7. *InSITE:* Western Jihadist Forums: The Monthly SITE Monitoring Service on Western Language Jihadist Websites, April-May 2009, accessed June 2009.

8. Gordon Corera, "Al-Qaeda's 007: The Extraordinary Story of the Solitary Computer Geek in a Shepherds Bush Bedsit Who Became the World's Most Wanted Cyber-Jihadist," *Times Online,* 16 January 2008, http://women.timesonline.co.uk/tol/life_and_style/women/the_way_we_live/article3191517.ece.

9. "US Army Says Blogging Site 'Twitter' Could Become Terrorist Tool." *Fox News,* 27 October 2008, accessed 11 March 2009.

10. Noah Shachtman, "Spy Fears: Twitter Terrorists, Cell Phone Jihadists." *Wired,* 24 October 2008, accessed 8 March 2009.

11. "Facebook terrorism investigation." *The Advertiser,* 5 April 2008, accessed 10 March 2009.

12. *InSITE:* "Western Jihadist Forums," ibid.

13. "Social Networking Explodes Worldwide as Sites Increase their Focus on Cultural Relevance." Press release. *ComScore.com.* 12 August 2008, accessed 15 March 2009.

14. Andrew Liepman, Violent Islamist Extremism: Al-Shabaab Recruitment in America. Hearing before the Senate Homeland Security and Governmental Affairs Committee, 11 March 2009.

15. "Cyber Terrorism: Perils of the Internet's Social Networks." *Middle East Times* [Washington D.C.] 8 September 2008.

16. *InSITE,* "ISI Supporters Group on Facebook," 21 August 2008.

17. "Jihadist Forum Suggests YouTube Invasion," *The Telegraph,* 4 December 2008, www.telegraph. co.uk/news/worldnews/northamerica/usa/3547072/Jihadist-forum-calls-for-YouTube-Invasion.html.

18. www.youtube.com/user/TamilEelamTigers.

19. The Internet and Terrorism: Hamas and Palutube "Global Terrorism." *Right Side News,* 6 April 2009.

20. www.tubetamil.com.

21. Maura Conway and Lisa McInerney, 2008. "Jihadi Video & Auto-Radicalisation: Evidence from an Exploratory YouTube Study," In Proceedings of the 1st European Conference on intelligence and Security informatics, Esbjerg, 3-5 December 2008.

22. Maura Conway, "Terrorism and the Internet: New Media-New Threat?" *Parliamentary Affairs* 59 (2006): 283-98.

KEY AND CHALLENGING WORDS

constrain, adherent, diaspora, iteration, logistical, viable, detrimental, opine, incitement, disseminate, configure, unwittingly, repository, paradoxically

QUESTIONS

1. Analyze the effectiveness of the introduction. What kind of introduction does Weimann use? What strategies does he use to attract interest and convey information?

2. a) What is the primary organizational method used in the essay? b) What kinds of secondary sources did Weimann use? Comment on their credibility, currency, variety, and other factors you consider relevant.

3. Identify three variants of the noun *jihad* in paragraphs 3 and 6. For two of them, write brief, one-sentence definitions based on their contexts; based on its context, write a brief definition of *Kuffar* (paragraph 12) or *mujahideen* (paragraph 13).

4. Identify one example of a primary source and evaluate its effectiveness in the paragraph in which it occurs.

5. a) Discuss the use the author makes of the Younes Tsouli case (paragraph 8); b) What does the author mean when he states, "other cyberterrorists learned from [Tsouli's] mistake."

6. Summarize paragraph 9, which discusses ways that "Twitter" could be utilized by terrorists.

7. Analyze the evidence presented in the section "YouTube and 'TheyTube,'" commenting on the ways that the author separates fact from conjecture. Why is it necessary to do this?

8. Analyze Weimann's conclusion. In your analysis, identify specific content (i.e., words, phrases, or sentences) repeated from the introduction. Is the conclusion successful?

POST-READING

1. *Collaborative or individual activity:* Discuss or debate one of the following questions: a) Do you believe that chat rooms or social networking sites like Facebook make Western nations more vulnerable to terrorist attacks? b) Of the various media discussed in the article, which do you consider the most useful for terrorist activities like recruitment, sharing information, and planning attacks?

   c) Are there feasible solutions to the problems discussed in the essay?

2. *Collaborative or individual activity:* What issues do you consider central to ensuring the safe and effective operation of social networking sites such as Facebook (e.g., privacy settings)? What specific steps would you take to ensure their safety?

RELATED WEBSITE OF INTEREST

SITE Intelligence Group (monitors and analyzes Internet terrorist sites):

www.siteintelgroup.com/

SOCIETY OF EXCESS

Pharmaceutical innovation: Can we live forever? A commentary on Schnittker and Karandinos

Joel Lexchin

(1,954 words)

Pre-reading

1. Access your library's database and read the abstract for "Methuselah's medicine: Pharmaceutical innovation and mortality in the United States, 1960–2000," the basis for Lexchin's commentary. Who was Methuselah? Summarize the article's abstract in two sentences.

2. Does the title suggest Lexchin's thesis or approach? Scan the first two paragraphs in order to determine this information and come up with a reading hypothesis.

---

1   If we discover enough new drugs can we live forever, or at least for a lot longer than we currently do? This is the thesis that Schnittker and Karandinos set out to explore in "Methuselah's Medicine: Pharmaceutical Innovation and Mortality in the United States, 1960–2000" in this issue of Social Science & Medicine (Schnittker & Karandinos, 2010). More specifically, they look at the relationship between pharmaceutical innovation and life expectancy between 1960 and 2000 in the United States (US). The amount of pharmaceutical innovation is measured by the number of new molecular entities (NME) approved by the Food and Drug Administration and mortality—life expectancy at birth and age-specific mortality—is examined as a function of NME approvals within a given year. In addition to drug approvals they also consider the role that per-capita gross domestic product (GDP) and health-specific spending play in increasing longevity. Although they find that GDP has a larger association with life expectancy than NME, they also conclude that their "study demonstrates a significant relationship between pharmaceutical innovation and life expectancy at birth" (Schnittker & Karandinos, 2010).

2   This paper joins a growing list of publications, chiefly from Frank Lichtenberg (2007), that argue that the more new drugs there are the better off we are. However, just as Lichtenberg has his critics (Baker & Fugh-Berman, 2009) so too there are issues with this present paper that need to be debated and clarified before its conclusions can be accepted. Before doing that, though, let us give some new drugs their due—the antiretroviral drugs for HIV/AIDS certainly have extended the lives of people with that disease; the antithrombolitics are extremely valuable for treating patients with acute myocardial infarctions.

Clearly, some new drugs are valuable but can that conclusion be generalized in the way that Schnittker and Karandinos have done?

3 All NMEs are not the same; the first angiotensin converting enzyme (ACE) inhibitor or the first proton pump inhibitor yielded significantly more benefits than the second or third or fourth in the class and many of the NMEs that have appeared in the 40 years being considered by the authors are "add-ons" to existing drug classes. Furthermore, many NMEs have nothing to do with increasing life expectancy. Terbinafine is a good drug for treating toenail fungal infections, but no one dies from infected toenails. Minoxidil has some benefit in male pattern alopecia, but baldness is not a fatal disease. What percent of NME introductions since 1960 have the potential for altering mortality patterns? That question is not explored in this present study.

4 The French drug bulletin, *La revue Prescrire*, analyzes the therapeutic value of new drugs (and new indications for older drugs) introduced into the French market. Out of 983 new drugs or new indications for existing drugs marketed between 1996 and 2006, only 4.1 per cent offered major therapeutic gains and an additional 10.8 per cent had some value but did not fundamentally change present therapeutic practice ("A look back at pharmaceuticals in 2006: aggressive advertising cannot hide the absence of therapeutic advances," 2007). Garattini and Bertele (2002) examined 12 new anticancer drugs approved in Europe between 1995 and 2000 which contained new molecular entities or known active principles with new indications and concluded that none of the 12 offered any significant improvement in action. Of the 61 new biotechnology products introduced in Europe between 1995 and 2003 for therapeutic purposes, only 2 were approved on the basis that they were superior to existing therapies using hard clinical endpoints (Joppi, Bertele, & Garattini, 2005). According to Schnittker and Karandinos (2010), the major benefit has come from the introduction of new drugs that treat cardiovascular disease and, as I acknowledged above, certain new drugs are extremely valuable in these conditions. But, on-the-other hand, the thiazide diuretics, some of which were introduced before 1960, are at least as good and possibly superior to the much newer ACE inhibitors

and calcium channel blockers in preventing the complications of hypertension (The ALLHAT officers and coordinators for the ALLHAT collaborative research group, 2002). Aspirin, which was available long before 1960, is a major factor in decreasing mortality from cardio and cerebrovascular disease.

5 The data presented by Schnittker and Karandinos show that mortality reduction is greatest in the 15–19 year age group (Schnittker & Karandinos, 2010). What are the major causes of mortality in that group? According to the US National Center for Injury Prevention and Control the three leading causes of death in the 15–19 age group are unintentional injury, homicide, and suicide (National Center for Injury Prevention and Control, 2009). Neither unintentional injury nor homicide is preventable by pharmacotherapy and the value of antidepressants in reducing deaths by suicide is far from clear (Jureidini & McHenry, 2009). The other 7 leading causes of death in this age group, which may be modifiable by drug treatment, account for little more than 12 per cent of mortality. Even if pharmaceuticals eliminated every death in each of these 7 causes, the overall impact on deaths would be minimal.

6 Schnittker and Karandinos note that their findings are for the US and that results in other countries may differ for a variety of reasons including how extensive health insurance is (eliminating financial barriers to prescription drugs) and the degree of innovation in the country. With these caveats in mind how do changes in life expectancy in the US compare to what has happened in other developed countries? Life expectancy in the United States in 1960 was 73.1 years for women and 66.6 years for men. In that year, the US ranked 14th among the Organisation for Economic Co-operation and Development countries for women and 20th for men. By 2000 US life expectancy for women and men was 79.5 and 74.1, respectively and the US ranked 22nd and 21st (Directorate for Employment, 2009). At the same time as the US is losing ground in life expectancy compared to European countries, the European Federation of Pharmaceutical Industries and Associations is complaining that innovation in Europe is lagging behind the US (European Federation of Pharmaceutical Industries and Associations, 2009) and other work shows that new drugs become available much faster in the US

than in other developed countries (Office of Fair Trading, 2007). Clearly there are other factors involved in changes in national mortality figures, but if new drugs are helping the US then they are significantly outweighed by these other considerations.

7   Schnittker and Karandinos state that "new drugs tend to be used promptly" and "this implies a relatively quick impact on mortality" (Schnittker & Karandinos, 2010). The first statement is certainly true, and this uptake is significantly fuelled by an annual $57.5 billion promotional budget (Gagnon & Lexchin, 2008). But there is good reason to question the latter claim. Knowledge about the safety of new drugs is minimal at best because they have only been tested in highly selective populations and in patient numbers that preclude identification of less common side effects. One indication of the unrecognized dangers from new drugs is that half of the drugs withdrawn from the US market for safety reasons occur within two years of marketing (Lasser et al., 2002). The example of what happened with rofecoxib should make us sceptical of claims that new drugs lead to rapid declines in mortality. Graham and colleagues estimate that in the five years that rofecoxib was on the US market there were between 88,000 and 140,000 excess cases of serious coronary heart disease with a case-fatality rate of 44 per cent (Graham et al., 2005).

8   Finally, and more generally, the paper by Schnittker and Karandinos (2010) buys into the notion that we will be saved by innovation. On a micro level, innovation is important and many people are better off due to technological advances, but on a population level, it is harder to prove that more innovation and technology is the most important reason for better health outcomes. The US has significantly more neonatologists and neonatal intensive care beds than Australia, Canada, or the United Kingdom but does not have better birth weight-specific mortality rates than these three other countries (Thompson, Goodman, & Little, 2002). A recent systematic review that I participated in compared health outcomes in the US and Canada for patients treated for similar underlying medical conditions; in effect we were comparing higher overall expenditures and more technology (US) with a universal public insurance plan where inpatient care is almost completely delivered by private not-for-profit institutions (Canada): "Studies addressed diverse problems, including cancer, coronary artery disease, chronic medical illnesses, and surgical procedures. Of 10 studies that included extensive statistical adjustment and enrolled broad populations, five favoured Canada, two favoured the United States, and three showed equivalent or mixed results. Overall, results for mortality favoured Canada" (Guyatt et al., 2007, p. e27).

9   Drugs that are important advances in medical care are few and far between. We definitely need more of them and their development should be encouraged but, despite new drugs, I'm not counting on living to 150.

Social Science & Medicine.
2010. (70).

References

A look back at pharmaceuticals in 2006: aggressive advertising cannot hide the absence of therapeutic advances. (2007). *Prescrire International, 16,* 80–86.

Baker, D., & Fugh-Berman, A. (2009). Do new drugs increase life expectancy? A critique of a Manhattan institute paper. *Journal of General Internal Medicine, 24,* 678–682.

Directorate for Employment, Labout, and Social Affairs. (2009). *OECD health data 2008-frequently requested data.* Organisation for Economic Co-operation and Development.

European Federation of Pharmaceutical Industries and Associations. (2009). *The pharmaceutical industry in figures: Key data – 2009 update.* Brussels: EFPIA.

Gagnon, M.-A., & Lexchin, J. (2008). The cost of pushing pills: a new estimate of pharmaceutical promotion expenditures in the United States. *PLoS Medicine, 5,*e1.

Garattini, S., & Bertele, V. (2002). Efficacy, safety, and cost of new anticancer drugs. British Medical Journal, 325, 269–271.

Graham, D. J., Campen, D., Hui, R., Spence, M., Cheetham, C., Levy, G., et al. (2005). Risk of acute myocardial infarction and sudden cardiac death in patients treated with cyclo-oxygenase 2 selective and non-selective non-steroidal anti-inflammatory drugs: nested case-control study. *Lancet, 365,* 475–481.

Guyatt, G. H., Devereaux, P. J., Lexchin, J., Stone, S. B., Yalnizyan, A., Himmelstein, D., et al. (2007). A systematic review of studies comparing health outcomes in Canada and the United States. *Open Medicine, 1,* E27–E36.

Joppi, R., Bertele, V., & Garattini, S. (2005). Disappointing biotech. *British Medical Journal, 331,* 895–897.

Jureidini, J. N., & McHenry, L. B. (2009). Key opinion leaders and paediatric antidepressant overprescribing. *Psychotherapy and Psychosomatics, 78*, 197–201.

Lasser, K. E., Allen, P. D., Woolhandler, S. J., Himmelstein, D. U., Wolfe, S. M., & Bor, D. H. (2002). Timing of new black box warnings and withdrawals for prescription medications. *JAMA, 287*, 2215–2220.

Lichtenberg, F. (2007). *Why has longevity increased more in some states than in others? The role of medical innovation and other factors.* New York: Manhattan Institute.

National Center for Injury Prevention and Control. (2009). *10 leading causes of death, United States 2006, all races, both sexes.* Atlanta: Centers for Disease Control and Prevention.

Office of Fair Trading. (2007). Annexe D: global overview of the pharmaceutical industry.

Schnittker, J., & Karandinos, G. (2010). Methuselah's Medicine: Pharmaceutical innovation and mortality in the United States, 1960–2000. *Social Science & Medicine, 70*, 961–968.

The ALLHAT officers and coordinators for the ALLHAT collaborative research group. (2002). Major outcomes in high-risk hypertensive patients randomized to angiotensin-converting enzyme inhibitor or calcium channel blocker vs diuretic: the antihypertensive and lipid-lowering treatment to prevent heart attack trial (ALLHAT). *JAMA, 288*, 2981–2997.

Thompson, L. A., Goodman, D. C., & Little, G. A. (2002). Is more neonatal intensive care always better? Insights from a cross-national comparison of reproductive care. *Pediatrics, 109*, 1036–1043.

KEY AND CHALLENGING WORDS

pharmaceutical, therapeutic, modifiable, caveat

QUESTIONS

1. What is the function of paragraph 1? How does it differ from introductions in the kinds of essays you might be asked to write?

2. a) What specific argumentative strategy does Lexchin use in paragraph 2? b) Paraphrase the last sentence in this paragraph.

3. Explain in your own words the problems with Schnittker and Karandinos's methodology and/or the assumptions on which part of the study is based (see paragraph 3), according to Lexchin.

4. Analyze the development of paragraph 6 (e.g., you could consider the rhetorical pattern, the placement of the topic sentence, use of deductive versus inductive development, etc.).

5. What kind of evidence does Lexchin use throughout the body paragraphs to support his claims? Pointing to at least one body paragraph show how his use of evidence provides support for his claim.

6. How does the claim in paragraph 8 differ from that of the other paragraphs? Why do you think he addresses this issue in his second-last paragraph rather than in an earlier paragraph?

7. Explain the extensive use of the Guyatt et al. study in paragraph 8.

POST-READING

1. *Collaborative activity:* a) Discuss or debate central issues related to health care in Canada versus in the US. b) Could the fact that the Schnittker and Karandinos study is based on US statistics affect its applicability to Canada? If so, how?

2. Access the Guyatt et al. study mentioned in paragraph 8. Note that it is found in the open access journal *Open Medicine* (www.openmedicine.ca/). a) What are open access sources? According to the website, why is open access publishing particularly important in the field of medicine? b) Summarize the "Discussion" section of the Guyatt et al. study in approximately 150 words (the section is 1,500 words).

3. In the same issue of *Social Science & Medicine* (volume 70, issue 7, 2010), Schnittker and Karandinos respond to Lexchin's commentary as well as to another commentary. Summarize Schnittker and Karandinos's response to Lexchin; then briefly explain whether you think it was an adequate response (make your summary and analysis 300–400 words).

ADDITIONAL READING

Young, S.M. (2005). Universities, governments and industry:
    Can the essential nature of universities survive the drive
    to commercialize? p. 196.

Did the banks go crazy?

Joseph Heath

(4,059 words)

Pre-reading

1. Using reliable sources, establish a timeline for the major events that led to the financial crisis of 2007–08.
2. Who is Joseph Heath? What makes him qualified to write an article like "Did the banks go crazy?"?

1   The great financial crisis of 2008 has provoked an extraordinary round of soul searching among economists. The reasons for this are not difficult to find. Not only did most members of the profession fail to predict the impending catastrophe, but many actively contributed to it, by aggressively rationalizing the very practices that gave rise to the collapse of the US investment banking system.

2   In the background was the assumption, widely shared among economists, that contractual arrangements entered into by private parties were efficient until proven otherwise—so that if a particular financial arrangement (say, a bank making a huge loan to a person with no money or job) looked like it was crazy, that was only because it had not been well enough understood. Look more carefully, and you can find the hidden rationale, the secret genius of the market at work.

3   Thus buckets of ink (or terabytes of keystrokes) were wasted, essentially intellectualizing

the work of financiers and bankers (much the way academics in the humanities intellectualize the work of artists and writers). The implosion on Wall Street was therefore a source of considerable embarrassment. Imagine an art historian, invited to offer impressions of a long-lost work by Duchamp. After waxing poetically for several minutes about its "transgressive" and "post-auratic" qualities, the historian is informed that a mistake has been made, and that the work in question is actually just a urinal. This is basically the situation that many academic economists found themselves in last fall.

4   The repercussions have been swiftly felt. While the public debate has been dominated by pointing fingers at a bewildering range of suspects, the debate in the economics profession has become quite narrowly focused on two rival theories.

5   Until recently, the dominant view of markets was that they were rational and efficient. These two virtues had always seemed to go together, like faith and hope. And yet in the fall of 2008 it became clear that financial markets had failed to perform efficiently. Two obvious explanations presented themselves. Some people, among them former US Federal Reserve chair Alan Greenspan, suggested that banks had simply gone crazy. According to this view, rationality and efficiency are still an inseparable duo; it is just that banks and investors failed to act rationally.

6   The other possibility is that no one went crazy, but that rationality and efficiency do not actually go together quite as neatly as many had assumed. Perhaps individually rational action, even in reasonably well-structured markets, is able to produce outcomes that are collectively self-defeating.

7   The first theory is the easier sell. It is the theory that everyone wants to believe. Unfortunately, it is the second theory that is correct.

I

8   Why does anyone start a small business? According to Statistics Canada, one half of all new small businesses fail before the end of their third year, and only one in five survives a decade or more. In other words, starting a small business and thinking you are going to make money is far less plausible

than getting married and thinking you will not get divorced. So why does anyone do it?

9   Self-deception is one answer. In the case of marriage, it is a fairly persuasive explanation. You are in love. You're not thinking straight. Emotions are clouding your judgement. But what about small businesses? Perhaps entrepreneurs are just incurable romantics. Yet isn't it strange to think that our economic system might depend upon this sort of irrationality?

10   John Maynard Keynes was not one to shrink from this conclusion. He argued that an essential ingredient of entrepreneurship was what he called the "animal spirits" of investors. The typical business plan contains about as much wishful thinking as the prospectus for "an expedition to the South Pole," he said. "Individual initiative will only be adequate when reasonable calculation is supplemented and supported by animal spirits, so that the thought of ultimate loss which often overtakes pioneers . . . is put aside as a healthy man puts aside the expectation of death."

11   The phenomenon that Keynes put his finger on is by now quite well documented. It is referred to as optimism bias. People tend to paint a rosy picture of things. To say that we all suffer from this tendency would be misleading, simply because "suffering from it" may well be an essential component of psychological well-being.

12   According to Keynes, this makes markets vulnerable to mood swings. Much of everyday economic activity depends upon our willingness to play along with the illusion that everything will work out well in the end. When something happens that challenges this assumption, it can have an arresting effect upon the economic system as a whole.

13   One can see this moodiness on display in Garth Turner's recent book, *After the Crash: How to Guard Your Money in These Turbulent Times*, where the one-time investment guru now recommends not just withdrawal from the market, but from most of western civilization. In this delightfully nutty jeremiad, Turner walks the reader step by step through the process of withdrawing all money from the bank, getting the house off the grid, stockpiling toilet paper, and otherwise preparing for the collapse of civilization. Animal spirits indeed. The book could just as well have been called "How to Make Things Worse."

14   Of course, the reference to animal spirits was something of a throwaway line for Keynes, not central to his diagnosis of the crisis tendencies of capitalism. But it has since become a catchphrase for a movement in contemporary economics that seeks to dislodge rationality from its traditional place of honour, in favour of a more accurate picture of human psychology with all of its foibles and flaws. For partisans of this new "behavioural" approach to economics, such as George Akerlof and Robert Shiller, authors of *Animal Spirits: How Human Psychology Drives the Economy, and Why It Matters for Global Capitalism*, the unexpectedness of the financial crisis reveals a fundamental methodological flaw in the way that economists have approached their subject. Far from being perfectly rational, people are subject to "changing confidence, temptations, envy, resentment and illusions." What triggered the market collapse? Essentially a mood swing.

II

15   Economists never really believed that people are perfectly rational. After all, they get up in the morning and go to work in the same world and you and I do. What they believed—and what many continue to believe—is that irrationality can safely be ignored when it comes to making predictions about the behaviour of the economy. Why?

16   Historically, many have been comforted by the thought that irrationality would produce mainly noise, or random deviation from the dominant tendency. If this were true, then irrationality could safely be disregarded whenever one was aggregating across a large enough number of people. Consider an analogy: when voting, some people no double make a mistake and tick off the wrong box on their ballot. But is this worth worrying about? Should we revise our assumptions that when people vote, they are expressing their true preferences? Of course not, because not only are these mistakes likely to be uncommon, but they are also likely to cancel each other out.

17   When it comes to the economy, the same thing applies. Sure, there are some bozos out there. But bozos, it was claimed, precisely due to the bozoness of their choices, tend to cancel each other out.

18   Furthermore, you cannot count on people making mistakes. Think about playing chess. Naturally, your opponent will sometimes make mistakes. But you can't build a strategy on that. You can't expect the person to overlook an obvious opportunity, despite the fact that people often do precisely that. When you are playing chess you have to treat your opponent as rational and not overly prone to error.

19   The same thing goes for the economy. Money, like chess, tends to focus the mind. People do not like losing it. So when you're entering into an adversarial market relationship—where your gain is someone else's loss—you should treat it like a chess game. You should assume the best about people. This in turn will make market behaviour as a whole more rational.

20   Of course the idea that deviations from the ideal of rationality would be random has taken something of a beating over the past few decades. What studies of optimism bias and other such psychological quirks have revealed is a set of extremely common errors that are not random, but typically push in the same direction. People get far more upset about losses than about foregone gains. People discount the future in a way that assigns exaggerated significance to the near term. People underestimate the probability of boring events, and overestimate the probability of exciting ones. And so on.

21   This suggests that we cannot afford to ignore irrationality.

22   But here is the killer counter-argument, and the lynchpin of the much-derided efficient markets hypothesis. If people exhibit systematic biases in their reasoning, then they will be predictably irrational. If their irrationality is predictable, then it will be easy to make money off them. Irrationality, as they say on Wall Street, creates arbitrage opportunities.

23   For example, Lisa Kramer, writing in *The Finance Crisis and Rescue: What Went Wrong? Why? What Lessons Can Be Learned?* (an instabook put together by professors at the University of Toronto's Rotman School of Management), argues that the 2008 crisis exposes the need for a new, behavioural approach to understanding finance. She offers as an example the fact that investors suffer from seasonal affective disorder, and so tend to ditch high-risk

stocks as the number of daylight hours declines. But if this were true, the obvious recommendation would be to buy these stocks in the late fall or winter, not the spring or summer. Yet if people started doing this, the trend that Kramer claims to observe would disappear.

24   This observation points to a fundamental asymmetry between rationality and irrationality. The fact that some people are rational does not create a buying opportunity for the irrational, whereas the fact that some people are irrational does create such opportunities. Thus irrationality summons up countervailing forces that tend to press for its elimination. This countervailing force will have two effects—first, it will have a tendency to adjust prices to their "correct" level, and, second, it will drive irrational players out of the market.

25   Thus the idea that economic actors will behave rationally is not just a fantasy dreamed up by ivory tower intellectuals, or a methodological bias imposed by the desire of economists to use fancy mathematics. Even if we are irrational, the discovery that we are will tend to correct the situation. The only stable outcome is one in which everyone is rational.

III

26   Economists are not mistaken in thinking that when we take any particular instance of seemingly irrational behaviour, we can often find a rational explanation for it. To take a paradigm instance on financial markets, consider the case of a bank run. This occurs when a large number of depositors try to withdraw their money from a bank simultaneously. Of course, this is lemming-like behaviour, since the attempt at simultaneous withdrawal guarantees the failure of the bank and therefore makes withdrawal impossible. (One may recall the famous run-on-the-bank scene in *Mary Poppins*.)

27   One way of understanding banks is to think of them as firms whose core business model consists of borrowing short and lending long. Richard Posner, in *A Failure of Capitalism: The Crisis of '08 and the Descent into Depression*, provides a lucid exposition of the basic structure. Banks make their money from the interest rate spread, since borrowers are willing to pay

more for long-term than for short-term loans. How is this a sustainable business? Because of the law of large numbers. Banks borrow short term from many, many people (the depositors) and make long-term loans to a smaller number of people (e.g. businesses, homeowners). While every day some depositors will need to be paid back, the number is likely to be small, and in any case, is likely to be offset by new deposits.

28   Thus the greatest enemy of banking is the enemy of all risk-pooling arrangements—correlation. If withdrawals are independent of one another, then the bank is stable. But if one person's withdrawal prompts someone else to withdraw, then the two events are no longer independent. They are correlated. Once that happens, the fundamental business model of a bank simply does not work.

29   This is why, back in the salad days of laissez-faire capitalism, the stability of banks was hostage to public sentiment. Rumours were able to generate extraordinary displays of crowd behaviour. The mere whiff of trouble at a bank could bring a stampede of depositors, clamouring for their money back. Furthermore, bank runs often gave rise to bank panics, when depositors, knowing that some banks were failing but not knowing which ones, tried to withdraw their money from all banks simultaneously. Compared to bank runs, bank panics were positively bacchanalian.

30   Akerlof and Shiller duly present bank runs as a paradigm instance of irrational mass behaviour. Indeed, it seems like an easy target. But it does not serve very well as an illustration of the madness of crowds. On the contrary, what is striking about the actions of depositors in the case of a bank run is that their actions are perfectly rational. While it may be the case that the simultaneous withdrawal of deposits has the effect of destroying the bank, the fact remains that those who get there first do succeed in redeeming their deposits. So if your bank is going to fail, the best thing to do is to run down there and get your money out as soon as possible, devil take the hindmost.

31   In other words, there is a purely rational explanation for bank runs; one need not appeal to animal spirits. Two things make bank runs seem irrational. First, because what each person does depends upon what that person thinks that everyone else is going to do, the interaction is subject to very dramatic tipping-point effects. Second, once the run

gets started it is collectively self-defeating, or inefficient. The best course of action for each individual
generates an outcome that is worse for everyone.

32   But neither of these two features adds up to
genuine irrationality. Indeed, if bank runs were
irrational it is not obvious what one could do to fix
them. And yet the introduction of deposit insurance
during the New Deal era all but eliminated bank runs
in the conventional banking sector. It did so by
changing the incentives faced by depositors (so that
there was no particular disadvantage associated with
being among the hindmost).

33   One can see here the problem with the animal
spirits view. It caters to popular prejudice in an
unhelpful way, by distracting attention away from the
structure of incentives that individuals face. It suggests that our problems are a consequence of human
nature, rather than of human institutions.

IV

34   The animal spirits theory of the financial crisis
is, so far, the one that has made the greatest headway.
It appeals to the outrage of the public and the desire to
condemn the eggheads who got us into this mess. But
it also satisfies the desire of the eggheads to redirect
blame. One need only consider Greenspan's remarks
to the House Committee on Oversight and Government Reform this past October to see the self-exculpatory dimension of the view. His only mistake, he said,
was trusting the banks to advance their own interests.

35   This all sounds plausible, until one stops to
wonder how the Federal Reserve could possibly operate
without that assumption. Indeed, if the problem is that
banks periodically go crazy, how could the situation
ever be corrected? What would a regulatory solution
look like? We design roads based on the assumption
that drivers are trying not to run into one another. Similarly, we design the system of financial regulations
based on the assumption that firms want to stay solvent. It is not clear how we could approach either
design question in the absence of these assumptions.

36   The model of the bank run—individually
rational, collectively inefficient—provides a much better set of tools for thinking about the current crisis. At
the heart of the subprime mortgage debacle were two

significant innovations, both of which were entirely
non-crazy.

37   The first was the securitization of mortgage
loans. Banks are by nature conservative when it comes
to making loans. They have to be, not only because of
their underlying business model, but because they
lend on fixed terms. Thus the upside of mortgage
loans is not all that great—you get repaid your money
with interest, at a fairly modest rate, and you pocket
the difference between that and what you are paying
your depositors. The downside, however, is enormous. Not only may you never see any of the interest
you are owed, but you can also lose a substantial portion of the principle you lent out.

38   Equality lenders, on the other hand, such as
shareholders, have a much greater upside to their
investments. If the value of the asset goes up, they get
a share of the profits. This is why investors in the
stock market are willing to take much bigger risks
than traditional banks. Unfortunately for the average
homeowner, going to the stock market to raise money
to purchase is not possible.

39   This suggests that there is a group of people out
there who want loans, and another group of people
who would be willing to make them those loans.
Banks are in a position to bring these two groups
together, by making the loans, then bundling them
up and selling the right to collect the payments to
investors. This is the essence of securitization, and it
is an idea that, in the case of mortgage loans, makes a
certain amount of sense.

40   The second non-crazy innovation involved the
creation of the now infamous collateralized debt
obligations. Once you start bundling up a whole
bunch of mortgage loans and reselling them to
investors, a question arises about how defaults should
be handled. When a single bank holds a mortgage,
any failure to repay simply becomes a loss for the
bank. But when the mortgage is held by a group of
investors, the loss can be divided up in all sorts of different ways. The brilliant idea at the heart of CDOs
was to divide up the investors into different
"tranches," and to have all the losses absorbed by the
most "junior" tranches first.

41   Thus buying into a senior tranche of a CDO typically gave the investor not merely the right to collect
payments from a bunch of different loans, but also

the right to collect payments from the best of these loans. This is why lenders began to relax their standards. When you take one single individual with perhaps a patchy credit history and unstable employment, the risk of default of a loan is quite high. But suppose you could take one hundred such individuals, or a thousand. While some will no doubt have trouble making their payments, the chances that more than a quarter will default are actually quite low.

42   Thus a lot of the behaviour that on the surface seemed quite crazy did have an underlying rationale. (One can find an admirably clear explanation of the basic mechanics in John Hull's contribution to *The Finance Crisis and Rescue*.) This is not to say that it was wise, but merely to say that it was not crazy.

43   Of course, there was an Achilles heel to all this, and it was the same Achilles heel that threatens the integrity of banks—correlation. If the chance of one person defaulting on a home loan is substantially independent of the chance of others defaulting, then the law of large numbers will insulate those at the senior levels of a CDO from all losses. But if one default starts to cause more defaults, then the whole model stops working, which is exactly what happened a year ago.

44   The problem—and this is a problem quite specific to the US housing market—is that most mortgages in the United States are so-called non-recourse loans. This means that if you default on your mortgage, the bank can seize your house, but it cannot seize any of your other assets. As Hull puckishly observes, this means that banks, in making zero-downpayment loans to homeowners, were essentially selling them a put option on their properties. (Selling someone a put consists in agreeing to buy some asset at a predetermined price in the future—in this case, the price was the market value of the house at the time of purchase.)

45   When house prices began to decline in the US, homeowners started exercising this put option (by defaulting on their mortgages, thereby "selling" the house back to the bank at the price they paid for it). As a result, the type of insurance offered by CDOs against credit default became either sketchy or worthless. Banks and investors, not knowing how much exposure anyone had to this now toxic debt, stopped lending to each other. Catastrophe ensued.

46   Again, the same features that one finds in an old-fashioned bank panic can be seen at work here: a dramatic tipping-point effect that creates volatility, along with a vicious cycle of collectively self-defeating behaviour. But this does not mean that any of the individuals involved acted irrationally, or that global finance is nothing but a castle built out of thin air. It just means that the market for credit default risk failed, for a variety of prosaic and fairly well-understood reasons.

V

47   Why then did so many economists miss all the warning signs? The problem is not that they assumed people were rational. The problem stemmed from what Harvard law professor Robert C. Clark once described as "facile optimism about the optimality of existing institutions."

48   "Thinking like an economist" is an ideal that harbours significant ambiguity. One way of doing so is to assume that everyone is egoistic and bloody-minded. Think of this as the Machiavellian strain. Another way is to assume that all agreements entered into by private parties are mutually beneficial, and that all outcomes produced by free markets are efficient. Think of this as the Panglossian strain.

49   All the rhetoric over the years about the invisible hand of the market has persuaded many people that there is no great tension between these strains. This is what led to mistakes. In the context of a properly structured capitalist economy, egoism and bloody-minded behaviour are capable of generating mutual benefit. But when that structure is less than perfect, the two have the capacity to come apart in spectacular ways.

50   Consider the earlier dust-up over stock options and executive compensation. A person of Machiavellian temperament looking at this would be inclined toward the view that CEOs were just ripping off shareholders, taking advantage of information asymmetries and collective action problems that resulted in weak oversight. Since this analysis happens to coincide with the verdict of common sense, many people would be surprised to discover how strongly it was resisted by academics in economics, finance, and corporate law.

51   What apologists for CEO pay—and they are legion—proposed instead were all sorts of baroque schemes through which these compensation

arrangements could be seen as in the best interests of all. Corruption, for instance, was interpreted as merely an implicit form of executive compensation, and therefore part of the "tacit" employment contract agreed to by shareholders.

52   Why would anyone think this? Because everything is for the best in the best of all possible worlds.

53   Similarly, when more cautious souls began to sound the alarm about the run-up in housing prices in the US, or the complexity and opacity of the derivatives that were being traded, the Panglossians responded in force. These bankers are clever people, they said, and they know what they are doing.

54   This turned out to be true. Most of them were clever, and they did know what they were doing. Unfortunately, there was never any reason to think that the sum of all this individual cleverness would be stable in the long term, but much less beneficial for society as a whole.

Literary Review of Canada.
2009. September 17 (7).

KEY AND CHALLENGING WORDS

repercussion, jeremiad, partisan, adversarial, foregone, arbitrage, asymmetry, countervailing, paradigm, bacchanalian, duly, self-exculpatory, solvent (adj.), debacle, volatility, prosaic, optimality, apologist, baroque, opacity

QUESTIONS

1.   a) Paraphrase the two major explanations for the financial crisis, according to Heath (paragraphs 5 and 6). b) What is Heath's thesis? c) Of the two explanations, which do you think is most reassuring to investors? Why?

2.   Using a reliable source, write a one-paragraph biography of noted economist John Maynard Keynes. Of what use does Heath make of his theories in paragraphs 9–13 and in other paragraphs?

3.   a) Discuss Heath's use of analogies, referring specifically to the analogy in paragraph 3 or 16; b) Identify one other analogy used in the essay; c) Identify one other rhetorical pattern used extensively in his essay.

4.   Explain why Heath considers the model of the bank run more convincing for analyzing the financial crisis than the "animal spirits" model.

5.   Heath synthesizes several book sources in his essay. Analyze his use of two of these sources, showing how each illustrates a different purpose for synthesizing sources (i.e., to introduce a point or concept, to expand on a point, or to disagree with a point).

6.   Choose one important definition in the essay and put it in your own words.

7.   Referring specifically to at least two passages, explain Heath's audience. Has he written for the specialist or non-specialist reader?

8.   Provide descriptive (content) headings for each of the numbered sections in the essay.

POST-READING

1.   Write a rhetorical analysis of Heath's essay, considering his argumentative strategies and their effectiveness.

2.   *Collaborative or individual activity:* Discuss similarities and differences between "Did the banks go crazy?" and other academic essays you have read.

RELATED WEBSITE OF INTEREST

The Economist (terms applicable to business and economics):

www.economist.com/research/economics/

Note: other related resources, such as *Oxford Reference Online*, can be accessed through your library.

ADDITIONAL LIBRARY READING

Many articles related to the financial crisis have appeared in major US and Canadian magazines, such as *The Economist*, *Business Week*, *Canadian Business Review*, and *Financial Post*, along with many newspapers. The following scholarly articles are among those that analyze the causes of the financial crisis of 2008:

Clark, C.M.A. (2010). Practical wisdom and understanding the economy. *Journal of Management Development, 29*(7/8), 678–685. doi:10.1108/02621711011059112

Ohanian, L.E. (2010). Understanding economic crises: The Great Depression and the 2008 recession. *Economic Record, 86*, 2–6. doi:10.1111/j.1475-4932.2010.00667.x

Siegel, L.B. (2010). Black swan or black turkey? The state of economic knowledge and the crash of 2007–2009. *Financial Analysts Journal, 66*(4), 1–4.

Life in metropolitan areas: Dependence on cars in urban neighbourhoods

Martin Turcotte

(6,229 words)

Pre-reading

1. This article was published in *Canadian Social Trends*, available through a library's database or online at the Statistics Canada website: www.statcan.gc.ca. Access this periodical in order to answer the following questions: What is the purpose/mission of *Canadian Social Trends*? What kinds of articles are published and who are they written for? Where do the statistics come from? What is the range of subjects covered?
2. What do you think is the main function of the headings in the article? How do they differ from headings in Type A essays? From Type B essays?

---

1   To get around easily in today's big cities, especially in their sparsely populated suburbs, access to a private motor vehicle is not only very convenient but sometimes absolutely essential. Parents with young children know this only too well, since they often have to commute to work and back, drive the

children to the daycare centre or evening activities, go to an appointment, shop for dinner and do other things besides—all in the same day.

2   While many Canadians simply could not do without their cars, the automobile is associated with numerous problems, as we are all aware. In Canada and other Western countries, road transportation is a big contributor to greenhouse gas (GHG) emissions.[1] A significant proportion of the increase in GHG emissions in recent years can be attributed to the growing popularity of pickup trucks and sport utility vehicles.[2]

3   Besides adding to GHG emissions, driving our cars every day is responsible for much of the pollution that generates smog.[3] In addition, the widespread use of automobiles by workers commuting to work instead of using public transit is a major factor in the traffic congestion that affects most metropolitan areas in North America[4] and leads to high costs for building and repairing roads.

4   In these circumstances, it is hardly surprising that many people are calling for an end to the excessive use of cars and for greater reliance on more environment-friendly means of transportation,

What you should know about this study

This article is based on data collected by the 2005 General Social Survey (GSS). The GSS is an annual survey that monitors changes and emerging trends in Canadian society. For the fourth time in Canada, the GSS has collected national level time use data. In addition to the time use diary, the 2005 questionnaire covers perceptions of the time crunch, social networks, transportation, and cultural and sports activities.

The time use estimates in this report are based on data from the time use diary portion of the (GSS). The diary provides a detailed record of the time spent on all activities in which respondents participated on the designated day. In addition, information was collected on where the activities took place (e.g., in a car as the driver, on public transit) and who the respondent was with (e.g., spouse, children, family, friends).

This study includes all trips made by people aged 18 and over on the reference day. Since age restrictions on automobile use may vary from province to province, people aged 15 to 17 were excluded from the study population.

Only people who made at least one trip regardless of mode of transportation on reference day were selected for the study. A few respondents reported total travel time of more than 720 minutes (12 hours); because these extreme cases could have had an excessive impact on the estimates, they were also excluded from the analysis.

In 2005, 85 per cent of Canadians aged 18 and over made at least one trip on their designated day. The proportion was roughly the same in low-density neighbourhoods as in high-density neighbourhoods and as high in central neighbourhoods as in peripheral neighbourhoods. Therefore, the differences in automobile dependence between types of neighbourhoods cannot be attributed to the fact that residents of certain types of neighbourhoods were more or less likely to have made at least one trip during their day.

According to 2005 GSS data, the factor that was most strongly associated with the probability of having made a trip on that day was age: 72 per cent of people aged 65 to 74 and 61 per cent of people aged 75 and over made at least one trip, compared with 91 per cent of people aged 18 to 24.

Delimiting the city centre, the periphery, and low- and high-density neighbourhoods

In this study, the city centre is the census tract that contains the city hall of the central municipality; hence, the distance from the city centre is the distance between the neighbourhood of residence and the central municipality's city hall. Central neighbourhoods are neighbourhoods that are less than five kilometres from census tract (CT) containing the city centre. Other neighbourhoods are referred to as peripheral neighbourhoods, and are differentiated by their distance from the city centre; for example, neighbourhoods that are between five and nine kilometres from the city centre are regarded as part of the near periphery.

The density level of neighbourhoods is based on the type of dwellings they contain. We established three main categories of neighbourhoods:

such as car-pooling, public transit, walking, and bicycling.

5   As much as they want to do something, many people probably feel helpless when confronted with such suggestions. One of the underlying reasons for these feelings may lie in the fact that the types of neighbourhoods and municipalities in which people live simply do not lend themselves to modes of travel other than the automobile—in part because businesses, places of work, and residences are located in different areas.

6   In this article, we focus on the relationship between the types of neighbourhoods in which people live and the use of cars for daily travel. How much do residents of peripheral areas and low-density neighbourhoods depend on cars in their daily lives compared with residents of more "urban" neighbourhoods? To what extent can residents of central neighbourhoods go about their day-to-day business without using a car? In which metropolitan areas is exclusive use of the automobile most common?

7   At the same time, we are interested in identifying the characteristics of people who use cars. For example, are people who live alone less inclined to drive and more likely to walk than couples with children?

Low-density neighbourhoods, which contain single, semi-detached, and mobile homes and dwellings. Such dwellings are considered to be traditional suburban dwellings. Specifically, low-density neighbourhoods are neighbourhoods in which at least 66.6 per cent of the dwellings are traditional suburban dwellings.

High-density neighbourhoods, which are essentially composed of apartment and condominium buildings (whether high-rise or low-rise) and row houses. Such dwellings are characteristic of traditional urban neighbourhoods. High-density neighbourhoods are neighbourhoods in which less than 33.3 per cent of the dwellings are traditional suburban dwellings.

Medium-density neighbourhoods are characterized by mid-level concentrations of 33.3 per cent to 66.6 per cent traditional suburban dwellings. For more details on how these criteria were defined, see "The city/suburb contrast: How can we measure it?" in *Canadian Social Trends*, 85.

Definitions

CMA: Census Metropolitan Area. A CMA is an area consisting of one or more adjacent municipalities situated around a major urban core. A CMA must have a population of at least 100,000, and the urban core must have a population of at least 50,000.

Eight largest CMAs: This category includes Toronto, Montreal, Vancouver, Ottawa–Gatineau, Calgary, Edmonton, Québec City, and Winnipeg.

Medium CMAs: This category includes Hamilton, London, Kitchener, St Catharines–Niagara, Halifax, Victoria, Windsor, and Oshawa.

Smaller CMAs: This category includes Saskatoon, Regina, St John's, Greater Sudbury, Chicoutimi–Jonquière, Sherbrooke, Abbotsford, Kingston, Trois-Rivières, Saint John, and Thunder Bay.

Predicted probability model

To calculate the predicted probabilities, we kept constant a number of characteristics to simulate a "typical" reference person. In the context of this analysis, this reference person is a man aged 35 to 44 years old, born in Canada, who has a job and holds a college diploma, has a household income of $60,000 to $99,999 but has no children living in the household, and he lives in the CMA of Toronto. We then ask the following question: if a person having all these characteristics moved from a high-density neighbourhood to a low- or medium-density neighbourhood, how would it change the probability that he would use a car to make all his daily trips?

Please note

The differences between the central municipalities and other constituent municipalities of CMAs are presented for information purposes only. The 2005 General Social Survey used the CMA and municipality boundaries for 2001. Consequently, any boundary changes made between 2001 and 2005 (especially in Quebec) are not reflected in the municipal data.

8   To answer these questions, we will use data from the 2005 General Social Survey (GSS) on time use to examine motor vehicle use by Canadians aged 18 and over who made at least one trip commuting and/or running errands on the survey reference day. Data from the 2001 Census were also used to differentiate the more central neighbourhoods of census metropolitan areas (CMAs) from the more peripheral ones, and low-density from high-density neighbourhoods (for more information, see "What you should know about this study").

Going by car is even more common now

9   Even though there is a growing tendency for the population to congregate in large urban centres and people have access to better public transportation services, dependence on the automobile increased between 1992 and 2005. According to data from the General Social Survey (GSS) on time use, the proportion of people aged 18 and over who went everywhere by car—as either a driver or a passenger—rose from 68 per cent in 1992, to 70 per cent in 1998 and then 74 per cent in 2005.

10   Conversely, the proportion of Canadians who made at least one trip under their own power by bicycle or on foot appears to have declined between 1998 and 2005. In 2005, 19 per cent of people 18 and over walked or pedalled from one place to another, down from 26 per cent and 25 per cent in 1992 and 1998 respectively. How can we explain why Canadians, most of whom live in large metropolitan regions, now need their cars more than ever to go about their daily business?

Distance from the city centre results in greater use of cars

11   Part of the explanation lies in the fact that many residents of metropolitan regions live a significant distance from the city centre. There are very clear links between living in a peripheral neighbourhood and depending on the automobile as the primary mode of transportation for day-to-day travel. The farther people live from the city centre, the more time they spend behind the wheel (Table 1).

12   For Canadians aged 18 and over who made at least one trip on the survey reference day, those who lived 25 kilometres from the centre of a census metropolitan area (CMA) spent an average of one hour and 23 minutes per day in the car. In comparison, those who lived within five kilometres of the centre of their CMA spent an average of just 55 minutes travelling by car, whether as the driver or a passenger.

13   In view of these differences, it is not surprising to find that the greater the distance from the centre, the higher the proportion of people who used a car for at least one of their trips. Specifically, 61 per cent of people living in a central neighbourhood got behind the wheel, compared with 73 per cent of people living between 10 and 14 kilometres from the city centre and 81 per cent of people living 25 kilometres or more from the centre.

14   In census agglomerations (CAs are smaller urban areas) and in rural areas and small towns, people behaved in much the same way as residents of neighbourhoods farthest from the CMA city centre. However, average travel times as a driver were lower for residents of small towns and rural areas that were farthest from the CA city centre.[5]

Neighbourhood density is important

15   Even more revealing relationships emerge if we ignore distance and instead categorize people according to the density of the neighbourhood in which they live. For example, over 80 per cent of residents comprising exclusively or almost exclusively suburban-type housing of very neighbourhoods made at least one trip by car (as the driver) during the day. By comparison, less than half of people living in very high-density neighbourhoods did so.

16   In addition, travelling exclusively by driving was far more common in low-density neighbourhoods. Only about one-third of residents in very high-density neighbourhoods were at the wheel for all of their trips during the day, compared with almost

TABLE 1   THE MORE SUBURBAN THE NEIGHBOURHOOD, THE MORE TIME PEOPLE SPENT IN A CAR ON THE REFERENCE DAY

| | Population aged 18 and over making at least one trip by car | | | |
| | As a driver | | As a driver or passenger | |
	%	Average duration in minutes	%	Average duration in minutes
Total (Canada)	**74**	**56**	**87**	**68**
Census metropolitan areas (CMAs) †	71	55	85	68
Census agglomeration	78*	53	91*	64
Rural areas in a strong metropolitan influence zone (MIZ)	82*	66*	93*	80*
Rural areas in a moderate, weak, or non-existent MIZ	77*	58	92*	74*
Distance from city centre (CMA only)				
Less than 5 km†	61	43	76	55
5 to 9 km	68*	50*	82*	62*
10 to 14 km	73*	56*	86*	69*
15 to 19 km	75*	60*	90*	74*
20 to 24 km	78*	60*	92*	71*
25 km or more	81*	70*	93*	83*
Percentage of suburban-type housing[1] in neighbourhood (CMA only)				
Less than 5†	44	30	60	41
5 to 9	49*	34	68*	49
10 to 19	53*	39*	70*	52*
20 to 29	62*	43*	81*	57*
30 to 39	63*	52*	78*	65*
40 to 49	69*	52*	85*	64*
50 to 59	71*	50*	83*	60*
60 to 69	76*	59*	89*	71*
70 to 79	77*	57*	91*	71*
80 to 89	80*	60*	82*	73*
90 to 94	82*	68*	94*	87*
95 to 100	84*	74*	94*	87*

[1] Single, semi-detached and mobile homes
† Reference category
* Statistically significant difference from reference category at p < 0.05

Note: Metropolitan area boundaries used in the 2005 General Social Survey are those established in the 2001 Census. Also see "What you should know about this study" for more information

Source: Statistics Canada, General Social Survey, 2005

two-thirds of those who lived in very low-density neighbourhoods (Chart 1).

Difference between large and smaller CMAs

17   Together, Canada's eight largest metropolitan areas—the CMAs of Toronto, Montreal, Vancouver, Ottawa-Gatineau, Calgary, Edmonton, Québec City, and Winnipeg—account for nearly half of the country's population (49 per cent according to the 2006 Census). They differ from many other CMAs in the size of their population, their geographic size and their very rapid growth.

18   Not surprisingly, there are significant differences between these large CMAs and their smaller counterparts with regard to dependence on automobiles. For example, 81 per cent of the residents of smaller CMAs with a population under 250,000 in 2001 went everywhere by car—as either the driver or a passenger—on the reference day, compared with 69 per cent of residents in the eight largest CMAs.

19   These differences between larger and smaller CMAs can be attributed to a number of factors. In CMAs such as Toronto, Montreal, and Vancouver, especially in their more central neighbourhoods, public transit provides better service and is therefore used more often; parking is not as readily available for downtown workers, which discourages them from driving; and higher density makes it easier for people to walk or bicycle than to drive (higher density favours public transit, but it also tends to increase traffic congestion).[6]

20   Conversely, in smaller CMAs, even neighbourhoods close to the centre have characteristics that make them similar in some ways to traditional postwar suburban neighbourhoods. In 2001, for example, 45 per cent of the dwellings in the central neighbourhoods of smaller CMAs were single-detached houses, whereas the proportions of that dwelling type were much lower in the central neighbourhoods of Toronto (13 per cent), Montreal (4 per cent), and Vancouver (21 per cent). Because of the high cost and scarcity of land in the centre of most big cities, very few single-detached houses are built there.

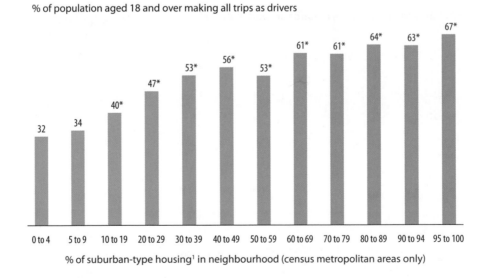

% of population aged 18 and over making all trips as drivers

% of suburban-type housing[1] in neighbourhood (census metropolitan areas only)

CHART 1   ABOUT TWO-THIRDS OF PEOPLE LIVING IN THE MOST SUBURBAN NEIGHBOURHOODS DROVE THEIR CARS TO MAKE ALL THEIR TRIPS ON THE REFERENCE DAY

[1] Single, semi-detached, and mobile homes
* Statistically significant difference from 0 to 4% at $p < 0.05$

Source: Statistics Canada, General Social Survey, 2005.

Making all trips by car is less common in Montreal's central neighbourhoods

21   In 2005, of the people living in the eight largest CMAs, Calgary and Edmonton residents were the most likely to have made all their trips on the reference day exclusively by car as either the driver or a passenger (75 per cent and 77 per cent, respectively). In contrast, Montreal residents were least likely to have done so (65 per cent). The difference may be due to the fact that more people live in low-density neighbourhoods in the two Alberta CMAs than in Montreal and other large urban areas. As we have seen, there is a correlation between lower population density and greater reliance on cars.[7]

The fact that Montreal is an older city that was well-established before the automobile became as ubiquitous as it is today may shed some light on this difference (Table 2).

22   Differences in automobile use also exist between the central neighbourhoods of the eight largest CMAs. Specifically, the proportion of central neighbourhood residents who travelled everywhere by car was 29 per cent in Montreal, compared with 43 per cent in Toronto, 56 per cent in Vancouver, and 66 per cent in Calgary. In the smaller CMAs, 75 per cent of the residents of central neighbourhoods travelled exclusively by car.

23   Despite these regional differences, the overall patterns are very similar in CMAs of all sizes: the greater the distance from the city centre, and the greater the prevalence of traditional suburban

TABLE 2   DEPENDENCE ON AUTOMOBILES DIFFERS CONSIDERABLY BETWEEN CMAs, BUT ONE OF THE MOST IMPORTANT REASONS IS HOUSING DENSITY

	% of population aged 18 and over making all trips by car (as a driver or a passenger on the reference day, by census metropolitan area (CMA)									
	Toronto	Montreal	Vancouver	Ottawa–Gatineau	Calgary	Edmonton	Quebec City	Winnipeg	Medium CMAs	Smaller CMAs
Total	**66**	**65**	**69**	**71**	**75**	**77**	**74**	**72**	**75**	**81**
Housing Density										
High†	52	50	51	51	46ᴱ	58	53	60	58	66
Medium	63*	69*	74*	68*	76*	77*	78*	63	70*	77*
Low	73*	80*	77*	83*	77*	80*	82*	77*	80*	87*
Distance from city centre										
Less than 5 km†	43	29	56	48	66	64	51	65	67	75
5 to 9 km	51	54*	57	69*	72	78*	75*	73	78*	83*
10 to 15 km	61*	66*	64	76*	79	80*	76*	78*	81*	91*
15 km or more	74*	78*	83*	82*	79	82*	89*	91*	81*	92*
Administrative Boundaries										
Suburban municipalities	76*	73*	75*	78*	89*	82*	78*	91*	—	—
Central municipality†	55	43	55	68	73	74	57	71	—	—

— not available for a specific reference period
ᴱ use with caution
† Reference category
* Statistically significant difference from reference category at p < 0.05

Notes: Metropolitan area boundaries used in the 2005 General Social Survey are those established in the 2001 Census. See "What you should know about this study" for a list of the CMAs comprising the medium and smaller CMA categories.

Source: Statistics Canada, General Social Survey, 2005.

dwellings, the higher the proportion of people who made their trips by car as the driver or a passenger.

Characteristics of the neighbourhood, or of the people who live in it?

24   The correlations described above between place of residence and reliance on cars for day-to-day travel appear to be very robust. There is a possibility, however, that a portion of these differences is due to the fact that characteristics differ considerably between people who live in higher- versus lower-density neighbourhoods, or neighbourhoods that are closer to or farther from the city centre.[8]

25   Many characteristics, aside from place of residence, are associated with lesser or greater automobile use (Table A.1). In order to confirm the robustness of the association between the use of a car and a place of residence, we performed a statistical analysis taking account of a number of variables at the same time (in other words, the effect of age, sex, income, and so on were held constant). Since we are primarily interested in the correlations between neighbourhood characteristics and automobile use for daily travel, only residents of CMAs were considered.

26   The results show a clear correlation between the density of the neighbourhood of residence and the probability that at least one trip during the day was made by car. For example, controlling for other factors associated with automobile use, the odds that a person drove on at least one of their trips during the day was 2.5 times higher for residents of low-density neighbourhoods than for residents of high-density neighbourhoods (Table 3, Model 1).

27   The conclusion was the same when we examined the other two cases: making *all* of the day's trips as a driver, and making *all* of the day's trips by car as either the driver or a passenger. That is, when we kept all other factors constant, the odds that a resident of a low-density neighbourhood made all of their trips by car was 2.8 times higher than the odds for a resident of a high-density neighbourhood.

28   When the influence of factors such as income, age, and so on, is removed, the distance between neighbourhood of residence and the centre of the CMA is also associated with an increase in automobile dependence. For example, if we keep all those other factors constant, the odds that someone drove their car on all trips during the day was 3.0 times higher for people who lived 25 kilometres or more from the city centre than for people who lived less than five kilometres from the centre (Table 3, Model 2).

Density, distance or both?

29   In many cases, high-density neighbourhoods are also central neighbourhoods, and peripheral neighbourhoods are usually low-density neighbourhoods.[9] So far, our analysis has not shown whether, at an equal distance from the city centre, a higher-density neighbourhood will exhibit less dependence on cars, and vice versa for lower-density neighbourhoods. This is an important question, since land is scarce and expensive in central neighbourhoods and since most new construction takes place in peripheral neighbourhoods.

30   The answer is provided by a supplementary analysis (Chart 2). Keeping constant all factors associated with automobile use, we find that in central and near-peripheral neighbourhoods five to nine kilometres from the city centre, living in a lower-density neighbourhood is associated with a higher predicted probability of using a car for all trips.

31   Above 10 kilometres from the city centre, however, the impact of neighbourhood density on automobile use dwindles until it almost vanishes.[10] If the effects of other factors are kept constant, the predicted probability that person living in a *medium-* or *high-*density neighbourhood made all trips by car was not statistically different from that of a person living in a *low*-density neighbourhood. In other words, beyond 10 kilometres from the city centre, the fact that a neighbourhood was mainly composed of single family or semi-detached houses rather than apartments was not correlated with greater or less automobile use.

32   This situation may be due to a number of factors, including the fact that neighbourhoods in peripheral areas, whether they are low-density or not, are

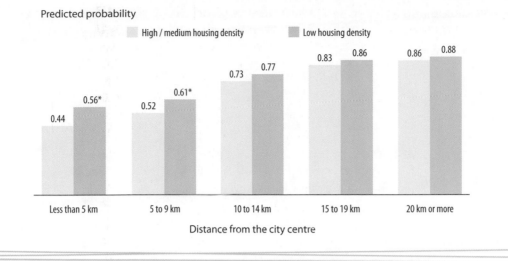

Predicted probability

High / medium housing density   Low housing density

Distance from the city centre

| Less than 5 km | 5 to 9 km | 10 to 14 km | 15 to 19 km | 20 km or more |

0.44 / 0.56* • 0.52 / 0.61* • 0.73 / 0.77 • 0.83 / 0.86 • 0.86 / 0.88

CHART 2   AT 10 OR MORE KILOMETRES FROM THE CITY CENTRE, THE HOUSING DENSITY OF A NEIGHBOURHOOD HAS NO EFFECT ON RESIDENTS' USE OF CARS

* Stastistically significant difference from high/medium housing density at p < 0.05

Note: A predicted probability of 1.0 indicates that a person had a 100% chance of having used a car to make all their trips during the reference day; a predicted probability of 0 indicates that a person had zero chance. The predicted probabilities measure the magnitude of the association between place of residence and car use, net of the effects of other variables.

Source: Statistics Canada, General Social Survey, 2005.

usually zoned for only one purpose (residential, commercial, or industrial) rather than multiple uses simultaneously.[11] Because of that, and because the activities in which most people take part during a day are often farther apart, it is difficult to use any means of transportation other than a car.[12] This is especially true since many locations in suburban neighbourhoods, such as shopping centres, movie theatres, office buildings, and other places of work, are difficult or impossible to get to on foot or by public transit.

33   In contrast, the central neighbourhoods of large cities are generally characterized by a greater mix of residential, commercial and industrial uses and by greater density, two conditions that favour adequate public transportation and travel on foot.[13]

Suburban men take their cars

34   Statistical analysis shows that a number of personal characteristics, other than the type and location of the neighbourhood in which one lives, are also strongly correlated with automobile use during a given day.

35   Age and sex are among the factors that have a substantial impact on the probability of driving. On the reference day in 2005, 81 per cent of Canadian men aged 18 and over made at least one trip behind the wheel of a car. The corresponding figure for women was just 66 per cent (Table A.1). This difference, which remains statistically significant when all additional factors are kept constant, is probably attributable to the fact that women are more likely to take public transit and that they are often passengers when they travel by car. In 2005, 31 per cent of women made at least one trip by car as a passenger, compared with only 11 per cent of men.

36   Baby boomers between ages 45 and 54 were particularly likely to have driven their cars during the day, a finding that remained statistically significant even when all other factors were controlled for. For example, when the density of the neighbourhood of residence and the other factors in the statistical model were kept constant, the odds that people aged 45 to 54 drove a car on all the trips they made in a given day was 2.5 times higher than the odds for 18- to 24-year-olds (Table 3).

TABLE 3   NEIGHBOURING HOUSING DENSITY IS STRONGLY ASSOCIATED WITH CAR DEPENDENCE, EVEN WHEN OTHER FACTORS LIKE INCOME, AGE AND PRESENCE OF CHILDREN ARE ACCOUNTED FOR

	Model 1			Model 2		
	Number of trips as driver		All trips as driver or passenger	Number of trips as driver		All trips as driver or passenger
	At least one	All trips		At least one	All trips	
			Odds ratios			
Housing density						
High[†]	1.0	1.0	1.0	—	—	—
Medium	1.7*	1.8*	1.9*	—	—	—
Low	2.5*	2.2*	2.8*	—	—	—
Distance from city centre (CMA only)						
Less than 5 km[†]	—	—	—	1.0	1.0	1.0
5 to 9 km	—	—	—	1.5*	1.3*	1.6*
10 to 14 km	—	—	—	2.1*	1.8*	2.1*
15 to 19 km	—	—	—	2.6*	2.1*	3.2
20 to 24 km	—	—	—	3.5*	2.5*	3.4*
25 km or more	—	—	—	3.9*	3.0*	4.4*
Sex						
Female[†]	1.0	1.0	1.0	1.0	1.0	1.0
Male	2.0*	2.2*	1.3*	2.1*	2.2*	1.3*
Age						
18 to 24 years[†]	1.0	1.0	1.0	1.0	1.0	1.0
25 to 34 years	1.8*	1.9*	1.8*	1.8*	1.8*	1.8*
35 to 44 years	2.1*	2.3*	2.2*	2.2*	2.3*	2.2*
45 to 54 years	2.6*	2.5*	2.6*	2.6*	2.5*	2.6*
55 to 64 years	2.6*	2.4*	2.5*	2.6*	2.3*	2.5*
65 to 74 years	2.6*	2.7*	3.2*	2.5*	2.6*	3.1*
75 years or more	1.5*	1.6*	1.5*	1.4*	1.6*	1.4*
Immigration status						
Born in Canada[†]	1.0	1.0	1.0	1.0	1.0	1.0
Immigrant (before 1990)	0.9	1.1	1.0	0.9	1.1	1.1
Recent immigrants (1990 to 2005)	0.5*	0.8*	0.9	0.5*	0.7*	0.8
Presence of activity limitations						
Yes/sometimes	0.8*	0.9	0.9	0.8*	0.8*	0.9
Yes/often	0.8*	0.8*	0.8*	0.8*	0.8*	0.8*
No[†]	1.0	1.0	1.0	1.0	1.0	1.0
Highest level of educational attainment						
No secondary diploma[†]	1.0	1.0	1.0	1.0	1.0	1.0
Secondary completion	1.5*	1.3*	1.3*	1.5*	1.3*	1.3*
College or trade diploma	1.6*	1.2*	1.2	1.6*	1.2	1.1
University degree	1.5*	1.1	0.9	1.6*	1.1	1.0

TABLE 3   CONTINUED

	Model 1			Model 2		
	Number of trips as driver		All trips as driver or passenger	Number of trips as driver		All trips as driver or passenger
	At least one	All trips		At least one	All trips	
			Odds ratios			
Household income						
Less than $20,000[†]	1.0	1.0	1.0	1.0	1.0	1.0
$20,000 to $39,999	1.5*	1.4*	1.7*	1.5*	1.4*	1.7*
$40,000 to $59,999	2.0*	1.6*	2.0*	2.1*	1.7*	2.1*
$60,000 to $99,999	2.7*	1.6*	2.2*	2.9*	1.7*	2.4*
$100,000 and more	2.6*	1.6*	2.0*	2.7*	1.7*	2.2*
Main activity for the last 7 days						
Employed/looking for work[†]	1.0	1.0	1.0	1.0	1.0	1.0
Caring for children/keeping house	0.7*	0.6*	0.9	0.7*	0.6*	0.9
Retired	0.8	0.8	0.9	0.8	0.8	0.9
Student	0.6*	0.5*	0.5*	0.6*	0.5*	0.5*
Other activity	1.0	1.0*	1.0*	1.0	1.0*	1.0*
Presence of a child under 5						
No[†]	1.0	1.0	1.0	1.0	1.0	1.0
Yes	1.0	1.0	1.0	1.0	1.0	0.9
Presence of a child aged 5 to 12						
No[†]	1.0	1.0	1.0	1.0	1.0	1.0
Yes	1.6*	1.1	1.0	1.6*	1.1	1.0
CMA of residence (Census Metropolitan Area)[1]						
CMA of Toronto	0.5*	0.6*	0.5*	0.3*	0.4*	0.2*
CMA of Montreal	0.6*	0.7*	0.6*	0.3*	0.4*	0.2*
CMA of Vancouver	0.7*	0.7*	0.6*	0.4*	0.5*	0.3*
CMA of Ottawa–Gatineau	0.6*	0.7*	0.6*	0.4*	0.5*	0.4*
CMA of Calgary	0.8	0.8	0.6*	0.7*	0.7*	0.5*
CMA of Edmonton	0.7*	0.9	0.7	0.6*	0.7*	0.6
CMA of Quebec	0.9	0.7*	0.7	0.6*	0.6*	0.5
CMA of Winnipeg	0.6*	0.7*	0.5*	0.6*	0.7*	0.5*
Medium CMAs	0.7*	0.8*	0.7*	0.7*	0.8*	0.6*
Small CMAs[†]	1.0	1.0	1.0	1.0	1.0	1.0
Worked on the reference day						
No[†]	1.0	1.0	1.0	1.0	1.0	1.0
Yes	1.4*	1.4*	1.0	1.4*	1.4*	1.0

— not applicable

[1] Metropolitan area boundaries used in the 2005 General Social Survey are those established in the 2001 Census. See "What you should know about this study" for a list of the CMAs comprising the medium and smaller CMA categories.

[†] Reference group

* Statistically significant difference from reference group at p < 0.05

Note: This table presents the odds that a respondent used a car on the reference day, relative to the odds that the reference group did the same thing, when the effect of all other factors shown in the table are controlled for. An odds ratio close to 1.0 for the comparison group means that there is little or no difference between the comparison and the reference groups.

Source: Statistics Canada, General Social Survey, 2005.

37   Similarly, people with children aged 5 to 12 also had odds 1.6 times higher than people without children that age to have driven on at least one trip. These parents were also more likely to have made trips during the day, regardless of the mode of transportation. Also among the other characteristics associated with a greater probability of driving during the day were being employed and living in a small CMA.

Summary

38   This article suggests that the physical and geographic characteristics of urban neighbourhoods are pivotal factors in Canadians' dependence on cars for their routine trips to work, to run errands and so on. It found that neighbourhoods composed primarily of typically suburban dwellings and located far from the city centre were characterized by an appreciably higher level of automobile dependence. This confirms a number of facts that are already known about low-density peripheral neighbourhoods.[14]

39   These results also reveal some new factors, elements that are not considered as often. For instance, the study shows that beyond a certain distance from the city centre, the housing density of a neighbourhood is not likely to have much impact on automobile use.

40   These findings are important in view of what we know about new neighbourhoods. A large proportion of the housing stock built since 1991 is found far from the city centre in low-density neighbourhoods. As we have seen, these are the neighbourhoods with the highest level of automobile dependence.

Canadian Social Trends. Statistics Canada
—Catalogue No. 11-008.

Notes

1. Environment Canada (2006). *National Inventory Report—Greenhouse Gas Sources and Sinks in Canada, 1990-2004*. Ottawa: Minister of the Environment.

2. Environment Canada (2006).

3. Statistics Canada (2006). *Canadian Environmental Sustainability Indicators*. Catalogue no.16-251-XWE. Ottawa: Minister of Industry. Specifically, this publication refers to fine particulate matter, to volatile organic compounds and to nitrogen oxides. For details about the links between automobile usage and polluting emissions, see also H. Frumkin, Frank, L. and Jackson, R. 2004). *Urban Sprawl and Public Health*. Washington: Island Press.

4. Downs, A. (2002). *Still Stuck in Traffic—Coping with Peak-hour Road Congestion*. Washington: Brookings Institution Press.

5. Technically, these little towns and rural areas belonging to the metropolitan influence zones (MIZ) surrounding census metropolitan areas and census agglomerations are said to be in moderate, weak or no influence MIZ.

6. Downs (2002); Newman and Kenworthy (1999). *Sustainability and Cities. Overcoming Automobile Dependence*. Washington: Island Press.

7. Turcotte, M. (2008). The difference between city and suburb: How can we measure it? *Canadian Social Trends*, 85. Catalogue no. 11-008-XIE, Ottawa: Minister of Industry.

8. Turcotte (2008).

9. See Turcotte, M. (2008). for more details about the relationship between distance to the city core and neighbourhood density.

10. Although the chart appears to show that neighbourhoods with low density are different than those with medium/high density at more than 10 kilometres from the city core, this difference is not statistically significant.

11. Duany, A., Plater-Zyberk, E. and Speck, J. (2000). *Suburban Nation—The Rise and Sprawl and the Decline of the American Dream*. New York: North Point Press.

12. Gillham, O. (2002). *The Limitless City—A Primer on the Urban Sprawl Debate*. Washington: Island Press.

13. Downs (2002); Newman and Kenworthy (1999).

14. It is impossible to account for all the characteristics of persons who live in different types of neighbourhoods and in particular for all the reasons leading a person to choose one neighbourhood rather than another. For example, it is possible that people wh o like to travel by car are more likely to establish themselves in peripheral suburbs of low density, while those people who like to walk choose a downtown location. In these cases, it is personal preferences that have a greater influence on the choice of transportation than the physical characteristics of the place of residence. Although this possibility has not been completely discarded by researchers, almost all recent studies seem to suggest that urban development has had a direct impact on the level of automobile dependence (see Cao, X., Mokhtarian, P.L. and Handy, S.L. (2007). *Examining the Impacts of Residential Self-selection on Travel Behavior: Methodologies and Empirical Findings*. Davis: Institute of Transportation Studies. In this article, the authors summarize and comment upon existing studies on this topic.) When people are choosing a neighbourhood in which to live, among other factors they consider are location of their workplace, access to schools and other services, geographic proximity to other family members, and so on. When these criteria are foremost in the choice of neighbourhood, the purchase and use of an automobile can become mandatory for most people.

TABLE A.1   CHARACTERISTICS ASSOCIATED WITH TYPE OF TRANSPORTATION USED FOR DAILY TRIPS BY PEOPLE LIVING IN A CENSUS METROPOLITAN AREA (CMA)[1], 2005

	% persons aged 18 and over making. . .				% persons aged 18 and over making. . .		
	At least one trip as a driver	All trips as a driver	All trips by car		At least one trip as a driver	All trips as a driver	All trips by car
Sex				**Presence of a child under 5**			
Women[†]	66	49	72	No[†]	73	59	74
Men	81*	69*	76*	Yes	76*	59	75
Age				**Presence of a child aged 5 to 12**			
18 to 24 years[†]	57	41	57	No[†]	72*	58*	73*
25 to 34 years	74*	58*	73*	Yes	81	63	77
35 to 44 years	80*	65*	77*	**Household income**			
45 to 54 years	82*	66*	80*	Less than $20,000[†]	50	39	55
55 to 64 years	77*	62*	79*	$20,000 to $39,999	68*	55*	70*
65 to 74 years	70*	57*	78*	$40,000 to $59,999	75*	61*	76*
75 years or more	55	45	67	$60,000 to $99,999	83*	64*	79*
Immigration status				$100,000 and more	83*	65*	77*
Born in Canada[†]	76	60	75	**Main activity for the last 7 days**			
Immigrant (before 1990)	74	61	75	Employed/looking for work[†]	80	65	77
Recent immigrants (1990 to 2005)	55*	45*	60*	Caring for children/ keeping house	61*	43*	73*
Presence of activity limitations				Retired	68*	55*	75
Yes/sometimes	69*	54*	71*	Student	45*	31*	44*
Yes/often	69*	56*	75	Other activity	65*	51*	72*
No[†]	75	60	74	**Day of the Week**			
Highest level of educational attainment				Weekday	75*	60*	72*
No secondary diploma[†]	64	54	73	Weekend[†]	71	55	79
Secondary completion	72*	58*	74	**Worked outside the home on the reference day**			
College or trade diploma	79*	62*	77*	No[†]	68*	52*	73*
University degree	77*	59*	71	Yes	81	67	75

[1] Metropolitan area boundaries used in the 2005 General Social Survey are those established in the 2001 Census.
[†] Reference group.
* Statistically different from the reference category (p < 0.05).

Source: Statistics Canada, General Social Survey, 2005.

TABLE A.2   PERCENTAGE OF PERSONS AGED 18 AND OVER USING PUBLIC TRANSIT FOR AT LEAST ONE OF THEIR TRIPS ON THE REFERENCE DAY, 2005

	Toronto	Montreal	Vancouver	Ottawa–Gatineau	Calgary	Edmonton	Quebec City	Winnipeg	Medium CMAs	Smaller CMAs
					percent					
All Census Metropolitan Areas (CMA)	16	18	12	15	12	9	9	10	7	3
Housing Density										
High	23	26	20	20	14	22	15	23	10	8
Medium	19	15	10	22	12	9	4	13	9	5
Low	12	10	7	6	12	6	3	9	4	2
Distance from city centre										
Less than 5 km	26	34	22	21	11	16	13	15	11	5
5 to 9 km	31	25	20	21	11	7	7	10	6	3
10 to 14 km	22	17	12	14	11	11	2	8	5	F
15 km or more	11	11	3	6	18	1	3	3	4	F
Administrative boundaries										
Suburban municipalities	9	14	7	10	5	3	5	F	—	—
Central municipality	25	30	23	17	13	11	9	12	—	—

— not available for a specific reference period
F too unreliable to be published

Notes: Metropolitan area boundaries used in the 2005 General Social Survey are those established in the 2001 Census. See "What you should know about this study" for a list of the CMAs comprising the medium and smaller CMA categories.

Source: Statistics Canada, General Social Survey, 2005.

KEY AND CHALLENGING WORDS

peripheral, constituent, congregate, agglomeration, ubiquitous, attributable, pivotal

QUESTIONS

1. In the introduction to the essay, identify the topic and the three main areas of discussion. Briefly identify the study's methodology.

2. What is the function of the section "What you should know about this study"? What section does it correspond to in a Type B essay? Who might be particularly interested in the information in this section?

3. What two main factors are associated with an increased use of cars?

4. Explain how the author uses specific strategies for coherence in the section "Difference between large and smaller CMAs."

5. a) Identify one example of consecutive paragraphs in which Turcotte begins by summarizing a statistical finding before trying to account for the finding in the next paragraph; b) Summarize the paragraph in which he accounts for the result.

6. a) Explain the rationale for the kinds of headings that accompany the tables and charts, using one specific

example; b) For Table A.1, explain its numbering and its placement in the article; c) Why do you think a chart, rather than a table, was used to represent the findings discussed in paragraphs 30–31?

7. In your own words, explain the percentages in the row "Less than 5 km" in Table 2 for Montreal, Calgary, and Smaller CMAs; how could the percentages for Vancouver and Ottawa–Gatineau be explained? Explain the percentages for the same cities in the row "15 km or more."

8. How is the "Summary" section similar to the concluding section of a Type B essay? How is it different?

POST-READING

1. *Collaborative activity:* Do you think city planners are doing enough to help reduce the use of cars in large CMAs? Medium or smaller CMAs? What could be done to alleviate the problem?

2. *Collaborative or individual activity:* In the section "Suburban men take their cars," the author cites other statistics related to the increased use of cars, referring to Table A.1 and Table 3. Analyze two of these categories (for example, sex or age) from Table A.1, inferring reasons for the statistical results.

3. Write an analytical report that makes recommendations to a municipal committee studying vehicle use; begin with a statement of the problem (for example, you might briefly outline why it is necessary to reduce car use), and refer to some of the results in "Dependence on cars in urban neighbourhoods"; conclude by making recommendations for reducing use of cars. Use as your target city one of the cities for which statistics are given in Table 2 or A.2, though you can, of course, also refer to statistics from other cities or in other tables and charts. You can also use a medium or smaller CMA as your target city, in which case you can use the statistics for the appropriate columns in the Table 2 or A.2.

4. In essay or report format, explore the uses and importance of census-taking in Canada, using the Statistics Canada website and other relevant sources. Questions you could attempt to answer include the following: What kind of information has been obtained and how has it been used? Who benefits from the census? What are its origins? How has gathering information from the census changed over the years? What do Canadians think about the census? What issues are relevant to census-taking today?

Fast food and deprivation in Nova Scotia

Jennifer Jones, BSc, Mikiko Terashima, MSc, and Daniel Rainham, PhD

(3,476 words)

Abstract

Objective: To examine the relationship between density of fast food restaurants and measures of social and material deprivation at the community level in Nova Scotia, Canada.

Methods: Census information on population and key variables required for the calculation of deprivation indices were obtained for 266 communities in Nova Scotia. The density of fast food restaurants per 1,000 individuals for each community was calculated and communities were divided into quintiles of material and psychosocial deprivation. One-way analysis of variance was used to investigate associations between fast food outlet densities and deprivation scores at the community level.

Results: A statistically significant inverse association was found between community-level material deprivation and the mean number of fast food restaurants per 1,000 people for Nova Scotia (p < 0.000).

Significant positive relationships were found between density of fast food restaurants and psychosocial deprivation (p < 0.000). Both associations were principally linear with greater fast food outlet density occurring as material deprivation decreased and as psychosocial deprivation increased.

Interpretation: Community-level deprivation in Nova Scotia is associated with fast food outlet density and lends support for environmental explanations for variations in the prevalence of obesity. Such findings are valuable to population health intervention initiatives targeting the modification of environmental determinants of obesity.

Key words: Psychosocial deprivation; material deprivation; obesity; fast food; mapping

*

1   In Canada the prevalence of objectively measured obesity, defined as a Body Mass Index (BMI) of ≥30.0, has increased by more than 10 per cent since 1979 with the largest increase among youth (12–17

years of age).[1,2] As of 2004, 23.1 per cent of all Canadians were classified as obese and 36.1 per cent as overweight ($25 \geq$ BMI < 30).[3] Children in Atlantic Canada are more likely to be overweight than children in other regions of Canada.[4] The rapidity of increasing obesity prevalence has been attributed to environmental more so than genetic influences[5,6] and has led to the development of research into obesogenic environments.

2   Multilevel cross-sectional and ecological studies have been employed to explore the environmental factors related to increasing overweight and obesity prevalence. A number of studies have shown a positive association between community deprivation and prevalence of overweight and obesity, even after adjusting for a range of socio-economic and demographic factors.[7–9] Environmental mediators of overweight and obesity may be more common in more deprived communities.[10] Deprivation refers to a measure of relative social and/or material disadvantage.[11] Theoretically, individuals in more deprived communities may have worse health due to fewer collective resources, particularly if adjacent geographically to similarly deprived communities.[12] In Canada, higher levels of material and social deprivation were associated with decreased life expectancy, increased mortality from tobacco use, as well as increased rates of hospitalization for mental illness.[13] Environmental mediators of overweight and obesity in Nova Scotia may be more prevalent in more deprived communities; consequently it has been hypothesized that deprived communities may have an excess of unhealthy food retailers, specifically fast food restaurants.[14]

3   Canadians spend almost $400 annually per capita on fast food, and increasing demands have led to growth in the supply of fast food restaurants with annual sales of approximately $35.1 billion.[15,16] The increasing availability of low-cost, high-energy, high-fat foods, and growth in serving sizes during consumption of food outside the home, suggest that fast food may play a significant role in overall dietary energy intake and quality.[17,18] Fast food is high in calories, saturated fat, and cholesterol, and fast food intake has been correlated with lower dietary quality and higher body mass index.[19–22]

4   While it is frequently suggested that more deprived communities have less access to healthy food, there is a paucity of research on whether community deprivation is associated with the prevalence of fast food restaurants and thus opportunities to consume unhealthy foods. Socio-economic status as an indicator of deprivation has been shown to be inversely associated with the number of fast food restaurants among communities studied in Australia and the United States.[23,24] Recent studies using deprivation measures have shown mixed results. A study using small census areas in England and Scotland found a higher density of McDonald's restaurants per thousand population in more deprived areas.[25] A subsequent study of neighbourhoods in Glasgow found no evidence that restaurants, including fast food chains, were more likely to be found in particularly deprived areas.[26]

5   Nova Scotia has a high prevalence of overweight and obesity which has often been attributed to poor lifestyle choices and dietary behaviours.[27,28] The objective of this study was to investigate the association between the density of fast food restaurants and indices of material and social deprivation among communities in Nova Scotia, Canada.

Methods

6   We obtained the address with full postal code of every McDonald's©, Wendy's©, Kentucky Fried Chicken©, Burger King©, Harvey's©, Dairy Queen©, and Tim Horton's© restaurant in Nova Scotia (n=306) as of July 2006 using Canada411™. Each restaurant address was cross-referenced and any missing address information was supplemented using online store locators found on the website of each restaurant.

7   The Nova Scotia Community Counts database links public administrative data—such as Canadian Census, Taxfiler, and several provincial databases (Transportation and Public Works data, for example)—at a provincially-relevant level of geography for the purpose of public policy development and decision making. Nova Scotia Community Counts (2006) provided information on age,

gender, and several census variables required for the construction of deprivation indices recalibrated to community geography.

Derivation of deprivation indices

8   We calculated standardized scores for material and psychosocial deprivation for each community using procedures outlined in Pampalon & Raymond and Salmond & Crampton as guides.[13,29] The following data from the Canadian Census (2001) were abstracted for each community: average individual income (15+ years old), unemployment rate (25+ years old), less than high school diploma (25+ years old), proportion of single parents (15+ years old), divorced, separated or widowed (15+ years old), and proportion of people living alone (15+ years old). Each item was first age-sex standardized using the following formula:

$$\text{Standardized Ratio} = \frac{\sum_i^{12} n_i}{\sum_i^{12} p_i R_i}$$

where i indicates age (in one of six groups: 15–24, 25–34, 35–44, 45–54, 55–6 4, 65+) by sex (2) = 12 groups. For example, n is the number of single parents in the community, p is the "at risk population" or population size of the age group in the community, and R is the proportion of single parents in each age group in the province. Z-scores were calculated to standardize values in the six items with different units for principal components analysis (PCA)—a variable reduction method. Two components met our criteria of eigenvalue ≥ 1.[30] They explained close to 70 per cent of the total variance among the six variables. VARIMAX rotation was applied to identify which of the six variables were explained by these two factors. The result showed that material deprivation was best explained by average individual income, unemployment rate and less than high school variables. Psychosocial deprivation scores were based on the proportion of single parents, proportion of people living alone, those divorced, separated or widowed. Material and psychosocial deprivation scores were derived from the addition of the standardized variables scores multiplied by their respective weights. For a more detailed description of deprivation score calculations, please refer to Terashima.[31]

Community geography and restaurant geocoding

9   The geographic unit of analysis for this study is the "community" as identified by Nova Scotia Community Counts using the following general guidelines: a population greater than 1,000 persons, 100 per cent coverage of the provincial population, and natural population clusters (rather than reliance on existing legal boundaries). There are currently 278 communities in Nova Scotia, including 20 reserves, 2 national parks, and Sable Island. We excluded data from 12 communities (9 reserves, parks, and Sable Island) to preserve confidentiality due to small population sizes.

10   The fast food restaurant location database was imported into a geographic information system (Arc-GIS 9.1, ESRI Corp, Redlands, CA) for geocoding. Geocoding is a process of assigning geographic identifiers (latitude and longitude) that closely approximate true locations.[32] Nova Scotia CanMAP Street™ files (DMTI Spatial, Ottawa, ON) contain accurate location information for civic addresses and were used to match fast food restaurants using a semi-automated geocoding function in the GIS software. The function automatically adds accurate coordinate information to the fast food outlet database. Unmatched restaurants were manually assigned coordinates using Google Earth™. In some instances, restaurants were contacted by telephone to verify location. In two cases, we used a handheld global positioning system to assign location information.

Analyses

11   Geocoded fast food restaurant locations were linked to community-level geography using a spatial join function in the GIS, and a count of the total number of restaurants per community was calculated. Population data for each community from the Community Counts database were then used to calculate fast food outlet density measures. Quintiles of material and psychosocial deprivation (1 = most deprived, 5 = least deprived) were also created for each community. Communities with no fast food restaurants were included in the analysis; communities without deprivation scores were excluded. Data were analyzed using one-way analysis of variance (ANOVA)

using MINTAB version 14.[33] Fast food outlet and deprivation data were mapped to spatially assess the distribution to complement the statistical analysis.

Results

12   We identified 306 fast food restaurants, 276 of which were included in the study for an average of 0.99 restaurants per community, or 0.15 restaurants per 1,000 individuals per community. Figure 1 illustrates the geographic distribution of material and psychosocial deprivation in Nova Scotia at the community level. Material deprivation is more prevalent in more rural communities of the province; however, it is important when visualizing this information to note that the preponderance of material deprivation is somewhat artifactual due to the fact that rural communities tend to have much larger boundaries to maintain equal population coverage. Psychosocial deprivation is more prominent in urban communities and there are only a few communities that are deprived both materially and psychosocially, most of which are Aboriginal reserves.

13   Table 1 shows the mean number of fast food restaurants per 1,000 people by deprivation (material and psychosocial) quintile for Nova Scotia. There is a statistically significant (p < 0.000) inverse linear association between quintiles of material deprivation and mean number of fast food restaurants per 1,000 individuals. A statistically significant (p < 0.000) positive relationship between quintiles of psychosocial deprivation and mean number of fast food restaurants per 1,000 individuals was found. The prevalence of fast food restaurants is greater in communities with less material deprivation and more psychosocial deprivation.

Discussion

14   The purpose of this study was to describe the prevalence of fast food restaurants among communities with different levels of material and psychosocial deprivation. Fast food is generally lower in nutritional value and high in calories and saturated fats. Increased density of fast food restaurants may facilitate increased consumption of unhealthy foods and has been identified as a potential environmental mediator of overweight and obesity. Geographically, the density of fast food restaurants is generally higher in more urban communities, those with less material deprivation and more psychosocial deprivation.

15   In Nova Scotia, there is a geographical gradient of material and psychosocial deprivation among urban and rural communities; material deprivation is greater and psychosocial deprivation is lower in rural communities whereas the pattern is reversed in urban communities. This is not to say that material deprivation does not exist in urban communities; rather, the analysis relies on aggregate data thus concealing the reality of urban poverty. In contrast, psychosocial deprivation is largely an urban reality. Similar geographical patterns of deprivation have been found elsewhere in Canada.[13]

16   Some of our results contrast with those of earlier studies that demonstrated higher concentrations of fast food restaurants in low-income or more materially-deprived communities.[23-25] To the contrary, we found more than double the number of fast food outlets in the most affluent communities when compared to the second-most affluent communities. In this regard, our results are consistent with at least one other study which demonstrated a predominance of fast food restaurants in less materially-deprived communities.[26] The prevalence of more fast food restaurants in urban centres may be due to demographic and marketing strategies that take advantage of higher demand, especially those arising from the density of schools and universities as well as youth activities and events.

17   Our results highlight the possibilities of distinguishing community-level environmental mediators of overweight and obesity for population health intervention. Community-level deprivation profiles allow for targeted health promotion and prevention strategies to communities with the greatest levels of deprivation. Geocoding and geographic display of fast food establishments, while useful for the determination of community density measures, would also be quite valuable in healthy urban planning initiatives and in developing geographic restrictions on access to fast food restaurants near schools, other publicly-funded institutions such as hospitals and universities, or vulnerable populations.

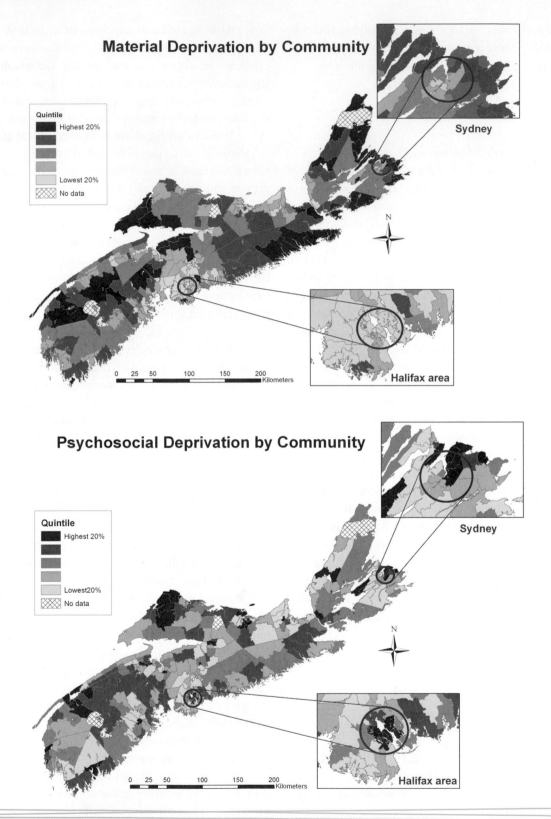

FIGURE 1   MAPS OF COMMUNITY-LEVEL MATERIAL AND PSYCHOSOCIAL DEPRIVATION IN NOVA SCOTIA, 2006

TABLE 1   MEAN NUMBER OF FAST FOOD RESTAURANTS PER 1,000 PEOPLE BY DEPRIVATION QUINTILES

Quintile	Material Deprivation		Psychosocial Deprivation	
	Mean	n	Mean	n
1 (Most Deprived)	0.0473	53	0.4081	53
2	0.0855	53	0.1470	54
3	0.0823	65	0.0556	63
4	0.1283	53	0.0575	53
5 (Least Deprived)	0.3573	52	0.0379	53
Total	0.1401	276	0.1412	276
p value (ANOVA)	0.0000		0.0000	

* Quintiles contain 266 communities.

ANOVA = analysis of variance.

18   This study has several important limitations. First, only fast food restaurants from well-known national chains were identified and included for analysis. Many local establishments have expedited food service but are not connected to fast food chains. Many single-site, mobile, and local "chain" fast food establishments identified as serving pizza, fried chicken, donairs, and similar high calorie foods found in larger fast food chains were not included and could have the effect of minimizing the significance of the associations between fast food restaurants and deprivation. It is possible that more rural communities would have a preponderance of independently-owned fast food restaurants as opposed to national or international chains. Moreover, there is also a possibility that rural communities lack the population density required by the location algorithms used by national fast food enterprises to site economically viable operations. Nevertheless, it is unlikely that the number of restaurants were undercounted disproportionately based on demographic and social characteristics of communities.

19   Second, it is important to note our adoption of an ecological cross-sectional study design in the analysis. While the design is not inherently a limitation for the interpretation of our analysis, it is restricted to a discussion of the relationships between fast food restaurant density and deprivation at the community level and not among individuals. Consequently, we do not presume causality between the prevalence of fast food restaurants and measures of deprivation, even after standardizing for age and gender—two important determinants of population health.

20   Third, census-based deprivation indices, like the one used in our study, are subject to the weakness of potentially concealing important variations within areas. Methodological improvements to minimize loss of information due to coarse aggregation used in census—such as by combining local knowledge of medical health officers through a survey—have been suggested.[34]

21   Fourth, despite our finding of an association between fast food restaurant density and deprivation, the directionality of the relationship is equivocal. For example, community characteristics could be shaped by the type of food outlets and other services available which make the community more or less desirable. Likewise marketers and restaurant owners may establish restaurants in communities with specific demographic and socio-economic profiles with the aims of reaching target consumers and maximizing profits.

22   Finally, our study is focused on one province and limits the generalizability of the results. The association between fast food restaurant density and deprivation measures may exist as a result of the unique characteristics of the region.

23   The rapid increase in the prevalence of overweight and obesity points to the role of obesogenic environments and specifically the health risks arising from increased access to unhealthy fast foods. Material affluence and psychosocial deprivation are associated with a greater prevalence of fast food restaurants across communities in Nova Scotia. Future research should incorporate additional environmental variables, such as exposure to television, access to amenities for physical activity, and other health-promoting attributes of the built environment. Our findings reinforce the potential for population health intervention strategies to modify the environmental determinants of overweight and obesity at the community level.

Canadian Journal of Public Health.
2009. January/February 100 (1).

References

1. Statistics Canada. Measured Obesity: Adult Obesity in Canada. Nutrition: Findings from the Canadian Community Health Survey. Issue no. 1. Ottawa, ON: Statistics Canada, Catalogue no. 82-620-MWE, 2005.
2. Statistics Canada. Measured Obesity: Overweight Canadian Children and Adolescents. Nutrition: Findings from the Canadian Community Health Survey. Issue no. 1. 2005b. (Catalogue no. 82-620-MWE). Ottawa, ON.
3. Tjepkema M. Adult obesity. *Health Reports* 2006;17(3): 9–25.
4. Willms JD, Tremblay MS, Katzmarzyk PT. Geographic and demographic variation in the prevalence of overweight Canadian children. *Obesity Res* 2003;11(5):668–73.
5. Hill J, Peters J. Environmental contributions to the obesity epidemic. *Science* 1998;280:1371–74.
6. Tremblay MS, Williams JD. Is the Canadian childhood obesity epidemic related to physical inactivity? *Int J Obes* 2003;27:1100–5.
7. Ellaway A, Anderson A, Macintyre S. Does area of residence affect body size and shape. *Int J Obes Relat Metab Disord* 1997;21:304–8.
8. Reijneveld SA. The impact of individual and area characteristics on urban socioeconomic differences in health and smoking. *Int J Epidemiol* 1998;27:33–40.
9. Sundquist J, Malmstrom M, Johansson SE. Cardiovascular risk factors and the neighbourhood environment: A multilevel analysis. *Int J Epidemiol* 1999;28:841–45.
10. Van Lenthe FJ, Mackenbach JP. Neighbourhood deprivation and overweight: The GLOBE study. *Int J Obesity* 2002;26:234–40.
11. Townsend P. Deprivation. *J Soc Policy* 1987;16(2):125–46.
12. Stafford M, Marmot M. Neighbourhood deprivation and health: Does it affect us all equally? *Int J Epidemiol* 2003;32:357–66.
13. Pampalon R, Raymond G. A Deprivation Index for Health and Welfare Planning in Quebec. *Chron Dis Can* 2000; 21(3):104–13.
14. Sooman A, Macintyre S, Anderson A. Scotland's health - A more difficult challenge for some? The price and availability of healthy foods in socially contrasting localities in the West of Scotland. *Health Bull* 1993;51:276–84.
15. Agriculture and Agri-Food Canada. The Food Marketing and Distribution Sector in Canada (1999). Available online at: www4.agr.gc.ca/AAFCAAC/display-afficher.do?id=1170960704448 (Accessed September 24, 2007).
16. Euromonitor International. Consumer Food Service in Canada. September 2007. London, UK.
17. Lin BH, Guthrie J, Frazáo E. Nutrition contributions of foods away from home. In: Frazáo E (Ed.), *America's Eating Habits: Changes and Consequences.* USDA/ERS, 1999;213–42.
18. Block JP, Scribner RA, DeSalvo KB. Fast food, race/ethnicity, and income. A geographic analysis. *Am J Prev Med* 2004;27(3):211–17.
19. Biing-Hwan L, Frazao E. Nutritional quality of foods at and away from home. Food review. US Government Printing Office, USDA/ERS, 1997;33–40.
20. Veugelers PJ, Fitzgerald AL, Johnston E. Dietary intake and risk factors for poor diet quality among children in Nova Scotia. *Can J Public Health* 2005;96(3):212–16.
21. Jeffrey R, French S. Epidemic obesity in the United States: Are fast foods and television viewing contributing? *Am J Public Health* 1998;88:277–80.
22. French SA, Harnack L, Jeffrey RW. Fast food restaurant use among women in the Pound of Prevention study: Dietary, behavioral and demographic correlates. *Int J Obesity Related Metabolic Disorders* 2000;24:1353–59.
23. Reidpath DD, Burns C, Garrard J, Mahoney M, Townsend M. An ecological study of the relationship between social and environmental determinants of obesity. *Health & Place* 2002;8:141–45.
24. Block JP, Scribner RA, DeSalvo KB. Fast food, race/ethnicity, and income. *Am J Prev Med* 2004;27:211–17.
25. Cummins S, McKay L, Macintyre S. McDonald's restaurants and neighbourhood deprivation in Scotland and England. *Am J Prev Med* 2005;29(4):308–10.
26. Macintyre S, McKay L, Cummins S, Burns C. Out-of-home food outlets and area deprivation: Case study on Glasgow, UK. *Int J Behav Nutr Physical Activity* 2005;2:16.
27. Katzmarzyk PT, Ardern CI. Overweight and obesity mortality trends in Canada, 1985-2000. *Can J Public Health* 2004;95(1):16–20.
28. Fitzgerald AL, Maclean DR, Veugelers PJ. Dietary reference intakes: A comparison with the Nova Scotia Nutrition Survey. *Can J Dietetic Pract Res* 2002;63(4):176-83.
29. Salmond C, Crampton P. NZDep2001 Index of Deprivation. Department of Public Health, Wellington School of Medicine and Health Sciences, 2002.
30. SAS Institute Inc. SAS/STAT 9.1 User's Guide. Cary, NC: SAS Institute Inc., 2004.

31. Terashima M, Geographical Public Health Analysis Team. Nova Scotia Multiple Deprivation Mapping Project. Available online at: www.gov.ns.ca/ finance/community-counts/resources.asp (Accessed July 2, 2007).

32. McElroy JA, Remington PL, Trentham-Dietz A, Robert S, Newcomb PA. Geocoding addresses from a large population-based study: Lessons learned. *Epidemiology* 2003; 14(4):399–407.

33. Minitab Inc. Meet MINITAB. Release 14 for Windows. State College, PA: Minitab Inc., 2003.

34. Bell N, Schuurman N, Oliver L, Hayes MV. Towards the construction of place-specific measures of deprivation: A case study from the Vancouver metropolitan area. *The Canadian Geographer* 2007;51(4):444–61.

KEY AND CHALLENGING WORDS

demographic, paucity, complement (v.), preponderance, artifactual, gradient, expedited, causality, equivocal

QUESTIONS

1. Identify the justification for the study. Of the studies that comprise the literature review section, which ones would you consider the most relevant to this study's objective?

2. Why might Nova Scotia be a good place to conduct a study like this one?

3. Hypotheses are common in empirical studies. Why do you think the authors of this study did not make a prediction (hypothesis) about the relationship between the prevalence of fast food outlets and population deprivation? (For a study with a hypothesis, see "Intended and unintended effects of an eating disorder educational program," p. 366.)

4. What were the variables used to determine material deprivation in this study? What were the variables used to determine psychosocial deprivation?

5. Why was it essential that precise location information was inputted into the geographic information system? What methods were used to ensure accuracy?

6. In two sentences, summarize the results of the study as given in paragraph 12.

7. Provide a structural breakdown of the Discussion section by adding subheadings (you should include four or five subheadings altogether).

8. Paraphrase paragraph 16, in which the authors compare their findings with those of other similar studies.

9. Suggest a possible follow-up study based on one of limitations discussed in paragraphs 18–22, clearly outlining the purpose of the study and a hypothesis.

POST-READING

1. *Group activity:* Would food zoning be a good or a bad thing? Discuss or debate this issue as it could be applied to your community (i.e., your city or town, or your immediate surroundings, such as your school or neighbourhood). What other environmental measures could be proposed in order to reduce the prevalence of obesity in your community?

RELATED WEBSITES OF INTEREST

Canadian Obesity Network:
www.obesitynetwork.ca/

Statistics Canada (studies, reports, surveys, and tables on subject of obesity):
www.statcan.gc.ca/stcsr/query.html?qt=obesity

ADDITIONAL LIBRARY READING

Kingston, A., & Köhler, N. (2008, August 25). L.A.'s fast food drive-by. *Maclean's, 121*(33), 37–40.

Vanasse, A., Demers, M., Hemiari, A., & Courteau, J. (2006). Obesity in Canada: Where and how many? *International Journal of Obesity, 30,* 677–683. doi:10.1038/sj.ijo.0803168

Roadblocks to laws for healthy eating and activity

Nola M. Ries and Barbara von Tigerstrom

(1,971 words)

Pre-reading

1. Scan the essay to try to determine where the most important information can be found. How does the essay's structure differ from that of most academic essays?
2. Find examples in the first four paragraphs of *jargon*, language used in particular disciplines that helps members communicate.

1   Modern environments promote overeating and sedentary behaviour, and the resulting epidemic of chronic disease is a major public health challenge of the early twenty-first century. Governments and experts around the world are sounding the alarm about the medical, economic, and social costs of escalating rates of obesity, diabetes, cardiovascular disease, and cancer, and are demanding concerted action, including legislative measures, to promote healthier nutrition and physical activity. A recent report from the World Cancer Research Fund and the American Institute for Cancer Research asserts:

Key points

- Modern environments promote overeating and sedentary behaviour and have created an epidemic of chronic disease.
- Legal measures are one policy tool that can be used to promote healthier eating and more physical activity.
- In Canada, jurisdictional wrangling, the threat of legal challenges, ideological opposition, and questions about effectiveness may stall adoption of novel legislation.
- Ongoing evaluation of legislative measures can provide evidence-based guidance on how to proceed.

"The increase in consumption of sugary drinks and of convenient processed and 'fast food,' the decline in physical activity, and the consequent rapid rise in overweight and obesity . . . now amounts to a global public health emergency that requires government intervention. . . . Specifically, government intervention needs to take the form of appropriate legal and fiscal measures designed to make healthy choices more affordable, accessible, and acceptable."[1]

2   Health reports from Canada and other countries are uniform in their calls for coordinated and comprehensive measures—including legal measures—to promote healthier diets and physical activity (Table 1).[2–11] Many jurisdictions in the United States regulate food and physical activity standards in schools, and 20 states require measurements of body mass index or other weight-related screening of schoolchildren.[12] Thirty states have implemented taxes on soft drinks and foods of low nutritional value, and a

TABLE 1   SUMMARY OF RECOMMENDATIONS FROM REPORTS FOR LEGISLATION ON OBESITY

Report	Food labelling	Food advertising	Food content	Pricing and economic incentives	Food and physical activity in school and child care
Canada, Standing Committee on Health[2]	Legislate labels on front of prepackaged foods	Assess effectiveness of regulation and self-regulation; explore ways to regulate Internet advertising	Establish regulations to limit trans fatty acid content while not increasing saturated fat content		Facilitate healthy food and physical activity standards and programs, and provide them in First Nations schools under federal jurisdiction
British Columbia, Select Standing Committee on Health[3]	Develop (in cooperation with industry) "warning labels" for foods high in fat, sugar, and sodium	"Enhance" self-regulation of advertising to children under 12 years of age	Negotiate voluntary reductions in fat, sugar, and sodium content	Remove sales tax exemption for candies and confectionary, soft drinks, and foods not recommended under food guidelines for schools; investigate new "junk food taxes"	Order removal from vending machines and food outlets of products not recommended in food guidelines for schools; prohibit sales of these foods by outlets in government properties
Ontario, Chief Medical Officer of Health[4]	Extend requirement for nutrition labels to fresh meat, poultry and fish; require large chain restaurants to disclose basic nutrition facts	Explore options to control food advertising that targets children	Phase out trans fatty acids from processed foods	Investigate impact of decreasing food prices, especially for communities where healthy foods are expensive	Ensure healthy food and physical activity in daycare settings, and that schools and school boards have guidelines on food
New Brunswick, Select Committee on Wellness[5]		Address the impact of marketing that promotes unhealthy behaviours		Investigate policies to make healthy foods more affordable	Make physical education mandatory for all grades and for graduation
United States, Institute of Medicine Committee on Prevention of Obesity in Children and Youth[6]	Prominently display energy content on nutrition facts labels; exercise more flexibility in allowing nutrition and health claims relevant to obesity	Authorize and provide resources to Federal Trade Commission to monitor compliance with advertising practices			Develop and implement standards for foods in schools and policies restricting advertising in schools; ensure minimum physical activity during school day; assess, and share with parents, students' weight and body mass index

TABLE 1   CONTINUED

Report	Food labelling	Food advertising	Food content	Pricing and economic incentives	Food and physical activity in school and child care
United Kingdom, Cross-Government Obesity Unit[7]	Adopt labelling system following evaluation	Review advertising codes and restrictions on advertising to children; review impact of best practice principles for websites	Work with industry to reduce saturated fat and added sugar content and decrease portion sizes		Ensure schools have guidelines on school food; cooking to be part of compulsory curriculum
Australia, Preventative Health Taskforce[8]	Include retailers and restaurants in national system of food labelling	Limit television advertising of foods high in calories, low in nutrition to children	Regulate trans fatty acid, saturated fat, sodium and sugar content	Consider food pricing strategies (e.g., taxing unhealthy foods); promote active forms of commuting and recreation through subsidies and taxation	Support school initiatives on healthy eating and physical activity; ensure that school policies and environments help students to maintain healthy weights, healthy diets and physical activity
New Zealand, Health Committee[9]	Develop (and regulate if necessary) "traffic light" or similar labelling	Extend current restriction on advertising during children's television programs; restrict or set targets for regulating marketing of unhealthy food and drink to children	Set targets for reformulation of foods high in calories		Remove unhealthy food and beverage products from schools (majority); include promotion of healthy eating and physical activity in performance evaluations for schools and early childhood centres
Commission of the European Communities[10]	Harmonize regulation of health claims; consider amending food labelling regulation	Consider measures to restrict advertising if self-regulation fails to give satisfactory results			
World Health Organization[11]	Consider requiring nutritional information; disallow misleading health claims	Work with consumer groups and private sector to develop approaches to deal with marketing to children, sponsorship, promotion, and advertising	Consider measures to encourage reductions in sodium, hydrogenated oil, and sugar content	Consider using taxation, subsidies, or direct pricing to encourage healthy eating and physical activity; take healthy nutrition into account in agricultural policy	Adopt policies to support healthy diets at school and limit availability of products high in sodium, sugar, and fat

growing number of states and local governments require that chain restaurants post nutritional information on menus. The province of Quebec and Sweden and Norway have restricted advertising to children for many years, and the telecommunications regulator in the United Kingdom now restricts food advertising aimed at children.

3   Despite the recommendations in Canadian government reports and legal precedents elsewhere, governments in Canada have taken little legislative action to promote healthy eating and physical activity (Table 2). Legal measures are sparse, with little consistency across the country. Three factors might explain this reticence: concern about legislative authority, ideological opposition to government regulation, and questions about the impact of legislation.

4   Debate about lawmaking authority may stall legislative initiatives. After the Parliamentary Standing Committee on Health produced its report on childhood obesity, Bloc Québécois members criticized the committee for "extending the study to areas that

TABLE 2   SUMMARY OF CANADIAN LEGISLATIVE INITIATIVES FOR HEALTHY EATING AND PHYSICAL ACTIVITY

Jurisdiction	Legislative initiatives
Federal	
Information disclosure	Food and Drugs Act and Regulations require a nutrition facts table on most prepackaged foods that provides information about calorie content and certain nutrients, including fats, sugars, and sodium
Advertising	Bill C-324, An Act to Amend the Competition Act and the Food and Drugs Act, a private member's bill, would prohibit commercial food advertising aimed at children younger than 13
Food content	Bill C-251, An Act to Amend the Food and Drugs Act, a private member's bill, would restrict trans fatty acid content in oils and fats intended for human consumption
Physical activity	Children's Fitness Tax Credit provides a tax credit (up to $500) for eligible fitness expenses paid by parents to register a child in a prescribed program of physical activity
Alberta	
Physical activity	Bill 206, Alberta Personal Income Tax (Physical Activity Credit) Amendment Act, passed a fitness tax credit (up to $500) in November 2008, but it has not been implemented (not funded in the April 2009 budget)
British Columbia	
Food service establishments	Proposed restrictions of trans fatty acid content in prepared foods in food service establishments, including restaurants and schools, are to be implemented by regulation under the new Public Health Act, which authorizes regulation of conditions, things, or activities that constitute a "health impediment"
Public health plans	New Public Health Act, effective Mar. 31, 2009, authorizes the Minister of Health to order public bodies to establish plans to "identify, prevent and mitigate the adverse effects of health impediments," which include factors that cause chronic disease or whose cumulative effects adversely affect health
Manitoba	
Food in schools	Bill 2, Public Schools Amendment Act (Trans Fat and Nutrition), although not yet in force, requires that each school establish a written policy about food and nutrition and report on progress in implementing the policy in the annual school plan; it also restricts artificial trans fatty acid content in foods provided by or sold in schools
	Healthy Child Manitoba Act guides "the development, implementation and evaluation of the Healthy Child Manitoba strategy," a prevention and early intervention strategy to promote healthy eating and physical activity; it also addresses such topics as parenting skills, daycare programs, fetal alcohol spectrum disorder, and healthy school environments
New Brunswick	
Physical activity in Schools	Healthy Students Act, proposed in 2005 (Bill 33) and 2006 (Bill 44), would have required a healthy students advisory committee to promote physical activity in schools and ensure that students receive 150 minutes per week of physical education
Nova Scotia	
Physical activity	Financial Measures Act, effective Jan. 1, 2009, provides a healthy living tax credit of up to $500 for sports or recreational activities; previous private member's bill (Bill 106, Income Tax Act Amendment) proposed a tax credit for recreational and physical activities, specifically for people aged 65 and older
Physical activity in schools	Bill 115, An Act to Amend the Education Act, a private member's bill, would require at least 30 minutes of physical activity each school day; previous private member's bill in 2006 (Bill 90, Student Fitness Act) sought to create a provincial healthy students advisory committee that would require 150 minutes of physical education per week

TABLE 2 CONTINUED

Jurisdiction	Legislative initiatives
Ontario	
Advertising	Bill 53 (2008), An Act to Amend the Consumer Protection Act, 2002 would prohibit "commercial advertising for food or drink that is directed at persons under 13 years of age"
Food in schools	Bill 8, Healthy Food for Healthy Schools Act, 2008 amends Education Act to establish policies and guidelines for school nutrition standards and for food and beverages available in schools; it also regulates trans fatty acid content of food in schools
Food service establishments	Bill 156, Healthy Decisions for Healthy Eating Act, 2009 would require food service establishments (fast food) with total gross annual revenues of more than $5 million to disclose certain nutritional information for foods and beverages; it would also limit trans fatty acid content
Public health standards	Provincial Public Health Standards, issued under the Health Protection and Promotion Act, are "guidelines for the provision of mandatory health programs and services;" the standards impose obligations on boards of health to monitor and promote healthy eating, physical activity and other health-related behaviours; the boards work with schools, workplaces, municipalities, and community partners in comprehensive health promotion programs and services
Quebec	
Advertising	Since 1980, Consumer Protection Act has prohibited commercial advertising directed at children younger than age 13
Financial measures	An Act to Establish the Fund for the Promotion of a Healthy Lifestyle, enacted in 2007, establishes a fund for programs that promote healthy eating and physical activity; part of the funding ($20 million/yr) is through revenue collected under the Tobacco Tax Act

are outside the federal government's jurisdiction."[2] When a private member's bill in Ontario proposed to regulate trans fatty acid content and disclosure of nutritional information on restaurant menus, the provincial premier responded by stating that the federal government should take the lead.[13]

Potential roadblocks

5   Lack of authority is not a significant bar to action, however, because both federal and provincial governments have constitutional powers to enact health-related laws.[14] This shared jurisdiction allows government to act in complementary ways, but it could be a source of delay while one level of government waits for another to act. The legislative initiatives described in Table 2 could serve as models for more consistent adoption across the country. Taxation and spending powers can be used by both levels of government: they could offer tax credits for physical activity but tax food and beverages that are high in

calories and low in nutritional value. Advertising can be restricted through federal authority over broadcast media and provincial authority over business regulation and consumer protection. With constitutional authority over education, the provinces can use school legislation to impose mandatory requirements for nutrition and physical activity. Provincial public health statutes also confer power to protect and promote health; notably, British Columbia's new Public Health Act includes the power to regulate factors implicated in chronic disease.[15] Under its criminal law jurisdiction, the federal government can prohibit or regulate health hazards and impose labelling requirements or advertising restrictions that discourage the consumption of hazardous products.

6   Governments may be concerned about legal challenges from the food industry. The most likely claim against advertising restrictions or labelling legislation would be infringement of freedom of expression, but such laws are defensible if they target a serious health or social problem in a reasonable way. The Supreme Court of Canada upheld Quebec's

ban on advertising directed at children under age 13[16] and federal tobacco legislation, including advertising restrictions and labelling requirements,[17] as justifiable restrictions on commercial speech.

7   In addition to these legal concerns, ideological opposition to the so-called "nanny state" (whereby governments assume a paternalistic role) may dissuade governments from adopting potentially controversial laws. The Lalonde report, so influential in advancing a "social determinants of health model" three decades ago, squarely stated the point: "The ultimate philosophical issue . . . is whether, and to what extent, government can get into the business of modifying human behaviour, even if it does so to improve health."[18] This debate persists today. A member of Ontario's legislature expressed classic opposition to public health intervention in his criticism of the proposed law to disclose trans fatty acid content and nutritional value on menus: "I believe in legislation, generally speaking, that protects me from you and you from me. I don't like legislation that purports to protect me from myself, and that's what this kind of legislation is."[19]

8   Those who accept a government role for regulation may nonetheless question the efficacy of legal measures in influencing healthier behaviour. A member of Alberta's Legislative Assembly criticized a proposed tax credit for physical activity in that province: ". . . we're kidding ourselves if we think a small monetary reward will be an incentive for Albertans to change their lives in such a drastic way. A comprehensive approach is needed if a tax incentive is going to ultimately produce results."[20]

9   It is true that, as lessons in tobacco control show, a "portfolio of policies" is needed to combat chronic diseases stemming from unhealthy modern environments.[21] However, a comprehensive approach must be built piece by piece, and it would be a mistake to allow skepticism about the impact of single legislative or policy interventions to preclude any action at all. Massive shifts have occurred in the conditions in which people live, work, and play, and it will be difficult to isolate and assess the role of the law in countering the unhealthy impact of these shifts. Yet, evidence about environments and behaviour can help identify defensible legislative interventions. For example, the amount of food consumed outside the home suggests that requiring information disclosure in food service establishments is a potential policy option. Evidence from areas such as behavioural economics can provide some insight on how consumers might react to higher prices for snack foods with low nutritional value or tax credits for physical activity. It is important to assess the results of specific legislative measures; researchers are already making concerted efforts to study the impact of laws on public health.[22] Early evaluations of novel approaches in the US and elsewhere can help identify strengths and weaknesses, and promising interventions can be adapted to Canada's social and cultural context.

10   With ongoing assessment, legislation can be adjusted over time to ensure that the objectives of public health are promoted. The personal and social harm associated with the increasing burden of chronic disease is a matter of urgent public concern. In an area so complex and controversial, not everyone will agree on the best way forward; however, the use of legal measures to promote healthier nutrition and physical activity, especially among children, deserves more attention and action from Canadian legislators.

*

Contributors: Both authors contributed to the conception of and research for the article. Nola Ries prepared the first draft of this article. Barbara von Tigerstrom conducted the research and analysis for information summarized in Table 1, and Nola Ries did so for Table 2. Both authors contributed equally to the revision of the article and approved the final version submitted for publication.

Funding: The authors acknowledge funding from the Canadian Institutes of Health Research, grant MOP81162. Nola Ries also receives funding from the Alberta Cancer Prevention Legacy Fund, Alberta Health Services.

CMAJ. 2010. April 182 (7).

References

1. *Policy and action for cancer prevention—food, nutrition, and physical activity: a global perspective.* Washington (DC): World Cancer Research Fund/American Institute for Cancer Research; 2009. p. 86. Available: www.dietand cancerreport .org (accessed 2010 Jan. 5).

2. Standing Committee on Health. *Healthy weights for healthy kids.* Ottawa (ON): House of Commons; 2007. p. 57. Available: www.ccfn.ca/pdfs/HealthyWeightsForHealthy Kids.pdf (accessed 2010 Jan. 5).

3. Select Standing Committee on Health. *A strategy for combatting childhood obesity and physical inactivity in British Columbia.* Victoria (BC): Legislative Assembly of British Columbia; 2006. Available: www.leg.bc.ca/CMT/38thparl/ session2 /health/reports/RptHealth38229Nov2006/Rpt Health38229Nov2006COOBC.htm (accessed 2010 Jan. 12).

4. Chief Medical Officer of Health. *2004 Chief Medical Officer of Health report: healthy weights, healthy lives.* Toronto (ON): Ministry of Health and Longterm Care; 2004. Available: www.health.gov.on.ca/english/public/pub/ ministry_reports/cmoh04_report/healthy_weights_ 112404.pdf (accessed 2010 Jan. 12).

5. Select Committee on Wellness. *Wellness . . . we each have a role to play: final report of the Select Committee on Wellness.* Fredericton (NB): The Committee; 2008. Available: www. gnb.ca/legis/Promos/Wellness/pdf/FinalReportWellnesse. pdf (accessed 2010 Jan. 12).

6. Institute of Medicine Committee on Prevention of Obesity in Children and Youth. Koplan JP, Liverman CT, Kraak VA, editors. In: *Preventing childhood obesity: health in the balance.* Washington (DC): National Academies Press; 2005.

7. CrossGovernment Obesity Unit. *Healthy weight, healthy lives: a crossgovernment strategy for England.* Department of Health and Department of Children, Schools and Families; 2008. Available: www.dh.gov.uk/prod_consum_dh/ groups/dh_digital assets/documents/digitalasset/dh_ 084024.pdf (accessed 2010 Jan. 12).

8. Preventative Health Taskforce. *Obesity in Australia: a need for urgent action.* Commonwealth of Australia; 2008. Available: www.preventativehealth.org.au /internet/ preventativehealth/publishing.nsf/Content/E233F869 5823F16CCA2574D D00818E64/$File/obesityjul09.pdf (accessed 2010 Jan. 12).

9. Health Committee. *Inquiry into obesity and type 2 diabetes in New Zealand.* New Zealand: House of Representatives; 2007. Available: www.parliament.nz/NR/rdonlyres/47F5 2D0D013242EFA2976AB08980C0EA/62831/DBSCH_ SCR _3868_5337.pdf (accessed 2010 Jan. 12).

10. Commission of the European Communities. *Promoting healthy diets and physical activity: a European dimension for the prevention of overweight, obesity and chronic diseases.* Brussels (Belgium): The Commission; 2005.

11. World Health Organization. *European Ministerial Conference on Counteracting Obesity: conference report.* Copenhagen (Denmark): World Health Organization Regional Office for Europe; 2007. Available: www.euro.who.int/ document/E90143.pdf (accessed 2010 Jan. 12).

12. *Supplement to "F as in fat: how obesity policies are failing America, 2009" obesity related legislation action in States, update.* Washington (DC): Trust for America's Health. Available: http://healthyamericans.org/reports/obesity2009/ StateSupplement 2009.pdf (accessed 2010 Jan. 5).

13. Canadian Press. *Ottawa should lead on childhood obesity: McGuinty.* Toronto (ON): CTV News; April 8, 2009. Available: www.ctv.ca/servlet/ArticleNews /story/CTVNews/ 20090408/mcguinty_obesity_090408/20090408?hub=H ealth&s _name= (accessed 2010 Jan. 5).

14. Ries NM. Legal foundations of public health law. In: Bailey TM, Caulfield T, Ries NM, editors. *Public health law & policy in Canada,* 2nd ed. Markham (ON): LexisNexis Canada; 2008. p. 736.

15. *Public Health Act,* S.B.C., 2008, c. 28.

16. *Irwin Toy Ltd.* v. *Quebec (Attorney General),* [1989] 1 S.C.R. 927.

17. *Canada (Attorney General)* v. *JTIMacdonald Corp.,* [2007] S.C.C. 30.

18. Lalonde M. *A new perspective on the health of Canadians.* Ottawa (ON): Government of Canada; 1981.

19. *Canada HC Debates. 391.* Available: http://hansardindex. ontla.on.ca/hansardeissue /391/l135.htm (accessed 2010 Jan. 5).

20. *Debates of the Legislative Assembly of Alberta.* 27th Legislature, First Session; November 17, 2008. Available: www. assembly.ab.ca/ISYS/LADDAR_files/docs /hansards/han/ legislature_27/session_1/20081117_1330_01_han.pdf (accessed 2010 Jan. 5).

21. *Foresight—tackling obesities: future choices, project report.* London (UK): Government Office for Science; 2007. Available: www.foresight.gov.uk/OurWork/ActiveProjects/ Obesity/Obesity.asp (accessed 2010 Jan. 5).

22. Moulton AD, Mercer SL, Popovic T, et al. The scientific basis of law as a public health tool. *Am J Public Health* 2009;99:1724.

KEY AND CHALLENGING WORDS

jurisdiction, reticence, ideological, paternalistic, efficacy, preclude, defensible

QUESTIONS

1. What is the function of the lengthy direct quotation in paragraph 1?

2. How is the information in Table 1 used to support the main point in paragraph 2? Do you think it was a good idea to provide support by relying on the content of a table?

3. Turning to Table 1, analyze its effectiveness in conveying content. Is its structure logical and consistent, and is the information easily accessible? Can you suggest any improvements or additions?

4. Identify the essay's thesis and main organizational method. Is it apparent from the first three paragraphs whether the essay will focus on exposition or argument? What rhetorical pattern do the authors use most frequently to develop their points?

5. Do the authors consider the issue of "legislative authority" a realistic or valid obstacle in enacting laws promoting activity and healthy eating? Explain your reasoning in one paragraph.

6. Using a reliable source, such as a news or scholarly article or government website, summarize in one to two sentences the significance of the *Lalonde Report* (see paragraph 7), citing your source. Why do the authors use the phrase "classic opposition" to describe the legislative member's objection?

7. How is the information in Table 2 used to support the main point in paragraph 3?

8. Analyze the rhetorical effectiveness of paragraph 9, showing how it provides a transition between paragraph 8 and the concluding paragraph.

POST-READING

1. *Collaborative activity:* Do you believe that people sometimes need to be protected from themselves (see paragraph 7) through legal means? Under what circumstances? Do you believe that freedom of choice should always prevail and that people should be free to make good or bad choices? Discuss or debate these questions.

2. The Report of the Standing Committee on *Health, Healthy Weights for Healthy Kids*, was published in 2007 (it is mentioned in paragraph 4 and referenced in note 2). a) Write a one- to two-page summary of this report in paragraph form (i.e., do not use bullets or point form). Your summary should include a brief overview of the major sections of the report with the main focus on the synthesis and recommendations sections. Also, include a representative summary of witnesses who appeared before the report's committee (not individual names but the kinds of organizations that were represented e.g., professional organizations, cultural groups, etc.); *OR* b) Take one of the thirteen recommendations in the report and analyze its feasibility. The report can be accessed online: e.g., www.ccfn.ca/pdfs/HealthyWeightsForHealthyKids.pdf.

THE HUMAN FACE OF SCIENCE

Most people are not WEIRD

Joseph Henrich, Steven J. Heine, and Ara Norenzayan

(900 words)

Pre-reading

1. What can you determine about the essay from its title? From the heading? After scanning the topic sentences (first sentences in the paragraphs) come up with a reading hypothesis consisting of a two- or three-sentence summary of what you expect the essay to be about.
2. Can you infer anything about the authors' credibility by scanning the brief list of references?

---

1 Much research on human behaviour and psychology assumes that everyone shares most fundamental cognitive and affective processes, and that findings from one population apply across the board. A growing body of evidence suggests that this is not the case.

2 Experimental findings from several disciplines indicate considerable variation among human populations in diverse domains, such as visual perception, analytic reasoning, fairness, cooperation, memory, and the heritability of IQ.[1,2] This is in line with what anthropologists have long suggested: that people from Western, educated, industrialized, rich, and democratic (WEIRD) societies—and particularly American undergraduates—are some of the most psychologically unusual people on Earth.[1]

3 So the fact that the vast majority of studies use WEIRD participants presents a challenge to the understanding of human psychology and behaviour. A 2008 survey of the top psychology journals found that 96 per cent of subjects were from Western industrialized countries—which house just 12 per cent of the world's population.[3] Strange, then, that research articles routinely assume that their results are broadly representative, rarely adding even a cautionary footnote on how far their findings can be generalized.

4 The evidence that basic cognitive and motivational processes vary across populations has become increasingly difficult to ignore. For example, many studies have shown that Americans, Canadians, and western Europeans rely on analytical reasoning strategies—which separate objects from their contexts and rely on rules to explain and predict behaviour—substantially more than non-Westerners. Research also indicates that Americans use analytical thinking more than, say, Europeans. By contrast, Asians tend to reason holistically, for example by considering people's behaviour in terms of their situation.[1] Yet many long-standing theories of how humans perceive, categorize, and remember emphasize the centrality of analytical thought.

5 It is a similar story with social behaviour related to fairness and equality. Here, researchers often use one-shot economic experiments such as the ultimatum game, in which a player decides how much of a fixed amount to offer a second player, who can then

accept or reject this proposal. If the second player rejects it, neither player gets anything. Participants from industrialized societies tend to divide the money equally, and reject low offers. People from non-industrialized societies behave differently, especially in the smallest-scale nonmarket societies such as foragers in Africa and horticulturalists in South America, where people are neither inclined to make equal offers nor to punish those who make low offers.[4]

6   Recent developments in evolutionary biology, neuroscience, and related fields suggest that these differences stem from the way in which populations have adapted to diverse culturally constructed environments. Amazonian groups, such as the Piraha, whose languages do not include numerals above three, are worse at distinguishing large quantities digitally than groups using extensive counting systems, but are similar in their ability to approximate quantities. This suggests the kind of counting system people grow up with influences how they think about integers.[1]

Costly generalizations

7   Using study participants from one unusual population could have important practical consequences. For example, economists have been developing theories of decision-making incorporating insights from psychology and social science—such as how to set wages—and examining how these might translate into policy.[5] Researchers and policy-makers should recognize that populations vary considerably in the extent to which they display certain biases, patterns, and preferences in economic decisions, such as those related to optimism.[1] Such differences can,

for example, affect the way that experienced investors make decisions about the stock market.[6]

8   We offer four suggestions to help put theories of human behaviour and psychology on a firmer empirical footing. First, editors and reviewers should push researchers to support any generalizations with evidence. Second, granting agencies, reviewers, and editors should give researchers credit for comparing diverse and inconvenient subject pools. Third, granting agencies should prioritize cross-disciplinary, cross-cultural research. Fourth, researchers must strive to evaluate how their findings apply to other populations. There are several low-cost ways to approach this in the short term: one is to select a few judiciously chosen populations that provide a 'tough test' of universality in some domain, such as societies with limited counting systems for testing theories about numerical cognition.[1,2]

9   A crucial longer-term goal is to establish a set of principles that researchers can use to distinguish variable from universal aspects of psychology. Establishing such principles will remain difficult until behavioural scientists develop interdisciplinary, international research networks for long-term studies on diverse populations using an array of methods, from experimental techniques and ethnography to brain-imaging and biomarkers.

10   Recognizing the full extent of human diversity does not mean giving up on the quest to understand human nature. To the contrary, this recognition illuminates a journey into human nature that is more exciting, more complex, and ultimately more consequential than has previously been suspected.

Nature. 2010. July 466 (1).

Notes

1.   Henrich, J., Heine, S.J. & Norenzayan, A. *Behav. Brain Sci.* doi:10.1017/S0140525X0999152X (2010).
2.   Henrich, J., Heine, S.J. & Norenzayan, A. *Behav. Brain Sci.* doi:10.1017/S0140525X10000725 (2010).
3.   Arnett, J. *Am. Psychol.* **63**, 602–614 (2008).
4.   Henrich, J. *et al. Science* **327**, 1480–1484 (2010).
5.   Foote, C.L., Goette, L. & Meier, S. *Policymaking Insights from Behavioral Economics* (Federal Reserve Bank of Boston, 2009).
6.   Ji, L.J., Zhang, Z.Y. & Guo, T.Y. *J. Behav. Decis. Making* **21**, 399–413 (2008).

KEY AND CHALLENGING WORDS

cognitive, holistically, empirical, judiciously, ethnography, consequential

QUESTIONS

1. In one sentence, summarize the claim in the first paragraph.

2. Why do the authors mention American undergraduate students in particular in their claim that people from "WEIRD" societies are "some of the most psychologically unusual people on Earth" (paragraph 2)? Specifically, what characteristics might make American undergraduates an unrepresentative or unreliable sample to generalize from? (Note: this question could be discussed as a group activity—see Post-reading, #3.)

3. How do the authors define "analytical reasoning"? How can it vary between cultures or societies, and why might variations be important to the study of human behaviour?

4. What fallacy or fallacies can be inferred from the authors' criticism of experiments using WEIRD participants; that is, what fallacies do such experiments illustrate/demonstrate? Is the use of these kinds of subjects essentially a failure in inductive or deductive reasoning? (See p. 121.)

5. Of the four recommendations mentioned in paragraph 8, which seems the most practical or realistic? Explain your reasoning.

6. Evaluate the evidence used to support the authors' claims. For example, is it sufficient, wide-ranging, and appropriate/relevant? Refer to specific examples.

POST-READING

1. Summarize the complete article in approximately 225 words.

2. The authors of this essay have published a much longer study to which other researchers have responded: Henrich, J., Heine, S.J., & Norenzayan, A. (2010). The weirdest people in the world? *Behavioral and Brain Sciences, 33* (2–3), 61–135. Access the main article (pp. 61–83) using a library database and read the abstract (you may want to scan the introduction as well). The same issue contains peer commentaries on and responses to the original article, each of which is preceded by an abstract (see pages 83–123 for the commentaries). Choose two of the commentaries and a) summarize them in one paragraph; b) in a separate paragraph, show how the commentary extends, modifies, or disputes the thesis of the main article.

3. *Collaborative activity:* Discuss or debate the following statement from Henrich, Heine, & Norenzayan (The Weirdest People in the World?, p. 82): "The sample of contemporary Western undergraduates that so overwhelms our database . . . . may represent the worst population on which to base our understanding of Homo sapiens."

Human dignity: A guide to policy making in the biotechnology era?

Timothy Caulfield and Roger Brownsword

(5,895 words)

Pre-reading

1. After reading the title, paraphrase its content in one sentence; your paraphrase should reflect your expectations of the essay's content. What is the significance of the question mark?
2. After reading the abstract, come up with your own one- or two-sentence definition of human dignity. Then, read Box 1 and consider which of the various connotations of the word "dignity" is closest to your own.

Abstract

This article explores the ways in which human dignity is used in debates about controversial biotechnologies, including biobanks, human gene patents, stem cell research, and human cloning. Increasingly, human dignity is used as a form of general condemnation and as blanket justification for regulatory restraint. However, this use of human dignity marks a significant departure from the traditional, human-rights informed view of human dignity that has dominated bioethics debates for decades. In addition, on its own, it stands as dubious justification for policies that are aimed at constraining controversial biotechnologies.

*

1   The concept of human dignity has emerged as a key point of reference for the regulation of modern science and technology, as evidenced by its use in recent policy debates on human genetics, human embryonic stem cell research, and human cloning.[1–3] But despite its frequent use, a practical definition of human dignity remains elusive.[4] Most would agree that the concept is closely related to the intrinsic worth of all humans—an idea enshrined in the 1948 Universal Declaration on Human Rights, which acknowledges the "inherent dignity" and "equal and inalienable rights of all members of the human family." In this reading, human dignity is an engine of individual empowerment, reinforcing individual autonomy and the right to self-determination.[5]

2   However, beyond statements such as the one in the Universal Declaration of Human Rights, there seems to be little clarity about the concept of human dignity. Indeed, it is increasingly used as a rationale for a wide variety of policy positions. For example, President George W. Bush has used it as a justification for a range of biomedical policies, including a ban on human cloning and embryonic stem cell research[6]. However, for some, respect for human dignity (as the underpinning of human rights) points in exactly the opposite direction. This confusion has led one commentator to assert that "[d]ignity is a useless concept in medical ethics and can be eliminated without any loss of content."[7] Others have argued that its inappropriate use can be an oppressive force, silencing open debate.[8]

3   Before this eruption of interest in human dignity, the fault-lines in bioethics were reasonably well defined: a dignity-informed rights perspective (for example, the right to self-determination) opposing a

utilitarian view (for example, an emphasis on the public good).[9] This rights-respecting use of human dignity remains an important part of research ethics and science policy, as exemplified by the debate surrounding human genetic databanks (where individual rights are contended for against larger public-health objectives). However, as the cloning and stem cell controversies highlight, the tensions in bioethics are now more complex; human dignity is increasingly used as a form of general condemnation.[10,11] Informed by a wide variety of religious and philosophical traditions, the 'dignitarian alliance' insists on regulatory restraint wherever biotechnology is seen as compromising human dignity.

4   Critics of the new dignitarianism complain that it serves as an 'all-purpose' justification, one that allows the user to invoke a "basketful of extraordinary meanings."[12] And often, the use of human dignity seems to amount to little more than an articulation of a general social unease with a given technology. When used in this manner, it seems to be little more than a politically palatable expression of the "yuck factor."[8]

5   Given its mixed pedigree, it is no surprise that dignitarianism represents a range of views, some with universalizing pretensions, others that are more local in character. For example, the principle of the sanctity of human life (interpreted broadly so that, *inter alia*, it protects human embryonic and fetal life), the principle that human life should not be commodified (interpreted as precluding sex selection, reproductive cloning, saviour siblings, and the like), and the principle that the human body should not be commercialized (precluding the sale of human bodies or body parts, prostitution, surrogacy, the patenting of human gene sequences, and so on) might be presented by dignitarians as universal principles. In other words, it is proclaimed that these activities should not be allowed because they infringe an idea of human dignity. However, as we discuss below, not all agree with many of the underlying values and/or conclusions that inform the various dignitarian positions. This does not mean that these are not valid positions worthy of public debate, but in a pluralistic society it is questionable whether they should be used as a foundation for a regulatory policy.

6   Here we consider how appeals to human dignity influence debates about bioscience policy. We make no attempt to cover every possible take on human dignity, for this is a concept with complex religious, moral, and political dimensions, as well as deep historical roots (BOX 1).[12-15] However, so far as the regulation of modern biotechnology is concerned, it is the tension between the empowerment and the constraint conceptions of human dignity that stands out as fundamental. As such, we focus our discussion on the use of human dignity from the human rights and dignitarian perspectives. Our goal here is not to critique the values that underlie these perspectives

BOX 1   DEFINING 'HUMAN DIGNITY'

Given its long history and varied use, it should be no surprise that a clear definition of human dignity does not exist. For human-rights theorists, human dignity refers to the inherent worth of every human and is the source of all human rights—as noted in documents such as the Universal Declaration of Human Rights. For example, because all humans have dignity, they have the right to self-determination (in bioethics, this is usually manifested in a respect for autonomy). This view of human dignity gained strength after the Second World War and, as a result of the Nazi atrocities, was used to "contain the power of states over persons."[5] But the term has been in existence much longer than the Universal Declaration of Human Rights. In ancient Rome the term dignity (*dignitas*) was used to refer to social status and individual prominence, primarily of the upper classes. The concept has also had an important role for religious philosophers. For example, Christian commentators have long used dignity to express, *inter alia*, the unique relationship humans have with God and the resultant special place humans have in the world order.[15] And academic philosophers have used and explained human dignity in very different ways,[13,16,17] including treating it as a virtue or as a description of personal conduct (dignified character).

(for example, the appropriate role of the ethical principle of autonomy or whether the embryo has a moral and legal status), but to consider how they relate to policy development in the biotechnology era.

Biobanks and consent

7   Numerous areas of genetic research have raised consent issues—from concerns about the testing of minors to the difficulties that are inherent in the communication of complex, probabilistic information. In recent years, one of the most pressing policy dilemmas has been the appropriateness of the consent processes that are associated with large-scale biobanks and population genetic studies.[16]

8   Traditional consent norms require consent to be obtained for each new research project, particularly when the genetic information is linked or linkable to the identity of the individual research participant. However, because large population projects, such as the UK Biobank and Iceland's deCODE initiative, involve the participation of a great number of individuals, obtaining consent for each new project is a challenge.[17,18] Several national and international entities acknowledge this dilemma. UNESCO (United Nations Educational, Scientific and Cultural Organization), for example, notes that "[a] system which required fresh consent would be extremely cumbersome and could seriously inhibit research."[19]

9   Most of the policy reforms that have been suggested to address this consent issue involve a departure and, in some cases, an erosion of traditional consent norms—such as the use of a blanket consent or, as in Iceland, the creation of a system of presumed consent. The requirement to obtain consent is one of the most fundamental in health law and bioethics. It flows directly, although not exclusively, from a rights-based concept of human dignity, such as that typified by the Universal Declaration of Human Rights. It is not surprising, then, that these projects have created a good deal of social controversy (recently, the Icelandic Supreme Court held that the country's database legislation was unconstitutional).[20] A WHO (World Health Organization) report, *Genetic Databases: Assessing the Benefits and Impact on Human and Patient Rights*, summarizes the policy quandary:

"We have, then, a fundamental tension between the possibility of considerable public good on the one hand, and the potential for significant individual and familial harm on the other. The basic interests that lie in the balance are those between human dignity and human rights as against public health, scientific progress, and commercial interests in a free market."[21]

10   Contemporary views about the need to obtain consent, particularly in the context of research, are built on a concept of human dignity that is predominantly informed by post-Holocaust human-rights deliberations—flowing from the Universal Declaration of Human Rights and the Nuremberg Code, through the Helsinki Declaration and into most current iterations of national research ethic policy.[22] Individuals have rights, such as the right to make autonomous decisions, because they have dignity. And these rights can only rarely be overridden—as exemplified by article 5 of the Helsinki Declaration: "In medical research on human subjects, considerations related to the well-being of the human subject should take precedence over the interests of science and society."[23]

11   In relation to consent and genetic databanks, human dignity is predominantly used in what can be considered the traditional human-rights perspective. In the legal arena, rightly or not, this is the most common application of human dignity—that is, as the foundation for specific legal entitlements, such as informed consent.[24] It is the least contentious use of the concept of human dignity. Few would disagree that, at some level, human dignity relates to the inherent worth of humans and that the right to self-determination flows from this principle. The use of dignity language might not be a necessary part of the biobanking debate,[8] but it does remind us about the historical context of the right to self-determination and consent. It reminds us of what is at stake.

Commercialization and patenting

12   Human dignity has also been a central element of the debate about the appropriateness of patents on human genetic material. Indeed, before the emergence of the more concrete issues that are associated

with human gene patents, such as their possible impact on the research environment, dignity arguments were a dominant theme in public and political deliberations.

13   The concern is that patents on human genetic material will promote a lack of respect for human life and, with that, a devaluation of human dignity.[25] Human dignity, it is said, is infringed by the commercialization and instrumentalization of humans. Arguments along these lines were put forward (although unsuccessfully) by dignitarians in the *Relaxin* opposition (BOX 2), the first serious ethical challenge to the patentability of human genetic material heard at the European Patent Office.[26,27] These dignity issues have also emerged in various national and international policy documents. In Canada, for example, the Parliamentary Standing Committee on Health suggested that the patenting of human genes is "repugnant" and "entails their commodification." This thinking led the committee to recommend that "patents be denied in relation to human material."[28]

14   Although not explicit about how dignity might be implicated by human gene patents, article 4 of the UNESCO Universal Declaration on the Human Genome and Human Rights (a document that is expressly founded on human dignity) states: "the human genome in its natural state shall not give rise to financial gain."[29] Likewise, France has long taken a relatively aggressive stance against the commercialization of the human body, as exemplified by its "refusal to ratify [that is, implement] the 1998 European biotechnology directive sanctioning most forms of patenting of the human genome."[30] Here the inference seems to be that any association with market forces is ethically inappropriate. Allowing patents on human genetic material invites the language of property and the forces of private markets into the realm of human tissue.[30,31] And, according to some, this will inevitably lead to an inappropriate commodification of human tissue and, ultimately, humans themselves.

15   Most would probably agree that patenting could, theoretically, implicate dignity issues. However, concerns about human dignity will be rather different for those who emphasize a human-rights perspective to the way that they will be for the dignitarian alliance.

16   Broadly speaking, if we take a human-rights view, our concerns about human gene patents will relate: first, to any direct violation of rights (for example, in the *Relaxin* opposition, there was a question about whether the pregnant women who donated biological samples to the researchers did so on the basis of a free and fully informed consent);[26,32]

BOX 2   THE RELAXIN OPPOSITION

In the *Relaxin* case at the European Patent Office (EPO), the opponents of the patent, relying on the morality exclusion in article 53(a) of the European Patent Convention, argued (unsuccessfully) that a patent on a human gene sequence, or a copy of a human gene sequence that has been isolated from the body, should not be allowed because it compromises human dignity.[26,32] This was a straightforward dignitarian challenge.

The opposition division of the EPO, rejecting the challenge, gave some quite detailed responses that aimed to show that the opponents misunderstood the nature of the relevant science and of the patent. For example, the opposition division emphasized that the patent in question would not imply anything that is analogous to enslavement of persons. The key to the opposition division's approach is that it understands human dignity within a human-rights framework. Accordingly, it cannot see what is wrong with the patent because the pregnant women who supplied the tissue and samples for the researchers did so on the basis of informed consent.

However, this response misses the opponents' point. From a human-rights perspective, whether or not the pregnant women gave their consent is a fundamental issue; but from the standpoint of the dignitarian alliance, where it is axiomatic that the commercial exploitation of human tissue compromises human dignity, it is irrelevant. Like ships passing in the night, these arguments and responses slide past one another.

and second, to any indirect threat to respect for rights, including the creation of a social ethos that will encourage an inappropriate commodification of humans.

17   In line with this analysis, commentators have suggested that most of the human-rights concerns that are associated with human gene patents are relatively theoretical and "have to do with possible threats to human dignity, not violations of human dignity."[33] There is nothing about gene patenting *per se* that violates conventional, dignity-based rights (provided that each relevant individual is fully informed, and consents to the use of his/her genetic material and to the patenting of any inventions that follow from that use, there can be no direct infringement of human dignity).[34]

18   What about the indirect effects of gene patenting? Patents, it will be said, do help to facilitate the introduction of market forces in the context of human tissue.[35] If this led to a world in which humans were treated as a commodity, this would certainly infringe an almost uniformly accepted aspect of human dignity—the belief that humans should not be used as mere means. This is, however, a rather speculative concern. Indeed, unlike the consent issues that are associated with databanks, the dignity concerns are far more indefinite and are open to interpretation. As a result, it is easy to see why members of the human-rights community still disagree about the degree to which human gene patents create or promote an environment that will lead to the eventual commodification of humans.[35]

19   By contrast, the dignitarian alliance is not concerned with debating speculative, indirect, consequences. For them, patenting human genetic material in itself compromises human dignity.

20   Such a concern might be seen as being more symbolic. Although human gene patents might not directly implicate individual, dignity-based rights, gene patents are nonetheless inappropriate, the dignitarians reason, because they involve the commercialization of material that is representative of humanity—or, as recently noted by the Danish Council of Ethics, the "impermissible reduction of something vested with its own sovereign integrity."[36] This position is also consonant with article 1 of the UNESCO declaration, which states: "The human genome underlies the fundamental unity of all members of the human family, as well as the recognition of their inherent dignity and diversity. In a symbolic sense, it is the heritage of humanity."[37]

21   Such symbolic concerns about human dignity cannot be addressed by simply ensuring that all those who provide genetic material consent to the patenting process. The instrumentalization of human tissue is, for those who hold these concerns, a detriment in itself. Moreover, it might lead to a more widespread degradation of human dignity. The question for policy makers, then, is whether these concerns are sufficient justifications for dignity-based policy action in relation to gene patents.

22   Unlike the biobanking debate, this question requires more than a weighing of clear dignity-based rights (for example, self-determination) against utilitarian-based counter-arguments (for example, the social worth of gene patents as a means of stimulating the innovation process). The concerns can be traced to a broadly accepted principle that is associated with the idea of human dignity (for example, that it is unacceptable to treat humans as a commodity). However, these concerns are also tied to views that remain contentious. For example, numerous commentators have noted that: "it is not so much the legal status of the human person that is at issue as it is the status of the body and body parts. The two are not necessarily the same."[38] Indeed, not all agree that genes hold special symbolic value or that gene patents are a particularly problematic form of property.[33,39]

23   Until now, these dignity-based concerns have had little impact on patenting policy in relation to human genes.[40] The dignity-based recommendation by the Canadian Parliamentary Standing Committee was largely ignored. Even in the EC (European Commission) Directive on the Legal Protection of Biotechnological Inventions, where the morality exclusion against patentability (in article 6) is designed to satisfy dignitarian concerns, article 5(2) explicitly provides for the patentability of "an element isolated from the human body or otherwise produced by means of a technical process, including the sequence or partial sequence of a gene. . . ."[41] And, more generally in Europe, concerns about human dignity have done little to alter a relatively permissive gene-patent policy (France being the exception).

24   Dignity-based commodification concerns have had an effect on policies that relate to embryonic stem cell patents. Indeed, dignity and commodification interests are at the heart of recent decisions by the European Patent Office to exclude embryonic stem cell patents,[42] therefore signalling that, at least in Europe, dignitarian concerns can, despite their contentious nature, have a tangible impact on the development of patent policy.

Human cloning and stem cell research

25   As noted in the introduction, the concept of human dignity is increasingly used as a nonnegotiable, one-line, reason for prohibiting some proposed application of biotechnology. One of the most striking features of this dignitarian objection is a concern not that the technology might be unsafe or might be abused but that it might work. For the dignitarian alliance, the damage is done not when the biotechnology goes wrong but when it goes right. Nowhere do we find this more clearly highlighted than in the debates about human reproductive cloning.

26   The possibility of human reproductive cloning is almost universally condemned. Although there are numerous reasons why reproductive cloning is a bad idea, many official documents rely on the protection of human dignity as the primary reason for regulatory prohibition. For example, the recently adopted United Nations Declaration on Human Cloning calls on members "to prohibit all forms of human cloning inasmuch as they are incompatible with human dignity and the protection of human life."[43] The drafting of this declaration gives members at least three interpretive opportunities to narrow the scope of the cloning prohibition (by taking "inasmuch as" to mean 'to the extent that' rather than 'for the reason that'; by adopting the empowerment rather than the constraint conception of human dignity; and by reading human life through a human-rights lens).[44] But it was a concern for human dignity, understood as the dignitarian alliance has it, that provided the real momentum for this declaration.

27   Although all 191 members of the UN support a prohibition on human reproductive cloning, it has not been possible to achieve a consensus on the regulation of all uses of cloning technology (reproductive and therapeutic). When the UN General Assembly finally voted on the declaration there were only 84 members in favour, with 34 against and 37 abstentions. Although rival concepts of human dignity converge in relation to human reproductive cloning, the paths start to diverge once the question turns to the regulation of therapeutic cloning and human embryonic stem cell research.[9]

28   Around the world, various provisions have been made to regulate therapeutic cloning and the use of human embryos for research.[45] In some jurisdictions there are outright prohibitions; in others the position is permissive but heavily qualified (for example, restricting researchers to the use of human embryos left over from IVF treatment); and, in others, the regulation is relatively liberal (notably, in the United Kingdom the regulators have recently granted a licence to Ian Wilmut to undertake therapeutic cloning of human embryos with a view to understanding more about the early development of motor neuron disease).

29   Many factors contribute to generating particular regulatory responses. As a matter of principle, those regulators who take a permissive approach to therapeutic cloning and stem cell research see no negative impingement on human dignity. From a human-rights perspective this is an understandable position. There is no direct compromising of human dignity because the human embryo is not yet a bearer of human rights; eggs are collected and embryos are derived from rights-holders on the basis of their free and informed consent. Neither is there evidence of indirect threats to rights-holders or of researchers becoming more casual about respect for the rights of fellow rights-holders. By contrast, from the perspective of the dignitarian alliance, the destruction of human embryos to derive stem cells is a direct violation of human dignity.

Concluding remarks

30   The rhetoric of human dignity is widely used in debates about biotechnology policies. However, as we move away from the conventional, rights-based

concept of human dignity—which, to a large degree, is manifested in a respect for individual autonomy and self-determination—things become less clear. This is not to say that this is the only legitimate conception of human dignity, but it is the one that has the most universally accepted foundation—the inherent worth of all humans.

31   As we see from this discussion, the effect of a human-rights concept of dignity will differ depending on the context. In the area of biobanking, human dignity emphasizes the importance of individual consent, and, as a result, might frustrate attempts to create large, population-based, research initiatives. In the context of embryonic stem cell research, however, the use of a human-rights based view of dignity seems less appropriate—at least from the perspective of regulatory policy.

32   The policy-making role of human dignity becomes more questionable when it is used as a form of general condemnation. Indeed, there are two principal reasons (one concerning regulatory effectiveness, the other regulatory legitimacy) why it becomes ever more problematic to use human dignity as a basis for government action.

33   First, it is a pre-condition of effective regulation that the rationale and purpose of the regulation are clearly stated. However, so long as human dignity is a contested concept, which is open to different interpretations, regulatory references to "respect for human dignity" cannot possibly give a clear steer to regulators and regulatees. In a culture in which researchers and funding bodies are anxious to achieve regulatory compliance, such uncertainty can operate as a chilling factor—not to mention creating problems for those whose task it is to interpret and apply the regulation.

34   Second, most liberal democracies are pluralistic societies. If regulators declare a position that reflects the views of only the dignitarian alliance (for example, by prohibiting therapeutic cloning), this will seem partial and undemocratic—particularly if more compelling justifications are absent. This is not to say that the beliefs that inform this position are not legitimate (such as a belief in the moral status of the embryo). But they are not beliefs that are held by all. As such, not all will agree that human dignity is necessarily engaged. It seems likely that such an approach will affect the perceived legitimacy of the

regulatory response. For example, when President Bush says that embryonic stem cell research infringes human dignity, he is not making a statement to which all North Americans can sign up.

35   There is a further point that is implicit in these comments about the regulation of biotechnology in modern pluralistic democracies. If public debate is to be framed in terms of issues that relate to human dignity, the public will only become fully engaged with the key questions if the advocates of respect for human dignity are absolutely clear in declaring their meaning.[4]

36   In some regulatory arenas, however, the vagueness of human dignity is undoubtedly viewed as an asset—at least from a political perspective. Human dignity, precisely because it is understood in so many ways, facilitates the drafting of international aspirational statements. For example, when the General Conference of UNESCO resolved that preparatory work on a Declaration on Universal Norms on Bioethics should continue, it was agreed that it was "opportune and desirable to set universal standards in the field of bioethics with due regard for human dignity and human rights and freedoms, in the spirit of cultural pluralism inherent in bioethics." Predictably, from that point on, the drafters have persisted in underlining the importance of respect for human dignity. Not only that, the drafters might reasonably say that they resist attempts to clarify or concretize the concept of human dignity because they know that, once they try to do that, they risk losing either the human-rights constituency or the dignitarian alliance. In some contexts, then, human dignity might be seen to function as a constructive ambiguity, keeping rival constituencies on board.[46]

37   Given the potential for fudging, equivocation, and confusion, would human-rights theorists be better off without human dignity? Clearly we should continue to re-examine the ways in which genetic research challenges our fundamental ethical concepts, such as the current paramountcy of autonomy and self-determination. For example, many commentators have made compelling arguments that genetic research, particularly in relation to biobanking and population genetics, raises questions about the adequacy and appropriateness of existing consent models.[47] These are important questions. But in a

community that is committed to human rights (which is how liberal democracies are framed), could such questions be effectively addressed without having to excavate the idea of human dignity?

38   Against such a temptation, various considerations might give us pause. The cause of human rights would be done few favours if the idea of human dignity were to be handed over to the dignitarian alliance. Not only would this abrogate a fundamental part of the history of human rights, it would mean that in debates such as those that concern gene patenting, cloning, and stem cells, the only apologists for human dignity would be the dignitarian alliance. In addition, human-rights theorists still need to offer a convincing account of the sense in which human rights are predicated on respect for human dignity. For some commentators in the human-rights tradition, modern biotechnology might present longer-term dangers to a rights-respecting community and more attention to human dignity might help to clarify our thinking at this level.[48,49]

39   In the end, the ambiguity that surrounds the concept of human dignity makes its value as a regulatory tool relatively limited. For example, without more content about how and why human dignity is engaged, documents such as the UNESCO declaration[29] will provide only minimal guidance to researchers and policy makers. Indeed, when it is claimed that a given research activity infringes human dignity, our first reaction should be to ask for specifics as to why this is so. Is the concern based on a morally contested social value, such as the moral status of the embryo, or a more universally accepted view, such as the inherent worth of all humans? In a pluralistic society, there needs to be room to discuss and debate all perspectives that inform the content of human dignity. However, not all perspectives should serve as a justification for science policy.

40   The concept of human dignity has been part of bioethics for decades. And, rightly or not, it seems likely to remain a central theme in future debates about controversial biotechnologies. But for it to be a legitimate, useful policy tool, regulators need to be clear about how and why human dignity is implicated. Without such clarity, the concept of human dignity is in danger of devolving into a hollow rhetorical slogan.

Nature. 2006. January (6).

Notes

1. Fukuyama, F. *Our Posthuman Future* (Profile Books, New York, 2002).
2. The President's Council on Bioethics. Human cloning and human dignity: an ethical inquiry. *The President's Council on Bioethics web site* [online], <www. bioethics.gov/reports/cloningreport/fullreport.html> (2002).
3. Caulfield, T. Human cloning laws, human dignity and the poverty of the policy making dialogue. *BMC Med. Ethics* 4, e3 (2003).
4. Verspieren, P. in *The Discourse of Human Dignity* (eds A mmicht-Quinn, R. *et al.*) 13–22 (SCM Press, London, 2003).
5. Brownsword, R. in *Human Rights* (ed. Brownsword, R.) 203–234 (Hart, Oxford, 2004).
6. Bush, G.W. President Bush calls on Senate to back human cloning ban; remarks by the President on human cloning legislation. *The White House web site* [online], <www.whitehouse.gov/news/releases/2   002/04/20020410-4.html> (2002).
7. Macklin, R. Dignity is a useless concept. *Br. Med. J.* 327, 1419–1420 (2003).
8. Caulfield, T. & Chapman, A. Human dignity as a criterion for science policy. *PLoS Med. 2*, e244 (2005).
9. Brownsword, R. Stem cells and cloning: where the regulatory consensus fails. *New Engl. Law Rev.* 39, 535–571 (2005).
10. Beyleveld, D. & Brownsword, R. *Human Dignity in Bioethics and Biolaw* (Oxford Univ. Press, Oxford, 2001).
11. Brownsword, R. Three bioethical approaches: a triangle to be squared. *The international conference on the patentability of biotechnology* [online], <www. ipgenethics.org/conference/transcript/session3.doc> (2004).
12. Horton, R. Rediscovering human dignity. *Lancet* 364, 1081–1085 (2004).
13. Shannon, T. Grounding human dignity. *Dialog* 43, 113–117 (2004).
14. Shultziner, D. Human dignity—functions and meanings. *Global Jurist Topics* 3, 1–21 (2003).
15. Harris, J. & Sulston, J. Genetic equity. *Nature Rev. Genet.* 5, 796–800 (2004).
16. Arnason, G., Nordel, S. & Arnason, V. (eds) *Blood and Data: Ethical, Legal and Social Aspects of Human Genetics Databases* (Univ. Iceland Press and Centre for Ethics, Reykjavik, 2004).
17. Cambon-Thomsen, A. The social and ethical issues of post-genomic human biobanks. *Nature Rev. Genet.* 5, 866–873 (2004).
18. Austin, M. A., Harding, S. & McElroy, C. Genebanks: a comparison of eight proposed international genetic databases. *Community Genet.* 6, 37–45 (2003).
19. UNESCO. *Draft Report on Collection, Treatment, Storage and Use of Genetic Data* (UNESCO, Paris, 2001).

20. Gertz, R. An analysis of the Icelandic Supreme Court judgement on the Health Sector Database Act. *SCRIPT-ed* **1**, 290–306 (2004).

21. World Health Organization. *Genetic Databases: Assessing the Benefits and the Impact on Human and Patient Rights* (World Health Organization, Geneva, 2003).

22. Medical Research Council of Canada *et al.* Tri-council policy statement: ethical conduct for research involving humans. *Interagency Advisory Panel on Research Ethics web site* [online], <www.pre.ethics.gc.ca/english/policystatement/policystatement.cfm> (1998; with 2000, 2002, 2005 ammendments).

23. World Medical Association. *Declaration of Helsinki—Ethical Principles for Medical Research Involving Human Subjects* (World Medical Association, Edinburgh, 2000).

24. *Reibl v. Hughes*, 114 DLR 3rd 1 Supreme Court of Canada (1980).

25. Australian Law Reform Commission. Genes and ingenuity: gene patenting and human health. *ALRC Report 99* [online], <www.austlii.edu.au/au/other/alrc/publications/reports/99/> (2004).

26. Brownsword, R. The *Relaxin* opposition revisited. *Jahrb. Recht Ethik; Annu. Rev. Law Ethics* **9**, 3–19 (2001).

27. Dworkin, G. Should there be property rights in genes? *Philos. Trans. R. Soc. Lond. B* **352**, 1077–1086 (1997).

28. Standing Committee on Health. Assisted reproduction: building families. *House of Commons, Canada* [online], <www.parl.gc.ca/InfoComDoc/37/1/HEAL/Studies/Reports/healrp01e.htm> (2001).

29. UNESCO International Bioethics Committee. *Universal Declaration on the Human Genome and Human Rights* (UNESCO, Paris, 1997).

30. Dickenson, D. The new French resistance: commodification rejected? *Med. Law Int.* **7**, 41–63 (2005).

31. Gold, R. Owning our bodies: an examination of property law and biotechnology. *San Diego Law Rev.* **32**, 1167–1247 (1995).

32. *Howard Florey v. Relaxin*, EPOR 541 (opposition division) (1995).

33. Resnik, D.B. DNA patents and human dignity. *J. Law Med. Ethics* **29**, 152–165 (2001).

34. Beyleveld, D. & Brownsword, R. Human dignity, human rights, and human genetics. *Mod. Law Rev.* **61**, 661–680 (1998).

35. Brown, B. The case for caution—being protective of human dignity in the face of corporate forces taking title to our DNA. *J. Law Med. Ethics* **29**, 166–169 (2001).

36. Danish Council on Ethics. *Patenting Human Genes and Stem Cells* (Danish Council on Ethics, Copenhagen, 2004).

37. UNESCO International Bioethics Committee. *International Declaration on Human Genetic Data* (UNESCO, Paris, 2003).

38. Gilmour, J. 'Our' bodies: property rights in human tissue. *Can. J. Law Soc.* **8**, 113 –138 (1993).

39. Kieff, F. S. Perusing property rights in DNA. *Adv. Genet.* **50**, 125–151; discussion 507–510 (2003).

40. Caulfield, T., Gold, E.R. & Cho, M.K. Patenting human genetic material: refocusing the debate. *Nature Rev. Genet.* **1**, 227–231 (2000).

41. Beyleveld, D., Brownsword, R. & Llewelyn, M. in *Pharmaceutical Medicine, Biotechnology and European Law* (eds Goldberg, R. & Lonbay, J.) 157–181 (Cambridge Univ. Press, New York, 2000).

42. European Group on Ethics in Science and New Technologies. *The Ethical Aspects of Patenting Inventions Involving Human Stem Cells: Opinion to the European Commission* (European Group on Ethics in Science and New Technologies, Brussels, 2002).

43. Fifty-Ninth General Assembly. General Assembly adopts United Nations Declaration on Human Cloning by vote of 84-34-37. *82nd Meeting (AM) Press Release* [online], <www.un.org/News/ Press/docs/2005/ga10333.doc.htm> (2005).

44. Brownsword, R. in *The Impact of Biotechnologies on Human Rights* (ed. Francioni, F.) (Hart, Oxford, 2006).

45. Pattinson, S.D. & Caulfield, T. Variations and voids: the regulation of human cloning around the world. *BMC Med. Ethics* **5**, e9 (2004).

46. Wijnberg, B. Intergovernmental activities in bioethics worldwide. *8th European Conference of National Ethics Committees* [online], <www.coe.int/T/E/ Legal_affairs/Legal _co-operation/Bioethics/COMETH/ACTES%208e%20COMETH.pdf> (2005).

47. Chadwick R. & Berg, K. Solidarity and equity: new ethical frameworks for genetic databases. *Nature Rev. Genet.* **2**, 318–321 (2001).

48. Habermas, J. *The Future of Human Nature* (Polity Press, Malden, Massachusetts, 2003).

49. Brownsword, R. Regulating human genetics: new dilemmas for a new millennium. *Med. Law Rev.* **12**, 14–39 (2004).

Acknowledgements

T.C. would like to thank M. Sharp for his insight and help, the anonymous reviewers for the useful comments and Genome Canada, the Stem Cell Network and the Alberta Heritage Foundation for Medical Research for funding support.

KEY AND CHALLENGING WORDS

autonomy, utilitarian, palatable, pluralistic, probabilistic, quandary, iteration, autonomous, commodification, ethos, consonant, detriment, contentious, jurisdiction, advocates (n.), opportune, equivocation, paramountcy, excavate, abrogate, apologist, predicate

QUESTIONS

1. What do the authors see as the main problem in coming up with a definition of human dignity? How has the problem affected the field of bioethics?

2. What two distinct approaches or viewpoints are major "players" in the bioethics debate today? Summarize these contrastive viewpoints in one sentence each.

3. What is the authors' thesis? Referring to specific passages in the introduction, consider the authors' objectivity. (You can consider their statements and sources, as well as linguistic matters, such as word choice.)

4. Why did the authors use the order of points that they did, starting with biobanks?

5. Why could the use of precedent be especially appropriate in this essay (see p. 120)?

6. Analyze the effectiveness of the authors' attempts to represent the two sides of the debate about gene patenting in paragraphs 15–21; refer to specific strategies promoting coherence.

7. What is the significance of "The *Relaxin* opposition" (Box 2) to the gene patent debate? Paraphrase the authors' analysis in the third paragraph of Box 2.

8. How do the authors undercut the "dignitarian" approach in paragraph 25?

9. Come up with a heading to replace "Concluding remarks" that would sum up this section's main focus. Summarize paragraph 36.

10. What rhetorical purpose is served by the following statement in paragraph 34: "This is not to say that the beliefs that inform [the dignitarian alliance] position are not legitimate"? Find other statements in the concluding and/or introductory sections of the essay that serve a similar function.

11. At the end of their essay, the authors acknowledge funding from three sources. Access one of the first two sources given below under "Websites of interest" in order to determine the purpose and reliability of the organization. Do either of these factors affect your reading of the essay? Why or why not?

POST-READING

1. Reconsider your original definition in pre-reading question 2, ensuring that it is applicable to concepts in biotechnology today, such as stem cell research.

2. Analyze the essay from a rhetorical and stylistic standpoint, considering the presentation and effectiveness of the argument. What specific strategies were used? In general, do you think the authors were able to express their points objectively and fairly?

3. In groups, a) discuss the following question: "[W]ould human-rights theorists be better off without human dignity?" (paragraph 37) OR b) discuss practical approaches to the human dignity debate that could help it become a useful tool in future regulation.

RELATED WEBSITES OF INTEREST

Genome Canada:
www.genomecanada.ca/

Stem Cell Network:
www.stemcellnetwork.ca/

UK Biobank:
www.ukbiobank.ac.uk

UN Website: *The Universal Declaration of Human Rights:*
www.un.org/en/documents/udhr/index.shtml

UNESCO.ORG: *Universal Declaration on the Human Genome and Human Rights:*
http://portal.unesco.org/en/ev.php-URL_ID=13177&URL_DO=DO_TOPIC&URL_SECTION=201.html

Where are we going with preimplantation genetic diagnosis?

Timothy Krahn

(1,591 words)

Pre-reading

1. Using a reliable source, such as a medical encyclopedia or dictionary or an online source like IVF Canada (www.ivfcanada.com/services/index.cfm), find background information on pre-implantation genetic diagnosis (PGD) and related areas (e.g., in-vitro fertilization, assisted reproduction). Come up with a one-sentence definition (paraphrase) of PGD and include a citation.

1   In Canada, preimplantation genetic diagnosis is governed by the Assisted Human Reproduction Act,[1] which received royal assent on 29 March 2004. Regulations for preimplantation genetic diagnosis in accordance with the act are currently being developed after a series of ongoing public consultations. To regulate uncertain and controversial public policy issues, such as assisted human reproduction, the Canadian government has an established history of taking its bearings from the best practises, policy precedents, and relevant regulatory structures in the United Kingdom.[2,3] In light of this history, it is fitting for us to pay attention to recent developments in the United Kingdom.

2   On 10 May 2006, the United Kingdom's Human Fertilisation and Embryology Authority published its decision to license preimplantation genetic diagnosis for hereditary breast and ovarian cancer (BRCA1 and BRCA2 mutations) and hereditary non-polyposis colorectal cancer.[4] These conditions

are distinct from those previously licensed to be tested for in the United Kingdom because of a combination of 3 factors: they have a later age of onset, they are lower penetrance conditions (up to 80 per cent,[5] compared to the previous threshold of more than 90 per cent penetrance[6]) and they are potentially treatable. Before this decision, the Human Fertilisation and Embryology Authority had licensed preimplantation genetic diagnosis for conditions for which 1, or at most 2, of these 3 factors applied. By permitting preimplantation genetic diagnosis for these hereditary adult-onset cancers, the Human Fertilisation and Embryology Authority has effectively downgraded its criteria for "significant risk of being affected by a serious inherited genetic condition."[7] The purpose of this commentary is to consider the moral dangers associated with this ruling in terms of its potential resonating effects on the normative fabric of our culture.

3   In much of the Western world, where parents are having fewer children, where some parents are having children after the experience of infertility and where prenatal diagnosis and preimplantation genetic diagnosis are promoted as part of good prenatal care, we are developing a culture that is overly directed by the interests of some well-intentioned, but perhaps misguided, prospective parents (and possibly more exacting clinicians) committed to having healthy children. The underlying beliefs are as follows: Because parents are having fewer children, it is both common sense and in the best interests of the children that they be given the "best" genetic prospects. Moreover, from a societal perspective, if the health care system and social services are unable to assume the full burden of treating serious genetic conditions, then it seems only just that the present generation uses all reasonable means of preventing these conditions. Indeed, such reasoning probably explains a certain societal sympathy for people who want to test their embryos for potentially heritable conditions. The moral danger does not lie with the people who seek the testing; rather, the danger lies in how this testing could promote further stigmatization of and discrimination against people with "genetic impairments"[8–10] or their parents.[11] Indeed, testing could entrench a culture of prevention and perfectionism and promote a culture of intolerance.

4   As the number of genetic tests for conditions with lower penetrance increases and these tests become more widely available, parents may have increased expectations of having "normal and healthy" (i.e., unaffected) offspring. This desire could subtly shift parents' attitudes toward their embryos (and eventually their children) if their embryos are treated more and more like consumer products subject to a process of quality control.

5   One serious limitation of preimplantation genetic diagnosis is that it focuses narrowly on evidence of genetic anomalies (deviations from the norm that may not even be expressed). The risk is that evidence of genetic conditions or predispositions may become the overriding or sole factor in the process of embryo selection and that decision-makers may value only that which they can test for as dictated by the current state of available technology. In the end, this practice of selecting against certain genetic characteristics could further upgrade the standards of "normality" and compress the spectrum of "healthy," with the result that many human imperfections might become "less tolerated and less likely to be accepted as normal human variation."[12]

6   Widespread efforts at prevention and perfectionism could seed a culture of intolerance. Of particular concern is the risk of exacerbating social problems for people with conditions for which genetic testing is available. Increases could be seen in resources that are directed at finding ways to diagnose and screen embryos for genetic conditions by preimplantation genetic diagnosis. Correspondingly, reductions could be seen in resources to provide health care support and treatment for people living with these same conditions.[13,14] Even the practice of labelling and singling out certain genetic conditions as "serious" and therefore test-worthy holds the danger of giving medical validation to some of our deepest fears and prejudices about what it is to live with, or to support people with, cognitive or physical impairments. Some have even suggested that we cannot brake on this slippery slope by applying more stringent criteria of what counts as a significant risk for a "serious" genetic condition (i.e., a condition valued negatively by the medical profession and society that is deemed worthy of screening against for reasons that extend beyond parental preference). From

this perspective, to better avoid the prejudice and stigmatization of "impairment" associated with screening for serious conditions, it may be preferable to have parental choice alone as the sole justification required for screening. Otherwise, by marking off a special class of genetic conditions as serious we risk making it seem like the decision against having a child with a "serious" condition is prima facie more legitimate than the decision to resist this entrenched prejudice in our society.[14]

7   The recent decision by the Human Fertilisation and Embryology Authority has put us on an undetermined path where we could lose sight of, or even come to have contempt for, people who are "genetically disadvantaged." Given what we as Canadians can learn from British policy and practice in these matters, we need to ask ourselves: Where are we going with these new genetic technologies? Should we be so sanguine about having preimplantation genetic diagnosis take us there? What are we sacrificing to gain control over genetic conditions? Doesn't authentic control include knowing not only where to start, but also where to stop?

8   As archeologists know, future generations can learn about the values and norms of previous generations as much by examining their garbage as by examining their achievements. Given this analogy, what might our descendants learn about our culture by observing not only which policy choices are taken up, but also by which ones are discarded? Abby Lippman reminds us that "There are choices to be made and the choices will reflect our values and ideology. How we choose our culture (by the routes we take) is no less problematic than how we choose our children, and consequences from both will be among our legacies."[15] We would do well to heed her admonition.

CMAJ. 2007. May 176 (10).

*

Acknowledgements: I would like to thank Françoise Baylis, Olga Kits, and Lynette Reid for their comments on earlier drafts of this commentary.

This work was supported by a grant from the Canadian Institutes of Health Research (CIHR).

References

1. Assisted Human Reproduction Act, *SC* 2004, c 2, S10(2), 40(1).
2. Jones M, Salter B, Pigeon N. RES-000-22-0987 – Policy transfer in risk governance: lessons from the UK biotechnology framework. London (UK): Economic and Social Research Council; 2006. Available: www.esrcsocietytoday.ac.uk/ESRCInfoCentre/Plain_English_Summaries/work_organisation/innovation_change/index27.aspx?ComponentId=15624&SourcePageId=1707 (accessed 2007 Mar 30).
3. Jones M. What can one nation learn from another? Exploring policy choice in the new Canadian framework for assisted human reproduction. London (UK): BioNews.org.uk; 2005 Oct 3. Available: www.bionews.org.uk/commentary.lasso?storyid=2765 (accessed 2007 Mar 16).
4. Human Fertilisation and Embryology Authority. Authority decision on the use of PGD for lower penetrance, later onset inherited conditions. London (UK):The Authority; 2006. Available: www.hfea.gov.uk/docs/The_Authority_decision__Choices_and_boundaries.pdf (accessed 2007 April 2).
5. Human Fertilisation and Embryology Authority. Choices & boundaries report 2006: a summary of responses to the HFEA public discussion. London (UK): The Authority; 2006. Available: www.hfea.gov.uk/cps/rde/xbcr/SID-3F57D79B-8FC36EC9/hfea/Choices_and_boundaries_Report_2006.pdf (accessed 2007 Mar 9).
6. Human Fertilisation and Embryology Authority. Choices and boundaries: Should people be able to select embryos free from an inherited susceptibility to cancer? London (UK): The Authority; 2005. Available: www.hfea.gov.uk/cps/rde/xbcr/SID-3F57D79B-5A0CC17F/hfea/Choices_and_Boundaries.pdf (accessed 2007 Mar 30).
7. Human Fertilisation and Embryology Authority. Code of practice. 6th ed. London (UK): The Authority; 2003. Available: www.hfea.gov.uk/cps/rde/xbcr/SID-3F57D79B-FAAAF985/hfea/Code_of_Practice_Sixth_Edition_-_final.pdf (accessed 2007 Mar 9).
8. Harris M, Winship I, Spriggs M. Controversies and ethical issues in cancer-genetics clinics. *Lancet Oncol* 2005;6: 301-10.
9. Asch A. Disability equality and prenatal testing: Contradictory or compatible? *Fla State Univ Law Rev* 2003;30: 315-42.
10. Matloff ET, Shappell H, Brierley K, et al. What would you do? Specialists' perspectives on cancer genetic testing, prophylactic surgery and insurance discrimination. *J Clin Oncol* 2000;18:2484-92.
11. Marteau TM, Drake H. Attributions for disability: the influence of genetic screening. *Soc Sci Med* 1995;40: 1127–32.
12. Beeson D. Social and ethical challenges of prenatal diagnosis. Med Ethics (Burlington, Mass) 2000 Winter;1–2,8.

Available: www.lahey.org/Pdf/Ethics/Winter_2000.pdf
(accessed 2007 Mar 30).

13. Holtzman NA, Shapiro D. Genetic testing and public
policy. *BMJ* 1998;316:852–6.

14. Wasserman D, Asch A. American Medical Association. The
uncertain rationale for prenatal disability screening. Virtual
Mentor. 2006; 8: 53–56. Available: www.ama-assn.org/ama/
pub/category/print/15809.html (accessed 2007 Mar 9).

15. Lippman A. Prenatal genetic testing and screening: constructing needs and reinforcing inequities. *Am J Law Med*
1991;17:15–50.

KEY AND CHALLENGING WORDS

normative, stigmatization, entrench, anomaly, exacerbate, stringent, sanguine, admonition

QUESTIONS

1. What is Krahn's purpose in mentioning the date of the
   Assisted Human Reproduction Act and the current
   (2007) public consultations? How could the decision of
   the UK's Human Fertilisation and Embryology Authority
   affect Canadians?

2. Identify the author's thesis and account for its placement
   in the essay.

3. In paragraph 3, Krahn addresses the opposing viewpoint. Do you think he discusses these views reasonably
   and impartially? Do you believe this discussion helps his
   argument or weakens it? Why?

4. Several hypothetical outcomes of focusing too much on
   genetic anomalies are mentioned in paragraph 6. Taking
   one of these possible outcomes, in a minimum of one
   paragraph evaluate its plausibility or validity.

5. Why does the author state "it may be preferable to have
   parental choice alone as the sole justification required
   for screening" (paragraph 6)?

6. Who is Abby Lippman, quoted in the essay's final paragraph? Do you think the ending is effective? Why or why
   not?

7. Analyze the effectiveness of Krahn's argument overall by
   considering such factors as the essay's organization,
   points, and support, the use of emotional or ethical
   appeals, or logical or emotional fallacies.

POST-READING

1. *Collaborative activity:* What are other controversial issues
   related to in-vitro fertilization that you have heard of?
   The discussion could focus on several of these issues, or
   one of the related issues could be debated (e.g., Beautiful
   People.com website).

2. *Collaborative or individual activity:* In a 2009 article (referenced below) in the same journal where Krahn's essay
   was published, the authors provide an overview of issues
   related to the genetic diagnosis of embryos, arguing that
   exaggerated rhetoric or unfounded fears could impact
   research and public policy. Do you believe that this article undermines or calls into doubt Krahn's argument?

3. Using the criteria for determining source credibility discussed on pp. 145–147, evaluate one of the following
   secondary sources mentioned in Krahn's essay: Beeson,
   D. Social and ethical challenges of prenatal diagnosis;
   available: www.lahey.org/Pdf/Ethics/Winter_2000.pdf;
   or Wasserman D., & Asch A. The uncertain rationale for
   prenatal disability screening; Available: www.ama-assn.
   org/ama/pub/category/print/15809.html.

RELATED WEBSITES OF INTEREST

Assisted Human Reproduction Canada:

www.ahrc-pac.gc.ca/index.php?lang=eng

Novel Tech Ethics, Dalhousie University:

www.noveltechethics.ca/

ADDITIONAL LIBRARY READING

Bouffard, C., Viville, S., & Knoppers, B.M. (2009). Genetic diagnosis of embryos: Clear explanation, not rhetoric, is needed. *CMAJ, 181*, 6–7. doi:10.1503/cmaj.080658.

It may also be available online at www.cmaj.ca/cgi/content/full/181/6-7/387

Handyside, A. (2010). Let parents decide. *Nature, 464*, 978–979.

Psychology's essential role in alleviating the impacts of climate change

Robert Gifford

(5,347 words)

Pre-reading

1. Scan the abstract, introduction, and headings in order to determine the essay's purpose (expository or argumentative?) and intended audience. From this information, formulate a reading hypothesis.
2. How might the IPCC Report, mentioned in the first sentence, have affected the timing of Gifford's essay?

Climate change is occurring: where is psychology? The conventional wisdom is that amelioration of the impacts of climate change is a matter for earth and ocean science, economics, technology, and policy-making. This article presents the basis for psychological science as a key part of the solution to the problem and describes the challenges to this both from within psychology and from other points of view. Minimizing the personal and environmental damage caused by climate change necessarily is a multidisciplinary task, but one to which psychology not only should, but must contribute more than it has so far.

Keywords: climate change, role of psychology, Canada

*

1   By now, the issue of whether or not climate change is occurring has been resolved for quite some time, and the fourth report of the Intergovernmental

Panel on Climate Change (IPCC), in November 2007 has reiterated its conclusion. It is happening. Some may wish to debate the relative extent of natural and human causes of the change, but little doubt exists that human activities have been, and continue to be, one important force driving climate change. One can imagine that climate change might have some positive consequences for some people in some places, but according to many experts, climate change already is having, and will have many more, negative consequences for many people in many places.

2   The present thesis is that psychology, in concert with other disciplines, has an important role to play in easing the pain caused by climate change. Were this thesis widely recognized, the present article would be unnecessary. Unfortunately, the thesis is not broadly acknowledged. Anecdotally, I can report that I sat through a recent meeting of scientists from a variety of disciplines concerned with climate change and heard a leading natural scientist state that the large interdisciplinary grant proposal being discussed should not include any input from "fluff," by which he apparently meant the social sciences. More formally, the emerging discipline of sustainability science, clearly a first cousin to climate-change studies, has been advocated and defined by some authors (e.g., Clark & Dickson, 2003) without the slightest reference to possible contributions by psychologists. Are these assertions and omissions justified?

A Bit of Background

3   Each person on the planet, whether as an individual or as part of an organization, curates a stream of natural resources that are converted into products; the conversion process often creates greenhouse gases. Thus, as psychologists have long recognized, the fundamental unit of analysis for the human-caused portion of climate change is the person (Ehrlich & Kennedy, 2005; Gifford, 1987). Thus, ultimately, amelioration of that part of environmental problems such as climate change over which we have some potential control occurs at the individual level (Clayton & Brook, 2005).

4   Psychologists have long been concerned with individuals' behaviour that contributes to climate change.[1] In particular, environmental psychology, a child of 1960s idealism, was conceived to solve environment-related problems through scientific evidence-based research. Research on energy conservation and other environmental problems has been going on for 35 years (e.g., Buckhout, 1972; Pallak & Cummings, 1976; Seligman & Darley, 1977). Derived in part from Kurt Lewin's mantra that nothing is so practical as a good theory, it has always been an approach that seeks to combine quality research with applications aimed at personal and organizational change. In doing so, it has developed a wide range of theories, models, and principles that can be used to design action research techniques for changing behaviour (e.g., Bechtel & Churchman, 2002; Gifford, 2007). A stream of special issues in journals on environmental problems has appeared since the 1980s (see Vlek & Steg, 2007, for a list), and they are the tip of an iceberg that includes hundreds of individual journal articles. In 40 years of existence, environmental psychologists have developed an extensive toolbox of ideas and techniques (e.g., Bechtel, Marans, & Michelson, 1987). They are based on hundreds of articles published in its two primary journals, the *Journal of Environmental Psychology* and *Environment and Behaviour*, and numerous allied journals, which form a very extensive information base for designing programmes and solutions to a variety of problems (Gifford, 2002b), including sustainability problems.

So Why Then Has Psychology Not Been a Climate-Change Player?

5   Discourse on climate change in the media and amongst policy-makers is virtually silent on the role of psychology. The conventional wisdom in the wider world of climate-change thought is that psychology has no important role to play. Why?

---

[1] Ironically, this probably precedes the concern for climate change on the part of most of the 2000 or so natural scientists whose work was used by the Intergovernmental Panel on Climate Change, and thus basked in the shared glory of the 2007 Nobel Prize, with the notable exception of Al Gore himself.

6   First, we must lay the blame in part on our selves. Psychology, in general, has been accused of ignoring the environment by treating people as if they existed in a vacuum (nicely embodied in the blank four walls of the laboratory). As noted by Kidner (1994), the psychological scientist too often "perpetuates and legitimizes a world view in which the individual is seen as separate from the environment" (p. 362). Even environmental psychologists have largely kept their focus on individual-level influences on environment-related behaviour: values, attitudes, motives, intentions, goals, social comparison, habits, and similar constructs. We have left the making of connections between these constructs—which *are* important, and policy—which is essential—to others. We write in our discussion sections that "someone" should take into account these important findings of ours. However, unfortunately, for the most part policymakers and natural scientists do not read our discussion sections. This is one reason sustainability science can be defined without reference to psychology.

7   Second, the kinds of effort needed to combat the consequences of climate change do not suit the academic context in which most established psychologists work. In this forum I need not elaborate on the ways and means needed to find an academic position, earn tenure, and win grants: usually it is to conduct many parametric experiments in laboratories with those handy introductory psychology students. This is not to blame graduate students and young PhDs who find themselves in this situation: the levers to success were not created by them.

8   Third, most policymakers in ministries and departments concerned with environmental problems were not trained in the behavioural sciences. Reser and Bentrupperbaumer (2001) estimate that functionaries in resource-related government agencies and departments trained in the natural sciences outnumber those trained in the social sciences by at least 50 to 1. With less or no social-science experience, these policymakers are unlikely to understand what the social sciences have to offer, and even if they were sympathetic to the idea, they would have difficulty understanding many of the concepts and results. This leads to fundamental misunderstandings of such concepts as values, valuation, and social impacts (Reser & Bentrupperbaumer, 2001). Some excellent

but isolated progress has been made toward finding ways for natural and social scientists to communicate (e.g., Miller, 1985), but uneven numbers and inadequate communication and understanding remain serious problems.

9   Fourth, the role of psychology in climate change has so far been particularly neglected in Canada. Although discourse on the role of psychological science and climate change has been less than robust anywhere, it has at least existed in the United States and Germany (Oskamp, 2000; Schmuck & Schultz, 2002; Stern, 1993), Australia (Reser, 2007), the Netherlands (Vlek, 2000), Sweden (Lundqvist & Biel, 2007), and the United Kingdom (Uzzell, 2007). I am unaware of any substantive previous discussion of psychology's role by a Canadian psychologist concerning the Canadian context. The leading proponent of environmental action in Canada was trained as a geneticist in a fruit-fly lab. How can psychologists expect to be players when we are silent?

The Basis for Psychology's Role

10   Each person, whether an average citizen or a CEO, has some level of choice and control over sustainability-related behaviours and actions. As Paul Stern (2005) has pointed out, these choices often are heavily constrained by contextual factors and one's own habits. Stern posits a hierarchical set of forces in which structural factors above or external to the individual usually are much more powerful influences on behaviour than individual-level influences.

11   Although one must acknowledge the power of context, and that Stern's hierarchy often accurately describes environmental behaviour choices, I maintain that individuals truly are the ultimate key to climate-change amelioration: policies, programmes, and regulations themselves do not change anything. For one thing, to be acceptable and efficacious to individuals; policies must be "bought into" by individuals. In short, policy beckons or even commands, but persons accept or refuse its demands. Behavioural change does not occur until this happens.

12   Many people do resist the temptation to engage in self-serving behaviours that contribute to climate change. Yet, admittedly, many do yield to the

temptation. What will it take to change these people's behaviour? As a start—but only a start—understanding environment-related motivations, attitudes, social and organizational perceptions, rationales, biases, habits, barriers to change, life-context, and trust in government will help. Certainly, psychologists are already engaged in the effort on their own. For example, some have investigated the psychological dimensions of global warming (e.g., Dresner, 1989–90; Heath & Gifford, 2006; Nilsson, von Borgstede, & Biel, 2004). However, the major thesis of the present article is that we psychologists must do more.

13   I do not wish to argue that environmental psychology is, or even could be, a stand-alone panacea. For example, Schmuck and Vlek (2003) advocate that we work more closely with environmental scientists. However, I believe that we must work with at least four other groups to be effective: natural scientists, technical experts, policy experts, and local citizens' committees.

14   Fortunately, environmental psychologists have a history of interdisciplinary collaboration, beginning with geography and architecture, embodied in the collaborations between Robert Sommer, Humphry Osmond, and Kiyo Izumi in 1950s Saskatchewan (Sommer, 1983), or between Raymond Studer and David Stea in the United States (1966). More recently, and more pertinent to current concerns, fruitful collaborative work is being done in sustainability research (e.g., Schoot Uiterkamp & Vlek, 2007), including some collaborations that represent new bridges. Schoot Uiterkamp and Vlek (2007) describe five instances of collaborations, and their account is particularly valuable for its advice about the practicalities of engaging in multidisciplinary studies. This collaboration trend has been influenced, one suspects, by policies at national and international grant agencies that, for better or worse, virtually require interdisciplinary collaboration. In terms of influencing policy, collaborative efforts not only have "face credibility" based on the very breadth of their approach, but also success that is legitimately based on the increased validity of policy suggestions that emerge from studying a given problem with multiple valuable perspectives.

15   Gattig and Hendrickx (2007) bring perspectives from economics and behavioural decision theory into the mix. Discounting, the tendency to reduce the importance of an outcome with greater "distance" (temporally, socially, geographically, and probabilistically), is seen to be an important component of thinking about sustainability-related thinking. Fortunately, environmental problems appear to be less subject to discounting than some other matters. Although they incorporate some concepts from economics, Gattig and Hendrickx demonstrate why using those concepts in the same way that traditional economists do could lead to ineffective policies (cf. Stern, 1986). "Rational" discount rates are not the same as those of the public which, to its credit, seems to discount environmental impacts less than in other domains. This helps to illustrate why other disciplines need psychology as much as psychology needs them.

16   Turning the policy issue upside down, some psychologists are examining the effects of policy strategies, as opposed to conducting studies that they hope will inform policy. Jager and Mosler (2007) are amongst those who use modeling to understand the outcomes of different policy choices. This form of active modeling offers the attractive advantage of trying out various policies before they are implemented and understanding why they might or might not work, thereby potentially avoiding expensive mistakes in policy-making. As Jager and Mosler point out, modeling can also be used to train policymakers. The very act of modeling encourages the idea that many policy alternatives exist, when often only a few may occur to a policymaker.

Technosalvation?

17   Technology is often promoted as the solution to many problems, including those related to climate change. Amongst these are biofuels, wind power, and solar power. Suspicion about the value of technology (e.g., Frank, 1966; Osborn, 1948) is longstanding and is justifiable in part. For example, growing biofuels requires the use of pesticides, reduces biodiversity, creates atmospheric pollution when burned, and has already caused large increases in food prices. Wind power creates noise, kills many birds, is unsightly, and negatively affects the rural lifestyle. Solar power requires the manufacture of photovoltaic

cells, which creates a waste stream of cadmium, lead, and other heavy metal by-products. The downside of technology (pollution, health impacts, landfill contributions, accidents, energy consumed in production, and impacts on flora and fauna) is often overlooked in the touting of its benefits. As just one example that is not widely recognized, air pollution kills about 800,000 people each year (Kenworthy & Laube, 2002), and most air pollution is caused by technology in one form or another.

18   Of course, technology has another side to it, and as Midden, Kaiser, and McCalley (2007) clearly show, psychological scientists must deal with it because it is very unlikely to go away. It will not disappear because, despite its negative effects on people and the environment, it undoubtedly has improved the quality of life for millions of other people, particularly when one thinks in terms of decades and centuries past (Simon, 1981). Assuming individuals have the motivation and appropriate skills, technology can assist in the goal of reducing greenhouse gas emissions. However, Midden et al.'s (2007) quite valid point is that the mere introduction of some new technology does not guarantee that it will be accepted and used by citizens, or that further investigation will not reveal that the cure is worse than the disease. Thus, policies aimed at facilitating the use by citizens of salutary technology must be encouraged, and the basis for such policies lies with research by environmental psychologists, who have the tools to understand why, whether, and when technology is accepted or not by citizens.

Three Models and Some Other Contributions of Psychology to Policy

19   Environmental psychologists share an interest in modeling with scientists in some other disciplines. The value of models is that they postulate relations amongst key influences and help to represent complex systems in understandable ways. They can stimulate investigation of the properties of the system and suggest predictions of future outcomes.

20   One such approach, Stern's (2000) values-beliefs-norms model (see Figure 1), postulates that behaviour is determined in part by a causal sequence that begins with deep-seated and quite-stable values, which strongly influence the more-mutable beliefs that one has, which set up the person's behavioural norms.

21   A second general approach is the social dilemma paradigm, which originated with Robyn Dawes' (1980) seminal article and has been expanded by Charles Vlek (1996). In essence, this paradigm asserts that individuals may act in self-interest or in the community interest; if they are amongst a few who act in self-interest they will prosper, but if many or most people act in self-interest, the environment (and they themselves) will suffer.

22   For the last several years, I have set myself the goal of integrating the many influences on, and outcomes of, social dilemmas into a coherent and comprehensive model (Gifford, 2002a, 2008). Initially, I considered that influences on proenvironmental

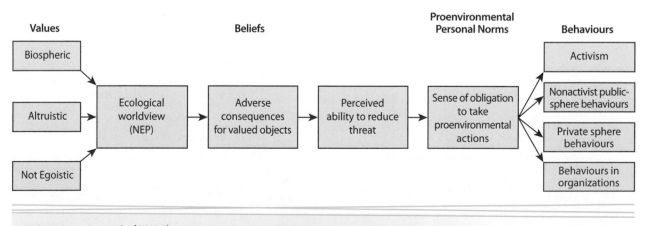

FIGURE 1   STERN'S (2000) VALUES-BELIEFS-NORMS MODEL.

behaviour could be grouped into those associated with (a) the natural resource itself, such as its abundance or regeneration rate, (b) the decision-makers, such as their values and experience, (c) relations amongst decision-makers, such as trust and communication, and (d) the structure of the dilemma, such as the rules that govern environment-related actions (Gifford, 1987). Since then, the model has been expanding and relations amongst these categories of influence have been described and investigated (see Figure 2). In a meta-analysis Donald Hine and I (1991) conducted, about 30 different influences could be identified. This gradually led to the attempt to create a more comprehensive and organized model.

23   The model includes five categories of antecedent influences on a person's decisions, as shown in Figure 2: geophysical, governance (policies), interpersonal, decision-maker characteristics, and

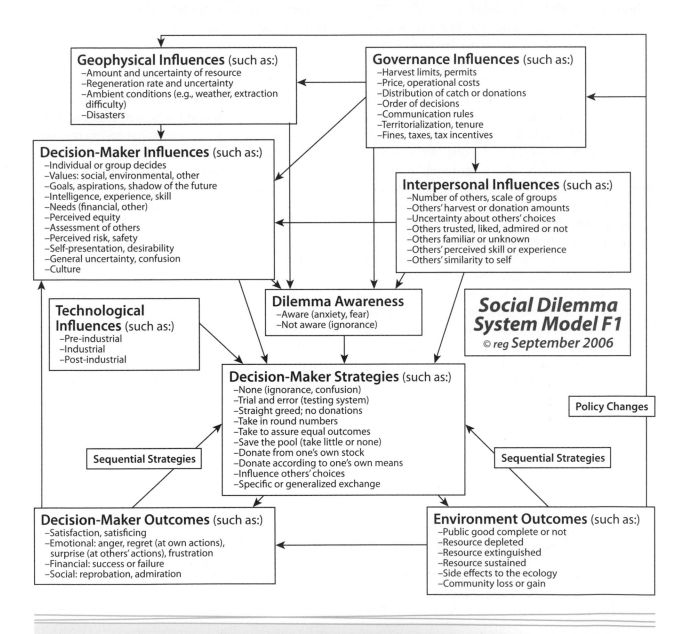

FIGURE 2   A MODEL OF THE SOCIAL DILEMMA APPROACH TO ENVIRONMENTAL PROBLEMS THAT FOCUSES ON THE DECISION-MAKING OF INDIVIDUALS (GIFFORD, 2008).

problem awareness. These influences are presumed to determine the different strategies or heuristics that individuals as decision-makers actually employ. Finally, two kinds of outcomes may be distinguished: those for decision-makers and their intimates, and those for the environment (the resource itself, the environment in general, and for other people in the community). Each element in the model includes numerous specific influences, which may be seen in Figure 2. A complete description of these influences may be found elsewhere (Gifford, 2007).

24   A mere listing of influences and outcomes is fairly straightforward; postulating and testing links amongst them is both more interesting and more challenging. For example, some decision-makers' strategy is geared toward sending a message to other decision-makers; the explicit message of some participants in our resource dilemma studies has been, for example: "Look, I am making sustainable choices, and I want you to do the same." Hence, a causal link exists between decision-maker strategies and interpersonal influences. At the larger social scale, consequences for climate change (environmental outcomes) often are reflected in changes in policies or regulations (governance influences). These hypothesized links between categories, and the conditions under which influence occurs or does not occur, represent the heuristic value of the model. Other direct and feedback links amongst the model's elements could be hypothesized and tested by psychologists, who alone amongst the climate-change players possess the necessary methodological tools to do so.

25   One recent example of this is provided by the work of Eek and Garling (2008). Social values (decision-maker influences) generally are thought to be associated with cooperative choices in resource dilemmas. One school of thought is that cooperation is actualized by a person's goals or aspirations (another decision-maker influence) that results in maximized outcomes for self and other (decision-maker outcomes). However, Eek and Garling convincingly make the case that a different goal, namely equal outcomes for all decision-makers, often is more influential than the joint maximization goal. Thus, choices presumably are a function of social values and goals, reflecting the model's implicit assertion that climate-change actions are multi-determined.

26   Another possibility is that over the course of time, different influences are regnant at different times (Gifford & Hine, 1997). This is reflected in the "sequential strategy" note in the model. Nevertheless, however helpful a comprehensive model might be for visualizing the big picture in the model, the challenge for psychologists is to find ways to encourage those influences that promote behaviours that result in less greenhouse gas emissions.

27   Decision-makers usually are investigated as individuals by environmental psychologists, but in the everyday world decisions are sometimes, perhaps usually, made by groups such as boards of directors or government committees. Groups may be largely unified in their goals and decisions, or not, which opens the door to group dynamics researchers, who often are psychologists. For example, Kazemi and Eek (2008) demonstrate the importance of considering the group as a decision-maker. Group goals (as well as individual goals) can affect the decisions made in the face of environmental problems. Clearly, given the ecological validity of the group as a decision-maker, this is an important direction for research to take. The model's decision-maker influences category obviously must include groups as well as individuals as the decision-makers. Its decision-maker strategies category includes several popular strategies used by decision-makers, and a link is necessary from that category to the interpersonal influences category, thereby postulating that strategies used by decision-makers will influence such within-group factors as trust, admiration, and perceived similarity to self.

The Challenges

28   Even a sustainability science that does include psychology must deal with several important human-nature challenges. The first is what has been called in other contexts mindlessness (Langer, Blank, & Chanowitz, 1978) or proximal cognition (Björkman, 1984), or what Dawes (1980) described in a more relevant context as limited-processing theory. Each of these constructs broadly asserts that humans often act without much reflection or rational planning. A few years earlier, I reported a little study in which university students were forced to navigate a path

through some classroom desks that had been deliberately arranged to be difficult to navigate as they entered and left a classroom. Virtually all the students struggled through the desks, squeezing and turning, but when interviewed afterward, were almost completely unaware of their struggles. Their attention was largely allocated to thinking about the laboratory assignment they were conducting and probably other matters. I called this phenomenon "environmental numbness" (Gifford, 1976).

29   The notion of environmental numbness probably can be extended to the current climate-change crisis, in that most people, most of the time, simply are not thinking at all about climate change. Instead, they are (understandably) thinking about their work, their friends and family, or the big game. The crucial challenges are to get as many people around the world as possible actively thinking about climate change, and to stimulate informed, evidence-based policy that creates accepted structural solutions, so that greenhouse gas emissions can be reduced whilst the rest of the people march, numb to the environment, through their days.

30   A second challenging element of the social dilemma is trust, or the lack of it (e.g., Brann & Foddy, 1987; Foddy & Dawes, 2008). When decision-makers remove less of the resource than they could have, or donors make a sizable contribution, many of them are trusting in a norm of fairness and reciprocity that, unfortunately, is not always shared by other decision-makers. Defectors or free-riders sometimes then see an opportunity for personal gain, and by acting in self-interest they harm the climate-change cause. For example, laboratory studies show that stealing from others in the commons is frequent (Edney & Bell, 1984). Lack of trust leads easily to reactance and denial. Read any online newspapers story about climate change, and below it will be comments deriding the scientific consensus that climate change is happening.

31   Third, a sense of community or group identity is important (Dawes & Messick, 2000). Where it is lacking, and around the globe it is tragically lacking, cooperation in our planetary commons is imperilled. For example, in one lab study, when harvesters thought of themselves more as individuals than as group members, they were more likely to overharvest

the resource (Tindall & O'Connor, 1987). Another lab study did suggest that not much is required to create enough group identity to improve cooperation. In it, the only difference between "high-identity" and "low-identity" participants was that the high-identity participants came to the lab and received their instructions as a group (as opposed to singly), yet the high-identity harvesters cooperated more (Samuelson & Hannula, 2001). Unfortunately, given human history and current events, one is forced to wonder about the ecological validity of this encouraging finding. In December, 2007, China was rejecting mandatory emissions cuts because it said that the wealthy nations created the problem (Casey, 2007); this shows that people can have a strong identity (, e.g., with their nation), but lack sufficient identity with the environment to avoid destructive attitudes and behaviour.

32   A fourth challenge is that of human aspiration. Before we condemn the defectors and free-riders in our commons, we must confess that self-improvement is an essential part of human nature. This is the motive that Julian Simon (1981) celebrated as the solution to human problems. The "ultimate resource" that he believed in essentially was human ingenuity. When combined with the improvement motive, it has led to all the wonderful inventions that we enjoy today. However, in others, it also leads to venal self-aggrandizement (aided and abetted, of course, by the vast apparatus of persuasion that has been constructed in the modern consumption-oriented society). What to do? Use psychological science to reframe aspiration toward climate-amelioration ends. The other disciplines in sustainability science do not have the tools for this task, so it is up to us.

33   The fifth serious challenge problem is uncertainty, which can take several forms, such as in the absolute or relative amount of one's greenhouse gas emissions, the intentions of other decision-makers, the number of other decision-makers, the correct cost of a carbon credit, and so forth (e.g., Hine & Gifford, 1997). In fact, uncertainty can be a factor in every part of the model, from uncertainty about geophysical influences to uncertainty about quantitative and qualitative outcomes. For example, if someone drives 100 km in a particular car, it would not be difficult to measure the amount of greenhouse gases

emitted. However, uncertainty about the effect of this emission on the atmosphere or whether the driver was wrong to drive at all is not easily decided. In sum, certainty may exist only under highly specific or highly aggregated conditions. For that reason, ecological validity in this area demands more studies of uncertainty in all the categories of the model.

34   A sixth challenge is that of perceived equity and justice, and the procedures designed to achieve these goals. Probably every researcher in the area, and certainly myself, has heard at least figurative and sometimes literal cries of revenge or anguish from participants who found the actions of others reprehensible. Therefore, justice-related issues cannot be ignored in social dilemma contexts. Four justice systems may be discerned: distributive, procedural, restorative, and retributive (Schroeder, Bembenek, Kinsey, Steel, & Woodell, 2008). Each system may be imposed from above (governance influences), or agreed-upon by decision-makers (interpersonal influences) but then are implemented as rules and regulations, thus creating a link between those two categories. Schroeder et al. (2008) believe that procedural justice systems will be more stable and cooperation-inducing than distributive justice systems, and explicitly argue that although such systems are best created through communication and agreements amongst those most affected (the decision-makers), they should become instituted as structural (i.e., rules and regulations) solutions to the eternal problem of transgressions in the commons. Clayton and Opotow (2003) discuss how justice is related to group and individual identity, and suggest that group identity promotes intergroup conflict, whereas its absence may allow individuals to experience their relation to nature as direct, which should lead to more pro-environmental behaviour.

35   The seventh challenge is the heavy weight of momentum. Although many people speak of changing their lives, the reality is that many people fail to achieve their goal of altering their behaviour patterns. Habit is not an exciting concept, but it is one important reason for the well-known gap between attitude and behaviour.

36   The eighth challenge is a widespread lack of a sense of efficacy, or perceived behavioural control. Many are hampered by the belief that they alone cannot change the global situation by anything that they do. Some acknowledge the truth that "every vote counts" without being able to muster the motivation (and often, the increased cost or inconvenience) of changing their behaviour in ways that would help to slow the forces that drive climate change.

37   The ninth challenge, and a potentially fatal one, is that of population size; this was central to Hardin's (1968) perspective, and current social scientists (e.g., McGinnis & Ostrom, 2008) quite naturally ask whether the often optimistic results obtained by those who work at the small-group level on common-resource problems would apply at larger scales. Of course, this question has been haunting psychologists for many years (e.g., Edney, 1981), particularly when many studies show a decline in cooperation as the size of the harvesting group grows, even in fairly small groups (by societal standards) of 3 versus 7 (e.g., Sato, 1989). Nearly every study of group size has found that behaviour in resource management tends increasingly toward self interest as group size increases. Cooperation declines both as the number of decision-makers rises and as the number of groups within a commons with a constant total membership rises (Komorita & Lapworth, 1982). Good reasons for this are easy to list. As group size increases, the harm from any one participant's greed is spread thinner amongst the other participants: no single other decision-maker is badly hurt. Also, violations of sustainability or failures to donate are often less visible to others in larger groups. In addition, in large groups, the effect of the harm done to other decision-makers often is less visible to the violator (Edney, 1981); it is easier to inflict pain if one does not have to watch the victim experience pain. Finally, negative feedback or sanctions to violators or free-riders are increasingly difficult to manage in larger groups.

The Opportunities and Imperatives

38   If psychological science is to become recognized as an essential part of sustainability science and as an important player in the struggle to ameliorate the impacts of climate change, it must move toward a more serious engagement with the problem. If we do

not, we run the danger of being viewed from the perspective of future citizens as the science that fiddled whilst the planet burned. One can either adopt the pessimistic view expressed by Garrett Hardin (1968) in his famous *Science* article, which most environmental psychologists have implicitly rejected by continuing to try to solve environmental problems, or one can adopt the view expressed in a more recent *Science* piece by Paul Ehrlich and Donald Kennedy (2005) that we "can organize fair and sustainable rules" (p. 563) to solve the problem.

39   Here is what we should do. First, obviously, we should conduct more research that bears directly on the many problems described above. Probably the central area of psychology for this task is environmental psychology, but we are a small group (about 650 worldwide who self-identify at least in part as environmental psychologists, according to a census I have undertaken this year, with only about two dozen in Canada). Other psychologists can help: how do people make climate-change-related decisions (cognitive and decision-science psychologists)? How can aspirations be reframed from owning more and more material goods to defining "improvement" as adopting climate-change amelioration behaviours (consumer psychologists)? How can helpful attitudes and lifestyles be more effectively taught (health psychologists)? How is acceptance of change related to the life cycle (life span psychologists)?

40   Second, we must engage policymakers (Clayton & Brook, 2005). A number of psychologists (e.g., Paul Stern) already are fully occupied in this crucial enterprise, and others have strongly advocated it (e.g., Vlek, 2000), but not enough of us are stepping off campus to do it. Green and green-leaning politicians now exist in much larger numbers in many countries, and these legislators both want and need quantified, substantiated information that they can use to enact more enlightened legislation. "Brown" politicians too should be our targets, perhaps more than green ones. Fritz Steele's (1980) notion of environmental competence includes knowing which political buttons to push, and psychologists have not done much button-pushing on climate change so far. The admirable fad in governments today is "evidence-based" policy (e.g., Davies, Nutley, & Smith, 2000). This new hunger for evidence-based policy is a huge opportunity for psychology, because of our methodological and research experience.

41   Because much in the way of needed change will occur (or not) at the level of individual citizens, environmental psychology is essential. Psychologists can serve as the key link between individuals—our traditional level of analysis—and policymakers. We can, and should, do the fundamental research on individuals and climate change, assess the acceptability of proposed policy and structural changes, and assess the impact of these changes on the behaviour, well-being, stress, and quality of life of individuals.

42   Third, we must seek out and interact with the other sustainability science players. We must tell the economists, technologists, and climate modellers what psychology can do. The climate scientists are merely the messengers, the technologists merely make machines, and the economists still think largely in terms of pricing. Without the help of psychological science, these disciplines, although valuable in their own ways, will not be able to ameliorate the impacts of climate change.

Canadian Psychology. 2008. 49 (4).

*

I wish to acknowledge the contributions of Paul Stern, Joseph Reser, and Charles Vlek to my thinking on this issue. Naturally, however, I take responsibility for any views or fallacies expressed in this article that would not flatter them. I thank Donald Hine for his unintended challenge, and Brenda McMechan, Reuven Sussman, Leila Scannell, and Mary Gick for their comments and suggestions.

References

Bechtel, R. B., & Churchman, A. (2002). *Handbook of environmental psychology.* New York: Wiley.

Bechtel, R. B., Marans, R. W., & Michelson, W. (1987). (Eds.), *Methods in environmental and behavioral research.* New York: Van Nostrand Reinhold.

Björkman, M. (1984). Decision making, risk taking and psychological time: Review of empirical findings and psychological theory. *Scandinavian Journal of Psychology, 25,* 31–49.

Brann, P., & Foddy, M. (1987). Trust and the consumption of a deteriorating common resource. *Journal of Conflict Resolution, 31,* 615–630.

Buckhout, R. (1972). Pollution and the psychologist: A call to action. In J. F. Wohlwill & D. H. Carson (Eds.), *Environment and the social sciences* (pp. 75–81). Washington, DC: American Psychological Association.

Casey, M. (2007). China rejects mandatory emissions cuts. *The Globe and Mail,* December 8, p. A21.

Clark, W. C., & Dickson, N. M. (2003). Sustainability science. *Proceedings of the National Academy of Sciences, USA, 100,* 8059–8061.

Clayton, S., & Brook, A. (2005). Can psychology help save the world? A model for conservation psychology. *Analyses of Social Issues and Public Policy, 5,* 87–102.

Clayton, S., & Opotow, S. (2003). Justice and identity: Changing perspectives on what is fair. *Personality and Social Psychology Review, 7,* 298–310.

Davies, H. T. O., Nutley, S. M., & Smith, P. C. (2000). *What works? Evidence-based policy and practice in public services.* Bristol, United Kingdom: Policy Press.

Dawes, R. M. (1980). Social dilemmas. *Annual Review of Psychology, 31,* 169–193.

Dawes, R. M., & Messick, D. M. (2000). Social dilemmas. *International Journal of Psychology, 35,* 111–116.

Dresner, M. (1989–1990). Changing energy end-use patterns as a means of reducing global-warming trends. *Journal of Environmental Education, 21,* 41–46.

Edney, J. J. (1981). Paradoxes on the commons: Scarcity and the problem of equality. *Journal of Community Psychology, 9,* 3–34.

Edney, J. J., & Bell, P. A. (1984). Sharing scarce resources: Group-outcome orientation, external disaster, and stealing in a simulated commons. *Small Group Behavior, 15,* 87–108.

Eek, D., & Garling, T. (2008). A new look at the theory of social value orientations: Prosocials neither maximize joint outcomes nor minimize outcome differences but prefer equal outcomes. In A. Biel, D. Eek, T. Garling, & M. Gustaffson (Eds.). *New issues and paradigms in research on social dilemma* (pp. 10–26). New York: Springer.

Ehrlich, P. R., & Kennedy, D. (2005). Millennium assessment of human behavior. *Science, 309,* 562–563.

Foddy, M., & Dawes, R. M. (2008). Group-based trust in social dilemmas. In A. Biel, D. Eek, T. Garling, & M. Gustaffson (Eds.), *New issues and paradigms in research on social dilemma* (pp. 57–71). New York: Springer.

Frank, J. D. (1966). Galloping technology, a new social disease. *Journal of Social Issues, 12,* 1–14.

Gattig, A., & Hendrickx, L. (2007). Judgmental discounting and environmental risk perception: Dimensional similar-

ities, domain differences, and implications for sustainability. *Journal of Social Issues, 63,* 21–39.

Gifford, R. (1976). Environmental numbness in the classroom. *Journal of Experimental Education, 44,* 4–7.

Gifford, R. (1987). *Environmental psychology: Principles and practice* (1st ed.). Newton, MA: Allyn & Bacon.

Gifford, R. (2002a). *Managing natural resources: A matter of life and death.* Keynote address to the International Congress of Applied Psychology, Singapore, July.

Gifford, R. (2002b). Making a difference: Some ways environmental psychology has improved the world. In R. Bechtel & A. Churchman (Eds.), Handbook of environmental psychology (2nd ed.). New York: Wiley.

Gifford, R. (2007). *Environmental psychology: Principles and practice* (4th ed.). Colville, WA: Optimal Books.

Gifford, R. (2008). Toward a comprehensive model of social dilemmas. In A. Biel, D. Eek, T. Gärling, & M. Gustaffson (Eds.), *New issues and paradigms in research on social dilemmas* (265–280). New York: Springer.

Gifford, R., & Hine, D. W. (1997). Toward cooperation in commons dilemmas. *Canadian Journal of Behavioural Sciences, 29,* 167–179.

Hardin, G. (1968). The tragedy of the commons. *Science, 162,* 1234–1248.

Heath, Y., & Gifford, R. (2006). Free-market ideology and environmental degradation: The case of beliefs in global climate change. *Environment & Behavior, 38,* 48–71.

Hine, D. W., & Gifford, R. (1991). *The commons dilemma: A quantitative review.* Canadian Psychological Association annual meetings, Calgary, June.

Hine, D. W., & Gifford, R. (1997). Individual restraint and group efficiency in commons dilemmas: The effects of two types of environmental uncertainty. *Journal of Applied Social Psychology, 26,* 993–1009.

Jager, W., & Mosler, H.-J. (2007). Simulating human behavior for understanding and managing environmental resource use. *Journal of Social Issues, 63,* 97–116.

Kazeemi, A., & Eek, D. (2008). Promoting cooperation in social dilemmas via fairness norms and group goals. In A. Biel, D. Eek, T. Garling, & M. Gustaffson (Eds.), *New issues and paradigms in research on social dilemmas* (pp. 72–92). New York: Springer.

Kenworthy, J., & Laube, F. (2002). Urban transport patterns in a global sample of cities and their linkages to transport infrastructures, land use, economics and environment. *World Transport Policy and Practice, 8,* 5–20.

Kidner, D. W. (1994). Why psychology is mute about the environmental crisis. *Environmental Ethics, 16,* 359–376.

Komorita, S. S., & Lapworth, C. W. (1982). Cooperative choice among individuals versus groups in an N-person dilemma situation. *Journal of Personality and Social Psychology, 42,* 487–496.

Langer, E., Blank, A., & Chanowitz, B. (1978). The mindlessness of ostensibly thoughtful action: The role of "placebic" information in interpersonal interaction. *Journal of Personality and Social Psychology, 36,* 635–642.

Lundqvist, L. J., & Biel, A. (2007). From Kyoto to the town hall: Making international and national climate policy work at the local level. Sterling, VA: Stylus.

McGinnis, M., & Ostrom, E. (2008). Will lessons from small-scale scale up?. In A. Biel, D. Eek, T. Garling, & M. Gustaffson (Eds.), *New issues and paradigms in research on social dilemmas* (pp. 189–211). New York: Springer.

Midden, C., Kaiser, F., & McCalley, T. (2007). Technology's four roles in understanding individuals' conservation of natural resources. *Journal of Social Issues, 63*, 155–174.

Miller, A. (1985). Cognitive styles and environmental problem-solving. *Journal of Environmental Studies, 26*, 535–541.

Nilsson, A., von Borgstede, C., & Biel, A. (2004). Willingness to accept climate change strategies: The effect of values and norms. *Journal of Environmental Psychology, 24*, 267–277.

Osborn, F. (1948). *Our plundered planet.* Boston: Little, Brown.

Oskamp, S. (2000). The psychology of promoting environmentalism: Psychological contributions to achieving an ecologically sustainable future for humanity. *Journal of Social Issues, 56*, 378–390.

Pallak, M. S., & Cummings, W. (1976). Commitment and voluntary energy conservation. *Personality and Social Psychology Bulletin, 2*, 27–30.

Reser, J. (2007). Psychology and the natural environment: *A position paper for the Australian Psychological Society.* Melbourne, Australia: Australian Psychological Society.

Reser, J. P., & Bentrupperbaumer, J. M. (2001). "Social science" in the environmental studies and natural science arena: Misconceptions, misrepresentations, and missed opportunities. In G. Lawrence, V. Higgins, & S. Lockie (Eds.), *Environment, society, and natural resource management: Theoretical perspectives from Australasia and the Americas.* Northampton, MA: Edward Elgar.

Samuelson, C. D., & Hannula, K. A. (2001). *Group identity and environmental uncertainty in a sequential resource dilemma.* Unpublished manuscript, Department of Psychology, Texas A&M University.

Sato, K. (1989). Trust and feedback in a social dilemma. *Japanese Journal of Experimental Social Psychology, 29*, 123–128.

Schmuck, P., & Schultz, W. P. (Eds.) (2002). *Psychology of sustainable development,* London: Kluwer Academic.

Schmuck, P., & Vlek, C. (2003). Psychologists can do much to support sustainable development. *European Psychologist, 8*, 66–76.

Schoot Uiterkamp, A. J. M., & Vlek, C. (2007). Practice and outcomes of multidisciplinary research for environmental sustainability. *Journal of Social Issues, 63*, 175–197.

Schroeder, D. A., Bembenek, A. F., Kinsey, K. M., Steel, J. E., & Woodell, A. J. (2008). A recursive model for changing justice concerns in social dilemmas. In A. Biel, D. Eek, T. Gärling, & M. Gustaffson (Eds.), *New issues and paradigms in research on social dilemmas* (pp. 142–158). New York: Springer.

Seligman, C., & Darley, J. M. (1977). Feedback as a means of decreasing residential energy conservation. *Journal of Applied Social Psychology, 62*, 363–368.

Simon, J. (1981). *The ultimate resource.* Princeton, NJ: Princeton University Press. Sommer, R. (1983). *Social design: Creating buildings with people in mind.* Englewood Cliffs, NJ: Prentice Hall. Steele, F. (1980). Defining and developing environmental competence. In C. P. Alderfer & C. L. Cooper (Eds.), *Advances in experiential social processes* (Vol. 2), 225–244.

Stern, P. C. (1986). Blind spots in policy analysis: What economics doesn't say about energy use. *Journal of Policy Analysis and Management, 5*, 220–227.

Stern, P. C. (1993). A second environmental science: Human-environment interactions. *Science, 260*, 1897–1899.

Stern, P. C. (2000). Towards a coherent theory of environmentally significant behavior. *Journal of Social Issues, 56*, 407–424.

Stern, P. C. (2005, September 21). *Psychological research and sustain-ability science.* Keynote address to the 6th Biennial Conference on Environmental Psychology, Bochum, Germany.

Studer, R., & Stea, D. (1966). Architectural programming and human behavior. *Journal of Social Issues, 12*, 1–14.

Tindall, D. B., & O'Connor, B. (1987, June). *Attitudes, social identity, social values, and behavior in a commons dilemma.* Presentation at the Canadian Psychological Association Conference, Vancouver, BC.

Uzzell, D. (2007). How the science of psychology can make a contribution to sustainable development. Working paper, British Psychological Society.

Vlek, C. (1996). Collective risk generation and risk management: The unexploited potential of the social dilemmas paradigm. In W. B. G. Liebrand & D. M. Messick (Eds.), *Frontiers in social dilemmas research* (pp. 11–38). New York: Springer-Verlag.

Vlek, C. (2000). Essential psychology for environmental policy making. *International Journal of Psychology, 35*, 153–167.

Vlek, C., & Steg, L. (2007). Human behavior and environmental sustain-ability: Problems, driving forces, and research topics. *Journal of Social Issues, 63*, 1–19.

KEY AND CHALLENGING WORDS

amelioration, parametric, functionary, substantive, salutary, postulate (v.), antecedent, heuristics, regnant, reciprocity, deride, venal, aggrandizement, retributive

QUESTIONS

1. What is the function of the section "A Bit of Background"?
2. Why is it important to study the behaviour of individuals in a global phenomenon like climate change?
3. What is environmental psychology? How could it be a "player" in climate change policies? Why has it not been?
4. "We write in our discussion sections that 'someone' should take into account these important findings of ours. However, unfortunately, for the most part policymakers and natural scientists do not read our discussion sections" (paragraph 6): a) Why do you think Gifford included this criticism of psychologists? b) What are stereotypes that are applied to psychologists? To what extent do you believe these stereotypes are responsible for the lack of credibility Gifford addresses in this paragraph?
5. Summarize paragraphs 10–11 in which the author explains his disagreement with Stern.
6. In no more than two sentences provide a more complete caption for Figure 2, using the explanation in paragraph
23. Then, in about two additional sentences explain the nature of the relationship between any two parts of the diagram, using one of the examples that refer to Figure 2 in paragraphs 24–27.
7. Analyze one of the paragraphs in the section "The Challenges," showing how the writer creates a coherent, unified, and well-developed paragraph (do not analyze paragraphs 29, 35, or 36, as they are too short.
8. Which do you consider are the two most crucial challenges for psychologists among the nine discussed in this section? Write one paragraph each explaining why you believe it is so important in alleviating the effects of climate change.
9. In one or two paragraphs, analyze the rhetorical effectiveness of the concluding section, "The Opportunities and Imperatives," referring to specific passages.

POST-READING

1. *Collaborative or individual activity:* "The Tragedy of the Commons" (see paragraph 38) refers to an analogy used by Garrett Hardin of an open pasture in which herdsmen overuse a resource by applying a process of "rational" (though selfish) thinking. According to Hardin, each herdsman attempts to maximize his own profit by asking, "What is the utility *to me* of adding one more animal to my herd?" His reasoning is that if he adds one animal to the pasturage, he will be able to sell an additional animal at the market, whereas the group cost will be shared among all the herdsmen. Hardin concludes that "Each man is locked into a system that compels him to increase his herd without limit—in a world that is limited," which creates the tragedy. Hardin believed that humans are doomed by the tragedy of the commons, which makes it impossible to solve all such problems of the commons, like that of world overpopulation.

    Discuss the apparent strengths and flaws in this concept, using, if possible, realistic examples from your own

experience or observation about shared resources (for example, car-pooling lanes). Before discussing or debating this issue, you could read Hardin's essay, accessing it through a library database or at the address given below.
2. Do you believe the gap mentioned between academic studies and policymakers first mentioned in paragraphs 7 and 8 applies to social science research in general? Write a response to one of the following prompts: a) Social science research done at universities is remote from the concerns of everyday life; *OR* b) Research in the social sciences done at universities could be made more relevant to everyday life and/or could affect policy decisions if. . . .
3. *Collaborative activity:* Do you believe that individuals are, in fact, the key to addressing climate change or that the key lies with politicians and other policymakers, rather than with individuals? What can individuals do to help alleviate climate change?

RELATED WEBSITES OF INTEREST

Climate Change 2007: Synthesis Report Summary for Policymakers (a 22-page summary of the IPCC Fourth Assessment Report):
www.ipcc.ch/pdf/assessment-report/ar4/syr/ar4_syr_spm.pdf

Canada's Action on Climate Change (federal government site):
www.climatechange.gc.ca/default.asp?lang=En&n=E18C8F2D-1

The Pembina Institute (non-profit Canadian institute focused on sustainable energy policies):
http://climate.pembina.org/

Garrett Hardin, "The Tragedy of the Commons":
www.sciencemag.org/cgi/content/full/162/3859/1243

ADDITIONAL LIBRARY READING

Mark Van Vugt, M. (2009). Averting the tragedy of the commons: Using social psychological science to protect the environment. *Current Directions in Psychological Science, 18*(3), 169–173.

Muir, H. (2008). Let science rule: The rational way to run societies. *New Scientist, 198*(2657), 40–43.

Climate change, health, and vulnerability in Canadian northern Aboriginal communities

Christopher Furgal and Jacinthe Seguin

(5,300 words)

Pre-reading

1.   From the abstract and the first two paragraphs, determine the essay's methodology. That is, what method(s) did the authors use to obtain information for their study?

Background: Canada has recognized that Aboriginal and northern communities in the country face unique challenges and that there is a need to expand the assessment of vulnerabilities to climate change to include these communities. Evidence suggests that Canada's North is already experiencing significant changes in its climate—changes that are having negative impacts on the lives of Aboriginal people living in these regions. Research on climate change and health impacts in northern Canada thus far has brought together Aboriginal community members, government representatives, and researchers and is charting new territory.

Methods and results: In this article we review experiences from two projects that have taken a community-based dialogue approach to identifying and assessing the effects of and vulnerability to climate change and the impact on the health in two Inuit regions of the Canadian Arctic.

Conclusions: The results of the two case projects that we present argue for a multi-stakeholder, participatory framework for assessment that supports the necessary analysis, understanding, and enhancement of capabilities of local areas to respond and adapt to the health impacts at the local level.

Key words: Aboriginal, adaptive capacity, Arctic, climate change, Inuit, vulnerability.

*

1   There is strong evidence that Canada's North is already experiencing significant changes in its climate (e.g., McBean et al. 2005). The climatic and environmental changes that have been observed during the last century require greater understanding and involvement by individuals and institutions to define effective adaptation strategies. Through signing the 1992 United Nations Framework Convention on Climate Change (2006) and ratifying the Kyoto Protocol (2006), Canada has shown its commitment to the global effort to slow the rate of warming, reduce emissions, conduct research, and initiate action at the national and regional levels to develop adaptation strategies to minimize the impact throughout the country (Government of Canada 2003). Canada has recognized that Aboriginal and northern communities face unique challenges and that it is necessary to expand the assessment of vulnerabilities to effects of climate change to all areas of Canada, including the North (Government of Canada 2003). This work is essential for the development of effective adaptive strategies to protect the health of Canadians in all regions of the country.

2   Assessing the impacts that these climate changes are having or may have on people's lives requires

a combination of disciplinary approaches and methods (Patz et al. 2000). Research on climate change and health impacts in northern Canada is in its infancy (Furgal et al. 2002). It uses and focuses particularly on indigenous knowledge and local observations of environmental change along with scientific assessments of the impacts associated with these and other forms of change. In this article, we review experiences from projects that used a community-based dialogue-oriented approach to identifying and assessing potential health impacts and vulnerabilities to climate change in two Inuit regions of Canada's North. These experiences build a strong case for a multi-stakeholder, qualitative, and participatory approach to identifying and assessing risks while enhancing the capacity of local areas to respond to the impacts of climate change.

The Canadian North

3   A common definition of Canada's North that we use here includes the three territorial administrative regions north of 60° latitude (Yukon, Northwest Territories, and Nunavut) as well as the region of Nunavik, north of 55° in the province of Québec and the Inuit settlement region of Nunatsiavut within Labrador. The latter two regions comprise communities with large Aboriginal populations and share many bio-geographic characteristics with the territorial Arctic. Together, this region covers approximately 60 per cent of Canada's land mass (Figure 1).

4   The vast coastline, islands, and permanent multi-year ice found in Canada's North are rich in geography and biodiversity. The diversity of the regions' ecosystems, climate, and cultures forms a socio-ecologic collage across the top of the country (Canadian Arctic Contaminants Assessment Report II 2003). Communities are spread along Canada's northern coastline and interior, and the land and sea provide northern residents with a primary source of nutrition and form a central part of their livelihoods and cultures (Van Oostdam et al. 2005).

5   Northerners have witnessed profound environmental, social, political, and economic changes in recent decades (Damas 2002; Wonders 2003). Research on contaminants, and more recently on

climate change, has uncovered what many northerners have known for some time: the Arctic environment is stressed, and irreversible changes are occurring. At the same time, many communities are transitioning economically, having become more permanent than they were 40 years ago. Many communities now have a mixed economy of traditional or land-based activities and wage employment, with many of the wage employment opportunities now associated with large-scale development of non-renewable natural resources (e.g., mining). These increases in development and cash income have resulted in changes in local economies and increased accessibility to many market items typically available in urban centres to the south. Further, dramatic political changes have resulted in Aboriginal groups in many regions now leading regionally based forms of self-government or being currently engaged in negotiations to establish such arrangements that include land claim and resource settlements. One example of this arrangement is the establishment of the Territory of Nunavut in 1999 (Indian and Northern Affairs Canada [INAC] 1993).

6   Just over half of the approximately 100,000 northern residents are Aboriginal and belong to distinct cultural groups, including the Yukon First Nations (Yukon), Dene, Métis, and Gwich'in (Northwest Territories), and Inuit (Nunavut, Nunavik, the new Inuit land claim area of Nunatsiavut within the region of Labrador, and the Inuvialuit Settlement Region of the Northwest Territories). Many of the communities are characterized by an increasingly young and rapidly growing population: 54 per cent of the population of Nunavut is under 15 years of age, compared with the national average of 25 per cent (Statistics Canada 2001). Many still experience lower health status than their southern counterparts. For example, life expectancy among Aboriginal people in some regions, such as Nunavik, is as much as 12 years lower than the national average for both sexes (Statistics Canada 2001). In addition, many remote communities are challenged by limited access to health services, lower average socio-economic status, crowding and poor-quality housing, and concerns regarding basic services such as drinking water quality (Statistics Canada 2001). Despite these challenges, all northern cultures retain

a close relationship with the environment and a strong knowledge base of their regional surroundings. Even today, the environment and the country foods that come from the land, lakes, rivers, and sea remain central to the way of life, cultural identity, and health of northern Aboriginal people (Van Oostdam et al. 2005). More than 70 per cent of northern Aboriginal adults harvest natural resources through hunting and fishing, and of those, > 96 per cent do so for subsistence purposes (Statistics Canada 2001). This strong relationship with their environment plays a critical role in the ability of northern Aboriginal peoples to observe, detect, and anticipate changes in their natural environment.

Climate Changes in Canada's North

7   The breadth of scientific research on the Canadian northern environment has grown significantly in recent decades. Scientific research, monitoring, and observations, and the knowledge we have acquired from Aboriginal people have resulted in an awareness that changes are taking place. Observed trends vary depending on the region and period analyzed. For example, the western and central Arctic have experienced a general warming over the past 30–50 years of approximately 2–3°C (Weller et al. 2005). This warming is more pronounced in winter months. It is not until the last 15 or so years that this same warming trend, although not to the same extent, has been observed in eastern regions of the Canadian Arctic. Observed impacts associated with these changes include a significant thinning of sea and freshwater ice, a shortening of the winter ice season, reduction in snow cover, changes in wildlife and plant species distribution, melting permafrost, and increased coastal erosion of some shorelines (Cohen 1997; Huntington and Fox 2005; Ouranos 2004; Weller et al. 2005). According to the Arctic Climate Impact Assessment (ACIA 2005) designated climate models, the predictions are for increased warming and precipitation throughout the Canadian Arctic. Annual mean warming in the west is projected to range between 3 and 4°C and upwards of 7°C in winter months. Winter warming is expected to be

greatest in the more centrally located areas of southern Baffin Island and Hudson Bay (3–9°C). A 30 per cent increase in precipitation is predicted by the end of the twenty-first century, with the greatest increases occurring in areas of greatest warming (Weller et al. 2005). The predicted impacts on the environment, regional economies, and people are far-reaching. Recent research projects have begun to identify specific local vulnerabilities and risk management measures/adaptation strategies that are already in place or that can be planned (e.g., Berkes and Jolly 2002; Ford et al. 2006; Nickels et al. 2002); however, very little attention has been given to health impacts and adaptations in this region to date.

Assessing Health Impacts and Vulnerability

8   Health data series and regional scale assessments in the Canadian North are limited. However, recent qualitative studies examining the potential health impacts of environmental change provide new insights with which to focus research and proactively develop response strategies. They show the need for community participation in filling information gaps and increasing our understanding of factors that enhance or inhibit adaptive capabilities (Furgal et al. 2002; Nickels et al. 2002). The cases we review below present some of these experiences.

Climate change and health in Nunavik and Labrador

9   The project Climate Change and Health in Nunavik and Labrador: What We Know from Science and Inuit Knowledge (Furgal et al. 2001) was conducted in the communities of Kuujjuaq, Nunavik (Québec), and Nain, Nunatsiavut (Labrador) in 2000–01. The project was initiated by members of regional Aboriginal (Inuit) agencies in charge of local environmental health issues in cooperation with a university researcher (C. Furgal, Laval University, Québec City, Québec, Canada). The project was conducted to establish a baseline understanding of the relationship between environmental changes observed in the communities and the potential impacts of these changes on health, as perceived by participants and reported in the health sciences literature.

10   Nunavik is home to approximately 9,000 Inuit residents living in 14 villages distributed along the coasts of Ungava Bay, Hudson Strait, and the eastern shore of Hudson Bay (Figure 1). In 2005 the autonomous Inuit region of Nunatsiavut was established via a tripartite agreement between the federal and provincial governments and the Inuit of Labrador. This region is situated within the mainland boundary of the province of Newfoundland and Labrador. The region is home to approximately 4,800 Inuit living in five coastal communities (Figure 1). Despite recent economic, political, and social changes in the regions of Nunavik and Nunatsiavut over the past decades, residents remain close to their traditions, and many aspects of a land-based traditional lifestyle are still commonly practised.

11   To identify potential impacts of observed climate-related changes on health, the project gathered information from various sources. Investigators reviewed the available scientific literature, conducted expert consultations with northern health and environment professionals and researchers, and documented Inuit knowledge and perspectives via focus groups with 16 Inuit hunters, elders, and women in the two communities. A process of thematic content analysis was then performed on the qualitative data, and common groups or categories of environmental changes and human impacts were developed (Tesch 1990). This analysis of the collective base of information identified a series of potential direct and indirect health impacts associated with climatic changes observed in Nunavik and Nunatsiavut (Table 1; Furgal et al. 2002).

12   Most observations and impacts were common between the two regions. For the purposes of the discussion here to present the scope of changes and impacts observed to date, the results of these two regions are combined. Participants in the two regions identified changes in climatic conditions over the past 10 years not previously experienced or reported in the region. Some changes were identified as having a direct impact on the health of individuals. Respiratory stress was reported among elderly participants and those with decreased respiratory health in

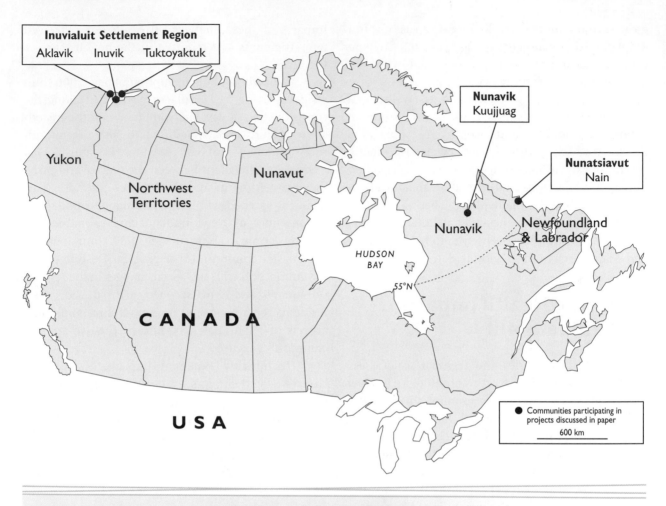

FIGURE 1   MAP SHOWING TERRITORIES AND REGIONS OF THE CANADIAN NORTH. COMMUNITIES ENGAGED IN PROJECTS SUCH AS THOSE DISCUSSED IN FURGAL ET AL. (2002), NICKELS ET AL. (2002), AND THIS PRESENT ARTICLE ARE IDENTIFIED.

association with an increase in summer temperature extremes that now exceed 30°C in both regions. The reported increase in uncharacteristic weather patterns and storm events had significant impacts on travel and hunting/fishing safety. As one focus group participant reported:

> it changes so quick now you find. Much faster than it used to. . . last winter when the teacher was caught out it was perfect in the morning. . . then it went down flat and they couldn't see anything. . . . Eighteen people were caught out then, and they almost froze, it was bitterly cold. (Nunatsiavut focus group participant, unpublished data, 2001)

13   Significantly more indirect associations between climate-related changes and health were reported by local residents and by northern environment and health professionals or were found in the pertinent scientific literature (Table 2). For example, warming winter temperatures in the areas around both communities were reported to have changed the timing of ice freeze-up and decreased its thickness and stability. For Inuit communities, sea ice travel is critical for accessing wildlife resources and travelling between communities during winter months. There are anecdotal reports of an increase in the number of accidents and drownings associated with poor or uncharacteristic ice conditions during times of the year that are

predictable and typically very safe. More events are reported each year, such as that occurring in 2003 when two young Inuit men went through the ice on their skidoos and drowned near their community as a result of a strange thinning ice phenomenon that was reported to have been "becoming more common in recent years" (Nelson 2003). With a young and increasingly sedentary population spending more time in communities engaged in wage employment and less time on the land, a combination of factors appears to make this group more vulnerable to the climate-related changes being reported in many northern regions today. Moreover, changes in the timing of the ice season are reported to impact the frequency and timing of hunting activities in communities, as indicated by the following comment:

> This year and last year, we have been stopped when we were going to go fishing. The ice broke up quickly. We would have gone fishing more in the past. (Nunavik focus group participant, unpublished data, 2001)

14   The implications of these changes on food security and potential implications on nutritional health among these populations, which receive significant energy and nutrient contributions to their total diet from these country foods, is only now being investigated. In fact, a number of focused research projects have been initiated with the communities involved in this present study and others in these regions. For example, work on climate and water quality, hunting behaviour, women's health, and emerging and chronic diseases in the North are currently under way.

15   In general, the impacts identified by local residents in this project were supported primarily by scientific evidence and the published literature, although, in some cases, the effects represented new findings. Many impacts were based on individuals' experiences in relation to observed climate-related changes in the local area. Other impacts were identified as "potential," as they were logical extrapolations for residents considering the observed patterns of change in regional climate variables and the perceived relationship between Inuit health and the environment (Tables 1 and 2).

Inuit community workshops on climate change

16   In response to growing concern among Inuit communities about environmental changes being observed, the national Inuit organization in Canada, Inuit Tapiriit Kanatami, initiated a project in cooperation with regional Inuit organizations and Canadian research institutions to document changes and impacts experienced in communities and to discuss how communities currently are adapting or may adapt in the future. In the first series of workshops in January and February 2002, a research team involving regionally based Inuit representatives visited three of the six communities in the Inuvialuit Settlement Region of the Northwest Territories (Tuktoyaktuk, Aklavik, and Inuvik, Northwest Territories; Figure 1). Community workshops occurred over two days in each community, and research team members documented Inuit residents' observations of environmental changes

TABLE 1   SUMMARY OF POTENTIAL DIRECT CLIMATE-RELATED HEALTH IMPACTS IN NUNAVIK AND LABRADOR

Identified climate-related change	Potential direct-health impacts
Increased (magnitude and frequency) temperature extremes	Increased heat- and cold-related morbidity and mortality
Increase in frequency and intensity of extreme weather events (e.g., storms)	Increased frequency and severity of accidents while hunting and travelling, resulting in injuries, death, psychosocial stress
Increase in uncharacteristic weather patterns	
Increased UV-B exposure	Increased risks of skin cancers, burns, infectious diseases, eye damage (cataracts), immuno-suppression

UV-B, ultraviolet B. Adapted from Furgal et al. (2002)

TABLE 2   SUMMARY OF POTENTIAL INDIRECT CLIMATE-RELATED HEALTH IMPACTS IN NUNAVIK AND LABRADOR

Identified climate-related change	Potential direct-health impacts
Increased (magnitude and frequency) temperature	Increase in infectious disease incidence and transmission, psychosocial disruption
Decrease in ice distribution, stability, and duration of coverage	Increased frequency and severity of accidents while hunting and travelling, resulting in injuries, death, psychosocial stress
	Decreased access to country food items; decreased food security; erosion of social and cultural values associated with country foods preparation, sharing, and consumption
Change in snow conditions (decrease in quality of snow for igloo construction with increased humidity)	Challenges to building shelters (igloo) for safety while on land
Increase in range and activity of existing and new infective agents (e.g., biting flies)	Increased exposure to existing and new vectorborne diseases
Change in local ecology of waterborne and foodborne agents (introduction of new parasites and perceived decrease in quality of natural drinking water sources)	Increase in incidence of diarrheal and other infectious diseases
	Emergence of new diseases
Increased permafrost melting, decreased structural stability	Decreased stability of public health, housing, and transportation infrastructure
	Psychosocial disruption associated with community relocation (partial or complete)
Sea-level rise	Psychosocial disruption associated with infrastructure damage and community relocation (partial or complete)
Changes in air pollution (contaminants, pollens, spores)	Increased incidence of respiratory and cardiovascular diseases; increased exposure to environmental contaminants and subsequent impacts on health development.

Adapted from Furgal et al. (2002)

and the reported effects they were experiencing in association with these changes. At the same time, communities began to identify existing strategies or develop potential adaptation strategies for local-level response (Table 3; Nickels et al. 2002). The processes used for the workshop drew on participatory analysis and planning techniques, including Participatory Rural Appraisal (PRA) and Objectives Oriented Project Planning (ZOPP) (Chambers 1997; Deutsche Gesellschaft für Technische Zusammenarbeit [German Agency for Technical Cooperation] 1988).

17   The communities of the Inuvialuit Settlement Region (ISR) have been observing changes associated with warming in their region for a longer period than those living in the eastern Arctic communities. Changes in the ISR appear more pronounced. For example, increased mean summer and winter temperatures, temperature extremes, an increase in uncharacteristic weather patterns and storm events, a decrease in precipitation, and changes in the characteristics of the ice season similar to those reported in the eastern communities (Furgal et al. 2002) were discussed in ISR community workshops (Nickels et al. 2002). These changes affect the health of individuals and communities, and in some cases communities are already beginning to respond (Table 3).

18   For example, in association with summer warming, residents are reporting an increase in the number and species of biting flies and insects, including bees. Many residents are concerned because of the potential for spread of disease or potential allergic reactions to stings, as many of these insects have never been seen before in this region. Consequently, a public education process was recommended by workshop participants to inform people about what action could be taken to minimize the risk of being

TABLE 3   EXAMPLES OF ENVIRONMENTAL CHANGES, EFFECTS, AND COPING STRATEGIES/ ADAPTATIONS REPORTED BY COMMUNITY RESIDENTS IN THE INUVIALUIT SETTLEMENT REGION TO MINIMIZE NEGATIVE HEALTH IMPACTS OF CLIMATE CHANGE.

Observation	Effect	Copying strategy/adaptation
Warmer temperatures	Not able to store country food properly while hunting; food spoils quicker; less country foods are consumed	Return to community more often in summer while hunting to store food safely (in cool temperatures) Needed: investment of more funds for hunting activities Decrease amount of future hunting and storage with fewer places to store extra meat Needed: re-investment in government-supported community freezer program
Warmer temperatures in summer	Can no longer prepare dried/ smoked fish in the same way: "It gets cooked in the heat" Less dried/smoked fish eaten	Alter construction of smoke houses: build thicker roofs to regulate temperature Adapt drying and smoking techniques
Lower water levels in some areas and some brooks/creeks drying up	Decrease in sources of good natural (raw) drinking water available while on the land Increased risk of waterborne illnesses	Bottled water now purchased and taken on trips
More mosquitoes and other (new) biting insects	Increased insect bites Increasing concern about health effects of new biting insects not seen before	Use insect repellent, lotion, or sprays Use netting and screens on windows and entrances to houses Needed: information and education on insects and biting flies to address current perception/fear
Changing animal travel/migration routes	Makes hunting more difficult (requires more fuel, gear, and time) Some residents (e.g. elders) cannot afford to hunt, thus consuming less country foods	Initiation of a community program for active hunters to provide meat to others (e.g. elders) who are unable to travel/hunt under changing conditions Needed: financial and institutional support to establish program

Adapted from Nickels et al. (2002)

bitten and to alleviate public fear. Currently, little information on these topics exists or is available in the communities (Table 3).

19   Locally appropriate strategies were suggested to address climate-related impacts on animal distribution and decreased human access to important country food sources (e.g., caribou and geese). Furgal et al. (2002) reported that some people (e.g., elders and those with limited equipment and financial resources) were challenged in their access to country food species, particularly during fall and spring because of changes in ice conditions, water levels, or shifts in animal migrations. These changes were resulting in increased costs and time associated with travelling longer distances to procure these foods and a decrease in consumption of these items for some members of the community. Because of these problems, it was recommended that a community hunting and sharing program be formalized to ensure access to these foodstuffs for all (Table 3).

20   Currently, more reactive than proactive strategies are in place to adapt to climate-related health impacts in these communities. Changes in hunting behaviour, increased investments in equipment or infrastructure (e.g., smoke houses, freezers), and the importance of increased education and information exchange were identified. As in the eastern Arctic communities, these initial workshops have led to the

establishment of a variety of projects that address specific issues. Some of these projects will potentially lead to proactive primary adaptations to reduce exposure (Casimiro et al. 2001).

Understanding the Capacity of Canada's North for Health Adaptation

21   A summary of examples of adaptive strategies from the work presented in table 3 is indicative of the inherently adaptive nature of Inuit society and northern Aboriginal cultures in general (Adger et al. 2003; Nickels et al. 2002; Reidlinger and Berkes 2001). However, the ability to respond varies among communities and regions and is influenced by some common critical factors. The World Health Organization framework for health adaptation (Grambsch and Menne 2003) identifies seven elements that influence vulnerability and adaptation to climate-related health impacts, many of which are applicable to the northern communities discussed here.

22   The ability to overcome changes in access to or availability of country food resources, which are important for nutritional and socio-cultural well-being, is significantly influenced by an individual's access to economic resources and technology. The ability to invest more in the required tools and equipment for hunting and travelling, or the access to other forms of transportation (e.g., snow machine, four-wheel all-terrain vehicle, flat-bottom or larger boat) allows individuals to adapt more easily to changing environmental conditions (Duhaime et al. 2002; Ford et al. 2006).

23   Similarly, the generation and sharing of local or traditional knowledge of regional environments and the relationship between the environment and humans further support this ability to adapt while on the land and safely navigate increasingly dangerous and uncharacteristic conditions. The ability to shift species, alter hunting behaviours, and read environmental cues (e.g., weather prediction, ice safety) all increase hunting and travel safety and success. The importance of this knowledge is gaining recognition among scientific and policy communities (e.g., Huntington and Fox

2005); however, its generation is being challenged locally with shifts toward a more "Western lifestyle" involving more time spent in communities engaged in indoor wage-based economic activities and less time on the land (Chapin et al. 2005).

24   The support provided through institutional or formal arrangements for aspects of traditional lifestyles and health may become increasingly important with climate change in Arctic regions. As many communities begin to represent more pluralistic societies in terms of livelihoods and lifestyles, establishing country food collection, storage, and distribution programs and economic support for the pursuit of traditional activities become important in reducing the vulnerabilities to and enhancing adaptive capabilities for climate-related changes. Also important is the formalization of traditional knowledge documentation and sharing mechanisms through the establishment of such things as community-based ice monitoring programs (Lafortune et al. 2004).

25   With warming temperatures and the potential for the introduction of new water and food-borne agents and permafrost melting, which threatens built structures in coastal communities, some basic public health infrastructures (e.g., water treatment and distribution, emergency transportation) are increasingly vulnerable. The security of basic public health infrastructure in small remote communities that are already challenged regarding provision of some basic services is a significant determinant of adaptive ability in these locations.

26   Finally, existing health status issues in Inuit populations (e.g., nutritional deficiencies, increasing rates of diabetes and some cancers associated with shifts toward a more "Western diet" and sedentary lifestyle, and rates of respiratory illness) appear to be further exacerbated by changes in local climate. The combination of environmental change, basic health needs, limited economic choices, and shifts in northern society and lifestyle appears to increase vulnerability and limit the ability of some Arctic communities to respond. When many of these factors overlap and the population is already facing some critical health issues, the impact of climate change is greater because of the population's vulnerability (e.g., small remote communities, with a limited natural and economic resource base).

Discussion

27   Indigenous populations are often more vulnerable to climatic changes because of their close relationship with the environment, their reliance on the land and sea for subsistence purposes, and the fact that they are more likely to inhabit areas of more severe impact such as coastal regions, often have lower socio-economic status, are more socially marginalized, and have less access to quality health care services (Kovats et al. 2003). In the public health sector, this combination of the current exposure-response relationship, the extent of exposure, and the possible preventative measures in place creates a vulnerability baseline against which the effectiveness of future policies can be measured via changes in the burden of disease (Ebi et al. 2003). The dialogue approach we present here shows the value of establishing this baseline and engaging Arctic Aboriginal communities on these issues by a process very similar to that outlined by Ebi et al. (2006).

28   The findings presented in these two small studies are supported by others (e.g., Ford et al. 2006; Krupnik and Jolly 2002). A workshop with northern health professionals, community leaders, and Aboriginal representatives from across the North reported similar results (Health Canada 2002). Critical issues identified included challenges related to northern home design and a lack of ventilation causing heat stress among elderly on increasingly warm days; impacts to food security because of changes in sea-ice access routes to hunting areas or ice-road stability and effects on reliable transport of market foodstuffs; combined impacts on mental health due to reduced ability of individuals to practise aspects of traditional lifestyles; and impacts to infrastructure and threats of community disruption or relocation (Health Canada 2002).

29   Although a regionally based analysis was not possible with the data available, variations in vulnerabilities and adaptive abilities appear to exist between and within regions on the basis of a number of common factors (see "Understanding the capacity of Canada's North for health adaptation"; Grambsch and Menne 2003). Similarly, both projects were conducted with Inuit communities, and hence, differences between Arctic cultural groups were not identified.

However, as each Aboriginal group is uniquely adapted to its geography and local ecology, it is reasonable to speculate that each group's socio-ecologic resilience and adaptive capacity for health issues is similarly unique. Observed climate changes, impacts, and response abilities of Yukon First Nations living in the interior of the western Arctic likely are very different from those of the Inuit communities presented here. It is therefore critical to conduct such assessments locally.

30   As in other regions of the world, enhancing adaptive capacity can be regarded as a "no regrets" option in the North, as it not only reduces vulnerability but also improves immediate resilience to current-day stresses (Yohe and Tol 2002). Strengthening access and availability to country foods throughout the year for communities or increasing public health education associated with environmental causes of disease are such examples. Establishing community freezer and distribution plans will help in addressing current nutritional and other food issues as well as increase the capability of an individual to access safe and healthy foods in the face of environmental changes. Increased knowledge and awareness of environmental causes of disease will address perceived risks and provide valuable information to empower individuals to continue to make healthy decisions.

31   Both the Nunavik-Nunatsiavut (Labrador) project and the workshops in the ISR are starting points in the collection of information to support community, regional, national, and international processes on climate change. Many new projects have since begun on components of the climate-health relationship in northern communities, and many of these are taking a similarly participatory approach (e.g., ArcticNet 2004). Arctic indigenous peoples have also participated in the international assessment of climate change impacts through their involvement in the ACIA with academic and government researchers (ACIA 2004). This level of engagement and contribution is a significant advance in environmental health impact and vulnerability research. Despite these advances, research on climate and health in northern Aboriginal populations is sparse (Berner and Furgal 2005), and the identification of the impacts on local populations and community adaptations is still in its

infancy and requires continued effort, with attention to thresholds and limits to adaptation (Berkes and Jolly 2002).

32   The studies presented here on populations in Canada's North and a review of other recent research in this region (e.g., ACIA 2005; Ford et al. 2006; Health Canada 2003) identify data gaps that we need to fill and methods that we need to use to increase our understanding of climate and health assessment, vulnerability, and the capacity to adapt in northern Aboriginal communities. They include the following:

Multiple-scale research and data. Community-based assessments and systematic research must be conducted on the issues of climate change impacts in the North and elsewhere in Canada. Local, regional, and national levels are interconnected in supporting and facilitating action on climate change; thus, data at multiple levels and research that link scales to understand these relationships are needed. Fine-scale meteorologic data is required in many northern regions and must be collected in a way that allows the data to be linked to existing and future health data sets. Models of change and impact must be linked with currently used global change scenarios.

Quality, comparable, standardized data. Innovative approaches to health and climate assessment are needed and should consider the role of socio-cultural diversity present among Arctic communities. This requires both qualitative and quantitative data and the collection of long-term data sets on standard health outcomes at comparable temporal and spatial levels. These data must include local observations and knowledge collected using reliable and standardized methods.

Integrated, interdisciplinary approaches to assessment. Assessments that take a multidisciplinary approach bringing together health scientists, climatologists, biologists, ecologists, social and behavioural scientists, and policy researchers and include demographic, socio-economic, and health and environmental data are required to develop an adequate understanding of impacts, vulnerabilities, and capabilities in Arctic communities.

Increased analysis of historical data. Historical data (climate, health, social, economic) from appropriate locations with climate systems similar to those projected for Canadian northern regions must be used for integrated and geographic analyses of the spread of disease relative to climate variables. These analyses would make efficient use of existing information and increase our understanding of these issues and their interconnected nature.

Improvement of scenarios and models for health assessment. Developing and improving regional scenarios is needed for areas projected to experience significant impacts, such as the western Arctic. Socio-economic scenarios to model and project impacts and changes within northern indigenous populations are needed. Such scenarios are currently sparse, poorly developed, and inadequate.

Conceptual and analytical understanding of vulnerability and capacity. Work is needed at both the conceptual and analytical levels to define and increase our understanding of vulnerability and community health, how best to measure these concepts, and the use of these concepts in making decisions about the health of the community and in risk management. This work should include local knowledge and informal institutions (e.g., cultural sharing networks) to best understand these concepts in Aboriginal communities.

Enhancement of local capacities to identify, conduct, and analyze data related to climate change and the impacts on health. To ensure success and sustainability of adaptation strategies, development of local and regional monitoring, analytical, and decision-making capabilities are needed to support cooperative and empowering approaches to research and action.

Conclusions

33   In the Canadian North, the debate is no longer solely about identifying and predicting effects of climatic change but rather about what can and should be done to adapt, as some communities are already reporting impacts. This research focuses on improving the understanding of the magnitude and timing

of the impacts of climate change, how individuals and communities cope with current and predicted changes, and what public institutions should do to actively support adaptation.

34   There is currently sparse information on the effectiveness of any current strategies for dealing with climate-related or environmental risks to health in the locations described here and in other areas of the country. This lack of information is an important gap in our understanding and ability to assess which, where, and when Canadians may be vulnerable to the effects of climate change. A significant component is the lack of an assessment of the Canadian health sector's ability at various levels and in various locations to cope with and plan for the impacts of climate change. The cooperative planning, development, and conduct of projects in Inuit communities bringing together scientists, northern environment and health professionals, and community residents and experts, as presented here, has been essential to the success of the projects described in this article.

The community-based, dialogue-focused approach has proven valuable in engaging communities and establishing a local baseline for understanding the changes, impacts, vulnerabilities, and ability to respond at the local scale. Such an approach may very well prove useful in establishing this baseline in other regions.

Environmental Health Perspectives.
2006. December 114 (12).

This article is part of the mini-monograph *Climate change and human health: National assessments of impacts and adaptation.*

We acknowledge the participation and contribution made by northern residents and organizations to this work to date. C.F. acknowledges Canadian Institutes of Health Research—Institute for Aboriginal Peoples' Health for support to his work provided through a grant to the Nasivvik Centre. Thanks are also extended to three anonymous reviews for their comments.

References

ACIA. 2004. Arctic Climate Impact Assessment. Overview Report. Cambridge, UK: Cambridge University Press.

ACIA. 2005. Arctic Climate Impact Assessment. Scientific Report. Cambridge, UK: Cambridge University Press.

Adger WN, Huq S, Brown K, Conway D, Hulme M. 2003. Adaptation to climate change in the developing world. Prog Dev Stud 3(3):179–195. ArcticNet. 2004. Network Centres of Excellence. Available: www.arcticnet.ulaval.ca [accessed 15 June 2006].

Berkes F, Jolly D. 2002. Adapting to climate change: social-ecological resilience in a Canadian western Arctic community. Conserv Ecol 5(2):18. Available: www.consecol.org/vol5/iss2/art18 [accessed 3 July 2006].

Berner J, Furgal C. 2005. Human health. In: Arctic Climate Impact Assessment (ACIA). Cambridge, UK: Cambridge University Press, 863–906.

Canadian Arctic Contaminants Assessment Report II. 2003. Canadian Arctic Contaminants Assessment Report II (Health, Biotic, Abiotic and Knowledge in Action). Ottawa, Ontario, CN: Northern Contaminants Program, Department of Indian and Northern Affairs.

Casimiro E, Calheiros JM, Dessai S. 2001. Human health. In: Climate Change in Portugal: Scenarios, Impacts and Adaptation Measures (Santos FD, Forbes K, Moita R, eds). Lisbon: Scenarios, Impacts and Adaptation Measures.

Chambers R. 1997. Whose Reality Counts? Putting the First Last. London: Intermediate Technology Publications.

Chapin FS. 2005. Polar systems. In: Millenium Ecosystem Assessment. Available: http://www.millenniumassessment.org/en/products.aspx [accessed 15 June 2006].

Cohen SJ. 1997. Mackenzie Basin Impact Study. Final Report. Ottawa, Ontario, CN: Environment Canada.

Damas D. 2002. Arctic Migrants/Arctic Villagers. Montréal, Québec, CN: McGill-Queen's University Press.

Deutsche Gesellschalt für Technische Zusammenarbeit (German Agency for Technical Cooperation). 1988. ZOPP (Objectives Oriented Project Planning: An Introduction to the Method). Eschborn, Germany: Deutsche Gesellschalt für Technische Zusammenarbeit.

Duhaime G, Chabot M and Gaudreault M. 2002. Food consumption patterns and socioeconomic factors among the Inuit of Nunavik. Ecol Food Nutr 41:91–118.

Ebi KL, Kovats RS, Menne B. 2006. An approach for assessing human health vulnerability and public health interventions to adapt to climate change. Environ Health Perspect 114:1930–1934.

Ebi KL, Mearns O, Nyenzi B. 2003. Weather and climate: changing human exposures. In: Climate Change and Health: Risks and Responses (McMichael AJ, Campbell-Lendrum OH, Corvalan CF, Ebi KL, Githeko A, et al., eds). Geneva: World Health Organization.

Ford JD, Smit B, Wandel J. 2006. Vulnerability to climate change in the Arctic: a case study from Arctic Bay, Canada. Global Environ Change 16:145–160.

Furgal C, Martin D, Gosselin P. 2002. Climate change and health in Nunavik and Labrador: lessons from Inuit knowledge. In: The Earth is Faster Now: Indigenous Observations of Arctic Environmental Change (Krupnik I, Jolly D, eds). Washington, DC: Arctic Research Consortium of the United States, Arctic Studies Center, Smithsonian Institute, 266–300.

Furgal C, Martin D, Gosselin P, Viau A, Labrador Inuit Association (LIA), Nunavik Regional Board of Health and Social Services (NRBHSS). 2001. Climate change in Nunavik and Labrador: what we know from science and Inuit ecological knowledge. Final Project Report prepared for Climate Change Action Fund. Beauport, Québec, CN: Centre hospitalier Universitaire du Québec Pavillon Centre hospitalier Université Laval.

Government of Canada. 2003. Climate Change Impacts and Adaptation: A Canadian Perspective. Available: www.adaptation.nrcan.gc.ca/perspective_e.asp [accessed 15 June 2006].

Grambsch A, and Menne B. 2003. Adaptation and adaptive capacity in the public health context. In: Climate Change and Health: Risks and Responses (McMichael AJ, Campbell-Lendrum DH, Corvalan CF, Ebi KL, Githeko A, Scheraga JD, et al., eds). Geneva: World Health Organization, 220–236.

Health Canada. 2002. Climate Change and Health and Well-Being in Canada's North. Report on the Public Health Planning Workshop on Climate Change and Health and Well-Being in the North, 6–7 July 2002, Yellowknife, Northwest Territories. Ottawa, Ontario, CN: Health Canada.

Health Canada. 2003. Climate Change and Health: Assessing Canada's Capacity to Address the Health Impacts of Climate Change. Prepared for the Expert Advisory Workshop on Adaptive Capacity, 27–28 November 2003, Mont Tremblant, Québec, CN. Ottawa, Ontario, CN: Climate Change and Health Office, Safe Environments Program, Health Environments and Consumer Safety Branch, Health Canada.

Huntington H, Fox S. 2005. The changing Arctic: indigenous perspectives. In: Arctic Climate Impact Assessment. Cambridge, UK: Cambridge University Press, 61–98.

Indian and Northern Affairs Canada (INAC). 1993. Agreement between the Inuit of the Nunavut Settlement Area and Her Majesty the Queen in Right of Canada. Ottawa, Ontario, CN: Indian Affairs and Northern Development Canada and the Tunngavik Federation of Nunavut.

Kovats S, Ebi KL, Menne B. 2003. Methods of assessing human health vulnerability and public health adaptation to climate change. In: Health and Global Environmental Change, Series no 1. Copenhagen: World Health Organization, World Meteorological Organization, Health Canada, United Nations Environment Programme.

Krupnik I, Jolly D. 2002. The Earth Is Faster Now: Indigenous Observations of Climate Change. Fairbanks, AK: Arctic Research Consortium of the United States.

Kyoto Protocol. 2006. Home Page. Available: http://unfccc.int/kyoto_protocol/items/2830. php [accessed 7 November 2006].

Lafortune V, Furgal C, Drouin J, Annanack T, Einish N, Etidloie B, et al. 2004. Climate Change in Northern Quebec: Access to Land and Resource Issues. Project report. Kuujjuaq, Québec, CN: Kativik Regional Government.

McBean G, Alekssev GV, Chen D, Forland E, Fyfe J, Groisman PY, et al. 2005. Arctic climate: past and present. In: Arctic Climate Impact Assessment. Cambridge, UK: Cambridge University Press, 21–60.

Nelson O. 2003. Two men drown in Inukjuak: snowmobile crashes through thin ice. Nunatsiaq News, 31 January 2003. Available: www.nunatsiaq.com/archives/nunavut 030131/news/nuunavik/30131_02.html [accessed 3 July 2006].

Nickels S, Furgal C, Castleden J, Moss-Davies P, Buell M, Armstrong B, et al. 2002. Putting the human face on climate change through community workshops: Inuit knowledge, partnerships, and research. In: The Earth is Faster Now: Indigenous Observations of Arctic Environmental Change (Krupnik I, Jolly D, eds). Washington, DC: Arctic Research Consortium of the United States, Arctic Studies Center, Smithsonian Institute, 300–344.

Ouranos. 2004. S'adapter aux changements climatiques. Bibliothèque nationale du Québec. Montréal, Québec, CN: Ouranos Climate Change Consortium.

Patz JA, Engelberg D, Last J. 2000. The effects of changing weather on public health. Annu Rev Public Health 21:271–307.

Reidlinger D, Berkes F. 2001. Responding to climate change in northern communities: impacts and adaptations. Arctic 54(1):96–98.

Statistics Canada. 2001. Aboriginal People's Survey 2001—Initial Findings: Well-Being of the Non-Reserve Aboriginal Population. Catalogue no. 89-589-XIE. Ottawa, Ontario, CN: Statistics Canada.

Tesch R. 1990. Qualitative research: analysis types and software tools. New York: Falmer.

United Nations Framework Convention on Climate Change. 2006. Home Page. Available: http://unfccc.int/2860.php [accessed 7 November 2006].

Van Oostdam J, Donaldson SG, Feeley M, Arnold D, Ayotte P, Bondy G, et al. 2005. Human health implications of environmental contaminants in Arctic Canada: a review. Sci Total Environ 351–352:165–246.

Weller G, Bush E, Callaghan TV, Corell R, Fox S, Furgal C, et al. 2005. Summary and Synthesis of the ACIA. In: Arctic Climate Impact Assessment. Cambridge, UK: Cambridge University Press, 989–1020.

Wonders W, ed. 2003. Canada's Changing North. Revised ed. Montréal: McGill-Queen's University Press.

Yohe G, Tol RSJ. 2002. Indicators for social and economic coping capacity—moving toward a working definition of adaptive capacity. Global Environ Change Hum Policy Dimen 12:25–40.

KEY AND CHALLENGING WORDS

autonomous, tripartite, anecdotal, extrapolation, alleviate, pluralistic, subsistence, resilience

QUESTIONS

1. Identify the essay plan. What could account for the absence of a separate literature review section?

2. What is the function of the section "The Canadian North"? What is meant by the phrase "a socio-ecologic collage" (paragraph 4)?

3. In two to three sentences for each study, summarize the purpose and methodology used in the two major studies that the authors focus on in this essay (under "methodology," consider the participants in the study and the methods used to collect and measure data—see, in particular, paragraphs 9–11 and 16).

4. How do "qualitative studies" differ from the "quantitative studies" that typify methods of evidence-gathering and presentation in Type B essays (see pages 23–24)? Why have qualitative methods been used so extensively to assess the impact of climate change in northern Aboriginal communities?

5. (a) Identify which paragraph(s) focus on the material presented in Table 1; identify which paragraph(s) focus on the material presented in Table 2. Is the more complete picture conveyed through the tables or through the corresponding sections of text? Explain why this might be the case by discussing the different functions of tables and text in this essay. (b) How is the focus of Table 3 different from that of tables 1 and 2? What accounts for the differing focus?

6. Explain the differences between "reactive" and "proactive" strategies (paragraph 20). In the long term, which could be considered more important?

7. Identify two general factors that can affect the capacity for health adaptation to climate change. Why is it important to establish a "vulnerability baseline" for Aboriginal groups experiencing the effects of climate change? For what other kinds of groups might it also be important?

8. What is the purpose of the list of "data gaps" mentioned in the "Discussion" section? Paraphrase one of the items in the list.

POST-READING

1. *Collaborative activity:* As a follow-up to question 4, discuss the pros and cons of using qualitative methods to investigate a problem or study a phenomenon (you could consider using qualitative methods only or combining them with quantitative ones—the "mixed method" approach). Then come up with one specific situation in which qualitative methods might be useful as a means of investigating a phenomenon. This could be a situation that exists at your university/college or within a particular student group. Along with describing the specific situation, identify which specific approach(es) or method(s) would be the most useful or appropriate (e.g., roundtable discussion, focus groups, workshops, direct observation, unstructured interview).

2. The authors mention the value of knowledge-sharing among members of groups or cultures who want to maintain a traditional lifestyle but state that the generation of this knowledge "is being challenged locally with shifts toward a more 'Western lifestyle'" (paragraph 23). Write a response (300 to 500 words) that addresses central issues around the maintenance of traditional lifestyles in the face of cultural pressures to conform to mainstream values or practices.

3. Write a brief (500- to 750-word) evaluative report (stressing assessment) or informational report (stressing content) on a website dedicated to the study of climate change in the Canadian Arctic. One such site mentioned in the article is ArcticNet; this site also contains links to similar sites that you could consider. Organize your report by appropriate formal or descriptive categories. Formal categories could include introduction, methods (basis of your evaluation), results, and conclusion. You could consider the website's purpose, credibility, main menu, links, navigation aids, accessibility, organization, visual appeal, quality and depth of information, use of charts to enhance understanding, and so on.

RELATED WEBSITES OF INTEREST

Network Environments for Aboriginal Health Research (NEAHR):
www.cihr-irsc.gc.ca/e/27071.html

Centre for Inuit Health and Changing Environments:
www.nasivvik.ulaval.ca/

ADDITIONAL LIBRARY READING

Lougheed T. (2010). The changing landscape of Arctic traditional food. *Environmental Health Perspectives, 118*, 386–393. doi:10.1289/ehp.118-a386

Nickels, S., Furgal, C., & Buell, M. (2005). *Unikkaaqatigiit: Putting the human face on climate change – perspectives from Inuit in Canada* [Ebook, National Aboriginal Health Organization].

Food security: The challenge of feeding 9 billion people

H. Charles J. Godfray, John R. Beddington, Ian R. Crute, Lawrence Haddad,
David Lawrence, James F. Muir, Jules Pretty, Sherman Robinson,
Sandy M. Thomas, and Camilla Toulmin

(5,911 words)

Pre-reading

1. How would you define "food security"? After you've written a short definition, check a reliable source, rewriting your definition if necessary.

2. Do an online search to obtain information about the organizations cited in notes 1–3: *The World Bank*: www.worldbank.org/ and *Food and Agriculture Organization of the United Nations*: www.fao.org/. Write a one-paragraph profile of each that includes purpose/objectives, organizational structure (including affiliation with other major organizations or countries, if applicable), and current projects and plans. Some of this information might be available via an "About Us" or "Who Are We?" page.

1   The past half-century has seen marked growth in food production, allowing for a dramatic decrease in the proportion of the world's people that are hungry, despite a doubling of the total population (Fig. 1) (*1*, *2*). Nevertheless, more than one in seven people today still do not have access to sufficient protein and energy from their diet, and even more suffer from some form of micronutrient malnourishment (*3*). The world is now facing a new set of intersecting challenges (*4*). The global population will continue to grow, yet it is likely to plateau at some 9 billion people by roughly the middle of this century. A major correlate of this deceleration in population growth is increased wealth, and with higher purchasing power comes higher consumption and a greater demand for processed food, meat, dairy, and fish, all of which add pressure to the food supply system. At the same time, food producers are experiencing greater competition for land, water, and energy, and the need to curb the many negative effects of food production on the environment is becoming increasingly clear (*5*, *6*). Overarching all of these issues is the threat of the effects of substantial climate change and concerns about how mitigation and adaptation measures may affect the food system (*7*, *8*).

2   A threefold challenge now faces the world (*9*): Match the rapidly changing demand for food from a larger and more affluent population to its supply; do so in ways that are environmentally and socially sustainable; and ensure that the world's poorest people are no longer hungry. This challenge requires changes in the way food is produced, stored, processed, distributed, and accessed that are as radical as those that occurred during the eighteenth- and nineteenth-century Industrial and Agricultural Revolutions and the twentieth-century Green Revolution. Increases in production will have an important part to play, but they will be constrained as never before by the finite resources provided by Earth's lands, oceans, and atmosphere (*10*).

3   Patterns in global food prices are indicators of trends in the availability of food, at least for those who can afford it and have access to world markets. Over the past century, gross food prices have generally fallen, leveling off in the past three decades but punctuated by price spikes such as that caused by the 1970s oil crisis. In mid-2008, there was an unexpected rapid rise in food prices, the cause of which is still being debated, that subsided when the world economy went into recession (*11*). However, many (but not all) commentators have predicted that this spike heralds a period of rising and more volatile food prices driven primarily by increased demand from rapidly developing countries, as well as by competition for resources from first-generation biofuels production (*12*). Increased food prices will stimulate greater investment in food production, but the critical importance of food to human well-being and also to social and political stability makes it likely that governments and other organizations will want to encourage food production beyond that driven by simple market mechanisms (*13*). The long-term nature of returns on investment for many aspects of food production and the importance of policies that promote sustainability and equity also argue against purely relying on market solutions.

4   So how can more food be produced sustainably? In the past, the primary solution to food shortages has been to bring more land into agriculture and to exploit new fish stocks. Yet over the past five decades, while grain production has more than doubled, the amount of land devoted to arable agriculture globally has increased by only ~9 per cent (*14*). Some new land could be brought into cultivation, but the competition for land from other human activities makes this an increasingly unlikely and costly solution, particularly if protecting biodiversity and the public goods provided by natural ecosystems (for example, carbon storage in rainforest) are given higher priority (*15*). In recent decades, agricultural land that was formerly productive has been lost to urbanization and other human uses, as well as to desertification, salinization, soil erosion, and other consequences of unsustainable land management (*16*). Further losses, which may be exacerbated by climate change, are likely (*7*). Recent policy decisions to produce first-generation biofuels on good quality agricultural land have added to the competitive pressures (*17*). Thus, the most likely scenario is that more food will need to be produced from the same amount of (or even less) land. Moreover, there are no major new fishing grounds: Virtually all capture fisheries are fully exploited, and most are overexploited.

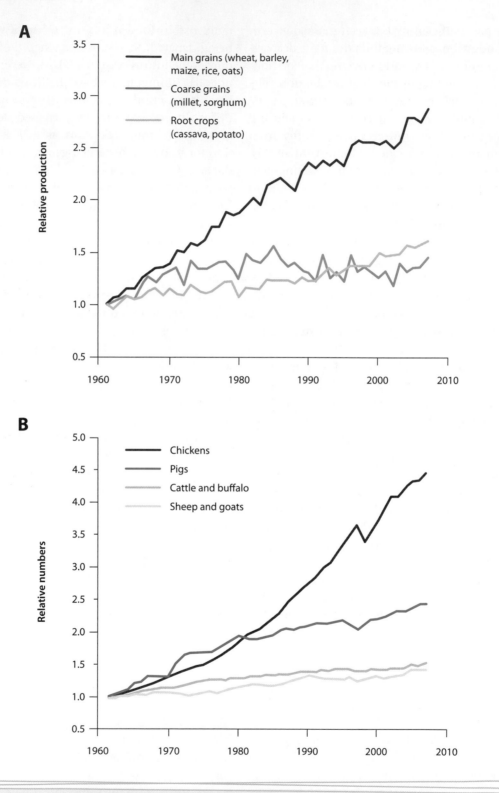

FIGURE 1 CHANGES IN THE RELATIVE GLOBAL PRODUCTION OF CROPS AND ANIMALS SINCE 1961 (WHEN RELATIVE PRODUCTION SCALED TO 1 IN 1961). (A) MAJOR CROP PLANTS AND (B) MAJOR TYPES OF LIVESTOCK.

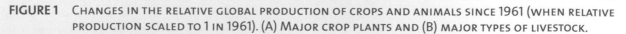

[Source: (2)]

5   Recent studies suggest that the world will need 70 to 100 per cent more food by 2050 (*1, 18*). In this article, major strategies for contributing to the challenge of feeding 9 billion people, including the most disadvantaged, are explored. Particular emphasis is given to sustainability, as well as to the combined role of the natural and social sciences in analyzing and addressing the challenge.

Closing the Yield Gap

6   There is wide geographic variation in crop and livestock productivity, even across regions that experience similar climates. The difference between realized productivity and the best that can be achieved using current genetic material and available technologies and management is termed the "yield gap." The best yields that can be obtained locally depend on the capacity of farmers to access and use, among other things, seeds, water, nutrients, pest management, soils, biodiversity, and knowledge. It has been estimated that in those parts of Southeast Asia where irrigation is available, average maximum climate-adjusted rice yields are 8.5 metric tons per hectare, yet the average actually achieved yields are 60 per cent of this figure (*19*). Similar yield gaps are found in rain-fed wheat in central Asia and rain-fed cereals in Argentina and Brazil. Another way to illustrate the yield gap is to compare changes in per capita food production over the past 50 years. In Asia, this amount has increased approximately twofold (in China, by a factor of nearly 3.5), and in Latin America, it has increased 1.6-fold; in Africa, per capita production fell back from the mid-1970s and has only just reached the same level as in 1961 (*2, 20*). Substantially more food, as well as the income to purchase food, could be produced with current crops and livestock if methods were found to close the yield gaps.

7   Low yields occur because of technical constraints that prevent local food producers from increasing productivity or for economic reasons arising from market conditions. For example, farmers may not have access to the technical knowledge and skills required to increase production, the finances required to invest in higher production (e.g., irrigation, fertilizer, machinery, crop-protection products, and soil-conservation measures), or the crop and livestock varieties that maximize yields. After harvest or slaughter, they may not be able to store the produce or have access to the infrastructure to transport the produce to consumer markets. Farmers may also choose not to invest in improving agricultural productivity because the returns do not compare well with other uses of capital and labor.

BOX 1   SUSTAINABLE INTENSIFICATION

Producing more food from the same area of land while reducing the environmental impacts requires what has been called "sustainable intensification" (*18*). In exactly the same way that yields can be increased with the use of existing technologies, many options currently exist to reduce negative externalities (*47*). Net reductions in some greenhouse gas emissions can potentially be achieved by changing agronomic practices, the adoption of integrated pest management methods, the integrated management of waste in livestock production, and the use of agroforestry. However, the effects of different agronomic practices on the full range of greenhouse gases can be very complex and may depend on the temporal and spatial scale of measurement. More research is required to allow a better assessment of competing policy options. Strategies such as zero or reduced tillage (the reduction in inversion ploughing), contour farming, mulches, and cover crops improve water and soil conservation, but they may not increase stocks of soil carbon or reduce emissions of nitrous oxide. Precision agriculture refers to a series of technologies that allow the application of water, nutrients, and pesticides only to the places and at the times they are required, thereby optimizing the use of inputs (*48*). Finally, agricultural land and water bodies used for aquaculture and fisheries can be managed in ways specifically designed to reduce negative impacts on biodiversity.

8   Exactly how best to facilitate increased food production is highly site-specific. In the most extreme cases of failed states and nonfunctioning markets, the solution lies completely outside the food system. Where a functioning state exists, there is a balance to be struck between investing in overall economic growth as a spur to agriculture and focusing on investing in agriculture as a spur to economic growth, though the two are obviously linked in regions, such as sub-Saharan Africa, where agriculture typically makes up 20 to 40 per cent gross domestic product. In some situations, such as low-income food-importing countries, investing purely in generating widespread income growth to allow food purchases from regions and countries with better production capabilities may be the best choice. When investment is targeted at food production, a further issue is the balance between putting resources into regional and national infrastructure, such as roads and ports, and investing in local social and economic capital (21, 22).

9   A yield gap may also exist because the high costs of inputs or the low returns from increased production make it economically suboptimal to raise production to the maximum technically attainable. Poor transport and market infrastructure raise the prices of inputs, such as fertilizers and water, and increase the costs of moving the food produced into national or world markets. Where the risks of investment are high and the means to offset them are absent, not investing can be the most rational decision, part of the "poverty trap." Food production in developing countries can be severely affected by market interventions in the developed world, such as subsidies or price supports. These need to be carefully designed and implemented so that their effects on global commodity prices do not act as disincentives to production in other countries (23).

10   The globalization of the food system offers some local food producers access to larger markets, as well as to capital for investment. At the aggregate level, it also appears to increase the global efficiency of food production by allowing regional specialization in the production of the locally most appropriate foods. Because the expansion of food production and the growth of population both occur at different rates in different geographic regions, global trade is necessary to balance supply and demand across

regions. However, the environmental costs of food production might increase with globalization, for example, because of increased greenhouse gas emissions associated with increased production and food transport (24). An unfettered market can also penalize particular communities and sectors, especially the poorest who have the least influence on how global markets are structured and regulated. Expanded trade can provide insurance against regional shocks on production such as conflict, epidemics, droughts, or floods—shocks that are likely to increase in frequency as climate change occurs. Conversely, a highly connected food system may lead to the more widespread propagation of economic perturbations, as in the recent banking crisis, thus affecting more people. There is an urgent need for a better understanding of the effects of globalization on the full food system and its externalities.

11   The yield gap is not static. Maintaining, let alone increasing, productivity depends on continued innovation to control weeds, diseases, insects, and other pests as they evolve resistance to different control measures, or as new species emerge or are dispersed to new regions. Innovation involves both traditional and advanced crop and livestock breeding, as well as the continuing development of better chemical, agronomic, and agro-ecological control measures. The maximum attainable yield in different regions will also shift as the effects of climate change are felt. Increasing atmospheric CO_2 levels can directly stimulate crop growth, though within the context of real agricultural production systems, the magnitude of this effect is not clear (7). More important will be the ability to grow crops in places that are currently unsuitable, particularly the northern temperate regions (though expansion of agriculture at the expense of boreal forest would lead to major greenhouse gas emissions), and the loss of currently productive regions because of excessively high temperatures and drought. Models that couple the physics of climate change with the biology of crop growth will be important to help policy-makers anticipate these changes, as well as to evaluate the role of "agricultural biodiversity" in helping mitigate their effects (25).

12   Closing the yield gap would dramatically increase the supply of food, but with uncertain impacts on the environment and potential feedbacks

that could undermine future food production. Food production has important negative "externalities," namely effects on the environment or economy that are not reflected in the cost of food. These include the release of greenhouse gases [especially methane and nitrous oxide, which are more damaging than CO2 and for which agriculture is a major source (26)], environmental pollution due to nutrient run-off, water shortages due to over-extraction, soil degradation and the loss of biodiversity through land conversion or inappropriate management, and ecosystem disruption due to the intensive harvesting of fish and other aquatic foods (6).

13   To address these negative effects, it is now widely recognized that food production systems and the food chain in general must become fully sustainable (18). The principle of sustainability implies the use of resources at rates that do not exceed the capacity of Earth to replace them. By definition, dependency on nonrenewable inputs is unsustainable, even if in the short term it is necessary as part of a trajectory toward sustainability.

14   There are many difficulties in making sustainability operational. Over what spatial scale should food production be sustainable? Clearly an overarching goal is global sustainability, but should this goal also apply at lower levels, such as regions (or oceans), nations, or farms? Could high levels of consumption or negative externalities in some regions be mitigated by improvements in other areas, or could some unsustainable activities in the food system be offset by actions in the nonfood sector (through carbon-trading, for example)? Though simple definitions of sustainability are independent of time scale, in practice, how fast should we seek to move from the status quo to a sustainable food system? The challenges of climate change and competition for water, fossil fuels, and other resources suggest that a rapid transition is essential. Nevertheless, it is also legitimate to explore the possibility that superior technologies may become available and that future generations may be wealthier and, hence, better able to absorb the costs of the transition. Finally, we do not yet have good enough metrics of sustainability, a major problem when evaluating alternative strategies and negotiating trade-offs. This is the case for relatively circumscribed activities, such as crop production on individual farms, and even harder when the complete food chain is included or for complex products that may contain ingredients sourced from all around the globe. There is also a danger that an overemphasis on what can be measured relatively simply (carbon, for example) may lead to dimensions of sustainability that are harder to quantify (such as biodiversity) being ignored. These are areas at the interface of science, engineering, and economics that urgently need more attention (see Box 1). The introduction of measures to promote sustainability does not necessarily reduce yields or profits. One study of 286 agricultural sustainability projects in developing countries, involving 12.6 million chiefly small-holder farmers on 37 million hectares, found an average yield increase of 79 per cent across a very wide variety of systems and crop types (27). One-quarter of the projects reported a doubling of yield. Research on the ability of these and related programs to be scaled up to country and regional levels should be a priority (Fig. 2).

15   Strategies designed to close the yield gap in the poorest countries face some particular challenges (28). Much production is dominated by small-holder agriculture with women often taking a dominant role in the workforce. Where viable, investment in the social and economic mechanisms to enable improved small-holder yields, especially where targeted at women, can be important means of increasing the income of both farm and rural nonfarm households. The lack of secure land rights can be a particular problem for many poor communities, may act as a disincentive for small holders to invest in managing the land more productively, and may make it harder to raise investment capital (29). In a time of rising prices for food and land, it can also render these communities vulnerable to displacement by more powerful interest groups. Where the political will and organizational infrastructure exist, title definition and protection could be greatly assisted by the application of modern information and communication technologies. Even so, there will be many people who cannot afford to purchase sufficient calories and nutrients for a healthy life and who will require social protection programs to increase their ability to obtain food. However, if properly designed, these programs can help stimulate local agriculture by providing small holders with increased certainty about the demand for their products.

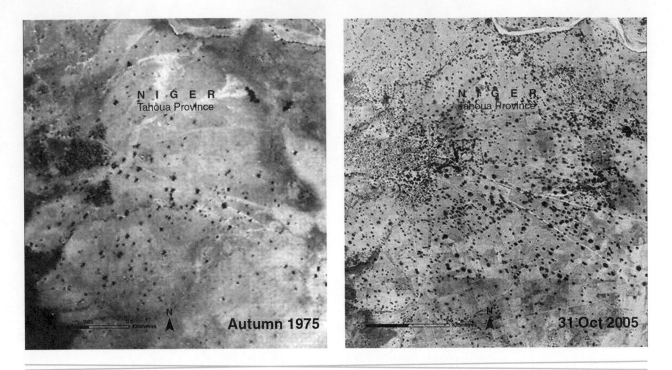

FIGURE 2   AN EXAMPLE OF A MAJOR SUCCESSFUL SUSTAINABLE AGRICULTURE PROJECT. NIGER WAS STRONGLY
AFFECTED BY A SERIES OF DROUGHT YEARS IN THE 1970S AND 1980S AND BY ENVIRONMENTAL
DEGRADATION. FROM THE EARLY 1980S, DONORS INVESTED SUBSTANTIALLY IN SOIL AND WATER
CONSERVATION. THE TOTAL AREA TREATED IS ON THE ORDER OF 300,000 HA, MOST OF WHICH WENT
INTO THE REHABILITATION OF DEGRADED LAND. THE PROJECT IN THE ILLELA DISTRICT OF NIGER
PROMOTED SIMPLE WATER-HARVESTING TECHNIQUES. CONTOUR STONE BUNDS, HALF MOONS, STONE
BUNDING, AND IMPROVED TRADITIONAL PLANTING PITS (ZAÏ) WERE USED TO REHABILITATE BARREN,
CRUSTED LAND. MORE THAN 300,000 HA HAVE BEEN REHABILITATED, AND CROP YIELDS HAVE
INCREASED AND BECOME MORE STABLE FROM YEAR TO YEAR. TREE COVER HAS INCREASED, AS SHOWN
IN THE PHOTOGRAPHS. DEVELOPMENT OF THE LAND MARKET AND CONTINUED INCREMENTAL
EXPANSION OF THE TREATED AREA WITHOUT FURTHER PROJECT ASSISTANCE INDICATE THAT THE
OUTCOMES ARE SUSTAINABLE (51, 52).

16   There is also a role for large-scale farming operations in poor-country agriculture, though the value
and contexts in which this is feasible are much
debated (30). This debate has been fanned by a substantial increase in the number of sovereign wealth
funds, companies, and individuals leasing, purchasing, or attempting to purchase large tracts of agricultural land in developing countries. This external
investment in developing-country agriculture may
bring major benefits, especially where investors bring
considerable improvements to crop production and
processing, but only if the rights and welfare of the
tenants and existing resource users are properly
addressed (31).

17   Many of the very poorest people live in areas
so remote that they are effectively disconnected from
national and world food markets. But for others, especially the urban poor, higher food prices have a direct
negative effect on their ability to purchase a healthy
diet. Many rural farmers and other food producers
live near the margin of being net food consumers and
producers and will be affected in complex ways by
rising food prices, with some benefitting and some
being harmed (21). Thus, whereas reducing distorting
agricultural support mechanisms in developed countries and liberalizing world trade should stimulate
overall food production in developing countries, not
everyone will gain (23, 32). Better models that can

more accurately predict these complex interactions are urgently needed.

Increasing Production Limits

18   The most productive crops, such as sugar cane, growing in optimum conditions, can convert solar energy into biomass with an efficiency of ~2 per cent, resulting in high yields of biomass (up to 150 metric tons per hectare) (33). There is much debate over exactly what the theoretical limits are for the major crops under different conditions, and similarly, for the maximum yield that can be obtained for livestock rearing (18). However, there is clearly considerable scope for increasing production limits.

19   The Green Revolution succeeded by using conventional breeding to develop F1 hybrid varieties of maize and semi-dwarf, disease-resistant varieties of wheat and rice. These varieties could be provided with more irrigation and fertilizer (20) without the risk of major crop losses due to lodging (falling over) or severe rust epidemics. Increased yield is still a

major goal, but the importance of greater water- and nutrient-use efficiency, as well as tolerance of abiotic stress, is also likely to increase. Modern genetic techniques and a better understanding of crop physiology allow for a more directed approach to selection across multiple traits. The speed and costs at which genomes today can be sequenced or resequenced now means that these techniques can be more easily applied to develop varieties of crop species that will yield well in challenging environments. These include crops such as sorghum, millet, cassava, and banana, species that are staple foods for many of the world's poorest communities (34).

20   Currently, the major commercialized genetically modified (GM) crops involve relatively simple manipulations, such as the insertion of a gene for herbicide resistance or another for a pest-insect toxin. The next decade will see the development of combinations of desirable traits and the introduction of new traits such as drought tolerance. By mid-century, much more radical options involving highly polygenic traits may be feasible (Table 1). Production of cloned animals with engineered

TABLE 1   EXAMPLES OF CURRENT AND POTENTIAL FUTURE APPLICATIONS OF GM TECHNOLOGY FOR CROP GENETIC IMPROVEMENT.

Time Scale	Target crop trait	Target crops
Current	Tolerance to broad-spectrum herbicide	Maize, soybean, oilseed brassica
	Resistance to chewing insect pests	Maize, cotton, oilseed brassica
Short-term (5–10 years)	Nutritional bio-fortification	Staple cereal crops, sweet potato
	Resistance to fungus and virus pathogens	Potato, wheat, rice, banana, fruits, vegetables
	Resistance to sucking insect pests	Rice, fruits, vegetables
	Improved processing and storage	Wheat, potato, fruits, vegetables
	Drought tolerance	Staple cereal and tuber crops
Medium-term (10–20 years)	Salinity tolerance	Staple cereal and tuber crops
	Increased nitrogen-use efficiency	
	High-temperature tolerance apomixis	
Long-term (>20 years)	Nitrogen fixation	Staple cereal and tuber crops
	Denitrification inhibitor production	
	Conversion to perennial habit	
	Increased photosynthetic efficiency	

[Source: (18, 49)]

innate immunity to diseases that reduce production efficiency has the potential to reduce substantial losses arising from mortality and subclinical infections. Biotechnology could also produce plants for animal feed with modified composition that increase the efficiency of meat production and lower methane emissions.

21   Domestication inevitably means that only a subset of the genes available in the wild-species progenitor gene pool is represented among crop varieties and livestock breeds. Unexploited genetic material from land races, rare breeds, and wild relatives will be important in allowing breeders to respond to new challenges. International collections and gene banks provide valuable repositories for such genetic variation, but it is nevertheless necessary to ensure that locally adapted crop and livestock germplasm is not lost in the process of their displacement by modern, improved varieties and breeds. The trend over recent decades is of a general decline in investment in technological innovation in food production (with some notable exceptions, such as in China and Brazil) and a switch from public to private sources (1). Fair returns on investment are essential for the proper functioning of the private sector, but the extension of the protection of intellectual property rights to biotechnology has led to a growing public perception in some countries that biotech research purely benefits commercial interests and offers no long-term public good. Just as seriously, it also led to a virtual monopoly of GM traits in some parts of the world, by a restricted number of companies, which limits innovation and investment in the technology. Finding ways to incentivize wide access and sustainability, while encouraging a competitive and innovative private sector to make best use of developing technology, is a major governance challenge.

22   The issue of trust and public acceptance of biotechnology has been highlighted by the debate over the acceptance of GM technologies. Because genetic modification involves germline modification of an organism and its introduction to the environment and food chain, a number of particular environmental and food safety issues need to be assessed. Despite the introduction of rigorous science-based risk assessment, this discussion has become highly politicized and polarized in some countries, particularly those in Europe. Our view is that genetic modification is a potentially valuable technology whose advantages and disadvantages need to be considered rigorously on an evidential, inclusive, case-by-case basis: Genetic modification should neither be privileged nor automatically dismissed. We also accept the need for this technology to gain greater public acceptance and trust before it can be considered as one among a set of technologies that may contribute to improved global food security.

23   There are particular issues involving new technologies, both GM and non-GM, that are targeted at helping the least-developed countries (35, 36). The technologies must be directed at the needs of those communities, which are often different from those of more developed country farmers. To increase the likelihood that new technology works for, and is adopted by, the poorest nations, they need to be involved in the framing, prioritization, risk assessment, and regulation of innovations. This will often require the creation of innovative institutional and governance mechanisms that account for socio-cultural context (for example, the importance of women in developing-country food production). New technologies offer major promise, but there are risks of lost trust if their potential benefits are exaggerated in public debate. Efforts to increase sustainable production limits that benefit the poorest nations will need to be based around new alliances of businesses, civil society organizations, and governments.

Reducing Waste

24   Roughly 30 to 40 per cent of food in both the developed and developing worlds is lost to waste, though the causes behind this are very different (Fig. 3) (16, 37–39). In the developing world, losses are mainly attributable to the absence of food-chain infrastructure and the lack of knowledge or investment in storage technologies on the farm, although data are scarce. For example, in India, it is estimated that 35 to 40 per cent of fresh produce is lost because neither wholesale nor retail outlets have cold storage (16). Even with rice grain, which can be stored more readily, as much as one-third of the harvest in

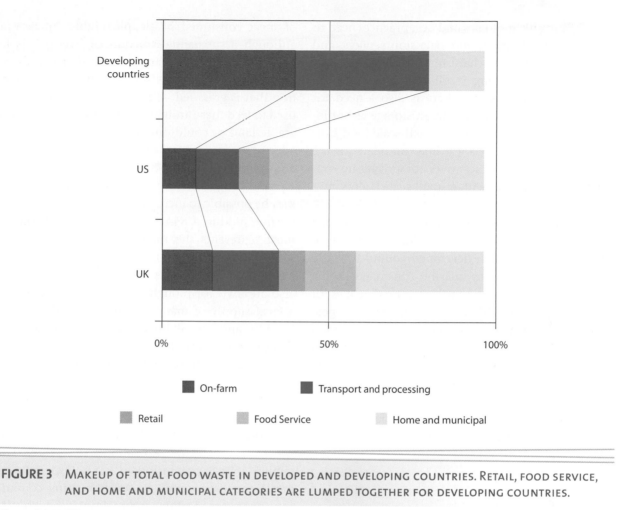

0%   50%   100%

■ On-farm   ■ Transport and processing

■ Retail   ■ Food Service   ■ Home and municipal

FIGURE 3   MAKEUP OF TOTAL FOOD WASTE IN DEVELOPED AND DEVELOPING COUNTRIES. RETAIL, FOOD SERVICE, AND HOME AND MUNICIPAL CATEGORIES ARE LUMPED TOGETHER FOR DEVELOPING COUNTRIES.

[Source: (*16, 37–39*)]

Southeast Asia can be lost after harvest to pests and spoilage (*40*). But the picture is more complex than a simple lack of storage facilities: Although storage after harvest when there is a glut of food would seem to make economic sense, the farmer often has to sell immediately to raise cash.

25   In contrast, in the developed world, pre-retail losses are much lower, but those arising at the retail, food service, and home stages of the food chain have grown dramatically in recent years, for a variety of reasons (*41*). At present, food is relatively cheap, at least for these consumers, which reduces the incentives to avoid waste. Consumers have become accustomed to purchasing foods of the highest cosmetic standards; hence, retailers discard many edible, yet only slightly blemished products. Commercial pressures can encourage waste: The food service industry frequently

uses "super-sized" portions as a competitive lever, whereas "buy one get one free" offers have the same function for retailers. Litigation and lack of education on food safety have led to a reliance on "use by" dates, whose safety margins often mean that food fit for consumption is thrown away. In some developed countries, unwanted food goes to a landfill instead of being used as animal feed or compost because of legislation to control prion diseases.

26   Different strategies are required to tackle the two types of waste. In developing countries, public investment in transport infrastructure would reduce the opportunities for spoilage, whereas better-functioning markets and the availability of capital would increase the efficiency of the food chain, for example, by allowing the introduction of cold storage (though this has implications for greenhouse gas emissions)

(*38*). Existing technologies and best practices need to be spread by education and extension services, and market and finance mechanisms are required to protect farmers from having to sell at peak supply, leading to gluts and wastage. There is also a need for continuing research in postharvest storage technologies. Improved technology for small-scale food storage in poorer contexts is a prime candidate for the introduction of state incentives for private innovation, with the involvement of small-scale traders, millers, and producers.

27   If food prices were to rise again, it is likely that there would be a decrease in the volume of waste produced by consumers in developed countries. Waste may also be reduced by alerting consumers to the scale of the issue, as well as to domestic strategies for reducing food loss. Advocacy, education, and possibly legislation may also reduce waste in the food service and retail sectors. Legislation such as that on sell-by dates and swill that has inadvertently increased food waste should be reexamined within a more inclusive competing-risks framework. Reducing developed-country food waste is particularly challenging, as it is so closely linked to individual behavior and cultural attitudes toward food.

Changing Diets

28   The conversion efficiency of plant into animal matter is ~10 per cent; thus, there is a prima facie case that more people could be supported from the same amount of land if they were vegetarians. About one-third of global cereal production is fed to animals (*42*). But currently, one of the major challenges to the food system is the rapidly increasing demand for meat and dairy products that has led, over the past 50 years, to a ~1.5-fold increase in the global numbers of cattle, sheep, and goats, with equivalent increases of ~2.5- and ~4.5-fold for pigs and chickens, respectively (*2*) (Fig. 1). This is largely attributable to the increased wealth of consumers everywhere and most recently in countries such as China and India.

29   However, the argument that all meat consumption is bad is overly simplistic. First, there is substantial variation in the production efficiency and environmental impact of the major classes of meat consumed by people (Table 2). Second, although a substantial fraction of livestock is fed on grain and other plant protein that could feed humans, there remains a very substantial proportion that is grass-fed. Much of the grassland that is used to feed these animals could not be converted to arable land or could only be converted with major adverse environmental outcomes. In addition, pigs and poultry are often fed on human food "waste." Third, through better rearing or improved breeds, it may be possible to increase the efficiency with which meat is produced. Finally, in developing countries, meat represents the most concentrated source of some vitamins and minerals, which is important for individuals such as young children. Livestock also are used for ploughing and transport, provide a local supply of manure, can be a vital source of income, and are of huge cultural importance for many poorer communities.

30   Reducing the consumption of meat and increasing the proportion that is derived from the most efficient sources offer an opportunity to feed more people and also present other advantages (*37*). Well-balanced diets rich in grains and other vegetable products are considered to be more healthful than those containing a high proportion of meat (especially red meat) and dairy products. As developing countries consume more meat in combination with high-sugar and -fat foods, they may find themselves having to deal with obesity before they have overcome undernutrition, leading to an increase in spending on health that could otherwise be used to alleviate poverty. Livestock production is also a major source of methane, a very powerful greenhouse gas, though this can be partially offset by the use of animal manure to replace synthetic nitrogen fertilizer (*43*). Of the five strategies we discuss here, assessing the value of decreasing the fraction of meat in our diets is the most difficult and needs to be better understood.

Expanding Aquaculture

31   Aquatic products (mainly fish, aquatic molluscs, and crustaceans) have a critical role in the food system, providing nearly 3 billion people with at least 15 per cent of their animal protein intake (*44*).

TABLE 2   CᴏᴍᴘᴀRɪSᴏN ᴏF THE ɪᴍᴘACT ᴏF GRAZɪNG AND ɪNTENSɪVE (CᴏNFɪNED/ɪNDᴜSTRɪALɪZED) GRAɪN-FED
LɪVESTᴏCK SYSTEMS ᴏN WATER ᴜSE, GRAɪN REQᴜɪREMENT, AND METHANE PRᴏDᴜCTɪᴏN. SERVɪCE
WATER ɪS THAT REQᴜɪRED FᴏR CLEANɪNG AND WASHɪNG LɪVESTᴏCK HᴏᴜSɪNG AND ᴏTHER FACɪLɪTɪES.
DASHES ɪNDɪCATE CᴏMBɪNATɪᴏNS FᴏR WHɪCH Nᴏ DATA ARE AVAɪLABLE (EɪTHER BECAᴜSE ɪT CANNᴏT
BE MEASᴜRED ᴏR BECAᴜSE THE CᴏMBɪNATɪᴏN DᴏES NᴏT EXɪST). THɪS TABLE DᴏES NᴏT ɪNCLᴜDE ᴏTHER
ɪMPACTS ᴏF DɪFFERɪNG LɪVESTᴏCK MANAGEMENT SYSTEMS SᴜCH AS (ɪ) NᴜTRɪENT RᴜN-ᴏFF AND
PᴏLLᴜTɪᴏN Tᴏ SᴜRFACE AND GRᴏᴜNDWATER, (ɪɪ) PRᴏTᴏZᴏAN AND BACTERɪAL CᴏNTAMɪNATɪᴏN ᴏF
WATER AND FᴏᴏD, (ɪɪɪ) ANTɪBɪᴏTɪC RESɪDᴜES ɪN WATER AND FᴏᴏD, (ɪV) HEAVY METAL FRᴏM FEED ɪN
SᴏɪLS AND WATER, (V) ᴏDᴏR NᴜɪSANCE FRᴏM WASTES, (Vɪ) ɪNPᴜTS ᴜSED FᴏR FEED PRᴏDᴜCTɪᴏN AND
LᴏST Tᴏ THE ENVɪRᴏNMENT, (Vɪɪ) LɪVESTᴏCK-RELATED LAND-ᴜSE CHANGE.

Water	Measure of water use	Grazing	Intensive
		Litres day^{-1} per animal at 15°C	
Cattle	Drinking water: all	22	103
	Service water: beef	5	11
	Service water: dairy	5	22
Pigs (lactating adult)	Drinking water	17	17
	Service water	25	125
Sheep (lactating adult)	Drinking water	9	9
	Service water	5	5
Chicken (broiler and layer)	Drinking water	1.3–1.8	1.3–1.8
	Service water	0.09–0.15	0.09–0.15
Feed required to produce 1 kg of meat		**kg of cereal per animal**	
Cattle		—	8
Pigs		—	4
Chicken (broiler)		—	1
Methane emissions from cattle		**kg of CH$_4$ per animal year^{-1}**	
Cattle: dairy (US, Europe)		—	117–128
Cattle: beef, dairy (US, Europe)		53–60	—
Cattle: dairy (Africa, India)		—	45–58
Cattle: grazing (Africa, India)		27–31	—

[Source: (7, 50)]

32   In many regions, aquaculture has been sufficiently profitable to permit strong growth; replicating this growth in areas such as Africa where it has not occurred could bring major benefits. Technical advances in hatchery systems, feeds and feed-delivery systems, and disease management could all increase output. Future gains may also come from better stock selection, larger-scale production technologies, aquaculture in open seas and larger inland water bodies, and the culture of a wider range of species. The long production cycle of many species (typically six to 24 months) requires a financing system that is capable of providing working capital as well as offsetting risk. Wider production options (such as temperature and salinity tolerance and disease resistance) and cheaper feed substrates (for instance, plant material with enhanced nutritional features) might also be accessed with the use of GM technologies.

33   Aquaculture may cause harm to the environment because of the release into water bodies of

organic effluents or disease treatment chemicals, indirectly through its dependence on industrial fisheries to supply feeds, and by acting as a source of diseases or genetic contamination for wild species. Efforts to reduce these negative externalities and increase the efficiency of resource use [such as the fish in-to-fish out ratio (45)] have been spurred by the rise of sustainability certification programs, though these mainly affect only higher-value sectors. Gains in sustainability could come from concentrating on lower-trophic level species and in integrating aquatic and terrestrial food production, for example, by using waste from the land as food and nutrients. It will also be important to take a more strategic approach to site location and capacity within catchment or coastal zone management units (46).

Conclusions

34   There is no simple solution to sustainably feeding 9 billion people, especially as many become increasingly better off and converge on rich-country consumption patterns. A broad range of options, including those we have discussed here, needs to be pursued simultaneously. We are hopeful about scientific and technological innovation in the food system, but not as an excuse to delay difficult decisions today.

35   Any optimism must be tempered by the enormous challenges of making food production sustainable while controlling greenhouse gas emission and conserving dwindling water supplies, as well as meeting the Millennium Development Goal of ending hunger. Moreover, we must avoid the temptation to further sacrifice Earth's already hugely depleted biodiversity for easy gains in food production, not only because biodiversity provides many of the public goods on which mankind relies but also because we do not have the right to deprive future generations of its economic and cultural benefits. Together, these challenges amount to a perfect storm.

36   Navigating the storm will require a revolution in the social and natural sciences concerned with food production, as well as a breaking down of barriers between fields. The goal is no longer simply to maximize productivity, but to optimize across a far more complex landscape of production, environmental, and social justice outcomes.

Science. 2010. February 327.

References and Notes

1. World Bank, *World Development Report 2008: Agriculture for Development* (World Bank, Washington, DC, 2008).
2. FAOSTAT, http://faostat.fao.org/default.aspx (2009).
3. Food and Agriculture Organization of the United Nations (FAO), *State of Food Insecurity in the World 2009* (FAO, Rome, 2009).
4. A. Evans, *The Feeding of the Nine Billion: Global Food Security* (Chatham House, London, 2009).
5. D. Tilman *et al.*, *Science 292*, 281 (2001).
6. Millenium Ecosystem Assessment, *Ecosystems and Human Well-Being* (World Resources Institute, Washington, DC, 2005).
7. Intergovernmental Panel on Climate Change, *Contribution of Working Group II to the Fourth Assessment Report of the Intergovernmental Panel on Climate Change*, M. L. Parry *et al.*, Eds. (Cambridge Univ. Press, Cambridge, 2007).
8. J. Schmidhuber, F. N. Tubiello, *Proc. Natl. Acad. Sci. U.S.A. 104*, 19703 (2007).
9. J. von Braun, *The World Food Situation: New Driving Forces and Required Actions* (International Food Policy Research Institute, Washington, DC, 2007).
10. G. Conway, *The Doubly Green Revolution* (Penguin Books, London, 1997).
11. J. Piesse, C. Thirtle, *Food Policy 34*, 119 (2009).
12. Royal Society of London, *Sustainable Biofuels: Prospects and Challenges* (Royal Society, London, 2008).
13. R. Skidelsky, *The Return of the Master* (Allen Lane, London, 2009).
14. J. Pretty, Philos. *Trans. R. Soc. London Ser. B Biol. Sci. 363*, 447 (2008).
15. A. Balmford, R. E. Green, J. P. W. Scharlemann, *Global Change Biol. 11*, 1594 (2005).
16. C. Nellemann *et al.*, Eds., *The Environmental Food Crisis* [United Nations Environment Programme (UNEP), Nairobi, Kenya, 2009].
17. J. Fargione, J. Hill, D. Tilman, S. Polasky, P. Hawthorne, *Science 319*, 1235 (2008); published online 7 February 2008 (10.1126/science.1152747).
18. Royal Society of London, *Reaping the Benefits: Science and the Sustainable Intensification of Global Agriculture* (Royal Society, London, 2009).
19. K. G. Cassman, *Proc. Natl. Acad. Sci. U.S.A. 96*, 5952 (1999).
20. R. E. Evenson, D. Gollin, *Science 300*, 758 (2003).
21. P. Hazell, L. Haddad, *Food Agriculture and the Environment Discussion Paper 34*, (International Food Policy Research Institute, Washington, DC, 2001).
22. Forum for Agricultural Research in Africa, *Framework for African Agricultural Productivity* (Forum for Agricultural Research in Africa, Accra, Ghana, 2006).
23. K. Anderson, Ed., *Distortions to Agricultural Incentives, a Global Perspective 1955-2007* (Palgrave Macmillan, London, 2009).

24. J. N. Pretty, A. S. Ball, T. Lang, J. I. L. Morison, *Food Policy* 30, 1 (2005).
25. G. C. Nelson *et al.*, *Climate Change: Impact on Agriculture and Costs of Adaptation* (International Food Policy Research Institute, Washington, DC, 2009).
26. N. Stern, *The Economics of Climate Change* (Cambridge Univ. Press, Cambridge, 2007).
27. J. N. Pretty *et al.*, *Environ. Sci. Technol.* 40, 1114 (2006).
28. P. Hazell, S. Wood, *Philos. Trans. R. Soc. London Ser. B Biol. Sci.* 363, 495 (2008).
29. K. Deininger, G. Feder, *World Bank Res. Obs.* 24, 233 (2009).
30. P. Collier, *Foreign Aff.* 87, 67 (2008).
31. L. Cotula, S. Vermeulen, L. Leonard, J. Keeley, *Land Grab or Development Opportunity? Agricultural Investment and International Land Deals in Africa* [International Institute for Environment and Development (with FAO and International Fund for Agricultural Development), London, 2009].
32. A. Aksoy, J. C. Beghin, Eds., *Global Agricultural Trade and Developing Countries* (World Bank, Washington, DC, 2005).
33. R. A. Gilbert, J. M. Shine Jr., J. D. Miller, R. W. Rice, C. R. Rainbolt, *Field Crops Res.* 95, 156 (2006).
34. IAASTD, *International Assessment of Agricultural Knowledge, Science and Technology for Development: Executive Summary of the Synthesis Report*, www.agassessment.org/index.cfm?Page=About_IAASTD&ItemID=2 (2008).
35. P. G. Lemaux, *Annu. Rev. Plant Biol.* 60, 511 (2009).
36. D. Lea, *Ethical Theory Moral Pract.* 11, 37 (2008).
37. Cabinet Office, *Food Matters: Towards a Strategy for the 21st Century* (Cabinet Office Strategy Unit, London, 2008).
38. Waste and Resources Action Programme (WRAP), *The Food We Waste* (WRAP, Banbury, UK, 2008).
39. T. Stuart, *Uncovering the Global Food Scandal* (Penguin, London, 2009).
40. FAO, www.fao.org/english/newsroom/factfile/IMG/FF9712-e.pdf (1997).
41. California Integrated Waste Management Board, www.ciwmb.ca.gov/FoodWaste/FAQ.htm#Discards (2007).
42. FAO, *World Agriculture Towards 2030/2050* (FAO, Rome, Italy, 2006).
43. FAO, *World Agriculture Towards 2030/2050* (FAO, Rome, Italy, 2003).
44. M. D. Smith *et al.*, *Science* 327, 784 (2010).
45. A. G. J. Tacon, M. Metian, *Aquaculture* 285, 146 (2008).
46. D. Whitmarsh, N. G. Palmieri, in *Aquaculture in the Ecosystem*, M. Holmer, K. Black, C. M. Duarte, N. Marba, I. Karakassis, Eds. (Springer, Berlin, Germany, 2008).
47. P. R. Hobbs, K. Sayre, R. Gupta, *Philos. Trans. R. Soc. London Ser. B Biol. Sci.* 363, 543 (2008).
48. W. Day, E. Audsley, A. R. Frost, *Philos. Trans. R. Soc. London Ser. B Biol. Sci.* 363, 527 (2008).
49. J. Gressel, *Genetic Glass Ceilings* (Johns Hopkins Univ. Press, Baltimore, 2008).
50. FAO, *Livestock's Long Shadow* (FAO, Rome, Italy, 2006).
51. C. P. Reij, E. M. A. Smaling, *Land Use Policy* 25, 410 (2008).
52. UNEP, *Africa: Atlas of Our Changing Environment* (UNEP, Nairobi, Kenya, 2008).
53. The authors are members of the U.K. Government Office for Science's Foresight Project on Global Food and Farming Futures. J.R.B. is also affiliated with Imperial College London. D.L. is a Board Member of Plastid AS (Norway) and owns shares in AstraZeneca Public Limited Company and Syngenta AG. We are grateful to J. Krebs and J. Ingrahm (Oxford), N. Nisbett and D. Flynn (Foresight), and colleagues in Defra and DfID for their helpful comments on earlier drafts of this manuscript. If not for his sad death in July 2009, professor Mike Gale (John Innes Institute, Norwich, UK) would also have been an author of this paper.

KEY AND CHALLENGING WORDS

correlate (n.), volatile, exacerbate, suboptimal, aggregate (adj.), propagation, perturbation, agronomic, mitigate, trajectory, circumscribe, polygenic, repository, salinity, substrate, effluent, catchment

QUESTIONS

1. How is the problem of people who "do not have access to sufficient protein and energy from their diet" different from those who "suffer from some form of micronutrient malnourishment" (paragraph 1)?
2. Paraphrase the section of paragraph 2 that introduces today's three challenges in food production and distribution. (A paraphrase includes all of the original information.)
3. Using a dictionary/encyclopedia entry (e.g., from Oxford Reference Online or SAGE Reference Online), a) write a short summary that focuses on the significance of the Industrial Revolution, the Agricultural Revolution, or the Green Revolution (see paragraph 2), considering how this revolution affected the food production cycle, and b) speculate on how those changes differ from the kinds of changes that apply to today's world.
4. What is the primary organizational (rhetorical) pattern of the essay? Which patterns are used to develop the following paragraphs: 4, 10, 24–25?
5. In your own words, define "yield gap" (paragraph 6) and "poverty trap" (paragraph 9).

6. Explain the function of Box 1 and Figure 2. Why do you think the authors chose not to incorporate the content into the text of the essay itself? Summarize the explanation in either Box 1 or Figure 2.

7. a) In the authors' view do the benefits of GM technologies outweigh the costs? Explain; b) Why do the authors use the first-person voice in paragraph 22? Do you believe it was a good choice?

8. How many challenges involved in feeding 9 billion people do the authors discuss? Which challenge appears the most crucial? Which do they believe is the most difficult? Which depends the most on public trust?

9. Using a reliable source, explain the main objective of the Millennium Development Goal. Why do the authors refer to this international agreement in their conclusion?

POST-READING

1. *Collaborative activity:* Discuss or debate practical strategies for reducing food waste at the retail and individual level. (This could also be assigned as an evaluation report that includes recommendations.)

2. *Collaborative activity:* Discuss or debate the benefits of vegetarianism; you could focus on issues of personal health, larger global concerns, or both. You could also consider realistic measures that governments could take to reduce the Western consumption of meat and/or if this would be a worthwhile goal.

RELATED WEBSITES OF INTEREST

Food and Agriculture Organization of the United Nations:
www.fao.org/

World Hunger Programme:
www.wfp.org/

International Food Policy Research Institute:
www.ifpri.org/

Millennium Project:
www.unmillenniumproject.org/

The World Bank:
www.worldbank.org/

LIBRARY RESOURCES

Journals sometimes focus on a single topic, combining related studies and perspectives in "special issues" or special sections, which may include editorials, forums, literature reviews, and original research in an area of concern to both specialists and non-specialists. For example, a section in the 13 August 2010 issue of *Science* focused on alternative energy sources. "Food security: The challenge of feeding 9 billion people" is part of a special section on food security in the 12 February 2010 issue of *Science*. Many other opinions on and approaches to the problem are discussed in this section.

APPENDIX A
A Note on Statistics

The Active Voice

What Do Students Need to Know about Statistics?

There are two main types of research: qualitative and quantitative. Both types help us to describe or explain a phenomenon (e.g., the experience of war veterans); however, each method goes about describing the situation in very different ways. Qualitative research uses non-numerical data, such as words or pictures, in order to describe a phenomenon. In-depth interviews and/or extensive observations are typically used in order to collect this type of data. An interview with a war veteran about his experience during the war is an example of a qualitative research approach. Quantitative research, on the other hand, uses numbers in order to describe or explain a phenomenon and typically investigates the relationship between variables (e.g., the relationship between war veterans and depression). Quantitative research typically includes questionnaires with large samples of participants and uses a strict methodology in order to control all factors that are related to the data and therefore may affect the interpretation of that data. A questionnaire mailed out to a random sample of 500 male war veterans across Canada between the ages of 65 and 85 who have no family history of depression is an example of a quantitative research approach.

The decision to use qualitative versus quantitative methods depends on the research question that you ask and the type of information you want to obtain. Qualitative research provides rich and detailed words to describe a phenomenon, but the data is situation- and context-specific. By contrast, quantitative research provides numerical data to describe the relationship between variables, and these relationships may be generalized to the population as a whole. In this essay, we will describe why and how quantitative research methods may be used to answer a research question.

In the social sciences, we conduct research because we are interested in better understanding human behaviour (e.g., frequency of drinking, reaction time, level of intelligence). Most of the time, however, we do not limit ourselves to describing just that behaviour, but we also want to know whether it is related (and how) to some other feature of the person or the situation. For example, suppose you are interested in studying the level of intelligence (IQ) of undergraduate students in linguistics. You might be wondering whether female and male students will have, on average, the same IQ or whether it varies depending on gender. That is, do female students have higher or lower IQ than males? In this case, IQ is what we call the dependent variable, and the feature in your study that you think has an influence on it—gender—is the independent variable.

Mean and variance

Now suppose you recruit 10 male and 10 female students from one of your classes to answer this question. After administering an intelligence test to your 20 participants (N=20), you realize that each has a different IQ level. For some participants, their IQ value is 100, for others 130, and for still others 110. Because you want to compare the IQ of two groups (females vs. males), you need a unique value, representative of each group, that would allow you to make this comparison. The best way to create that value is by averaging the individual IQ values within each group, creating the mean IQ for each group.

Because the mean is only an average of individual IQ values, it will not tell us much about each value from which it was calculated. For example, suppose the mean IQ of both the male and female groups is the same (e.g., 115). The single values used to compute those means could nonetheless be very different. Some males, for example, may have values of 90 and others 130, averaging out to 100, whereas the IQ values of females may be in general closer to the mean (e.g., some 115 and others 120) but also averaging out to 100. In other words, the group of males may have more variation in their IQ values than the group of females.

As you can probably infer by now, the mean becomes less trustworthy as an estimate of the group's IQ when the variation is greater. Therefore, it is useful to have information about how much the single values used to calculate the mean differ from this mean (i.e., a general measure of how spread these values are from the mean). You can obtain this information by calculating the variance.

Once you have the information about the mean IQ and the variance for each of your groups, you can use a statistical test of inference to determine whether the means of the two groups are actually different from each other. Recall that you were interested in determining whether, on average, females in your class have higher or lower IQ than males. If the mean IQ for males and females is exactly the same, you would intuitively conclude that females and males are equally smart (as measured by IQ). If they differ by one or two points, your conclusion would probably be the same, because you would consider those one or two points to be random and unimportant. However, what would you conclude if the two means differed by 10 points? How would you determine whether the two means are meaningfully different and that their difference is not just due to chance?

Researchers consider two means to be significantly different when there is a very small probability (less than 0.05 or less than five in 100 times) that these two means are different only by chance. In order to determine this probability there are a number of statistical tests you can use (see below, "Correlation and prediction"). Returning

to our example, if the mean IQ for female students was 130 and the mean IQ for male students was 120, and if the test you used indicated that there was less than a five in 100 probability that these two values differed by chance, then you could (sadly or happily) say that the girls in your class have a significantly higher IQ value than the boys. The standard of five in 100 for "statistical significance" is an arbitrary but useful convention in research. It does not refer to the social or practical significance of the result, because that is not a statistical issue.

If you had obtained the 20 participants from your class (i.e., your sample) using a random procedure, you could generalize the results of your study to your entire class (in this case, your population). However, notice that very rarely do researchers randomly select subjects to participate in their studies and, instead, the selection depends on other factors (e.g., those people who agree to participate in the study).

Correlation and prediction

Say we want to know the relationship between high school GPA and college GPA. Our research question could be, What is the relationship between GPA in high school and GPA in college? A simple bivariate correlation can be used to answer this question. Correlations describe the extent to which two variables co-vary (e.g., as high school GPA goes up, so does college GPA).

However, say we determine that mothers' college GPA, fathers' college GPA, age, gender, and parents' income are also related (correlated) to GPA, and we want to know which factors influence college GPA the most. We can use multiple regression to answer this question. In multiple regression, all of the variables are entered into a regression (mathematical) equation, which then determines which factors most strongly influence college GPA when controlling for all other factors that were entered into the equation. Let's say fathers' college GPA and mothers' college GPA are revealed as the strongest factors influencing a college GPA. We can then use this information to screen and/or predict who will do the best in college based on their scores on the predictor variables. For example, if a student's mother and father had a high college GPA, we would predict that the student would have a high college GPA.

Another common statistical procedure is called an ANOVA (analysis of variance), which allows us to compare groups. Say we want to compare basketball players, volleyball players, and soccer players on their GPA. A t-test can be used to compare two groups (e.g., basketball players and volleyball players); however, an ANOVA will allow us to compare 2+ groups (e.g., basketball, volleyball, and soccer players).

For many people, statistics seem intimidating and overwhelming. However, the importance of statistics cannot be understated. At the most basic level of statistics, there are means, medians, modes, and percentages that tell us basic descriptive information (e.g., can describe the current situation). At the more complex level of statistical analysis used by most researchers, statistics allow us to answer some very interesting questions and to make important predictions about human behaviour.

Rachel Dean, Ph.D., and Agustin Del Vento, M.Sc.
Department of Psychology, University of Victoria

APPENDIX B

Characteristics of Type A, Type B, and Type C Essays

Feature	Type A	Type B	Type C
Methodology	qualitative (concerns, ideas, values, qualities); may have theoretical base	usually quantitative; centred on data that are generated, observed, and recorded	qualitative: organizes studies by categories, such as approaches to subject; summarizes and analyzes them
Author	often single author	often two or more authors	varies
Abstract?	sometimes	yes	sometimes
Purpose	variable: may inform, generate new knowledge, or seek to interpret knowledge in a new way	generates new knowledge	evaluates what has been written; finds gaps in the research and suggest future directions
Audience	other scholars and advanced students in the humanities	other scholars/researchers and advanced students in the social sciences and sciences	other scholars/researchers and advanced students in all disciplines, especially the social sciences; other educated and interested readers
Length	variable; tend to be longer than Type B and C; paragraphs may be lengthy due to discursive nature	variable; "Methods" may be longest and "Results" shortest; qualitative studies are often longer than quantitative ones	variable
Structure	may use content headings as structural markers	formal, standardized headings and sections	may use content headings
Introduction	includes thesis, key question(s), or essay plan; justifies need for study and often includes literature review; claim is interpretive[1]	includes hypothesis to be tested or question to be answered; justifies need for study and includes literature review; claim is fact-based[1]	essay plan, key question(s), or thesis; justifies need for review but no special review section as the entire article reviews the literature; claim is fact-based
Primary sources	interprets/analyzes them; often uses direct quotation	generates raw (numerical) data in order to test hypothesis, arrive at conclusions; primary sources often appear in tables/charts	focuses on results/conclusions of studies, but may refer to primary sources

[1] In an interpretive claim, the author weighs and interprets the evidence of the primary or secondary sources, using close analysis and sound reasoning. In a fact-based claim, the author presents his or her hypothesis and proceeds to test it under controlled conditions. An interpretive claim could use factual material as evidence; similarly, the evidence in a fact-based claim could be interpreted various ways.

Feature	Type A	Type B	Type C
Secondary sources	interprets/analyzes them; uses both direct quotation and summary	refers to them in literature review; uses summary	refers to/analyzes secondary sources (studies) throughout; uses summary more than direct quotation
Source treatment	uses analysis and synthesis throughout essay	uses analysis in "Results" and/or "Discussion" section; uses synthesis in literature review and may use it in "Discussion" or "Conclusion"	uses synthesis throughout; analyzes and critically evaluates studies, often using compare and contrasting pattern; definition and division are also common
Voice	variable: may be relatively detached (humanities) or involved (some social science research involving group observation, for example); active voice preferred	objective, detached; may use passive voice	objective; may use passive voice
Style	variable: may be discursive and complex; longer sentences and paragraphs; sentence variety; moderate/difficult language level	straightforward, direct; simple sentence structure	variable: straightforward, direct; simple sentence structure; may at times be discursive in analyzing/evaluating studies
Terminology	specialized diction but may borrow terms from other disciplines and define their specific usage in essay; may use terms applicable to a particular theory	specialized diction; assumes reader familiarity with terms as well as experimental and statistical processes	specialized diction; may explain key terms
Ancillary material	may be included in some disciplines, such as history or Greek and Roman studies; illustrations may be used in book chapters	charts, graphs, tables, figures, photos, appendices are common	sometimes includes graphics
Conclusion	may summarize or focus on implications of the study's findings	indicates whether hypothesis is proved/disproved or how question has been answered; often suggests practical applications/further research directions	may summarize and/or suggest future research directions or specific ways to apply the studies reviewed; may make recommendations

Credits

Anderson, Christopher G. "The senate and the fight against the 1885 Chinese Immigration Act." *Canadian Parliamentary Review* 30 (Summer 2007), pp. 21–6.

Attaran, Amir. "The ugly Canadian." *The Literary Review of Canada*, 17.5 (2009), pp. 3–6.

Barron, Christine, and Dany Lacombe. "Moral panic and the Nasty Girl." *Canadian Review of Sociology and Anthropology* 42.1 (2005), pp. 51–69.

Bernstein, Michael J., Steven G. Young, Christina M. Brown, Donald F. Sacco, and Heather M. Claypool. "Adaptive responses to social exclusion: Social rejection improves detection of real and fake smiles." *Psychological Science* 19 (October 2008) 981–983.

Binkley, Peter. "Wikipedia grows up." First published in the Canadian Library Association publication, *Feliciter*, vol. 52, No. 2 and is used with permission of the Canadian Library Association.

Caulfield, Timothy, and Roger Brownsword. "Human dignity: A guide to policy making in the biotechnology era?" *Nature* Vol. 7 (January 2006), pp. 72–6.

Chapin, Paul H. "Into Afghanistan: The transformation of Canada's international security policy since 9/11." *American Review of Canadian Studies* 40.2 (2010): 189–99.

Dunae, Patrick A. "Sex, charades and census records: Locating female sex trade workers in a Victorian city". *Histoire sociale/Social History*, 42 (2009), pp. 267–97.

Fiske, Susan T., Lasana T. Harris, and Amy J.C. Cuddy. "Why ordinary people torture enemy prisoners." *Science* Vol. 306 no. 5701 (26 November 2004), pp. 1482–1483.

Furgal, Christopher, and Jacinthe Seguin. "Climate change, health, and vulnerability in Canadian northern Aboriginal communities. Reproduced with permission from *Environmental Health Perspectives*.

Gecelovsky, Paul. "Canadian cannabis: Marijuana as an irritant/problem in Canada–U.S. relations." *The American Review of Canadian Studies* 38.2 (2008), pp. 207–12.

Gidengil, Elisabeth, André Blais, Richard Nadeau, and Neil Nevitte. "Enhancing democratic citizenship." Reprinted with permission of the Publisher from *Citizens* by Elisabeth Gidengil et al. ©University of British Columbia Press 2004. All rights reserved by the publisher.

Gifford, Robert. "Psychology's essential role in alleviating the impacts of climate change." *Canadian Psychology* 49.4 (2008), pp. 273–80.

Gillam, Ken, and Shannon R. Wooden. "Post-princess models of gender: The new man in Disney/Pixar." *Journal of Popular Film & Television* 36 (2008), pp. 2–8.

Gliksman, Louis, E. Adlaf, A. Demers, and B. Newton-Taylor. "Heavy drinking on Canadian campuses." *Canadian Journal of Public Health* 2003, 94(1): 17–21.

Godfray, H. Charles J. et al. "Food security: The challenge of feeding 9 billion people." *Science* Vol. 327 (12 Feb. 2010), pp. 812–18.

Griffiths, Mark. "Online video gaming: What should educational psychologists know?" *Educational Psychology in Practice*, Vol. 26, No. 1, March 2010, pp. 35–40.

Hadwin, Allyson F., Mika Oshige, Mariel Miller, and Peter Wild, "Examining student and instructor task perceptions in a complex engineering design task." (2009, July). Paper proceedings presented for the Sixth International Conference on Innovation and Practices in Engineering Design and Engineering Education (CDEN/C2E2), McMaster University, Hamilton, Ont., Canada.

Heath, Joseph. "Did the banks go crazy?" *Literary Review of Canada* 17.7 (2009), pp. 3–5.

Henrich, Joseph, Steven J. Heine, and Ara Norenzayan. "Most people are not WEIRD." *Nature* 466 (1 July 2010), p. 29.

Jacobs, Beverley. "Response to Canada's apology to residential school survivors." *Canadian Woman Studies* Vol. 26 3/4 (2008), pp. 223–5.

Jones, Jennifer, Mikiko Terashima, and Daniel Rainham, "Fast food and deprivation in Nova Scotia." *Canadian Journal of Public Health* 100.1 (2009), pp. 32–5.

Krahn, Timothy. "Where are we going with preimplantation genetic diagnosis?" *CMAJ* 176.10 (2007), pp. 1445–6.

Lexchin, Joel. "Pharmaceutical innovation: Can we live forever? A commentary on Schnittker and Karandinos." *Social Science & Medicine* 70 (2010), pp. 972–3.

Maticka-Tyndale, Eleanor. "Sexuality and sexual health of Canadian adolescents: Yesterday, today and tomorrow." *The Canadian Journal of Human Sexuality* 17.3 (2008), pp. 85–95.

McMurtry, John. "University wars: The corporate administration vs. the vocation of learning." *CCPA Monitor* 16.3, 2009.

Miller, Jim. "Which 'native' history? By whom? For whom?" *Canadian Issues* (Autumn 2008), pp. 33–5.

Nikiforuk, Andrew. "Tarmageddon: Dirty oil is turning Canada into a corrupt petro-state." *CCPA Monitor* 17.1 (2010), pp. 10–11.

Ouellette, Laurie. "Reality TV gives back: On the civic functions of reality entertainment." *Journal of Popular Film & Television* (2010), pp. 67–71. DOI: 10.1080/01956051.2010.483347

Ries, Nola M., and Barbara von Tigerstrom, "Roadblocks to laws for healthy eating and activity." *CMAJ* 182.7 (2010), pp. 687–91.

Robidoux, Michael A. "Imagining a Canadian identity through sport: A historical interpretation of lacrosse and hockey." Published in *Journal of American Folklore*, 115.456 (2002), pp. 209–25.

Ruby, Tabassum F. "Listening to the voices of *hijab*." *Women's Studies International Forum* 29 (2006), pp. 54–66.

Saul, John Ralston. "Listen to the North" (first published in *The Literary Review of Canada* October 2009). Copyright ©2009 John Ralston Saul. With permission of the author.

Schwartz, Marlene B., Jennifer J. Thomas, Kristin M. Bohan, and Lenny R. Vartanian. "Intended and unintended effects of an eating disorder educational program: Impact of presenter identity." *International Journal of Eating Disorders* (2007) 40(2).

Sills, Jennifer, ed. "Climate change and the integrity of science." *Science*, Vol. 328 no. 5979 (7 May 2010), pp. 689–90.

Snow, Catherine E. "Academic language and the challenge of reading for learning about science." *Science* vol. 328 (23 April 2010), pp. 450–2.

Turcotte, Martin. "Life in metropolitan areas: Dependence on cars in urban neighbourhoods." Adapted from Statistics Canada publication *Canadian Social Trends*, Catalogue 11-008-XWE2008001, no. 85, http://www.statcan.gc.ca/pub/11-008-x/2008001/article/10503-eng.htm.

Walker, Carol M., Beth Rajan Sockman and Steven Koehn. "An exploratory study of cyberbullying with undergraduate university students." *TechTrends* 55.2 (2011): 31–8.

Weimann, Gabriel. "Terror on Facebook, Twitter, and Youtube." *Brown Journal of World Affairs* 16.2 (2010), pp. 45–54.

Wicks, Ann, and Raylene Lang-Dion. "Women in politics: Still searching for an equal voice." *Canadian Parliamentary Review* 31 (Spring 2008), pp. 34–7.

Young, Simon N. "Universities, governments and industry: Can the essential nature of universities survive the drive to commercialize?" *Journal of Psychiatry and Neuroscience*, volume 30, issue 3, 2005.

Subject Index

The Subject Index includes essays in *The Active Reader* organized by 25 subject categories.

Index

Classification of Readings by Rhetorical Mode/Pattern

Most essays in *The Active Reader* employ the problem–solution rhetorical pattern; in addition, virtually all essays use some form of analysis and most use examples. However, writers utilize other rhetorical patterns to develop their main points. These patterns are listed below. Readings may make use of other patterns than just those listed.